TUTORIAL.
SOFTWARE DESIGN STRATEGIES second edition

GLENN D. BERGLAND
RONALD D. GORDON

Bell Laboratories
Murray Hill, New Jersey

IEEE Catalog No. EH0184-2
Library of Congress No. 81-84179
IEEE Computer Society Order No. 389
ISBN 0-8186-0389-5

ADDITIONAL COPIES AVAILABLE FROM:

IEEE COMPUTER SOCIETY

THE INSTITUTE OF ELECTRICAL AND ELECTRONICS ENGINEERS, INC.

IEEE COMPUTER SOCIETY
P.O. Box 80452
Worldway Postal Center
Los Angeles, CA 90080

IEEE SERVICE CENTER
445 Hoes Lane
Piscataway, N.J. 08854

IEEE Catalog No. EH0184-2
Library of Congress No. 81-84179
IEEE Computer Society Order No. 389
ISBN 0-8186-0389-5 (paper)
ISBN 0-8186-4389-7 (microfiche)

Order from: IEEE Computer Society
Post Office Box 80452
Worldway Postal Center
Los Angeles, CA 90080

IEEE Service Center
445 Hoes Lane
Piscataway, NJ 08854

 The Institute of Electrical and Electronics Engineers, Inc.

PREFACE

New software design techniques exist that can reduce the problems of software analysis, development, and maintenance and lead to inexpensive, reliable programs. Unfortunately, for many people the benefits of these techniques have remained either nebulous or elusive.

In this tutorial text, we attempt to clarify and focus on aspects of software design that have a direct effect on the structure of the final program. Because the structure of the program itself is the single most important determinant of the life cycle costs of a software project, a major portion of the tutorial is devoted to methods of structured program design.

Several major design strategies are developed and compared, including: traditional forms of functional decomposition, the data-structure design method of Michael Jackson, the data-flow design method of Larry Constantine, and the programming calculus of Edsger Dijkstra.

The process of organizing and coordinating the efforts of the design team is also studied. In particular, the practices of top-down development, code walkthroughs, and design reviews are presented and evaluated.

Finally, several of the program design tools that are currently in use within industry are introduced. Included in this survey are: the TOPD system, the PSL/PSA documentation and analysis system, the structured analysis and design technique, and program development languages.

We hope that this tutorial will be useful to software managers and practitioners in the field. Managers and designers alike should benefit from the overview of the major software development techniques presented within the chapter introductions.

For a brief overview, we suggest you read the chapter introductions and "Software Management Survey of the Practice in 1980"[1] followed by "Top-Down Design and Testing."[5] You may want to continue with "Structured Programming in a Production Programming Environment"[7] and "The Programmer's Workbench—A Machine for Software Development."[25]

Software designers unfamiliar with this material could benefit by reading the light overview, "A Guided Tour of Program Design Methodologies"[22] before plunging into "Designing Software for Ease of Extension and Contraction,"[8] "Constructive Methods of Program Design,"[9] and "Transform Analysis."[15]

Experienced structured designers should start by reading "Information Systems: Modelling, Sequencing and Transformations,"[10] and "Two Pairs of Examples in the Jackson Approach to System Development."[11] You can then move on to "Transaction Analysis,"[16] "Distributed Processes: A Concurrent Programming Concept."[21] More difficult reading, but a follow up to the above articles, is the paper by Gries, "An Illustration of Current Ideas on the Derivation of Correctness Proofs and Correct Programs."[17]

Software practitioners will find that this tutorial text provides an update of the most widely used software design strategies. Although much of the material may be familiar to some professionals, our objective is to provide a broad cross-section of significant strategies being used today.

For those who are concerned with programming environments, the introduction to UNIX[†] provided by "The Programmer's Workbench—A Machine for Software Development"[25] is must reading. You will also be interested in the ambitious undertaking for supporting the design and development of real-time programs that is outlined in "Software Requirements Engineering Methodology (SREM) at the Age of Four."[26]

Several good texts exist for the most established software design techniques and management practices. The Program Design Library section of this tutorial provides the needed references for those readers who wish to obtain more detailed information. This field is rapidly changing, and much pertinent information is available only through published papers in a wide variety of technical publications. To assist those readers who need more information beyond the scope of this tutorial, we provide a permuted title index at the end of the book that lists relevant papers published during the last two years.■

---

† UNIX is a Trademark of Bell Laboratories.

iii

Table of Contents

INTRODUCTION

This book was prepared as the text for a tutorial course on Software Design Strategies. It presents structured design methodologies, software development techniques, and software tools that are representative of current solutions to the problems associated with large software development projects. Current papers are presented that describe state-of-the-art approaches to today's software development problems.

In addition to explaining and demonstrating some of the best techniques available, we have included some comparisons of different design strategies. We hope that this approach will make you aware of the new software technology and will help you to take a significant step toward writing correct, maintainable programs.

A lot of design strategies have been proposed. However, most are, as yet, untested in any large development effort. Most strategies that have been used extensively are introduced in this book with one or more reprints. In addition, several survey papers are included which indicate some movement toward a rational approach to comparing design methodologies.

Management techniques also exist that assist in organizing and tracking the design and development effort. We have included papers that describe some of these current management strategies.

One format for discussing recent advances in the field of software engineering is to consider their effect on each phase of the software development cycle. That is, you could consider: the effect of program teams and walk-throughs on problem specification, the effect of data abstractions on design, the effect of high-level languages on implementation, etc.

Software engineering techniques have been divided into three different categories in this book (see Figure 1). The first category has to do with software project management techniques for improving the program development process. A number of organizational and management oriented techniques are described that can make a significant difference if the original design has been done properly. Without a proper design, however, these techniques run the risk of becoming inefficient, ineffective, and expensive to administer.

Figure 1. Software Techniques Hierarchy.

The second category concerns deriving a well-structured program that is an accurate model of the problem being solved and its environment. This is the single most important goal of the software design process. If the program has a structure with many random interfaces that do not properly model reality, no amount of effort or money spent in walk-throughs, high-level languages, or development support systems can keep that program out of trouble. It is only within the context of a well-structured program that walk-throughs, code reading, programmer teams, and development support libraries can be properly exploited.

Once methods for achieving proper designs have been found and a process for implementing these designs has been achieved, only then should these procedures be automated and enforced within one's programming environment, the third category. Software tools that automate the most routine parts of the program design and development process are presented.

Each of the categories of software engineering techniques highlighted above is represented by a major chapter within this tutorial. Each chapter, in turn, has an introduction that underlines the concepts being discussed and introduces the papers that have been reprinted. Where possible, we attempt to discuss the motivation, application, and potential problems associated with each technique. While we tend to fare much better in the role of historians than as prophets, we point out what we consider to be likely future trends.

Unfortunately, even though "structured programming" has been with us for well over a decade, we are still far from knowing all of the answers or, for that matter, even all of the questions! While it is clear that progress has been made, (and we hope that this tutorial will reinforce that view), there is still much to be done.■

SOFTWARE PROJECT MANAGEMENT

Many software engineering techniques focus on improving the software development *process* rather than on improving the *software* developed by the process. The techniques often consist of a collection of management and organizational strategies plus procedures for integrating and testing the final software product. Those techniques discussed here tend to complement the design strategies developed in the next section of the tutorial. That is, given a good design strategy that results in a good program structure, software development techniques exist that can be applied fruitfully to obtain a "correct" program faster. However, when these techniques are not used in the context of a good program structure they can become both cumbersome and unmanageable.

The first paper by Jack Distaso, **"Software Management—A Survey of the Practice in 1980,"** summarizes the many problems that hinder software development activities. It presents a brief survey of the strategies, tools, and management practices that have evolved to combat these problems. Four critical problem areas are addressed: developing satisfactory software requirements, software cost estimation, realizing improvements in productivity, and maintaining management control and visibility. This survey puts into perspective the role of development tools and the contribution of program design methodologies from a manager's point of view.

THE SOFTWARE LIFE CYCLE

The successful development of large software systems can be viewed as a problem of properly controlling the system life cycle and maintenance resource consumption functions. The resource consumption expenditure functions evolve from management control of the project to achieve an appropriate return on investment. This is the viewpoint of William C. Cave and Alan B. Salisbury in their paper, **"Controlling the Software Life Cycle—The Project Management Task."**

A quantitative measure of software quality is proposed. This measure is used by management to assure a desirable level of software functionality consistent with the consumption of resources for the project. Resulting in a rough measure of overall system quality, the quantitative function attempts to gauge the functional availability of the system in relation to its observed maintenance and development costs.

Even before a system is operational, the success of a project depends on the judicious and controlled expenditure of resources during enhancement and maintenance. In order to maximize his return on investment, a successful manager must understand the factors that influence the resource consumption functions.

The most significant characteristic of the resource consumption curve is the steep rate of consumption that occurs prior to the system's initial operational capability. This large outlay must be ultimately recovered during the useful life of the system. This period, however, is limited by advances in technology and system obsolescence. Increasing the rate of resource consumption prior to initial operational capability may serve to lengthen the useful life of the product and capture a greater market share. Yet such a course requires much greater management skill and control.

Successful life cycle planning requires an environment that affords proper management control and response coupled with enforceable management procedures for maintaining project control. Fundamentally, it is the responsibility of management to define the system requirements accurately and completely. Only in this way can the development of user-oriented software be assured. Development of a measurable set of project milestones and standards provides the foundation for maintaining project control through all phases of the system's life cycle.

The concepts presented by Cave and Salisbury should serve to identify the key factors that must be controlled to achieve long-term economic success in a competitive environment.

The software life cycle may be decomposed into requirements engineering, design, coding, testing, and maintenance. Software management impacts each of these areas and is the most significant factor that contributes to the success or failure of a project.

EHO184-2/81/000/0003$00.75 © 1981 IEEE

Many tools have been developed for use within each phase of the software life cycle. In addition to reducing much of the clerical operations needed to produce software and its supporting documents, these tools provide a convenient means of monitoring the progress of the development effort. A more detailed description of many applicable tools will be found in the third section of our tutorial, "Software Development Environments."

In "**Software Engineering**"[3] by Barry W. Boehm, many of the design strategies now in widespread use are placed in context within the software life cycle. Software requirements engineering, testing, and maintenance are addressed in this survey, as well. Several notable approaches are introduced, including the hierarchical decomposition design technique of *SofTech,* the TRW software development methodology, SDC's *Software Factory,* and the *System Design Laboratory* developed at the Naval Electronics Laboratory.

Boehm's paper provides an excellent overview of the many factors that influence the production of quality software. An extensive set of references serves to cover in much greater detail the techniques that have evolved.

PROGRAMMING TEAMS

Critical to the success of any software management strategy is the integration of software technology and managerial principles. One of the most well known of these integrated approaches is IBM's top-down structured programming technique that makes use of chief programmer teams. This concept is discussed in F. Terry Baker's paper, "**Structured Programming in a Production Programming Environment,**"[7] which appears later in this tutorial.

Programming teams can complement the hierarchical program design with a hierarchical people organization. Given any organization that must work toward a common goal, a certain number of interactions must occur among the people doing the work. As shown in Figure 1, the number of interactions required within a given team is a function of team size. As the number of people who must interact gets larger, the number of potential interactions grows quadratically and can take a larger and larger portion of each person's time. Teams of three to five people have generally been regarded as "about right," while teams of 10 to 12 have usually been regarded as "too large."

The concept of assigning programming teams to particular functional modules within a large system localizes most of the people interactions to the team itself and minimizes the communication required between teams. If the program structure has low coupling between modules, the program teams require few

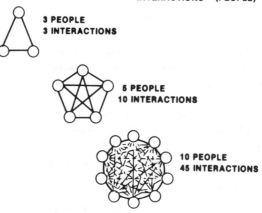

INTERACTIONS ~ (PEOPLE)^2

3 PEOPLE
3 INTERACTIONS

5 PEOPLE
10 INTERACTIONS

10 PEOPLE
45 INTERACTIONS

Figure 1. Programming Team Interactions.

interactions with other teams. Conversely, a program module that is coupled tightly to many other modules will place a significant communication burden on each implementation team.

In most cases, simple programming teams are staffed with graduate engineers and computer scientists who have long-term career potential with the company. These people are often supported by program librarians or programming secretaries who perform the clerical and administrative functions, freeing the programmers to solve the technical problems.

This partitioning of work is carried even further in a "chief programmer team" (see Reprint 7). Part of the motivation behind chief programmer teams is that the requirements and design part of the job, using structured programming techniques, far overshadows the coding part of the job. Thus, many people have moved away from the concept of having one designer feed work to three or four less qualified coders. Coding now represents less than 15 percent of the total effort and, in many cases, it is easier to do one's own than to delegate. This is especially true when the capabilities of the designer and the implementors differ by nearly an order of magnitude.

The "chief programmer team" concept sounds nice in theory, but most structured programming teams tend to be teams of peers, with the possible exception of a team leader and a program librarian. This team, as a group, is encouraged to identify with the total job, not individually with pieces of tricky code or a particular personal part of the job.

4

In projects where this approach is not taken, an individual is often assigned the responsibility for maintaining a particular segment of code. These people become experts at living with and fielding questions about the idiosyncrasies of their own particular segment of code. In this organizational structure only the person responsible for the code must know how to read the program, so there is no strong incentive to make it understandable to others. A poorly written piece of code tends to stay with its creator for a long period of time. Since changing assignments would require costly apprenticeships, people become relatively immobile. In this environment, comments concerning the quality of a particular program are usually viewed as reflecting directly on the quality of the programmer.

This approach contrasts with the concept of having a team responsible for a major program subsystem, thus allowing one to move more toward what G. M. Weinberg refers to in his book, *The Psychology of Computer Programming*,[1] as "egoless" programming. Under this policy, everybody is expected to know and be able to read all the programs in their subsystem. The team works to make all of the programs easy to understand and easy to modify for the sake of both new users and new team members. People outside the team are encouraged and supported in the use of the programs. Since a single team can carry a new feature from specification through to its first application, this concept tends to provide a good environment and, as R. N. Ford describes "motivation through the work itself."[2]

A concept that has some similarities with "egoless teams" is called the "buddy system." Here, a group of people is responsible for a group of programs, as before, but no one person follows any given program all the way through the development cycle. A person on the team might design one program, code another, and test a third. Thus, of necessity, a program must be designed and written so that it can be understood by at least two other "buddies."

WALK-THROUGHS

Walk-throughs were one of the first techniques used by most organizations in trying to adopt structured programming. In several large organizations, it quickly seemed as if every hour of every day, some kind of walk-through was being held by someone.

A typical scenario involved some poor programmer trying dutifully to explain his or her program to a dozen or more people who couldn't care less. Soon the size of the audiences diminished, but still it was a painful time for all.

Programming walk-throughs build on having clearly understandable specifications, program designs, and code to walk through. They complement the concept of working in programming teams. In "**Structured Walk-Throughs: A Project Management Tool**,"[4] the activities that make up a successful walk-through are discussed and several pitfalls are identified.

The program walk-through process is shown in Figure 2 as preparing for and holding a series of meetings in' which problems are identified but not resolved. These meetings are normally held when system requirements have been determined, when the system design is completed, and when the code has been written. Walk-throughs are normally called by members of each programming team, with only those people directly involved in the topic at hand being invited.

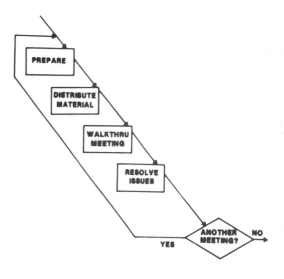

Figure 2. The Walk-through Process.

The major concern of the walk-through is to identify problems early in the project so that they can be resolved when the cost of correcting them is lowest. The earlier an error is found, the easier it is to correct, and the less it impedes the rest of the program development process. A secondary benefit of program walk-throughs results from the interactions within the walk-through meetings themselves. A new kind of informal classroom situation often develops. The atmosphere of the meeting should be open, frank, and friendly. Management does not attend the walk-through, and the action list produced is not used to measure the performance of the employee. In many cases, the older, more experienced programmers can give the benefit of their experience to the newer programmers; and the newer programmers can share the recent advances in computer science that they just learned in school with the older programmers.

Several walk-throughs may be conducted at various stages during the project. The author of a system element to be reviewed is responsible for scheduling the walk-through and selecting attendees who will be best able to evaluate the work product. Users, analysts, programmers, testers, etc., may be assembled to inspect and identify errors, inconsistencies, or omissions.

Four to six people generally participate in the walk-through. A recording secretary is appointed to document all problems that are uncovered. After receiving initial evaluations from the reviewers, the author walks through the function under investigation. Enough detail is presented so that concerns raised during the initial evaluations can be addressed. Specifications, design, algorithms, interfaces, coding method, and documentation are studied as appropriate to the nature of the work under review.

As noted earlier, there is a potential hazard in holding program walk-throughs if the size of the group attending is too large. Just going to the meetings associated with the walk-throughs can be a very time consuming activity for the program development team members. One guard against this is to adhere strictly to the rule that problems are only identified and not resolved in the meeting. The second safeguard relies on having a well-structured program. If the program is structured in a fashion that minimizes connectivity and maximizes independence, then the number of people involved in any given program walk-through will be small.

Given a hierarchical design, the people who have major interfaces with any given program are relatively easy to identify; thus, the number of people involved can be kept small. A program that can be characterized as "spaghetti" coding would require that larger audiences be present at each walk-through, since any given program is capable of directly affecting a large number of other programs.

Edward Yourdon emphasized the need for an integration of program structuring and the walk-through process, yielding a review technique he calls "the structured walk-through." His book, *Structured Walk-Throughs,*[3] is a good handbook for organizations planning to use this type of review mechanism.

Program walk-throughs, management reviews, and project checkpoints all share the aim of trying to find errors early in the development cycle to reduce development costs. The relative cost of finding errors at different stages in the development process is shown in Figure 3 (see Boehm[4]). Other studies show even higher ratios.[5]

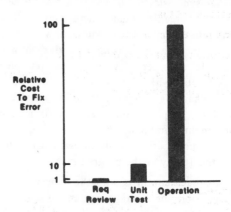

Figure 3. The Relative Cost of Errors.

Walk-throughs are a useful project management tool that serves to improve the communication between project members and to help ensure the quality of the final product. They have been applied successfully in conjunction with other strategies, including structured coding, programmer teams, top-down design, parallel testing, and development support libraries.

TOP-DOWN STRATEGIES

Top-down implementation and testing and top-down design are completely separate issues. The first procedure concerns order of implementation and the second is a design strategy.

Top-down implementation reportedly can reduce the effort required for program integration and program testing. It is a testing and integration philosophy that can capitalize on the modular hierarchical design discussed earlier.

Given a hierarchical program design, one can implement the program by starting at the bottom of the hierarchy (that is, by implementing the leaves of the tree structure), writing drivers to exercise these modules, and gradually working one's way up by considering larger and larger subtrees. The problem with this approach is that one often starts by testing and working on the most detailed, change-prone modules first. Naturally, a series of small changes in the requirements will occur steadily throughout the life of the project. Since the most detailed modules are implemented first, they must be modified the most over the longest period of time. This can lead to severe compatibility problems later in the program integration phase. It also requires that a significant number of program drivers (that are not deliverable software) be produced, debugged, and tested along with the main program.

In top-down development, the idea is to write and execute the most critical high-level code first and to provide stubs for functions that are not yet completed. This is shown schematically in Figure 4. The advantages of this approach are that:

(1) No separate drivers are required.

(2) The critical programs are tested the most.

(3) The code that is the least likely to change is developed first instead of last.

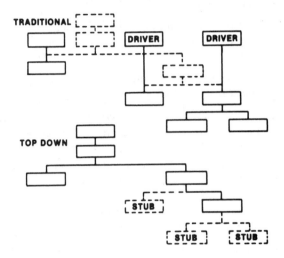

Figure 4. Top-Down Implementation.

Top-down design not only yields benefits that do not result when traditional bottom-up methods are applied, but also presents unique problems and difficulties as well. After a brief overview of the technical concepts behind the top-down approach, the reprint **"Top-Down Design and Testing,"**[5] an excerpt from Edward Yourdon's book *Managing the Structured Techniques,* reviews the management-oriented benefits and pitfalls that can be expected when implementing and administering such an approach.

It is important to distinguish between the concepts "structured programming" and the "top-down" approach. The former refers to the disciplined use of control-flow structures (sequencing, selection, and iteration) while the latter can be described as a procedure that divides, then subdivides the problem into components of manageable complexity.

The important applications of the top-down

approach can be identified as design, coding, and testing. Top-down design provides an organized method of breaking the original problem into successively smaller problems that can be understood and solved. Top-down coding allows high-level system components to be written and executed before subordinate routines are coded, perhaps even before they are designed. During top-down testing, the system is exercised to verify the operation of the high-level modules that have been coded.

Application of the top-down approach varies depending on how much of the system design is completed prior to coding and testing. At one end of the spectrum, all the design is completed in a top-down manner before top-down coding and testing begins. At the other end, coding and testing begin as soon as the highest level of design has been completed. The most successful approach lies somewhere in between. Deciding which end of the spectrum is to be favored is a management decision that should be based on the environment in which the project is being developed.

Since major interfaces must be designed and tested early in the project life, several advantages may be realized as a result of applying the top-down approach.

- Users can see a working demonstration of the system, and managers are better able to assess the progress being developed.

- Because partial versions of the system are available early, deadlines are met with at least some functions operational.

- Programmers' morale is higher because they have an opportunity to begin programming and can see the results of their efforts sooner.

- Debugging is also easier, and the demand for machine time is more evenly distributed over the life of the project.

Problems may arise, however, since the system equipment and machine time are required earlier in the development cycle. The gradual buildup of staff that occurs naturally in a top-down application may conflict with the sudden expansion that is typical for some organizations when a new project is initiated. Programmers may be concerned that the top-down approach will fail as a result of problems that may arise only after the lowest system elements are coded. Misunderstanding of top-down strategy may cause system-level integration or testing to be performed bottom-up. Or it may result in versions that do not represent complete (although skeletal), implementations of the system.

The benefits that can result when the top-down approach is properly applied and managed are significant. By recognizing the needs that must be met to provide a suitable environment for the top-down approach and guarding against the problems and difficulties that can arise, managers can expect to achieve these benefits.

PHASED BUILDS

A related implementation strategy to top-down development goes under the name "phased builds." With some planning, program modules can be implemented in an order that allows partial processing of certain inputs almost immediately. More complicated inputs are handled in succeeding versions (see Figure 5).

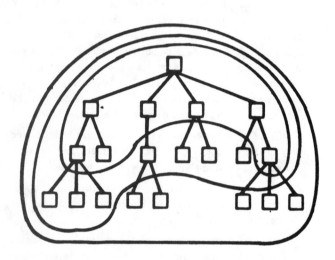

Figure 5. Phased Builds.

With this approach, useful work can be seen from the beginning, and progress can be monitored by viewing the types of inputs and outputs that are currently still stubbed. The integration testing is done incrementally.

A phased approach to a payroll system[6] could start by reading in a list of employees and printing out a $100 paycheck for each of them with the output figure appearing in octal format. Version 2 could pay all the employees their correct salaries. Version 3 could be enhanced to print their pay check in decimal notation so they could actually cash it.

This approach has two advantages. First, one has a subset of the system running almost immediately, and further progress consists simply of integrating more detailed functions into an already working program. This eliminates the need for that dreaded day of truth and turmoil called "program integration."

A second advantage is that progress on the project is visible and demonstrable early. Many projects have been killed or had funding severely restricted because there were no visible signs of progress.

REFERENCES

1. Weinberg, G. M., *The Psychology of Computer Programming*. Van Nostrand Reinhold Company, New York, 1969.

2. Ford, R. N., *Motivation Through the Work Itself*. American Management Association, Inc., New York, 1969.

3. Yourdon, Edward, *Structured Walk-Throughs*. Yourdon, Inc., New York, 1978.

4. Boehm, Barry, "Software Engineering: R&D Trends and Defense Needs," Research Directions in Software Technology Proceedings, Brown University, October, 1977.

5. Cammack, W. B., and Rodgers, J. J., Jr., "Improving the Programming Process," IBM Poughkeepsie, New York, TR 00.2483, October 19, 1973.

6. Yourdon, Edward, and Constantine, L. L., *Structured Design*. Yourdon, Inc., New York, 1975.

Reprinted from *Proceedings of the IEEE*, Volume 68, Number
9, September 1980, pages 1103-1119. Copyright © 1980 by The
Institute of Electrical and Electronics Engineers, Inc.

Software Management—A Survey of the Practice in 1980

JACK R. DISTASO, MEMBER, IEEE

Abstract—The primary thrust of this paper is to explore many of the
problems currently plaguing software development activities and to
propose how some of the recently developed management practices
may be employed in dealing with them. The practices described range
from people organizations (e.g., chief programmer teams) to fully
automated engineering tools (e.g., software requirements engineering
methodology). A number of techniques are presented. These include
methods for coping with communications problems in the requirements
definition activity, for evolving a facility which will help increase the
productivity of software designers and programmers, and for maintaining
a high degree of visibility during the elusive unit design code and test
phase of a project.

Manuscript received March 24, 1980; revised May 6, 1980.
The author is with TRW Defense and Space Systems, One Space Park,
Redondo Beach, CA 90278.

A very practical view of the management problems and suggested
approaches is presented. Key principles, potential "pitfalls," and unresolved concerns are addressed from a viewpoint of where the state
of the art is today and where the industry appears to be heading in the
mid-1980's.

I. INTRODUCTION

DURING the 1970's, several major studies were accomplished toward the orderly evolution of a software
management methodology. Advanced methods for
defining requirements, achieving productivity improvements,
and improving the control and visibility of the software
development process were introduced and utilized in many
places. This paper presents a summary of several of the approaches developed, with emphasis on how these practices
may help address many of the real issues facing the software

9

EHO184-2/81/0000/0009$00.75 © 1980 IEEE

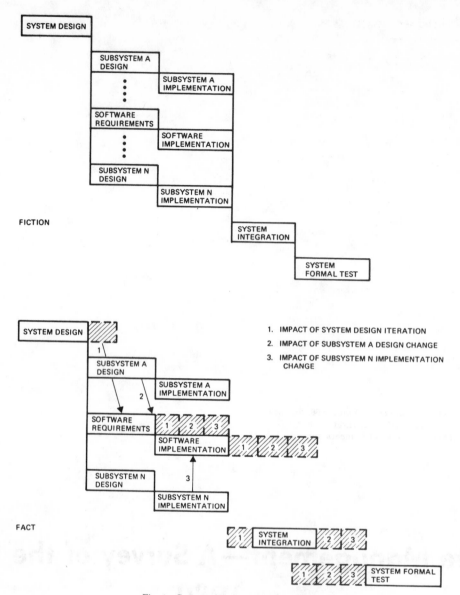

Fig. 1. System development schedule.

development manager of the 1980's. Four principal problem areas are addressed

1) obtaining satisfactory software requirements;
2) improving the art of software cost estimating;
3) achieving significant productivity improvements;
4) maintaining control and visibility of software developments.

Finally, a brief look is taken at some issues that are likely to become key problems in the 1980's.

II. REQUIREMENTS

Obtaining satisfactory software requirements remains the single largest obstacle to software project success.

The problem of generating complete, consistent, unambiguous, testable software requirements continues to plague the software industry and remains management's most serious challenge to bring order to the software development process [1]. It is important to understand why this problem, which has been debated, analyzed, and researched for years, is in-

variably the critical factor in project success or failure for most projects of significant size. The key elements of this problem are the following:

1) continually changing user needs;
2) scheduling difficulties of major system developments;
3) communication barriers among users, system designers and software designers;
4) lack of use of new generalized methodologies;
5) misapplication of simulation.

A. User Needs

Few of us would be inclined to make a significant purchase for a product (car, house, etc.) that does not exist and for which there is not even an artist's conception available. Similarly, we would not likely invest in a product for which the only description that exists is a few block diagrams of its basic functions, plus perhaps some equations or other descriptions of its fundamental operating principles. On the other hand, a building contractor who was continuously expected to construct buildings without the square footage, the numbers of

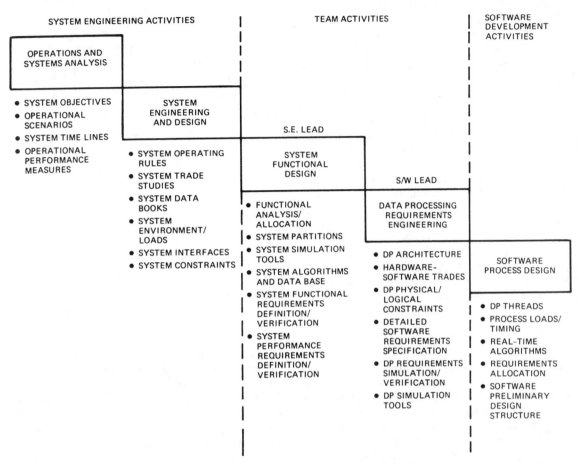

Fig. 2. Team approach to software requirements definition.

floors, and the locations for walls and windows specified, would quickly consider another line of business. Yet, these scenarios still reasonably reflect the situations which data processing users and developers are commonly faced with at the start of a major software development activity. J. B. Munson [2] stated that the software industry still has not come up with any "pictures" of its products. Users of major new complex systems are asked to generate precise specifications for a product which they can neither "see" nor fully understand. User's responses are predictable. They want a specification that leaves them some options, does *not* lock them forever to their initial thoughts, and provides some freedom to better express their needs as they see the product evolve.

For the developer, the growing size and complexity of systems, coupled with users' inability to express their needs, is increasingly going to impact the developer's ability to scope and produce his system. The software industry is one of the few remaining builders of one-of-a-kind systems, and until we can provide a better prespective of our product, the problem of software requirements will remain with us.

B. System Schedules

For major embedded computer systems, another phenomenon serves to make the software requirements definition task difficult. This is the fact that software requirements definition requires a stable overall system design—but schedules rarely permit adequate time for the systems engineering and subsystem design tasks to stabilize before software requirements are needed. For embedded systems, the software provides the control logic (i.e., the glue) that holds the system together and causes it to work as a system. Consequently, functional, control or interface changes in virtually every other subsystem typically have an impact (often major) on the system control software. This is particularly pronounced early in the program when the design of these subsystems are undergoing major fluctuations in attempting to meet their own specifications. It also continues at a lower level throughout the development such that the software continually must adjust to the changing requirements of the subsystems it controls (see Fig. 1).

Consequently, the software requirements are both initially delayed and changed frequently during this time of subsystem design iteration. Unfortunately, to support integration of these same subsystems, portions of the software must be developed and ready at the time of functional integration of these components into the system. The net effect is that the software development must be initiated early enough to support the integration schedule, but runs the risk of major requirements changes if it starts before the system design has settled down sufficiently.

C. Communication Barriers

There exist real communication barriers among typical systems users/operators, hardware systems engineering personnel and software designers/programmers. With the growing application of computer technology into many realms of endeavors, it is not feasible for the average software designer to learn the language and technology of all the potential applications of his product. Conversely, the current explosion of hardware/software computer technology has made it impossible for anyone not continually involved in this arena to keep up with the terminology, let alone the full range of technical implications. Consequently, even though much progress has been made in the education of society in uses and applications of the computer [3], a continually growing communication gap exists among the key organizations needed to configure a major new system. With the increasing specialization required to cope with the complexities in all facets of both the applications and the data processing technology, a new breed of specialists is required who can bridge the gap between the other specialists. The problem with this "generalized" specialist is that his useful life (~5 years) in this role, before he is outdated by the disciplines he serves, is very short relative to the time it takes to gain the experience needed to perform in that role. Currently, the best approach to overcoming these communication barriers is the assembly of a team of systems engineers and data processing designers working together closely to perform the system functional analyses and to prepare the detailed software requirements specifications. As shown in Fig. 2, the systems engineers should take the lead during the functional analysis, and the software designers should direct the detail requirements definition activity. From these teams, hopefully, the "generalized" specialists of the future will emerge.

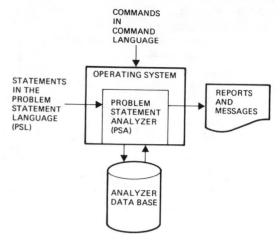

Fig. 3. PSL/PSA system [6].

D. Methodology

Until recently, methodologies for generation of software requirements have been quite informal. Requirements analyses using functional flow block diagrams, N^2-charts, processing flow analyses, and the like have been employed to understand the problem. In this mode, traditional manual free-form English language statements (i.e., the program shall . . .) are used to document the requirements. As Boehm [4] notes, these require virtually no training—but their ambiguity and lack of organization generally lead to serious problems with incompleteness, inconsistency, and misunderstanding among the people using them. While there are now other options available, manual specifications are still the overwhelming majority among forms of current specifications. Boehm [4] and Miller [5] describe four other categories of methodologies

1) forms based: special purpose forms are used to provide the basic structures of the specification;
2) automated assistance: automated interaction with the user is provided to help rapidly construct a specification that adheres to built-in consistency rules;
3) automated: integrated tools that help in generation and validation of complete and consistent specifications;
4) formal: specifications are expressed in a precise mathematical form, with both syntax and semantics rigorously defined.

Two major automated tools which have received probably the most usage the past few years are problem statement language (PSL)/problem statement analyzer (PSA) [6] and software requirements engineering methodology (SREM) [7]. PSL/PSA is a computer-aided structured documentation and analysis technique that was developed for analysis and documentation of requirements and preparation of functional processing specifications. As shown in Fig. 3, this system has the capability to describe an information system, record that description in a computerized data base, incrementally modify the data-base description and produce reports and documentation on the system. PSL expresses the system description in eight aspects: system input/output flow, system structure,

data structure, data derivation, system size, system dynamics, system properties, and project management. The software package PSA records this description in the data base, modifies it, performs analysis, and generates reports under direction of the user command language. PSL/PSA has continued to evolve and has added more powerful consistency and completeness checks, plus better user-oriented data entry and output reports.

SREM is a complete methodology for generation of software requirements for large real-time processing systems. As shown in Fig. 4, it employs a nomenclature called requirements networks (RNet's) to unambiguously represent all processing paths in a system while maintaining precedence/successor relationships but without imposing design constraints. It uses a formal requirements statement language (RSL) to reduce ambiguity and to facilitate the automation of the methodology. Automated tools, integrated into a requirements engineering and validation system (REVS) using RSL statements as input, check the requirements for completeness and consistency, maintain traceability to originating requirements and models and generate simulations to validate the correctness of the requirement. SREM has become available on a number of host computers and has been utilized on a number of defense, business, and distributed processing applications.

Several other tools such as SADT [8], SAMM [9], etc., are also in various stages of development and usage. The area of semiautomated and automated requirements generation tools represents one of the major accomplishments of software engineering in the last decade. Yet, at this time, the usage of these tools represents a very small percentage of their potential application. An obvious reason for this is their general lack of availability in many places and the time it takes to learn to use them effectively. Another reason, however, is that these tools generally require a data processing/computer science orientation. Yet, many of the large system software requirements activities are managed and staffed with system analysts/engineers who have relatively little of this orientation and often resist the learning required by these kinds of approaches. This resistance is somewhat akin to that experienced during the early days of structured programming, and a determined customer/management encouragement will probably be required for these tools to gain widespread acceptance.

E. Simulation

Simulation has been used for several years now in the requirements specification process to bring quantification and preci-

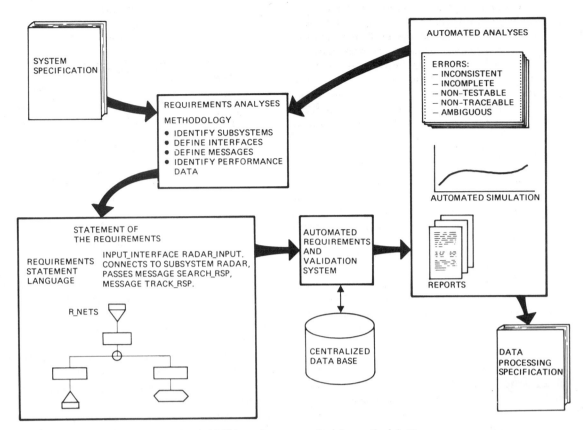

Fig. 4. SREM requirements engineering methodology.

sion to the statement of performance requirements. However, experience has shown that simulation is just as likely to be improperly used as it is to be used effectively. Some questions which should be asked when deciding whether to employ simulation are the following.

1) Is the problem supportive of simulation? Systems which are essentially open loop, steady state, or deterministic in nature rarely require simulation to accurately define their performance characteristics. Conversely, closed-loop nonlinear systems or systems requiring rapid response to step events often do require modeling to adequately define their performance parameters. In particular, systems requiring responses to certain stimuli within a small time factor (<10) to the average module dispatch time or running time will usually require fairly detailed modeling of the data-processing hardware and software process.

2) Is there adequate schedule, cost, and data available to model the system to the required fidelity? This is probably the single area where most simulation efforts run into trouble. There is always a level of fidelity below which the simulation is essentially worthless for the task it is being called to do. Yet, frequently, there is either insufficient cost/schedule available to build the simulation or there is insufficient data on the system or environment to model it to the level of detail necessary. In either case, it is prudent to take a hard look at whether any simulation work should be performed, or whether simpler analytic techniques could achieve essentially equivalent results.

3) Is the system design stabilized sufficiently for simulation? Although simulation is frequently used in the requirements definition process, it is important to remember that it is design that must be modeled—not requirements, *per se*. If a system requires modeling in great detail to achieve the required simulation fidelity, then changes to that system design will be dev-

astating to the simulation effort. In these cases, the simulation often cannot be done in sufficient time to be useful to the requirements definition process, and again a simpler means of obtaining performance parameters must be utilized.

If the answer to all three of these questions is yes, then simulation is usually the best means to obtain precise, quantifiable system/software performance parameters. To obtain the data necessary to define data-processing requirements (e.g., timing, instruction rates, throughput, etc.) usually will require a functional (e.g., event driven) simulation of the data-processing hardware and software, an accurate representation of the process control algorithms, and a realistic model of the external input–output environment.

III. COSTING

Software cost estimating is, at best, an imprecise art. Estimates are generally clouded by questions of instruction counts and complexity factors, and universally not believed.

Why are software cost estimates generally considered to be consistently poor? In most endeavors, the first time through a new experience is typically a time of difficulty and error. To improve one's probability of success, generally a period of intense planning, preliminary design and laboratory breadboarding is spent. Few building contractors would bid on a house without a set of plans showing the size, material, and layout required. Rarely is a new piece of engineering hardware (whether a jet engine or an electronic communications set) costed without a significant research and development effort which scopes the magnitude, performance, and environment of the equipment. Yet, major software procurements frequently occur without any research or even meaningful preliminary design of the products to be developed.

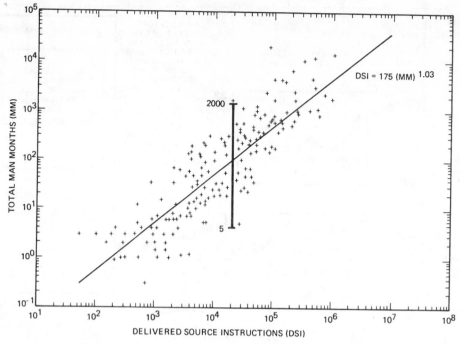

Fig. 5. Correlation of software effort with number of instructions.

A principal reason for this is that a customer or system designer can usually specify a few performance parameters (e.g., radar range, pulse rate, frequency, signal-to-noise, etc.) to characterize a piece of hardware sufficient for a hardware designer to design, scope and bid the equipment. For software, no such parameters currently exist. Software can only be characterized by the detailed functions it must perform to carry out the requirements of the system, and often these must all be specified by the system designer. Frequently major systems are defined and bid before the detailed functional sequences of these systems are specified. Consequently, the software estimates for these systems reflect the lack of design definition necessary for accuracy.

Costing of software is further complicated by the metrics involved. (See Curtis [35], this issue.) RADC [10] has shown that the number of machine instructions provides the best single correlation with program cost (Fig. 5). Yet, even from this data, errors of almost 1000:1 are possible using only this factor as an estimator. Thus it becomes necessary to include such qualitative factors as complexity, requirements volatility, experience, etc., to get a better picture of the true potential cost. This is in sharp contrast to most hardware developments where a few simpler metrics (e.g., numbers of components, drawers, etc.) can usually estimate the effort to a reasonable degree.

Unfortunately, even knowing the factors involved does not guarantee a credible estimate since both the relative value of a given factor and the sensitivity of a particular job to that factor must also be estimated. Several efforts have been made over the past fifteen years to quantify these factors and sensitivities in a form that can be related to a particular software task. Two models which are being maintained and updated are the RCA PRICE-S [11] and TRW SCEP [12]. Although most previous cost models have been generated by curve-fitting cost data from previous developments, both PRICE-S and SCEP attempt to construct the estimate by accounting for the effect of each sensitivity and factor and combining these into a total estimate. Both models have used previous developments for validation and refinement.

PRICE-S uses 42 representative factors (Fig. 6) to represent the software development environment. The principal inputs to the model are grouped into 7 categories

1) project magnitude—how much code to be produced;
2) program application—type of project (e.g., MIS, C^2, etc.);
3) level of new design and code—not available from existing inventory;
4) resources-experience/skill level of developers;
5) hardware limitations—timing/memory constraints;
6) customer specifications and reliability requirements—measure of reliability, testing and documentation required;
7) development environment—what complicating factors exist.

The basic metric for project magnitude is number of delivered executable machine instructions (DEMI's) to be developed. Program application is the model's approach to provide weights for the relative difficulty of different types of software (from 11.0 for operating systems to 0.9 for routine mathematical operations). Organizational capabilities and experience, including labor categories, productivity rates, computer operations, etc., are modeled by the resources variable. Other complexity parameters can be accounted for under development environment, where special factors such as parallel hardware developments, new languages, highly changing requirements, etc., may be addressed.

RCA PRICE-S is a supported model, accessed on commercial time sharing computers and available under monthly leasing agreements. Another similar commercial software cost estimation model is the Putman SLIM model [13].

TRW software cost estimating program (SCEP) is a model which uses 16 factors to encompass the cost estimating range. These are grouped into

1) program size—number of DEMI's and data items;
2) program attributes—complexity, type, language;
3) hardware attributes—storage/timing constraints, concurrent hardware developments;

PROJECT SIZE
PROJECT TYPE (MIS, RADAR,
   TELEMETRY, ETC.)
OPERATIONAL CUSTOMER ENVIRONMENT
HARDWARE CONSTRAINTS (SYSTEM LOADING)
EXISTING DESIGN
EXISTING CODE
EXTERNAL INTERFACES (TYPE AND
   QUANTITY)
HIERARCHICAL DESIGN FUNCTIONAL
   FLOW STRUCTURE
NUMBER OF FUNCTIONS PERFORMED
AMOUNT OF CODE PER FUNCTION
SCHEDULE CONSTRAINTS, LEAD TIMES
   AND OVERLAPS
RESOURCE CONSTRAINTS
ECN EFFECTS
ECONOMIC TRENDS
TECHNOLOGY GROWTH
FEE, PROFIT, AND G & A
COMPUTER OPERATION COSTS
OVERHEAD
ORGANIZATIONAL EFFICIENCY
SKILLS
PROJECT FAMILIARITY

INTENSITY OF EFFORT
CHANGING REQUIREMENTS
PROGRAMMING LANGUAGE
COMPILER POWER AND EFFICIENCY
DEVELOPMENT LOCATION
   (IN-HOUSE OR ON-SITE)
PROJECT COMPLEXITY
ENGINEERING REQUIREMENTS
PROGRAMMING REQUIREMENTS
CONFIGURATION CONTROL
DOCUMENTATION
PROGRAM MANAGEMENT
DESIGN PHASE ACTIVITIES
IMPLEMENTATION ACTIVITIES
TEST AND INTEGRATION ACTIVITIES
INTEGRATION AND INDEPENDENT PROJECTS
VERIFICATION AND VALIDATION
MULTIPLE TEST BEDS INSTALLATIONS
GOVERNMENT FURNISHED SOFTWARE
PURCHASED SOFTWARE (E.G., SUBCONTRACTS)
DESIGN-TO-COST
RESOURCE ALLOCATION WITH RESPECT TO
   TIME

Fig. 6. Factors accounted for by price S.

FACTOR	RATING	RQTS. ANALYSES	PRELIM. DESIGN	DETAIL DESIGN	CODE & UNIT TEST	INTEG. & TEST
1. REQUIRED QUALITY	VERY LOW	• LITTLE DETAIL • MANY TBD'S • LITTLE VALID'N • MINIMAL PLANS (QA, CM, ACCEPT.) • MINIMAL SRR	• LITTLE DETAIL • MANY TBD'S • LITTLE VERIF'N • MINIMAL QA, CM, STDS. • MINIMAL PDR • NO DRAFT USER MAN.	• BASIC DESIGN INFO. • MINIMAL UDF'S • MINIMAL QA, CM • MINIMAL CDR • NO DRAFT USER MAN.	• MINIMAL U.T. PLAN • MINIMAL FCL'S, PATH TEST, STDS CHECK • MINIMAL QA, CM • MINIMAL I/O AND OFF-NOMINAL TESTS • MINIMAL USER MAN.	• MINIMAL TEST PLANS • NO TEST PROCEDURES • MANY RQTS, UNTESTED • MINIMAL QA, CM • MINIMAL STRESS, OFF-NOMINAL TESTS • MINIMAL AS-BUILT DOC'N
	LOW	• BASIC INFO. VALID'N • FREQUENT TBD'S • BASIC PLANS (QA, CM, ACCEPT.) • BASIC SRR	• BASIC INFO. VERIF'N • FREQUENT TBD'S • BASIC QA, CM, STDS • BASIC PDR • MINIMAL USER MAN.	• MODERATE DETAIL • BASIC UDF'S, PA, CM, CDR • MINIMAL USER MAN.	• BASIC U.T. PLAN • PARTIAL FCL'S, PATH TEST, STDS CHECK • BASIC QA, CM, U.M. • PARTIAL I/O AND OFF-NOMINAL TESTS	• BASIC TEST PLANS • MINIMAL TEST PROCED. • FREQUENT RQTS UNTESTED • BASIC QA, CM, U.M. • PARTIAL STRESS, OFF-NOMINAL TESTS
	AVG.	FULL TRW POLICIES	FULL TRW POLICIES	FULL TRW POLICIES	FULL TRW POLICIES	FULL TRW POLICIES
	HIGH	• DETAILED VALID'N PLANS, SRR	• DETAILED VERIF'N, QA, CM, STDS, PDR, DOC'N	• DETAILED VERIF'N, QA, CM, STDS, CDR DOC'N	• DETAILED U.T. PLAN, FCL'S, QA, CM, DOC'N CODE WALK THRUS • EXTENSIVE OFF-NOMINAL TESTS	• DETAILED TEST PLANS, PROCEDURES, QA, CM, DOC'N • EXTENSIVE STRESS, OFF-NOMINAL TESTS
	VERY HIGH	• DETAILED VALID'N, PLANS, SRR • IV&V INTERFACE (SUPPORT, RESPONSE)	• DETAILED VERIF'N, QA, CM, STDS, PDR, DOC'N • IV&V INTERFACE	• DETAILED VERIF'N, QA, CM, STDS, CDR, DOC'N • IV&V INTERFACE	• DETAILED U.T. PLAN, (FCL'S, QA, CM, DOC'N) CODE WALK-THRUS • VERY EXTENSIVE OFF-NOMINAL TESTS • IV&V INTERFACE	• VERY DETAILED TEST PLANS, PROC'S, QA, CM, DOC'N • VERY EXTENSIVE STRESS, OFF-NOMINAL TESTS • IV&V INTERFACE

Fig. 7. Example of factor/rating definitions: TRW SCEP model.

4) project attributes—personnel quality, experience;
5) environmental attributes—requirements volatility, required quality, computer access.

A major thrust of the SCEP model was to define subjective parameters (e.g., complexity, required quality) in terms relatable to the problem being solved. Fig. 7 shows an example of the different rating values for required quality. In this table, quality is defined relative to "full TRW policies." This rating refers to a standard set of policies for TRW software development projects, which provide another foundation block for

reliable software cost estimation. As in PRICE-S, the principal metric for SCEP is the number of DEMI's to be developed. The fidelity of the model was demonstrated by comparisons with twenty completed projects (see Fig. 8) and this validation is continuing as further project completion data is made available.

The principal considerations for someone using these or similar models for costing are: ability to accurately estimate program size, ability to define the project environment and characteristics (e.g., personnel quality, requirements volatility, relative complexity, etc.) and the ability of the model to accurately

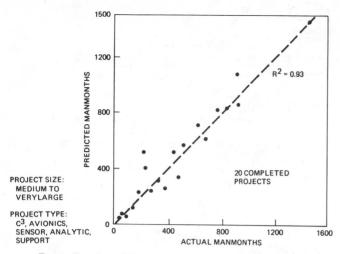

Fig. 8. Example of TRW software cost model performance.

estimate the cost. For a new development, errors in estimating program size of 100 percent are not unusual. Unless the program requirements are reasonably stable and a thorough preliminary design is performed (to a level where either algorithms can be scoped or unit sizes compared with previous experiences), the likelihood of significantly misestimating program size is quite high. One's ability to accurately assess the program environment will vary greatly from project to project. For an environment where the requirements are available or self-generated, the programming team defined and in place, and the task homogeneous and well understood, the environment should be readily defined. Many business systems projects fit this description. The opposite end of the spectrum would be a large new tactical command and control system where the man–machine interface and operational algorithms are only vaguely understood, the processor capacity limited by size/weight considerations, and a large increase of staff necessary to obtain the needed development personnel. For this latter class of projects, it will be necessary to continue the estimating process well into the development itself until many of the parameters have settled down. For many projects, it may be as late as the software preliminary design review (PDR) before an accurate assessment can be made. However, it is usually better to recognize the budget problems that exist at this time (before the main project expenditures are committed) then to jump into the main development effort unaware of the potential cost implications.

IV. Productivity

Techniques for obtaining the large software productivity improvements needed to meet the data processing demands of the 1980's are neither currently available nor even on the near horizon.

During the last decade, the industry experienced continually increasing productivity, primarily through the use of higher order languages and software implementation/test tools and the employment of modern programming practices. Estimates on the long-term productivity improvement rate of programmers range from 3 to 7 percent/year [14]–[16]. While this is not without merit, the demands of the 1980's is for 10, 50, or 100:1 improvement [1]. This demand for order of magnitude improvements is being driven by three forces: the advent of complex "super systems" created by netting of multiple distrib-

uted systems, the scarcity of trained software personnel, and the explosive growth of the computer hardware/microprocessor industry which has put data processing hardware within the cost reach of most organizations.

It can be said that the software industry has managed to automate virtually every field except its own. In fact, Tanaka [16] sees information processing becoming the most labor intensive of all industries by 1985 if better methods are not employed.

The greatest likelihood for obtaining substantial productivity improvements lies in better automated tooling for the software designer just as computer aided design/manufacturing (CAD/ CAM) has significantly improved the productivity of hardware designers. The techniques most commonly discussed are the software production facility, libraries of primitives, new applications-oriented languages, integrated systems of development tools, etc. A problem with most of these approaches is that they focus on the implementation phase of the development, while much of the software cost and schedule is embedded in the requirements, design, and system test phases. Further research to tie requirements methodologies, design languages, and automated test generation/verification tools, together with the implementation tools will be necessary before the degrees of desired improvements can be approached.

An example of a specialized computing facility dedicated to support large software development projects is the programmers's workbench (PWB) [17] in use at Bell Laboratories. The PWB is based on the concept that program development and execution of the resulting programs are two radically different functions, and much can be gained by assigning each function to a computer best suited for it. The software development is done on a PWB computer dedicated to that task, while execution occurs on another computer—the "target" machine. Thus the PWB presents a single uniform interface to its users, even though it may be supporting several target systems. The Bell Labs PWB is currently implemented on a network of PDP-11's operating under the UNIX time-sharing systems. Some capabilities of the PWB are

1) convenient interactive computing services;
2) a file structure oriented to interactive use;
3) a set of tools for scanning and editing text files;
4) a flexible command language;
5) extensive document preparation facilities;
6) facilities to support small data base management problems.

The PWB is a reasonably good example of a program production facility which generally features interactive programming, automated tools and word processing. The range of possibilities for such a facility (Fig. 9) is a function of the tooling provided. This can range from a few text editing capabilities to a complete set of development, test, quality assurance, and configuration management tools to a set of tools plus an entire library of primitives which can be called and inserted into a program via the interactive programming features. The key to gaining significant productivity improvements from these techniques is the provision of those tools and primitives which the users are familiar with and believe are useful. This generally means starting the production facility simply, with the interactive features, and a few well chosen tools. Then additions to the tooling can be made as the demand for them increases (i.e., when the users become comfortable with the environment). This will also serve to spread out the capital investments needed to furnish this kind of a facility.

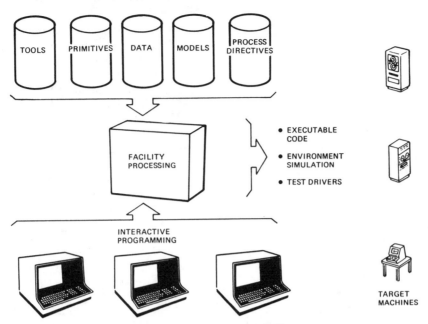

Fig. 9. Program production facility.

PAGE	DOCUMENT	SPECIFICATION PARAGRAPH	DESIGN SOLUTION			CHANGE STATUS	TEST PROCEDURE ALLOCATION			NOTES
			FUNCT-ION	TASK	ROUTINE		UNIT	SUB-SYSTEM	SYSTEM	
153	SPEC. #1439765	3.2.2.1.3.4.2.1a	JBCR1	TRQ1	R173 R174				SP 2110	
153	SPEC. #1439765	3.2.2.1.3.4.2.1b	JBCR1	TRQ1	R173	ECP #49	173-6			*MAY BE IMPACTED BY ECP #84a
153	SPEC. #1439765	3.2.2.1.3.4.2.2	JBCR1	TRQ1	R194 R195			IP 1003		
154	SPEC. #1439765	3.2.2.1.3.4.2.3a	JBCR1	TRQ1	R173	ECP #49			SP 2110	
154	SPEC. #1439765	3.2.2.1.3.4.2.3b	JBCR1	TRQ2 TBR3	R265 R397			IP 1003		
155	SPEC. #1439765	3.2.2.1.3.5	JBD	TCB	R541	ECP #49	541-3			
155	SPEC. #1439765	3.2.2.1.3.5.1	JBD	TCB	R541	ECP #49	541-7			
155	SPEC. #1493765	3.2.2.1.3.5.1.1a	JBD	TCB	R547 R552 R539				SP 2479	
156	SPEC. #1439765	3.2.2.1.3.5.1.2a	JBD	TCC	R012 R438	ECP #12		IP 1123		*SEE ICD #43179
156	SPEC. #1439765	3.2.2.1.3.5.1.2b	JBD	TCC	R012 R823	ECP #12		IP 1123		*SEE ICD #43179
156	SPEC. #1439765	3.2.2.1.3.5.2	JBDA	TCC	R019 R051 R018	ECP #12		IP 1124		
157	SPEC. #1439765	3.2.2.1.3.5.3.d	JBDA	TAC2	R043 R047				SP 2217	
158	SPEC. #1439765	3.2.2.1.3.5.3.a	JBDA	TAC1	R049		49-4 49-5			*REFERENCE DPR-AC1
159	SPEC. #1439765	3.2.2.1.3.5.3.3	JBDA	TAJS	R691			IP 1271		
159	SPEC. #1439765	3.2.2.1.3.5.4	JBDA	TAJS TQJ3	R692 R247 R248 R249			IP 1271		

Fig. 10. Example of requirements tracebility matrix.

V. CONTROL

The key to effective control is to break up the development into a number of small measurable steps and then to rigorously audit the satisfactory completion of those steps.

The 1970's are noted for the introduction of several excellent approaches for bringing order into the software development process. The initial work which started this trend was the structured programming/top-down design concepts presented by Dijkstra [18]. Many others have since contributed elements of these approaches, generally referred to as "modern programming practices." This paper would like to discuss some of these techniques, which are believed necessary for controlling the development of the large software based systems of the 1980's.

A. Requirements Traceability

While it is often most difficult to obtain an adequate requirements specification for a large operational real-time system, it is mandatory that once obtained, those requirements be controlled, mapped to the design, and verified in some formal auditable fashion, in order to have any measure of confidence that the product will meet the intent for which it is being developed. While this is relatively straightforward for small

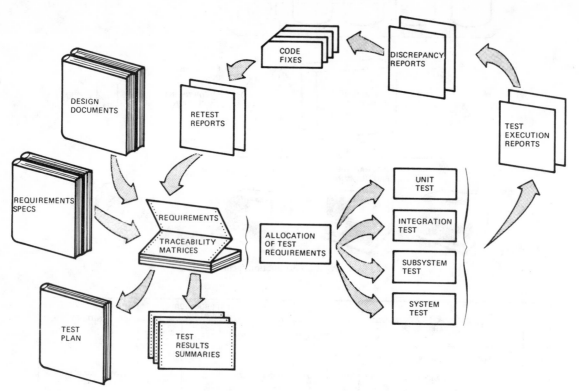

Fig. 11. Requirements tracebility process.

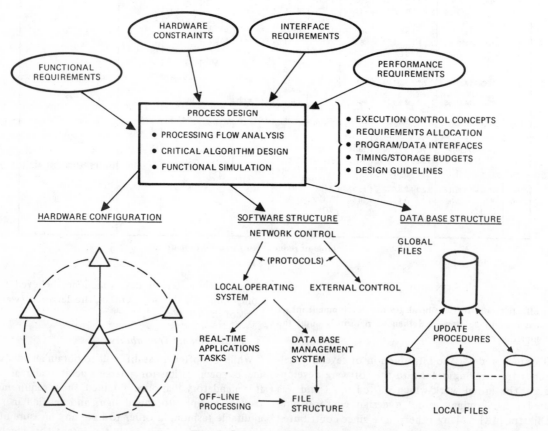

Fig. 12. Process design approach.

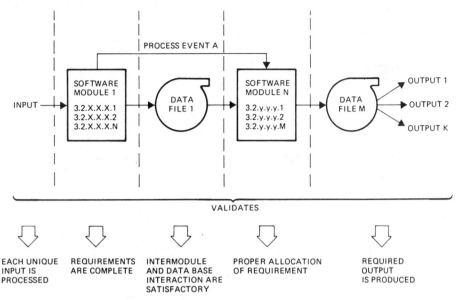

Fig. 13. Mapping of system inputs—requirements—outputs.

projects, it is often a major consideration for large projects with thousands of requirements, many of which are undergoing significant change throughout the development. To control this process, it is advisable to maintain a record for each requirement showing its origin, change status, design allocation, test allocation, verification method, and authority. The origin of an individual requirement can range from a uniquely identified paragraph in a requirements specification to an element in a table of an interface control document. It is mandatory to collect each real requirement (whatever its source), give it a unique identification (usually referenced to source document, paragraph, section, etc.) and establish a control record for it which is maintained throughout the project. Fig. 10 shows an example of the type of information needed in this process. In [19], Krause and Diamant discuss a specific tool to perform this task which was used successfully to control and monitor the testing of a program with over 10 000 requirements.

As shown in Fig. 11, the key elements in successfully tracking the requirements allocation and testing process are to

1) uniquely identify every individual processing requirement (including subparagraphs or sections);
2) allocate design solution to lowest level(s) possible;
3) maintain status of latest authority governing that requirement (specification, interface document, change notice, etc.);
4) allocate verification of that requirement to specific test procedure (at either unit, subsystem or system level);
5) maintain record of test/retest results;
6) continuously audit the process to be sure all data is up to date.

B. Process Design

The concept of process design grew out of the ballistic missile defense processing requirement for large scale, high reliability, ultra-high-speed real-time processing of complex algorithms, and the associated need to have some assurance that the problem was solvable during the early stages of the major development. Davis and Vick [20], Gaulding and Lawson [21], Dreyfus and Karacsony [22] have each discussed different aspects of the approach. Yeh and Zave [36] present a view of process specification from the perspective of software requirements generation. The purpose of process design is to iterate the system requirements, hardware/software architecture, and data-base structure to evolve a baseline hardware configuration and software design structure. The tools of process design are processing flow analysis, functional simulation and critical algorithm design/benchmarking. Fig. 12 depicts the basic engineering approach. Conceptually, process design considers a real-time system as a set of transformations on the system stimuli to produce the proper system responses. These transformations may initially be represented in any of several different forms (RNet's, threads, Petri-net, etc.) but must eventually provide a direct mapping which shows how the allocated processing requirements operate on the system inputs to provide both the proper external outputs and internal state changes (see Fig. 13). Critical algorithm benchmarking is used to "size" (timing, memory) those key functions which have large uncertainties associated with them. Functional simulation is used to model the entire process, aid in iterating the potential design solutions, and then to test the baseline structure to demonstrate its predicted performance under varying loads and external environments.

C. Incremental Development

The purpose of incremental development (Fig. 14) is to reduce risk in the project by obtaining an early determination of the performance of key tools, procedures and software. Williams [23] discusses the need to "hear the process talk" many months before a complete set of capabilities would otherwise be available. The partitioning of a software implementation can significantly affect the entire system development process and needs to be considered as a fundamental step in the initial scheduling of a program. Some of the key factors which should be considered in defining an incremental development approach are as follows.

1) Preliminary design of the entire software package must be completed before initiation of any incremental development activity. Each increment must proceed in a straightforward manner from the preliminary design structure. Budgets for timing, storage, accuracy, etc., allocated at preliminary design must be rigorously adhered to and demonstrated in

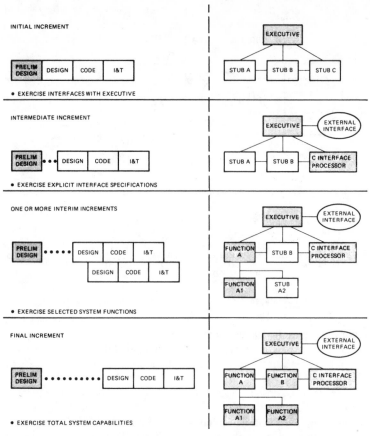

Fig. 14. Incremental development and top-down integration.

each increment, so that late increments do not have to "make-up" for the lack of control of earlier increments.

2) Functional capabilities which are well defined but considered high risk should be developed early.

3) System capabilities which are poorly defined or likely to change should be implemented as late as possible. This includes software functions supporting other subsystems which themselves are undergoing change.

4) Organize increments to minimize breakage. Where possible include complete functions with clear interface delineations.

McGowan [24] suggests that for large projects the following 4 increments should be provided in the indicated order.

1) "An *initial* increment to exercise all interfaces with executive software." This can be done using a "dummy" or "stub" version of the applications code to execute the operating system features in a realistic environment.

2) "An *intermediate* increment to exercise explicit interface specifications." This is exceptionally valuable when the software system must interface with newly built hardware or nonstandard interface protocols. Most interface bugs can usually be worked out during this increment.

3) One or more "*interim* increments to exercise selected system functions." This is where function selection based on potential requirements or software breakage should be carefully addressed.

4) "A *final* increment to exercise total system functions." By this time most of the system capabilities will have been demonstrated. Therefore, this increment can focus on demonstrating system performance under varying environments and loads.

As seen, top-down integration is readily served by incremental development, as the process can evolve from a first increment consisting of an operating system plus "dummy" application programs (i.e., application modules represented by stubs simulating the module interfaces) to a set of module control routines with either stubs or real functional software (depending on the specific increment) supporting them to a final capability where all stubs are replaced by operational software.

D. Structured Development

In early 1970's, Baker [25], Mills [26], Brooks [27] and others, reporting on the lessons learned at IBM, presented a software development methodology which included the concepts on top-down design, chief programmer teams, structured programming, and the like. These concepts received widespread acclaim in the literature, but did not as readily become accepted practices within the industry. Although a 1977 study by Holton [28] implied a lack of the widespread usage of these approaches at that time, Munson [2] demonstrated at a 1979 workshop on software management that at least most aerospace and defense system contractors now use some version of these practices as a matter of policy. A brief summary of the key concepts is given below.

Chief Programmer Team: A team of 4–8 software developers consisting of a chief programmer, backup programmer, librarian, and task programmers. The chief programmer is the team leader who is responsible for both the development of critical modules and the review of noncritical modules assigned to the task programmers. The backup programmer is also a senior programmer who supports the development of critical modules and is available to take over as chief programmer, if required.

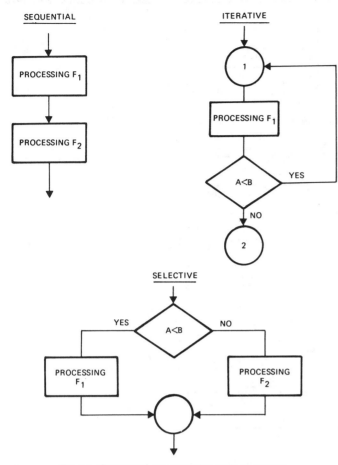

SEQUENTIAL

PROCESSING F$_1$

PROCESSING F$_2$

ITERATIVE

1

PROCESSING F$_1$

A<B — YES

NO

2

SELECTIVE

YES — A<B — NO

PROCESSING F$_1$

PROCESSING F$_2$

Fig. 15. Structured programming basic constructs.

The librarian maintains the support processes for updating code libraries and test data libraries, supports program compilation, binding and execution, and maintains status on program discrepancies and fixes.

Top-Down Design: Following allocation of requirements to individual modules, the system is further decomposed in a series of steps starting from the module control level to a set of simpler and simpler functions until the lowest level routines are defined. Program design and coding is then started at the top level. Testing occurs with stubs for lower level routines. The "stubs" are then replaced as each lower level routine is completed. Top-down integration proceeds similarly.

Structured Design: This approach enhances the modularity of a system by providing techniques for dividing large programs into modules. It provides a methodology for decomposition of a system into independent modules, such that changes to any given module will have minimal effect on other modules of the system.

Structured Programming: This concept serves to define a system by programs having only single points of entry and exit. This is accomplished by virtual elimination of branching statements, or conversely, by limitation of program constructs to sequential, iterative (DO-UNTIL), and selective (IF-THEN-ELSE) structures (Fig. 15). This process eliminates the source of many programming errors, provides a formal mechanism for reducing individual routine size to less than a single page of listing (thus complementing program modularity), and eliminates the possibility of generating complicated hard-to-understand (and debug) "spaghetti" code. This technique is usually implemented along with source listing logic indentation to improve readability. By expanding this concept into design language or flowcharts, every system can be represented by a series of one-page descriptions with single entry and exit.

Design Walk Through: This walk through is a peer-level design review with the emphasis on program error detection. It is conceptually a low-key nondefensive review where the participants work to help the reviewer find potential errors in the design and code. There has been much discussion on whether management could or should attend. The quality and intensity of the review is potentially higher with some management attendance—but the thrust of the review must still be to find errors, not to impress the boss. Thus any management participation must be limited to those capable of understanding and contributing to the detail review process.

E. Software Design Language

The application of tools to allow English-like languages to be used in designing and documenting software is becoming more widespread. One such automated tool is the program design language (PDL) of Caine *et al.* [29]. A design in PDL is written in structured English for processing by the PDL processor. The processor generates design documents which include formatted sequence listings, program calls and call cross references. The PDL output can be formatted so as to remove the need for separate program flowcharts. Updates are accommodated by changes to the structured English input.

PDL is commercially available and is currently supported on a number of different computers.

F. Unit Development Folders

Most software organizations use some sort of project notebook, development workbook, design folder, etc., to collect and maintain the multiplicity of data generated during a large development project. One of the most effective devices of this kind is the unit development folder (UDF) described by Ingrassia [30]. The UDF is a notebook associated with each unit of software in a development project. The notebook is organized by sections (shown in Fig. 16) and provides a uniform collection point for all documentation and code associated with that unit. The principle features of the UDF that differentiate it from many of the other notebooks are

1) it is both a working document and an audited controlled document;
2) it provides management with detailed visibility into the progress and performance of each unit on the project;
3) it aids individual discipline in the establishment and attainment of scheduled milestones;
4) it provides a consistent project-wide approach for unit development and status assessment;
5) it produces the deliverable documentation associated with a given unit or an as-you-go basis.

The UDF is "opened" upon allocation of specific requirements to units, usually at the completion of preliminary design. A unit can be any level of software from a routine to a collection of routines (performing a specific function) which can be developed by one individual. Upon initiation, the responsible manager or chief programmer assigns the allocated requirements and establishes the date for completion of testing for this unit in accordance with the project schedule. These are recorded on the UDF cover sheet (Fig. 17). The assigned programmer then defines his own intermediary milestones and initiates the design activity. When each section is completed,

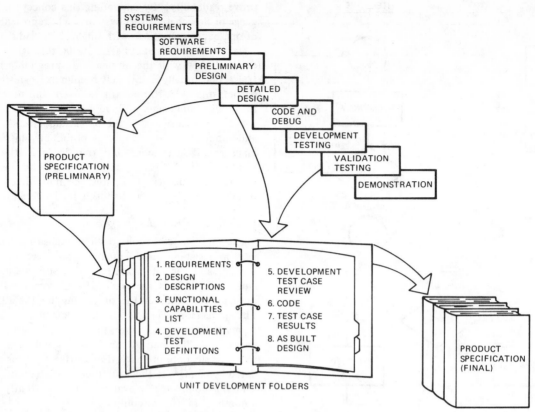

Fig. 16. Unit development folder organization.

the responsible designer signs and dates the section. The review authority (manager, chief programmer, or other reviewers) then reviews the section for completeness and accuracy and approves it. Thus each unit is reviewed frequently for adequacy of development and progress. Additionally, each UDF is continually accounted for and maintained in a location accessible by quality assurance personnel for standards compliance auditing as well as other designers for interface review. The as-built design description is maintained in the exact format specified for delivery to the customer. Thus the large majority of the deliverable documentation is made available by copying that section from all UDF's on the project. A separate "notes" section may be kept with the UDF to record memos, analyses, or other pertinent data relative to that unit.

G. Quality Assurance/Configuration Management

Quality assurance (QA)/configuration management (CM) play an important role for the software project manager in the auditing of on-going activities, status accounting of configured items and change specifications. The QA manager acts as the project manager's "hired gun" to verify that standards are adhered to, procedures are followed, documentation is kept up to date, etc. Generally, well-defined logical standards, rigorously enforced, are well accepted by most programmers. An excellent approach for accomplishing this is to automate as much of the audit as possible. Code standards, structured programming rules, commentary requirements, etc., are readily amenable to automated verification. Often programmers will use these tools themselves during development to assure their passing of the audit at code turnover. At this time, documentation must still be manually audited; however, use of the UDF allows much of this audit to be done during the develop-

ment, rather then all just prior to documentation release. The role of configuration management is to maintain the current status of all configured items and documentation. For a large project, a requirements or interface change can have a significant ripple effect through much of the remaining documentation and code releases. Controlled updating of both upon incorporation of changes is mandatory for software development sanity. Inevitably, however, it will be necessary to get some "fix" incorporated before all the paperwork reviews and approval are complete. A streamlined quick fix procedure which provides fast test turnaround is mandatory to avoid having the project wrapped up in its own paper. However, this must be done within the framework of a release-based CM system; it must provide a mechanism for identification of all changes (quick or permanent) attached to a released baseline; and it must facilitate the incorporation (or replacement) of the "quick" fix as a permanent, fully documented change.

H. Life-Cycle Maintenance

As the investment in large software systems continues at its exponentially increasing rate, the interest in maintaining these systems at reasonable costs is also increasing. In a recent survey, Lientz–Swanson [31] showed that for business data-processing systems maintenance costs now exceed development costs. DeRoze [32] estimated in 1976 that 60–70 percent of the Department of Defense software dollars are being spent after the software has been tested and delivered by the development contractor. According to Swanson [33], maintenance resources are generally applied to three classes of efforts: corrective—correction of latent problems; perfective—program/ documentation improvements; and adaptive—changes to the

MNEMONIC ___TFAST___   CUSTODIAN ___Bradley___

SECTION NO.	DESCRIPTION	DUE DATE	DATE COMPLETED	ORIGINATOR	REVIEWER/ DATE
1	REQUIREMENTS	14 Nov 1975	12-23-75 RMB	Bradley	Norman Ŋ.N. 1/7/76
2	DESIGN DESCRIPTION INITIAL: CODE TO:	19 Dec 1975	12-29-75 RMB	Bradley	Norman Ŋ.N. 1/7/76
3	FUNCTIONAL CAPABILITIES LIST	19 Dec 1975	12-23-75 RMB	Bradley	Norman JN. 1/7/76
4	DEVELOPMENT TEST DEFINITIONS	29 Dec 1975	1-22-76 RMB	Norman 1-22-76 Jjm	Bradley 1-22-76
5	DEVELOPMENT TEST CASE REVIEW	6 Jan 1976	2-16-76	Bradley	Norman Jjm 2-16-76
6	UNIT CODE	9 Jan 76 / 12 Mar 76	1-16-76 RMB / 3-1-76	Bradley / Bradley	1-23-76 Jjm / Norman 3-8-76 Jjm
7	TEST CASE RESULTS	2 Feb 1976	2-4-76 RMB	Judson	Norman 2-11-76 Jjm
8	AS BUILT DETAIL DESIGN DESCRIPTION	9 Feb 1976	3-1-76 Jjm	Bradley	Norman 3-8-76 Jjm

Fig. 17. Unit development folder cover sheet.

environment. Unlike hardware components, software repair is a relatively small part of the maintenance activity. According to the Lientz-Swanson survey, maintenance efforts were roughly distributed as follows:

1) correction of problems—22 percent;
2) Program/documentation improvements—51 percent;
3) changes to data, files, and environment—27 percent.

Consequently, unlike hardware, improving software reliability will not, of itself, drastically reduce software maintenance costs. Munson [34] provides some practical guidelines for consideration of life-cycle problems during the requirements and development activities. Some further thoughts for dealing with each of the classes of maintenance efforts are

Corrective:
1) test every branch and instruction during unit testing;
2) track and verify the demonstration of all requirements during some level of testing;
3) perform both nominal and stress testing whenever possible;
4) perform comprehensive regression tests after each significant change is incorporated.

Perfective:
1) many of these changes occur because the requirements specification was incomplete or unclear; look for potential holes in the specification;
2) provide feedback to the user as early as possible during development as to the capabilities and interface he will have with the systems; enhancements are frequently needed in the user interface area.

Adaptive:
1) build maintainable code; use coding and documentation standards, such as structured programming, to facilitate a maintenance programmer easily following the logic of the developed program;
2) build modular code; simplify interfaces; limit code and data interface functions to control routines;

3) keep documentation up to date; do not allow a new code release into the system until all documentation is complete;
4) maintain the same level of control on the data base as on the code; Use automated, centralized control whenever possible.

VI. DIRECTIONS

The software industry is currently experiencing unparallelled growth, recognition and influence, but there are some worried concerns on how the train can be kept "on track."

As the 1970's were completed, the software industry could rightly point to having overcome many of the problems headlined the decade before. Many large projects are being completed on schedule and within cost; a methodology for controlling large developments is being employed in many places; and reliable cost models are being demonstrated and validated. Although examples to the contrary still abound, it is realistically possible today to estimate, develop and field a large operational software system with a high probability of success. Certainly, overly ambitious estimates in a competitive environment, continually changing requirements, poor management, lack of qualified personnel, etc., can still undermine any project, but given reasonable development conditions, successful developments of monolithic systems should start becoming the norm. Unfortunately, the processing demands of the 1980's will not likely allow this utopian condition to last for long. Some of the areas which software managers should watch for in the 1980's include the following.

Requirements Definition: All of the requirements methodologies in the world cannot overcome a customer (user or system designer) who continually changes his specification. While many software users have become educated as to the penalties of this process, the rapid growth of data processing into new fields of endeavor only means more potential customers who will have to learn the price the hard way.

Distributed Processing: Many of the procedures and techniques established for monolithic systems are not readily transferable or upgradable to distributed systems. The multiplication of possible paths, problems of intraprocess timing and deadlock, synchronization of data bases, and nondeterminism of the programming problem provide several dimensions of new complexity to an already difficult problem. Yet, the real hardware cost savings available will drive the industry in this direction at a continually accelerating rate.

Microprocessing: The advent of the very low cost, high performance microcomputer is causing the introduction of digital processing modules in areas previously limited to electromechanical or other pure hardware solutions. In many ways, the lessons learned in the 1960's regarding the need for higher level languages, structured developments, integration principles, etc., are being relearned. It appears we have become so complacent with our newly gained methodologies and techniques that we cannot see many of the same old problems when they reappear in a slightly different form.

Personnel: The data-processing industry is growing at such an accelerated pace into areas of such increased complexity that the availability of trained personnel has been almost completely exceeded. While software development remains one of the most labor intensive of industries (with no real change in sight) the capability of meeting the continually growing processing demands of the 1980's is greatly threatened. Additionally, the increased complexity of most new systems makes lowering of the qualifications for personnel a virtual impossibility. Greatly increased research into means for significantly improving productivity and for simplifying the development processes is mandatory to keep from falling too far behind the demand.

Super Systems: Very large data systems are being configured and then linked with other large systems to create super-system networks to cope with the data problems (e.g., FET, communication, command, and control, etc.) in today's society. These systems, by their very size and nature, are beyond the scope of understanding of any person or team of persons. Yet, the data-processing industry must demonstrate a capability to rationally evolve this class of systems to provide the services demanded by society while respecting the concerns of society for privacy and protection against "big government/business."

Government Regulations: As software receives a higher and higher percentage of the costs of new systems, the attention it is receiving at all levels of government (e.g., House Government Operation Committee) is also increasing. The solution of government to this perceived "problem" is likely more regulation and standardization. While this is not necessarily bad (the industry itself is continually attempting to standardize on key approaches, languages, etc.), the potential effect of over-regulation at a time when innovation is required could be devastating. Recent studies have shown that one impact of the "Brooks Bill" has been to impede the acquisition by the government of new computing equipment. Similar impediments on software by imposition of overly detailed standards or auditing processes could create an environment which is not supportive of increased productivity.

VII. CONCLUSIONS

The field of software engineering and management is still very young as an engineering discipline. However, the rapid expansion of the data-processing industry will not allow a quiet time to grow and bring to maturity the technologies and practices needed to smoothly evolve the large systems of the future. The processes and techniques needed to guide future developments must be developed and proven themselves right along with the systems they are being used to support. The ideas and approaches presented in this paper represent a snapshot in time of some of the key principles evolved during the last decade. The complexity of the systems of the 1980's will require significant advancements in most of these approaches to keep pace with the demands for improved productivity while dealing with problems of increased dimensionality.

Ten years ago, no one would have predicted that the art of software engineering and management would have achieved its present state of maturity this soon. Consequently, this author is not going to predict that the ingenuity and intensity of effort needed to meet the challenges of the 1980's will not be forthcoming. However, it will not be a smooth and easy road.

REFERENCES

[1] J. R. Distaso, J. B. Munson, J. H. Manley, and L. G. Stucki, "Software technology—Key issues of the '80s," *Digest of Papers COMPCON '80*, Feb. 1980, pp. 387-389.
[2] J. B. Munson, "Lessons learned in the application of some modern programming practices," presented at the 1979 IEEE Lake Arrowhead Workshop, Lake Arrowhead, CA, Sept. 5-7, 1979.
[3] R. H. Austing and G. L. Engel, "Computers and society: Report of a workshop," in *Proc. COMPSAC '8*, pp. 801-813, Nov. 1978.
[4] B. W. Boehm, "Software engineering—As it is," in *Proc. 4th Int. Conf. Software Engineering*, pp. 11-21, Sept. 1979.
[5] E. Miller, "Tutorial: Automated tools for software engineering," in *Proc. COMPSAC 79*, pp. 29-31, Nov. 1979.
[6] D. Teichrow and E. A. Hershey III, "PSL/PSA: A computer-aided technique for structured documentation and analysis of information processing systems," *IEEE Trans. Software Eng.*, vol. SE-3, pp. 41-48, Jan. 1977.
[7] M. W. Alford, "A requirements engineering methodology for real-time processing requirements," *IEEE Trans. Software Eng.*, vol. SE-3, pp. 60-69, Jan. 1977.
[8] D. T. Ross and K. E. Scherman, Jr., "Structured analysis for requirements definition," *IEEE Trans. Software Eng.*, vol. SE-3, pp. 6-15, Jan. 1977.
[9] S. S. Lamb, V. G. Loch, L. J. Peters, and G. L. Smith, "SAMM: A modeling tool for requirements and design specifications," in *Proc. COMPSAC 78*, pp. 48-53, Nov. 1978.
[10] R. Nelson, "Software data collection and analysis," Draft Rep., RADC, Sept. 1978.
[11] F. R. Freiman and R. E. Park, "PRICE software model—Version 3, and overview," in *Proc. Workshop Quantitative Software Models*, pp. 32-41, Oct. 1979.
[12] B. W. Boehm and R. W. Wolverton, "Software cost modeling: Some lessons learned," in *Proc. 2nd Software Life Cycle Management Workshop*, pp. 129-132, Aug. 1978.
[13] L. H. Putnam and A. Fitzsimmons, "Estimating software costs," *Datamation*, Sept.-Nov. 1979.
[14] W. Myers, "The need for software engineering," *Comput.*, Feb. 1978.
[15] J. M. Henson, "Computer Applications: Applications, trends, and directions," presented at *COMPCON Fall 77*, Sept. 1977.
[16] N. French, "Programmer productivity rising too slowly: Tanaka," *Computerworld*, 1977, 11(32) p. 1.
[17] T. A. Dolotta and J. R. Mashey, "An introduction to the programmer's workbench," in *Proc. 2nd Int. Conf. Software Engineering*, pp. 164-168, Oct. 1976.
[18] E. W. Dijkstra, "Programming considered as a human activity," in *Proc. IFIP Congr. 1965*.
[19] K. W. Krause and L. W. Diamant, "A management methodology for testing software requirements," in *Proc. COMPSAC 78*, Nov. 1978, pp. 749-754.
[20] C. G. Davis and C. R. Vick, "The software development system," *IEEE Trans. Software Eng.*, vol. SE-3, pp. 69-84, Jan. 1977.
[21] S. N. Gaulding and J. D. Lawson, "Process design engineering—A methodology for real-time software requirements," in *Proc. 2nd Int. Conf. Software Engineering*, pp. 80-85, Oct. 1976.
[22] J. M. Dreyfus and P. J. Karacsony, "The preliminary design as a key to successful software development," in *Proc. 2nd Int. Conf. Software Engineering*, pp. 206-213, Oct. 1976.
[23] R. D. Williams, "Managing the development of reliable software," in *Proc. 1975 Int. Conf. Reliable Software*, pp. 3-8, Apr. 1975.
[24] C. L. McGowan, "Management planning for large software projects," in *Proc. COMPSAC 78*, pp. 90-92, Nov. 1978.
[25] F. T. Baker, "Chief programmer team management of production

programming," *IBM Syst. J.*, vol. 11, no. 1, pp. 56–73, 1972.

[26] H. D. Mills, "Top-down programming in large systems," in *Debugging Techniques in Large Systems*, R. Rustin, Ed. Englewood Cliffs, NJ: Prentice Hall, 1971, pp. 41–55.

[27] F. P. Brooks, Jr., *The Mythical Man-Month: Essays on Software Engineering*. Reading, MA: Addison-Wesley Publishing, 1974, 195 pp.

[28] J. B. Holton, "Are the new programming techniques being used," *Datamation*, pp. 97–103, July 1977.

[29] S. H. Caine and E. R. Gordon, "PDL—A tool for software design," in *Proc. Nat. Computer Conf.*, pp. 271–276, 1975.

[30] F. S. Ingrassia, "Combating the 90% complete syndrome," *Datamation*, pp. 171–176, Jan. 1978.

[31] B. P. Lientz and E. B. Swanson, "Software maintenance: A user/management tug-of-war," *Data Management*, pp. 26–30, Apr. 1979.

[32] B. C. DeRoze, "The United States defense systems software management program," in *Proc. AIAA Government Initiatives Software Management Conf. II*, 1976.

[33] E. B. Swanson, "The dimension of maintenance," in *Proc. 2nd Int. Conf. Software Engineering*, pp. 492–497, Oct. 1976.

[34] J. B. Munson, "Software maintainability; a practical concern for life-cycle costs," in *Proc. COMPSAC 78*, pp. 54–59, Nov. 1978.

[35] B. Curtis, "Measurement and experimentation in software engineering," this issue, pp. 1144–1157.

[36] R. T. Yeh and P. Zave, "Specifying software requirements," this issue, pp. 1077–1085.

Reprinted from *IEEE Transactions on Software Engineering*. Volume
SE-4. Number 4. July 1978, pages 326-334. Copyright © 1978 by
The Institute of Electrical and Electronics Engineers, Inc.

Controlling the Software Life Cycle—The Project Management Task

WILLIAM C. CAVE AND ALAN B. SALISBURY, SENIOR MEMBER, IEEE

Abstract—This paper describes project management methods used for controlling the life cycle of large-scale software systems deployed in multiple installations over a wide geographic area. A set of management milestones is offered along with requirements and techniques for establishing and maintaining control of the project. In particular, a quantitative measure of software quality is proposed based upon functional value, availability, and maintenance costs. Conclusions drawn are based on the study of several cases and are generally applicable to both commercial and military systems.

Index Terms—Life cycle, software development, software management, software quality, system management.

Manuscript received June 15, 1977; revised December 3, 1977 and January 1, 1978.
W. C. Cave is with Prediction Systems, Inc., Manasquan, NJ 08736.
A. B. Salisbury is with the Research Directorate, National Defense University, Washington, DC 20319.

I. INTRODUCTION

THIS paper is the result of an effort to investigate project management methods which were used successfully in the development of several large software systems. As used herein, "success" implies the delivery of a quality product, on time and within budget, resulting in a high degree of user satisfaction.

A number of systems spanning a significant range of applications were examined during the course of this effort. Examples include an automated engineering design system, a stock transfer accounting system, and a real-time military command and control system. Sizes ranged from 340 000 to 700 000 bytes of object code, and assembly language examples were considered in addition to higher order languages (Fortran and Cobol). All of the systems studied had the common property of deployment at multiple geographically dispersed locations, ranging from 6 to 15 in number.

Two key differences between hardware and software have been examined. One is the shape of the life-cycle resource consumption function, and the other is the maintenance function. In addition, considerations of vendor warranties and maintenance of software have led to the development of a measure of quality of the end product. This measure points out the need for formal user involvement in functional requirements specification.

Review of case histories of successfully managed projects has led to elements considered essential to their success. These elements are characterized in terms of management experience, the environment in which management must operate, and management methods. The management methods are classified into those used to establish control and those for maintaining control. The need for good management policies, procedures, and standards which can be practically enforced becomes evident.

The results of this study and the conclusions reported in this paper should be applicable to most large software development projects. Whether the system is being developed in a competitive environment by a commercial vendor with a profit motive or, alternatively, in-house (or under contract) with an operational savings or improved effectiveness motive, many similar conclusions can be drawn. These conclusions will be identified in the discussions that follow.

II. DEFINING THE PM LIFE-CYCLE CONTROL PROBLEM

A. Measuring Project Size and Level of Difficulty

Definition of the system life-cycle management problem is highly dependent upon the environment under consideration. This is particularly true when judging methods of managing software development, since the scope of problems encountered is subject to considerable variation. For example, the following factors can place radically differing demands on management approaches:

1) the number of geographically separate installations to be maintained;

2) the number of different types of users expected to interact with the system;

3) the level of automation previously implemented for the application;

4) the requirements on system availability; and

5) the level of system complexity.

Most of the factors which the project manager must consider appear to be subfactors of two major elements which are critical. These are quality (of the end product) and risk (of project failure). As in other markets, product quality and profits go hand in hand. Quality of the end product depends upon availability of system functions required by the user and the cost to maintain that availability. Naturally, the developer will be taking measures to "predict" and "control" quality from inception of the system life cycle. However, in practice, the final measure of quality cannot be determined until the system is deployed in the hands of real users in multiple live operational environments.

Risk, as used here, is generally the risk of failing to turn a profit or achieve a savings. Alternatively, for military systems,

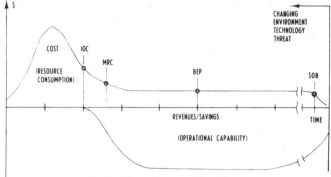

Fig. 1. Typical system life cycle.

it might be the risk of not achieving an adequate performance level. In either case we are concerned with minimizing this risk or keeping it at an acceptable level.

In measuring risk, one must consider the percent of a given organization's resources to be consumed in getting a product to the payoff point. In addition, time to achieve the payoff point, expected return on investment (ROI), and probability of staying on schedule with regard to time and resources are all factors to be considered in assessing risk. It is the project manager's task to determine when quality and risk are not at acceptable levels and make judgments on how, if at all, his organization should proceed with the project.

In the commercial systems investigated, the software vendors did not anticipate profitable revenues until multiple installations were successful in live operation. In particular, one system did not turn profitable until the fifth installation was in production. The vendor covered total costs of development starting from market concept and user interviews through to a financial break-even point well into the installation and maintenance phase. Performance of the vendor and his project management were clearly measurable across the entire system life cycle. Corporate memory of how time and cost estimates were made is well preserved to cut future risk.

In a multiple installation environment, requirements on reliability and maintainability are of major importance. As the number of installations and corresponding costs go up, reliability and maintainability requirements get multiplied. This type of maintenance environment amplifies the need for design quality. Add to this a competitive requirement to fully satisfy user needs under warranty[1] and the result is an environment which places the highest demands on product quality and formal management control. This is the principal environment investigated here.

B. Defining the Life-Cycle Control Problem

To start, consider a theoretically "ideal" way of describing the life-cycle control problem as depicted in Fig. 1 (see [4]). Assume that operational capability can be measured in the same way as resources consumed so that a clear measure (dollars and cents) of ROI performance can be achieved. Such

---

[1] In the commercial software vendor environment, it is difficult to sell software products without long-term warranties. Warranties are also beginning to appear in defense systems.

a measure can be precisely determined in the case of a software vendor marketing a packaged product. This measure is also valid for projects where savings can be clearly determined. In the case of military operational capability, there appears to be little doubt that the methods and conclusions drawn are directly applicable, although their evaluation may be more subjective.

The curves shown in Fig. 1 represent a general solution to the software life-cycle control problem. The solution is a general one since, for a given software problem, there can be an infinite set of possible solution curves. Their actual shape will depend upon judgements of the project manager as well as many other factors across the life cycle. The technical problem objective is to shape these curves in such a way as to maximize ROI.

There are many external constraints which the manager of such a project must face. First, he must determine the period of time during which there is expected to be a real market for the product. In other words, he must determine the period during which revenues for the system will flow or savings accrue. He must consider the changing environment, changing technology, and his competition. In the military case, this corresponds to the period during which a real operational capability can exist prior to being overcome by a changing enemy threat. At sometime in the future, the market or military requirement will become obsolete.

If a market already exists for the system, then the initial operational capability (IOC) will depend only upon development time to achieve that goal. Thus, the total period for revenues is bounded by IOC and system obsolescence (SOB). Obviously, if more money is spent up-front to shorten the time to IOC, revenues will start to come in earlier. However, the experienced project manager is well aware that there is no even dollar for dollar tradeoff relationship and, in fact, the cost to do things faster can rise exponentially.

Additional external financial constraints which must also be considered are maximum resource consumption (MRC) and break-even point (BEP). MRC occurs when revenues or savings finally exceed current expenses. There must be enough financial resources available at the rate required to cover those utilized to MRC. BEP occurs when total expenses have been recovered via revenues or savings.[2] Vendor profits cannot be realized until this point, except through long-term capitalization of the up-front peak costs. In any event, if a vendor is facing many years to BEP, he will also be considering where else he can invest his resources.

In summary, the software life-cycle control problem is reduced to one of shaping the curves in Fig. 1 in such a way that maximizes ROI while meeting constraints on factors such as quality, risk, MRC, time to IOC, and BEP.

III. Determining Software Quality

As an aid to defining the life-cycle control problem, we offer a measure of software quality. As defined here, software

[2]The payoff point is clearly the break-even point for systems producing revenues or quantifiable savings. For military systems it may again be subjective, varying from IOC to some other time according to the definition of the user.

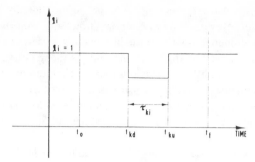

Fig. 2. Level of availability of function f_i.

quality can only be *measured* after IOC in a live operational environment. Prior to IOC, software quality can be *predicted* and controlled by measuring factors that affect it. However, the measure of quality offered here is considered essential in correlating the effects of such factors.

We start with the intuitive notion that quality is proportional to system availability A and inversely proportional to the cost of maintaining that availability M.[3]

$$Q = \frac{A}{1 + M}. \qquad (1)$$

The cost to maintain a system is directly measurable in the environments considered. To define availability as used in (1), we first define factors f_i which describe the relative importance of all system functions as judged by the user. These factors can be normalized such that

$$\sum_{i=1}^{n} f_i = 1, \qquad (2)$$

where n is the number of functions which must be available to the user. We define l_i as the level of availability of function i such that

$$0 \le l_i \le 1. \qquad (3)$$

If l_i is one (zero), then the system is totally available (unavailable), and levels can take on binary or continuous values. If all system functions are totally available, then

$$\sum_i f_i \cdot l_i = \sum_i f_i = 1. \qquad (4)$$

It is the user who must define the relative importance of functions of the system as well as their level of availability at any point in time.

We now define instantaneous system availability as

$$A(t) = \sum_i f_i \cdot l_i(t) \qquad (5)$$

noting that software quality changes with time. (While quality as we have defined it may fluctuate up and down, in the long run it generally improves.) To measure availability practically, a reasonable time increment must be selected. Referring to Fig. 2, consider that we will take measurements over successive time intervals of length $t_f - t_0$. A practical increment may be

[3]The unit is added only because the cost of maintenance could theoretically vanish.

1 month. During these intervals we will continually measure the availability level of each system function. We assume that all functions are totally available unless it is determined that their availability level falls below unity. For example, in Fig. 2, at time t_{kd}, the level of availability of function i drops to some value less than 1. At time t_{ku}, the problem is corrected and the function is totally available to the user. For ease of defining average availability over the interval (t_0, t_f), we define unavailability as

$$u_i = 1 - l_i. \tag{6}$$

We can now obtain average availability for the total system over the period (t_0, t_f) as

$$A = 1 - \frac{1}{t_f - t_o} \sum_i \sum_k f_i u_{ki} \tau_{ki} \tag{7}$$

where u_{ki} is the kth malfunction of function f_i and τ_{ki} is the duration of the kth malfunction from time of discovery to time of correction. We thus have a measure of average system availability over a given time interval. Knowing the cost of maintenance over the same time interval, we can then compute a value for quality.

As an alternative, it may be meaningful to define M' as a relative cost of restorative maintenance where

$$M' = \frac{\text{support budget consumed by restorative maintenance}}{\text{total support budget}} \tag{8}$$

leading to

$$Q' = \frac{A}{1 + M'} \tag{9}$$

as a more universal measure of quality, ranging between 0 and 1.[4] This approach is based on the experience that the budgeted cost of restorative maintenance is normally small compared to the total support budget allotted for changes and enhancements.

The measures of quality offered are not intended to be absolute. Their shortcomings, such as interdependencies among functions, can be overcome by good judgment in determining the levels of availability. If a log is kept of individual values of functional availability, then one can compute a new set of quality factors upon changing the relative weights of functional importance. However, the significance of the measures lies with their interpretation. Note that availability can be improved by shortening the time it takes to bring a reduced level of availability back to unity. However, such efforts can increase the cost of maintenance and thereby offset potential improvements in the overall measure of quality.

In the commercial vendor environment, prospective buyers of a software system will want to talk with existing users about the availability of desired system functions. This is the quality of the product as seen by the user. However, it is only part of the picture as seen by a developer maintaining a system

[4]Suggested by R. McHenry, IBM Corporation, in private communication.

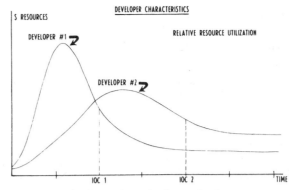

Fig. 3. Comparison of software developers.

under warranty. From the developer's perspective, he must consider cost of maintenance in determining ROI. To be a high quality product, the software system must also be inexpensive to maintain.

In order to build a high quality product as defined above, the developer must invest more time and money during development, prior to IOC. It is left to the project manager to determine an adequate level of availability, below which the risk of losing anticipated revenues or savings becomes too high. Project management judgment of such an acceptable level of quality will certainly depend much more on user needs and the capability of the competition than on numbers one might obtain from the equation derived above. However, the prudent software developer will not disregard such measures since, as users become more sophisticated, such measures will become more meaningful.

IV. MEASURING SUCCESS IN A COMPETITIVE ENVIRONMENT

Having defined the problem theoretically, we now consider how the project manager can achieve practical solutions. Questions to be answered are: What are the controls that shape the curves? How can we predict their responses? How can we validate our predictions in a changing environment? We approach these questions by comparing software vendors in a competitive environment (see Fig. 3). Before going into specific case studies some general conclusions can be drawn from our observations.

1) Certain software developers have been consistently more successful than others.

2) There is a common view that risk can be reduced by going slowly, particularly if management is inexperienced. However, going slowly may not minimize risk in the way defined above and, in fact, can decrease ROI dramatically.

3) The steep rate of resource utilization by developer 1 requires a knowledge of how to effectively use those resources—in other words, management experience.

4) It is important to understand how and where software fits into the life cycle of total systems and to what degree software life-cycle management influences total system management.

In the Introduction, it was indicated that software is different from hardware. Probably the most significant difference is the shape of the resource utilization curve across the

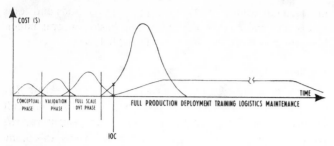

Fig. 4. Hardware life cycle consumption function: the Army life-cycle management model.

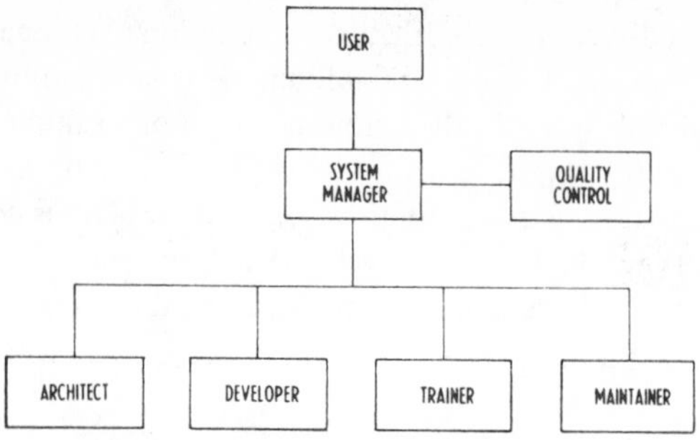

Fig. 5. Formal system manager interfaces.

life cycle. Fig. 4 indicates the consumption of resources across the life cycle for a typical Army hardware system. Note that the peak occurs well after IOC. In typical software life cycles which have been characterized elsewhere ([4], [5]), the peak occurs substantially prior to IOC. When software consumes a major portion of the system life cycle resources, it is necessary to get top management understanding and approval of early peak resource utilization. If this is not done, and the same IOC is attempted to be met, that IOC will be premature. This results in a fictitious operational capability wherein the user is led to believe that a real operational capability exists, when in fact it does not. Continuing software development while under live operation can cause trauma unless it was specifically planned.

In addition to the resource consumption function being different from that of hardware, the software life cycle has a different set of natural intrinsic milestones. Unless these are mapped properly into the total system life cycle, and made clearly visible, then the software part of the system will not be properly controlled.

It turns out that the set of hardware system life-cycle milestones, activities, and events within the Army do not require much change in terms of names and general achievement in order to be used for software. What they do require are proper interpretation and a different set of specific measurement criteria for their attainment. This requirement for management milestones and standards[5] peculiar to software is very important to recognize.

V. A Typical Case History

Product quality as described above can and must be designed and built into a system from its inception. This can only be achieved through a formal management discipline which must be introduced at many points throughout the system life cycle. The ease with which such a discipline can be invoked and enforced depends upon the understanding, perspective, and experience of all contributors to the project with regard to the need for formality and discipline. It also depends upon the environment in which management must operate and the means for practical enforcement.

The requirement for a formal discipline exists at interfaces between the system manager and other elements involved in

[5]*Note:* the term standards will be used throughout in a management sense.

the system life cycle as indicated in Fig. 5. To facilitate understanding of the discipline required at these interfaces, consider the following typical vendor predicament. A system has moved to the installation and maintenance phase of its life cycle, with installation under way at the seventh user location. Three users in the field are calling for a software change which they claim will provide a substantial reduction in personnel skills required at an important human interface. This change appears trivial to the user but will ripple through a major part of the system. It is determined that 35 percent of the potential user market will want the change, and prospects are talking to existing users as well as competitors. Finally, marketing is trying to encourage maintenance to make a "quick-fix" at their showplace installation, so they can prove to prospects that the change is in.

In the vendor environment described, it is important that decisions on such changes be made on a sound economic basis. If a decision is made to implement such a change, it must be done under tight control or system quality can be badly degraded and future market losses incurred. Prior to giving birth to a new version of the system, consideration must be given to the following:

1) Can a single system identity be preserved, or will it be necessary to maintain separate versions for different market segments, and at what cost?

2) What will the costs be for design, documentation, development, and formal testing?

3) What will the cost be for upgrading all existing installations if a unique identity is to be preserved?

4) How will testing, training, and maintenance procedures be affected and at what cost?

The quality of the total system product will weigh heavily in the on-going costs of installation, training, and maintenance, and this is particularly true when software implements user policies and procedures.

VI. Defining the Software Product

In the vendor environment considered, the software product consists of three libraries. These are the external documentation library, program library, and test library. Of these three, the most important is the external documentation library shown in Fig. 6. In a well disciplined environment, the external documentation is completed prior to programming. Any coding done before completion of this library is for validation of approach, not for production. This discipline

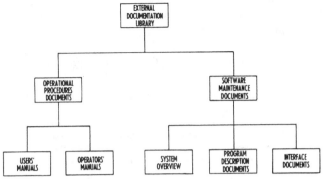

Fig. 6. External documentation library.

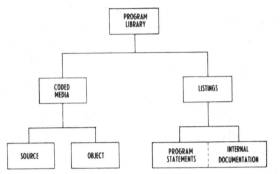

Fig. 7. Program library.

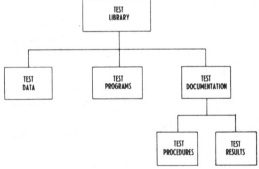

Fig. 8. Test library.

forces an orderly approach to the system design process which is embodied in the development of the external documentation in increasing layers of detail. The program library, Fig. 7, and the test library, Fig. 8, can be developed concurrently once the external documentation library is complete.

The formality and discipline used to develop and maintain these libraries will impart a major influence on their quality and, therefore, the quality of the software end product.

VII. Elements Essential to Success

It is our conclusion that there are three elements essential to a successful software life cycle. These elements are experienced management, an environment which affords proper

management control, and good supporting methods and tools to execute and control the work. The basic concepts underlying these essential elements are offered below.

A. Management

The development of user oriented software systems is first and foremost a management problem. This is a difficult premise to have accepted because poor management reflects right to the top of any organization. Nevertheless, this premise is key, since project failures are generally the result of improper or inexperienced management and not a lack of technical ability. Recognition of this premise is the most essential element required to bring about the successful development of a highly user oriented software system.

This conclusion has been drawn from the following observations:

1) Many project failures are the result of inaccurately or incompletely specified requirements. Anything not explicitly defined by the user is implicitly left to the software developer to define. The reason, which is not readily apparent, is that the very nature of software development—creating and implementing a decision process—forces this responsibility upon those doing the creating. The software product in and of itself defines the policies and procedures of the user, or, in the military sense, it is doctrine! It is fundamentally a management problem to ensure that the product will in fact be what the user wants.

2) It is apparent that good knowledge, experience, and judgment are most effective when provided with a high enough level of visibility. Without this visibility, decisions to avoid major mistakes in policy and effect successful direction cannot be made.

B. Environment

The success of an organization whose responsibility is the development of user oriented systems is ultimately measured by the willingness on the part of prospective clients to order and pay for services rendered on a long-term continuing basis. An essential element within organizations with outstanding long-term profit records is the presence of an environment which places heavy emphasis on responsiveness to user requirements and their satisfaction, on time and within budget.

When dollar control flows directly from the end user down through the ranks of the developer, management ability is more frequently measured by the bottom line. This creates a greater willingness to call on outside expertise, eliminating the not invented here (NIH) factor. It creates a need for accurate performance measurement as well as a steering capability through management emphasis so that response to direction can be achieved. Without an environment which affords proper control and response, the most capable managers will be stifled!

C. Methods

There is no simple set of methods for development of the types of software systems discussed here. What has been used successfully in practice is a set of management policies, procedures, and standards for acquiring and maintaining project control, see [2]. Some of these methods are outlined in the next two sections.

VIII. Establishing Control

A. Life-Cycle Planning

Successful life-cycle planning must provide for an incremental commitment of resources. Increment size can be determined by the time frame and resources required to achieve a measurable milestone and the risk of not achieving that milestone. A set of milestones based on those which have been used successfully in the past by various software developers are offered below. These milestones segment the software development cycle into sequential phases. Each phase should be terminated with thorough documentation of work completed, a critical review, a detailed plan for the next phase, and an updated overall plan for the remainder of the project. A go-no go decision can then be made regarding commitment of resources for the next phase. If a go decision is made, changes resulting from review are formally incorporated into a continuation plan and the next phase is initiated.

B. Risk Increments and Management Milestones

The following set of management milestones for controlling software life cycles is offered:

1) *Project Definition:* The problem to be solved must be defined in general terms. Basic user objectives and constraints must be agreed upon along with an overall plan and gross estimate of resources required for their satisfaction. This plan must include sufficient resource commitments from the user, or his representatives, to participate in the effort required to specify in complete detail the functional and performance requirements of the system.

2) *Functional Analysis and Specification:* User functional requirements must be analyzed and detailed functional specifications developed for the system in a manner which is easily understood by the end user. This may require mockup demonstrations using terminal equipments and throw-away software to simulate man–machine or intersystem interfaces. Proper completion of this milestone is heavily dependent upon the user's commitment of resources to the task.

3) *Environment Analysis and Specification:* Implementation and development requirements, such as equipment configuration, languages, and support software to be used for both the development and operational environments, must be produced. Again, throw-away software for bench mark testing may be required here. The software development/maintenance environment specified during this phase is a major factor in determining the shape of the life-cycle consumption function.

4) *System Design:* A detailed system design must be completed to the module level. A detailed documentation set and a detailed development and testing schedule must also be completed. Substantial throw-away software may be required to complete the detailed design. The documentation and test plans and procedures are the most important products of this phase.

5) *Program Development:* All programs must be coded and integrated into a working system. A regression test set must

be completed and available for quality control of future modifications. A training package must also be completed. The system is fully tested in the development environment.

6) *Operational Testing:* Initial users utilize the complete system in a carefully maintained live operational environment. Quality control procedures, (e.g., regression testing, independent acceptance testing, and configuration control over all libraries) are fully implemented.

7) *Installation and Maintenance:* The system is operationally deployed and maintained for multiple live installations which may be geographically separated. The training package is used for bringing up live installations. The system is corrected, refined, and enhanced until obsolescence using strict quality control procedures.

C. Establishing a Proper Management Environment

Software life-cycle project control must be established with the acceptance of a formal management plan based on measurable milestones such as those offered above. This formal management plan must contain realistic estimates of time and resources required across the system life cycle. However, accurate estimates cannot be expected to be derived during the initial phase of the project. It is therefore essential that both user and developer top management understand the incremental approach which is based on minimizing the risk of wasting resources.

In a highly competitive vendor environment, decisions to terminate work on future product line systems are not uncommon due to changing market emphasis and technology. If each phase is properly documented at its termination point, projects can be shelved for periods and then restarted at the next phase with minimum loss of continuity. While one may believe that the level of documentation can be lessened to some degree to minimize time delays for urgently needed systems, it should never be eliminated in the name of expediency. The best solution in such a case is to apply additional resources to achieve the required schedule while insuring adequate quality of the end product.

Managers must be constantly reminded that the decision to continue a project under uncertain terms definitely places the responsibility for failure on their shoulders. Major decisions should only be based on well documented facts. This formality puts performance measurement and enforcement of discipline on a practical basis. Practical enforcement ultimately lies with management review of the written record! Unless a clear set of specifications, documentation, and plans for the next phase are formally written, reviewed, and approved, the next phase should not be started.

IX. Maintaining Control

A good management plan is essential to establishing project control. Equally important are good management policies, procedures, and standards for maintaining project control and, particularly, control of the software product.

A. Measuring Milestone Achievement

An integrated set of software development standards is the best way to measure milestone achievement. The following typical set of standards is considered essential to successful software system development and maintenance.

1) Specification Standards: These standards should be followed in specifying the system functional performance and environmental requirements.

2) Documentation Standards: These standards specify the format, structure, and content of the external documentation set, i.e., system documentation external to the source listings.

3) Programming Standards: Separate programming standards should be adopted for each language to be used in developing the system (see for example [3]).

4) Quality Control Standards: Standards for testing and maintaining the software product should be formally adopted.

B. Predicting and Tracking Progress

There is no substitute for good judgment and experience in estimating the time and resources required for software development. However, there are available today practical quantitative methods for aiding the project manager in this task. Norden [4] has characterized the software life-cycle resource consumption function. Putnam [5] has extended this work to estimate time and resource requirements via regression analysis.

It appears that Putnam's method is directly applicable to prediction of the consumption function based on the milestones offered above in the following way. If, instead of using the slope of the function at a particular point of time, one were to use the area under the curve required to complete initial phases of the life cycle, it should be possible to apply similar regression analysis to determining areas required for future phases.

Probably the best way to track progress is by rate charting as described by Snyder [7]. Rate charting has the distinct advantage that the project manager can track rate of change of progress in addition to status. This provides an excellent means for flagging activities which are falling behind at an increasing rate. It provides information which can allow resources to be shifted on a priority basis from activities which are ahead and gaining to those which are falling behind. Rate charting is a practical method for preventing a crisis management situation.

C. Controlling System Quality

"Software quality control has been a major contributing factor in producing and sustaining the high reliability and quality of software in the Bell System's Number 1 Electronic Switching System (ESS)" [1].

Control of system quality starts at the beginning of the life cycle. The initial project plan must provide proper resources necessary to insure that good specification, documentation, programming, and quality control standards will be adhered to. During the course of the project, the documentation, program, and test libraries which make up the software product must be constantly audited, not just reviewed. Formal audit procedures and reports are the only way to practically enforce standards.

It is the opinion of the authors that configuration management and regression testing become even more important in the deployment and maintenance phase of the life cycle ([6]). Unless proper configuration management controls and regression test procedures are developed with this in mind, the system can easily go out of control as multiple installations start to go live. The reason is that software, unlike hardware, requires that the product specification and design be changed every time software maintenance is performed. In addition, one uses software because of the economic advantages involved in making changes. No one would conceive of building in hardware everything that has been built in software. The costs would be too great.

D. Making Decisions in a Changing Environment

The development of large software systems with long life cycles must take into account changing requirements and technology. Such change can and must be planned for. By breaking resource commitment into risk increments as defined above, project managers are afforded time to anticipate and make decisions in a changing environment.

Structuring of the overall software development cycle into sequential phases as described affords the following advantages:

1) allowance for incremental learning experience to be gained in successive phases with a particular application so that subsequent phases can be planned more carefully and realistically;

2) allowance for review and justification to proceed with a modified plan after each phase, allowing maximum management control;

3) allowance for changes in

    project emphasis
    project time frame
    project environment
    available resources
    personnel assignments

with minimal loss of project coherence;

4) allowance for gaps between phases due to

    personnel acquisition
    hardware acquisition
    market justification/priority; and

continual user interaction, refinement, and review of specifications and documentation on an increasing detail basis before each phase commits more resources.

X. Conclusion

In summary, the successful development of large software systems can be achieved in a consistent manner. Essential elements necessary to achieve success are experienced management, an environment which affords proper management control and response, and enforceable management procedures and standards for maintaining project control. It is our conclusion that these elements are essential for the achievement of long-term operational and economic success in the development of software systems in either a military or commercial environment. In addition, we anticipate that these same elements will permit software developers to continue to derive maximum benefits from a rapidly changing computer technology.

REFERENCES

[1] S. Bloom *et al.*, "Software quality control," in *1973 IEEE Symp. Comput. Software Rel., Rec.*, New York, 1973.

[2] W. C. Cave, *The Incremental Method for Management Control of Software Development*. Manasquan, NJ: Shalmar Corp., 1975.

[3] H. F. Ledgard and W. C. Cave, "COBOL under control," *Commun. Ass. Comput. Mach.*, vol. 19, pp. 601-608, Nov. 1976.

[4] P. V. Norden, "Useful tools for project management," in *Management of Production*, M. K. Starr, Ed. Baltimore, MD: Penguin, 1970, pp. 71-101.

[5] L. H. Putnam, "A macro-estimating methodology for software development," in *Dig. Papers, Fall COMPCON '76, Thirteenth IEEE Computer Soc. Int. Conf.*, Sept. 1976, pp. 138-143.

[6] A. L. Sherr, "Developing and testing a large programming system," in *Program Test Methods*, W. C. Hetzel, Ed. Englewood Cliffs, NJ: Prentice-Hall, 1972.

[7] T. R. Snyder, "Rate charting," *Datamation*, pp. 44-47, Nov. 1976.

William C. Cave received the B.S.E.E. degree from the Pennsylvania State University, University Park, and the M.S.E.E. degree from New York University, New York City. He has done additional graduate work at both the Polytechnic Institute of New York, Brooklyn, and Stevens Institute of Technology, Hoboken, NJ.

He entered the computer field in 1958 and was employed by the U.S. Army Electronics Research and Development Laboratories where he directed in-house projects for the development of a general-purpose digital computer, a multiprocessor system architecture, digital circuit research, and computer aided design/optimization. From 1968 to 1973 he was president of Optimal Systems Research, Inc. During this period, the company developed three large software systems which are presently operational in more than twenty major corporations throughout the United States. He has been a Vice President of Martin Marietta Corp., consulted for various commercial/industrial companies, and provided seminars on management methods for software development and automated engineering design. He is now President of Prediction Systems, Inc., Manasquan, NJ, whose principle product is software for market prediction.

Mr. Cave is a member of Eta Kappa Nu and TIMS.

Allan B. Salisbury (S'71-M'73-SM'77) received the B.S. degree from the United States Military Academy, West Point, NY, in 1958, and the M.S.E.E. and Ph.D. degrees from Stanford University, Stanford, CA, in 1964 and 1973, respectively.

He is currently a Senior Research Fellow at the National Defense University, Washington, DC. His recent assignments include Project Manager, Position Location Reporting System (1976-1977) and Director, Center for Tactical Computer Sciences, Fort Monmouth, NJ (1975-1976). In addition, he has taught electrical engineering and computer science at the United States Military Academy, American University, Washington, DC, the New York Institute of Technology, Old Westbury, and Fairleigh Dickinson University, Rutherford, NJ. He is the author of *Microprogrammable Computer Architectures* (Elsevier, 1976).

Software Engineering

BARRY W. BOEHM

Reprinted from *IEEE Transactions on Computers*, Volume C-25, Number 12, December 1976, pages 1226-1241. Copyright © 1976 by the Institute of Electrical and Electronics Engineers, Inc.

Abstract—This paper provides a definition of the term "software engineering" and a survey of the current state of the art and likely future trends in the field. The survey covers the technology available in the various phases of the software life cycle—requirements engineering, design, coding, test, and maintenance—and in the overall area of software management and integrated technology-management approaches. It is oriented primarily toward discussing the domain of applicability of techniques (where and when they work), rather than how they work in detail. To cover the latter, an extensive set of 104 references is provided.

Index Terms—Computer software, data systems, information systems, research and development, software development, software engineering, software management.

I. INTRODUCTION

THE annual cost of software in the U.S. is approximately 20 billion dollars. Its rate of growth is considerably greater than that of the economy in general. Compared to the cost of computer hardware, the cost of software is continuing to escalate along the lines predicted in Fig. 1 [1].[1] A recent SHARE study [2] indicates further that software demand over the years 1975–1985 will grow considerably faster (about 21–23 percent per year) than the growth rate in software supply at current estimated growth rates of the software labor force and its productivity per individual, which produce a combined growth rate of about 11.5–17 percent per year over the years 1975–1985.

In addition, as we continue to automate many of the processes which control our life-style—our medical equipment, air traffic control, defense system, personal records, bank accounts—we continue to trust more and more in the reliable functioning of this proliferating mass of software. *Software engineering* is the means by which we attempt to produce all of this software in a way that is both cost-effective and reliable enough to deserve our trust. Clearly, it is a discipline which is important to establish well and to perform well.

This paper will begin with a definition of "software engineering." It will then survey the current state of the art of the discipline, and conclude with an assessment of likely future trends.

II. DEFINITIONS

Let us begin by defining "software engineering." We will define software to include not only computer programs, but also the associated documentation required to develop, operate, and maintain the programs. By defining software in this broader sense, we wish to emphasize the necessity of considering the generation of timely documentation as an integral portion of the software development process. We can then combine this with a definition of "engineering" to produce the following definition.

Software Engineering: The practical application of scientific knowledge in the design and construction of computer programs and the associated documentation required to develop, operate, and maintain them.

Three main points should be made about this definition. The first concerns the necessity of considering a broad enough interpretation of the word "design" to cover the extremely important activity of software requirements engineering. The second point is that the definition should cover the entire software life cycle, thus including those activities of redesign and modification often termed "software maintenance." (Fig. 2 indicates the overall set of activities thus encompassed in the definition.) The final point is that our store of knowledge about software which can really be called "scientific knowledge" is a rather small base upon which to build an engineering discipline. But, of course, that is what makes software engineering such a fascinating challenge at this time.

The remainder of this paper will discuss the state of the art of software engineering along the lines of the software life cycle depicted in Fig. 2. Section III contains a discussion of software requirements engineering, with some mention of the problem of determining overall system requirements. Section IV discusses both preliminary design and detailed design technology trends. Section V contains only a brief discussion of programming, as this topic is also covered in a companion article in this issue [3]. Section VI covers both software testing and the overall life cycle concern with software reliability. Section VII discusses the highly important but largely neglected area of software maintenance. Section VIII surveys software management concepts and techniques, and discusses the status and trends of integrated technology-management approaches to software development. Finally, Section IX concludes with an assessment of the current state of the art of software engineering with respect to the definition above.

Each section (sometimes after an introduction) contains a short summary of current practice in the area, followed by a survey of current frontier technology, and concluding with a short summary of likely trends in the area. The survey is oriented primarily toward discussing the domain of applicability of techniques (where and when they work)

Manuscript received June 24, 1976; revised August 16, 1976.

The author is with the TRW Systems and Energy Group, Redondo Beach, CA 90278.

[1] Another trend has been added to Fig. 1: the growth of software maintenance, which will be discussed later.

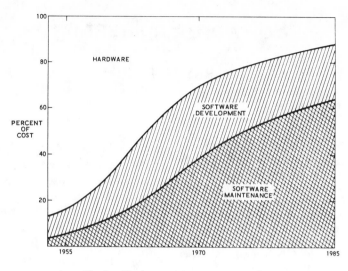

Fig. 1.   Hardware–software cost trends.

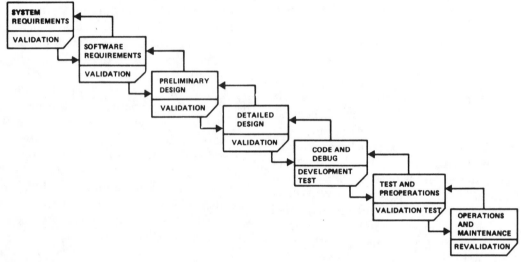

Fig. 2.   Software life cycle.

rather than how they work in detail. An extensive set of references is provided for readers wishing to pursue the latter.

III. SOFTWARE REQUIREMENTS ENGINEERING

A. Critical Nature of Software Requirements Engineering

Software requirements engineering is the discipline for developing a complete, consistent, unambiguous specification—which can serve as a basis for common agreement among all parties concerned—describing *what* the software product will do (but *not how* it will do it; this is to be done in the design specification).

The extreme importance of such a specification is only now becoming generally recognized. Its importance derives from two main characteristics: 1) it is easy to delay or avoid doing thoroughly; and 2) deficiencies in it are very difficult and expensive to correct later.

Fig. 3 shows a summary of current experience at IBM

[4], GTE [5], and TRW on the relative cost of correcting software errors as a function of the phase in which they are corrected. Clearly, it pays off to invest effort in finding requirements errors early and correcting them in, say, 1 man-hour rather than waiting to find the error during operations and having to spend 100 man-hours correcting it.

Besides the cost-to-fix problems, there are other critical problems stemming from a lack of a good requirements specification. These include [6]: 1) top-down designing is impossible, for lack of a well-specified "top"; 2) testing is impossible, because there is nothing to test against; 3) the user is frozen out, because there is no clear statement of what is being produced for him; and 4) management is not in control, as there is no clear statement of what the project team is producing.

B. Current Practice

Currently, software requirements specifications (when they exist at all) are generally expressed in free-form English. They abound with ambiguous terms ("suitable,"

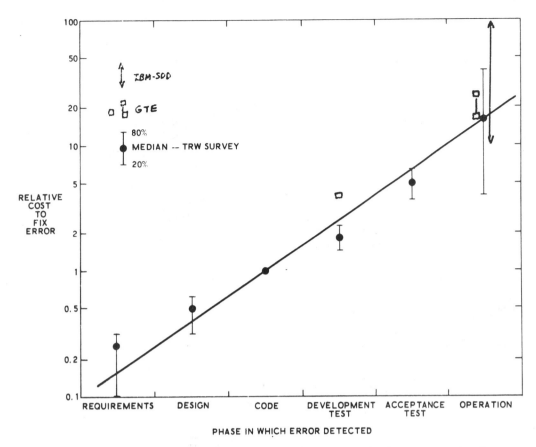

Fig. 3. Software validation: the price of procrastination.

"sufficient," "real-time," "flexible") or precise-sounding terms with unspecified definitions ("optimum," "99.9 percent reliable") which are potential seeds of dissension or lawsuits once the software is produced. They have numerous errors; one recent study [7] indicated that the first independent review of a fairly good software requirements specification will find from one to four nontrivial errors per page.

The techniques used for determining software requirements are generally an ad hoc manual blend of systems analysis principles [8] and common sense. (These are the good ones; the poor ones are based on ad hoc manual blends of politics, preconceptions, and pure salesmanship.) Some formalized manual techniques have been used successfully for determining business system requirements, such as accurately defined systems (ADS), and time automated grid (TAG). The book edited by Couger and Knapp [9] has an excellent summary of such techniques.

C. Current Frontier Technology: Specification Languages and Systems

1) ISDOS: The pioneer system for machine-analyzable software requirements is the ISDOS system developed by Teichroew and his group at the University of Michigan [10]. It was primarily developed for business system applications, but much of the system and its concepts are applicable to other areas. It is the only system to have passed a market and operations test; several commercial,

aerospace, and government organizations have paid for it and are successfully using it. The U.S. Air Force is currently using and sponsoring extensions to ISDOS under the Computer Aided Requirements Analysis (CARA) program.

ISDOS basically consists of a problem statement language (PSL) and a problem statement analyzer (PSA). PSL allows the analyst to specify his system in terms of formalized entities (INPUTS, OUTPUTS, REAL WORLD ENTITIES), classes (SETS, GROUPS), relationships (USES, UPDATES, GENERATES), and other information on timing, data volume, synonyms, attributes, etc. PSA operates on the PSL statements to produce a number of useful summaries, such as: formated problem statements; directories and keyword indices; hierarchical structure reports; graphical summaries of flows and relationships; and statistical summaries. Some of these capabilities are actually more suited to supporting system design activities; this is often the mode in which ISDOS is used.

Many of the current limitations of ISDOS stem from its primary orientation toward business systems. It is currently difficult to express real-time performance requirements and man–machine interaction requirements, for example. Other capabilities are currently missing, such as support for configuration control, traceability to design and code, detailed consistency checking, and automatic simulation generation. Other limitations reflect deliberate, sensible design choices: the output graphics are crude, but they are produced in standard 8 ½ × 11 in size on any standard line printer. Much of the current work on ISDOS/CARA is oriented toward remedying such limitations, and extending the system to further support software design.

2) SREP: The most extensive and powerful system for software requirements specification in evidence today is that being developed under the Software Requirements Engineering Program (SREP) by TRW for the U.S. Army Ballistic Missile Defense Advanced Technology Center (BMDATC) [11]–[13]. Portions of this effort are derivative of ISDOS; it uses the ISDOS data management system, and is primarily organized into a language, the requirements statement language (RSL), and an analyzer, the requirements evaluation and validation system (REVS).

SREP contains a number of extensions and innovations which are needed for requirements engineering in real-time software development projects. In order to represent real-time performance requirements, the individual functional requirements can be joined into stimulus-response networks called R-Nets. In order to focus early attention on software testing and reliability, there are capabilities for designating "validation points" within the R-Nets. For early requirements validation, there are capabilities for automatic generation of functional simulators from the requirements statements. And, for adaptation to changing requirements, there are capabilities for configuration control, traceability to design, and extensive report generation and consistency checking.

Current SREP limitations again mostly reflect deliberate design decisions centered around the autonomous, highly real-time process-control problem of ballistic missile defense. Capabilities to represent large file processing and man–machine interactions are missing. Portability is a problem: although some parts run on several machines, other parts of the system run only on a TI-ASC computer with a very powerful but expensive multicolor interactive graphics terminal. However, the system has been designed with the use of compiler generators and extensibility features which should allow these limitations to be remedied.

3) Automatic Programming and Other Approaches: Under the sponsorship of the Defense Advanced Research Projects Agency (DARPA), several researchers are attempting to develop "automatic programming" systems to replace the functions of currently performed by programmers. If successful, could they drive software costs down to zero? Clearly not, because there would still be the need to determine what software the system should produce, i.e., the software requirements. Thus, the methods, or at least the forms, of capturing software requirements are of central concern in automatic programming research.

Two main directions are being taken in this research. One, exemplified by the work of Balzer at USC-ISI [14], is to work within a general problem context, relying on only general rules of information processing (items must be defined or received before they are used, an "if" should have both a "then" and an "else," etc.) to resolve ambiguities, deficiencies, or inconsistencies in the problem statement. This approach encounters formidable problems in natural language processing and may require further restrictions to make it tractable.

The other direction, exemplified by the work of Martin at MIT [15], is to work within a particular problem area, such as inventory control, where there is enough of a general model of software requirements and acceptable terminology to make the problems of resolving ambiguities, deficiencies, and inconsistencies reasonably tractable.

This second approach has, of course, been used in the past in various forms of "programming-by-questionnaire" and application generators [1], [2]. Perhaps the most widely used are the parameterized application generators developed for use on the IBM System/3. IBM has some more ambitious efforts on requirements specification underway, notably one called the Application Software Engineering Tool [16] and one called the Information Automat [17], but further information is needed to assess their current status and directions.

Another avenue involves the formalization and specification of required properties in a software specification (reliability, maintainability, portability, etc.). Some success has been experienced here for small-to-medium systems, using a "Requirements-Properties Matrix" to help analysts infer additional requirements implied by such considerations [18].

D. Trends

In the area of requirements statement languages, we will see further efforts either to extend the ISDOS-PSL and SREP-RSL capabilities to handle further areas of application, such as man–machine interactions, or to develop language variants specific to such areas. It is still an open question as to how general such a language can be and still retain its utility. Other open questions are those of the nature, "which representation scheme is best for describing requirements in a certain area?" BMDATC is sponsoring some work here in representing general data-processing system requirements for the BMD problem, involving Petri nets, state transition diagrams, and predicate calculus [11], but its outcome is still uncertain.

A good deal more can and will be done to extend the capability of requirements statement analyzers. Some extensions are fairly straightforward consistency checking; others, involving the use of relational operators to deduce derived requirements and the detection (and perhaps generation) of missing requirements are more difficult, tending toward the automatic programming work.

Other advances will involve the use of formal requirements statements to improve subsequent parts of the software life cycle. Examples include requirements-design-code consistency checking (one initial effort is underway), the automatic generation of test cases from requirements statements, and, of course, the advances in automatic programming involving the generation of code from requirements.

Progress will not necessarily be evolutionary, though. There is always a good chance of a breakthrough: some key concept which will simplify and formalize large regions of the problem space. Even then, though, there will always remain difficult regions which will require human insight and sensitivity to come up with an acceptable set of software requirements.

Another trend involves the impact of having formal, machine-analyzable requirements (and design) specifications on our overall inventory of software code. Besides improving software reliability, this will make our software much more portable; users will not be tied so much to a particular machine configuration. It is interesting to speculate on what impact this will have on hardware vendors in the future.

IV. SOFTWARE DESIGN

A. The Requirements/Design Dilemma

Ideally, one would like to have a complete, consistent, validated, unambiguous, machine-independent specification of software requirements before proceeding to software design. However, the requirements are not really validated until it is determined that the resulting system can be built for a reasonable *cost*—and to do so requires developing one or more software *designs* (and any associated hardware designs needed).

This dilemma is complicated by the huge number of degrees of freedom available to software/hardware system designers. In the 1950's, as indicated by Table I, the designer had only a few alternatives to choose from in selecting a central processing unit (CPU), a set of peripherals, a programming language, and an ensemble of support software. In the 1970's, with rapidly evolving mini- and microcomputers, firmware, modems, smart terminals, data management systems, etc., the designer has an enormous number of alternative design components to sort out (possibilities) and to seriously choose from (likely choices). By the 1980's, the number of possible design combinations will be formidable.

The following are some of the implications for the designer. 1) It is easier for him to do an outstanding design job. 2) It is easier for him to do a terrible design job. 3) He needs more powerful analysis tools to help him sort out the alternatives. 4) He has more opportunities for designing-to-cost. 5) He has more opportunities to design and develop tunable systems. 6) He needs a more flexible requirements-tracking and hardware procurement mechanism to support the above flexibility (particularly in government systems). 7) Any rational standardization (e.g., in programming languages) will be a big help to him, in that it reduces the number of alternatives he must consider.

B. Current Practice

Software design is still almost completely a manual process. There is relatively little effort devoted to design validation and risk analysis before committing to a par-

TABLE I
Design Degrees of Freedom for New Data Processing Systems
(Rough Estimates)

Element	Choices (1950's)	Possibilities (1970's)	Likely Choices (1970's)
CPU	5	200	100
Op-Codes	fixed	variable	variable
Peripherals (per function)	1	200	100
Programming language	1	50	5–10
Operating system	0–1	10	5
Data management system	0	100	30

ticular software design. Most software errors are made during the design phase. As seen in Fig. 4, which summarizes several software error analyses by IBM [4], [19] and TRW [20], [21], the ratio of design to coding errors generally exceeds 60:40. (For the TRW data, an error was called a design error if and only if the resulting fix required a change in the detailed design specification.)

Most software design is still done bottom-up, by developing software components before addressing interface and integration issues. There is, however, increasing successful use of top-down design. There is little organized knowledge of what a software designer does, how he does it, or of what makes a good software designer, although some initial work along these lines has been done by Freeman [22].

C. Current Frontier Technology

Relatively little is available to help the designer make the overall hardware–software tradeoff analyses and decisions to appropriately narrow the large number of design degrees of freedom available to him. At the micro level, some formalisms such as LOGOS [23] have been helpful, but at the macro level, not much is available beyond general system engineering techniques. Some help is provided via improved techniques for simulating information systems, such as the Extendable Computer System Simulator (ECSS) [24], [25], which make it possible to develop a fairly thorough functional simulation of the system for design analysis in a considerably shorter time than it takes to develop the complete design itself.

1) Top-Down Design: Most of the helpful new techniques for software design fall into the category of "top-down" approaches, where the "top" is already assumed to be a firm, fixed requirements specification and hardware architecture. Often, it is also assumed that the data structure has also been established. (These assumptions must in many cases be considered potential pitfalls in using such top-down techniques.)

What the top-down approach does well, though, is to provide a procedure for organizing and developing the control structure of a program in a way which focuses early attention on the critical issues of integration and interface definition. It begins with a top-level expression of a hierarchical control structure (often a top level "executive" routine controlling an "input," a "process," and an "out-

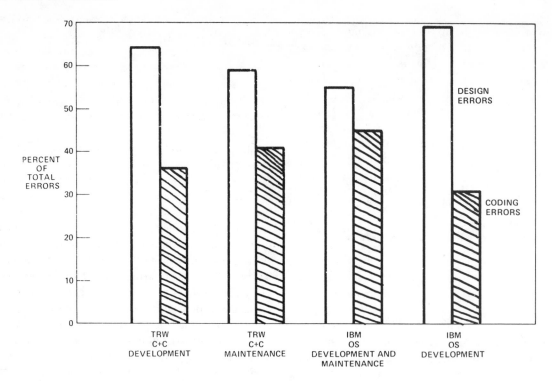

Fig. 4. Most errors in large software systems are in early stages.

put" routine) and proceeds to iteratively refine each successive lower-level component until the entire system is specified. The successive refinements, which may be considered as "levels of abstraction" or "virtual machines" [26], provide a number of advantages in improved understanding, communication, and verification of complex designs [27], [28]. In general, though, experience shows that some degree of early attention to bottom-level design issues is necessary on most projects [29].

The technology of top-down design has centered on two main issues. One involves establishing guidelines for *how to perform* successive refinements and to group functions into modules; the other involves techniques of *representing* the design of the control structure and its interaction with data.

2) Modularization: The techniques of structured design [30] (or composite design [31]) and the modularization guidelines of Parnas [32] provide the most detailed thinking and help in the area of module definition and refinement. Structured design establishes a number of successively stronger types of binding of functions into modules (coincidental, logical, classical, procedural, communicational, informational, and functional) and provides the guideline that a function should be grouped with those functions to which its binding is the strongest. Some designers are able to use this approach quite successfully; others find it useful for reviewing designs but not for formulating them; and others simply find it too ambiguous or complex to be of help. Further experience will be needed to determine how much of this is simply a learning curve effect. In general, Parnas' modularization criteria and guidelines are more straightforward and widely used than the levels-of-binding guidelines, although they may also be becoming more complicated as they address such issues as distribution of responsibility for erroneous inputs [33]. Along these lines, Draper Labs' Higher Order Software (HOS) methodology [34] has attempted to resolve such issues via a set of six axioms covering relations between modules and data, including responsibility for erroneous inputs. For example, Axiom 5 states, "Each module controls the rejection of invalid elements of its own, and only its own, input set."[2]

3) Design Representation: Flow charts remain the main method currently used for design representation. They have a number of deficiencies, particularly in representing hierarchical control structures and data interactions. Also, their free-form nature makes it too easy to construct complicated, unstructured designs which are hard to understand and maintain. A number of representation schemes have been developed to avoid these deficiencies.

The hierarchical input-process-output (HIPO) technique [35] represents software in a hierarchy of modules, each of which is represented by its inputs, its outputs, and a summary of the processing which connects the inputs and outputs. Advantages of the HIPO technique are its ease of use, ease of learning, easy-to-understand graphics, and disciplined structure. Some general disadvantages are the ambiguity of the control relationships (are successive lower

---

[2] Problems can arise, however, when one furnishes such a *design choice* with the power of an *axiom*. Suppose, for example, the input set contains a huge table or a master file. Is the module stuck with the job of checking it, by itself, every time?

level modules in sequence, in a loop, or in an if/else relationship?), the lack of summary information about data, the unwieldiness of the graphics on large systems, and the manual nature of the technique. Some attempts have been made to automate the representation and generation of HIPO's such as Univac's PROVAC System [36].

The structure charts used in structured design [30], [31] remedy some of these disadvantages, although they lose the advantage of representing the processes connecting the inputs with the outputs. In doing so, though, they provide a more compact summary of a module's inputs and outputs which is less unwieldy on large problems. They also provide some extra symbology to remove at least some of the sequence/loop/branch ambiguity of the control relationships.

Several other similar conventions have been developed [37]–[39], each with different strong points, but one main difficulty of any such manual system is the difficulty of keeping the design consistent and up-to-date, especially on large problems. Thus, a number of systems have been developed which store design information in machine-readable form. This simplifies updating (and reduces update errors) and facilitates generation of selective design summaries and simple consistency checking. Experience has shown that even a simple set of automated consistency checks can catch dozens of potential problems in a large design specification [21]. Systems of this nature that have been reported include the Newcastle TOPD system [40], TRW's DACC and DEVISE systems [21], Boeing's DECA System [41], and Univac's PROVAC [36]; several more are under development.

Another machine-processable design representation is provided by Caine, Farber, and Gordon's Program Design Language (PDL) System [42]. This system accepts constructs which have the form of hierarchical structured programs, but instead of the actual code, the designer can write some English text describing what the segment of code will do. (This representation was originally called "structured pidgin" by Mills [43].) The PDL system again makes updating much easier; it also provides a number of useful formatted summaries of the design information, although it still lacks some wished-for features to support terminology control and version control. The program-like representation makes it easy for programmers to read and write PDL, albeit less easy for nonprogrammers. Initial results in using the PDL system on projects have been quite favorable.

D. Trends

Once a good deal of design information is in machine-readable form, there is a fair amount of pressure from users to do more with it: to generate core and time budgets, software cost estimates, first-cut data base descriptions, etc. We should continue to see such added capabilities, and generally a further evolution toward computer-aided-design systems for software. Besides improvements in determining and representing control structures, we should see progress in the more difficult area of data structuring.

Some initial attempts have been made by Hoare [44] and others to provide a data analog of the basic control structures in structured programming, but with less practical impact to date. Additionally, there will be more integration and traceability between the requirements specification, the design specification, and the code—again with significant implications regarding the improved portability of a user's software.

The proliferation of minicomputers and microcomputers will continue to complicate the designer's job. It is difficult enough to derive or use principles for partitioning software jobs on single machines; additional degrees of freedom and concurrency problems just make things so much harder. Here again, though, we should expect at least some initial guidelines for decomposing information processing jobs into separate concurrent processes.

It is still not clear, however, how much one can formalize the software design process. Surveys of software designers have indicated a wide variation in their design styles and approaches, and in their receptiveness to using formal design procedures. The key to good software design still lies in getting the best out of good people, and in structuring the job so that the less-good people can still make a positive contribution.

V. Programming

This section will be brief, because much of the material will be covered in the companion article by Wegner on "Computer Languages" [3].

A. Current Practice

Many organizations are moving toward using structured code [28], [43] (hierarchical, block-oriented code with a limited number of control structures—generally SEQUENCE, IFTHENELSE, CASE, DOWHILE, and DOUNTIL—and rules for formatting and limiting module size). A great deal of terribly unstructured code is still being written, though, often in assembly language and particularly for the rapidly proliferating minicomputers and microcomputers.

B. Current Frontier Technology

Languages are becoming available which support structured code and additional valuable features such as data typing and type checking (e.g., Pascal [45]). Extensions such as concurrent Pascal [46] have been developed to support the programming of concurrent processes. Extensions to data typing involving more explicit binding of procedures and their data have been embodied in recent languages such as ALPHARD [47] and CLU [48]. Metacompiler and compiler writing system technology continues to improve, although much more slowly in the code generation area than in the syntax analysis area.

Automated aids include support systems for top-down structured programming such as the Program Support Library [49], Process Construction [50], TOPD [40], and

COLUMBUS [51]. Another novel aid is the Code Auditor program [50] for automated standards compliance checking—which guarantees that the standards are more than just words. Good programming practices are now becoming codified into style handbooks, i.e., Kernighan and Plauger [52] and Ledgard [53].

C. Trends

It is difficult to clean up old programming languages or to introduce new ones into widespread practice. Perhaps the strongest hope in this direction is the current Department of Defense (DoD) effort to define requirements for its future higher order programming languages [54], which may eventually lead to the development and widespread use of a cleaner programming language. Another trend will be an increasing capability for automatically generating code from design specifications.

VI. SOFTWARE TESTING AND RELIABILITY

A. Current Practice

Surprisingly often, software testing and reliability activities are still not considered until the code has been run the first time and found not to work. In general, the high cost of testing (still 40–50 percent of the development effort) is due to the high cost of reworking the code at this stage (see Fig. 3), and to the wasted effort resulting from the lack of an advance test plan to efficiently guide testing activities.

In addition, most testing is still a tedious manual process which is error-prone in itself. There are few effective criteria used for answering the question, "How much testing is enough?" except the usual "when the budget (or schedule) runs out." However, more and more organizations are now using disciplined test planning and some objective criteria such as "exercise every instruction" or "exercise every branch," often with the aid of automated test monitoring tools and test case planning aids. But other technologies, such as mathematical proof techniques, have barely begun to penetrate the world of production software.

B. Current Frontier Technology

1) Software Reliability Models and Phenomenology: Initially, attempts to predict software reliability (the probability of future satisfactory operation of the software) were made by applying models derived from hardware reliability analysis and fitting them to observed software error rates [55]. These models worked at times, but often were unable to explain actual experienced error phenomena. This was primarily because of fundamental differences between software phenomenology and the hardware-oriented assumptions on which the models were based. For example, software components do not degrade due to wear or fatigue; no imperfection or variations are introduced in making additional copies of a piece of software (except possibly for a class of easy-to-check copying errors); repair of a software fault generally results in a different software configuration than previously, unlike most hardware replacement repairs.

Models are now being developed which provide explanations of the previous error histories in terms of appropriate software phenomenology. They are based on a view of a software program as a mapping from a space of inputs into a space of outputs [56], of program operation as the processing of a sequence of points in the input space, distributed according to an operational profile [57], and of testing as a sampling of points from the input space [56] (see Fig. 5). This approach encounters severe problems of scale on large programs, but can be used conceptually as a means of appropriately conditioning time-driven reliability models [58]. Still, we are a long way off from having truly reliable reliability-estimation methods for software.

2) Software Error Data: Additional insights into reliability estimation have come from analyzing the increasing data base of software errors. For example, the fact that the distributions of serious software errors are dissimilar from the distributions of minor errors [59] means that we need to define "errors" very carefully when using reliability prediction models. Further, another study [60] found that the rates of fixing serious errors and of fixing minor errors vary with management direction. ("Close out all problems quickly" generally gets minor simple errors fixed very quickly, as compared to "Get the serious problems fixed first.")

Other insights afforded by software data collection include better assessments of the relative efficacy of various software reliability techniques [4], [19], [60], identification of the requirements and design phases as key leverage points for cost savings by eliminating errors earlier (Figs. 2 and 3), and guidelines for organizing test efforts (for example, one recent analysis indicated that over half the errors were experienced when the software was handling data singularities and extreme points [60]). So far, however, the proliferation of definitions of various terms (error, design phase, logic error, validation test), still make it extremely difficult to compare error data from different sources. Some efforts to establish a unified software reliability data base and associated standards, terminology, and data collection procedures are now under way at USAF Rome Air Development Center, and within the IEEE Technical Committee on Software Engineering.

3) Automated Aids: Let us sketch the main steps of testing between the point the code has been written and the point it is pronounced acceptable for use, and describe for each stop the main types of automated aids which have been found helpful. More detailed discussion of these aids can be found in the surveys by Reifer [61] and Ramamoorthy and Ho [62] which in turn have references to individual contributions to the field.

a) Static code analysis: Automated aids here include the usual compiler diagnostics, plus extensions involving more detailed data-type checking. Code auditors check for standards compliance, and can also perform various type-checking functions. Control flow and reachability analysis is done by structural analysis programs (flow charters have been used for some of the elementary checks here, "structurizers" can also be helpful). Other useful static analysis tools perform set-use analysis of data elements, singularity analysis, units consistency analysis, data base consistency checking, and data-versus-code consistency checking.

b) *Test case preparation:* Extensions to structural analysis programs provide assistance in choosing data values which will make the program execute along a desired path. Attempts have been made to automate the generation of such data values; they can generally succeed for simple cases, but run into difficulty in handling loops or branching on complex calculated values (e.g., the results of numerical integration). Further, these programs only help generate the *inputs;* the tester must still calculate the expected outputs himself.

Another set of tools will automatically insert instrumentation to verify that a desired path has indeed been exercised in the test. A limited capability exists for automatically determining the minimum number of test cases required to exercise all the code. But, as yet, there is no tool which helps to determine the most appropriate sequence in which to run a series of tests.

c) *Test monitoring and output checking:* Capabilities have been developed and used for various kinds of dynamic data-type checking and assertion checking, and for timing and performance analysis. Test output post-processing aids include output comparators and exception report capabilities, and test-oriented data reduction and report generation packages.

d) *Fault isolation, debugging:* Besides the traditional tools—the core dump, the trace, the snapshot, and the breakpoint—several capabilities have been developed for interactive replay or backtracking of the program's execution. This is still a difficult area, and only a relatively few advanced concepts have proved generally useful.

e) *Retesting (once a presumed fix has been made):* Test data management systems (for the code, the input data, and the comparison output data) have been shown to be most valuable here, along with comparators to check for the differences in code, inputs, and outputs between the original and the modified program and test case. A promising experimental tool performs a comparative structure analysis of the original and modified code, and indicates which test cases need to be rerun.

f) *Integration of routines into systems:* In general, automated aids for this process are just larger scale versions of the test data management systems above. Some additional capabilities exist for interface consistency checking, e.g., on the length and form of parameter lists or data base references. Top-down development aids are also helpful in this regard.

g) *Stopping:* Some partial criteria for thoroughness of testing can and have been automatically monitored. Tools exist which keep a cumulative tally of the number or percent of the instructions or branches which have been exercised during the test program, and indicate to the tester what branch conditions must be satisfied in order to completely exercise all the code or branches. Of course, these are far from complete criteria for determining when to stop testing; the completeness question is the subject of the next section.

4) *Test Sufficiency and Program Proving:* If a program's input space and output space are finite (where the input space includes not only all possible incoming inputs, but also all possible values in the program's data base), then one can construct a set of "black box" tests (one for each point in the input space) which can show conclusively that the program is correct (that its behavior matches its specification).

In general, though, a program's input space is infinite; for example, it must generally provide for rejecting unacceptable inputs. In this case, a finite set of black-box tests is not a sufficient demonstration of the program's correctness (since, for any input x, one must assure that the program does not wrongly treat it as a special case). Thus, the demonstration of correctness in this case involves some formal argument (e.g., a proof using induction) that the dynamic performance of the program indeed produces the static transformation of the input space indicated by the formal specification for the program. For finite portions of the input space, a successful exhaustive test of all cases can be considered as a satisfactory formal argument. Some good initial work in sorting out the conditions under which testing is equivalent to proof of a program's correctness has been done by Goodenough and Gerhart [63] and in a review of their work by Wegner [64].

5) *Symbolic Execution:* An attractive intermediate step between program testing and proving is "symbolic execution," a manual or automated procedure which operates on symbolic inputs (e.g., variable names) to produce symbolic outputs. Separate cases are generated for different execution paths. If there are a finite number of such paths, symbolic execution can be used to demonstrate correctness, using a finite symbolic input space and output space. In general, though, one cannot guarantee a finite number of paths. Even so, symbolic execution can be quite valuable as an aid to either program testing or proving. Two fairly powerful automated systems for symbolic execution exist, the EFFIGY system [65] and the SELECT system [66].

6) *Program Proving (Program Verification):* Program proving (increasingly referred to as program verification) involves expressing the program specifications as a logical proposition, expressing individual program execution statements as logical propositions, expressing program branching as an expansion into separate cases, and performing logical transformations on the propositions in a way which ends by demonstrating the equivalence of the program and its specification. Potentially infinite loops can be handled by inductive reasoning.

In general, nontrivial programs are very complicated and time-consuming to prove. In 1973, it was estimated that about one man-month of expert effort was required to prove 100 lines of code [67]. The largest program to be proved correct to date contained about 2000 statements [68]. Again, automation can help out on some of the complications. Some automated verification systems exist, notably those of London *et al.* [69] and Luckham *et al.* [70]. In general, such systems do not work on programs in the more common languages such as Fortran or Cobol. They work in languages such as Pascal [45], which has (unlike Fortran or Cobol) an axiomatic definition [71] allowing clean expression of program statements as logical propositions. An excellent survey of program verification technology has been given by London [72].

Besides size and language limitations, there are other factors which limit the utility of program proving techniques. Computations on "real" variables involving truncation and roundoff errors are virtually impossible to analyze with adequate accuracy for most nontrivial programs. Programs with nonformalizable inputs (e.g., from a sensor where one has just a rough idea of its bias, signal-to-noise ratio, etc.) are impossible to handle. And, of course, programs can be proved to be consistent with a specification which is itself incorrect with respect to the system's proper functioning. Finally, there is no guarantee that the proof is correct or complete; in fact, many published "proofs" have subsequently been demonstrated to have holes in them [63].

It has been said and often repeated that "testing can be used to demonstrate the presence of errors but never their absence" [73]. Unfortunately, if we must define "errors" to include those incurred by the two limitations above (errors in specifications and errors in proofs), it must be admitted that "program proving can be used to demonstrate the presence of errors but never their absence."

7) Fault-Tolerance: Programs do not have to be error-free to be reliable. If one could just detect erroneous computations as they occur and compensate for them, one could achieve reliable operation. This is the rationale behind schemes for fault-tolerant software. Unfortunately, both detection and compensation are formidable problems. Some progress has been made in the case of software detection and compensation for hardware errors; see, for example, the articles by Wulf [74] and Goldberg [75]. For software errors, Randell has formulated a concept of separately-programmed, alternate "recovery blocks" [76]. It appears attractive for parts of the error compensation activity, but it is still too early to tell how well it will handle the error detection problem, or what the price will be in program slowdown.

C. Trends

As we continue to collect and analyze more and more data on how, when, where, and why people make software errors, we will get added insights on how to avoid making such errors, how to organize our validation strategy and tactics (not only in testing but throughout the software life cycle), how to develop or evaluate new automated aids, and

how to develop useful methods for predicting software reliability. Some automated aids, particularly for static code checking, and for some dynamic-type or assertion checking, will be integrated into future programming languages and compilers. We should see some added useful criteria and associated aids for test completeness, particularly along the lines of exercising "all data elements" in some appropriate way. Symbolic execution capabilities will probably make their way into automated aids for test case generation, monitoring, and perhaps retesting.

Continuing work into the theory of software testing should provide some refined concepts of test validity, reliability, and completeness, plus a better theoretical base for supporting hybrid test/proof methods of verifying programs. Program proving techniques and aids will become more powerful in the size and range of programs they handle, and hopefully easier to use and harder to misuse. But many of their basic limitations will remain, particularly those involving real variables and nonformalizable inputs.

Unfortunately, most of these helpful capabilities will be available only to people working in higher order languages. Much of the progress in test technology will be unavailable to the increasing number of people who find themselves spending more and more time testing assembly language software written for minicomputers and microcomputers with poor test support capabilities. Powerful cross-compiler capabilities on large host machines and microprogrammed diagnostic emulation capabilities [77] should provide these people some relief after a while, but a great deal of software testing will regress back to earlier generation "dark ages."

VII. SOFTWARE MAINTENANCE

A. Scope of Software Maintenance

Software maintenance is an extremely important but highly neglected activity. Its importance is clear from Fig. 1: about 40 percent of the overall hardware–software dollar is going into software maintenance today, and this number is likely to grow to about 60 percent by 1985. It will continue to grow for a long time, as we continue to add to our inventory of code via development at a faster rate than we make code obsolete.

The figures above are only very approximate, because our only data so far are based on highly approximate definitions. It is hard to come up with an unexceptional definition of software maintenance. Here, we define it as "the process of modifying existing operational software while leaving its primary functions intact." It is useful to divide software maintenance into two categories: software *update,* which results in a changed functional specification for the software, and software *repair,* which leaves the functional specification intact. A good discussion of software repair is given in the paper by Swanson [78], who divides it into the subcategories of corrective maintenance (of processing, performance, or implementation failures),

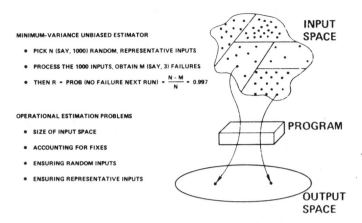

MINIMUM-VARIANCE UNBIASED ESTIMATOR

• PICK N (SAY, 1000) RANDOM, REPRESENTATIVE INPUTS

• PROCESS THE 1000 INPUTS, OBTAIN M (SAY, 3) FAILURES

• THEN R = PROB (NO FAILURE NEXT RUN) = $\frac{N - M}{N}$ = 0.997

OPERATIONAL ESTIMATION PROBLEMS

• SIZE OF INPUT SPACE

• ACCOUNTING FOR FIXES

• ENSURING RANDOM INPUTS

• ENSURING REPRESENTATIVE INPUTS

Fig. 5. Input space sampling provides a basis for software reliability measurement.

adaptive maintenance (to changes in the processing or data environment), and perfective maintenance (for enhancing performance or maintainability).

For either update or repair, three main functions are involved in software maintenance [79].

Understanding the existing software: This implies the need for good documentation, good traceability between requirements and code, and well-structured and well-formatted code.

Modifying the existing software: This implies the need for software, hardware, and data structures which are easy to expand and which minimize side effects of changes, plus easy-to-update documentation.

Revalidating the modified software: This implies the need for software structures which facilitate selective re-test, and aids for making retest more thorough and efficient.

Following a short discussion of current practice in software maintenance, these three functions will be used below as a framework for discussing current frontier technology in software maintenance.

B. Current Practice

As indicated in Fig. 6, probably about 70 percent of the overall cost of software is spent in software maintenance. A recent paper by Elshoff [80] indicates that the figure for General Motors is about 75 percent, and that GM is fairly typical of large business software activities. Daly [5] indicates that about 60 percent of GTE's 10-year life cycle costs for real-time software are devoted to maintenance. On two Air Force command and control software systems, the maintenance portions of the 10-year life cycle costs were about 67 and 72 percent. Often, maintenance is not done very efficiently. On one aircraft computer, software development costs were roughly $75/instruction, while maintenance costs ran as high as $4000/instruction [81].

Despite its size, software maintenance is a highly neglected activity. In general, less-qualified personnel are assigned to maintenance tasks. There are few good general principles and few studies of the process, most of them inconclusive.

Further, data processing practices are usually optimized

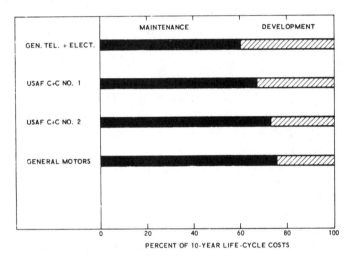

Fig. 6. Software life-cycle cost breakdown.

around other criteria than maintenance efficiency. Optimizing around development cost and schedule criteria generally leads to compromises in documentation, testing, and structuring. Optimizing around hardware efficiency criteria generally leads to use of assembly language and skimping on hardware, both of which correlate strongly with increased software maintenance costs [1].

C. Current Frontier Technology

1) Understanding the Existing Software: Aids here have largely been discussed in previous sections: structured programming, automatic formatting, and code auditors for standards compliance checking to enhance code readability; machine-readable requirements and design languages with traceability support to and from the code. Several systems exist for automatically updating documentation by excerpting information from the revised code and comment cards.

2) Modifying the Existing Software: Some of Parnas' modularization guidelines [32] and the data abstractions of the CLU [48] and ALPHARD [47] languages make it easier to minimize the side effects of changes. There may be a maintenance price, however. In the past, some systems with highly coupled programs and associated data structures have had difficulties with data base updating. This may not be a problem with today's data dictionary capabilities, but the interactions have not yet been investigated. Other aids to modification are structured code, configuration management techniques, programming support libraries, and process construction systems.

3) Revalidating the Modified Software: Aids here were discussed earlier under testing; they include primarily test data management systems, comparator programs, and program structure analyzers with some limited capability for selective retest analysis.

4) General Aids: On-line interactive systems help to remove one of the main bottlenecks involved in software maintenance: the long turnaround times for retesting. In addition, many of these systems are providing helpful capabilities for text editing and software module management. They will be discussed in more detail under "Management and Integrated Approaches" below. In general, a good deal more work has been done on the maintainability aspects of data bases and data structures than for program structures; a good survey of data base technology is given in a recent special issue of *ACM Computing Surveys* [82].

D. Trends

The increased concern with life cycle costs, particularly within the U.S. DoD [83], will focus a good deal more attention on software maintenance. More data collection and analysis on the growth dynamics of software systems, such as the Belady–Lehman studies of OS/360 [84], will begin to point out the high-leverage areas for improvement. Explicit mechanisms for confronting maintainability issues early in the development cycle, such as the requirements-properties matrix [18] and the design inspection [4] will be refined and used more extensively. In fact, we may evolve a more general concept of software quality assurance (currently focussed largely on reliability concerns), involving such activities as independent reviews of software requirements and design specifications by experts in software maintainability. Such activities will be enhanced considerably with the advent of more powerful capabilities for analyzing machine-readable requirements and design specifications. Finally, advances in automatic programming [14], [15] should reduce or eliminate some maintenance activity, at least in some problem domains.

VIII. SOFTWARE MANAGEMENT AND INTEGRATED APPROACHES

A. Current Practice

There are more opportunities for improving software productivity and quality in the area of management than anywhere else. The difference between software project successes and failures has most often been traced to good or poor practices in software management. The biggest software management problems have generally been the following.

Poor Planning: Generally, this leads to large amounts of wasted effort and idle time because of tasks being unnecessarily performed, overdone, poorly synchronized, or poorly interfaced.

Poor Control: Even a good plan is useless when it is not kept up-to-date and used to manage the project.

Poor Resource Estimation: Without a firm idea of how much time and effort a task should take, the manager is in a poor position to exercise control.

Unsuitable Management Personnel: As a very general statement, software personnel tend to respond to problem situations as designers rather than as managers.

Poor Accountability Structure: Projects are generally organized and run with very diffuse delineation of responsibilities, thus exacerbating all the above problems.

Inappropriate Success Criteria: Minimizing development costs and schedules will generally yield a hard-to-maintain product. Emphasizing "percent coded" tends to get people coding early and to neglect such key activities as requirements and design validation, test planning, and draft user documentation.

Procrastination on Key Activities: This is especially prevalent when reinforced by inappropriate success criteria as above.

B. Current Frontier Technology

1) Management Guidelines: There is no lack of useful material to guide software management. In general, it takes a book-length treatment to adequately cover the issues. A number of books on the subject are now available [85] –[95], but for various reasons they have not strongly influenced software management practice. Some of the books (e.g., Brooks [85] and the collections by Horowitz [86], Weinwurm [87], and Buxton, Naur, and Randell [88] are collections of very good advice, ideas, and experiences, but are fragmentary and lacking in a consistent, integrated life cycle approach. Some of the books (e.g., Metzger [89], Shaw and Atkins [90], Hice *et al.* [91], Ridge and Johnson [92], and Gildersleeve [93], are good on checklists and procedures but (except to some extent the latter two) are light on the human aspects of management, such as staffing, motivation, and conflict resolution. Weinberg [94] provides the most help on the human aspects, along with Brooks [85] and Aron [95], but in turn, these three books are light on checklists and procedures. (A second volume by Aron is intended to cover software group and project considerations.) None of the books have an adequate treatment of some items, largely because they are so poorly understood: chief among these items are software cost and resource estimation, and software maintenance.

In the area of software cost estimation, the paper by Wolverton [96] remains the most useful source of help. It is strongly based on the number of object instructions (modified by complexity, type of application, and novelty) as the determinant of software cost. This is a known weak spot, but not one for which an acceptable improvement has surfaced. One possible line of improvement might be along the "software physics" lines being investigated by Halstead [97] and others; some interesting initial results have been obtained here, but their utility for practical cost estimation remains to be demonstrated. A good review of the software cost estimation area is contained in [98].

2) Management-Technology Decoupling: Another difficulty of the above books is the degree to which they are decoupled from software technology. Except for the Horowitz and Aron books, they say relatively little about the use of such advanced-technology aids as formal, machine-readable requirements, top-down design approaches, structured programming, and automated aids to software testing.

Unfortunately, the management-technology decoupling works the other way, also. In the design area, for example, most treatments of top-down software design are presented as logical exercises independent of user or economic considerations. Most automated aids to software design provide little support for such management needs as configuration management, traceability to code or requirements, and resource estimation and control. Clearly, there needs to be a closer coupling between technology and management than this. Some current efforts to provide integrated management-technology approaches are presented next.

3) Integrated Approaches: Several major integrated systems for software development are currently in operation or under development. In general, their objectives are similar: to achieve a significant boost in software development efficiency and quality through the synergism of a unified approach. Examples are the utility of having a complementary development approach (top-down, hierarchical) and set of programming standards (hierarchical, structured code); the ability to perform a software update and at the same time perform a set of timely, consistent project status updates (new version number of module, closure of software problem report, updated status logs); or simply the improvement in software system integration achieved when all participants are using the same development concept, ground rules, and support software.

The most familiar of the integrated approaches is the IBM "top-down structured programming with chief programmer teams" concept. A good short description of the concept is given by Baker [49]; an extensive treatment is available in a 15-volume series of reports done by IBM for the U.S. Army and Air Force [99]. The top-down structured approach was discussed earlier. The Chief Programmer Team centers around an individual (the Chief) who is responsible for designing, coding, and integrating the top-level control structure as well as the key components of the team's product; for managing and motivating the team personnel and personally reading and reviewing all their code; and also for performing traditional management and customer interface functions. The Chief is assisted by a Backup programmer who is prepared at anytime to take the Chief's place, a Librarian who handles job submission, configuration control, and project status accounting, and additional programmers and specialists as needed.

In general, the overall ensemble of techniques has been quite successful, but the Chief Programmer concept has had mixed results [99]. It is difficult to find individuals with enough energy and talent to perform all the above functions. If you find one, the project will do quite well; otherwise, you have concentrated most of the project risk in a single individual, without a good way of finding out whether or not he is in trouble. The Librarian and Programming Support Library concept have generally been quite useful, although to date the concept has been oriented toward a batch-processing development environment.

Another "structured" integrated approach has been developed and used at SofTech [38]. It is oriented largely around a hierarchical-decomposition design approach, guided by formalized sets of principles (modularity, abstraction, localization, hiding, uniformity, completeness, confirmability), processes (purpose, concept, mechanism, notation, usage), and goals (modularity, efficiency, reliability, understandability). Thus, it accommodates some economic considerations, although it says little about any other management considerations. It appears to work well for SofTech, but in general has not been widely assimilated elsewhere.

A more management-intensive integrated approach is the TRW software development methodology exemplified in the paper by Williams [50] and the TRW Software Development and Configuration Management Manual [100], which has been used as the basis for several recent government in-house software manuals. This approach features a coordinated set of high-level and detailed management objectives, associated automated aids—standards compliance checkers, test thoroughness checkers, process construction aids, reporting systems for cost, schedule, core and time budgets, problem identification and closure, etc.—and unified documentation and management devices such as the Unit Development Folder. Portions of the approach are still largely manual, although additional automation is underway, e.g., via the Requirements Statement Language [13].

The SDC Software Factory [101] is a highly ambitious attempt to automate and integrate software development technology. It consists of an interface control component, the Factory Access and Control Executive (FACE), which provides users access to various tools and data bases: a project planning and monitoring system, a software development data base and module management system, a top-down development support system, a set of test tools, etc. As the system is still undergoing development and preliminary evaluation, it is too early to tell what degree of success it will have.

Another factory-type approach is the System Design Laboratory (SDL) under development at the Naval Electronics Laboratory Center [102]. It currently consists primarily of a framework within which a wide range of aids to software development can be incorporated. The initial installment contains text editors, compilers, assemblers, and microprogrammed emulators. Later additions are envisioned to include design, development, and test aids, and such management aids as progress reporting, cost reporting, and user profile analysis.

SDL itself is only a part of a more ambitious integrated approach, ARPA's National Software Works (NSW) [102]. The initial objective here has been to develop a "Works Manager" which will allow a software developer at a terminal to access a wide variety of software development tools on various computers available over the ARPANET. Thus, a developer might log into the NSW, obtain his source code from one computer, text-edit it on another, and perhaps continue to hand the program to additional computers for test instrumentation, compiling, executing, and postprocessing of output data. Currently, an initial version of the Works Manager is operational, along with a few tools, but it is too early to assess the likely outcome and payoffs of the project.

C. Trends

In the area of management techniques, we are probably entering a consolidation period, particularly as the U.S. DoD proceeds to implement the upgrades in its standards and procedures called for in the recent DoD Directive 5000.29 [104]. The resulting government-industry efforts should produce a set of software management guidelines which are more consistent and up-to-date with today's technology than the ones currently in use. It is likely that they will also be more comprehensible and less encumbered with DoD jargon; this will make them more useful to the software field in general.

Efforts to develop integrated, semiautomated systems for software development will continue at a healthy clip. They will run into a number of challenges which will probably take a few years to work out. Some are technical, such as the lack of a good technological base for data structuring aids, and the formidable problem of integrating complex software support tools. Some are economic and managerial, such as the problems of pricing services, providing tool warranties, and controlling the evolution of the system. Others are environmental, such as the proliferation of minicomputers and microcomputers, which will strain the capability of any support system to keep up-to-date.

Even if the various integrated systems do not achieve all their goals, there will be a number of major benefits from the effort. One is of course that a larger number of support tools will become available to a larger number of people (another major channel of tools will still continue to expand, though: the independent software products marketplace). More importantly, those systems which achieve a degree of conceptual integration (not just a free-form tool box) will eliminate a great deal of the semantic confusion which currently slows down our group efforts throughout the software life cycle. Where we have learned how to talk to each other about our software problems, we tend to do pretty well.

IX. CONCLUSIONS

Let us now assess the current state of the art of tools and techniques which are being used to solve software development problems, in terms of our original definition of software engineering: the practical application of *scientific knowledge* in the design and construction of software.

TABLE II
Applicability of Existing Scientific Principles

Dimension	Software Engineering	Hardware Engineering
Scope Across Life Cycle	Some principles for component construction and detailed design, virtually none for system design and integration, e.g., algorithms, automata theory.	Many principles applicable across life cycle, e.g., communication theory, control theory.
Scope Across Application	Some principles for "systems" software, virtually none for applications software, e.g., discrete mathematical structures.	Many principles applicable across entire application system, e.g., control theory application.
Engineering Economics	Very few principles which apply to system economics, e.g., algorithms.	Many principles apply well to system economics, e.g., strength of materials, optimization, and control theory.
Required Training	Very few principles formulated for consumption by technicians, e.g., structured code, basic math packages.	Many principles formulated for consumption by technicians, e.g., handbooks for structural design, stress testing, maintainability.

Table II presents a summary assessment of the extent to which current software engineering techniques are based on solid scientific principles (versus empirical heuristics). The summary assessment covers four dimensions: the extent to which existing scientific principles apply across the entire software life cycle, across the entire range of software applications, across the range of engineering-economic analyses required for software development, and across the range of personnel available to perform software development.

For perspective, a similar summary assessment is presented in Table II for hardware engineering. It is clear from Table II that software engineering is in a very primitive state as compared to hardware engineering, with respect to its range of scientific foundations. Those scientific principles available to support software engineering address problems in an area we shall call *Area 1: detailed design and coding* of *systems software* by *experts* in a relatively *economics-independent* context. Unfortunately, the most pressing software development problems are in an area we shall call *Area 2: requirements analysis design, test, and maintenance* of *applications software* by *technicians* [3] in an *economics-driven* context. And in Area 2, our scientific foundations are so slight that one can seri-

[3] For example, a recent survey of 14 installations in one large organization produced the following profile of its "average coder": 2 years college-level education, 2 years software experience, familiarity with 2 programming languages and 2 applications, and generally introverted, sloppy, inflexible, "in over his head," and undermanaged. Given the continuing increase in demand for software personnel, one should not assume that this typical profile will improve much. This has strong implications for effective software engineering technology which, like effective software, must be well-matched to the people who must use it.

ously question whether our current techniques deserve to be called "software engineering."

Hardware engineering clearly has available a better scientific foundation for addressing its counterpart of these Area 2 problems. This should not be too surprising, since "hardware science" has been pursued for a much longer time, is easier to experiment with, and does not have to explain the performance of human beings.

What is rather surprising, and a bit disappointing, is the reluctance of the computer science field to address itself to the more difficult and diffuse problems in Area 2, as compared with the more tractable Area 1 subjects of automata theory, parsing, computability, etc. Like most explorations into the relatively unknown, the risks of addressing Area 2 research problems in the requirements analysis, design, test and maintenance of applications software are relatively higher. But the prizes, in terms of payoff to practical software development and maintenance, are likely to be far more rewarding. In fact, as software engineering begins to solve its more difficult Area 2 problems, it will begin to lead the way toward solutions to the more difficult large-systems problems which continue to beset hardware engineering.

REFERENCES

[1] B. W. Boehm, "Software and its impact: A quantitative assessment," *Datamation,* pp. 48–59, May 1973.
[2] T. A. Dolotta *et al., Data Processing in 1980–85.* New York: Wiley-Interscience, 1976.
[3] P. Wegner, "Computer languages," *IEEE Trans. Comput.,* this issue, pp. 1207–1225.
[4] M. E. Fagan, "Design and code inspections and process control in the development of programs," IBM, rep. IBM-SDD TR-21.572, Dec. 1974.
[5] E. B. Daly, "Management of software development," *IEEE Trans. Software Eng.,* to be published.
[6] W. W. Royce, "Software requirements analysis, sizing, and costing," in *Practical Strategies for the Development of Large Scale Software,* E. Horowitz, Ed. Reading, MA: Addison-Wesley, 1975.
[7] T. E. Bell and T. A. Thayer, "Software requirements: Are they a problem?," *Proc. IEEE/ACM 2nd Int. Conf. Software Eng.,* Oct. 1976.
[8] E. S. Quade, Ed., *Analysis for Military Decisions.* Chicago, IL: Rand-McNally, 1964.
[9] J. D. Couger and R. W. Knapp, Eds:, *System Analysis Techniques.* New York: Wiley, 1974.
[10] D. Teichroew and H. Sayani, "Automation of system building," *Datamation,* pp. 25–30, Aug. 15, 1971.
[11] C. G. Davis and C. R. Vick, "The software development system," in *Proc. IEEE/ACM 2nd Int. Conf. Software Eng.,* Oct. 1976.
[12] M. Alford, "A requirements engineering methodology for real-time processing requirements," in *Proc. IEEE/ACM 2nd Int. Conf. Software Eng.,* Oct. 1976.
[13] T. E. Bell, D. C. Bixler, and M. E. Dyer, "An extendable approach to computer-aided software requirements engineering," in *Proc. IEEE/ACM 2nd Int. Conf. Software Eng.,* Oct. 1976.
[14] R. M. Balzer, "Imprecise program specification," Univ. Southern California, Los Angeles, rep. ISI/RR-75-36, Dec. 1975.
[15] W. A. Martin and M. Bosyj, "Requirements derivation in automatic programming," in *Proc. MRI Symp. Comput. Software Eng.,* Apr. 1976.
[16] N. P. Dooner and J. R. Lourie, "The application software engineering tool," IBM, res. rep. RC 5434, May 29, 1975.
[17] M. L. Wilson, "The information automat approach to design and implementation of computer-based systems," IBM, rep. IBM-FSD, June 27, 1975.
[18] B. W. Boehm, "Some steps toward formal and automated aids to software requirements analysis and design," *Proc. IFIP Cong.,* 1974, pp. 192–197.
[19] A. B. Endres, "An analysis of errors and their causes in system programs," *IEEE Trans. Software Eng.,* pp. 140–149, June 1975.
[20] T. A. Thayer, "Understanding software through analysis of empirical data," *Proc. Nat. Comput. Conf.,* 1975, pp. 335–341.
[21] B. W. Boehm, R. L. McClean, and D. B. Urfrig, "Some experience with automated aids to the design of large-scale reliable software," *IEEE Trans. Software Eng.,* pp. 125–133, Mar. 1975.
[22] P. Freeman, "Software design representation: Analysis and improvements," Univ. California, Irvine, tech. rep. 81, May 1976.
[23] E. L. Glaser *et al.,* "The LOGOS project," in *Proc. IEEE COMPCON,* 1972, pp. 175–192.
[24] N. R. Nielsen, "ECSS: Extendable computer system simulator," Rand Corp., rep. RM-6132-PR/NASA, Jan. 1970.
[25] D. W. Kosy, "The ECSS II language for simulating computer systems," Rand Corp., rep. R-1895-GSA, Dec. 1975.
[26] E. W. Dijkstra, "Complexity controlled by hierarchical ordering of function and variability," in *Software Engineering,* P. Naur and B. Randell, Eds. NATO, Jan. 1969.
[27] H. D. Mills, "Mathematical foundations for structured programming," IBM-FSD, rep. FSC 72-6012, Feb. 1972.
[28] C. L. McGowan and J. R. Kelly, *Top-Down Structured Programming Techniques.* New York: Petrocelli/Charter, 1975.
[29] B. W. Boehm *et al.,* "Structured programming: A quantitative assessment," *Computer,* pp. 38–54, June 1975.
[30] W. P. Stevens, G. J. Myers, and L. L. Constantine, "Structured design," *IBM Syst. J.,* vol. 13, no. 2, pp. 115–139, 1974.
[31] G. J. Myers, *Reliable Software Through Composite Design.* New York: Petrocelli/Charter, 1975.
[32] D. L. Parnas, "On the criteria to be used in decomposing systems into modules," *CACM,* pp. 1053–1058, Dec. 1972.
[33] D. L. Parnas, "The influence of software structure on reliability," in *Proc. 1975 Int. Conf. Reliable Software,* Apr. 1975, pp. 358–362, available from IEEE.
[34] M. Hamilton and S. Zeldin, "Higher order software—A methodology for defining software," *IEEE Trans. Software Eng.,* pp. 9–32, Mar. 1976.
[35] "HIPO—A design aid and documentation technique," IBM, rep. GC20-1851-0, Oct. 1974.
[36] J. Mortison, "Tools and techniques for software development process visibility and control," in *Proc. ACM Comput. Sci. Conf.,* Feb. 1976.
[37] I. Nassi and B. Schneiderman, "Flowchart techniques for structured programming," *SIGPLAN Notices,* pp. 12–26, Aug. 1973.
[38] D. T. Ross, J. B. Goodenough, and C. A. Irvine, "Software engineering: Process, principles, and goals," *Computer,* pp. 17–27, May 1975.
[39] M. A. Jackson, *Principles of Program Design.* New York: Academic, 1975.
[40] P. Henderson and R A. Snowden, "A tool for structured program development," in *Proc. 1974 IFIP Cong.,* pp. 204–207.
[41] L. C. Carpenter and L. L. Tripp, "Software design validation tool," in *Proc. 1975 Int. Conf. Reliable Software,* Apr. 1975, pp. 395–400, available from IEEE.
[42] S. H. Caine and E. K. Gordon, "PDL: A tool for software design," in *Proc. 1975 Nat. Comput. Conf.,* pp. 271–276.
[43] H. D. Mills, "Structured programming in large systems," IBM-FSD, Nov. 1970.
[44] C. A. R. Hoare, "Notes on data structuring," in *Structured Programming,* O. J. Dahl, E. W. Dijkstra, and C. A. R. Hoare. New York: Academic, 1972.
[45] N. Wirth, "An assessment of the programming language Pascal," *IEEE Trans. Software Eng.,* pp. 192–198, June 1975.
[46] P. Brinch-Hansen, "The programming language concurrent Pascal," *IEEE Trans. Software Eng.,* pp. 199–208, June 1975.
[47] W. A. Wulf, *ALPHARD: Toward a language to support structured programs,* Carnegie-Mellon Univ., Pittsburgh, PA, internal rep., Apr. 30, 1974.
[48] B. H. Liskov and S. Zilles, "Programming with abstract data types," *SIGPLAN Notices,* pp. 50–59, April 1974.
[49] F. T. Baker, "Structured programming in a production programming environment," *IEEE Trans. Software Eng.,* pp. 241–252, June 1975.
[50] R. D. Williams, "Managing the development of reliable software," *Proc., 1975 Int. Conf. Reliable Software* April 1975, pp. 3–8, available from IEEE.
[51] J. Witt, "The COLUMBUS approach," *IEEE Trans. Software*

Eng., pp. 358–363, Dec. 1975.

[52] B. W. Kernighan and P. J. Plauger, *The Elements of Programming Style*. New York: McGraw-Hill, 1974.

[53] H. F. Ledgard, *Programming Proverbs*. Rochelle Park, NJ: Hayden, 1975

[54] W. A. Whitaker *et al.*, "Department of Defense requirements for high order computer programming languages: 'Tinman,' " Defense Advanced Research Projects Agency, Apr. 1976.

[55] *Proc. 1973 IEEE Symp. Comput. Software Reliability*, Apr.–May 1973.

[56] E. C. Nelson, "A statistical basis for software reliability assessment," TRW Systems, Redondo Beach, CA, rep. TRW-SS-73-03, Mar. 1973.

[57] J. R. Brown and M. Lipow, "Testing for software reliability," in *Proc. 1975 Int. Conf. Reliable Software*, Apr. 1975, pp. 518–527.

[58] J. D. Musa, "Theory of software reliability and its application," *IEEE Trans. Software Eng.*, pp. 312–327, Sept. 1975.

[59] R. J. Rubey, J. A. Dana, and P. W. Biche, "Quantitative Aspects of software validation," *IEEE Trans. Software Eng.*, pp. 150–155, June 1975.

[60] T. A. Thayer, M. Lipow, and E. C. Nelson, "Software reliability study," TRW Systems, Redondo Beach, CA, rep. to RADC, Contract F30602-74-C-0036, Mar. 1976.

[61] D. J. Reifer, "Automated aids for reliable software," in *Proc. 1975 Int. Conf. Reliable Software*, Apr. 1975, pp. 131–142.

[62] C. V. Ramamoorthy and S. B. F. Ho, "Testing large software with automated software evaluation systems," *IEEE Trans. Software Eng.*, pp. 46–58, Mar. 1975.

[63] J. B. Goodenough and S. L. Gerhart, "Toward a theory of test data selection," *IEEE Trans. Software Eng.*, pp. 156–173, June 1975.

[64] P. Wegner, "Report on the 1975 International Conference on Reliable Software," in *Findings and Recommendations of the Joint Logistics Commanders' Software Reliability Work Group*, Vol. II, Nov. 1975, pp. 45–88.

[65] J. C. King, "A new approach to program testing," in *Proc. 1975 Int. Conf. Reliable Software*, Apr. 1975, pp. 228–233.

[66] R. S. Boyer, B. Elspas, and K. N. Levitt, "Select—A formal system for testing and debugging programs," in *Proc. 1975 Int. Conf. Reliable Software*, Apr. 1975, pp. 234–245.

[67] J. Goldberg, Ed., *Proc. Symp. High Cost of Software*, Stanford Research Institute, Stanford, CA, Sept. 1973, p. 63.

[68] L. C. Ragland, "A verified program verifier," Ph.D. dissertation, Univ. of Texas, Austin, 1973.

[69] D. I. Good, R. L. London, and W. W. Bledsoe, "An interactive program verification system," *IEEE Trans. Software Eng.*, pp. 59–67, Mar. 1975.

[70] F. W. von Henke and D. C. Luckham, "A methodology for verifying programs," in *Proc. 1975 Int. Conf. Reliable Software*, pp. 156–164, Apr. 1975.

[71] C. A. R. Hoare and N. Wirth, "An axiomatic definition of the programming language PASCAL," *Acta Informatica*, vol. 2, pp. 335–355, 1973.

[72] R. L. London, "A view of program verification," in *Proc. 1975 Int. Conf. Reliable Software*, Apr. 1975, pp. 534–545.

[73] E. W. Dijkstra, "Notes on structured programming," in *Structured Programming*, O. J. Dahl, E. W. Dijkstra, and C. A. R. Hoare. New York: Academic, 1972.

[74] W. A. Wulf, "Reliable hardware-software architectures," *IEEE Trans. Software Eng.*, pp. 233–240, June 1975.

[75] J. Goldberg, "New problems in fault-tolerant computing," in *Proc. 1975 Int. Symp. Fault-Tolerant Computing*, Paris, France, pp. 29–36, June 1975.

[76] B. Randell, "System structure for software fault-tolerance," *IEEE Trans. Software Eng.*, pp. 220–232, June 1975.

[77] R. K. McClean and B. Press, "Improved techniques for reliable software using microprogrammed diagnostic emulation," in *Proc. IFAC Cong.*, Vol. IV, Aug. 1975.

[78] E. B. Swanson, "The dimensions of maintenance," in *Proc. IEEE/ACM 2nd Int. Conf. Software Eng.*, Oct. 1976.

[79] B. W. Boehm, J. R. Brown, and M. Lipow, "Quantitative evaluation of software quality," in *Proc. IEEE/ACM 2nd Int. Conf. Software Eng.*, Oct. 1976.

[80] J. L. Elshoff, "An analysis of some commercial PL/I programs," *IEEE Trans. Software Eng.*, pp. 113–120, June 1976.

[81] W. L. Trainor, "Software: From Satan to saviour," in *Proc.*, *NAECON*, May 1973.

[82] E. H. Sibley, Ed., *ACM Comput. Surveys (Special Issue on Data Base Management Systems)*, Mar. 1976.

[83] *Defense Management J. (Special Issue on Software Management)*, vol. II, Oct. 1975.

[84] L. A. Belady and M. M. Lehman, "The evolution dynamics of large programs," IBM Research, Sept. 1975.

[85] F. P. Brooks, *The Mythical Man-Month*. Reading, MA: Addison-Wesley, 1975.

[86] E. Horowitz, Ed., *Practical Strategies for Developing Large-Scale Software*. Reading, MA: Addison-Wesley, 1975.

[87] G. F. Weinwurm, Ed., *On the Management of Computer Programming*. New York: Auerbach, 1970.

[88] P. Naur and B. Randell, Eds., *Software Engineering*, NATO, Jan. 1969.

[89] P. J. Metzger, *Managing a Programming Project*. Englewood Cliffs, NJ: Prentice-Hall, 1973.

[90] J. C. Shaw and W. Atkins, *Managing Computer System Projects*. New York: McGraw-Hill, 1970.

[91] G. F. Hice, W. S. Turner, and L. F. Cashwell, *System Development Methodology*. New York: American Elsevier, 1974

[92] W. J. Ridge and L. E. Johnson, *Effective Management of Computer Software*. Homewood, IL: Dow Jones-Irwin, 1973.

[93] T. R. Gildersleeve, *Data Processing Project Management*. New York: Van Nostrand Reinhold, 1974.

[94] G. F. Weinberg, *The Psychology of Computer Programming*. New York: Van Nostrand Reinhold, 1971.

[95] J. D. Aron, *The Program Development Process: The Individual Programmer*. Reading, MA: Addison-Wesley, 1974.

[96] R. W. Wolverton, "The cost of developing large-scale software," *IEEE Trans. Comput.*, 1974.

[97] M. H. Halstead, "Toward a theoretical basis for estimating programming effort," in *Proc. Ass. Comput. Mach. Conf.*, Oct. 1975, pp. 222–224.

[98] *Summary Notes, Government/Industry Software Sizing and Costing Workshop*, USAF Electron. Syst. Div., Oct. 1974.

[99] B. S. Barry and J. J. Naughton, "Chief programmer team operations description," U. S. Air Force, rep. RADC-TR-74-300, Vol. X (of 15-volume series), pp. 1-2-1-3.

[100] *Software Development and Configuration Management Manual*, TRW Systems, Redondo Beach, CA, rep. TRW-SS-73-07, Dec. 1973.

[101] H. Bratman and T. Court, "The software factory," *Computer*, pp. 28–37, May 1975.

[102] "Systems design laboratory: Preliminary design report," Naval Electronics Lab. Center, Preliminary Working Paper, TN-3145, Mar. 1976.

[103] W. E. Carlson and S. D. Crocker, "The impact of networks on the software marketplace," in *Proc. EASCON*, Oct. 1974.

[104] "Management of computer resources in major defense systems," Department of Defense, Directive 6000.29, Apr. 1976.

Barry W. Boehm received the B.A. degree in mathematics from Harvard University, Cambridge, MA, in 1957, and the M.A. and Ph.D. degrees from the University of California, Los Angeles, in 1961 and 1964, respectively.

He entered the computing field as a Programmer in 1955 and has variously served as a Numerical Analyst, System Analyst, Information System Development Project Leader, Manager of groups performing such tasks, Head of the Information Sciences Department at the Rand Corporation, and as Director of the 1971 Air Force CCIP-85 study. He is currently Director of Software Research and Technology within the TRW Systems and Energy Group, Redondo Beach, CA. He is the author of papers on a number of computing subjects, most recently in the area of software requirements analysis and design technology. He serves on several governmental advisory committees, and currently is Chairman of the NASA Research and Technology Advisory Committee on Guidance, Control, and Information Systems.

Dr. Boehm is a member of the IEEE Computer Society, in which he currently serves on the Editorial Board of the IEEE TRANSACTIONS ON SOFTWARE ENGINEERING and on the Technical Committee on Software Engineering.

STRUCTURED WALK-THROUGHS: A PROJECT MANAGEMENT TOOL

IBM CORPORATION

Abstract: This document describes the structured walk-through, a tool being used within the IBM Systems Development Division. Experience to date indicates that there are major benefits to its use both the programming project team, and for the quality of the software they produce.

This description of structured walk-throughs represents the collected work of many people with the Systems Development Division. Special acknowledgements are expressed to William B. Cammack, David R. McRitchie, David E. Fishlock, and Henry J. Rodgers, Jr.

1. STRUCTURED WALK-THROUGHS

Project management has long recognized the need for periodic reviews as a vehicle for determining where the project stands in relation to its schedule, and for identifying areas that require special attention. Generally, however, these exercises have been looked upon with misgivings by those who must submit themselves to the review.

The situation which classically arises during the review is one of conflict and hostility. The review takes on the appearance of a witch hunt and the reviewer finds himself in the position of inquisitor. At best the reviewees feel they have little to gain from this encounter and most probably feel that they will come out of the review with a list of "to-dos" which will only serve to put them farther behind in their development schedules. More damaging still is their belief that the longer the list, the longer the indictment against them. They feel that they will learn nothing in the review which will help them attack their unique problems; and moreover, they feel that they will spend a large and unproductive portion of the meeting just bringing the reviewer up from ground zero.

The structured walk-through described here increases the value of these reviews beyond a determination of schedule variance and problem identification, and eliminates many of the negative aspects. Within IBM the structured walk-through is:

1. A positive motivator for the project team.

2. A learning experience for the team.

3. A tool for analyzing the functional design of a system.

4. A tool for uncovering logic errors in program design.

5. A tool for eliminating coding errors before they enter the system.

6. A framework for implementing a testing strategy in parallel with development.

7. A measure of completeness.

A structured walk-through is a generic name given to a series of reviews, each with different objectives and each occurring at different times in the application development cycle. The basic characteristics of the walk-through are:

1. It is arranged and scheduled by the developer (reviewee) of the work product being reviewed.

2. Management does not attend the walk-through and it is not used as a basis for employee evaluation.

3. The participants (reviewers) are given the review materials prior to the walk-through and are expected to be familiar with them.

4. The walk-through is structured in the sense that all attendees know what is to be accomplished and what role they are to play.

5. The emphasis is on error detection rather than error correction

6. All technical members of the project team, from most senior to most junior, have their work product reviewed.

2. MECHANICS

The objectives of the structured walk-through will be different at different stages of the project. The basic mechanics will, however, remain the same. The reviewee, the person whose work product is being reviewed, is responsible for arranging the meeting. Several days prior to the meeting the reviewee selects the attendees he feels are required, distributes his work product to them, states what the objectives of the walk-through will be, and specifies what roles the reviewers are to play.

Although there are no hard and fast rules as to who the reviewers should be, the idea is for the reviewee to pick those interested parties who can detect deviations, inconsistencies, and violations within the work product or in the way that it interacts with its environment. Typically, but not necessarily, the reviewers will be project teammates of the reviewee. For example, early in the project, when a major objective is to ensure that the system is functionally complete, the reviewee might want user representatives. Or, if programmers and analysts are functionally separated, and the objective of the walk-through is to ensure that the programmer's internal specifications match the analyst's external specifications, then the programmer would want the analyst to attend. Within IBM, it is not uncommon for a programmer to reschedule a walk-through several times in order to ensure that a particular reviewer will be available.

A typical walk-through will include four to six people and will last for a pre-specified time, usually one or two hours. If at the end of that time the objectives have not been met, another walk-through is scheduled for the next convenient time. Someone is designated as the recording secretary. This person records all the errors, discrepancies, exposures and inconsistencies that are uncovered during the walk-through. This record becomes an action list for the reviewee and a communication vehicle with the reviewers.

In addition to the substantive questions which will hopefully arise in the reviewer's mind prior to the walk-through, he will undoubtedly detect minor mistakes such as typos, spelling, grammatical and coding syntax errors. These can be handled several ways. One way is to instruct each reviewer to make an error list and pass it to the recording secretary at the beginning of the walk-though. Another way is for each reviewer to cover these errors with the reviewee offline. Or, the reviewers can annotate their copies of the work product and return it to the reviewer at the end of the walk-through. The important point is that the walk-through should be concerned with problems of greater substance (i.e., ambiguous specifications, basic design flaws, poor logic, inappropriate or inefficient coding techniques).

Mechanically, what takes place during the structured walk-through? First, the reviewers are requested to comment on the completeness, accuracy and general quality of the work product. Major concerns are expressed and identified as areas for potential follow-up. The reviewee then gives a brief tutorial overview of the work product. He next "walks" the reviewers through the work product in a step-by-step fashion which simulates the function under investigation. He attempts to take the reviewers through the material in enough detail so that the major concerns which were expressed earlier in the meeting will either be explained away, or brought into focus. New thoughts and concerns will arise during this "manual execution" of the function, and the ensuing discussion of these points will crystallize everyone's thinking. Significant factors that require action are recorded as they emerge.

A key element regarding the structured walk-through is its relationship to the project test strategy. Within IBM, the structured walk-through is part and parcel of a parallel test strategy, and in fact, the "manual execution" is often driven by formalized test cases. This is discussed more fully in Section 4.

Immediately after the meeting, the recording secretary distributes copies of the handwritten action list to all the attendees. It is the responsibility of the reviewee to ensure that the points of concern on the action list are successfully resolved, and that the reviewers are notified of the actions and/or corrections that have been taken. (This latter point is important because many of the revelations which arise impact the reviewers, particularly if they and the reviewee are teammates.) Management does not double check the action list to ensure that the outstanding problems have been resolved, nor does it use this list as a basis for employee evaluation. Rather the action list is considered to be a tool used to improve the product.

3. AS PART OF NEW TECHNOLOGIES . . .

Structured walk-throughs have been implemented within IBM programming groups which are using structured programming, top-down development, development support libraries and team operations. In fact, the use of walk-through as described in this paper has evolved to its present position because of these new technologies.

The visibility inherent in structured programming, the idea that code is meant to be read by others, the enforced programming conventions, and the simplified program logic make it easy for the reviewer to be "walked through" code segments.

The use of HIPO as a top-down design and documentation tool lends itself well to the structured walk-through. HIPO's graphical representation of function gives the reviewee the luxury of something concrete and tangible through which he can take the reviewers in a step-by-step fashion at increasing levels of detail.

A development support library organizes and structures the emerging system so that the details can be easily reviewed. In addition, the librarian can also serve as the recording secretary for the walk-throughs.

The concept of a tightly knit team whose members possess unique skills and who are in close communication with each other, is logically supported by the idea of a walk-through. Since the chief programmer and the backup programmer already read code, the extension to everyone reading code is not a major jump. Additionally, there is value in the walk-through as an educational tool. Because the chief programmer and the backup programmer design and code the top of the system first, their initial walk-throughs serve as important learning experiences for the other team members-- both in terms of design and coding techniques, and as an introduction to the system.

Within an application development cycle, there are several major milestones and many minor milestones where the walk-through technique can be used. As an example, a manning curve for an application development cycle in which the new technologies are being used might look as shown in Figure 1. The management of this project could decide that one condition for successfully reaching the milestones listed in the left hand column of Figure 2, is that the items in the right hand column must have been reviewed in a structured walk-through. In this sense the walk-through tracks progress and serves as a meaningful measure of completeness. Major milestones where structured walk-throughs might be employed include end of system planning, end of system design and end of development.

4. PARALLEL TESTING

The structured walk-through can serve to establish a framework for parallel testing. Parallel testing implies: 1) the development of test cases and testing procedures in parallel with the development of the system, and 2) an independent tester who is responsible for implementing the test strategy.

When using team operations, the tester would logically be the backup programmer. In large, functionally separated, organizations the tester(s) might come from an independent group.

The tester builds a product in much the same manner as the developer does. They both start at the same place, with a set of functional specifications. The developer, however, looks at the specs as a builder might look at blueprints, while the tester looks at those specs in the way a building inspector might look at blueprints. The tester, like the inspector, attempts to ensure that the specifications meet certain standards, and that the product matches the specifications.

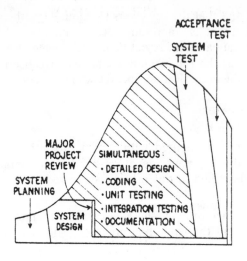

Figure 1. A typical manning curve for an application development cycle.

A functional program specification can be boiled down to a set of cause and effect relationships:

- "If the accumulated FICA deduction is equal to or greater than $10,800, then return the difference to net pay."

- "When the on-hand balance falls below the reorder point, transfer control to the EOQ routine."

- "Set the transmission line to inoperative and notify the network control operator if the retry procedure fails."

Initially the tester takes the functional specifications and breaks them down into a series of cause and effect statements. Rigorous testing means that each of these cause and effect relationships must be tested. That is to say, the tester, using some form of tabular or graphical assistance, must determine whether each cause has its desired effect. Unfortunately, this not always easy to do. If it were, testing would not be a problem and systems would be more error free. Cause and effect relationships tend to string together in complex logical chains. Therefore, it is not always obvious what is a cause and what is an effect. In addition, analysts an designers don't apply the same discipline to their specifications that the programmer must apply to his code. Rather, they tend toward free flowing prose, resplendent with inconsistencies.* Nevertheless, the product which the tester is creating will evolve into a formalized set of machine readable test cases, residing in a test library, which based on the quality of his efforts and the thoroughness with which he breaks down the functional specifications, will test the code.

Within IBM the tester plays a key role in those structured walk-throughs which relate to detailed design and programming. The tester views the walk-through as the vehicle which formally brings him together with the developer. After the reviewee walks the reviewers through the work product to bring everyone to a common level of understanding, he passes control of the meeting to the tester. The tester presents his test cases, one by one, to the reviewee. All participants observe as the reviewee walks each test case through the work product. Inconsistencies and errors are spotted in the work product

---

* The English language is not noted for its ability to express complex relationships with precision. Perhaps the future will see us evolve into structured specification languages. A step in that direction would be pseudo code narrative associated with structured programming.

PROJECT MILESTONES	ITEMS TO BE REVIEWED VIA A STRUCTURED WALK-THROUGH
End of System Planning	Project Plans System Definition Task Identification
Major Project Milestones	
Major Project Review "Technical"	Functional Specifications Work Assignments Schedules
Multiple Minor Milestones	
• Detailed Design	Internal Specifications HIPO Package
• Doding	Uncompiled Source Listings

• Documentation	User Guides
	Programmer Maintenance Manuals
	  • Internal Specifications
	  • HIPO Package

End of Development	Deliverable Product
	  • Code
	  • Documentation

Figure 2. The table shows items which might be reviewed using structured walk-throughs at various times during a project. The minor milestones would be repeated as the system grew.

and also in the test cases. The recording secretary is responsible for recording problems that relate to the product, and the tester is responsible for recording and correcting problems that relate to his test cases. The tester's goal is to produce a complete and non-overlapping library of test cases which will validate the final product.

The evolution of the test library proceeds in parallel with the system. While the system develops from functional specifications to internal program specifications and HIPO diagrams, to source code and finally to compiled code, the tester is independently developing the test library from the functional specifications, to cause and effect relationships, to manual test cases, and finally to machine readable test cases. By the time a subset of the system is ready to be compiled, the test cases will be included in the test library and can be driven against the compiled code.

This parallel evolution of the application and its test cases, synchronized at each development step by a structured walk-through, ensures a thoroughness and a discipline which cannot be achieved when testing is handled as a follow-on to development.

5. PSYCHOLOGY

The interested reader may wonder why management doesn't take a more active part in the walk-through; or more specifically, why management doesn't use the action list as a measure of employee performance. The answer is that management could, but only at the expense of losing some of the values of the walk-through.

An essential ingredient for a successful walk-through is an open and non-defensive attitude on the part of the participants. A productive atmosphere is one in which the reviewee makes it easy for the reviewers to find problems. He should welcome their feedback and should encourage their frankness. If, however, he feels that he is being evaluated by what occurs in the walk-through, and by the size of the action list, he will naturally tend to suppress criticisms. He will be defensive and unreceptive to new ideas. His ego will be staked to the work product and he will have little motivation to use the session as a learning experience. A successful walk-through, by comparison, is one in which many errors and inconsistencies are uncovered.

The role of the reviewers is one of preparation, non-malicious probing, and problem definition. If they are teammates of the reviewee, it will not be uncommon for them to discover that hidden relationships exist between what they are developing and what is being reviewed. Ambiguities will come to light which will require further clarification and definition. If for no other reason, management should value the walk-through for its contribution as a communication tool among the developers.

Setting the proper psychological atmosphere for structured walk-through is key. An organization utilizing team operations, top-down development, and structured programming can do it rather naturally. Since the chief programmer and the backup programmer will produce the initial design and the most critical code in the system, their work products will be the first under review. Because they are more senior and more closely attuned to management's desires (the design programmer may in fact be the manager), they are in a position to establish the proper framework and attitude surrounding the walk-through. In addition, these initial walk-throughs will serve as a learning experience for the team not only as to the walk-through mechanics, but with respect to the system itself.

6. SUMMARY

Our experience with structured walk-throughs has been most encouraging. Undoubtedly there are a number of ways they could be modified to fit other organizations. The central idea, however, should remain the same; i.e., to convert the classical project review into a productive working session which not only tracks progress but which makes a positive contribution to that progress. Outwardly management involvement appears low, but in reality structured walk-throughs provide management with a vehicle for catching errors in the system at the earliest possible time when the cost of correcting them is lowest and their impact is smallest. ∎

Top-Down Design and Testing

This chapter deals specifically with two related techniques: *top-down design* and *top-down testing*. The format of the chapter is simple: First, a brief overview of the technical concepts behind the top-down approach; second, a review of the management-oriented benefits of the approach; and third, a discussion of the problems and difficulties that you, as a manager, are likely to encounter when implementing the top-down approach in your organization.

4.1 An overview of the top-down approach

Top-down design and top-down testing have been practiced instinctively by many programmers for years. In academic circles, the top-down approach has been referred to as "systematic programming," "stepwise refinement," "levels of abstraction," and a variety of other names. The phrase "top-down," however, today seems to dominate the other buzz-words.

My purpose in this section is to provide you with enough of an understanding of these important concepts of design and implementation to enable you to discuss them intelligently with your technical people — and with other EDP managers. I am *not* trying to make you an expert on top-down design, and I certainly don't intend to say everything there is to be said on the subject (even if I were capable of doing so!). If you and/or your programmers require a more detailed discussion of the top-down approach, the references at the end of this chapter should prove helpful.

Before discussing the approach, I should warn you that many EDP people use the phrase top-down rather loosely. For reasons that are largely historical in nature, top-down design and structured programming have long been discussed together. Indeed, you'll notice that many of the references at the end of this chapter emphasize structured programming, but that few include top-down in the title. There is nothing wrong with the association, but you should make sure that when *you* are discussing top-down design with one of your colleagues, he or she is not thinking about structured programming. The two are not synonymous, as you will see in our discussion of structured programming in Chapter 6.

Also, when you are discussing the top-down approach with a colleague, make sure that you're both discussing the same *aspect* of the top-down approach. We can identify three related, but distinct, aspects of top-down:

- *top-down design:* a design strategy that breaks large, complex problems into smaller, less complex problems — and then decomposes each of those smaller problems into even smaller problems, until the original problem has been expressed as some combination of many small, *solvable* problems.

- *top-down coding:* a strategy of coding high-level, executive modules as soon as they have been designed — and generally before the low-level, detail modules have been designed.

- *top-down testing* or *top-down implementation:* a strategy of testing the high-level modules of a system before the low-level modules have been coded — and possibly before they have been designed.

What a perfectly simple idea! Indeed, what more does one need to say to introduce the top-down approach? Well, perhaps a simple example would be useful to illustrate the top-down aspects of design, coding, and testing. Let us take as our example that most universal of all commercial data processing systems, the payroll system.

I had the opportunity a few years ago to participate in the development of a payroll system; we began the project by breaking the entire system into an edit, an update, a sort, and several print routines. ("What's so special about that?" you ask. "We've been doing that sort of thing for years!" Of course! That's just the point: Many organizations have followed some form of top-down design all along.) Having identified the edit, update, and print levels as top-level modules and having determined the next few levels of modules beneath them, we wrote code for the top-level modules — in many cases, writing code to call lower-level modules that we had not yet designed.

Our primary reason for writing this code was to make it possible to test — or exercise, as we preferred to call it, since the testing was not exhaustive — a preliminary version of the payroll system, but one that was, in a sense, a *complete* payroll system. Approximately six weeks after beginning the project, we produced what was referred to as "Version 1": a payroll system that accepted input transactions and a master file, and that produced paychecks.

Of course, our Version 1 payroll system had a few minor limitations. The user was required to provide error-free transactions, for our payroll system made no attempt to validate them. In addition, the user was required to provide transactions that already had been sorted, as our system was too lazy to do the sorting. Furthermore, our system was unwilling to allow the user to hire new employees, fire existing employees, give any employee a salary increase — or, for that matter, make *any* change to an employee's current status.

To add insult to injury, our payroll system uniformly paid everyone a salary of $100 per week, and withheld a uniform $15 in taxes from everyone's paycheck. It insisted that all employees be paid by check (instead of allowing the convenience of being paid by cash, or having one's paycheck deposited directly into a bank account). The final indignity: It printed all of the paychecks in octal.

Not a very exciting payroll system! On the other hand, it *did* involve all of the top-level modules. What made the system so primitive was the fact that all of the lower-level modules existed as "stubs," or "dummy routines." For example, the top-level module in the update portion of the system called a module to compute an employee's salary. For the Version 1 system, that module simply returned an output of $100. Similarly, the top-level module in the edit part of the system called a module to determine the validity of a specific transaction. For Version 1, that module simply returned with an indication that the transaction was valid — without going to any effort to *actually* validate the transaction.

Subsequent versions of the payroll system merely involved adding lower-level modules to the existing skeleton of top-level modules. A second version of the system, for example, allowed the user to hire and fire employees. It also sorted the transactions, and in a few very simple cases, it actually computed an employee's gross pay. However, Version 2 still made no attempt to validate the input transactions. In most cases, it still paid employees $100 per week. In all cases, it withheld $15 in taxes and printed paychecks in octal. Subsequent versions rectified these limitations, until a final version produced output that was satisfactory to the user.

That, in a nutshell, is the top-down approach. The concept of top-down *design* is very simple, and has been around for a long time. Indeed, one could argue that it is just a variation of Julius Caesar's "divide and conquer" strategy. Most intelligent programmers would argue that they've been doing top-down design all along, and most serious data processing managers would insist that they always have enforced top-down design in their departments.

However, my visits to several hundred organizations around the world during the past dozen years suggest otherwise. Many managers promote good design strategies in their standards manuals but fail to enforce them. Many programmers follow such a sloppy and informal version of top-down design that they are unable to take advantage of its benefits. Some programmers attempt to practice bottom-up design (that is, they first try to identify all of the bottom-level modules that will be required, and then try to figure out how to put them together). Finally, the majority of programmers do *no* design, but rather begin coding as soon as they have been given specifications.

Still, it probably is fair to say that many organizations attempt to practice top-down design. By contrast, very *few* organizations make any conscious attempt at top-down testing. The small number of organizations that have some kind of formal test plan unfortunately advocate a bottom-up strategy, as follows: First, the bottom-level modules are tested in isolation. Then, these are combined with modules at the next higher level to form programs, which are tested in isolation. Next, the programs are combined with modules at the next higher level to form subsystems, which are tested in isolation. Finally, all of the subsystems are combined to permit a *system test.*

So, if your programmers tell you that they already practice top-down design and top-down testing, beware! Look more closely at what they *really* are doing. For example, could they provide you with a payroll system that paid all employees $100 in octal shortly after the beginning of the project?

4.2 The benefits of the top-down approach

The benefits of top-down design should be immediately obvious. Most problems (whether in the data processing field or elsewhere) are too complex to be grasped in their entirety. Top-down design provides an organized method of breaking the original problem into smaller problems that we *can* grasp, and that we *can* solve with some degree of success.

The benefits of top-down testing are not so immediately apparent — particularly in organizations that have followed the bottom-up approach for the past ten or twenty years. Those benefits are summarized in the following sections.

4.2.1 Major interfaces are exercised at the beginning of the project

In the brief sketch drawn earlier of the payroll system, Version 1 demonstrated that the edit subsystem could communicate — to some limited extent — with the update subsystem, which in turn was capable of communicating with the sort subsystem, which in turn was capable of communicating with the various print routines.

In any major computer system, one usually can identify subsystems, *and interfaces between the subsystems.* Those interfaces may be implemented in the form of a magnetic tape file, or a disk file, or data passed from module to module through core memory. Typically, the interface will be documented by the designer(s) on paper: some documentation of the file layout, the intermodule calling sequence, or something of that nature. Unfortunately, individual programmers may interpret the interface documents slightly differently. They may code bugs into that portion of their program that passes information through the interface. The interface document may be blatantly incorrect (a common occurrence with certain information supplied by computer vendors!); or the interface document may be incomplete, failing to describe certain conditions, exceptions, or special situations.

What we are saying, then, is that the interface between modules and the interface between subsystems are common places for bugs to occur. In the bottom-up approach, *major* interfaces usually are not tested until the very end — at which point, the discovery of an interface bug can be disastrous! The presence of the interface bug may require that several modules be recoded; even worse, it often occurs the day before the final deadline — or the day *after* the final deadline!

By contrast, the top-down approach tends to force important, top-level interfaces to be exercised at an early stage in the project, so that if there are problems, they can be resolved while there still is the time, the energy, and the resources to deal with them. Indeed, we usually find that as we go further and further in the project, the bugs become simpler and simpler — that is, the interface problems become more and more localized.

We should emphasize that interface problems occur not only at the interfaces between major pieces of an application system, but also at the interfaces between the vendor's hardware and your applications, and between the vendor's software and your applications. Thus, one of my clients found that Version 1 of an on-line system represented a major test of a CRT terminal (with which they had no prior experience), a new modem, newly installed telephone lines, a recently acquired telecommunications monitor from a major software firm, a newly acquired database management system from a different software firm, the vendor's operating system, *and* several major application subsystems.

You can imagine the sort of things that were discovered in Version 1: The vendor's terminal worked, but the programming manual for the terminal left out some key details that would have caused major problems if their absence had not been detected at the outset. The modem had the nasty habit of dropping bits of data at random intervals. The telephone lines actually worked, but the telecommunications monitor gobbled up all available memory in the computer, fragmented the memory into small pieces, and then shut down the system because it could not obtain enough big chunks of memory. The database management package worked fine, but could only carry out one disk access at a time, a fact which would have caused major throughput problems if it had not been discovered at an early stage. All of the application subsystems had a variety of interface bugs. It was a wonder the client ever got Version 1 working at all — but when they did, it was relatively smooth sailing from there on!

4.2.2 Users can see a working demonstration of the system

Perhaps the single most important advantage of the top-down approach is that one can demonstrate a skeleton version of a system to a user at an early stage — *before* the programmers have wasted a great deal of time coding from fuzzy, inaccurate specifications.

This point brings up one of the most serious philosophical problems in the computer field today: the myth of perfect systems analysis, a point that I discussed briefly in the previous chapter. This is the belief that *if* one spends enough time talking to the user, or *if* one puts a user on the analysis team, or, conversely, *if* one makes the programmers work *in* the user department, or *if* one gets the user to formally sign and accept the functional specification, and *if* a few other well-intentioned gimmicks are implemented, then it will be possible to get *perfect* specifications, from which we can write perfect code that will make the user perfectly happy.

Humbug! There may be a few cases in which this has worked to some degree, but it largely is an exercise in futility. First, in any new, sophisticated computer system, the user does *not* know what he wants — and he *won't* know what he wants until he begins to see, in terms of something more tangible than a stack of paper, what he can get.

Second, one must recognize that communication problems between the user, the analyst, and the programmer are inevitable. The user will explain what he wants in a language that is incomplete, ambiguous, and imprecise. The analyst and the programmer will misinterpret the user's wishes in a variety of subtle ways — not to mention the simple human errors they are likely to make. Even with the improved graphic tools of structured analysis discussed in Chapter 3, there is still room for misunderstandings. The less experienced the user, the more likely this is to occur. And the more complex the system, the more likely the misunderstandings.

Finally, one must accept that in today's world, things often change more quickly than we can develop computer systems. I have seen a number of systems that were specified in 1973, and were scheduled to be installed in 1976. By 1976, most of the major premises upon which the systems were based had changed. The business had changed, the economy had changed, the technology had changed, the competition had changed. Indeed, even the user had changed — the "ultimate system" was delivered to a person other than the one who originally had ordered it.

All of these phenomena — of which you should be painfully aware in your own organization — argue strongly for a top-down approach. Even if the user seems to know what he wants, implement a top-level skeleton first — and make him look at it! Chances are, he'll want something deleted from the original specifications or something added. In general, it is easier to make changes *before* coding. In many cases, one can avoid the frustrating experience of writing beautiful code, only to throw it away because the user changed his mind!

4.2.3 Deadline problems can be dealt with more satisfactorily

Although this book is aimed at managers, and is concerned with problems of management, it is not a book on "project management." I say this because, with all of our experience, projects *still* are typically behind schedule and over budget.

Why? Partly, I suspect, because deadlines reflect political pressures more than they reflect the sober, rational judgment of a manager. The reason the deadline is January 1 is because someone insisted that the system must be operational by the beginning of the new year — and to hell with your PERT charts!

The other major reason for deadline problems is the occurrence of unforeseen events. If all of the programmers come down with the bubonic plague, the project probably will be late; if a tornado demolishes the computer room, things probably will fall behind schedule.

All of this is well known. Yet many of us persist in drawing neater, more accurate PERT charts — in the hopes that users and top management someday will allow us to schedule our projects on a rational basis. And many of us continue assuming that there will be no tornadoes and no bubonic plague epidemic — and that users and top management will someday be sympathetic to the problems of meeting a deadline with handicaps like these.

The point of all this is that when the deadline arrives, the classical bottom-up approach usually leaves us in a vulnerable position. Typically, we find that the design has been completed, most (or all) of the code has been written, and most (possibly all) of the modules have been tested individually. Unfortunately, when the modules are assembled together, they *don't* work. That is, when the deadline arrives, we find that we are in the middle of system testing — with 20,000 lines of code that don't *do* anything. Try to explain that to a user who doesn't know the difference between a line of code and a football.

And try to explain it to top managers who have been getting status reports all along indicating that things are on schedule! Chances are, you've been fooled, too. Your programmers probably began telling you on the second day of the project that they were 95 percent done — and on "deadline day," they *still* are 95 percent done! Sure, they reached the milestone of "design completed" on schedule — but what does that mean?

And they reached the milestone of "all modules coded" on schedule — but what does that mean?

Compare that with the top-down approach, but be sure to recognize that there is no magic in this world. Whether one works top-down or bottom-up, there *still* will be deadline problems. The system *still* may not be finished when the deadline arrives, and the users *still* will be irritated (even if you never committed your staff to meeting the deadline!).

However, you undoubtedly will be in a *much* stronger political position than you would be with the bottom-up approach — because you will have a skeleton version of the system that performs some demonstrable processing. Of course, this advantage must be viewed in the proper perspective, for if we present a payroll system that produces octal paychecks, the user is unlikely to be impressed with our efforts and might well send us off to the slave labor camps in Siberia. Consider the following dialogue, and you will see what I mean:

User: Good morning. Today's the deadline. . . . Where is my payroll system?

DP Manager: I'm sorry to say that we're not finished.

User: What? That's ridiculous! We agreed that you would be finished by January 1.

DP Manager: Actually, *you* agreed that it would be done on January 1. I told you all along that that date was optimistic. However, I do have a Version 3 payroll system that works and can be put into operation today.

User: Version 3? What does that mean?

DP Manager: Well, it's a payroll system that pays everyone by check; it won't pay anyone in cash, or by direct bank deposit. And if anyone works double overtime on a national holiday, the system still will pay $100 per week. And the system does not validate transactions that *decrease* salary, which means that an employee's salary might accidentally be reduced below zero. But, other than those minor details, the system works just fine.

User: That's ridiculous! That's unacceptable! I want the whole thing! I asked for the whole payroll system to be working by January 1.

DP Manager:	I know — but we didn't make it. In the meantime, you should be able to live with these minor restrictions. We'll have them fixed in another two weeks.
User:	Grumble, grumble . . . well, I suppose it's better than nothing.

4.2.4 *Debugging is easier*

One of the advantages of the top-down approach involves a technical process that really shouldn't concern you as a manager, but that nevertheless is a factor of which you should be aware: The process of debugging is easier when the top-down approach is used.

To explain this point, we need to clarify the distinction between testing and debugging. Loosely speaking, *testing* is the process one goes through to demonstrate the correctness (or incorrectness) of a program or system. It usually consists of supplying known inputs to the system and verifying that the outputs are correct. *Debugging*, on the other hand, is the black art of tracking down a bug once its existence has been made known. The existence of a bug usually is learned from a controlled test procedure — which is why testing and debugging are considered by most programmers to be almost synonymous. But when a production program blows up in the middle of the night, and the computer operator calls the responsible programmer — it's *debugging* that the poor, sleepy programmer is doing, not testing!

Given that distinction, we maintain that debugging tends to be easier in a top-down testing environment than in a bottom-up testing environment. Why? Because top-down testing tends to be *incremental* in nature. That is, it usually consists of adding one new module to an existing skeleton of modules, and then observing the behavior of the new system. If the new system misbehaves, common sense tells the programmer that the problem must be located in the new module — or in the interface between the new module and the rest of the system. Indeed, if the programmer gets desperate, he always has the option of a strategic retreat; that is, he can remove the new module, reinsert the dummy, or stub, in its place, and retreat to his office to contemplate the mystery of the bug.

By contrast, the bottom-up approach tends to be *phased* in nature. That is, one usually finds geometrically increasing numbers of modules being combined for the first time — any one of which (or any combination of which) may contain a bug. This is particularly evident during system testing, when hundreds (or even thousands) of modules are combined for the first time, and one of those modules contains a bug that ultimately destroys the entire system. Even worse, a bug in module A combines with a bug in module B to produce a subtly incorrect output that the programmer finds impossible to relate to any single module; or, a bug in module A cancels the effect of a bug in module B, thus leading to correct output — until the maintenance programmer innocently fixes the bug in module A!

4.2.5 Requirements for machine test time are distributed more evenly throughout a top-down project

It has been observed in many projects that the requirement for machine time rises almost exponentially toward the end of the project. By contrast, the requirement for machine time in a top-down project remains fairly constant during the lifetime of the project.

The differences between the two approaches can be shown graphically as follows:

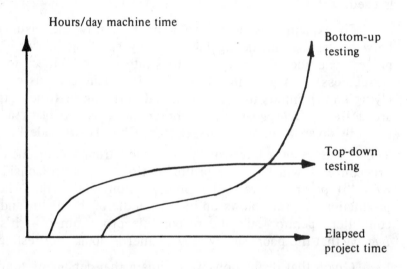

You should be able to anticipate the reasons for these two curves from what we have said about the top-down approach. The bottom-up approach generally does not begin using computer test time until the project is well underway, simply because the approach involves designing and coding all (or most) of the system before any testing begins. Once testing begins, the requirement for machine time rises rapidly as modules are combined into programs, programs into subsystems, and subsystems into systems.

By contrast, the top-down approach begins using machine time earlier. This is possible because one begins writing code before the design is finished. Normally, we find that the requirement for test time reaches a certain point, and then levels off — remaining relatively constant for the duration of the project. The reason for the constant requirement for test time is fairly simple: The incremental nature of the testing involves adding one new module to the system each day, and running roughly the same set of test data through the system. It should be noted that early use of machine time can cause some problems, which are discussed in Section 4.3.2.

4.2.6 Programmer morale is improved

A minor advantage of the top-down approach — but one that should not be ignored — is that the programmers are usually happier and better motivated. Why? For the same reasons that users and managers like the top-down approach: They can see tangible results of progress at an earlier stage. The morale boost associated with seeing an early version of a system can be a particularly effective way of avoiding the "mid-project slump" associated with most projects that go on for two or three years.

This can be a significant point. Programmers, for the most part, *do* like to program. They do *not* like to write detailed specifications, they do *not* like to prepare flowcharts, they do *not* like to become engrossed in the paperwork that is characteristic of the early stages of a typical project. Not being terribly enthusiastic about such work, they'll put in a 9-to-5 day, at best! However, when they get into the programming and testing — the *fun* part — *then* they begin to work the 16-hour days on which we have come to depend.

With the top-down approach, the programming usually begins much earlier in the project — which means that the programmer can begin, at an earlier stage, doing what he really enjoys doing. On top of this, he has the tremendous morale boost of seeing a Version 1 system actually work. It doesn't matter that the Version 1 payroll system is trivial and that it only produces octal paychecks. It is a *real* program that accepts *real* inputs and produces *real* outputs! That alone probably is sufficient to motivate the programmer to work 16-hour days to produce Version 2 of the system.

4.2.7 Top-down testing eliminates the need for test harnesses

Finally, there is a characteristic of top-down testing that is basically technical in nature, although it has some management overtones.

We observe that the classic bottom-up scheme usually requires the presence of a test driver, or test harness, that is, a program that can read test data from a file, pass the test data to the module being tested, capture the output from the module, and print the output on a suitable output device. A few organizations are disciplined enough to require their programmers to make use of a general-purpose test driver (along with a general-purpose test data generator, perhaps), but most organizations don't bother. That is, in most companies, each programmer writes a quick-and-dirty test driver for each module being tested.

The top-down approach eliminates the need for drivers, since the existing skeleton system can serve as a natural test driver for a new detail module being added to the system.

On the other hand, the top-down approach *does* require the use of stubs, or dummy routines. Such routines are substitutes for detailed modules that have not yet been coded, and their implementation usually consists of

1. immediate exit, with no processing

2. returning constant output — that is, returning $100 in the dummy version of the salary computation module in the payroll system example

3. returning a random number within some range

4. printing an output message, to inform the programmer that the dummy module was executed

5. executing a timing loop to consume N microseconds in a controlled fashion (useful in some real-time systems)

6. providing a primitive quick-and-dirty implementation of the *real* function of the module

7. asking for help from an on-line terminal (in which case a human being does the work that the module was supposed to do)

Although I see nothing fundamentally wrong with test drivers, it is worth observing that dummy routines usually are simpler to code than a corresponding driver routine. In the best case, the dummy routine consists of one statement: EXIT.

4.3 Management problems with the top-down approach

Based on the preceding discussion, you might be tempted to issue a memo to your programmers that says: "Troops! Starting tomorrow, I want all of you to design and test your systems in a top-down fashion!" Or maybe you should send all 300 of your programmers to a one-hour class on top-down implementation, and *then* issue the edict. . . .

As stated in Chapter 2, an approach like this is likely to lead to a certain degree of chaos and confusion. Indeed, even if you ease into top-down implementation slowly and gradually (and diplomatically), you may experience chaos and confusion. The troops, even with the best of intentions, are likely to do some silly things in the name of top-down implementation.

What sort of things? Well, companies vary, but the sort of problems that I have seen include

- a misunderstanding of radical top-down implementation versus conservative top-down implementation

- lack of sufficient test time

- lack of hardware for top-down testing

- staffing problems

- programmers' fears that changes to low-level modules will propagate to high-level modules

- common tendency to practice top-down *program* testing, combined with bottom-up *system* testing

- communication problems in multi-team projects

- difficulty in visualizing top-down versions

- difficulty in getting the user involved

- unwillingness to renegotiate schedules and budgets

A brief discussion of each of these potential problem areas follows.

4.3.1 Misunderstanding between radical top-down and conservative top-down

At this point, you may well be wondering, "What's conservative top-down? What's radical top-down?" Indeed, these concepts have not been discussed, but they cause many organizations trouble when they first attempt the top-down approach.

We could describe the radical top-down approach in the following manner: First, design the top level of a system — that is, recognize that the payroll system mentioned earlier will have a top-level edit module, a top-level update module, and a variety of top-level print modules. Having done this much design, *immediately* write the code for those modules, and test them as a Version 1 system. Next, design the second-level modules, those modules a level below the top-level modules just completed. Having designed the second-level modules, next write the code and test a Version 2 system, and so forth.

The conservative approach to top-down implementation consists of designing all the top-level modules, then the next level, then all third-level modules, and so on until the entire design is finished. Then code the top-level modules and implement them as a Version 1. From the experience gained in implementing Version 1, make any necessary changes to the lower levels of design, then code and test at the second level, and on down to the lowest level.

The important thing to realize is that the radical approach and the conservative approach represent the two extreme points on a spectrum. There are an infinite number of compromise top-down strategies that you can select, depending on your situation. You may decide, for example, to finish 75 percent of the design, and then begin coding and testing those modules that you have designed. (Obviously, the coding and testing would be done top-down.) Or you might decide to design 25 percent of the system — and then, with 75 percent of the system still quite fuzzy, start coding and implementing.

As you may have guessed, there is no single right answer. I cannot tell you whether the radical approach is better than the conservative approach for all possible projects. However, I *can* identify the primary factors that will help *you* decide just how radical or conservative you will want to be:

- *User fickleness.* If the user has no idea of what he wants, or has a tendency to change his mind, I would opt for the radical approach. Why waste time designing a great deal of detailed logic that will be thrown away? On the other hand, if the user knows precisely what he wants, I might attempt a complete design.

- *Design quality.* Committing oneself to code too early in the project may make it difficult to improve the design later. All other things being equal, we prefer to finish the entire design (see Section 4.3.5 below).

- *Time pressures.* If you are under extreme pressure from users or higher levels of management to produce some tangible output quickly, go for the radical approach. If your deadline is absolutely inflexible, i.e., if it is a case of "you bet your job," go for the radical approach. If you are not under much pressure, and if the deadline is flexible, go for the conservative approach.

- *Accurate estimates.* If you are required by your organization to provide accurate, detailed estimates of schedules, manpower, and other resources, then you should opt for the conservative approach. How can you estimate how long it will take to implement the system until you know how many modules it will contain?

All of this makes sense — at least, it *should* make sense. The reason that problems have occurred in this area is primarily because the top-down approach has been interpreted by some programmers, managers, and users as a kind of religion, but all three parties tend to interpret that religion differently.

To the user community, top-down means that they should have a working system on the second day of the project — and it should be a perfect design! The programmers sometimes interpret the religion as an official license to begin writing code on the second day of the project, which unfortunately degenerates into coding without *any* design!

In practice, hardly anyone follows the extreme radical approach described earlier. Most designers instinctively explore at least half of the design before committing themselves to code — even if much of that design is subconscious and undocumented! Unfortunately, many projects *do* seem to follow the extreme conservative approach, and while it may, in general, lead to better technical designs, it fails for two reasons: (a) on a large project, the user is incapable of specifying the details with any accuracy, and (b) on a large project, users and top management increasingly are unwilling to accept two or three years of effort by the EDP department with no visible, tangible output. Hence, the movement toward the radical approach.

The important thing for you, as a manager, is: Don't let the users intimidate you into taking a radical approach in situations in which that seems inappropriate. Don't let your project management textbooks convince you to follow the conservative approach in developing the perfect design when you know, in the pit of your stomach, that the user really is uncertain about what kind of system he wants.

And finally, *don't ever* let the programmers bamboozle you into thinking that top-down implementation means that they are automatically at liberty to begin generating code on the first day of the project.

4.3.2 *Lack of sufficient machine time*

In several of the organizations I have visited, the programmers have complained to me (sometimes privately, so that the boss wouldn't get irritated) that they get only one test shot a day. In other words, they have to wait twenty-four hours to see the output of any test run that they have submitted. In a few organizations, the programmers complain that they may get as little as one test shot a week.

In addition, the programmers sometimes state that they can't get *any* machine time when they need it. As we observed previously, the top-down approach requires machine availability earlier in the project life cycle than is traditional — and this may cause problems in organizations in which the assumption always is that programmers do not need any machine time until a project has been underway for six months.

In most organizations in which this problem has come up, the programmers have abandoned top-down testing partially or completely, often without even knowing it. Instead of adding only *one* new module to an existing skeleton and testing the system incrementally, the programmers begin adding *all* of the modules at a particular level (e.g., all of the second-level edit modules in the payroll system) and testing them en masse. In the worst case, the programmers will retreat to the bottom-up approach with which they are more familiar.

So, my advice to you is to ensure that your programmers have enough machine time to indulge in the top-down approach — at least for their first few projects, when they occasionally may be tempted to slip back into their old ways.

How *much* machine time should you allocate? Should one expect to use more machine time with the top-down approach than would have been used with the bottom-up approach? The honest answer is: We don't know. You probably will be safe if you allocate roughly as much test time as you would have allocated with your classical bottom-up techniques; and then use the experience of your first few pilot projects (a concept discussed in more detail in Chapter 12) to refine your estimates.

My experience has been that the *amount* of machine time is somewhat less important than the *frequency* of test shots. If the programmer knows that he is going to have only one test shot a week, it is almost impossible to resist the temptation to throw *all* of his modules into the machine at once and hope that they'll all work. On the other hand, if he knows that he'll get two or three test shots a day, he will be more inclined to follow the incremental approach of testing one new module at a time.

By the way, one reason for our inability to predict the amount of machine time needed in a top-down project is that very few projects (indeed, *none* that I have worked on) use *only* top-down implementation. Most organizations use top-down implementation, *plus* structured design, *plus* structured walkthroughs, *plus* . . . The overall result, generally, is much *less* machine time. If your programmers write code with no bugs, then they will need a modest amount of machine time to *verify* that they have no bugs — but, they will need no debugging time, and they will need no computer time for re-compiling and re-testing their programs.

4.3.3 Lack of hardware for testing

Not getting *enough* machine time for testing is one problem. Not getting *any* machine time for testing is a qualitatively different problem. The most extreme form of this phenomenon occurs in projects that have *no* available computer hardware during the system development phase.

Many of today's on-line systems run into this problem. In order to carry out top-down implementation, the programmers require access to terminals, modems, multiplexors, and communications lines, in addition to the conventional central site hardware. If this is the organization's *first* on-line system, the terminals and communications equipment may not exist; and management frequently is reluctant to install the communications equipment until the last possible moment.

The result? Bottom-up development, in one form or another. A great deal of application software will be written and tested in a batch environment, or, at best, in a simulated on-line environment — and an attempt will be made, sometimes on the day before the deadline, to interface all of this software with the newly arrived teleprocessing hardware/software.

The reason for management's reluctance is obvious: The teleprocessing equipment is expensive, and management is concerned that it will be idle for a substantial portion of the development phase of the project. In truth, my experience has been that the equipment will be idle *anyway*, while the programmers try to find their bugs. The only question is whether you would prefer to have the equipment installed and idle *before* the deadline, or *after* the deadline.

Obviously, compromises can be made in this area. If an on-line system eventually will have 1,000 terminals, we could expect to carry out a reasonable form of top-down implementation with three or four terminals and one or two communications lines. If certain pieces of hardware simply are *not* available (perhaps because they haven't been built), then simulator software is better than none.

4.3.4 Staffing problems

In some organizations, a full complement of programmers, designers, and analysts is assigned to a programming project *on the first day of the project.* Sometimes this is the result of contractual and billing procedures, particularly in dealings between a software consulting organization and a separate user organization. Sometimes, however, the problem is much more mundane. As a manager, for example, you know that you'll need Fred and Susy in the middle of the project. Unfortunately, if you don't grab them now — at the beginning of the project — they'll be occupied with something else when you need them. Rather than lose them, you may decide to bring them into your project, even though there is nothing for them to do.

The result of this kind of management decision should be obvious. In an attempt to keep Fred and Susy busy, someone will invent some bottom-level modules and *hope that they will be needed later on.* Fred and Susy then will be sent off to code these modules, and the rest of the team will continue to work on the *top* part of the system.

Of course, the problem is that subsequent design work may show that nobody really needs Fred's module after all, and that the interface that was specified for Susy's module is completely impractical. That's the risk one runs when combining top-down design with bottom-up design!

Two things should be observed here. First, it often is practical to have several programmer/analysts working on the top portion of the system — even if they function only as coders, reviewers (as in a structured walkthrough, discussed in Chapter 10), or librarians (as in Chapter 9). Thus, Fred and Susy might be very useful as participants in the top-level design — *more* useful, perhaps, than sending them off to code bottom-level modules that may never be needed.

Second, it is a good idea to complete all, or most, of the system's design before trying to figure out how many Freds and Susys will be required to code the individual modules. Thus, the normal problems of staffing and resource planning often provide a strong argument for the conservative top-down approach.

4.3.5 Programmers' fears that changes to low-level modules will propagate up to the top-level modules

It may not have occurred to you that programmers sometimes object to the top-down approach. Relatively few do object, but those who do frequently mention one major concern: The implementation of bottom-level modules, late in the project, may cause problems in top-level modules that already have been designed, coded, and tested.

In my experience, this concern usually is exaggerated. Yes, the implementation of bottom-level modules may suggest or even require changes to some of the higher-level modules, but this is usually fairly minor. It is *possible* that the implementation of the last bottom-level module will uncover design flaws that will be propagated throughout the rest of the system . . . but it's rather unlikely.

If it appears that this may be a serious problem on your project, or something that is going to bother your programmers, then you should opt for the conservative top-down approach. Finish the entire design before writing any code. This way, you'll be able to anticipate almost all of the potential design problems with bottom-level modules.

At the same time, note that this problem is identical to the one frequently observed in a bottom-up project. At the very end of the pilot, when two major subsystems are linked together for the first time, we find that the interface isn't right — subsystem A is passing the wrong kind of data to subsystem B (usually because someone misread or misunderstood the interface documentation). Correcting that interface problem may have a ripple effect all the way down to the bottom-level modules. My experience has been that problems of this sort are *much* worse than the problems discovered in the top-down approach.

Also, keep in mind that many of the problems will come from the user — and this is an argument for using a more radical top-down implementation. There is no point in finishing the entire design and letting the programmers reassure themselves that all of the interfaces are proper, and that the design is perfect, only to have half of the entire effort thrown out because the user changed his mind.

4.3.6 The mistake of combining top-down program testing and bottom-up system testing

This problem is characterized by the following kind of dialogue at the beginning of a project:

Boss: OK, troops, let's break the system down into a bunch of individual programs.

Troops: Right, boss.

Boss:	Fred, you take program #1. Susy, you take program #2. Charlie, you take program #3. And then I want all of you to use top-down testing, structured programmming, and the rest of that stuff.
Troops:	Right, boss.
Boss:	And when you're done, let's all get back together — and then we'll merge the programs into a system.

As one might expect, this approach has many of the same problems as the original bottom-up approach. Fred, Susy, and Charlie find that their individual programming projects are quite easy — the problems occur when they get back together again. At that point, they find that Fred decided to change the interface specifications without telling anyone; Susy's program doesn't work with Charlie's program, and so forth.

In most cases, this problem is the result of a misunderstanding of the top-down concept. Sometimes, it is the result of other problems, such as lack of sufficient computer time.

Depending on the size of the project, this combination of top-down program development and bottom-up systems development may or may not be serious. If Fred, Susy, and Charlie are writing small programs that require only a day's effort, then their systems integration difficulties should be manageable. But if this situation occurs with 50 programmers who each spend a year developing their individual programs, chaos will reign supreme.

4.3.7 Communication problems in multi-team projects

On very large projects, the programming group is usually broken into smaller teams — each team being responsible for a program, or a subsystem, or some other unit of work. At that point, Mealy's Law* takes over: The eventual structure of the system reflects the structure of the organization that builds the system. For example, if two teams have difficulty communicating with each other (because of personality clashes or political problems), then their subsystems probably will have difficulty communicating.

In particular, I have found that each team tends to isolate itself from other teams. Early integration of the top-level skeleton of one team's subsystem with the top-level skeleton of another team's subsystem often is regarded as a hassle — and both teams avoid it. As a result, there is a tendency to use the

---

*So named after George Mealy, one of the architects of IBM's OS/360.

approach discussed in the previous section: top-down program development and bottom-up systems integration.

Why is it a hassle interfacing two subsystems at an early stage? Because the interfaces are fuzzy! Team A hasn't defined precisely what data it requires from team B — and as a result, it's very difficult to put the two subsystems into the machine and make them communicate. But that is *exactly* what the top-down approach is trying to accomplish: *forcing* the precise definition of major interfaces, and forcing those interfaces to be coded and exercised in a computer to ensure that they work!

In other words, you should *expect* problems in this area. The larger your project, the more problems there will be. Rather than avoiding the problems, you should confront them directly. This is what the top-down approach is all about.

4.3.8 *Difficulty visualizing top-down versions*

Visualizing systems versions proves to be a common problem — and certainly is most serious. Many people, particularly programmers, seem to have a very confused notion of the sequence of implementation in a top-down project.

In our example of a payroll system, many programmers seem to think that top-down implementation means the following: Version 1 of the system will do all of the editing, but nothing else; Version 2 will combine all of the editing and all of the update logic (and thus all of the salary computations, tax calculations, and so forth); Version 3 will combine all of the editing, all of the update logic, and the sorting; and Version 4 will throw in the printing.

I don't know why some programmers have had such difficulty visualizing a skeleton version of a *complete* system — for example, visualizing a payroll system that incorporates the top-level logic of the edit *and* the update *and* the printing. I can only warn you that this difficulty is likely to be a problem — so watch out for it!

4.3.9 *Difficulty getting the user involved*

One of the major objectives of top-down testing is to involve the user in the early skeleton versions of the system. If something is wrong with the system (from the user's point of view), it is better to discover the problem as early as possible. Unfortunately, this is not always easy to accomplish. Sometimes the user is too busy to participate in early versions of the system. He may, in effect, say to you, "Leave me alone! I'm swamped with work — that's why I need a new system! Don't talk to me until you've got the entire system finished!"

Such a user deserves what he gets — just as a customer who refuses to look at a custom-built house until it's finished deserves what he gets. Unfortunately, the architect (or EDP project manager) often gets the blame even if the customer is wrong.

The moral: Make an extra effort to get your user involved in early versions of your system, even if he thinks it's a waste of time. He'll thank you for it later.

4.3.10 Unwillingness to renegotiate schedules and budgets

It's possible — indeed, highly likely — that when the user sees Version 1 of his new EDP system, he will want to make major changes. He may decide that certain processing capabilities that he never mentioned in the functional specification are now absolutely essential. And other features that he previously considered essential now are deemed useless. Still other features of the system may be modified drastically.

In other words, it's likely to be a whole new ball game. And when Version 2 of his system is demonstrated to the user, the game may change again. Indeed, *each* version of a top-down system may bring changes to the specification.

Unfortunately, the user (and the EDP project manager) sometimes fails to appreciate that these changes require a re-evaluation of the timetable, the manpower staffing plan, and the budget for the project. And when it's brought to his attention, the user may be reluctant to agree to any changes in the project schedule or budget. "Why, these are just small changes," he'll say. "You should be able to work these into the system without any real fuss or bother."

Or, if he's clever, your user may say to you, "I thought all this top-down development stuff was supposed to make it easier for me to get what I want, and easier to make changes. Now you're telling me that you can't make any changes!"

In fact, you *can* accommodate a number of minor changes to the original specifications without changing the schedule or budget — the increased productivity associated with the structured techniques helps you in that respect. But if it's a *major* change that the user wants, it's obvious that something will have to give.

More important, it's a mistake to let the user think that he can arbitrarily change the specifications for his system without having to worry about the additional time and money it may cost. So you should go through the negotiation process even if you *can* accommodate the change with no extra work.

Chapter 4: Bibliography

1. Baker, F.T. "Chief Programmer Team Management of Production Programming." *IBM Systems Journal,* Vol. 11, No. 1 (January 1972), pp. 56-73.

   This classic article on the so-called New York Times System gives an illustration of top-down design as well as of several other important structured techniques.

2. Dahl, O.J., E.W. Dijkstra, and C.A.R. Hoare. *Structured Programming.* Englewood Cliffs, N.J.: Prentice-Hall, 1972.

   Another formal, scholarly view of top-down design.

3. Dijkstra, E. "Structured Programming." *Software Engineering, Concepts and Techniques.* eds. J.M. Buxton, P. Naur, and B. Randell. New York: Petrocelli/Charter, 1976.

   One of the first discussions to refer to top-down design as levels of abstraction.

4. McGowan, C.L., and J.R. Kelly. *Top-Down Structured Programming.* New York: Petrocelli/Charter, 1975.

   A discussion of structured programming and top-down design, discussed primarily in terms of PL/I.

5. Mills, H.D. "Top-Down Programming in Large Systems." *Debugging Techniques in Large Systems.* Englewood Cliffs, N.J.: Prentice-Hall, 1971.

   Mills is one of IBM's foremost advocates of top-down design, top-down implementation, and other related structured techniques.

6. Wirth, N. *Systematic Programming.* Englewood Cliffs, N.J.: Prentice-Hall, 1973.

   A more theoretical and academic view of the "stepwise refinement" (Wirth's phrase for top-down design) process by one of the world's leading computer science scholars.

7. Yourdon, E. *Techniques of Program Structure and Design.* Englewood Cliffs, N.J.: Prentice-Hall, 1975.

   Chapter 2 of this book discusses the top-down approach, in terms meant to be understood by programmers, designers, and analysts.

8. _____, and L.L. Constantine. *Structured Design: Fundamentals of a Discipline of Computer Program and Systems Design.* Englewood Cliffs, N.J.: Prentice Hall, 1979.

   Chapter 20 discusses top-down implementation in great detail.

SOFTWARE DESIGN STRATEGIES

The title of this chapter is *software design strategies* and **not** *software design methodologies* or *algorithms* or *procedures*. None of the existing software design techniques truly gives a procedure for system design that can be followed step by step, from start to finish, like a recipe in a cookbook. Rather, the techniques represent alternative plans of attack whose success or failure is (in large measure) determined by the skill and experience of the designer. These strategies may work well for one class of problems but may fail miserably for another. Unfortunately, this is the state of the programming "art." Each method, successfully used by others, is just another tool in our programming workshop.

Software structure, or the lack of it, is the most significant factor affecting the life cycle cost of computer software.

Software design strategies that determine the structure of a program form the foundation for choosing and applying all the other software engineering techniques. The development process can be structured to exploit a clear and modular design. Development support tools can allow us to concentrate on real structural design issues instead of more peripheral issues such as packaging, scheduling, documentation, etc.

MODULAR PROGRAMMING

When modular programming became fashionable in the 1960s, it was characterized as:[1]

Construction of a complete software system from a number of small functional units where there is a formal set of standards that control the characteristics of those units.

That formal set of standards usually included requirements like:

(1) Modules implement a single independent function.

(2) Each module performs a single logical task.

(3) Modules have a single entry and a single exit point.

(4) Modules are separately testable.

(5) Modular programs are constructed entirely of modules.

In many cases, the objective was to define a set of powerful, reusable modules that had the freedom and flexibility of a very high-level programming language. The hope was to build on the work of others. Unfortunately, in most cases programmers were all too happy to share their modules with others, but they seldom sought out other people's programs to use themselves. In Weinberg's words,

"Program libraries are most unusual. Everyone wants to put something in but nobody wants to take anything out."[2]

An attitude survey of people using modular programming was reported in 1973.[1] Benefits perceived by users of modular programming in that survey are summarized in Figure 1.

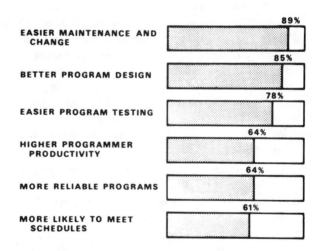

Figure 1. Modular Programming Benefits.

The percentage of those responding in each category is shown by the horizontal bar graph. Perceived disadvantages are shown in Figure 2. These figures are based on

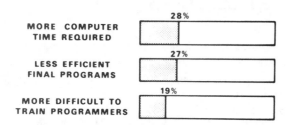

Figure 2. Modular Programming Disadvantages.

questionnaires that were sent to all known users of third-generation computers in the United Kingdom. The 1770 questionnaires that were sent out resulted in 905 useful replies, of which 47 percent of the respondents professed to be using modular programming.

In general, respondents did not achieve their major hope of producing a library of reusable modules. Those who did achieve some success in reusing modules tended to restrict their activities to providing specific reusable task programs for one system or to reusing specialized modules within one program.

STRUCTURED PROGRAMMING

The next phase of structured programming started at a more microscopic level. That is, it addressed questions like, "Is the code within a module easier to read, write, and maintain when it is constructed out of a limited number of control constructs that do not permit wild **gotos**?" It was shown that the three basic constructs of sequence, iteration, and selection were sufficient to implement the most complex programs. In fact they formed the basis for writing more understandable, correct programs. Figure 3 shows the most popular control-flow constructs, including iteration constructs, with both a *pre* and a *post* test, a selection between two parts, and a selection of one out of *n* parts.

A major structured-coding controversy occurred in the late 1960s and the early 1970s. Dijkstra responded to this controversy in 1972 in his widely acclaimed Turing Lecture.[3] While much of this controversy (in retrospect) was blown out of proportion, it did serve to publicize the fact that the "software problem" might be amenable to change after all.

During this period, the term *structured programming* became a household word that was much used and abused. The word *structured* became synonymous with *good* and therefore had multiple definitions. David Gries, in his paper, **"On Structured Programming,"**[6]

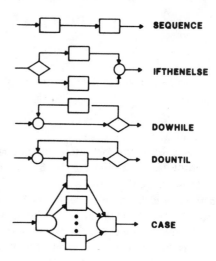

Figure 3. Structured Coding Constructs.

later commented on this state of affairs.

Gries properly credits Dijkstra with both coining the term and failing to properly define it. Gries goes on to list 13 impressions, gleaned from a number of people, of what structured programming means. In our opinion, most of the views on the list still simply represent what different people mean by *good*.

Gries does, however, go on to functionally decompose structured programming into four related topics. These are: programming methodology, program notation, program correctness, and program verification. Each of these concepts is more easily interpreted, but we are sure that the term *structured programming* will outlast them all.

The interest in structured programming became more than academic with its first widely acclaimed success story. The secrets of success were revealed in skeleton form by F. Terry Baker in his article, **"Structured Programming in a Production Programming Environment."**[7]

In his article, Baker stated that structured coding techniques alone do not significantly impact the overall quality of large software systems. This must be so because structured programming, by itself, affects only a small portion of the effort spent during the entire software production schedule. To be most beneficial, a development methodology should provide a coherent blend of technique, organization, and tools.

Such a methodology is presented and its successful application is documented by Baker. He combines structured coding and the project direction motivated by top-down development with an effective organization, the chief programmer team. The development support library is the tool that brings these elements together and, in a real sense, provides the foundation upon which they operate and interact.

The development support library is a file maintenance tool used to store all the source and object code, job control language, test data, and results for the project. Combined with machine and office procedures, it keeps current project status visible and makes it possible for the team librarian to do a majority of the clerical work.

Structured coding is used for the disciplined application of control-flow constructs during program development. The structures SEQUENCE, IF-THEN-ELSE, and DO-WHILE, plus two optional forms, DO-UNTIL and CASE, are provided to use standard coding or preprocessors that translate to an appropriate language for compilation. Instruction, along with a set of programming guidelines, helps to introduce structured coding concepts to both new and experienced programmers.

Built around a small nucleus of experienced programmers, the chief programmer team is a specific programming organization. It consists of a chief programmer who holds complete technical responsibility for the project. The chief must be the interface between the team and management and the customer organization. As well, the chief must provide the overall architecture and design of critical system components. In all these tasks, the chief is assisted by a peer, the backup programmer, with whom all designs can be freely reviewed. The backup programmer (as the name implies) also provides for the successful continuation of the project in the absence of the chief. Other programmers are added to the team as the system framework and functions are defined by the chief and backup programmers.

Top-down development provides the direction for the programming team that makes the most efficient use of the project organization. By scheduling in parallel the design and development of program systems containing multiple components, top-down development allows a project to effectively utilize the expertise of the chief and backup programmers and the efforts of the other programmers on the team. By providing the user and development personnel with operational segments of major high-level portions of the system much earlier, it eliminates gross errors before acceptance testing. Management planning is much different from what it would have been if bottom-up development were used, and a course acquainting managers with these differences is administered.

For Terry Baker, the combination of programming technique, organization, and tools has resulted in a useful software development methodology. Proper education and training allowed the method to be successfully introduced. Measurements taken indicated a significant increase in productivity and software reliability.

Baker's paper also provides an example of an integrated approach to software design management. By combining an organizational structure that is well suited to the technical requirements of software production, with methods for project control and tracking, successful project management is achieved.

Additional information is contained in the set of reprints collected by Basili and Baker, *Structured Programming: A Tutorial.*[4]

HIERARCHICAL MODULAR PROGRAMMING

The concept of hierarchical modular programming gained a following in the early 1970s since it was viewed as carrying the advantages of structured coding above the module level. A hierarchical modular program structure is perhaps ideal in the sense that the connectivity of program modules is clearly limited and delineated. Subsequent inspection or modification of the program can be made in a straightforward manner, since it is quite clear what parts of the program must be altered and affected. When diagramed, the structure of such a program resembles an inverted tree structure (see Figure 4). A faithfully implemented design will preserve this tree structure and with it will obtain many advantages that will ease subsequent modification. An implementation that commits "arboricide" (the killing of trees) results in a disordered "pile of leaves."

The modular part of hierarchical modular programming is applied in much the same manner discussed earlier. That is, while we are still interested in implementing single independent functions, performing single logical tasks, etc., all of these constraints are applied to subtrees rather than to single boxes on the structure diagram. In Figure 4, each dotted circle should be considered as a separate module. The chief difference lies in defining the problem and its solution as nested modules that can become arbitrarily complex, rather than as an interconnected sequence of modules. The importance of taking a hierarchical view was expressed by Dijkstra:

> "The sooner we learn to limit ourselves to hierarchical program constructs, the faster we will progress."[3]

This is true at the code level and at the module level. While this approach limits one's options, it promises great rewards in easing later modifications.

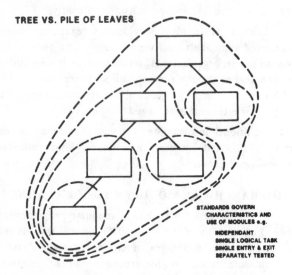

Figure 4. Hierarchical Modular Program Structure.

Note that many of the advantages of a hierarchical modular program structure are topological. The connectivity of the program is severely restricted. Each module (within a dotted circle) can be designed, tested, and modified independently. All connections with the rest of the system are clearly delineated and can be accounted for. An additional benefit is that the ripple effect of errors caused by program modifications can be dramatically reduced.

Note also that a final hierarchical modular program structure seldom reveals how it was derived. The following sections focus on strategies for deriving proper program structures.

BOTTOM-UP DESIGN

Bottom-up design is the process of enhancing the capabilities of your machine by successively giving it more and more powerful instructions that hide more and more of the detail. In effect, one builds up layers of virtual machines by forming data abstractions, resource abstractions, or high-level functional calls.

The concept of a data abstraction[5] is represented schematically in Figure 5. Note that the stack can be dealt with only through specially defined procedure calls (create, push, top, etc.). These procedure calls "know about" the location and format of the data stored within, but hide that information from user programs. If the physical implementation or layout of data within the stack is subsequently changed, only the procedure-call programs must be modified. Since the user programs

know nothing about the physical implementation of the stack, they are not affected.

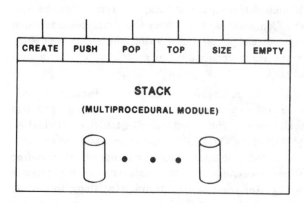

Figure 5. Data Abstraction of a Stack.

Other physical input/output or storage devices can also be viewed as abstract resources. Figure 6 shows a typical layered configuration of virtual machines in which an operating system kernel and operating system utilities insulate the user programs from dealing with the peculiarities of the hardware.

Figure 6. Levels of Virtual Machines.

Terminals, typically, are interfaced with user programs through "driver" programs. The concept of a virtual terminal that presents a uniform interface to application programs is an appealing one, since it can dramatically reduce the number of special cases with which the application program must deal. Clearly, an application programmer wants to write information to a terminal without knowing or caring whether it is displayed on a CRT screen or printed on paper. Thus, data abstractions are simply one example of abstract resources that are developed within the virtual machine seen by the application programmer.

The goal, in most cases, is to carry bottom-up design as far as possible while keeping a high degree of application independence. That is, the application programmer should build up a friendly virtual machine environment before solving any one application program in detail. If the virtual machine is designed properly, it can later facilitate moving (or porting) programs from one piece of hardware to another. Hopefully, the same virtual machine environment can be created on a number of physical machines, thus making the applications programs quite portable.

The whole concept of bottom-up design is very useful and powerful as long as one keeps in mind the fact that each program is modeling some aspect of the real world. One program should generally model only one type of terminal, and this model should be detailed enough to support the functions it will later be called upon to perform. A program that models two different kinds of terminals will have unnecessary cross coupling, control interactions, etc.

TOP-DOWN DESIGN

Proponents of top-down design will encourage you to start a design simply by defining one "super" instruction that will solve the whole problem and then implementing that instruction with less and less abstract semi-super instructions. Sooner or later, you get down to instructions that will actually execute on the physical machine. This procedure is usually called *functional decomposition,* meaning that the main function is decomposed into successively simpler and simpler components. Alternatively, one can think of performing stepwise refinement, meaning that the solution is successively refined into more and more detailed explanations of how that solution is to be brought about. In either case, the parallel objective is to identify reusable functional modules wherever possible. In an ideal world, a very high-level application-language or application-oriented virtual machine would be defined along the way.

While this is a very noble objective, in practice it is extremely difficult to identify reusable modules in a top-down fashion. What usually happens is that a fair amount of bottom-up design is done in parallel. This is as it should be. We believe that the user environment (virtual machine) can be defined most easily and effectively in a bottom-up manner, and that, therefore, top-down design should be preceded by as much bottom-up design as possible. This gives the top-down designer the tools needed to solve the problem and provides a certain separation of concerns. Implementing the virtual machine and solving the application problem should be addressed as separate concerns, even though they often have to be solved simultaneously.

In doing top-down design, two questions must be addressed immediately:

(1) What criterion do I use for identifying the top?

(2) What is the basis for partitioning the problem and its solution?

Strategies that have evolved for answering these questions in a reasonable way are discussed below.

FUNCTIONAL DECOMPOSITION

In using this approach, the top is defined as the ultimate function to be performed, and this function is divided into subfunctions by decomposing with respect to time order, data flow, logical groupings, access to a common resource, control flow, or some other criterion. The choice of "what to decompose with respect to" has a major impact on the "goodness" of the resulting program and is often controversial.

One attempt to formalize the procedure of functional decomposition using stepwise refinement was proposed very early by David Parnas.[6] His concepts are updated in his more recent article, "**Designing Software for Ease of Extension and Contraction.**"[8]

In the latter article, Parnas explains that when designing a software system, there is a tendency to attempt to develop *the* software for *the* problem as if there were only one specific problem and one program to do that job. Instead, one ought to design software in a manner that economically permits new features to be added or unused features to be removed for efficiency. The resulting family of program versions is simply subsets of all of the functions that are generic to the application.

Although any system may have a new feature added, the amount of effort required to add it may be out of proportion to the nature of the change. Often, it is nearly impossible to remove a feature and regain all of the efficiency and resources that support the no-longer-needed function. The inability of such systems to expand and contract as the application evolves stems from several design errors.

Knowledge about specific features or changeable aspects of the implementation may be distributed excessively throughout the system. Designing for change requires that this information be encapsulated within a module and hidden from the view of the other modules. An interface that is insensitive to anticipated changes provides controlled access to this information.

Chains of transformation processes may be difficult to remove when they reformat as well as process the data stream. When the process is not required for an application, a skeletal process that must reformat the data (as did the original transform process) is required. In such a situation, it is not possible to regain all the system efficiency without recoding other unrelated processes.

The use of hierarchies of virtual machines helps to avoid this problem. Instead of treating the system as a sequence of transformations, it is decomposed into multiple virtual machine levels. At each level, the system employs (possibly) complex virtual machine instructions that are made available by the next lower level. Unused instructions may be omitted whenever the application does not require them.

When decomposing a system into levels of abstract machines and modules, it is essential to consider a relation described by Parnas as the "uses" relation. Program A "uses" program B, if the correct execution of A depends on the correct execution of B. All the programs of a system may be placed into a "uses" relation hierarchy in which level $\emptyset$ contains all those programs which use no other and at each level i for $i \geq 1$, the programs use at least 1 program at level $i-1$ and no other program at a higher level than $i-1$. The preparation of the "uses" hierarchy is considered a major milestone of the system design.

Parnas proposes that systems which are amenable to functional expansion and contraction can be achieved if the system is structured so that A "uses" B only when all the following criteria are met:

(1) A is simpler because it "uses" B.

(2) B is not much more complex because it may not "use" A.

(3) There is a useful function subset containing B but not A.

(4) There is no useful function subset containing A but not B.

An example of such a design is detailed.

The concept of the "uses" relation is a very powerful extension of the simple technique of information hiding within modules.

The development of highly modular systems is complicated because the factoring that will yield a reliable and serviceable system is difficult to discern. Constantine states that to develop a successful modular system it is vital that the modules be relatively independent. In the books by Yourdon and Constantine, *Structured Design*,[7] and by Myers, *Reliable Software Through Composite Design*,[8] the degree of interdependence is referred to as *coupling*. The number and complexity of data connections determines the coupling between modules.

Equally important is the binding among the elements within a module. Modules that perform a single task are more cohesive than modules that perform multiple tasks. Several degrees of cohesiveness have been characterized, ranging from coincidental to functional.

Yourdon and Constantine have noted that there are at least seven criteria which can be used in functional decomposition of a system and have ranked them in terms of the perceived cohesion of the resulting program. Their levels of cohesion are shown in Figure 7.

THE ASSOCIATION BETWEEN ELEMENTS OF A MODULE

LEVELS OF COHESION

- FUNCTIONAL   ~ integral
- SEQUENTIAL   ~ data flow
- COMMUNICATIONAL   ~ common data
- PROCEDURAL   ~ flow chart
- TEMPORAL   ~ same time
- LOGICAL   ~ similar fctn
- COINCIDENTAL   ~ random

Figure 7. Levels of Cohesion.

The lowest level of cohesion results when the decomposition is done randomly. Similar functions, such as input routines, test routines, bug routines, etc., score slightly higher. Functions performed at the same time, such as the initialization routine, result in temporal cohesion. Flowchart thinking (do this, then do that, etc.) results in procedural cohesion. Communicational cohesion results when programs having access to common data are grouped together. (The procedure-call routines, described earlier as parts of a data abstraction, have communicational cohesion.) Programs that pass data between each other, like stations on an assembly line, result in sequential cohesion.

The decomposition of a function into a new set of functions which are integral to the problem is deemed to be both the "best cohesion" and the hardest to define. The square-root routine is usually used as an example of such a functionally cohesive module. On a scale of $\emptyset$ to 10, Yourdon rates coincidental, logical, and temporal cohesion lowest at approximately $\emptyset$, 1, and 3, respectively. Procedural cohesion is scored at 5. Communicational, sequential, and functional cohesion are rated highest at 7, 9, and 10, respectively.

The major advantage of functional decomposition is its general applicability. It has also been used by more people longer than any of the other methods discussed.

The disadvantages are its unpredictability and variability. The chances of two programmers independently solving a given problem in the same way are practically nil. Thus, each new person exposed to a program starts by saying, "This isn't the way I would have done it, but . . ."

JACKSON DESIGN

When the program structure is derived from the data structure, the relationship between different levels of the hierarchy tends to be a "is composed of" relationship. That is, an output report is composed of a header followed by a report body, followed by a report summary. This relationship is generally static and does not change during the execution of the program. Thus, a firm base for modeling the problem is formed.

Since a data-structure specification usually lends itself well to being viewed as correct or incorrect, the program structure, based on a data-structure specification, can likewise be viewed as correct or incorrect. Hence, two people solving the same problem should come up with (essentially) identical program structures.

The best known data-structure design method is that of Michael Jackson as described in his paper, "**Constructive Methods of Program Design.**"[9] The Jackson design methodology is a constructive method of program design. Based upon a formal description of a program's input and output data structures, the technique develops an executable program through a sequence of clearly defined and easily applied steps. The resulting program may take the form of a collection of cooperating processes that may later be transformed and combined to yield a single program task.

Michael Jackson, the inventor of the data structure design method, claims his method encourages a proper modeling of the problem environment and provides for a separation of concerns during the problem solution. Specifically, the programming process can be partitioned into the following steps:

(1) Model the real world.

(2) Define the data-stream structures.

(3) Derive and verify the program structures.

(4) Derive and allocate the elementary operations.

(5) Write the structured text.

The first step in applying the method is to form a model of the real world environment in sufficient detail to support the functions you will later want to implement.

The next step in applying the method is to precisely describe the structure of the input and output data. A graphic notation is used, and a static model of the data files is developed.

In the next step, the data-structure diagrams are combined to form the program structure. Components in this structure may result from correspondences identified by the problem statement between the input and output data elements. At this stage there are no executable operations; only the organization of the program has been determined. This structure is based upon the static properties of the data processed by the program and provides the framework upon which the program function will be applied. Although simply described, the preceding steps can involve a great deal of work for the designer. On the other hand, the problem has been decomposed since the consideration of dynamic properties has been delayed until a later stage of development.

A list of executable operations is next composed, starting from the output and working backwards to the system input. These operations are allocated to the program structure—a trivial task if the structure is properly constructed and is an adequate model of the data structures. The augmented program structure can be simply translated into structured text and finally into a programming language for execution.

It is not always possible to fit together the input and output data structures into a single program structure. This problem is called a *structure clash*. The situation is resolved by decomposing the problem into cooperating programs, each reflecting a non-conflicting portion of the data structures. The resulting programs interact through serial data files that effectively decouple the programs. And because these files are described by the input and output structures of the programs which access them, a precisely documented interface is provided.

Networks of cooperating programs, or concurrently executing processes, can be transformed in a systematic fashion in order to impose more optimal scheduling constraints, eliminate the intermediate files, and improve execution efficiency. It is crucial to note, however, that these transformations are performed only after the designer has completed the first stage in the design procedure, arriving at the correctly executing program network.

Effectively partitioning the design process as well as the problem solution, the steps in this whole procedure can usually be performed and verified independently. The resulting program structure for large problems is a network of hierarchies. That is, each simple program is implemented as a true hierarchical modular structure, but these simple programs are connected together in a data-flow network. The network can be placed into a "calls" or "is called by" hierarchy by a process called *program inversion,* but this is considered as a matter of scheduling that is independent of the structure of the program.

While the Jackson design methodology is a top-down method, it has been developed in a bottom-up manner by Jackson and his associates. Considerable time and effort went into making certain that they knew how to do program design before working their way up to systems design.

We're glad to say that during the last several years, progress has been made on extending the Jackson method to systems design. That work is documented here by Jackson's paper entitled, **"Information Systems: Modeling, Sequencing and Transformations,"**[10] and by John Cameron's paper, **"Two Pairs of Examples in the Jackson Approach to System Development."**[11]

Traditionally, designing an information processing system begins with the consideration of the system's function. Because the function is typically quite complex, methods have been developed to decompose the function of the system into more manageable pieces. In Jackson's paper, however, the role of function is considered secondary to modeling.

Functional design has three serious disadvantages. Functional decomposition is difficult for all but the most trivial problems and the most inspired designers. Often, an apparently small change in specification causes a large disruption in the overall system structure. There is a conceptual unification of the design process at all levels that blurs the distinction between system design decisions and implementation concepts.

Viewing the system as a model of the customer's world helps to lessen these disadvantages. Components may be more easily identified as independently active entities in the real world. These entities are modeled by asynchronous, concurrently executing processes, interacting with each other via serial data streams. Such a model is capable of supporting precisely those functions that deal with the entities modeled, functions that are readily formulated and allow the designer to more clearly assess the adequacy of the model in terms of possible future changes. Implementation of the model on currently available machines is possible by the application of specific transformations once the design has been completed.

Jackson's system design philosophy is viewed as separating model from function and design from implementation. Several examples are shown to illustrate these concepts. The form of the system, a network of communicating processes, is easily derived. Transformations that allow efficient implementation, although arduous to apply, may be automated, and thus liberate the programmer of this chore.

Cameron's paper carries these ideas one step further and uses two pairs of examples to demonstrate the emerging system development method.

Cameron explains Jackson's system development method as an enlargement of the program design method. Roughly, Jackson structured programming (JSP) addresses the programming phase of a conventional system life cycle. Jackson system development (JSD) addresses virtually the whole of the system life cycle, including requirements analysis, design, programming, but rearranges the life cycle in a fairly radical way so that there is no longer a programming phase, as commonly understood.

The first steps of the JSD approach are concerned with building a formal model of the external world that concerns the system. Later steps consist of transforming a formal specification into a running system. Finally, the processing functions are superimposed on this model to produce a running system.

The basic JSD life cycle is: (1) describe some abstraction of the real world, (2) add the functional requirement, and (3) implement the system by transformation.

Jackson System Development is truly a departure from conventional functional decomposition which is it's strength and it's weakness. The design process and the resulting program structures are different enough to present difficulties when JSD is mixed with other design strategies. The resulting program, however, may implement a truer model of the world, resulting in lower costs for maintenance and enhancement. Thus it may be worth taking that big step to JSD and reaping it's benefits.

At this point we believe that Jackson and Cameron's efforts have produced a program design methodology that is a first step toward a unified method of systems design. However, much work remains.

WARNIER-ORR DESIGN

Structured systems design based on Jean-Dominique Warnier's logical construction of programs is described in Kenneth Orr's paper entitled, **"Introducing Structured Systems Design."**[12] and in the chapter of his book entitled, **"Using Structured Systems Design."**[13]

Structured programming with Warnier-Orr diagrams is a program-design method that combines an output-oriented program construction technique with the disciplined application of control flow constructs. Because the design is derived from the output, the approach tends to produce consistent designs that closely model the problem.

The first step in the design procedure is to identify and formally describe the system output. For this, a graphical notation is used to detail the logical data structure. In order to develop the logical data base, this structure is augmented with the data elements that appear in the output.

Once the logical data base structure has been developed, the physical data base is designed. The impact of hardware and processing constraints is taken into account so that the efficiency of the final product will be satisfactory.

The process structure is derived from the logical data structure. In complex applications, the process structure represents the structure of all programs within the system. The structure is hierarchical with each level in the diagram corresponding to a logical level of procedure calls. The process structure is translated into a conventional programming language for execution. Structured coding is easily applied, since the graphic notation imposes the forms sequence, selection, and iteration.

Programs that result tend to use a minimal amount of memory and alternate program structures, produced when different people apply the method to a given problem, are isomorphic. As a result, the Warnier-Orr method yields a consistent design.

While this method uses a single graphical notation that is more easily automated, the derivation of the hierarchical data structures is not as clear nor as simply verified as with the Jackson approach. Lacking also are ways to identify and deal with structure clashes and recognition difficulties.

Orr extends Warnier's method in order to assist in system, data base, and procedure definition. He uses the notation of Warnier-Orr diagrams applied to represent complex logical structures as the basic tool. The hierarchical representation that results forms a conceptual link with data base management thinking.

Both Jackson's and Warnier's data structure design methods were first applied in the area of business data processing. Increasingly they are also being applied to a number of on-line problems, but they are still unproven for most real-time applications. For more detailed descriptions of the Jackson design methodology see Jackson's book, *Principles of Program Design*.[9] For a more thorough treatment of the Warnier-Orr method see Orr's book, *Structured Systems Development*.[10]

DATA FLOW DESIGN

The data-flow design method is essentially functional decomposition with respect to data flow. Each block of the structure diagram is viewed as a small "black box" that transforms an input data stream into an output data stream. When these streams are linked together appropriately, the computational process can be modeled and implemented much like an assembly line merging streams of input parts and outputting streams of final products.[7,8]

One strategy of decomposition based on data-flow is called *transform centered design*. This method is explained by Stevens, Myers, and Constantine in their paper, "**Structured Design**,"[14] and by Meilir Page-Jones in the chapter of his book entitled, "**Transform Analysis**."[15]

The goal of transform-centered design is to assist the programmer in developing a modular program that contains elements having minimal coupling and a maximum degree of cohesion. A structure chart is used to clearly display the connections that are present between modules. Each box in this graphic notation represents a module. Connections between boxes indicate that the module above calls the module below. The connections have labeled arrows that explicitly show the data passed between the modules. The structure chart is a useful means of displaying and assessing the degree of coupling present.

A data flow graph is another graphic tool that helps the designer to show the flow and transformation of data through the system. Circles or bubbles represent conceptual transformations on data streams, while arcs between such transformations detail the flow of information into and out of the transform. The purpose of the bubble chart is to clarify the program requirements and identify the major transformations that will become modules of the proposed system.

Bubble charts are partitioned in order to identify three different types of transforms. Afferent (input) modules are concerned with the function of accepting or developing the system input. Efferent (output) modules are concerned with delivering system output data. Between the afferent and efferent branches of the bubble chart is the central transform. The identification of the three portions of a bubble chart leads to the hierarchy of modules shown in the structure chart.

The designer iterates between bubble chart and structure chart in order to improve levels of coupling and cohesion and to factor the system into smaller and more manageable pieces.

An example that illustrates the application of structured design is included in the Page-Jones reprint. Consideration of the scope of control and effect and its impact on problem decomposition is also demonstrated. The resulting design is characteristic of the solutions that can result from a diligent application of the data-flow design considerations.

Proponents of data-flow design contend that the resulting systems contain fewer errors because the problem has been effectively factored. As well, subsequent efforts to change the program are minimized due to the independence of modules.

A possible problem with data-flow decomposition is that it inherently tends to produce a network and not a hierarchy of programs. This shortcoming can be solved simply by "picking" up the network in the middle and letting the input and output data streams "hang down" from the middle. At each level a module is then further decomposed into a "get" module, a "transform" module, or a "put" module.

In the data-flow context, the relation between modules was motivated by a "consumes/produces" relationship. This hierarchical transformation procedure results in modules that are related by a "calls / is called by" relationship. Thus, the artificial hierarchy formed is imposed by the scheduling and often has nothing to do with modeling the hierarchy of the real problem. This contrasts with the "uses" relationship of decomposition with respect to function, and the "is composed of" relationship that motivates a data structure design.

A second strategy for functional decomposition based on data-flow is called *transaction-centered design*. Page-Jones's chapter entitled, **"Transaction Analysis,"**[16] explains this method.

This technique is primarily applicable to programs that are transaction-processing systems. It permits many applications to be modeled in a stimulus-response form. That is, each stimulus triggers a set of responses within the system. Examples of stimulus-response might include programs that: add a new customer, delete an old customer, change a customer's address, or bill a customer. Every customer transaction entering the system would carry a transaction code (*e.g.*, ADD, DELETE, BILL) to indicate it's type. Referring to the transaction code, the system would know what processing each transaction required and would be able to verify that the transaction was properly handled. The organization of the resulting program would (presumably) be much easier to understand and change than a similar program organized around flags and switches.

Bell Telephone of Canada was the first company known to have used this method in a system called SAPTAD (for "System, Analysis, Program, Transaction, Action, and Detail").

When this method is used with transform-centered design, the resulting data-flow diagram includes transaction centers that form transaction-processing subsystems.

We feel that the system flow diagram, which forms the basis for decomposition with respect to data flow, is a very useful contribution. In fact, it may be the best approach currently available at the system design level. We are not convinced, however, that the second step of putting things into a "calls" hierarchy using "transform-centered design"[7] is as useful. It seems to produce a structure with a lot of data passing and with artificial "afferent" (input) and "efferent" (output) branches while reverting back to standard functional decomposition for decomposing the "central transform," the heart of the problem. It isn't clear that anything is gained over simply using functional decomposition from the start.

The concept of transaction-centered design would seem to be more unique. It provides a way of handling stimulus-response systems compactly when many other methods would likely result in an explosion of "special cases." Transaction centers seem to be a good complement to many other design strategies.

A PROGRAMMING CALCULUS

While a "proof of correctness" is disappointingly difficult to develop after a program has been written, the constructive proof-of-correctness discipline, taught by Dijkstra and Gries, is encouraging. Dijkstra's design discipline can be methodically applied to obtain a modest-sized "elegant" program with "a deep logical beauty." Using this method, the program is produced as a by-product of the correctness proof instead of vice versa.

The initial design task consists of formally representing the required result as an assertion stated in the predicate calculus. This result assertion is then "weakened" to form an invariant relation that must hold true throughout the computation. To the extent that both the result and invariant should be formed in stages by a sequence of stepwise refinements, this could be called a top-down design method. Any similarity with the other design methods ends quickly, however, since the design process consists of deriving a host of logical assertions that must be specified formally, using the predicate calculus.

An introduction to this new discipline of programming is given by David Gries in his paper, **"An Illustration of Current Ideas on the Derivation of Correctness Proofs and Correct Programs."**[17]

Gries states that a logical system for proving programs correct will also provide a set of axioms and inference rules that completely describe, in a formal way, the effect of statement types in a programming language, independent of their implementation. Such a system equips the programmer with the tools and techniques required, not only to prove programs correct, but also to derive (in a disciplined fashion) fashion a correct program from a formal specification of its behavior. Informally, the method enables one to more efficiently understand and develop programs.

In Gries's paper, axiom schemes and inference rules for assignment, composition, alternation, and iteration are presented in the form $\{P\}\ S\ \{R\}$ where P and R are assertions and S is some program text. Such a rule states that if the execution of S is begun when P is true, then upon termination, R will be true. The definitions are enhanced by introducing a rule for deriving the weakest precondition for which the execution of S will establish the desired postcondition, R.

Development of a correct program proceeds from the formal statement of the *postconditions* that are desired after execution is complete, backwards to the *preconditions* that exist prior to execution. Formally specifying these conditions is the first step in the program design process, and perhaps the most difficult, in light of the imprecise and inaccurate program requirements usually provided.

Beginning with the desired postconditions, useful relationships are identified that yield a sequence of assignment statements. The weakest precondition, under which the execution of these simple computations would establish the desired postconditions, is then determined. Because the program is treated as a mathematical object, this development proceeds solely by manipulating expressions.

The technique is applied to a realistic problem in order to demonstrate the derivation and concurrent proof of a program. Indeed, this is quite different from proving an arbitrary program correct, a task that may be much more difficult. The concept of an invariant relation for an iteration is presented, and its use in deriving the required loop initialization, iteration condition, and body is demonstrated.

Using this method, program development is very organized and formal. Although the programmer needs more mathematical skills in order to successfully apply the technique, training and practice can overcome this drawback. Significant benefits can then be realized, and, indeed, you will profit most from reading this article by taking pencil in hand and deriving the program components along with the author.

This introduction to program derivation techniques and correctness proofs may be expanded upon by studying Dijkstra's book, *A Discipline of Programming*.[11]

A second paper involving program proving is "**An Example of Hierarchical Design and Proof**"[18] by Spitzen, Levitt, and Robinson.

The authors point out that hierarchical design and implementation is a much more powerful means of structuring and partitioning large programs than by simply using structured coding techniques. For example, in order to solve a given problem, an abstract machine is designed on which it is easy to prepare the program required. The problem is then solved using this abstract machine, and if the abstract machine is realized on the computer hardware or compiler, the job is done. If not, a lower-level abstract machine is designed, and the abstract data types and operations provided by the high-level machine are implemented using the facilities of the lower-level machine.

This results in a hierarchy of abstract machines that divide the solution to the original problem on the real machine into an ordered set of smaller components. Although described simply as if top-down design and implementation were employed, a flexible mixture of top-down and bottom-up programming shapes the abstract machine hierarchy that results.

Each abstract machine is formally specified. In this paper, the language SPECIAL is used. The use of formal specifications enables one to prove important properties about the machines themselves and about programs that are written. The abstract data types and operations provided by an abstract machine are implemented using the facilities of the next-lower-level machine. The implementation language ILPL is used. The formal machine specifications make it possible to prove that the implementations of the machines are correct.

It is often possible to further partition an abstract machine into several modules. Such a module consists of a collection of operations and data. Formal specification of a module is based on a state model which abstracts the results of the sequences of operations that have been performed. The initial module data is formally specified by a set of V-functions that define the initial state of the model. Operations are specified by OV-functions that calculate a value and, in addition, describe the change of the module state.

Spitzen, Levitt, and Robinson illustrate the method of hierarchical design and proof by using an example program that maintains a representation of lists such that structurally isomorphic lists are identical. This nontrivial program clearly demonstrates the use of formal specification and functional program verification techniques.

It appears that the primary disadvantage of both of these approaches is that a relatively high degree of logical and mathematical proficiency is required for producing even "simple" programs. The mathematical proofs involved are often several times longer than the program derived.

A second, and perhaps equally important, disadvantage is that use of these methods admits the existence of multiple solutions to the same problem. Each different choice of an invariant assertion, while providing a solution, can lead to a different program structure. The resulting programs do not necessarily portray accurate and consistent models of the problem's environment or its solution. Thus, a "correct" program may still have the "wrong" structure.

In spite of these problems, we view programming calculus based design disciplines as an encouraging step forward on the road to developing correct programs. It is a method that you should be aware of, for it definitely holds promise for the future.

PROGRAMS AS PROCESSES

The concept of a "network of processes" is becoming an increasingly important idea as a means of decomposing large problems. In Kahn and MacQueen's paper, **"Coroutines and Networks of Parallel Processes,"**[19] a programming language is presented that allows a clear semantic presentation of process interaction.

Kahn and MacQueen describe a process as an autonomous program that communicates with adjacent modules as if they were input and output subroutines. Channels interconnect processes and buffer their communications. They carry information serially and in only one direction from a producer to one or more consumer processes.

The programming language which they develop provides a concise and flexible means for creating complex networks of processes. Process declarations specify call-by-value parameters and ports that are bound to communications channels. Conceptually, each process is thought of as executing on a separate machine so that it cannot communicate with other processes except through interconnecting channels. Thus all referenced global data must be treated as read-only.

Functions are provided to receive and transmit values via input and output channels, respectively. An attempt to receive information from a channel that is empty suspends the consumer process until an element is available.

During execution, the network of processes may be appropriately modified. Reconfiguration instructions are provided to permit new processes to be interposed on existing communications channels, thus, allowing the parent process to either continue execution or to leave the network and terminate. Splicing provides a simple mechanism that results in a newly configured network that outputs values on a channel previously bound to the output port of the parent process. Networks may also be created that contain cycles. Such a configuration saves significant time and space compared to networks that employ recursive processes.

The constructs provided are written using a functional notation that provides a concise way of expressing the relationships between processes. Programs are conceived functionally, and operational concerns such as scheduling do not enter into their design. Because the resulting networks exhibit time-independent behavior, program proofs can be developed at a level of abstraction that avoids the intricacies of dynamic behavior.

In Tony Hoare's paper entitled, **"Communicating Sequential Processes,"**[20] foundations for a programming language are proposed that attempt to provide a simple, unified solution for several fundamental programming problems. This paper suggests that input and output operations and concurrency of execution should be regarded as programming primitives that underlie many programming concepts.

Dijkstra's guarded commands are incorporated as sequential control structures to control nondeterminism. A parallel command specifies the execution of its constituent sequential commands as concurrently executed sequential processes.

Input and output commands are provided to support communication between explicitly named producer and consumer processes. A facility is provided to allow the consumer process to identify the structure of an input message. Information is transferred without buffering between two concurrently executing processes when: (1) an input command in one process specifies as its source the process name of the other process, (2) the first process is named as the destination in an output command of the second process, and (3) the structure of the target variable specified in the input command matches the structure denoted by the expression of the output command.

Input commands may appear within guards. As a result, consumer processes can specify alternate sources and types of input and behave accordingly. A repetitive command that specifies input commands as guards terminates when all of the named sources have terminated.

The elementary mechanisms provided are surprisingly versatile. Examples demonstrate the use of the proposed language mechanisms in order: to effect specific scheduling constraints, to realize conventional subroutine and function mechanisms, for recursion, for monitors, for semaphores, and for buffers. These primitive concepts provide a simple basis for more specific or complex language features. However, the fact that they can be used to create more complex mechanisms does not imply that these primitives should wholly replace them. Where a less general mechanism is frequently used, has properties that are more simply provable, and can be implemented more efficiently, there is a strong case for its inclusion within a programming language.

In Per Brinch Hansen's paper, **"Distributed Processes: A Concurrent Programming concept,"**[21] distributed processes is a language concept proposed for real-time applications that are controlled by microcomputer networks with distributed storage. A concurrent program in such a system consists of a fixed number of sequential processes that are executed simultaneously. To satisfy real-time constraints, each processor is dedicated to a single process.

Communication between processes is achieved by procedure calls. Thus a process may invoke common procedures embedded in either itself or in other processes, but may not communicate via common variables. Communication between processes is asymmetric, requiring only the process invoking a procedure to identify the process that defines the procedure.

Nondeterminism is controlled by guarded regions that may delay the execution of the process and guarded commands. Both regions specify a choice among possible alternatives based on the current state of local variables of the process. Much of the power of distributed processes stems from the ability to delay the execution of a process by means of Boolean expressions. These expressions involve global variables of a process and the input parameters from other processes. Quasi-concurrent processes within each processor manage this scheduling. Also permitted, are synchronizing conditions, written as expressions involving only global variables of a process. Periodic evaluation of the expression is required; but it does not represent a serious computational burden, because it involves only the local store of a single processor that has nothing else to do.

Several examples demonstrate the flexibility of the language facilities provided. Distributed processes form a common denominator for several programming concepts including: procedures, coroutines, classes, monitors, processes, semaphores, buffers, path expressions, and input/output functions. The proposed constructs constitute a first step toward a practical language for multiprocessor networks.

For additional information on processes and the use of concurrent programming facilities, you may wish to read Per Brinch Hansen's book, *The Architecture of Concurrent Programs.*[12]

COMPARISON AND SUMMARY

We have included three papers that provide a summary and comparison of the methods presented earlier. The first paper by Bergland entitled, **"A Guided Tour of Program Design Methodologies,"**[22] illustrates the application of functional decomposition, the data-flow approach, the data-structure design method, and the programming calculus. A modest example is solved using each technique.

The paper entitled **"Comparing Software Design Methodologies,"**[23] by Peters and Tripp, gives a brief overview of many of the methods treated, including higher-order software, logical construction of programs, and structured design.

A more in-depth comparison and summary is given by Griffiths in **"Design Methodologies—A Comparison."**[24] This report attempts to assess the present value of most of the major techniques as well as their future potential as design methodologies.

In summary, we believe that the most promising of the methods described are those that base program structure on the static structure of the input and output data processed. The Jackson Design Methodology pioneered by Michael Jackson in England, and the logical construction of programs developed by Jean-Dominique Warnier in France (and subsequently by Kenneth T. Orr in the United States), derive their program structures from the structure of the data. We feel that programs formed in this way can be designed consistently, have a more significant chance of being correct initially, and perhaps most importantly, best model the user's problem so that (as a result) the programs are more amenable to future specification changes.

A first step in extending these methods to encompass the problem of systems design has been taken. The Jackson design methodology derives the structure of systems by first developing models of real-world entities as seen from the user's perspective. The models, implemented as concurrently executing serial processes, may be transformed in order to realize more efficient implementations. Structured systems analysis and design, based on the logical construction of programs, extends those concepts in order to solve the system problem by using essentially the same basic tools and techniques applied to program construction.

Structured design, developed by Larry Constantine and Edward Yourdon, provides the necessary tools needed to construct effective, highly modular systems. Module cohesiveness and coupling are introduced as measures of the binding among the elements of and the interdependence among modules. By controlling these factors, successful programs can be developed.

Structured programming, an important technique, has been applied to improve the clarity and ultimately the precision of the programming activity. Viewed as a mathematical form, programs may be derived from a precise specification of their intended behavior. Applying such a constructive approach to program development in a top-down fashion will yield a hierarchy of abstract machines. These techniques play an important role in developing programs for which proofs of correctness may be possible.

Many design strategies decompose the problem solution into a network of cooperating processes. Notions of a coroutine and process networks are introduced. The fundamental concepts, useful in such an environment, may be represented by communicating sequential processes. A first attempt at providing a useful programming language and environment for the convenient execution of process networks is presented.

In the future, we still hope to see a movement toward generic solutions to generic problems. There is already a fair amount of agreement on how the operating system of a single-processor computer should be structured. Why not that same sort of consensus for standard application programs? Given these generic solution building blocks, we can concern ourselves with yet larger and more complex systems, calling out solutions to previously solved problems with a single statement. In the world of data processing we may head in this direction some day in the future.

Regarding real-time programming, we do not see as much progress. There are still many competing methodologies which result in many different partitionings of problems and their solutions. One hopeful "ray of light" that we have seen recently in this area is the work being done on SREM.[13]

Current and anticipated problems continue to be: (1) the ability to distinguish between good and bad program structures consistently (where bad means costly and difficult to enhance and maintain); (2) the ability to produce good program structures consistently; and (3) the ability to build on the previous work of others.

REFERENCES

1. Her Majesty's Stationery Office, *Implications of Using Modular Programming*, "Evaluation of Programming and Systems Techniques," British Central Computer Agency Guide No. 1, 1973.

2. Weinberg, G. M., *The Psychology of Computer Programming*, Van Nostrand Reinhold Company, New York, 1971.

3. Dijkstra, E. W., "The Humble Programmer," *Communications of the ACM*, October 1972, pp. 859-66.

4. Basili, Victor R., and Baker, Terry, *Structured Programming: A Tutorial*. IEEE, Inc., New York, 1977.

5. Liskov, B., and Zilles, S., "Programming with Abstract Data Types," Proc. ACM Conference on Very High-Level Languages, *SIGPLAN NOTICES*, Vol. 9, April 1974.

6. Parnas, D. L., "On the Criteria to be Used in Decomposing Systems into Modules." *Communications of the ACM*, December 1972.

7. Yourdon, E., and Constantine, L. L., *Structured Design*. Yourdon, Inc., New York, 1975.

8. Myers, G. J., *Reliable Software through Composite Design*, Petrocelli/Charter, New York, 1975.

9. Jackson, M. A., *Principles of Program Design*. Academic Press, New York, 1975.

10. Orr, Kenneth T., *Structured Systems Development*. Yourdon Press, New York, 1980.

11. Dijkstra, E. W., "*A Discipline of Programming*," Prentice-Hall, Inc., Englewood Cliffs, 1976.

12. Brinch Hansen, Per, *The Architecture of Concurrent Programs*. Prentice-Hall, Englewood Cliffs, 1977.

13. Alford, Mack W., "Software Requirements Engineering Methodology (SREM) at the Age of Four," *Computer Software and Applications Conference*, Chicago, Illinois (October 1980), pp. 866-874.

On Structured Programming

David Gries

What is structured programming?

The term *structured programming* (hereafter abbreviated *sp*) has been used with many different meanings since Edsger W. Dijkstra first coined the term. Actually, the term appeared in the title of his monograph Notes on structured programming [Dijkstra 77d*], but as far as I can determine not in the monograph itself! The lack of a precise definition has allowed, even encouraged, people to use it as they wished, to attribute to sp what they themselves learned from reading Notes on structured programming, however different this might have been from Dijkstra's intent. Taken out of context or viewed in the wrong light, some of the resulting definitions of sp that have appeared in the literature seem stupid (e.g., sp is programming without **gotos**), and it is quite understandable that programmers have looked askance when asked to learn and practice it. The matter has gotten so out of hand that some programmers and managers feel that sp is an attempt to "deskill" the profession—to put so many restrictions on the programmer that his task becomes trivial and can be performed by almost any person.

In discussing sp in [Denning 73], Peter Denning found the first five of the following impressions people seem to have of sp; I found the following eight. Taken together, they give a good general view of the subject.

1. It is a return to common sense.

2. It is the general method by which our leading programmers program.

3. It is programming without the use of **goto** statements.

4. It is the process of controlling the number of interactions between a given local task and its environment so that the number of interactions is some linear function of some parameter or parameters of the task.

5. It is top-down programming.

6. sp theory deals with converting arbitrarily large and complex flowcharts into standard forms so that they can be represented by iterating and nesting a small number of basic and standard control logic structures (these usually being sentencing, alternation, and iteration) [Mills 71].

7. sp is a manner of organizing and coding programs that makes the programs easily understood and modified [Donaldson 73].

8. The purpose of sp is to control complexity through theory and discipline [Mills 71].

9. sp should be characterized not by the absence of **gotos**, but by the presence of structure [Mills 72].

10. A major function of the structuring of the program is to keep a correctness proof feasible [Dijkstra 72d*].

11. Fundamental concept (of sp) is a proof of correctness [Karp 1974].

12. sp...allows verification of the correctness of all steps in the design process and, thus, automatically leads to a *self-explicable* and *self-defensive* programming style [Bauer 73].

13. sp is no panacea—it really consists of a formal notation for orderly thinking, *an attribute not commonly inherent in programmers or any other type* (my emphasis). It is a discipline which must be acquired and continuously reinforced through conscious effort. It is worth the trouble [Butterworth 74].

Let me give C. A. R. Hoare's definition, which I feel captures the essence of sp: "The task of organizing one's thought in a way that leads, in a reasonable time, to an understandable expression of a computing task, has come to be called sp."

I would add to this that one should always strive for simplicity and elegance. The simplest solution is always the easiest to understand. This does not mean that one must sacrifice efficiency; indeed, it is often only when we understand a problem and a solution that we can develop a more efficient one. Computer science already has its complexity theory; we might call sp the "art of simplicity" or "simplicity theory."

Research in structured programming

I think the reader will have a better understanding of sp if he understands the various areas of research on the subject. Research in sp involves four closely related topics: programming, methodology, program notation, program correctness, and program verification. I shall discuss each of these.

1. *Programming methodology*. The goals are to devise orderly, efficient methods for developing readable correct programs, to identify and explain tools and techniques for solving programming problems (or any problems for that matter), and to find out how to think clearly when programming. Some of the current buzz terms are: levels of abstraction, stepwise refinement, top-down programming, "solve a simpler problem first," and "find a related problem." But these buzz terms mean little by themselves; the only way to really understand what has been done so far is to study some of the discussions on the subject, most notably [Dijkstra 72d*].

It must be made clear that one technique will never suffice (for example, top-down programming). A programmer needs a bag of tricks, a collection of methods for attacking a problem. Secondly, if we are to raise the level of programming, each programmer (no matter how good he feels he is) must become more conscious of the tools and techniques he uses. It is not enough to just program; we must discover how and why we do it. Programming methodology is concerned with how we should program and why.

We *must* realize that programming is a difficult task, and we must be more receptive to new ideas; even the best programmer can learn to program more efficiently.

Computer science is in the *unique* position of trying to teach general problem solving to a large number of students. When a student finishes a programming course, we expect him to be able to program any problem in an area in which he is knowledgeable. Yet it is fair to say that almost none of the elementary programming books say anything about problem solving, about orderly thinking, about expressing algorithms clearly and simply. The only conclusion to draw is that the students are not being taught how to program; they are only being taught a programming language.

Teaching a programming methodology means that we ourselves must understand the programming process and how it can be made more orderly and efficient. Someone must isolate and explain the tools that are available, must give examples of their use, must try to determine why one way of looking at a problem may be more useful than another. Thus, it is not fair to criticize work in this area by saying, "That's obvious, I always program that way."

When touching programming, I am interested in explaining problem solving ideas, in teaching orderly thinking, in getting across a sense of simplicity, elegance, and style. The language that best suits my needs is one which is itself "clean," which has the control structures I feel are most useful in programming, and which can be taught in a modular fashion. Here FORTRAN is at a distinct disadvantage to ALGOL, ALGOL W, Pascal, and a limited subset of PL/1, and if a reasonably efficient implementation of any of these is available, I fail to see why anyone would pick FORTRAN. (We are of course partially limited in choice since others outside computer science often have a voice in the matter; because of this, for example, Cornell teaches a subset of PL/1 instead of Pascal or ALGOL W.) But anyone who has been taught programming (as opposed to a programming language) should be able to become fluent in FORTRAN, PL/1, ALGOL, etc., with relative ease.

2. *Program notation.* Language shapes the thought and culture of those who use it, Benjamin Whorf said; and this is certainly true in programming. A cluttered programming language can hinder us from thinking clearly; a restricted language can hide the best algorithm from us. Research in this area of sp is devoted to improving notation (1) by looking for better notation and language features which can help simplify the programming process, (2) by determining which control structures are best suited for describing algorithms correctly and clearly, and (3) by learning how to describe data structures in a cleaner fashion.

A restricted notation puts a programmer at a severe disadvantage. A prime example of this is the **do** I=1 ... loop notation. Even on some very simple problems, programmers with the **do** I=1 ... mentality do not find the simplest, most efficient solution because their idea of iteration is so limited.

This does not mean one shouldn't use FORTRAN. Sp methodology tells us not to program *in* a programming language, but *into* it. Express the algorithm in a notation that best fits the problem, then refine this algorithm into the programming language. Use any notation that fits the problem, and then use whatever is necessary—including **gotos**—to *simulate* that notation in the programming language, taking care of course to describe your intent in the program itself. This is often harder to do with FORTRAN, but there is no harm in it as long as you do not restrict your algorithmic thoughts to FORTRAN concepts.

3. *Program correctness.* The first 25 years of programming saw little emphasis on initial correctness and too much emphasis on debugging. But debugging can never show the absence of errors, only their presence. Current sp methodology suggests that one should try to develop a program and its proof of correctness hand in hand.

What is a proof? The broadest definition would allow any informal discussion that convinces at least one person (besides the author), and the narrowest would require a strictly formal, detailed analysis leading from a set of axioms to the theorem. To be *practical*, we want something that falls between these two extremes.

Most of the work on proving correctness has been quite formal and mathematical and is as yet of no use to the programmer. But some important *practical* ideas have arisen in the research on axiomatic approaches to programming language definition. One such idea is that we should not look so much at how a program changes values of variables, but instead at how relations among the variables remain the same.

The fact that one can prove a program correct using a mathematical definition of correctness, without reference to how a program is executed, is extremely valuable and insightful. It allows the programmer to separate his two main concerns—efficiency and correctness—and deal with each in turn. A significant advance is Hoare's invariant relation axiom for **while** loops. This axiom gives us finally a practical approach to understanding iteration; it bridges the gap between the static aspect of a loop (how we read it) and its dynamic aspect (how it gets executed).

The invariant relation axiom is practical enough to be used by any programmer willing to spend some time studying it. For more information read [Dijkstra 72d*; Wirth 73a*; Gries 73a*].

4. *Program verification.* No matter how hard we try to prove the correctness of a program there will be mistakes in it. Most of these will be syntactic mistakes; we have proven the correctness of the algorithm, and not its representation as a program. Thus there is still need for program verification.

I hesitate to call this phase of programming "debugging," for this seems to imply that mistakes are to be expected. Syntax mistakes, perhaps, but not logical mistakes. The attitude of "I'll just run it, find the bugs, and fix them" has caused much trouble.

Research is being done in this area (see for example [Hetzel 73]), but I feel that at this stage the other three areas of sp are more important.

Conclusion

Structured programming, then, is an approach to understanding the complete programming process. While it is true that some people go overboard on their belief in the preliminary results (don't ever use a **goto**, you must use only the conditional and while statements!), the majority of the people involved in sp are interested only in learning how to program better. sp research will have an important and lasting impact on computing because it will lead to a better understanding of programming.

If you are interested in learning more about what sp really is, I can give some suggestions. The first is to study the readings given below with an open mind; the second is to actually try to write several programs using the principles that have emerged from sp research. You will find it hard work, because you will have to be continually aware of your thought processes, and you will have to think differently than you're used to. If, after this study (and only then), you disagree with the principles, you are entitled to say they are not for you, and you are invited to propose your own principles.

I suggest you read several things: Polya's paperback entitled *How to Solve It* [Polya 71], and [Dijkstra 72d*; Gries 73*; Wirth 73*; Dijkstra 76*].

References

[Dijkstra 72d*] Dijkstra, E. W., "Notes on structured programming," in *Structured Programming*. Dahl, O.-J., Hoare, C. A. R., and Dijkstra, E. W., Academic Press, New York, 1972.

[Denning 73] Denning, P. J., "Letter to the editor," *SIGPLAN Notices* **8** (Oct 1973), 5-6.

[Mills 71] Mills, H., "Chief programmer team operations," IBM Tech. Rep. FSC 71-5108, 1971.

[Donaldson 73] Donaldson, J., "Structured programming," *Datamation* (Dec 1973), 53.

[Bauer 73] Bauer, F. L., "A course of three lectures on a philosophy of programming," Technische Univ., Muenchen, Oct 1973.

[Wirth 73a*] Wirth, N., *Systematic Programming: An Introduction*. Prentice-Hall, Englewood Cliffs, N.J., 1973.

[Gries 73a*] Gries, D., and Conway, R., *An Introduction to Programming: a Structured Approach Using PL/I and PL/C*. Winthrop, Cambridge, Mass., 1973. [2nd ed., 1975.]

[Hetzel 73] Hetzel, W. C., (ed.), *Program Test Methods*. Prentice-Hall, Englewood Cliffs, N. J., 1973.

[Polya 71] Polya, G., *How to Solve It*. Princeton Univ. Press, Princeton, N. J., 1971.

[Dijkstra 76*] Dijkstra, E. W., *A Discipline of Programming*. Prentice-Hall, Englewood Cliffs, N. J., 1976.

[Butterworth 74] Butterworth, D., "Letter to the Editor," *Datamation,* (March 1974), 158.

IEEE TRANSACTIONS ON SOFTWARE ENGINEERING, VOL. SE-1, NO. 2, JUNE 1975

Structured Programming in a Production Programming Environment

F. TERRY BAKER

Abstract—This paper discusses how structured programming methodology has been introduced into a large production programming organization using an integrated but flexible approach. It next analyzes the advantages and disadvantages of each component of the methodology and presents some quantitative results on its use. It concludes with recommendations based on this generally successful experience, which could be useful to other organizations interested in improving reliability and productivity.

Index Terms—Chief programmer teams (CPT's), development support libraries (DSL's), structured coding, structured programming, top-down development, top-down programming.

I. INTRODUCTION

AT this point in time, the ideas of structured programming have gained widespread acceptance, not only in academic circles, but also in organizations doing production programming. What is perhaps not so widely appreciated, however, is that the organizations, procedures, and tools associated with the implementation of structured programming are critical to its success. This is particularly true in production programming environments, where program systems (rather than single programs) are developed, and the attainment of reliable, maintainable software on time and within cost estimates is a prime management objective. In this environment, module level coding and debugging activities typically account for about 20 percent of the effort spent on software development [1]. Thus, narrow applications of structured programming ideas limited only to these activities have correspondingly limited benefits. It is therefore desirable to adopt an integrated but flexible approach incorporating the ideas into as many aspects of projects as possible to achieve maximum reliability improvements and cost savings.

II. BACKGROUND

The IBM Federal Systems Division (FSD) is an organization involved in production programming on a large scale. Although much of its software work is performed for federal, state, and local governmental agencies, the division also contracts with private business enterprises for complex systems development work. Work scope ranges from less than a man-year of effort on small projects to thousands of man-years spent on the development and maintenance of large, evolutionary, long-term systems such as the Apollo/Skylab ground support

software. Varying customer requirements necessitate the use of a wide variety of hardware, programming languages, software tools, documentation procedures, management techniques, etc. Problems range from software maintenance, through pure applications programming using commercially available operating systems and program products, to the concurrent development of central processors, peripherals, firmware, support software and applications software for avionics requirements. Thus, within this single organization can be found a wide range of software development efforts.

FSD has always been concerned with the development of more reliable programs through use of improved software tools, techniques and management methods. Most recently, FSD has been active in the development of structured programming techniques [2]. This has led to organizations, procedures and tools for applying them to production programming projects, particularly with a new organization called a chief programmer team (CPT) [3]. The team, a functional organization based on standard support tools and disciplined application of structured programming principles, had its first trial on a major software development effort in 1969–71 [4], [5]. In the three years since the completion of that experimental project, FSD has been incorporating structured programming techniques into most of its software development projects. Because of the scope and diversity of these projects, it was impossible to adapt any single set of tools and procedures or any rigid type of organization to all or even to a majority of them. And because of the ongoing nature of many of these systems, it was necessary to introduce these techniques gradually over a period of several years. It is believed that any software development organization can improve the reliability and reduce the costs of its software projects using an approach similar to that described herein.

III. PLAN

To introduce the ideas of structured programming into FSD work practices and to evaluate their use, a plan with four major components was implemented. First, a set of guidelines was established to define the terminology associated with the ideas with sufficient precision to permit the introduction and measurement of individual components of the overall methodology. These guidelines were published, and directives regarding their implementation were issued. Second, support tools and methodologies were developed, particularly for projects using commercial hardware and operating systems. For those projects

Manuscript received February 1, 1975.
The author is with IBM Federal Systems Division, Gaithersburg, Md. 20760.

97

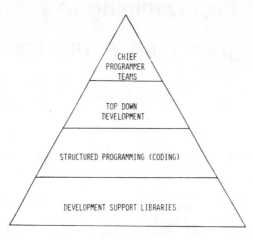

Fig. 1. Hierarchy of techniques.

where these were not employed, standards based on the developed tools enabled them to provide their own support. Third, documentation of the techniques and tools, and education in their use, were both carried out. These were done on a broad scale covering management techniques, programming methodologies, and clerical procedures. Fourth, a measurement program was established to provide data for technology evaluation and improvement. This program included both broad measurements which were introduced immediately, and detailed measurements which required substantial development work and were introduced later. The next four subsections cover the components of this plan and their implementation in detail.

A. Guidelines

A number of important considerations influenced the establishment of a set of guidelines for the application of structured programming technology within FSD. First and most important, they had to permit adaptation to the wide variety of project environments described above. This required that they be useful in program maintenance situations where unstructured program systems were already in being, as well as in situations where completely new systems were to be developed. Second, they had to allow for the range of processors and operating systems in use. This necessitated the description of functions to be provided instead of specific tools to be used. Third, they had to allow for differences in organizations and methodology (e.g., specifications, documentation, configuration management) required or in use on various projects.

The guidelines resulting from these considerations describe a hierarchical set of four components, graphically illustrated in Fig. 1. With one limited exception, use of the component at any level presupposes use of those below it, even though certain components could be used more independently. Thus, by beginning at a level which a project's environment and status permit, and then progressing upward, projects can evolve gradually toward full use of the technology.

1) Development Support Libraries (DSL's): The intro-

ductory level is the DSL which is a tool designed with two key principles in mind.

1) Keep current project status organized and visible at all times. In this way, any programmer, manager or user can find out the status or study an approach directly without depending on anyone else's interpretation.

2) Make it possible for a librarian to do the majority of library maintenance, thus separating clerical from intellectual activity.

A DSL is normally the primary responsibility of a secretary or clerk trained as a programming librarian. Programmers interface with the computer primarily through the library and the programming librarian. This allows better control of computer activity and ensures that the library is always complete and current, thus reducing misunderstandings and inconsistencies. In general, the library system is the prime factor in increasing the visibility of a developing project and thus reducing risk and increasing reliability.

The guidelines for a DSL are as follows.

1) A library system providing the capabilities described in Section III-B 1) below must be used.

2) The library system must be used throughout the development process, not just to store debugged source or object code, for example.

3) Visibility of the current status of the entire project, as well as past history of source code activities and run executions, should be provided by the external library.

4) The visibility of the code should be such that the code itself serves as the prime reference for questions of data formats, program operation, etc.

5) Filing procedures must be faithfully adhered to for all runs, whether or not setup is performed by a librarian. However, use of a trained librarian is recommended.

2) Structured Coding: In order to provide for use of structured programming techniques on maintenance as well as development projects, it was necessary to separate them into two components. In FSD, then, we distinguish between those practices used in system development (top-down development) and those used in

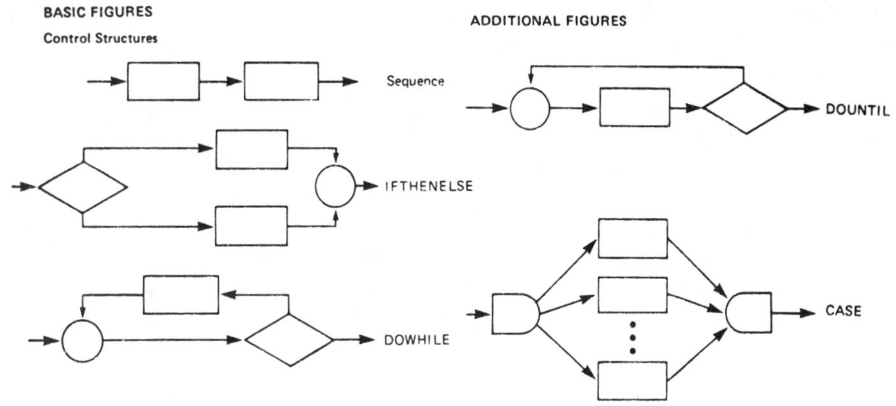

BASIC FIGURES

Control Structures

ADDITIONAL FIGURES

Sequence

IFTHENELSE

DOWHILE

DOUNTIL

CASE

Fig. 2.   Control structures.

coding individual program modules (structured coding). Our use of the term "structured coding" in the guidelines thus refers primarily to standards governing module organization and construction, and control flow within it. The three basic control flow figures and two optional ones shown in Fig. 2 are permitted. The guidelines also refer to a Guide [6] (see Section III-C below) which contains general information and standards for structured coding, as well as detailed standards for use of various programming languages. Finally, they require that code be reviewed by someone other than the developer. The detailed guidelines for structured programming are as follows.

1) The conventions established in the *Structured Programming Guide* should be followed. Exceptions to conventions must be documented. If a language is not covered in the Guide, then use of a locally generated set of conventions consistent with the rules of structured programming is acceptable.

2) The code should be reviewed for functional integrity and for adherence to the structured programming conventions.

3) A DSL must be used.

3) Top-Down Development: Top-down development refers to the process of concurrent design and development of program systems containing more than a single compilable unit. It requires development to proceed in a way which minimizes interface problems normally encountered during the integration process typical of "bottom-up development" by integrating and testing modules as soon as they are developed. Other opportunities provided are for the following.

1) A project to staff up more gradually and reduce the total manpower required.

2) Computer time requirements to be spread more evenly over the development period.

3) The user to work major portions of the system much earlier and identify gross errors before acceptance testing.

4) Most of the system to be used long enough by the time it is delivered that both the user and the developer have confidence in its reliability.

The term "top-down" may be somewhat misleading if taken too literally. What top-down development really implies in everyday production programming is that one builds the system in a way which ideally eliminates (or more practically, minimizes) writing any code whose testing is dependent on other code not yet written, or on data which are not yet available. This requires careful planning of the development sequence for a large system consisting of many programs and data sets, since some programs will have to be partially completed before other programs can be begun. In practice, it also recognizes that exigencies of customer requirements or schedule may force deviations from what would otherwise be an ideal development sequence. The guidelines for top-down development are as follows.

1) Code currently being developed should depend only on code already operational, except in those portions where deviations from this procedure are justified by special circumstances.

2) The project schedule should reflect a continuing integration, as part of the development process, leading directly to system test; as opposed to a development, followed by integration, followed by system test cycle.

3) The managers of the effort should have attended a structured programming orientation course (see Section III-C below).

4) Structured coding and a development support library system must be used. (Because ongoing projects may not be able to install a DSL, an implementation of only structured coding is acceptable in these cases.)

4) CPT's: A CPT is a functional programming organization built around a nucleus of three experienced persons doing well-defined parts of the programming development process using the techniques and tools described above. It is an organization uniquely oriented toward the techniques and tools and is a logical outgrowth of their introduction and use. Described in detail in [3]–[5], it has been used extensively in FSD on projects ranging up to approximately 100 000 lines of source code and is being experimented with on larger projects. The guidelines for CPT's are as follows.

1) One person, the chief programmer, should have complete technical responsibility for the effort. He should ordinarily be the manager of the other people.

2) There must be a backup programmer prepared to assume the role of chief programmer.

3) Top-level code segments and the critical control paths of lower level segments should be coded by the chief and backup programmers.

4) Other programmers should be added to the team only to code specific well-defined functions within a framework established by the chief and backup programmers.

5) The chief and backup programmers must review the code produced by other members of the team.

6) Top-down development, structured coding, and a DSL must be used.

B. Support

Support of several types is necessary in order to permit effective implementation of, and achieve maximum benefits from, the ideas of structured programming. Development support libraries, introduced above, are a recognized and required component of the methodology employed in FSD. Standards are necessary to ensure a consistent approach and to help realize benefits of improved project communications and manageability. Procedures are required for effective use of the tools and to permit functional breakup and improved overall efficiency in the programming process. Finally, other techniques of design, programming, testing, and management can be helpful in a structured programming environment as well as in a conventional one.

1) DSL's: The need for and value of DSL's both as a necessity for structured programming and as a vehicle for project communication and control, has been thoroughly covered in [3]–[7]. Early work on DSL's in FSD centered on the provision of libraries for projects using IBM's System/360 Operating System and Disk Operating System in batch programming development situations. Subsequent work on DSL's in FSD has extended the support to some of the non-System/360 equipment in use and also introduced interactive DSL's for use both by librarians and programmers [8]. Furthermore, a study of general requirements for DSL's has been performed under contract to the United States Air Force and has been published in [9]. DSL's are now available for and in use on most programming projects in FSD.

A DSL keeps *all* machine readable data on a project—source code, object code, linkage editor language, job control language, test data, and so on—in a series of data sets which comprise the internal library. Since all data are kept internally and are fully backed up, there is no need for programmers to generate or maintain their own personal copies. Corresponding to each type of data in the internal library, there is a set of current status binders which comprise the external library. These are filed centrally and used by all as a standard means of communication. There is also a set of archives of superseded status pages which are retained to assist in disaster recovery, and a set of run books containing run results. Together, these record the activities—current and historical—of an entire project and keep it completely organized.

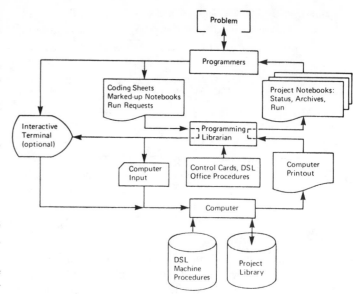

Fig. 3. DSL operations.

The machine procedures, as the name implies, are cataloged procedures which perform internal library initiation, updating, compilation and test, housekeeping and termination. Most of them are used by programming librarians by means of simple control cards they have been trained to prepare.

The office procedures are a set of "clerical algorithms" used by the programming librarian to invoke the machine procedures, to prepare the input and file the output. Once a new code has been created and placed in the library initially, a programmer makes additions and corrections to it primarily by marking up pages in the external library and giving them to the programming librarian to make up control and data cards to cause the corresponding changes or additions to be made to the internal library. As a result, clerical effort and wasted time on the part of the programmers are significantly reduced. Fig. 3 shows the work flow and the central role of the programming librarian in the process. Machine and office procedures for a typical DSL are documented for programmers in [6] and for librarians in [10].

2) Standards: To support structured coding in the various languages used, standards were required. These covered the implementation of the control flow figures in each language as well as the conventions for formatting and indenting programs in that language.

There are four approaches which can be taken to provide the basic and optional control flow figures in a programming language, and each was used in certain situations in FSD.

1) The figures may be directly available as statements in the language. In the case of PL/I, all of the basic figures were of this variety. In Cobol, the IFTHENELSE (with slight restrictions) and the DOUNTIL (as a PERFORM) were present.

2) The figures may be easily simulated using a few standard statements. The CASE statement may be readily

simulated in PL/I using an indexed GOTO and a LABEL array, with each case implemented via a DO-group ending in a GOTO to a common null statement following all cases.

3) A standard preprocessor may be used to augment the basic language statements to provide necessary features. The macro assembler has been used in FSD to add structuring features to System/360, System/370 and System/7 Assembler Languages.

4) A special precompiler may be written to compile augmented language statements into standard ones, which may then be processed by the normal compiler. This was done for the Fortran language, which directly contains almost none of the needed features.

The result of using these four approaches was a complete set of figures for PL/I, Cobol, Fortran, and Assembler. Using these as a base, similar work was also done for several special-purpose languages used in FSD.

To assist in making programs readable and in standardizing communications and librarian procedures, it was desirable that programs in a given language should be organized, formatted and indented in the same way. (This was true of the Job Control and Link Editor Languages as well as of the procedural languages mentioned above.) Coding conventions were developed for each covering the permitted control structures, segment formatting, naming, use of comments, labels, and indentation and formatting for all control flow and special (e.g., OPEN, CLOSE, DECLARE) statements.

3) Procedures: An essential aspect of the use of DSL's is the standardization of the procedures associated with them. The machine procedures used in setting up, maintaining and terminating the libraries were mentioned above in that connection. However, the office procedures used by librarians in preparing runs, executing them and filing the results are also quite extensive. These were developed and documented [10] in a form readily usable by nonprogramming oriented librarians.

4) Other: While the above constitute the bulk of the work originated by FSD, certain other techniques and procedures have been assimilated into the methodology in varying degrees. These include management techniques, hierarchy plus input-process-output (HIPO) diagrams and structured walk-throughs.

FSD has been active in the development of management techniques for programming projects. A book [1] resulting from a management course and guide used in FSD has become generally available. As top-down development and structured coding came into use, it became apparent that traditional management practices would have to be substantially revised (see Section IV-C below). An initial examination was done, and a report [12] was issued which has been very valuable in guiding managers into using the new methodology. Some of this material has now been added to a revised edition of the *FSC Programming Project Management Guide* [13] from which the book mentioned above was drawn.

A technique called HIPO diagrams [7], [14] developed by the IBM System Development Division (SDD) has proved valuable in design and documentation in top-down development. HIPO consists of a set of operational diagrams which graphically describe the functions of a program system from the general to the detail level. Not to be confused with flowcharts, which describe procedural flow, HIPO diagrams provide a convenient means of documenting the functions identified in the design phase of a top-down development effort.

Structured walk-throughs [7] were developed on an SDD CPT project as a formal means for design and code reviews during the development process. Using HIPO diagrams and eventually the code itself, the developer "walks through" his efforts for the reviewers. These latter may consist of the chief or backup programmer (or lead programmer if a CPT is not being employed), other programmers and a representative from the group which will formally test the programs. Emphasis is on error avoidance and detection, not correction, and the attitude is open and nondefensive on the part of all participants (today's reviewer will be tomorrow's reviewee). The reviewers prepare for the walk-through by studying the diagrams or code before the meeting, and follow-up is the responsibility of the reviewee, who must notify the reviewers of corrective actions taken.

C. Documentation and Education

Once the fundamental tools and guidelines were established, it was necessary to begin disseminating them throughout FSD. Much experimental work had already been done in developing the tools and guidelines themselves, so that a cadre of people familiar with them was already in being.

Most of the documentation has been referred to above. The primary reference for programmers was the *FSC Structured Programming Guide* [6]. In addition to the standards for each language and for use of DSL's, it contained general information on the use of top-down development and structured coding, as well as the procedures for making exceptions to the standards when necessary. It also contained provisions for sections to be added locally when special-purpose languages or libraries were in use. Distributed throughout FSD, the Guide has been updated and is still the standard reference for programmers. The *FSC Programming Librarian's Guide* serves a similar purpose for librarians and also has provisions for local sections where necessary. While the use of the macros for System/360 Assembler Language was included in the *Programming Guide*, additional documentation [15] was available on them if desired. Finally, management documentation in the form of [11]–[14] was also available.

It was recognized that providing documentation alone was not sufficient to permit most personnel to begin applying the techniques. A series of courses (one for each major language) was set up to train experienced FSD programmers in structured programming and DSL techniques. Lasting 25 hours, these courses provided instruction and, more importantly, practice problems which forced the programmers to begin the transition process. Once all programmers had been introduced to the ideas these courses were discontinued, and structured programming is now included as part of the basic programmer training courses given to newly hired personnel.

The same situation held true for managers as well as programmers. Because FSD wished to apply the methodology as rapidly as possible, it was desirable to acquaint managers with it and its potential immediately. Thus, one of the first actions taken was to give a half-day orientation course to all FSD managers. This permitted them to evaluate the depth to which they could begin to use it on current projects, and to begin to plan for its use on proposed projects. This was then followed up by a 12-hour course for experienced programming managers, acquainting them with management and control techniques peculiar to top-down development and structured coding. (It was expected that most of these managers would also attend one of the structured programming courses described above to acquire the fundamentals.) Again, now that most programming managers have received this form of update, the material has now been included in the normal programming management course given to all new programming managers.

D. Measurement

One of the problems of the production programming world is that it has not developed good measures of its activities. Various past efforts, most notably the System Development Corporation studies [16] have attempted to develop measurement and prediction techniques for production programming projects. The general results have been that a number of variables must be accurately estimated to yield even rough cost and schedule predictions, and that the biggest factors are the experience and abilities of the programmers involved. Nevertheless, it was felt in FSD that some measures of activity were needed, not so much for prediction as for evaluation of the degree to which the methodology was being applied, the reliability and productivity improvements which were achieved and the problems which were experienced in its use. To these ends, two types of measurements were put into effect.'

The first type of measurement, implemented immediately, was a monthly report required from each programming project. In addition to some quantitative data on his project, each manager was required to state the following:

1) the total number of programmers on the project;
2) the number currently programming;
3) the number using structured coding;
4) the number of programming groups on the project;
5) the number of CPT's;
6) whether a DSL was in use; and
7) whether top-down development was in use.

These figures were summarized monthly for various levels of FSD management and were a valuable tool in

ensuring that the methodology was indeed being introduced, as well as that the guidelines were being followed.

The second type of measurement was a much more comprehensive one. It required a great deal of research in its preparation, and eventually took the form of a questionnaire from which data were extracted to build a measurement data base. The questionnaire contains 105 questions organized into the following eight sections:

1) identification of the project;
2) description of the contractual environment;
3) description of the personnel environment;
4) description of the personnel themselves;
5) description of the technical environment;
6) definition of the size, type and reliability of the programs produced;
7) itemization of the financial, computer and manpower resources used in their development; and
8) definition of the schedule.

The questionnaire is administered at four points during the lifetime of every project. The first point is at the beginning, in which all questions are answered with estimates. The next administration is at the end of the design phase, when the initial estimates are updated as necessary. It is again filled out halfway through development, when actual figures begin to be known. And it is completed for the last time after the system has been tested and delivered, and all results are in. The four points provide for meaningful comparisons of estimates to actuals, and allow subsequent projects to draw useful guidance for their own planning. The data base permits reports to be prepared automatically and statistical comparisons to be made.

IV. IMPLEMENTATION EXPERIENCE

Each of the four components of the methodology which FSD has introduced has resulted in substantial benefits. However, experience has also revealed that their application is neither trivial nor trouble free. This section presents a qualitative analysis of the experience to date, describing both the advantages and the problems.

A. Development Support Libraries

Most projects of any size have historically gravitated toward use of a program library system of some type. This was certainly true in FSD, which had some highly developed systems already in place when the methodology was introduced. These were primarily used as mechanisms to control the code, so that differing versions of ongoing systems could be segregated. In some cases they provided program development services such as compilation, testing, and so forth. However, none were being used primarily to achieve the goals of improved communications or work functionalization which are the direct benefits of a DSL. In fact, the general attitude toward the services they provided was that they were there to be used when and if the programmers wished. Most code in them was presumed private, with the usual exceptions of macro and subroutine libraries.

One of the most difficult problems in the introduction of the DSL approach was to convince ongoing projects that their present library systems fulfilled neither the requirements nor the intents of DSL. A DSL is as much a management tool as a programmer convenience. A programming librarian's primary responsibility is to management, in the sense of supporting control of the project's assets of code and data—analogous to a controller's responsibility to management of supporting control of financial assets. The project as a whole should be entirely dependent on the DSL for its operation, and this, more than any other criterion, is the determining factor in whether a library system meets the guidelines as a DSL.

When all functions are provided, and a project implements a DSL, then a high degree of visibility is available. Programmers use the source code as a basic means of communication and rely on it to answer questions on interfaces or suggest approaches to their problems. Managers use the code itself (together with the summary features of more sophisticated DSL's) to determine the progress of the work. Users also benefit, even at an early stage of implementation, from the ready availability of the test data and the possibility of using part of the developing system on an experimental basis without interference with or from the rest.

The visibility in itself is valuable, even on a laissez-faire basis. But when it is coupled with well-managed code-reading procedures, it also provides reliability improvements. The walk-throughs described above, or equivalent procedures, ensure that someone in addition to the developer reviews the code, verifying that the specifications have been addressed, checking the planned test coverage, assisting in standards compliance and, last but not least, constructively criticizing the content. While the review procedure is obviously greatly facilitated by concomitant use of structured programming, it is possible without it and was included with the DSL guidelines to encourage its adoption.

The archives which are an integral part of a DSL provide an ability to refer to earlier versions of a routine—sometimes useful in tracing intent when a program is passed from hand to hand. More importantly, they give a project the ability to recover from a disaster in which part of its resources are destroyed. (It is perhaps obvious but worth mentioning that this will not be complete insurance unless project management sees to it that the backup data sets are stored physically separate from the working versions.) There was an initial tendency in FSD to over-collect and to over-formalize the archiving process. It appears unnecessary to retain more than a few generations of object code, run results and so forth. The source code and test data generally warrant longer retention, but even here it rapidly becomes impractical to save all versions. In general, sufficient archives should be retained to provide complete recovery capability when used in conjunction with the backup data sets, plus enough additional to provide back references.

The separation of function introduced by the DSL office procedures has two main benefits. The obvious one is of lowered cost through the use of clerical personnel instead of programmers for program maintenance, run setup and filing activities. A significant additional benefit comes about through the resulting more concentrated use of programmers. By reducing interruptions, librarians afford the programmers a work environment in which errors are less likely to occur. Furthermore, they permit programmers to work on more routines in parallel than typically is the case.

The last major benefit experienced from a DSL rests in its support of a programming measurement activity. By automatically collecting statistics of the types described above, they can enhance our ability to manage and improve the programming process. The early DSL's in FSD did not include measurement features, and the next generation is only beginning to come into use, so a full assessment of this support is not yet possible.

It was difficult to convince FSD projects in some cases that a well-qualified programming librarian could benefit a project as much as another programmer. In fact, there was an initial tendency to use junior programmers or programmer technicians to provide librarian support. This had two disadvantages and hence is not recommended. First, the use of programming-qualified personnel is not necessary because of the well-defined procedures inherent in the DSL's. Use of over-qualified individuals in some cases led to boredom and sloppy work with a resulting loss of reliability. Second, such personnel cannot perform other necessary functions when needed. One of the advantages of using secretaries as librarians is that they can use both skills effectively over the lifetime of a typical project. During design and documentation phases, they can provide typing and transcription services; while during coding and testing phases, they can perform the needed librarian work.

Related to this is the need to provide backup librarian services. In most cases this has been accomplished through informal cross-project sharing or through temporary assumption of the duties by programmers.

Two problems remain in defining completely the role of librarians. First, the increasing use of interactive systems for program development is forcing an evolution of librarian skills toward terminal operation and test support rather than coding of changes and extensive filing. The most effective division of labor between programmer and librarian in such an environment remains to be determined. It also appears possible to use librarians to assist in documentation, such as in preparation of HIPO diagrams. Second, FSD has a number of small projects in locations remote from the major office complexes and support facilities—frequently on customer premises. Here it is not always possible to use a librarian cost-effectively. In this situation, better definition of the programmer-librarian relationship in the interative system development environment may permit some degree of development and librarian support from the central facility instead of requiring all personnel to be on-site.

B. Structured Coding

Structured coding was separated from top-down development primarily to permit ongoing projects to use some of the methodology. Combined with usage of a DSL, it provides enhanced readability of code, enforces modularity (and thus encourages changeability) and maintainability, simplifies testing, and permits improved manageability and accountability. These are all well-known benefits and need not be elaborated on here. An additional, unplanned for, result of structured coding is that it tends to encourage the property of "locality of reference," which improves performance in a virtual systems environment.

The introduction of structured coding was not easily achieved in FSD. The broad variety of projects, languages and support has already been mentioned, and the development of DSL's, the Guides [6], [10], and the education program were necessary before widespread application of the methodology could take place. Furthermore, the ongoing nature of many of the systems meant that structured coding could take place only as modules were rewritten or replaced.

This gradual introduction created a problem of education timing. Practically, it was most expedient to have programmers attend the education courses between assignments. The nature of the courses was such that they introduced the techniques and provided some initial practice. Yet they required substantial work experience using the techniques to be fully effective. Structured coding requires the development of a whole new set of personal patterns in programming. Until old habits are unlearned and replaced by new ones, it is difficult for programmers to fully appreciate its advantages. For best results, this work experience and the overcoming of the natural reluctance to change habits should follow the training immediately. This was not always feasible and resulted in some loss of educational effectiveness.

A second problem arose because of the real-time nature of a significant fraction of FSD's programming business. Here the difficulty was one of demonstrating that structured coding was not detrimental to either execution speed or core utilization. While it is difficult to verify the advantages quantitatively, a working consensus based on experience has arisen and is supported by the results of one internal experiment on a real-time multiprocessing system. Simply stated, it is that the added time and thought required to structure a program pay off in better core utilization and improved efficiency which generally are comparable to the effects achieved in unstructured programs by extensive optimization of critical portions. It is also useful to note that even in "critical" programs, a relatively small fraction of the code is really time or core sensitive, and this fraction may not in fact be identifiable during coding. Hence it is probably a better

strategy to use structured coding throughout to begin with. Then, if performance bottlenecks do appear and cannot be resolved otherwise, at most small units of code must be hand tailored to remedy the problems. In this way the visibility, manageability, and maintainability advantages of structured coding are largely retained.

Perhaps the most difficult problem to overcome in applying structured coding is the purist syndrome, in which the goal is to write perfectly structured code in every situation. It must be emphasized that structured coding is not an end in itself, but is a means to achieving better, more reliable, more maintainable programs. In some cases (e.g., exiting from a loop when a search is complete, handling interrupt conditions), religious application of the figures allowed by the Guide may produce code which is less readable than that which might contain a GOTO (e.g., to the end of the loop block, or to return from the interrupt handler to a point other than the point of interrupt). Clearly the exceptions must be limited if discipline is to be maintained, but they must be permitted when desirable. To ensure that exceptions are justified, FSD requires documentation and management approval for each one.

C. Top-Down Development

As defined in Section III-A 3), top-down development is the sequencing of program system development to eliminate or avoid interface problems. This permits development and integration to be carried out in parallel and provides additional advantages such as early availability discussed there.

Top-down development is the most difficult of the four components to introduce, probably because it requires the heaviest involvement and changes of approach on the part of programming managers. Top-down development has profound effects on traditional programming management methodology. While the guidelines sound simple, they require a great deal of careful planning and supervision to carry out thoroughly in practice, even on a small project. The implementation of top-down development, unlike structured coding and DSL's, thus is both a management and a programming problem.

Let us distinguish at this point between what might be called "top-down programming" and true top-down development. While they were originally used interchangeably and the guidelines do not distinguish between them, the two terms are valuable in delineating levels of scope and complexity as use of the methodology increases.

Top-down programming is primarily a single-program-oriented concept. It applies to the development of a "program," typically consisting of one or a few load modules and a number of independently compilable units, which is developed by one or a few programmers. At this level of complexity the problems are primarily ones of program design, and approaches such as "levels of abstraction" [17] and Mills' Expansion Theorem [2] are used. Within this scope of development external problems and constraints are not as critical as in top-down development, and while management involvement is needed, it need not be so prevasive as in top-down development. Many of FSD's successful projects have used only top-down programming, and the experience gained on them has been most valuable.

Top-down development, on the other hand, is a multiple-program oriented idea. It applies to the development of a "program system," typically consisting of many load modules and perhaps a hundred or more independently compilable units, which is developed by one or more programming departments with five or more people in each. Now the problems expand to those of system architecture, and external problems and constraints become the major ones. The programs in the system are usually interdependent and have a large number of interfaces, perhaps directly but also frequently through shared data sets or communications lines. They may operate in more than one processor concurrently—for example, in a System/7 "front end" and a System/370 "host" or may involve hardware developed especially for the system.

The complexity of such a system makes management involvement in its planning and development essential even when external constraints are minimal. It involves all aspects of the project from its inception to its termination. For example, a proposal for a project to be implemented top-down should differ from one for a conventional (bottom-up) implementation in the proposed manning levels and usage of computer time. Functions must be carefully analyzed during the system design phase to ensure that the practical approach to top-down development (presented in Section III-A 3) above) of minimum code and data dependency is met and a detailed implementation sequence must be planned in accordance with the overall proposed plan and schedule. The design of the system very probably should differ significantly from what it would have been if bottom-up development were to be used. During implementation, progress must be monitored via the DSL to ensure that this sequence is being followed, and their schedules are being met. The early availability of parts of the system must be coordinated with the user if he intends to use these parts for experimentation or production. An entirely different type of test plan must be prepared, for incremental testing over the entire period. Rather than tracking individual components, the manager has the more difficult task of tracking the progress of the system as a whole. In a bottom-up development, the condition of the system is usually not known until the integration phase, when it suddenly becomes a critical item. In top-down work, the condition of the system must always be known, but this knowledge enables the manager to identify problems earlier and to correct them while there is still time to do so.

In typical system development environments such as those in FSD, however, external constraints are the rule rather than the exception. A user will have schedule requirements which must be met. A particular data set must be designed to interface with an existing system.

Special hardware may arrive late in a development cycle and may vary from that desired. These are typical of situations not directly under the developers' control which have profound effects on the sequence in which the system is produced. Now the manager's job becomes still more complex in planning and controlling development. Each of these external constraints may force a deviation from what would otherwise be a simple, no-dependency development sequence. Provision may have to be made for testing, documentation, and delivery of products at intermediate points in the overall cycle. This will typically change the schedule from the ideal one, and will probably increase the complexity of the management job. This is especially true on a very large project (several hundred thousand lines of source code or more), since any realistic schedule may well require that major subsystems be developed in parallel and integrated in a nearly conventional fashion (hopefully at an earlier point in time than the end of the project). Top-down development was carried out successfully on a project of 400 000 lines of source code, the largest known to the author to date.

When carried to its fullest extent, top-down development of a large system probably has greater effects on reliability (and thus, indirectly, on productivity) than any other component of the methodology. Even when competent management is fully devoted to its implementation, there are two other problems which can arise and must be planned for. These both relate to the overlapping nature of design, development and integration in a top-down environment.

The first of these concerns the nature of materials documenting the system design to be delivered to and reviewed by the user. Typically, a user receives a program design document at the end of the design phase and must express his concurrence before development proceeds. This is impractical in top-down development because development must proceed in some areas before design is complete in others. To give a user a comparable opportunity, a detailed functional specification is desirable instead. This describes all external aspects of a system, as well as any processing algorithms of concern to a user, but does not address the system's internal design. This type of specification is probably more readily assimilated by typical users, is more meaningful than a design document and should pose no problems in most situations. Where standardized procurement regulations (such as the United States Government Armed Services Procurement Regulations) are in effect, then efforts must be made to seek exceptions. (As top-down development becomes more prevalent, then it is hoped that changes to to such procedures will directly permit submission of this type of specification.)

The second problem is one of the most severe to be encountered in any of the components and is one of the most difficult to deal with. It has to do with the depth to which a design should be carried before implementation is begun. If a complete, detailed design of an entire system is done, and implementation of key code in all areas is carried out by the programmers who begin the project, then the work remaining for programmers added later is relatively trivial. In some environments this may be perfectly appropriate and perhaps even desirable: in others it may lead to dissatisfaction and poor morale on the part of the latecomers. It can be avoided by recognizing that design to the same depth in all areas of most systems is totally unnecessary. The initial system design work (the overworked term "architecture" still seems to be appropriate here) should concentrate on specifying all modules to be developed and all intermodule interfaces. Those modules which pose significant schedule, development or performance problems should be identified, and detailed design work and key code writing done only on these. This leaves scope for creativity and originality on the part of the newer programmers, subject obviously to review and concurrence through normal project design control procedures. On some projects, the design of entire support subsystems with interfaces to a main subsystem only through standard, straightforward data sets have been left until late in the project. Note that while this may solve the problems of challenge and morale, it also poses a risk that the difficulty has been underestimated. Thus, here again management is confronted with a difficult decision where an incorrect assessment may be nearly impossible to recover from.

D. CPT's

The introduction of CPT's should be a natural outgrowth of top-down development. This is because of the need to complete the system architecture and develop a nucleus before many programmers can work in parallel, and because of the reliance on a DSL, which suggest the use of a small, highly specialized team at the beginning evolving into a larger team later. The use of a smaller group based on a nucleus of experienced people tends to reduce the communications and control problems encountered on a typical project. Use of the other three components of the methodology enhances these advantages through standardization and visibility.

In order for a CPT to function effectively, the chief programmer must be given the time, responsibility, and authority to perform the technical direction of the project. In some environments this poses no problem; in FSD it is sometimes difficult to achieve because of other demands which may be levied upon the chief. In a contract programming environment he may be called upon to perform three distinct types of activities: technical management—the supervision of the development process itself, personnel management—the supervision of the people reporting to him, and contract management—the supervision of the relationships with the customer. The latter in particular can be a very time-consuming function and also is the simplest to secure assistance on. Hence, many FSD CPT's have a program manager who has the primary customer interface responsibility in all non-

technical matters. The chief remains responsibile for technical customer interface as well as the other two types of management; in most cases this makes the situation manageable, and if not then additional support can be provided where needed.

The backup programmer role is one that seems to cause people a great deal of difficulty in accepting, probably because there are overtones of "second-best" in the name. Perhaps the name could be improved, but the functions the backup performs are essential and cannot be dispensed with. One of the primary tenets of management is that every manager should identify and train his successor. This is no less true on a CPT and is a major reason for the existence of the backup position. It is also highly desirable for the chief to have a peer with whom he can freely and openly interact, especially in the critical stages of system design. The backup is thus an essential check and balance on the chief. Because of this, it is important that the chief have the right of refusal on a proposed backup; if he feels that an open relationship of mutual trust and respect cannot be achieved, then it is useless to proceed. The requirement that the backup be a peer of the chief also should not be waived, since it is always possible that a backup will be called on to take over the project and must be fully qualified to do so.

One of the limits on a CPT is the scope of a project it can reasonably undertake. It is difficult for a single CPT to get much larger than eight people and still permit the chief and backup to exercise the essential amount of control and supervision. Thus, even at the productivity rates achievable by CPT's it is difficult for a single team to produce much more than perhaps 20 000 lines of code in its first year and 30–40 000 lines after the architecture is complete and the team has grown to full size. Large projects must therefore look to multiple CPT's, which can be implemented in two ways. First, interfaces may be established and independent subsystems may be developed concurrently by several CPT's and then integrated. Second, a single CPT may be established to do architecture and nucleus development for the entire system. It then can spin off subordinate CPT's to complete the development of these subsystems. The latter approach is inherently more appealing, since it carries the precepts of top-down development through intact. It is also more difficult to implement; the experiment under way by the author was not fully successful because equipment being developed concurrently ran into definition problems and prevented true top-down development.

It is difficult to identify problems unique to CPT's which differ from those of top-down development discussed above. Perhaps the most significant one is the claim frequently heard that, "We've had chief programmer teams in place for years—there's nothing new there for us." While it is certainly true that many of the elements of CPT's are not new, the identification of the CPT as a particular form of functional organization using a disciplined, precise methodology suffices to make it unique. In particular, the emphasis on visibility and

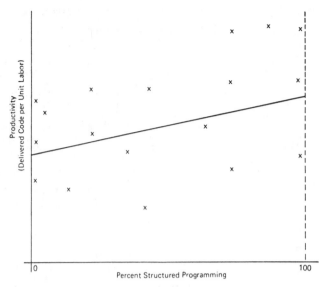

Fig. 4. Productivity trend.

	Technologies Used	Bytes of New Code (Millions)	Total Effort to Delivery (Man-months)	Productivity (Bytes Per Man-month)
Apollo				
Mission Operations Control	DSL	5.8	3748	1547
Ground Support Simulation	None	2.1	1809	1161
Skylab				
Mission Operations Control	DSL	1.4	1665	841
Ground Support Simulation	DSL SP TDD	4.0	1065	3756

Fig. 5. Productivity comparison.

control through management code review, formal structured programming techniques and DSL's differentiate true CPT's from other forms of programming teams [18]. And it is this same set of features which make the CPT approach so valuable in a production programming environment where close control is essential if cost and schedule targets are to be met.

V. MEASUREMENT RESULTS

It is not possible, because it would reveal valuable business data, to present significant amounts of quantitative information in this paper. At this time, the results of the measurement program do show substantial improvements in programming productivity where the new technology has been used. Fig. 4 is an idealized version of an actual graph where each point represents a completed FSD project. The horizontal axis records the percentage of structured code in the delivered product, and the vertical axis records the productivity. (The latter includes all effort on the project, including analysis, design, testing, management, support and documentation as well as coding and debugging. It also is based only on delivered code, so that effort used to produce drivers, code written but replaced, etc., tends to reduce the measured productivity.) A weighted least squares fit to the points on the graph shows a better than 1.5 to 1 improvement in the coding rate from projects which use no structured programming to those employing it fully. Since these data were derived from the monthly reports (see Section III-D above), there was no opportunity to test the effects of other factors such as languages or experience, but the results were nevertheless encouraging.

It is also possible, because the data have already been released elsewhere, to make one quantitative comparison between productivity rates experienced using various components of the technology on some of the programming support work which FSD performed for the National Aeronautics and Space Administration's Apollo and Skylab

projects. This comparison is especially significant because the primary identifiable change in approach was the degree to which the new methodology was used; the people, experience level, management and support were all substantially the same in each area. (Other factors may have varied also, but their effects are not clear, and they were not considered important by the participants.) Fig. 5 shows the productivity rates and the components of the technology used. In the Apollo project, a rate of 1161 bytes of new object code per man-month was experienced on the ground support simulation work. (Again, all numbers are based on overall project effort.) This work used none of the components described in this paper. In the directly comparable effort on the Skylab project, a DSL, structured coding, and top-down development were all employed, and a rate of 3756 bytes of new code per man-month was achieved—almost twice as much new code was produced with slightly more than half the effort. It is interesting also to remark that this was achieved on the planned schedule in spite of over 1100 formal changes made during the development of that product, along with cuts in both manpower and computer time. Finally, while the improvement may rest to some extent on the similar work done previously, this was not demonstrated in the parallel mission operations control work. There productivity dropped from 1547 to 841 bytes per man-month on comparable work which in neither case used anything other than a DSL.

In addition to making reliability measurements and determining productivity rates, the measurement activity has served a number of other useful purposes. First, it has built up a substantial data base of information about FSD projects. As new data are submitted, checks are made to ensure its validity, and questionable data are reviewed before being added. The result is an increasingly consistent and useful set of data. Second, it has enabled FSD to begin studies on the value of the components of the methodology. Third, and related, it also permits the study of other factors (e.g., environment, personnel) affecting project activity. Fourth, it is used to assist in reviewing ongoing projects, where the objective data it contains have proven quite valuable. And fifth, it is used in estimating for proposed projects, where it affords an opportunity to compare the new work against similar work done in the past, and to identify risks which may exist.

VI. CONCLUSIONS

Reflecting on the benefits of structured programming, one is struck by the fact that the techniques fundamentally are directed toward encouraging programming discipline. Historically, programming has been a very individualistic, undisciplined activity. Thus, introducing discipline (in the form of practices which most programmers recognize as beneficial), yields double rewards—the advantages inherent in the methodology itself, plus those due to better standardization and control.

It should be clear at this point that FSD's experience has been a very positive one. Work remains to be done, particularly in the management of top-down development and the formalization and application of CPT's. Nevertheless, FSD is fully committed to application of the methodology and is continuing to require its use.

In retrospect, the plan appears to have been a success and could serve as a model for other organizations interested in applying the ideas. The FSD experience shows that this is neither easy nor rapid. It takes substantial time and effort and, most important, commitments and support from management, to equip an organization to apply the methodology.

To summarize, it appears that once a base of tools, standards, and education exists, it is most appropriate to begin with use of DSL's, structured coding and top-down programming. Then, when the people, know-how, and opportunity exist, top-down development should be applied on a few large, complex projects to yield an experienced group of people and the required management techniques. It is likely that one or more of these may also present the opportunity to introduce a CPT. This is essentially the approach that FSD has taken, and it appears to be an excellent way to introduce structured programming.

REFERENCES

[1] B. W. Boehm, "Software and its impact: A quantitative assessment," *Datamation*, vol. 19, p. 52, May 1973.
[2] H. D. Mills, "Mathematical foundations for structured programming," IBM Corp., Gaithersburg, Md., Rep. FSC 71-6012, Feb. 1972.
[3] ——, "Chief programmer teams: Principles and procedures," IBM Corp., Gaithersburg, Md., Rep. FSC 71-5108, June 1972.
[4] F. T. Baker, "Chief programmer team management of production programming," *IBM Syst. J.*, vol. 11, no. 1, pp. 56–73, 1972.
[5] ——, "System quality through structured programming," in *1972 Fall Joint Comput. Conf., AFIPS Conf. Proc.*, vol. 41, part I. Montvale, N. J.: AFIPS Press, 1972, pp. 339–343.
[6] *Federal Systems Center Structured Programming Guide*, IBM Corp., Gaithersburg, Md., Rep. FSC 72-5075, July 1973 (revised).
[7] *Improved Technology for Application Development: Management Overview*, IBM Corp., Bethesda, Md., Aug. 1973.
[8] *TSO-3270 Structured Programming Facility (SPF) General Information Manual*, IBM Corp., Gaithersburg, Md., Form GH20-1638 (available through any IBM branch office).
[9] F. M. Luppino and R. L. Smith, "Programming support library (PSL) functional requirements," IBM Corp., Gaithersburg, Md., Final Rep., prepared under Contract F30602-74-C-0186 with the U.S. Air Force Rome Air Development Center, Griffiss Air Force Base, Rome, N. Y., July 1974 (release subject to approval of Contracting Officer, P. DeLorenzo).
[10] *Federal Systems Center Programming Librarian's Guide*, IBM Corp., Gaithersburg, Md., Rep. FSC 72-5074, Apr. 1972
[11] P. W. Metzger, *Managing a Programming Project*. Englewood Cliffs, N. J.: Prentice-Hall, 1973.
[12] R. C. McHenry, *Management Concepts for Top Down Structured Programming*. Gaithersburg, Md.: IBM Corp., Nov. 1972
[13] P. W. Metzger and F. R. Bliss, *Programming Project Management Guide*. Gaithersburg, Md.: IBM Corp., Form GA36-0005, July 1974 (available through any IBM branch office).
[14] *HIPO-Hierarchical Input-Process-Output Documentation Technique: Audio Education Package*, IBM Corp., Gaithersburg, Md., Form SR20-9413 (available through any IBM branch office).
[15] M. M. Kessler, *Assembly Language Structured Programming Macros*. Gaithersburg, Md.: IBM Corp., Sept. 1972.
[16] G. F. Weinwurm *et al.*, "Research into the management of computer programming: A transitional analysis of cost estimation techniques," System Development Corp., Santa Monica, Calif., Nov. 1965 (available from the Clearinghouse for Federal Scientific and Technical Information as AD 631 259).
[17] E. W. Dijkstra, "The structure of the THE multiprogramming system," *Commun. Ass. Comput. Mach.*, vol. 11, pp. 341–346, May 1968.
[18] G. M. Weinburg, *The Psychology of Computer Programming*. New York: Van Nostrand Reinhold, 1971.

F. Terry Baker was born in Waterbury, Conn., on January 4, 1935. He received the B.S. degree in mathematics from Yale University, New Haven, Conn., in 1956, and the S.M. degree in applied mathematics from Harvard University, Cambridge, Mass., in 1963.

He has been employed since 1956 by the IBM Corporation in various programming and programming management positions and is currently Manager of the NSDG Development Department, IBM Federal Systems Division, Gaithersburg, Md. He also, on military leave from IBM during the period from 1957 to 1960, served as a lieutenant at the HQ USAF Computer Center in Washington, D.C. Since 1969 he has been active in structured programming, with particular emphasis on its management and on its installation and use in large organizations.

Mr. Baker is a member of Phi Beta Kappa, Sigma Xi, and the Association for Computing Machinery.

Reprinted from *IEEE Transactions on Software Engineering*,
Volume SE-5, Number 2, March 1979, pages 128-137. Copy-
right © 1979 by the Institute of Electrical and Electronics
Engineers. Inc.

Designing Software for Ease of Extension and Contraction

DAVID L. PARNAS

Abstract—Designing software to be extensible and easily contracted is
discussed as a special case of design for change. A number of ways that
extension and contraction problems manifest themselves in current
software are explained. Four steps in the design of software that is
more flexible are then discussed. The most critical step is the design of
a software structure called the "uses" relation. Some criteria for design
decisions are given and illustrated using a small example. It is shown
that the identification of *minimal* subsets and *minimal* extensions can
lead to software that can be tailored to the needs of a broad variety of
users.

Index Terms—Contractibility, extensibility, modularity, software engineering, subsets, supersets.

Manuscript received June 7, 1978; revised October 26, 1978. The
earliest work in this paper was supported by NV Phillips Computer In-
dustrie, Apeldoorn, The Netherlands. This work was also supported by
the National Science Foundation and the German Federal Ministry for
Research and Technology (BMFT). This paper was presented at the
Third International Conference on Software Engineering, Atlanta, GA,
May 1978.

The author is with the Department of Computer Science, University
of North Carolina, Chapel Hill, NC 27514. He is also with the Information Systems Staff, Communications Sciences Division, Naval Research
Laboratory, Washington, DC.

I. INTRODUCTION

THIS paper is being written because the following com-
plaints about software systems are so common.

1) "We were behind schedule and wanted to deliver an early
release with only a <proper subset of intended capabilities>,
but found that that subset would not work until everything
worked."

2) "We wanted to add <simple capability>, but to do so
would have meant rewriting all or most of the current code."

3) "We wanted to simplify and speed up the system by removing the <unneeded capability>, but to take advantage of
this simplification we would have had to rewrite major sections of the code."

4) "Our SYSGEN was intended to allow us to tailor a system to our customers' needs but it was not flexible enough to
suit us."

After studying a number of such systems, I have identified
some simple concepts that can help programmers to design
software so that subsets and extensions are more easily obtained.
These concepts are simple if you think about software in the
way suggested by this paper. Programmers do not commonly
do so.

II. Software As a Family of Programs

When we were first taught how to program, we were given a specific problem and told to write one program to do that job. Later we compared our program to others, considering such issues as space and time utilization, but still assuming that we were producing a single product. Even the most recent literature on programming methodology is written on that basis. Dijkstra's *A Discipline of Programming* [1] uses predicate transformers to specify *the* task to be performed by *the* program to be written. The use of the definite article implies that there is a unique problem to be solved and but one program to write.

Today, the software designer should be aware that he is not designing a single program but a family of programs. As discussed in an earlier paper [2], we consider a set of programs to be a program family if they have so much in common that it pays to study their common aspects before looking at the aspects that differentiate them. This rather pragmatic definition does not tell us what pays, but it does explain the motivation for designing program families. We want to exploit the commonalities, share code, and reduce maintenance costs.

Some of the ways that the members of a program family may differ are listed below.

1) They may run on different hardware configurations.

2) They may perform the same functions but differ in the format of the input and output data.

3) They may differ in certain data structures or algorithms because of differences in the available resources.

4) They may differ in some data structures or algorithms because of differences in the size of the input data sets or the relative frequency of certain events.

5) Some users may require only a subset of the services or features that other users need. These "less demanding" users may demand that they not be forced to pay for the resources consumed by the unneeded features.

Engineers are taught that they must try to anticipate the changes that may be made, and are shown how to achieve designs that can easily be altered when these anticipated changes occur. For example, an electrical engineer will be advised that the world has not standardized the 60-cycle 110-V current. Television designers are fully aware of the differing transmission conventions that exist in the world. It is standard practice to design products that are easily changed in those aspects. Unfortunately, there is no magic technique for handling unanticipated changes. The makers of conventional watches have no difficulty altering a watch that shows the day so that it displays "MER" instead of "WED," but I would except a long delay for redesign were the world to switch to a ten day week.

Software engineers have not been trained to design for change. The usual programming courses neither mention the need to anticipate changes nor do they offer techniques for designing programs in which changes are easy. Because programs are abstract mathematical objects, the software engineers' techniques for responding to anticipated changes are more subtle and more difficult to grasp than the techniques used by designers of physical objects. Further, we have been led astray by the other designers of abstract objects—mathematicians who state and prove theorems. When a mathematician becomes aware of the need for a set of closely related theorems, he responds by proving a more general theorem. For mathematicians, a more general result is always superior to a more specialized product. The engineering analogy to the mathematician's approach would be to design television sets containing variable transformers and tuners that are capable of detecting several types of signals. Except for the U.S. armed forces stationed overseas, there is little market for such a product. Few of us consider relocations so likely that we are willing to pay to have the generality present in the product. My guess is that the market for calendar watches for a variable length week is even smaller than the market for the television sets just described.

In [2] I have treated the subject of the design of program families rather generally and in terms of text in a programming language. In this paper I focus on the fifth situation described above; families of programs in which some members are subsets of other family members or several family members share a common subset. I discuss an earlier stage of design, the stage when one identifies the major components of the system and defines relations between those components. We focus on this early stage because the problems described in the introduction result from failure to consider early design decisions carefully.

III. How Does the Lack of Subsets and Extensions Manifest Itself?

Although we often speak of programs that are "not subsetable" or "not extensible," we must recognize that phrase as inaccurate. It is always possible to remove code from a program and have a runable result. Any software system can be extended (TSO proves that). The problem is that the subsets and extensions are not the programs that we would have designed if we had set out to design just that product. Further, the amount of work needed to obtain the product seems all out of proportion to the nature of the change. The obstacles commonly encountered in trying to extend or shrink systems fall into four classes.

A. Excessive Information Distribution

A system may be hard to extend or contract if too many programs were written assuming that a given feature is present or not present. This was illustrated by an operating system in which an early design decision was that the system would support three conversational languages. There were many sections of the system where knowledge of this decision was used. For example, error message tables had room for exactly three entries. An extension to allow four languages would have required that a great deal of code be rewritten. More surprisingly, it would have been difficult to reduce the system to one that efficiently supported only two of the languages. One could remove the third language, but to regain the table space, one would have had to rewrite the same sections of code that would be rewritten to add a language.

B. A Chain of Data Transforming Components

Many programs are structured as a chain of components, each receiving data from the previous component, processing it (and changing the format), before sending the data to the next program in the chain. If one component in this chain is not needed, that code is often hard to remove because the output of its predecessor is not compatible with the input requirements of its successor. A program that does nothing but change the format must be substituted. One illustration would be a payroll program that assumed unsorted input. One of the components of the system accepts the unsorted input and produces output that is sorted by some key. If the firm adopts an office procedure that results in sorted input, this phase of the processing is unnecessary. To eliminate that program, one may have to add a program that transfers data from a file in the input format to a file in the format appropriate for the next phase. It may be almost as efficient to allow the original SORT component to sort the sorted input.

C. Components That Perform More Than One Function

Another common error is to combine two simple functions into one component because the functions seem too simple to separate. For example, one might be tempted to combine synchronization with message sending and acknowledgment in building an operating system. The two functions seem closely related; one might expect that for the sake of reliability one should insist on a "handshake" with each exchange of synchronization signals. If one later encounters an application in which synchronization is needed very frequently, one may find that there is no simple way to strip the message sending out of the synchronization routines. Another example is the inclusion of run-time type-checking in the basic subroutine call mechanism. In applications where compile-time checking or verification eliminates the need for the run-time type-check, another subroutine call mechanism will be needed. The irony of these situations is that the "more powerful" mechanism could have been built separately from, but *using*, simpler mechanisms. Separation would result in a system in which the simpler mechanism was available for use where it sufficed.

D. Loops in the "Uses" Relation

In many software design projects, the decisions about what other component programs to use are left to individual systems programmers. If a programmer knows of a program in another module, and feels that it would be useful in his program, he includes a call on that program in his text. Programmers are encouraged to use the work of other programmers as much as possible because, when each programmer writes his own routines to perform common functions, we end up with a system that is much larger than it need be.

Unfortunately, there are two sides to the question of program usage. Unless some restraint is exercised, one may end up with a system in which nothing works until everything works. For example, while it may seem wise to have an operating system scheduler use the file system to store its data (rather than use its own disk routines), the result will be that the file system must be present and working before any task scheduling is possible. There are users for whom an operating system subset without a file system would be useful. Even if

one has no such users, the subset would be useful during development and testing.

IV. STEPS TOWARDS A BETTER STRUCTURE

This section discusses four parts of a methodology that I believe will help the software engineer to build systems that do not evidence the problems discussed above.

A. Requirements Definition: Identifying the Subsets First

One of the clearest morals in the earlier discussion about "design for change" as it is taught in other areas of engineering is that one must anticipate changes before one begins the design. At a past conference [3] many of the papers exhorted the audience to spend more time identifying the actual requirements before starting on a design. I do not want to repeat such exhortations, but I do want to point out that the identification of the possible subsets is part of identifying the requirements. Treating the easy availability of certain subsets as an operational requirement is especially important to government officials who purchase software. Many officials despair of placing strict controls on the production methods used by their contractors because they are forbidden by law to tell the contractor how to perform his job. They may tell him what they require, but not how to build it. Fortunately, the availability of subsets may be construed as an operational property of the software.

On the other hand, the identification of the required subsets is not a simple matter of asking potential users what they could do without. First, users tend to overstate their requirements. Second, the answer will not characterize the set of subsets that might be wanted in the future. In my experience, identification of the potentially desirable subsets is a demanding intellectual exercise in which one first searches for the *minimal* subset that might conceivably perform a useful service and then searches for a set of *minimal* increments to the system. Each increment is small—sometimes so small that it seems trivial. The emphasis on minimality stems from our desire to avoid components that perform more than one function (as discussed in Section III-C). Identifying the minimal subset is difficult because the minimal system is not usually a program that anyone would ask for. If we are going to build the software family, the minimal subset is useful; it is not usually worth building by itself. Similarly, the maximum flexibility is obtained by looking for the smallest possible increments in capability: often these are smaller increments than a user would think of. Whether or not he would think of them before system development, he is likely to want that flexibility later.

The search for a minimal subset and minimal extensions can best be shown by an example. One example of a minimal subset is given in [4]. Another example will be given later in this paper.

B. Information Hiding: Interface and Module Definition

In an earlier section we touched upon the difference between the mathematician's concept of generality and an engineer's approach to design flexibility. Where the mathematician wants his product, a theorem or method of proof, to be as general as possible, i.e., applicable, without change, in as many situations as possible, an engineer often must tailor his product to the situation actually at hand. Lack of generality is necessary to make the program as efficient or inexpensive as possible. If he must develop a family of products, he tries to isolate the changeable parts in modules and to develop an interface between the module and the rest of the product that remains valid for all versions. The crucial steps are as follows.

1) Identification of the items that are likely to change. These items are termed "secrets."

2) Location of the specialized components in separate modules.

3) Designing intermodule interfaces that are insensitive to the anticipated changes. The changeable aspects or "secrets" of the modules are not revealed by the interface.

It is exactly this that the concept of information hiding [5], encapsulation, or abstraction [6] is intended to do for software. Because software is an abstract or mathematical product, the modules may not have any easily recognized physical identity. They are not necessarily separately compilable or coincident with memory overlay units. The interface must be general but the contents should not be. Specialization is necessary for economy and efficiency.

The concept of information hiding is very general and is applicable in many software change situations—not just the issue of subsets and extensions that we address in this paper. The ideas have also been extensively discussed in the literature [5]-[9]. The special implications for our problem are simply that, as far as possible, even the presence or absence of a component should be hidden from other components. If one program uses another directly, the presence of the second program cannot be fully hidden from its user. However, there is never any reason for a component to "know" how many other programs use it. All data structures that reveal the presence or number of certain components should be included in separate information hiding modules with abstract interfaces [10]. Space and other considerations make it impossible to discuss this concept further in this paper; it will be illustrated in the example. Readers for whom this concept is new are advised to read some of the articles mentioned above.

C. The Virtual Machine (VM) Concept

To avoid the problems that we have described as "a chain of data transforming components," it is necessary to stop thinking of systems in terms of components that correspond to steps in the processing. This way of thinking dies hard. It is almost certain that your first introduction to programming was in terms of a series of statements intended to be executed in the order that they were explained to you. We are goal oriented; we know what we start with and what we want to produce. It is natural to think in terms of steps progressing towards that goal. It is the fact that we are designing a family of systems that makes this "natural" approach the wrong one.

The viewpoint that seems most appropriate to designing software families is often termed the virtual machine approach. Rather than write programs that perform the transformation from input data to output data, we design software machine extensions that will be useful in writing many such programs. Where our hardware machine provides us with a set of instructions that operate on a small set of data types, the extended or virtual machine will have additional data types as well as "software instructions" that operate on those data types. These added features will be tailored to the class of programs that we are building. While the VM instructions are designed to be generally useful, they can be left out of a final product if the user's programs do not use them. The programmer writing programs for the virtual machine should not need to distinguish between instructions that are implemented in software and those that are hardware implemented. To achieve a true virtual machine, the hardware resources that are used in implementing the extended instruction set must be unavailable to the user of the virtual machine. The designer has traded these resources for the new data elements and instructions. Any attempt to use those resources again will invalidate the concept of virtual machine and lead to complications. Failure to provide for isolation of resources is one of the reasons for the failure of some attempts to use macros to provide a virtual machine. The macro user must be careful not to use the resources used in the code generated by the macros.

There is no reason to accomplish the transformation from the hardware machine to a virtual machine with all of the desired features in a single leap. Instead we will use the machine at hand to implement a few new instructions. At each step we take advantage of the newly introduced features. Such a step-by-step approach turns a large problem into a set of small ones and, as we will see later, eases the problem of finding the appropriate subsets. Each element in this series of virtual machines is a useful subset of the system.

D. Designing the "Uses" Structure

The concept of an abstract machine is an intuitive way of thinking about design. A precise description of the concept comes through a discussion of the relation "uses" [11], [12].

1) The relation "uses": We consider a system to be divided into a set of programs that can be invoked either by the normal flow of control mechanisms, by an interrupt, or by an exception handling mechanism. Each of these programs is assumed to have a specification that defines exactly the effect that an invocation of the program should have.

We say of two programs A and B that A uses B if correct execution of B may be necessary for A to complete the task described in its specification. That is, A uses B if there exist situations in which the correct functioning of A depends upon the availability of a correct implementation of B. Note that to decide whether A uses B or not, one must examine both the implementation and the specification of A.

The "uses" relation and "invokes" very often coincide, but uses differs from invokes in two ways:

a) Certain invocations may not be instances of "uses." If A's specification requires only that A invoke B when certain conditions occur, then A has fulfilled its specification when it has generated a correct call to B. A is correct even if B is incorrect or absent. A proof of correctness of A need only make assumptions about the way to invoke B.

b) A program A may use B even though it never invokes it. The best illustration of this is interrupt handling. Most programs in a computer system are only correct on the assumption that the interrupt handling routine will correctly handle the interrupts (leave the processor in an acceptable state). Such programs use the interrupt handling routines even though they never call them. *"Uses"* can also be formulated as *"requires the presence of a correct version of."*

Systems that have achieved a certain "elegance" (e.g., T.H.E. [5], Venus [6]) have done so by having parts of the system *"use"* other parts in such a way that the "user" programs were simplified. For example, the transput stream mechanism in T.H.E. *uses* the segmenting mechanism to great advantage. In contrast, many large and complex operating systems achieve their size and complexity by having "independent" parts. For example, there are many systems in which "spooling," virtual memory management, and the file system all perform their own backup store operations. Code to perform these functions is present in each of the components. Whenever such components must share a single device, complex interfaces exist.

The disadvantage of unrestrained "usage" of each others facilities is that the system parts become highly interdependent. Often there are no subsets of the system that can be used before the whole system is complete. In practice, some duplication of effort seems preferable to a system in which nothing runs unless everything runs.

2) The uses hierarchy: By restricting the relation *"uses"* so that its graph is loop free we can retain the primary advantages of having system parts *"use"* each other while eliminating the problems. In that case it is possible to assign the programs to the levels of a hierarchy by the following rules:

a) level 0 is the set of all programs that *use* no other program;

b) level i (i $\geqslant$ 1) is the set of all programs that *use* at least one program on level i - 1 and no program at a level higher than i - 1.

If such a hierarchical ordering exists, then each level offers a testable and usable subset of the system. In fact, one can get additional subsets by including only parts of a level. The easy availability of these subsets is very valuable for the construction of any software systems and is vital for developing a *broad* family of systems.

The design of the "uses" hierarchy should be one of the major milestones in a design effort. The division of the system into independently callable subprograms has to go on in parallel with the decisions about *uses*, because they influence each other.

3) The criteria to be used in allowing one program to use another: We propose to allow A *"uses"* B when all of the following conditions hold:

a) A is essentially simpler because it uses B;

b) B is not substantially more complex because it is not allowed to use A;

c) there is a useful subset containing B and not A;

d) there is no conceivably useful subset containing A but not B.

During the process of designing the "uses" relation, we often find ourselves in a situation where two programs could obviously benefit from using each other and the conditions above cannot be satisfied. In such situations, we resolve the apparent conflicts by a technique that we call "sandwiching." One of the programs is "sliced" into two parts in a way that allows the programs to "use" each other and still satisfy the above conditions. If we find ourselves in a position where A would benefit from using B, but B can also benefit from using A, we may split B into two programs: B1 and B2. We then allow A to use B2 and B1 to use A. The result would appear to be a sandwich with B as the bread and A as the filling. Often, we then go on to split A. We start with a few levels and end up with many.

An earlier report [11] introduced many of the ideas that are in this paper and illustrated them by proposing a "uses" relation for a family of operating systems. It contains several examples of situations where "sandwiching" led us from a "T.H.E.-like structure" [14] to a structure with more than twice as many levels. For example, the virtual memory mechanism was split into address translation and dynamic allocation of memory areas to segments.

The most frequent instances of splitting and sandwiching came because initially we were assuming that a "level" would be a "module" in the sense of Section IV-B. We will discuss this in the final part of this paper.

4) Use of the word "convenience": It will trouble some readers that it is usual to use the word "convenience" to describe a reason for introducing a certain facility at a given level of the hierarchy. A more substantial basis would seem more scientific.

As discussed in [11] and [13], we must assume that the hardware itself is capable of performing all necessary functions. As one goes higher in the levels, one can lose capabilities (as resources are consumed)—not gain them. On the other hand, at the higher levels the new functions can be implemented with simpler programs because of the additional programs that can be used. We speak of "convenience" to make it clear that one could implement any functions on a lower level, but the availability of the additional programs at the higher level is useful. For each function we give the lowest level at which the features that are useful for implementing that function (with the stated restrictions) are available. In each case, we see no functions available at the next higher level that would be useful for implementing the functions as described. If we implemented the program one level lower we would have to duplicate programs that become available at that level.

V. EXAMPLE: AN ADDRESS PROCESSING SUBSYSTEM

As an example of designing for extensibility and subsets, we consider a set of programs to read in, store, and write out lists of addresses. This example has also been used, to illustrate a different point, in [10] and has been used in several classroom experiments to demonstrate module interchangeability. This

The following items of information will be found in the addresses to be processed and constitute the only items of relevance to the application programs:

- Last name
- Given names (first name and possible middle names)
- Organization (Command or Activity)
- Internal identifier (Branch or Code)
- Street address or P.O. box
- City or mail unit identifier
- State
- Zip code
- Title
- Branch of service if military
- GS grade if civil service

Each of the above will be strings of characters in the standard ANSI alphabet, and each of the above may be empty or blank.

Fig. 1.

example is intended as an integral part of this paper; several statements in the final summation are supported only in this section.

A. Our Basic Assumptions

1) The information items discussed in Fig. 1 will be the items to be processed by all application programs.

2) The input formats of the addresses are subject to change.

3) The output formats of the addresses are subject to change.

4) Some systems will use a single fixed format for input and output. Other systems will need the ability to choose from several input or output formats at run-time. Some systems will be required in which the user can specify the format using a format definition language.

5) The representation of addresses in main storage will vary from system to system.

6) In most systems, only a subset of the total set of addresses stored in the system need be in main storage at any one time. The number of addresses needed may vary from system to system, and in some systems the number of addresses to be kept in main memory may vary at run-time.

B. We Propose the Following Design Decisions

1) The input and output programs will be table driven: the table will specify the format to be used for input and output. The contents and organization of these format tables will be the "secrets" of the input and output modules.

2) The representation of addresses in core will be the "secret" of an address storage module (ASM). The implementation chosen for this module will be such that the operations of changing a portion of an address will be relatively inexpensive, compared to making the address table larger or smaller.

3) When the number of addresses to be stored exceeds the capacity of an ASM, programs will use an address file module (AFM). An AFM can be made upward compatible with an ASM; programs that were written to use ASM's could operate using an AFM in the same way. The AFM provides additional

commands to allow more efficient usage by programs that do not assume the random access properties of an ASM. These programs are described below.

4) Our implementation of an AFM would use an ASM as a submodule as well as another submodule that we will call block file module (BFM). The BFM stores blocks of data that are sufficiently large to represent an address, but the BFM is not specialized to the handling of addresses. An ASM that is used within an AFM may be said to have two interfaces. In the "normal interface" that an ASM presents to an outside user, an address is a set of fields and the access functions hide or abstract from the representation. Fig. 2 is a list of the access programs that comprise this interface. In the second interface, the ASM deals with blocks of contiguous storage and abstract from the contents. There are commands for the ASM to input and output "addresses" but the operands are storage blocks whose interpretation as addresses is known only within the ASM. The AFM makes assumptions about the association between blocks and addresses but not about the way that an address's components are represented as blocks. The BFM is completely independent of the fact that the blocks contain address information. The BFM might, in fact, be a manufacturer supplied access method.

C. Component Programs

1) Module: Address Input

INAD: Reads in an address that is assumed to be in a format specified by a format table and calls ASM or AFM functions to store it.

INFSL: Selects a format from an existing set of format tables. The selected format is the one that will be used by INAD. There is always a format selected.

INFCR: Adds a new format to the tables used by INFSL. The format is specified in a "format language." Selection is *not* changed (i.e., INAD still uses the same format table).

INTABEXT: Adds a blank table to the set of input format tables.

INTABCHG: Rewrites a table in the input format tables using a description in a format language. Selection is not changed.

INFDEL: Deletes a table from the set of format tables. The selected format cannot be deleted.

INADSEL: Reads in an address using one of a set of formats. Choice is specified by an integer parameter.

INADFO: Reads in an address in a format specified as one of its parameters (a string in the format definition language). The format is selected and added to the tables and subsequent addresses could be read in using INAD.

2) Module: Address Output

OUTAD: Prints an address in a format specified by a format table. The information to be printed

Access Functions for "Normal Interface"

MODULE: ASM

NAME OF ACCESS PROGRAM*	INPUT PARAMETERS						OUTPUT	
*ADDTIT:	asm	X	integer	X	string	→	asm	•
ADDGN:	asm	X	integer	X	string	→	asm	•
ADDLN:	asm	X	integer	X	string	→	asm	•
ADDSERV:	asm	X	integer	X	string	→	asm	•
ADDBORC:	asm	X	integer	X	string	→	asm	•
ADDCORA:	asm	X	integer	X	string	→	asm	•
ADDSORP:	asm	X	integer	X	string	→	asm	•
ADDCITY:	asm	X	integer	X	string	→	asm	•
ADDSTATE:	asm	X	integer	X	string	→	asm	•
ADDZIP:	asm	X	integer	X	string	→	asm	•
ADDGSL:	asm	X	integer	X	string	→	asm	•
SETNUM:	asm	X	integer	→	asm	•		
FETTIT:	asm	X	integer	→	string			
FETGN:	asm	X	integer	→	string			
FETGN:	asm	X	integer	→	string			
FETLN:	asm	X	integer	→	string			
FETSERV:	asm	X	integer	→	string			
FETBORC:	asm	X	integer	→	string			
FETCORA:	asm	X	integer	→	string			
FETSORP:	asm	X	integer	→	string			
FETCITY:	asm	X	integer	→	string			
FETSTATE:	asm	X	integer	→	string			
FETZIP:	asm	X	integer	→	string			
FETGSL:	asm	X	integer	→	string			
FETNUM:	asm	→	integer					

*These are abbreviations: ADDTIT = ADD TITLE; ADDGN = ADD GIVEN NAME, etc.

Fig. 2. Syntax of ASM functions.

is assumed to be in an ASM and identified by its position in an ASM.

OUTFSL: Selects a format table from an existing set of output format tables. The selected format is the one that will be used by OUTAD.

OUTTABEXT: Adds a "blank" table to the set of output format tables.

OUTTABCHG: Rewrites the contents of a format table using information in a format language.

OUTFCR: Adds a new format to the set of formats that can be selected by OUTFSL in a format description language.

OUTFDEL: Deletes a table from the set of format tables that can be selected by OUTFSL.

OUTADSEL: Prints out an address using one of a set of formats.

OUTADFO: Prints out an address in a format specified in a format definition language string, which is one of the actual parameters. The format is added to the tables and selected.

3) Module: Address Storage (ASM)

FET: (Component Name): This is a set of functions used to read information from an address store. Returns a string as a value. See Fig. 2.

ADD: (Component Name): This is a set of functions used to write information in an address store. Each takes a string and an integer as parameters. The integer specifies an address within the ASM. See Fig. 2.

0BLOCK: Takes an integer parameter, returns a storage block as a value.

1BLOCK: Accepts a storage block and integer as parameters. Its effect is to change the contents of an address store—which is reflected by a change in the values of the FET programs.

ASMEXT: Extends an address store by appending a new address with empty components at the end of the address store.

ASMSHR: "Shrinks" the address store.

ASMCR: Creates a new address store. The parameter specifies the number of components. All components are initially empty.

ASMDEL: Deletes an existing address store.

4) Module: Block File Module

BLFET: Accepts an integer as a parameter and returns a "block."

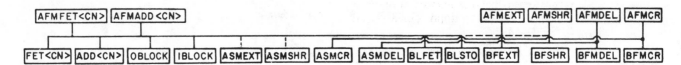

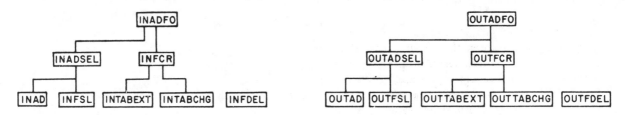

Fig. 3.

BLSTO: Accepts a block and an integer and stores the block.

BFEXT: Extends BFM by adding additional blocks to its capacity.

BFSHR: Reduces the size of the BFM by removing some blocks.

BFMCR: Creates a file of blocks.

BFMDEL: Deletes an existing file of blocks.

5) Module: Address File Module

This module includes implementations of all of the ASM functions except OBLOCK and IBLOCK. To avoid confusion in the diagram showing the uses hierarchy we have changed the names to:

AFMADD (Component Name) defined as in Fig. 2

AFMFET (Component Name) defined as in Fig. 1

AFMEXT defined as in BFM above

AMFSHR defined as in BFM above

AFMCR defined as in BFM above

AFMDEL defined as in BFM above.

D. Uses Relation

Fig. 3 shows the *uses* relation between the component programs. It is important to note that we are now discussing the implementation of those programs, not just their specifications. The *uses* relation is characterized by the fact that there are a large number of relatively simple, *single-purpose* programs on the lowest level. The upper level programs are implemented by means of these lower level programs so that they too are quite simple. This *uses* relation diagram characterizes the set of possible subsets.

E. Discussion

To pick a subset, one identifies the set of upper level programs that the user needs and includes only those programs that those programs use (directly or indirectly). For example, a user who uses addresses in a single format does not need the component programs that interpret format description lan-

guages. Systems that work with a small set of addresses can be built without any BFM components. A program that works as a query system and never prints out a complete address would not need any Address Output components.

The system is also easily extended. For example, one could add a capability to read in addresses with self-defining files. If the first record on a file was a description of the format in something equivalent to the format description language, one could write a program that would be able to read in that record, use INTABCHG to build a new format table, and then read in the addresses. Programs that do things with addresses (such as print out "personalized" form letters) can also be added using these programs and selecting only those capabilities that they actually need.

One other observation that can be made is that the upper level programs can be used to "generate" lower level versions. For example, the format description languages can be used to generate the tables used for the fixed format versions. There is no need for a separate SYSGEN program.

We will elaborate on this observation in the conclusion.

VI. SOME REMARKS ON OPERATING SYSTEMS: WHY GENERALS ARE SUPERIOR TO COLONELS

An earlier report [11] discusses the design of a "uses" hierarchy for operating systems. Although there have been some refinements to the proposals of that report, its basic contents are consistent with the present proposals. This section compares the approach outlined in this paper and the "kernel" approach or "nucleus" approach to OS design [18]-[20]. It is tempting to say that the suggestions in this paper do not conflict with the "kernel" approach. These proposals can be viewed as a refinement of the nucleus approach. The first few levels of our system could be labeled "kernel," and one could conclude that we are just discussing a fine structure within the kernel.

To yield to that temptation would be to ignore an essential difference between the approaches suggested in this paper and the kernel approach. The system kernels known to me are such that some desirable subsets cannot be obtained without major surgery. It was assumed that the nucleus must be in every system family member. In the RC4000 system the inability to separate synchronization from message passing has led some users to bypass the kernel to perform teletype handling functions. In Hydra as originally proposed [19], "type checking" was so intrinsic to the call mechanism that it appeared impossible to disable it when it was not needed or affordable.[1]

Drawing a line between "kernel" and the rest of the system, and putting "essential" services of "critical programs" in the nucleus yields a system in which kernel features cannot be removed and certain extensions are impractical. Looking for a *minimal* subset and a set of *minimal* independent incremental function leads to a system in which one can trim away unneeded features. I know of no feature that is always needed. When we say that two functions are *almost* always used together, we should remember that "almost" is a euphemism for "not."

VII. Summation

This paper describes an approach to software intended to result in systems that can be tailored to fit the needs of a broad variety of users. The points most worthy of emphasis are as follows.

1) The Requirements Include Subsets and Extensions: It is essential to recognize the identification of useable subsets as part of the preliminaries to software design. Flexibility cannot be an afterthought. Subsetability is needed, not just to meet a variety of customers' needs, but to provide a fail-safe way of handling schedule slippage.

2) Advantages of the Virtual Machine Approach: Designing software as a set of virtual machines has definite advantages over the conventional (flowchart) approach to system design. The virtual machine "instructions" provide facilities that are useful for purposes beyond those originally conceived. These instructions can easily be omitted from a system if they are not needed. Remove a jamor box from a flowchart and there is often a need to "fill the hole" with conversion programs.

3) On the Difference Between Software Generality and Software Flexibility: Software can be considered "general" if it can be used, *without change*, in a variety of situations. Software can be considered flexible, if it is *easily changed* to be used in a variety of situations. It appears unavoidable that there is a run-time cost to be paid for generality. Clever designers can achieve flexibility without significant run-time cost, but there is a design-time cost. One should incur the design-time cost only if one expects to recover it when changes are made.

Some organizations may choose to pay the run-time cost for generality. They build general software rather than flexible software because of the maintenance problems associated with maintaining several different versions. Factors influencing this decision include a) the availability of extra computer resources,

b) the facilities for program change and maintenance available at each installation, and c) the extent to which design techniques ease the task of applying the same change to many versions of a program.

No one can tell a designer how much flexibility and generality should be built into a product, but the decision should be a conscious one. Often, it just happens.

4) On the Distinction Between Modules, Subprograms, and Levels: Several systems and at least one dissertation [14]-[17] have, in my opinion, blurred the distinction between modules, subprograms, and levels. Conventional programming techniques consider a subroutine or other callable program to be a module. If one wants the modules to include all programs that must be designed together and changed together, then, as our example illustrates, one will usually include many small subprograms in a single module. If does not matter what word we use; the point is that the unit of change is not a single callable subprogram.

In several systems, modules and levels have coincided [14], [15]. This had led to the phrase "level of abstraction." Each of the modules in the example abstract from some detail that is assumed likely to change. In our approach there is no correspondence between modules and levels. Further, I have not found a relation, "more abstract than," that would allow me to define an abstraction hierarchy [12]. Although I am myself guilty of using it, in most cases the phrase "levels of abstraction" is an abuse of language.

Janson has suggested that a design such as this one (or the one discussed in [11]) contain "soft modules" that can represent a breach of security principles. Obviously an error in any program in one of our modules can violate the integrity of that module. All module programs that will be included in a given subset must be considered in proving the correctness of that module. However, I see no way that allowing the component programs to be on different levels of a "uses" hierarchy makes this process more difficult or makes the system less secure. The boundaries of our modules are quite firm and clearly identified.

The essential difference between this paper and other discussions of hierarchically structured designs is the emphasis on subsets and extensions. My search for a criterion to be used in designing the *uses* hierarchy has convinced me that if one does not care about the existence of subsets, it does not really matter what hierarchy one uses. Any design can be bent until it works. It is only in the ease of change that they differ.

5) On Avoiding Duplication: Some earlier work [21] has suggested that one needs to have duplicate or near duplicate modules in a hierarchically structured system. For example, they suggest that one needs one implementation of processes to give a fixed number of processes at a low level and another to provide for a varying number of processes at a user's level. Similar ideas have appeared elsewhere. Were such duplication to be necessary, it would be a sound argument against the use of "structured" approaches. One can avoid such duplication if one allows the programs that vary the size of a data structure to be on a higher level than the other programs that operate on that data structure. For example, in an operating system, the programs to create and delete processes need not be on the

[1] Accurate reports on the current status and performance of that system are not available to me.

117

same level as the more frequently used scheduling operations. In designing software, I regard the need to code similar functions in two separate programs as an indication of a fundamental error in my thinking.

6) Designing for Subsets and Extensions Can Reduce the Need for Support Software: We have already mentioned that this design approach can eliminate the need for separate SYSGEN programs. We can also eliminate the need for *special-*purpose compilers. The price of the convenience features offered by such languages is often a compiler and run-time package distinctly larger than the system being built. In our approach, each level provides a "language extention" available to the programmer of the next level. We never build a compiler; we just build our system, but we get convenience features anyway.

7) Extension at Run-Time Versus Extension During SYSGEN: At a later stage in the design we will have to choose data structures and take the difference between run-time extension and SYSGEN extension into consideration. Certain data structures are more easily accessed but harder to extend while the program is running; others are easily extended but at the expense of a higher access cost. These differences do not affect our early design decisions because they are hidden in modules.

8) On the Value of a Model: My work on this example and similar ones has gone much faster because I have learned to exploit a pattern that I first noticed in the design discussed in [11]. Low level operations assume the existence of a fixed data structure of some type. The operations on the next level allow the swapping of a data element with others from a fixed set of similar elements. The high level programs allow the creation and deletion of such data elements. This pattern appears several times in both designs. Although I have not designed your system for you, I believe that you can take advantage of a similar pattern. If so, this paper has served its purpose.

Acknowledgment

The ideas presented in this paper have been developed over a lengthy period and with the cooperation and help of many collaborators. I am grateful to numerous Philips employees for thought provoking comments and questions. Price's collaboration was invaluable at Carnegie-Mellon University. The help of W. Bartussek, G. Handzel, and H. Wuerges at the Technische Hochschule Darmstadt led to substantial improvements. Heninger, Weiss, and J. Shore at the Naval Research Laboratory helped me to understand the application of the concepts in areas other than operating systems. B. Trombka and J. Guttag both helped in the design of pilots of the address process system. Discussions with P. J. Courtois have helped me to better understand the relation between software structure and run-time characteristics of computer systems. Dr. E. Britton, H. Rettenmaier, L. Belady, Dr. D. Stanat, G. Fran, and Dr. W. Wright made many helpful suggestions about an earlier draft of this paper. If you find portions of this paper helpful, these people deserve your thanks.

References

[1] E. W. Dijkstra, *A Discipline of Programming.* Englewood Cliffs, NJ: Prentice-Hall, 1976.

[2] D. L. Parnas, "On the design and development of program families," *IEEE Trans. Software Eng.*, vol. SE-2, pp. 1-9, Mar. 1976.

[3] 2nd Int. Conf. Software Engineering, Oct. 13-15, 1976; also, *IEEE Trans. Software Eng.*, (Special Issue), vol. SE-2, Dec. 1976.

[4] D. L. Parnas, G. Handzel, and H. Würges, "Design and specification of the minimal subset of an operating system family," presented at the 2nd Int. Conf. Software Engineering, Oct. 13-15, 1976; also, *IEEE Trans. Software Eng.*, (Special Issue), vol. SE-2, pp. 301-307, Dec. 1976.

[5] D. L. Parnas, "On the criteria to be used in decomposing systems into modules," *Commun. Ass. Comput. Mach.*, Dec. 1972.

[6] T. A. Linden, "The use of abstract data types to simplify program modifications," in *Proc. Conf. Data: Abstraction, Definition and Structure*, Mar. 22-24, 1976; also, *ACM SIGPLAN Notices* (Special Issue), vol. II, 1976.

[7] D. L. Parnas, "A technique for software module specification with examples," *Commun. Ass. Comput. Mach.*, May 1972.

[8] ——, "Information distribution aspects of design methodology," in *1971 Proc. IFIP Congr.* Amsterdam, The Netherlands: North-Holland, 1971.

[9] ——, "The use of precise specifications in the development of software," in *1977 Proc. IFIP Congr.* Amsterdam, The Netherlands: North-Holland, 1977.

[10] ——, "Use of abstract interfaces in the development of software for embedded computer systems," Naval Res. Lab., Washington, DC, NRL Rep. 8047, June 1977.

[11] ——, "Some hypotheses about the 'uses' hierarchy for operating systems," Technische Hochschule Darmstadt, Darmstadt, West Germany, Tech. Rep., Mar. 1976.

[12] ——, "On a 'buzzword': Hierarchical structure," in *1974 Proc. IFIP Congr.* Amsterdam, The Netherlands: North-Holland, 1974.

[13] D. L. Parnas and D. L. Siewiorek, "Use of the concept of transparency in the design of hierarchically structured systems," *Commun. Ass. Comput. Mach.*, vol. 18, July 1975.

[14] E. W. Dijkstra, "The structure of the "THE"-multiprogramming system," *Commun. Ass. Comput. Mach.*, vol. 11, pp. 341-346, May 1968.

[15] B. Liskov, "The design of the Venus operating system," *Commun. Ass. Comput. Mach.*, vol. 15, pp. 144-149, Mar. 1972.

[16] P. A. Janson, "Using type extension to organize virtual memory mechanisms," Lab. for Comput. Sci., M.I.T., Cambridge, MA, MIT-LCS-TR167, Sept. 1976.

[17] ——, "Using type-extension to organize virtual memory mechanisms," IBM Zurich Res. Lab., Switzerland, Res. Rep. RZ 858 (#28909), August 31, 1977.

[18] P. Brinch Hansen, "The nucleus of the multiprogramming system," *Commun. Ass. Comput. Mach.*, vol. 13, pp. 238-241, 250, Apr. 1970.

[19] W. Wulf, E. Cohen, A. Jones, R. Lewin, C. Pierson, and F. Pollack, "HYDRA: The kernel of a multiprocessor operating system," *Commun. Ass. Comput. Mach.*, vol. 17, pp. 337-345, June 1974.

[20] G. J. Popek and C. S. Kline, "The design of a verified protection system," in *Proc. Int. Workshop Prot. In Oper. Syst.*, IRIA, pp. 183-196.

[21] A. R. Saxena and T. H. Bredt, "A structured specification of a hierarchical operating system," in *Proc. 1975 Int. Conf. Reliable Software*.

David L. Parnas received the B.S., M.S., and Ph.D. degrees in electrical engineering—systems and communications sciences from the Carnegie Institute of Technology, Pittsburgh, PA.

He held the position of Assistant Professor of Computer Science at the University of Maryland and at Carnegie-Mellon University. During the period 1969-1970 he was employed by Philips-Electrologica, Apeldoorn, The Netherlands, and at the MBLE Research Laboratory, Brussels, Belgium. He then returned to Carnegie-Mellon

University where he held the rank of Associate Professor until 1973. In June of 1973 he was appointed Professor and Head of the Research Group on Operating Systems I at the Technical University of Darmstadt, Germany, where he remained through August 1976. He is presently Professor in the Department of Computer Science, University of North Carolina, Chapel Hill. He is also with the Information Systems Staff, Communications Sciences Division, at the Naval Research Laboratory, Washington, DC. He has published papers in the areas of computer design languages and simulation techniques. His current interests are in the field of software engineering methods, computer system design, abstract specification for programs, verification that a program meets its specifications, and cooperating sequential processes.

CONSTRUCTIVE METHODS OF PROGRAM DESIGN

M. A. Jackson

Abstract Correct programs cannot be obtained by attempts to test or to prove incorrect programs: the correctness of a program should be assured by the design procedure used to build it.

A suggestion for such a design procedure is presented and discussed. The procedure has been developed for use in data processing, and can be effectively taught to most practicing programmers. It is based on correspondence between data and program structures, leading to a decomposition of the program into distinct processes. The model of a process is very simple, permitting use of simple techniques of communication, activation and suspension. Some wider implications and future possibilities are also mentioned.

1. Introduction

In this paper I would like to present and discuss what I believe to be *a more constructive method of program design*. The phrase itself is important; I am sure that no-one here will object if I use a LIFO discipline in briefly elucidating its intended meaning.

'Design' is primarily concerned with structure; the designer must say what parts there are to be and how they are to be arranged. The crucial importance of modular programming and structured programming (even in their narrowest and crudest manifestations) is that they provide some definition of what parts are permissible: a module is a separately compiled, parameterized subroutine; a structure component is a sequence, an iteration or a selection. With such definition, inadequate through they may be, we can at least begin to think about design: what modules would make up that program, and how should they be arranged? Should this program be an iteration of selections or a sequence of iterations? Without such definitions, design is meaningless. At the top level of a problem there are P^N possible designs, where P is the number of distinct types of permissible part and N is the number of parts needed to make up the whole. So, to preserve our sanity, both P and N must be small: modular programming, using tree or hierarchical structures, offers small values of N; structured programming offers, additionally, small values of P.

'Program' or, rather 'programming' I would use in a narrow sense. Modeling the problem is 'analysis'; 'programming' is putting the model on a computer. Thus, for example, if we are asked to find a prime number in the range 10^{50} to 10^{60}, we need a number theorist for the analysis; if we are asked to program discounted cash flow, the analysis calls for a financial expert. One of the major ills in data processing stems from uncertainty about this distinction. In mathematical circles the distinction is often ignored altogether, to the detriment, I believe, of our understanding of programming. Programming is about computer programs, not about number theory, or financial planning, or production control.

'Method' is defined in the Shorted OED as a 'procedure for attaining an object'. The crucial word here is 'procedure'. The ultimate method, and the ultimate is doubtless unattainable, is a procedure embodying a precise and correct algorithm. To follow the method we need only execute the algorithm faithfully, and we will be led infallibly to the desired result. To the extent that a putative method falls short of this ideal it is less of a method.

To be 'constructive', a method must itself be decomposed into distinct steps, and correct execution of each step must assure correct execution of the whole method and thus the correctness of its product. The key requirement here is that the correctness of the execution of a step should be largely verifiable without reference to steps not yet executed by the designer. This is the central difficulty in stepwise refinement: we can judge the correctness of a refinement step only be reference to what is yet to come, and hence only by exercising a degree of foresight to which few people can lay claim.

Finally, we must recognize that design methods today are intended for use by human beings: in spite of what was said above about constructive methods, we need, now and for some time to come, a substantial ingredient of intuition and subjectivity. So what is presented below does not claim to be fully constructive - merely to be 'more constructive'. The reader must supply the other half of the comparison for himself, measuring the claim against the yardstick of his own favored methods.

2. Basis of the Method

The basis of the method is described, in some detail, in (1). It is appropriate here only to illustrate it by a family of simple example problems.

Example 1

A cardfile of punched cards is sorted into ascending sequence of values of a key which appears in each card. Within this sequence, the first card for each group of cards with a common key value is a header card, while the others are detail cards. Each detail card carries an integer amount. It is required to produce a report showing the totals of amount for all keys.

Solution 1

The first step in applying the method is to describe the structure of the data. We use a graphic notation to represent the structures as trees:

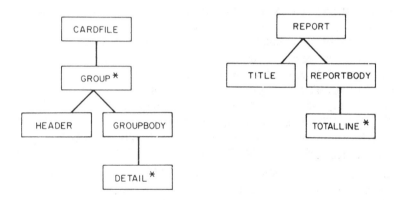

The above representations are equivalent to the following (in BNF with iteration instead of recursion):

$$<\text{cardfile}> ::= \{<\text{group}>\}_0^\infty$$
$$<\text{group}> ::= <\text{header}> <\text{groupbody}>$$
$$<\text{groupbody}> ::= \{<\text{detail}>\}_0^\infty$$
$$<\text{report}> ::= <\text{title}> <\text{reportbody}>$$
$$<\text{reportbody}> ::= \{<\text{totalline}>\}_0^\infty$$

The second step is to compose these data structures into a program structure:

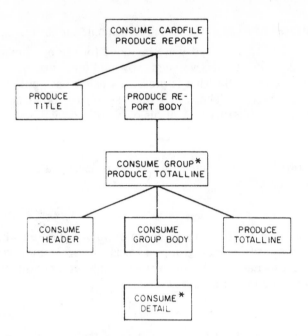

This structure has the following properties:

- It is related quite formally to each of the data structures. We may recover any one data structure from the program structure by first marking all nodes lying in a path from a marked node to the root.

- The correspondences (cardfile : report) and (group : totalline) are determined by the problem statement. One report is derivable from one cardfile; one totalline is derivable from one group, and the totallines are in the same order as the groups.

- The structure is vacuous, in the sense that it contains no executable statements: it is a program which does nothing; it is a tree without real leaves.

The third step in applying the method is to list the executable operations required and to allocate each to its right place in the program structure. The operations are elementary executable statements of the programming language, possibly after enhancement of the language by a bout of bottom-up design; they are enumerated, essentially, by working back from output to input along the obvious data-flow paths. Assuming a reasonably conventional machine and a line printer (rather than a character printer), we may obtain the list:

1. write title
2. write totalline (groupkey, total)
3. total := total + detail.amount
4. total := 0
5. groupkey := header.key
6. open cardfile
7. read cardfile
8. close cardfile

Note that every operation, or almost every operation, must have operands which are data objects. Allocation to a program structure is therefore a trivial task if the program structure is correctly based on the data structures. This triviality is a vital criterion of the success of the first two steps. The resulting program, in an obvious notation, is:

```
CARD-REPORT sequence
    open cardfile;
    read cardfile;
    write title;
    REPORT-BODY iteration until cardfile.eof
        total := 0;
        groupkey := header.key;
        read cardfile;
        GROUP-BODY iteration until cardfile.eof
                        or detail.key ≠ groupkey
            total := total + detail.amount;
            read cardfile;
        GROUP-BODY end
        write totalline (groupkey, total);
    REPORT-BODY end
    close cardfile;
CARDFILE-REPORT end
```

Clearly, this program may be transcribed without difficulty into any procedural programming language.

Comment

The solution has proceeded in three steps: First, we defined the data structures; second, we formed them into a program structure; third, we listed and allocated the executable operations. At each step we have criteria for the correctness of the step itself and an implicit check on the correctness of the steps already taken. For example, if at the first step we had wrongly described the structure of cardfile as

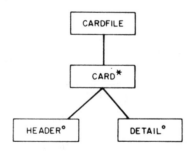

(that is: $<$cardfile$> ::= \{<$card$>\}_0^\infty$

$<$card$> ::= <$header$>|<$detail$>$),

we should have been able to see at the first step that we had failed to represent everything we knew about the cardfile. If nonetheless we had persisted in error, we would have discovered it at the second step, when we would have been unable to form a program structure in the absence of a cardfile component corresponding to a totalline in report.

The design has throughout concentrated on what we may think of as a static rather than a dynamic view of the problem: on maps, not on itineraries, on structures, not on logic flow. The logic flow of the finished program is a by-product of the data structures and the correct allocation of the 'read' operation. There is an obvious connection between what we have done and the design of a very simple syntax analysis phase in a compiler: the grammar of the input file determines the structure of the program which parses it. We may observe that the 'true' grammar of the cardfile is not context-free: within one group, the header and detail cards must all carry the same key value. It is because the explicit grammar cannot show this that we are forced to introduce the variable groupkey to deal with this stipulation.

Note that there is no error-checking. If we wish to check for errors in the input we must elaborate the structure of the input file to accommodate those errors explicitly. By defining a structure for an input file we define the domain of the program: if we wish to extend the domain, we must extend the input file structure accordingly. In a practical data processing system, we would always define the structure of primary input (such as decks of cards, keyboard messages, etc) to encompass all physically possible files: it would be absurd to construct a program whose operation is unspecified (and therefore, in principle, unpredictable) in the event of a card deck being dropped or a wrong key depressed.

Example 2

The cardfile of example 1 is modified so that each card contains a card-type indicator with possible values 'header', 'detail' and other. The program should take account of possible errors in the composition of a group: there may be no header card and/or there may be cards other than detail cards in the group body. Groups containing errors should be listed on an errorlist, but not totaled.

Solution 2

The structure of the report remains unchanged. The structure of the errorlist and of the new version of the cardfile are:

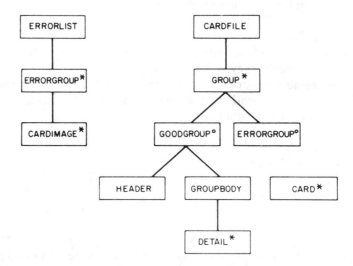

The structure of cardfile demands attention. Firstly, it is ambiguous: anything which is a goodgroup is also an errorgroup. We are forced into this ambiguity because it would be intolerably difficult - and quite unnecessary - to spell out all of the ways in which a group may be in error. The ambiguity is simply resolved by the conventions we use: the parts of a selection are considered to be ordered, and the first applicable part encountered in a left-to-right scan is chosen. So a group can be parsed as an errorgroup only if it has already been rejected as a goodgroup. Secondly, a goodgroup cannot be recognized by a left-to-right parse of the input file with any predetermined degree of lookahead. If we choose to read ahead R records, we may yet encounter a group containing an error only in the R+1'th card.

Recognition problems of this kind occur in many guises. Their essence is that we are forced to a choice during program execution at a time when we lack the evidence on which the choice must be based. Note that the difficulty is not structural but is confined to achieving a workable flow of control. We will call such problems 'backtracking' problems, and tackle them in three stages:

- Ignore the recognition difficulty, imagining that a friendly demon will tell us infallibly which choice to make. In the present problem, he will tell us whether a group is a goodgroup or an errorgroup. Complete the design procedure in this blissful state of confidence, producing the full program text.

- Replace our belief in the demon's infallibility by a sceptical determination to verify each 'land-mark' in the data which might prove him wrong. Whenever he is proved wrong we will execute a 'quit' statement which branches to the second part of the selection. Those 'quit' statements are introduced into the program text created in stage a.

- Modify the program text resulting from stage b to ensure that side-effects are repealed where necessary.

The result of stage a, in accordance with the design procedure used for example 1, is:

```
CFILE-REPT-ERR sequence
    open cardfile;
    read cardfile;
    write title;
    REPORT-BODY iteration until cardfile.eof
        groupkey := card.key;
        GROUP-OUTG select goodgroup
            total := 0;
            read cardfile;
            GOOD-GROUP iteration until cardfile.eof
                    or detail.key ≠ groupkey
                total := total + detail.amount;
                read cardfile;
            GOOD-GROUP end
            write totalline (groupkey, total);
        GROUP-OUTG or errorgroup
            ERROR-GROUP iteration until cardfile.eof
                    or card.key ≠ groupkey
                write errorline (card);
                read cardfile;
            ERROR-GROUP end
        GROUP-OUTG end
    REPORT-BODY end
    close cardfile;
CFILE-REPT-ERR end
```

Note that we cannot completely transcribe this program into any programming language, because we cannot code an evaluable expression for the predicate goodgroup. However, we can readily verify the correctness of the program (assuming the infallibility of the demon). Indeed, if we are prepared to exert ourselves to punch an identifying character into the header card of each goodgroup - thus acting as our own demon - we can code and run the program as an informal demonstration of its acceptability.

We are now ready to proceed to stage b, in which we insert 'quit' statements into the first part of the selection GROUP-OUTG. Also, since quit statements are not present in a normal selection, we will replace the words 'select' and 'or' by 'posit' and 'admit' respectively, thus indicating the tentative nature of the initial choice. Clearly, the landmarks to be checked are the card-type indicators in the header and detail cards. We thus obtain the following program:

```
CFILE-REPT-ERR sequence
    open cardfile;
    read cardfile;
    write title;
    REPORT-BODY iteration until cardfile.eof
        groupkey := card.key;
        GROUP-OUTG posit goodgroup
            total := 0;
            quit GROUP-OUTG if card.type ≠ header;
            read cardfile;
            GOOD-GROUP iteration until cardfile.eof
                    or card.key ≠ groupkey
                quit GROUP-OUTG if card.type ≠ detail;
                total := total + detail.amount;
                read cardfile;
            GOOD-GROUP end
            write totalline (groupkey, total);
        GROUP-OUTG admit errorgroup
            ERROR-GROUP iteration until cardfile.eof
                    or card.key ≠ groupkey;
                write errorline (card);
                read cardfile;
            ERROR-GROUP end
        GROUP-OUTG end
    REPORT-BODY end
    close cardfile;
CFILE-REPT-ERR end
```

The third stage, stage c, deals with the side-effects of partial execution of the first part of the selection. In this trivial example, the only significant side-effect is the reading of cardfile. In general, it will be found that the only troublesome side-effects are the reading and writing of serial files; the best and easiest way to handle them is to equip ourselves with input and output procedures capable of 'noting' and 'restoring' the state of the file and its associated buffers. Given the availability of such procedures, stage c can be completed by inserting a 'note' statement immediately following the 'posit' statement and a 'restore' statement immediately following the 'admit'. Sometimes side-effects will demand a more ad hoc treatment: when 'note' and 'restore' are unavailable there is no alternative to such cumbersome expedients as explicitly storing each record on disk or in main storage.

Comment

By breaking our treatment of the backtracking difficulty into three distinct stages, we are able to isolate distinct aspects of the problem. In stage a we ignore the backtracking difficulty entirely, and concentrate our efforts on obtaining a correct solution to the reduced problem. This solution is carried through the three main design steps, producing a completely specific program text: we are able to satisfy ourselves of the correctness of that text before going on to modify it in the second and third stages. In the second stage we deal only with the recognition difficulty: the difficulty is one of logic flow, and we handle it, appropriately, by modifying the logic flow, and we handle it, appropriately, by modifying the logic flow of the program with quit statements. Each quit statement says, in effect, 'It is supposed (posited) that this is a goodgroup; but if, in fact, this card is not what is ought to be then this is not, after all, a goodgroup'. The required quit statements can be easily seen from the data structure definition, and their place is readily found in the program text because the program structure perfectly matches the data structure. The side-effects arise to be dealt with in stage c because of the quit statements, producing discontinuities in the context of the computation and hence side-effects. The side-effects are readily identified from the program text resulting from stage b.

Note that it would be quite wrong to distort the data structures and the program structure in an attempt to avoid the dreaded four-letter word 'goto'. The data structures shown, and hence the program structure, are self-evidently the correct structures for the problem as stated: they must not be abandoned because of difficulties with the logic flow.

3. Simple Programs and Complex Programs

The design method, as described above, is severely constrained: it applies to a narrow class of serial file-processing programs. We may go further, and say that if defines such a class - the class of 'simple programs'. A 'simple program' has the following attributes:

- The program has a fixed initial state; nothing is remembered from one execution to the next.
- Program inputs and outputs are serial files, which we may conveniently suppose to be held on magnetic tapes. There may be more than one input and more than one output file.
- Associated with the program is an explicit definition of the structure of each input and output file. These structures are tree structures, defined in the grammar used above. This grammar permits recursion in addition to the features shown above; it is not very different from a grammar of regular expressions.
- The input data structures define the domain of the program, the output data structures its range. Nothing is introduced into the program text which is not associated with the defined data structures.
- The data structures are compatible, in the sense that they can be combined into a program structure in the manner shown above.
- The program structure thus derived from the data structures is sufficient for a workable program. Elementary operations of the program language (possibly supplemented by more powerful or suitable operations resulting from bottom-up designing) are allocated to components of the program structure without introducing any further 'program logic'.

A simple program may be designed and constructed with the minimum of difficulty, provided that we adhere rigorously to the design principles adumbrated here and eschew any temptation to pursue efficiency at the cost of distorting the structure. In fact, we should usually discount the benefits of efficiency, reminding ourselves of the mass of error-ridden programs which attest to its dangers.

Evidently, not all programs are simple programs. Sometimes we are presented with the task of constructing a program which operates on direct-access rather than on serial files, or which processes a single record at each execution, starting from a varying internal state. As we shall see later, a simple program may be clothed in various disguises which give it a misleading appearance without affecting its underlying nature. More significantly, we may find that the design procedure suggested cannot be applied to the problem given because the data structures are not compatible: that is, we are unable at the second step of the design procedure to form the program structure from the data structures.

Example 3

The input cardfile of example 1 is presented to the program in the form of a blocked file. Each block of this file contains a card count and a number of card images.

Solution 3

The structure of blockedfile is:

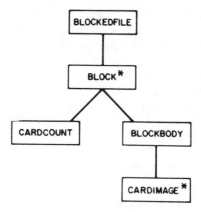

This structure does not, of course, show the arrangement of the cards in groups. It is impossible to show, in a single structure, both the arrangement in groups and the arrangement in blocks. But the structure of the report is still:

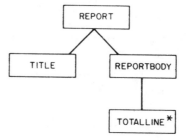

We cannot fit together the structures of report and blockedfile to form a program structure; nor would we be in better case if we were to ignore the arrangement in blocks. The essence of our difficulty is this: the program must contain operations to be executed once per block, and these must be allocated to a 'process block' component; it must also contain operations to be executed once per group, and these must be allocated to a 'process group' component; but it is impossible to form a single program structure containing both a 'process block' and a 'process group' component. We will call this difficulty a 'structure clash'.

The solution to the structure clash in the present example is obvious: more so because of the order in which the examples have been taken and because everyone knows about blocking and deblocking. But the solution can be derived more formally from the data structures. The clash is of a type we will call 'boundary clash': the boundaries of the blocks are not synchronized with the boundaries of the groups. The standard solution for a structure clash is to abandon the attempt to form a single program structure and instead decompose the problem into two or more simple programs. For a boundary clash the required decomposition is always of the form:

The intermediate file, file X, must be composed of records each of which is a cardimage, because cardimage is the highest common factor of the structures blockedfile and cardfile. The program PB is the program produced as a solution to example 1; the program PA is:

```
PA sequence
    open blockedfile;
    open fileX;
    read blockedfile;
    PABODY iteration until blockedfile.eof
        cardpointer := 1;
        PBLOCK iteration until cardpointer > block.cardcount
            write cardimage (cardpointer);
            cardpointer := cardpointer + 1;
        PBLOCK end
        read blockedfile;
    PABODY end
    close fileX;
    close blockedfile;
PA end
```

The program PB sees file X as having the structure of cardfile in example 1, while program PA sees its structure as:

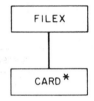

Comment

The decomposition into two simple programs achieves a perfect solution. Only the program PA is cognizant of the arrangement of cardimages in blocks; only the program PB of their arrangement in groups. The tape containing file X acts as a cordon sanitaire between the two, ensuring that no undesired interactions can occur: we need not concern ourselves at all with such questions as 'what if the header record of a group is the first cardimage in a block with only one cardimage?', or 'what if a group has no detail records and its header is the last cardimage in a block'; in this respect our design is known to be correct.

There is an obvious inefficiency in our solution. By introducing the intermediate magnetic tape file we have, to a first approximation, doubled the elapsed time for program execution and increased the program's demand for backing store devices.

Example 4

The input cardfile of example 1 is incompletely sorted. The cards are partially ordered so that the header card of each group precedes any detail cards of that group, but no other ordering is imposed. The report has no title, and the totals may be produced in any order.

Solution 4

The best we can do for the structure of cardfile is:

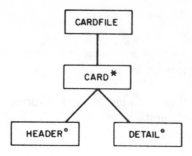

which is clearly incompatible with the structure of the report, since there is no component of cardfile corresponding to totalline in the report. Once again we have a structure clash, but this time of a different type. The cardfile consists of a number of groupfiles, each one of which has the form:

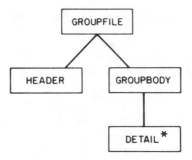

The cardfile is an arbitrary interleaving of these groupfiles. To resolve the clash (an 'interleaving clash') we must resolve cardfile into its constituent groupfiles:

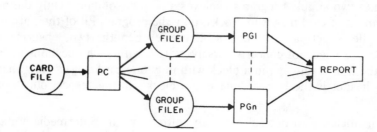

Allowing, for purposes of exposition, that a single report may be produced by the n programs PG1, ... PGn (each contributing one totalline), we have decomposed the problem into $n+1$ simple programs; of these, n are identical programs processing the n distinct groupfiles groupfile1, ... groupfilen; while the other, PC, resolves cardfile into its constituents.

Two possible versions of PC are:

```
    PC1 sequence
        open cardfile;
        read cardfile;
        open all possible groupfiles;
        PC1BODY iteration until cardfile.eof
            write record to groupfile(record.key);
            read cardfile;
        PC1BODY end
        close all possible groupfiles;
        close cardfile;
    PC1 end
```

and

```
    PC2 sequence
        open cardfile;
        read cardfile;
        PC2BODY iteration until cardfile.eof
            REC-INIT select new groupfile
                open groupfile(record.key);
            REC-INIT end
            write record to groupfile(record.key);
            read cardfile;
        PC2BODY end
        close all opened groupfiles;
        close cardfile;
    PC2 end
```

Both PC1 and PC2 present difficulties. In PC1 we must provide a groupfile for every possible key value, whether or not cardfile contains records for that key. Also, the programs PG1, ... PGn must be elaborated to handle the null groupfile:

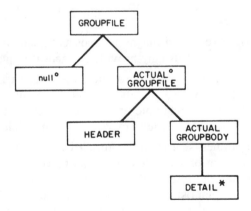

In PC2 we must provide a means of determining whether a groupfile already exists for a given key value. Note that it would be quite wrong to base the determination on the fact that a header must be the first record for a group: such a solution takes impermissible advantage of the structure of groupfile which, in principle, is unknown in the program PC; we would then have to make a drastic change to PC if, for example, the header card were made optional:

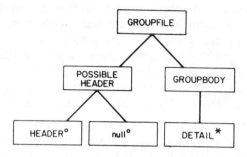

Further, in PC2 we must be able to run through all the actual key values in order to close all the groupfiles actually opened. This would still be necessary even if each group had a recognizable trailer record, for reasons similar to those given above concerning the header records.

Comment

The inefficiency of our solution to example 4 far outstrips the inefficiency of our solution to example 3. Indeed, our solution to example 4 is entirely impractical. Practical implementation of the designs will be considered below in the next section. For the moment, we may observe that the use of magnetic tapes for communication between simple programs enforces a very healthy discipline. We are led to use a very simple protocol: every serial file must be opened and closed. The physical medium encourages a complete decoupling of the programs: it is easy to imagine one program being run today, the tapes held overnight in a library, and a subsequent program being run tomorrow; the whole of the communication is visible in the defined structure of the files. Finally, we are strengthened in our resolve to think in terms of static structures, avoiding the notoriously error-prone activity of thinking about dynamic flow and execution-time events.

Taking a more global view of the design procedure, we may say that the simple program is a satisfactory high level component. It is a larger object than a sequence, iteration or selection; it has a more precise definition than a module; it is subject to restrictions which reveal to us clearly when we are trying to make a single program out of what should be two or more.

4. Programs, Procedures and Processes

Although from the design point of view we regard magnetic tapes as the canonical medium of communication between simple programs, they will not usually provide a practical implementation.

An obvious possiblity for implementation in some environments is to replace each magnetic tape by a limited number of buffers in main storage, with a suitable regime for ensuring that the consumer program does not run ahead of the producer. Each simple program can then be treated as a distinct task or process, using whatever facilities are provided for the management of multiple concurrent tasks.

However, something more like coroutines seems more attractive (2). The standard procedure call mechanism offers a simple implementation of great flexibility and power. Consider the program PA, in our solution to example 3, which writes the intermediate file X. We can readily convert this program into a procedure PAX which has the characteristics of an input procedure for file X. that is, invocations of the procedure PAX will satisfactorily implement the operations 'open file X for reading', 'read file X' and 'close file X after reading'.

We will call this conversion of PA into PAX 'inversion of PA with respect to file X'. (Note that the situation in solution 3 is symmetrical: we could equally well decide to invert PB with respect to file X, obtaining an output procedure for file X.) The mechanics of inversion are a mere matter of generating the appropriate object coding from the text of the simple program: there is no need for any modification to that text. PA and PAX are the same program, not two different programs. Most practicing programmers seem to be unaware of this identity of PA and PAX, and even those who are familiar with coroutines often program as if they supposed that PA and PAX were distinct things. This is partly due to the baleful influence of the stack as a storage allocation device: we cannot jump out of an inner block of

PAX, return to the invoking procedure, and subsequently resume where we left off when we are next invoked. So we must either modify our compiler or modify our coding style, adopting the use of labels and go to statements as a standard in place of the now conventional compound statement of structured programming. It is common to find PAX, or an analogous program, designed as a selection or case statement: the mistake is on all fours with that of the kindergarten child who has been led to believe that the question 'what is 5 multiplied by 3?' is quite different from the question 'what is 3 multiplied by 5?'. At a stroke the poor child has doubled the difficulty of learning the multiplication tables.

The procedure PAX is, of course, a variable state procedure. The value of its state is held in a 'state vector' (or activation record), of which a vital part is the text pointer; the values of special significance are those associated with the suspension of PAX for operations on file X—open, write and close. The state vector is an 'own variable' par excellence, and should be clearly seen as such.

The minimum interface needed between PB and PAX is two parameters: a record of file X, and an additional bit to indicate whether the record is or is not the eof marker. This minimum interface suffices for example 3: there is no need for PB to pass an operation code to PAX (open read or close). It is important to understand that this minimum interface will not suffice for the general case. It is sufficient for example 3 only because the operation code is implicit in the ordering of operations. From the point of view of PAX, the first invocation must be 'open', and subsequent invocations must be 'read' until PAX has returned the eof marker to PB, after which the final invocation must be 'close'. This felicitous harmony is destroyed if, for example, PB is permitted to stop reading and close file X before reaching the eof marker. In such a case the interface must be elaborated with an operation code. Worse, the sequence of values of this operation code now constitutes a file in its own right: the solution becomes:

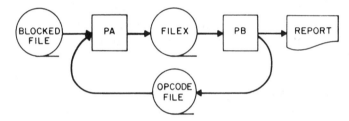

The design of PA is, potentially, considerably more complicated. The benefit we will obtain from treating this complication conscientiously is well worth the price: by making explicit the structure of the opcode file we define the problem exactly and simplify its solution. Failure to recognize the existence of the opcode file, or, just as culpable, failure to make its structure explicit, lies at the root of the errors and obscurities for which manufacturer's input-output software is deservedly infamous.

In solution 4 we created an intolerable multiplicity of files—groupfile1,... groupfilen. We can rid ourselves of these by inverting the programs PG1,...PGn with respect to their respective groupfiles: that is, we convert each of the programs PGi to an output procedure PGFi, which can be invoked by PC to execute operations on groupfilei. But we still have an intolerable multiplicity of output procedures, so a further step is required. The procedures are identical except for their names and the current values of their state vectors. So we separate out the pure procedure part—PGF—of which we need keep only one copy, and the named state vectors SVPGF1, ... SVPGFn. We must now provide a mechanism for storing and retrieving these state vectors and for associating the appropriate state vector with each invocation of PGF; many mechanisms are possible, from a fully-fledged direct-access file with serial read facilities to a simple arrangement of the state vectors in an array in main storage.

5. Design and Implementation

The model of a simple program and the decomposition of a problem into simple programs provides some unity of viewpoint. In particular, we may be able to see what is common to programs with widely different implementations. Some illustrations follow.

a. A conversational program is a simple program of the form:

The user provides a serial input file of messages, ordered in time; the conversation program produces a serial file of responses. Inversion of the program with respect to the user input file gives an output procedure 'dispose of one message in a conversation'. The state vector of the inverted program must be preserved for the duration of the conversation: IBM's IMS provides the SPA (Scratchpad Area) for precisely this purpose. The conversation program must, of course, be designed and written as a single program: implementation restrictions may dictate segmentation of the object code.

b. A 'sort-exit' allows the user of a generalized sorting program to introduce his own procedure at the point where each record is about to be written to the final output file. An interface is provided which permits 'insertion' and 'deletion' of records as well as 'updating'.

We should view the sort-exit procedure as a simple program:

To fit it in with the sorting program we must invert it with respect to both the sortedfile and the final output. The interface must provide an implementation of the basic operations: open sortedfile for reading; read sortedfile (distinguishing the eof marker); close sortedfile after reading; open finaloutput for writing; write finaloutput record; close finaloutput file after writing (including writing the eof marker).

Such concepts as 'insertion' and 'deletion' of records are pointless: at best, they serve the cause of efficiency, traducing clarity; at worst, they create difficulty and confusion where none need exist.

c. Our solution to example 1 can be seen as an optimisation of the solution to the more general example 4. By sorting the cardfile we ensure that the groups do not overlap in time: the state vectors of the inverted programs PGF1, ... PGFn can therefore share a single area in main storage. The state vector consists only of the variable total; the variable groupkey is the name of the currently active group and hence of the current state vector. Because the records of a group are contiguous, the end of a group is recognizable at cardfile.eof or at the start of another group. The individual groupfile may therefore be closed, and the totalline written, at the earliest possible moment.

We may, perhaps, generalize so far as to say that an identifier is stored by a program only in order to give a unique name to the state vector of some process.

d. A data processing system may be viewed as consisting of many simple programs, one for each independent entity in the real world model. By arranging the entities in sets we arrange the corresponding simple programs in equivalence classes. The 'master record' corresponding to an entity is the state vector of the simple program modelling that entity.

The serial files of the system are files of transactions ordered in time: some are primary transactions, communicating with the real world, some are secondary, passing between simple programs of the system. In general, the real world must be modelled as a network of entities or of entity sets; the data processing system is therefore a network of simple programs and transaction files.

Implementation of the system demands decisions in two major areas. First a scheduling algorithm must be decided; second, the representation and handling of state vectors. The extreme cases of the first are 'real-time' and 'serial batch'. In a pure 'real-time' system every primary transaction is dealt with as soon as it arrives, followed immediately by all of the secondary and consequent transactions, until the system as a whole becomes quiet. In a pure 'serial batch' system, each class (identifier set) of primary transactions is accumulated for a period (usually a day, week or month). Each simple program of that class is then activated (if there is a transaction present for it), giving rise to secondary transactions of various classes. These are then treated similarly, and so on until no more transactions remain to be processed.

Choosing a good implementation for a data processing system is difficult, because the network is usually large and many possible choices present themselves. This difficulty is compounded by the long-term nature of the simple programs: a typical entity, and hence a typical program, has a lifetime measured in years or even decades. During such a lifetime the system will inevitably undergo change: in effect, the programs are being rewritten while they are in course of execution.

e. An interrupt handler is a program which processes a serial file of interrupts, ordered in time:

Inversion of the interrupt handler with respect to the interrupt file gives the required procedure 'dispose of one interrupt'. In general, the interrupt file will be composed of interleaved files for individual processes, devices, etc. Implementation is further complicated by the special nature of the invocation mechanism, by the fact that the records of the interrupt file are distributed in main storage, special registers and other places, and by the essentially recursive structure of the main interrupt file (unless the interrupt handler is permitted to mask off secondary interrupts).

f. An input-output procedure (what IBM literature calls an 'access method') is a simple program which processes an input file of access requests and produces an output file of access responses. An access request consists of an operation code and, sometimes, a data record; an access response consists of a result code and, sometimes, a data record. For example, a direct-access method has the form:

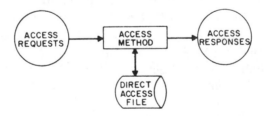

By inverting this simple program with respect to both the file of access requests and the file of access responses we obtain the desired procedure. This double inversion is always possible without difficulty, because each request must produce a response and that response must be calculable before the next request is presented.

The chief crime of access method designers is to conceal from their customers (and, doubtless, from themselves) the structure of the file of access requests. The user of the method is thus unable to determine what sequences of operations are permitted by the access method, and what their effect will be.

g. Some aspects of a context-sensitive grammar may be regarded as interleaved context-free grammars. For example, in a grossly simplified version of the COBOL language we may wish to stipulate that any variable may appear as an operand of a MOVE statement, while only a variable declared as numeric may appear as an operand of an arithmetic (ADD, SUBTRACT, MULTIPLY or DIVIDE) statement. We may represent this stipulation as follows:

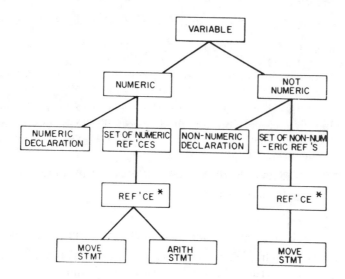

The syntax-checking part of the compiler consists, partly, of a simple program for each declared variable. The symbol table is the set of state vectors for these simple programs. The algorithm for activating and suspending these and other programs will determine the way in which one error interacts with another both for diagnosis and correction.

6. A Modest Proposal

It is one thing to propose a model to illuminate what has already been done, to clarify the sources of existing success or failure. It is quite another to show that the model is of practical value, and that it leads to the construction of acceptable programs. An excessive zeal in decomposition produces cumbersome interfaces and pointlessly redundant code. The "Shanley Principle" in civil engineering (3) requires that several functions be implemented in a single part; this is necessary for economy both in manufacturing and in operating the products of engineering design. It appears that a design approach which depends on decomposition runs counter to this principle: its main impetus is the separation of functions for implementation in distinct parts of the program.

But programs do not have the intractable nature of the physical objects which civil, mechanical or electrical engineers produce. They can be manipulated and transformed (for example, by compilers) in ways which preserve their vital qualities of correctness and modifiability while improving their efficiency both generally and in the specialized environment of a particular machine. The extent to which a program can be manipulated and transformed is critically affected by two factors: the variety of forms it can take, and the semantic clarity of the text. Programs written using today's conventional techniques score poorly on both factors. There is a distressingly large variety of forms, and intelligibility is compromised or even destroyed by the introduction of implementation-orientated features. The justification for these techniques is, of course, efficiency. But in pursuing efficiency in this way we become caught in a vicious circle: because our languages are rich the compilers cannot understand, and hence cannot optimize, our programs; so we need rich languages to allow us to obtain the efficiency which the compilers do not offer.

Decomposition into simple programs, as discussed above, seems to offer some hope of separating the considerations of correctness and modifiability from the considerations of efficiency. Ultimately, the objective is that the first should become largely trivial and the second largely automatic.

The first phase of design would produce the following documents:

- a definition of each serial file structure for each simple program (including files of operation codes!);
- the text of each simple program;
- a statement of the communication between simple programs, perhaps in the form of identities such as

$$\text{output } (p_i, f_r) \equiv \text{input } (p_j, f_s).$$

It may then be possible to carry out some automatic checking of self-consistency in the design—for instance, to check that the inputs to a program are within its domain. We may observe, incidentally, that the 'inner' feature of Simula 67 (4) is a way of enforcing consistency of a very limited case. More ambitiously, it may be possible, if file-handling protocol is exactly observed, and read and write operations are allocated with a scrupulous regard to principle, to check the correctness of the simple programs in relation to the defined data structures.

In the second phase of design, the designer would specify, in greater or lesser detail:

- the synchronization of the simple programs;
- the handling of state vectors;
- the dissection and recombining of programs and state vectors to reduce interface overheads.

Synchronization is already loosely constrained by the statements of program communication made in the first phase: the consumer can never run ahead of the producer. Within this constraint the designer may choose to impose additional constraints at compile time and/or at execution time. The weakest local constraint is to provide unlimited dynamic buffering at execution time, the consumer being allowed to lag behind the producer by anything from a single record to the whole file, depending on resource allocation elsewhere in the system. The strongest local constraints are use of coroutines or program inversion (enforcing a single record lag) and use of a physical magnetic tape (enforcing a whole file lag).

Dissection and recombining of programs becomes possible with coroutines or program inversion; its purpose is to reduce interface overheads by moving code between the invoking and invoked programs, thus avoiding some of the time and space costs of procedure calls and also, under certain circumstances, avoiding replication of program structure and hence of coding for sequencing control. It depends on being able to associate code in one program with code in another through the medium of the communication data structure.

A trivial illustration is provided by solution 3, in which we chose to invert PA with respect to file X, giving an input procedure PAX for the file of cardimages. We may decide that the procedure call overhead is intolerable, and that we wish to dissect PAX and combine it with PB. This is achieved by taking the invocations of PAX in PB (that is, the statements 'open fileX', 'read fileX' and 'close fileX') and replacing those invocations by the code which PAX would execute in response to them. For example, in response to 'open fileX' statement in PB can be replaced by the statement 'open blockedfile'.

A more substantial illustration is provided by the common practice of designers of 'real-time' data processing systems. Suppose that a primary transaction for a product gives rise to a secondary transaction for each open order item for that product, and that each of those in turn gives rise to a transaction for the open order of which it is a part, which then gives rise to a transaction for the open order of which it is a part, which then gives rise to a transaction for the customer who placed the order. Instead of having separate simple programs for the product, order item, order and customer, the designer will usually specify a 'transaction processing module': this consists of coding from each of those simple programs, the coding being that required to handle the relevant primary or secondary transaction.

Some interesting program transformations of a possibly relevant kind are discussed in a paper by Burstall and Darlington (5). I cannot end this paper better than by quoting from them:

"The overall aim of our investigation has been to help people to write correct programs which are easy to alter. To produce such programs it seems advisable to adopt a lucid, mathematical and abstract programming style. If one takes this really seriously, attempting to free one's mind from considerations of computational efficiency, there may be a heavy penalty in program running time; in practice it is often necessary to adopt a more intricate version of the program, sacrificing comprehensibility for speed. The question then arises as to how a lucid program can be transformed into a more intricate but efficient one in a systematic way, or indeed in a way which could be mechanized."

"...We are interested in starting with programs having an extremely simple structure and only later introducing the complications which we usually take for granted even in high level language programs. These complications arise by introducing useful interactions between what were originally separate parts of the program, benefiting by what might be called 'economies of interaction'." ■

References

1. Principles of Program Design; M A Jackson; Academic Press 1975.

2. Hierarchical Program Structures; O-J Dahl; in Structured Programming; Academic Press 1972.

3. Structured Programming with *go to* Statements; Donald E Knuth; in ACM Computing Surveys Vol 6 No 4 December 1974.

4. A Structural Approach to Protection; C A R Hoare; 1975.

5. Some Transformations for Developing Recursive Programs; R M Burstall & John Darlington; in Proceedings of 1975 Conference on Reliable Software; Sigplan Notices Vol 10 No 6 June 1975.

Information Systems: Modelling, Sequencing and Transformations

M. A. Jackson

Keywords: function, hierarchy, model, network optimisation, procedure, process, program transformation.

Abstract: Specification and design of an information system conventionally starts from consideration of the system *function*. This paper argues that consideration may more properly be given first to the system as a *model* of the reality with which it is concerned, the function being subsequently superimposed on the model.

The form of model proposed is a network of sequential processes communicating by serial data streams. Such a model permits a clear representation of change or activity over time, and it also prevents over-specification of sequencing by separating problem-oriented from solution-oriented sequencing constraints. The model, however, cannot be efficiently executed on uniprocessor hardware without transformation. Some relevant kinds of transformation are mentioned, and the derivation, by means of them, of conventional information system configurations from the proposed model.

1. Introduction

The design of an information system may be approached from a *functional* point of view. From the original question 'what is the system for?' we progress naturally to asking 'what should the system do?' or 'what should be the system's *function*?'. Since the system's function is usually very complicated, we seek a method of mastering its complexity, and we find that method in step-wise refinement, or in its homely country cousin, top-down design: a first, gross, statement of the system function is elaborated or refined in successive stages until a hierarchy of functions, subfunctions and sub-subfunctions has been constructed. The fundamental structuring device is the procedure invocation, and the design task ends when the lowest level procedures of the system hierarchy can be implemented by the elementary operations of the available hardware/software machine.

The functional view is readily extended from system design back to requirements analysis, and is widely accepted as the implicitly necessary basis for all thinking about systems development methodology(1). I would wish to argue that this functional view, even allowing for the considerable degree of over-simplification and perhaps caricature in the above description, has severe disadvantages, and that an alternative approach merits serious consideration.

The first disadvantage is that functional design is simply very difficult for all but the most trivial problems and the most inspired designers. By hypothesis, the total function is too complex to be grasped in every detail by a single mind at a single time: how then can the designer, as he makes his first refinement step, have confidence that unforeseen details will not invalidate his decisions? How can he decide which decisions to take now and which to postpone? Consider, for example, the small problem of printing out, in order, the prime numbers up to 1000. Should the first refinement be:

```
begin
    generate table of primes;
    print table of primes
end
```

or:

EHO184-2/81/0000/0139$00.75 © 1978 IEEE

```
for n := 2 step 1 until 100
    if n is prime then print n fi;
```

or:

```
begin
    n := 2;
    while n < = 1000
        do
            print n;
            generate next prime n
        od
end
```

or perhaps something altogether different? Only a prior acquaintance with the problem, or great foresight, or intuition, or good fortune, can guide the designer to the best decision. At the outset of the design activity, when the problem is not yet solved, the set of apparently possible solutions by functional refinement is too large, and there are few, if any effective criteria for choice.

The second disadvantage is that system function is subject to almost arbitrary change: as soon as the system is built, or earlier if we permit it, the customer is knocking on our door with requests for specification changes. Distressingly often an apparently small change in specification causes a large disruption in the system structure: it is not easy to anticipate these specification changes nor to design systems which are robust enough to withstand them. We need, at least, to be able to categorise all possible specification changes according to their expected cost; we need to be able to say to the customer 'these changes will be very expensive, those will be moderately expensive, and those will be cheap'. It is hard to see how this can be done on the basis of a purely functional design.

The third disadvantage appears at first in the guise of a benefit: there is a conceptual unification of the design process from the highest to the lowest level of the system. We may consider each level of the system to be, conceptually, a machine; at the lowest level we have the hardware machine providing elementary executable operations such as add and subtract, multiply and divide; at the next level up we have a software machine built of simple procedures providing such functions as sin, square root, arctan; at the highest level we have a software machine providing the operation 'solve this problem'. Although we may choose, at different stages, to engage in bottom-up or in top-down design, to raise the machine platform upwards towards the problem or to lower the problem level downwards towards the machine, the product of the design activity is the same for both directions: a hierarchy of functional procedures. The crucial disadvantage of this unification is that there is no clear point at which we lay down the designer's tools and take up those of the constructor, at which we abandon the pencil and circuit diagram and take up the wire-wrap gun. The software engineering practitioner always works with pencil and paper—or, if he is in fashion, with screen and keyboard. As a result, potentially valuable distinctions become blurred; decisions that properly belong to a late stage of construction are taken, perhaps unconsciously, in an early stage of design. This is particularly true of decisions about sequencing: the problem of scheduling a multiprocess system on a uniprocessing machine is often solved prematurely, before the processes to be scheduled have been fully understood.

1.1. Modelling

I suggest that these difficulties may be lessened by demoting the idea of 'function' to a secondary role. Instead of viewing the system as primarily a device for doing something, for computing its outputs from its inputs, we should view it primarily as a model of the reality with which it is concerned. The 'function' of the system is secondary, and is considered to be superimposed on the underlying model: a given model can support many functions. Of course, the choice of model must ultimately depend on the functions which the system is to provide, but it does not depend on them in detail; rather, it depends on the customer's view of his world, for it is that which we must model. Modelling has inevitably played an implicit part in all information system design. In simulation it plays an explicit part, and we sometimes find the separation of model from function also appears in a fully explicit form. For example, after describing a job-shop model, Dahl and Hoare (2) write:

'The model above should be augmented by mechanisms for observing its performance. We may for instance very easily include a "reporter" process, which will operate in "parallel" with the model components and give output of relevant state information at regular simulated time intervals.'

The following programming problem is a small illustration.

"An organisation provides resources for use by the public. (It might be, for example, that the resource is a time-sharing system, or boats on a pleasure lake). Each session of use by a customer has a starting time and an ending time, which are recorded, in chronological order, on a magnetic tape file. Each record of the file contains the session-identifier, a type code ('S' for start and 'E' for end) record, in that order, for each session in one day.

"It is desired to produce a report from the tape showing the total number of sessions of use and the average session time. Time for a session is computer as Te - Ts, where Te and Ts are the start and end times respectively for the session."

By considering the function of the program we arrive, with little difficulty, at the following text:

```
P: begin
      sessions := 0;
      totaltime := 0;
      open tape;
      read tape;
      while not eof(tape)
         do
             if code = 'S'
                 then begin
                     sessions := sessions + 1;
                     totaltime := totaltime - Ts
                 end
                 else totaltime := totaltime + Te
             fi
             read tape
         od
      print 'number of sessions = ', sessions;
      if sessions ≠ 0
         then print 'average session time = ',
                 (totaltime / sessions)
      fi
      close tape
P: end
```

This program certainly solves the problem in the sense that it satisfies the 'functional requirement'. But it is not based on any explicit model, and the implicit model, so far as we can discern it, is grossly inadequate. In the specification, informal as it was, a reality was described in which there were sessions of use of the organisation's resource, each session having an individual existence. These individual sessions should have been modelled in the program but have not been: there is nothing in the program which can be identified with an individual session.

The penalty for this failure in modeling is that the program is entirely incapable of modification to meet changed requirements. For example, if we are required to print out the longest session time of the day, or to split the report into two parts, one for sessions starting in the morning and one for sessions starting in the afternoon, or to accommodate an imperfect tape which may contain unreadable records—if we are faced with any of these requests we can only abandon the program and write a new one.

I am suggesting that modelling must not only be more explicit, but must be given a primary position in system design activity. The designer should start, not by considering the required function (what are the inputs and outputs of the system?) but by considering the reality to be modelled (what is a session? what is a customer?). The model is then designed and built in a basic form which is in principle, though not necessarily in practice, executable. The action of the model then reflects the action of the real world: as each session is a recognisable entity in the real world it is in the model; as each session has a beginning and ending in the real world, so it does in the model also. Then, and only then, the function of the system may be superimposed on the model: just as we might employ a human observer with a stopwatch to collect information from the real world, so we can employ a model observer to collect information from the model.

The functions that can be superimposed are, evidently, limited by the model: if the system does not model the individual customers, then we cannot obtain information about customers; if the system does not model the individual parts of the resource (for example, the individual boats on the pleasure lake), then we cannot obtain information about those. How, then, is it easier to deal with specification changes? It is easier because the model is explicit, and defines, as it were, the convex hull of all the functions it can possibly support. With the explicit model we can go to the system user and define the requirements which we can meet, now and in the future, in an easily intelligible way—we can say 'you will be able to get any information you want about sessions, but you will not be able to ask questions about individual customers or individual boats'. The set of functions thus described is readily formulated and readily understood; its simplicity is due to the fact that it is unrelated to considerations of system implementation.

The basic form of model is a network of processes, one process for each independently active entity in the real world. These processes communicate by writing and reading serial data streams or files, each data stream connecting exactly two processes; there is no process synchronisation other than by these data streams. Implementation of such a model on currently available uniprocessor or pauciprocessor machines, requires substantial transformation of the program texts.

In the body of this paper I would like first to describe the basic model in more detail, then to give some small examples of models and superimposed functions, and finally to discuss some transformations by which systems of a more conventional appearance are derivable from the basic model. Related transformations and equivalences among different conventional systems are discussed by Dwyer (3).

2. The basic model form

2.1. Entities

Each independently active entity in the real world is represented in the model by a process. Thus, if in the real world there are customers, orders, suppliers, parts and employees, then in the model there must be a process for each customer, for each order, for each supplier, for each part and for each employee. As the entity progresses through its lifetime in the real world, so the modelling process progresses through its program text; we may, in principle, follow the lifetime of the entity by following the text pointer of its program. If an order has been placed, but the ordered parts have not yet been allocated, then the text pointer of the order process will have a value lying between the part of the program text which models the placing of the order and the part which models the allocation of the parts.

A process may have local variables, which can represent attributes of the entity (for example, a customer's address) or summaries of its history (for example, a customer's current balance). A process is considered to be executing on a dedicated processor; there is therefore no notion of process scheduling or sharing of processors.

2.2. Process communication

Process communication is entirely effected by serial data streams; a process may have any number of input and output data streams, but each data stream is written by only one process and read by only one process. Each data stream consists of a sequence of records, each record being the object of a 'write' and a 'read' operation in the producing and consuming process respectively. The data stream itself is considered to be an infinitely expansible queue; the consuming process is blocked when it attempts to execute a read operation on any empty queue, but the producing process is never blocked by a write operation. The write operation models an action by the producing process which affects the consuming process; the read operation models the readiness of the consuming process to be appropriately affected. Kahn and MacQueen (4) and Hoare (5) discuss some of the implications of such a scheme.

2.3. System inputs and outputs

In addition to data streams which connect two processes, there are data streams which connect the system to the real world. In a pure model, with no superimposed functions, there are no system outputs: the data streams connecting the system to the real world are therefore written outside the system and read by processes within the system. The meaning of the records of these data streams is somewhat different from the meaning of the records of other data streams: they provide synchronisation and co-ordination of the model with the real world. Thus, for example, if the customer in the real world places an order, the customer process in the model must be stimulated to do the same; the data stream input which achieves this is not therefore an action affecting the customer, but rather an action to be performed by the customer himself.

Superimposed functions will, in general, produce outputs. These may be obtained either by suitable output operations embedded within the model processes themselves, or by the addition of reporting processes which are privileged to examine the local state variables of the model processes and to report on their values. We may refer to functions implemented in these two ways as *embedded* functions and *imposed* functions respectively.

2.4. Process classes

Each process may be considered to belong to a process *class* (6). For example, there may be a class of customer processes, a class of order processes, and so on. The class of a process determines its program text, and also determines how the process fits into the system network. Each data stream too may be considered to belong to a data stream class, which determines the possible sequences of records in the data stream: with each data stream class a grammar is associated, and each data stream of the class is a sentence in that grammar. More properly there are two grammars associated with each data stream class, one relevant to the producing process and the other relevant to the consuming process; a data stream of that class is a sentence in both of these grammars. The structure of the program text for a process class is based on the structures (ie grammars) of the data streams which it reads and writes (7).

A process may create a process of another class and communicate with it by data streams. Having created a process, it may subsequently terminate it, by executing a 'close' operation on the data stream read by the created process. A process which is created and terminated within the system in this way may be called a *child* process of its creator. Those process which are not children of other processes in the system must be created and terminated from outside the system, via the external data streams which they read from the outside world. The ideas of set membership and set ownership in database systems may be compared (8).

3. Some small examples

We may illustrate these rather informal ideas about modeling by some small examples.

Example 1

The system to be modelled consists only of a set of inert and unchanging objects: it is a collection of vehicle license numbers made by a young boy for no purpose beyond the simple joys of collecting.

The model is a set of degenerate processes, one for each license number in the collection. The local variables (actually, constants) of each process are the license number itself, the date it was spotted by the collector, and the make of vehicle. There are no data streams in the system and no connections among the degenerate processes. The program texts consist of no more than the declarations of the local data, there being no executable part.

Clearly, only imposed functions are possible in a system of this kind: embedded functions would never be activated. Since the model itself is merely a set of inert objects, with no interconnections, an imposed function may treat the collection as having any desired structure: the responsibility of traversing the set of license numbers according to the requirements of the desired structure lies with the imposed function, not with the model system.

Example 2

The system is a simple calendar in which the day of the week varies over an indefinite period which begins on a Sunday.

The whole system consists of a single process:

```
WEEKCAL: begin
            while true
                do
                    day := Sunday;
                    day := Monday;
                    ...
                    day := Saturday
                od
         WEEKCAL: end
```

This model is, in a sense, complete, but evidently it is not very useful: it is not a real-time model. It executes much faster than the real-world calendar, rather after the fashion of a spring-driven clock from which a naughty child has removed the escapement: as soon as we set it in motion, the wheels revolve without constraint, and hours pass in seconds. To make our model into a real-time model, we must slow it down. We therefore provide it with an input data stream, SRF, from which it will read a record each day. A record is written to SRF from outside the system at sunrise on each day. We may represent the configuration of the system diagrammatically as:

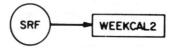

in which we follow the convention that circles represent data streams and rectangles represent processes.

The program text for WEEKCAL2 is as follows:

```
WEEKCAL2: begin
             open SRF;
             read SRF;
             while not eof(SRF)
                 do
                     day := Sunday; read SRF;
                     day := Monday; read SRF;
                     ...
                     day := Saturday; read SRF;
                 od
             close SRF
          WEEKCAL2: end
```

The records of SRF have no content; their purpose is purely to synchronise the model with the real world. Synchronisation is achieved because (a) the process WEEKCAL2 is blocked whenever it encounters a 'read SRF' operation and the next SRF record is not yet available (i.e. the sun has not yet risen on the next day), and (b) we assume that execution of a process which is not blocked is very fast in the context of the grain of time (in this case, a day) for which synchronisation is required.

We may note in passing that a useful embedded function can be superimposed on this model by elaborating the process to produce a reminder each morning of the day of the week:

```
day := Monday; print day; read SRF;
day := Tuesday; print day; read SRF;
day := Friday; print day; read SRF;
```

Example 3

A bank has a set of customers, each of whom has a balance in the bank's books. Each customer may incur debits (for example, by drawing cheques) and may effect credits (for example, by paying in cash or cheques).

The system consists of a process for each customer, each with its own data stream of input from the real world:

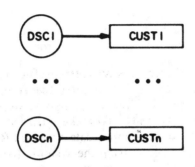

The grammar for the data streams DSC1, ... DSCn is:

    <dsc>::={<transaction>}*
    <transaction>::= <credit>|<debit>
    <credit>::=CR<amount>
    <debit>::=DR<amount>

The program text for each customer is:

```
CUST: begin
          balance := 0;
          open DSC;
          read DSC;
          while not eof(DSC)
              do
                  if CR
                      then balance := balance + amount;
                      else balance := balance - amount;
                  fi
                  read DSC
              od
          close DSC
CUST: end
```

Although there are several processes in the system, they are not connected in any way. Further, the timing of the individual processes is indeterminate, in that there is no well-defined grain of time to which the transactions can be allocated. For a superimposed function to report on the state of a single customer process, it will be convenient to make it an embedded function, reporting perhaps after each transaction or after any transaction which leaves the balance with a negative value. To report on the state of the whole system, however, an imposed function will be necessary: this imposed function, if it is to give valid results, must be executed when every process in the system is simultaneously blocked;

otherwise the reported state of the system may be one which has never in fact occurred.

Example 4

The problem is the same as in Example 3, with the additional requirement that if, at the end of any day's business, a customer has a debit balance of f50 or more then an interest charge of one fiftieth of one per cent is added to the balance.

At first sight, it appears that we need only add a calendar input data stream SRFC to each customer process: SRFC contains one record for each day, available in real time; these records are marked with a day number, and the records of DSC are similarly marked, thus permitting the two data streams to be collated by the process.

However, there is an immediate difficulty. In order to collate the two data streams, the process CUST must be able to examine the *next* record on each; but when the next record of SRFC is for day(n), the next record on DSC may be for day(n) or for any later day. The process CUST is thus unable to apply the interest charge until some indefinite time has passed and a subsequent transaction has occurred.

This only matters in a real-time system. If we are willing to wait, possibly until the end-file marker appears on DSC (that is, until CUST1 has ceased to be a customer), we may be satisfied with the CUST process in the form of a simple collate with lookahead on both input data streams. But this scheme does not satisfy even the weakest constraint of a real-time system: there is no point in time, t(i), earlier than termination of the whole system, at which we can guarantee that the state of the system will be up to date as at time t(j) for some value of $j \leq i$.

Nor do we obtain relief from the general form of this difficulty by permitting a process to test the availability of a next record on an input data stream. Suppose, for instance, that we establish the rule that any record of DSC for day(i) will be available before the SRFC record for day(i+1); the program text for CUST could then include something like:

```
        ...
        read SRFC;   (* SRFC record for day(i+1) *)
                if DSC record alread read   (* must be for day(i) *)
                    then deal with DSC record
                fi
X:              while DSC record available
                    do
                read DSC;
                        quit X if not record for day(i);
                deal with DSC record
                    od (* end of X *)
        ...
```

Ignoring the unattractiveness of this rather disagreeable and messy text, we observe that the expedient cannot be extended readily to the general case. Suppose, for example, that the process CUST1 writes an output data stream which is read by another process P; and suppose that P, like CUST1, is required to carry out certain operations at the end of each business day, and, like CUST1, has an input data stream SRFP. We ought to be able to treat the process P in exactly the same way as we treated CUST1, but we cannot. CUST1 cannot write its output for day(i), in general, until it has seen all of its input for day(i); it can be sure of having seen all its day(i) input only after reading the SRFC record for day(i+1). P's input for day(i) is not therefore available before its SRFP record for day(i+1). We could repair the situation by staggering the different SRF data streams, so that the SRFP record for day(i+1) is available to P later than the SRFC record is available to CUST1, by an amount of time dependent on the speed of the CUST1 processor. Such a solution is clearly unattractive: its complexity will increase with the complexity of the system network, and it forces us to take account of the absolute and relative speeds of the processors.

We will not therefore permit any process to test availability of input records (a conclusion reached also by Kahn and MacQueen (4)). Instead, we will introduce marker records into the data streams to indicate the end of each time interval. Thus, in the present example, we will write 'end-of-day' marker records on the data stream DSC1; the grammar of DSC1 is now:

> <dsc>::={<daygroup>}*
> <daygroup>::=<daygroupbody>ENDDAY
> <daygroupbody>::={<transaction>}*
> <transaction>::= ...

This data stream is readily collated with SRFC. Strictly, SRFC is now no longer required for correct execution of the process CUST1; however, it will often be advantageous to retain a calendar file such as SRFC to provide indications of time structure (such as months and years, or accounting periods) which are not conveniently indicated in other data streams.

Example 5

A lending library communicates with its customers by post. A customer may request a book; if it is available it will be sent to him, otherwise his name will be placed on a waiting list. After a customer has received, and subsequently returned, a requested book, he may request another book.

The system consists of a process for each customer and a process for each book; in addition, there will be a process for the librarian, whose responsibility it is to resolve conflicts among customers who request books on the same day.

The process for a single customer, say C1, has an input data stream DSC1, whose records are the customer actions RQ (request a book) and RN (return a book), interspersed with ED (end-of-day) records. It writes an output data stream DSC1L which is essentially a copy of DSC1, since the customer deals only through the librarian. The process L writes a data stream DSLC1 which is read by the process C1: the records of DSLC1 are the librarian actions BS (book sent) and WL (wait-listed), and ED (end-of-day). A diagrammatic representation of the communication between the customer C1 and the librarian shows:

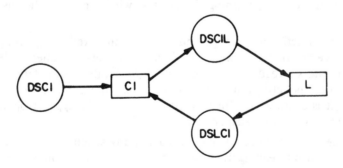

The grammar of DSC1 is:

> <dsc>::= <inactiveperiod> <dscbody>
> <dscbody>::={<loan>}*
> <loan>::=RQ<interval>RN<inactiveperiod>
> <interval>::={ED}*

The process C1 collates its input data streams DSC1 and DSLC1; as a result of this collation, a slightly more elaborate structure is imposed on <interval>, which is then divided into a <waitperiod> and a following <loanperiod>.

The restriction that a customer may not have more than one book on loan, or even request, at any time, makes it possible to design the system without a separate process for each loan. In a sense, there is a separate process for each loan, but it is a marsupial process: it remains in its mother's pouch. If the restriction is lifted, then the loan process must come outside the C process and live an independent life of its own.

The librarian process has an input data stream for each customer in the system, and an output data stream to each customer in the system. Similarly, it has an input and output data stream for each book in the system. The program text of the librarian process expresses whatever algorithm is chosen for allocating books when there is conflict among customers. The process for each book has an input data stream from the librarian and an output data stream to the librarian. It also has its wait list, which can take the form of a data stream which is both output from and input to the book process.

Various embedded functions can be imposed on this system. The customer program may be equipped with embedded operations to allow it to acknowledge requests, inform the customer when a book is not available and the request is wait-listed, send reminders for overdue books, enquire of customers who are inactive for long periods whether they wish to retain their membership of the library, prepare mailing labels for mailing out books, acknowledge return of books, and so on. The book program may be equipped to estimate waiting time (from the number of records in its wait-list), keep statistics on the book's popularity and usage, remind the librarian when a certain number of loans have been made and the book is a candidate for rebinding, and so on.

4. Transformations

4.1. Reducing the number of processors

Information systems do not conventionally have the appearance of the models described above. The most obvious difference is in the number of processors: instead of the hundreds, thousands or even millions of processors of our model, a conventional system has a single processor.

Transformation of a model system to execute on a single processor is straightforward, given a processor of adequate speed and storage capacity. The essential step is to provide a general-purpose operating system, which will manage the data stream queues and schedule execution of the individual processes by the single processor. To a substantial extent, such an operating system is provided in the execution-time support of those programming languages which permit the use of quasi-parallel processes.

Each individual process has an activation record and a re-entrant executable program text, the latter being shared with other processes of the same class. When a process is scheduled for execution, it is allowed to run until it encounters a read, write, open or close operation on a data stream, whereupon it is suspended. On suspension, its activation record will contain the current values of local variables, including the text pointer; it is also convenient to record explicitly the type of operation and the identity of the data stream which have caused suspension.

Assuming a processor of adequate speed and storage capacity, any scheduling algorithm in the operating will suffice which does not permit reading from an empty data stream queue and does not forever ignore a process waiting to read from a non-empty queue. For example, we might use the trivial algorithm:

```
while true
  do
      i := 1;
      while i < = maxprocess
        do
            if process(i) not blocked
              then activate process(i)
            fi
            i := i + 1;
        od
  od
```

In a real-time system in which the smallest grain of time is a day, to assume a processor of sufficient speed is to assume that each day the system would reach a *rest state* in which every process is blocked and further progress must wait until the next day's records become available in the external input data streams. The values of the activation records, in these states, depend only on the model system and its previous external inputs, and not on the scheduling algorithm or any other property of the operating system.

In conventional terminology, the activation record of, for instance, the customer process, is referred to as the 'customer record'. The value of the customer record at any rest state may be taken to represent the state of the customer: for example, the customer has submitted a request for a book, has been wait-listed, and has been waiting three days. Obviously, interpretation of the customer activation record depends on the customer program text, without which the customer activation record has no meaning.

If, as is usually the case, the storage required for the operating system, the model program texts and the process activation records exceeds the main storage available in the single machine, it becomes necessary to relegate model program texts and process activation records to backing storage such as disk, and to bring them into main storage only when they are needed. Hence an operating system must also, usually, include a program loader and a data management system.

A general-purpose operating system of the kind described above is not likely to be satisfactory in practice. The overhead costs of process activation and suspension and of program loading and data management will be severe; also the execution times of the individual processes become important when there are very large number of processes sharing a single processor.

One task of the system designer may be regarded as the resolution of this difficulty by distributing the operating system functions among the processes of the model system. In particular, the scheduling of processes can be wholly or partly determined at design time, and the scheduling decisions reflected in suitable transformations of the program texts. Consider, for example, the trivial case of a system consisting of only two processes:

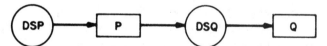

We may decide that the process Q is to be activated whenever process P is suspended at an operation on the data stream DSQ. Q is then implemented as a semi-coroutine (6) in which the 'read DSQ' operations are compiled as 'detach' operations; P is implemented with its 'write record to DSQ' operations compiled as 'call Q' or 'resume Q' operations. Equivalently, Q may be compiled as an 'inverted program' (7) which appears to P as a 'dispose of record of DSQ' procedure; P invokes Q whenever P wishes to execute an operation on the data stream DSQ.

The effect of this transformation is that the data stream DSQ itself requires no identifiable implementation, and that the processes P and Q appear to the operating system as a single process. It is, of course, possible, and it may be attractive, to treat P itself in the same way as we are treating Q, whereupon the model system would appear to the operating system as a 'dispose of record of DSP' procedure: the operating system could then schedule the use of the processor by systems other than the combined pairs of processes P and Q.

If, regarding each process and each data stream as a node, we can represent a system as a tree whose root is a process node, then the whole system can be reduced, by successive applications of the transformation described above, to a single process with a hierarchy of directly and indirectly invoked procedures.

A glaring and intolerable inefficiency in our modelling of a real-time system such as that of the lending library was the introduction of the end-of-day marker records. Although it simplified the programming of the processes, and avoided the need to introduce any dependency on processor speeds, it also burdened the system with a plethora of additional records on each data stream: in many systems, these additional marker records would greatly outnumber the other records.

The markers can be eliminated by suitable scheduling of the processes; one method of scheduling leads to a batch processing system, and another method leads to what would be called a real-time system in a conventional sense of that term. With some simplification, both may be regarded as transformations of a part of the system which has the configuration:

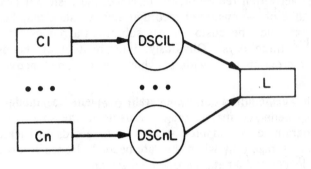

The first transformation, leading to a batch processing system, is to ensure that the process L is not activated until the end of each time period, at which point the data streams DSC1L, ... DSCnL will be known to contain all records generated by the processes C1, ... Cn for that period. The data streams may then be merged into whatever order corresponds to the other of the read operations in L. L can then read from this merged data stream with the normal look-ahead (of at least one record), and the absence of a potentially present record is detectable without any explicit end-markers other than the single end-file marker on the whole merged data stream.

The second transformation, leading to a real-time system in the conventional sense, requires that the process L be capable of accepting the records of its input data streams in whatever order they may be written by the processes C1, ... Cn. L is implemented as an inverted program, appearing to the processes C1, ... Cn as a 'dispose of next record of DSCL' procedure; the merging of the individual data streams to give the single data stream DSCL is accomplished by permitting L to be invoked by all the processes which contribute to DSCL.

If we adhere strictly to the hypothesis that the grain of time is a day, then even in the transformed system L cannot allocate books until the end of the day. It is usual to abandon the grain of time altogether, permitting L to respond to a request record in DSCL before reading the next record of DSCL. The beneficial effect of fast response is then accompanied by two other effects: the possible algorithms for allocating books are severely curtailed, and the action of the system will in some cases depend on the comparative speeds of its constituent processes.

4.2. Program dismembering

Even when the overhead of process activation and suspension has been reduced by distributing the operating system among the processes of the model, there is still a motive for further transformation of the program texts.

When a process is activated to deal with a record of an input data stream, it will execute operations which depend, in general, on the values of variables including the text pointer and the data record. Either or both of these may be already known to the process writing the record, and some improvement in efficiency may be obtained by making direct use of this knowledge.

Consider, for example, the system of two processes P and Q discussed in section 4.2 above. Suppose that the grammar of DSQ, as seen by both processes, is:

<dsq>::={<record>}*
<record>::=A | B

The program text of Q will be essentially the following:

```
Q: begin
      ...
      read DSPQ;
      while not eof(DSPQ)
          do
              if A
                  then operation_a
                  else operation_b
              fi
              read DSPQ
          od
Q: end
```

in which the type of record is evaluated to determine what operation should be carried out. But the program text of P will doubtless contain:

```
...
recordtype:=A; write record to DSPQ;
...
recordtype:=A; write record to DSPQ;
...
recordtype:=B; write record to DSPQ;
...
```

or something similar. There is an evident inefficiency in allowing process P to assign a value to record-type merely so that Q can immediately examine that value. Instead, therefore, of keeping the text of Q as a single 'dispose of next record of DSPQ' procedure, we may dismember Q into its constituent parts and distribute these into the text of P. Thus we would replace the operations

```
recordtype:=A; write record to DSPQ;
```

in the text of P by the operation 'operation_a'. and so on. The process Q would then effectively cease to exist as an identifiable process. It will also, of course, be necessary to replace the operation 'open DSPQ' in P by any operations which precede the loop in Q and the operation 'close DSPQ' by any operations which follow the loop in Q.

This dismembering transformation will not usually be so simple. Suppose, for example, that the grammar of DSPQ as seen by P is the trivial grammar above, but that the grammar as seen by Q is:

```
<qdspq>::=A{<record>}*
<record>::=A | B
```

and that the program text of Q is:

```
Q: begin
      ...
      read DSPQ;
      operation_a1;
      read DSPQ;
      while not eof(DSPQ)
          do
              if A
                  then operation_a2
                      ...
```

In the program text of Q, the determination whether to execute operation_a1 or operation_a2 is made automatically according to the value of the text pointer on activation. Once the program text of Q has been dismembered, P must make an explicit determination:

```
P: begin
    ...
    boolean firstA;
    firstA := true;
    ...
    if firstA
        then begin
            operation_a1;
            firstA := false
        end
        else operation_a2
    fi
    ...
```

in which the boolean variable firstA is a vestigial remnant of the text pointer of Q, pointing to a program text which no longer exists.

An additional motive for program dismembering is due to the limitation of main storage available for program text. It is not usually possible to keep all program texts in main storage simultaneously, even after some have been dismembered. Since program loading is expensive in time, it is necessary to partition the program texts of the whole system into *load modules* which correspond approximately to the text to be executed on a particular activation of the system. In an on-line system, for example, the classical partitioning is into 'transaction handling modules'. To achieve adequate response, the system is scheduled so that on receipt of a transaction record from an external data stream the reading process is immediately activated; as that process writes records to its output data streams the processes which read those data streams are activated; in turn they also produce records for which the reading processes are activated, and so on until the system is blocked. The program texts of the processes activated in this way are dismembered, and only those parts which can be executed directly or indirectly as a result of the incoming transaction type are included in the load module. The parts of the dismembered processes are thus distributed to many places in the resulting system.

The retrieval of activation records and their retention is a function of the operating system which is readily distributed among the processes of the model: each program text is made responsible for identifying the particular process which is being activated and for retrieving and updating the activation record explicitly.

Just as program texts may be dismembered to allow efficient program loading, so too activation records may be dismembered to allow efficient data management. Instead of keeping the activation record of a process as a single object within the data management scheme, the designer may fragment it into parts which can be more quickly retrieved from backing storage. These parts can be linked together in ways which reflect the scheduling of processes: broadly, where there is a data stream in the model system connecting two processes P and Q there will be a link between the fragments of the activation record of P and the fragments of the activation record of Q.

5. Conclusion

This paper has been a plea for the separation of two pairs of concerns: the separation of model from function, and the separation of design from implementation.

There is nothing new here. Separation of model from function is an almost necessary concomitant of simulation programming in one sphere and of database design in another; separation of design from implementation is advocated by many, especially in the fields of abstract data types (9) and program transformation (10).

The greatest difficulty appears to lie in the separation of design from implementation: the transformations involved are too arduous to be carried out by hand with reasonable effort and reasonable reliability, but the choice of transformation is too difficult to automate. Some interaction between the programmer and the machine seems desirable: the programmer's human intelligence chooses the transformations to apply, while the machine applies them with a reliable guarantee that correctness is preserved.

Acknowledgments

In a paper of this nature it is difficult to make proper acknowledgements: readers will be able to identify many sources from which ideas have been drawn consciously or unconsciously. The members of the IFIPS Working Group 2.3 on Programming Methodology have been a source of both enlightenment and stimulus. ▪

References

1. IEEE Transactions on Software Engineering; *Special Collection on Requirement Analysis;* SE-3, 1 January 1977.

2. Dahl O-J and Hoare C A R; *Hierarchical Program Structures;* in Structured Programming (O-J Dahl, E W Dijkstra and C A R Hoare) p219; Academic Press, 1972.

3. Dwyer B; *On the Relationship between Serial and Random Processing;* to be published, 1978.

4. Kahn G and MacQueen D; *Coroutines and Networks of Parallel Processes;* IRIA Rapport de Recherche No. 202, November 1976.

5. C A R Hoare; *Communicating Sequential Processes;* CACM 1978.

6. Dahl O-J and Hoare C A R; *op cit* (2); pp175-220.

7. Jackson M A; *Principles of Program Design;* Academic Press, 1975.

8. Martin J; *Computer Data-base Organisation;* Prentice-Hall, 1977.

9. Guttag J V et al; *The design of Data Type Specifications;* in Proc 2nd International Conference on Software Engineering pp414-420; IEEE, 1976.

10. Burstall R M and Darlington J; *Some transformations for Developing Recursive Programs;* in Proc International Conference on Reliable Software pp465-472; Sigplan Notices 10,6, June 1975.

Two Pairs of Examples in the Jackson Approach to System Development

John R. Cameron

Abstract. The Jackson System Development method develops formal system specifications in a number of distinct steps. The specifications are written in terms of sequential processes; the early steps make a description or model of the relevant external reality; the later steps add the functional requirement; the specifications are implemented in a series of mechanisable transformations. The method is illustrated by two pairs of examples; each pair having rather similar specifications, but different likely implementations.

1. Introduction

The purpose of this paper is to introduce the Jackson System Development method (JSD).

The approach taken is illustration by example; two pairs of examples are presented and their solutions sketched; in particular the comparisons within each pair are meant to be illuminating. Many details of the specifications are omitted, particularly from the second pair. Some important aspects of JSD are ignored. The aim has been to convey the flavour of the whole approach, and to illustrate at least the principal stages of a development.

The underlying principles and their justification are discussed more fully in reference (3).

JSD is closely related to the Jackson method of programming (often known as Jackson Structured Programming, JSP) (references 1,2). JSD can be regarded as an enlargement of JSP. Certainly it is in no sense a front end which attacks conventional analysis or design, delivering up specifications to be solved by JSP. Roughly JSP addresses the programming phase of a conventional system life cycle. JSD addresses virtually the whole of the system life cycle, including requirements analysis, design, programming, but rearranges the life cycle in a fairly radical way (ref. 3) so that there no longer is a programming phase, as commonly understood. Some knowledge of JSP is necessary for the understanding of this paper.

2. Scope of the Method

JSD addresses those systems which are concerned with objects and entities whose behavior and state vary over time. Almost all application systems satisfy this criterion.

JSD does not address the aras of feasibility study, business justification or project selection at the beginning of a development or the areas of installation and acceptance at the end. JSD does address the complete technical development of a system and its subsequent maintenance. JSD therefore does include such areas as requirements specification, functional specification, system design, program specification and program design. JSD is directly technical, but it has important implications for the management of development projects.

3. The Early JSD Steps: Modelling

The first steps of the approach are concerned with building a formal description of that part of the external world which concerns the system. This description is called the model and consists of a number of sequential processes. We will view the finished system as an information system about the real world which is described in the model.

The model description of any entity covers the complete period during which the entity is

This paper is the preliminary version of the document originally published in *Proceedings, 15th Annual Hawaii International Conference on System Sciences*, 1982. Copyright © 1982. Reprinted by permission of Hawaii International Conference on System Sciences.

of interest. Thus if a mortgage lasts for 25 years, the model describes all 25 years.

JSD models are running models. At build time we specify what can happen to an entity. As the system runs, input from the external world tells us what did happen and the model is coordinated with reality.

The system, then will consist of long running processes (e.g. 25 years); the corollary is that the system as specified will only be run once.

4. The Later JSD Steps: Transformation of Formal Specification into Runnable System

A JSD specification consists of a large number (for a DP system perhaps 10^3-10^8 processes) which run for a long time (maybe 10^4 days) and are infrequently activated (maybe 10^{-1} per day). The target environment has few processors (maybe 1) which run for short periods (maybe 10 days) but which can handle many transactions.

The later JSD steps — the implementation steps — manipulates the texts of the specified processes, and add new programs to schedule the specified processes and access their state vectors; these steps transform the specification into a runnable and efficient system.

5. The JSD Life Cycle: Model-Function-Implementation

A development method can be characterized by the order decisions are taken. The JSD life cycle differs markedly from the conventional. Many JSD modelling decisions are conventionally left until a programming phase; many conventional design decisions are late JSD implementation decisions. These differences are very significant.

The basic JSD lifecycle is: describe some abstraction of the real world;

6. The Car Rally Problem

In a car rally, drivers start at intervals from either checkpoint-1 or checkpoint-2 and drive the course shown without stopping. At each checkpoint there is a remote terminal. As each driver passes (or starts or finishes), an operator keys in the car-id; this causes a record to be sent to a single queue at a central computer; the record contains the car-id; the time and the checkpoint-id. a driver scores $A(t_1)+C(t_2)+D(t_3)+E(t_4)$ points or $B(t_1)+C(t_2)+D(t_3)+E(t_4)$ points (where t_j is the time taken for the jth section of the course and A,B,C,D,E are given functions) according to whether he started at CH-1 or CH-2. The program has to calculate each driver's total score and output it to a device which will display it on a scoreboard opposite the main grandstand. Assume that all drivers complete the course correctly.

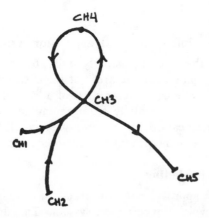

7. The Golden Handshake Problem

A company gives each employee a golden handshake when they retire; the amount depends on the length of time he or she has worked at the various jobs within the company. The career path of all employees is: start as office-boy or as a messenger; promoted to clerk; promoted to manager, demoted to clerk (usually some other title); retires. When an employee starts, is promoted, demoted and retires, a record containing his employee-id, the date and a code describing his new position (OB, ME, CL, MA, RE) is created and sent to the DP department. A program is required to compute the golden handshakes so that cheques can be written and presented at the official retirement party. The golden handshake is $\$(A(t_1)+C(t_2)+D(t_3)+E(t_4))$ or $\$(Bt_1)+C(t_2)+D(t_3)+E(t_4))$ according to whether he started as an office-boy or a messenger (and where t_j is the number of days spent in the jth company job and A,B,C,D,E are given functions). Assume that all employees follow this career path exactly.

8. Comparison of the Car Rally Problem and the Golden Handshake Problem

The problems are identical in almost every respect. The career path of an employee is the same as the route of the rally. In each case the input is a merged serial stream of records each of which has 3 fields, the car-id/employee-id, the ch-id/job-code and the time/date. The same calculation produces the output. Each problem even has a scheduling constraint — output must be produced quite quickly for the scoreboard/retirement party. The only difference between the problems is the calibration of the time dimension. In the Golden Handshake system things happen very much slower. In JSD the specification stages for these two problems are identical; there will probably be a significant difference in the implementation. Note that both systems are real time systems. In JSD a DP system is regarded as a very slow running real time system.

9. Modelling Steps for the Car Rally/Golden Handshake Systems

The terminology of the Car Rally problem is used, although the solution also applies to the Golden Handshake system.

Entities		Actions	
Driver	synonym of car	Start section (j)	SELECTED
Checkpoint	omb (outside model boundary)	End section (j)	SELECTED
		Start course	part synonym
Terminal	part of input collection	Pass checkpoint	synonym
Car	SELECTED		
Section	part of CAR's life		

In the first step, the nouns and verbs from the application area are listed and sifted. Decisions to include or exclude entities and actions are, at this stage, necessarily tentative.

An entity is a noun which performs or suffers actions of interest, in some time sequence. A system output is never an entity. Similarly, what the system does is never an action.

In the second step, the time sequencing of the action is described in one or more structure diagrams for each entity.

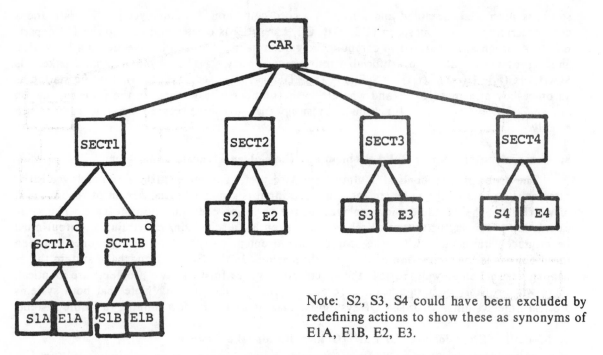

Note: S2, S3, S4 could have been excluded by redefining actions to show these as synonyms of E1A, E1B, E2, E3.

The description so far has been an abstraction of some part of the real world. In the 3rd modelling step, the realization of this abstraction is considered, at least in principle. For each structure in step 2, we aim to make an identical computer process, which is connected to the reality by either data stream or state inspection.

The suffix -O denotes the real world abstraction. The suffix -1 denotes the identical computer process. Here the data stream connection is realized by the operators who create records when a car starts or finishes a section. The level-O model kept separate the end and start of adjacent sections. In the level-1 model the distinct start record is not needed, and the operators do not create one.

At this realization step, the initial abstraction may have to be reconsidered; an unrealizable abstraction is not worth keeping. The analysis of errors also starts here. We have to acknowledge that the bridge between levelp-O and level-1 may be unreliable. These issues are, for reasons of space, not considered further in this paper.

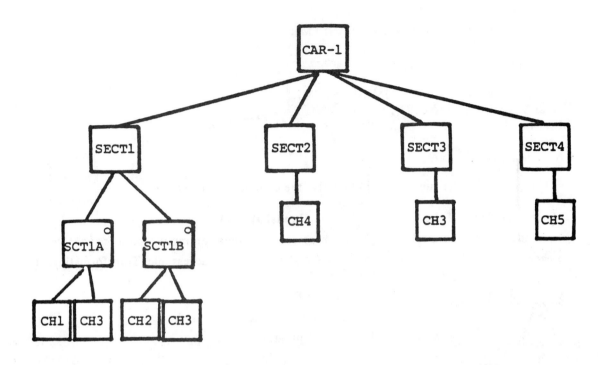

10. Function Steps in the Car Rally/Golden Handshake

The only function in this problem is the calculation and output of the total points scored by each car. This function can be added to the model by simple embedding. Operations, including output operations are allocated to the model process, exactly as in JSP (Jackson Structured Programming).

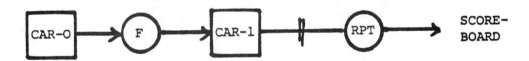

CAR-1 seq
  open F; read F; MARK:=0;
  SECT1 select (CH1)
    LASTTM:= INTIME; read F;
    MARK:= MARK + A(INTIME-LASTTM);
    LASTTM:= INTIME; read F;
  SECT1 alt (CH2)
    LASTTM:= INTIME; read F;
    MARK:= MARK + B (INTIME-LASTTM);
    LASTTM:= INTIME; read F;
  SECT1 end
  SECT2 seq
    MARK:= MARK + C(INTIME-LASTTM);
    LASTTM:= INTIME; read F;
  SECT2 end
  SECT3 seq

The double bars indicate multiplicity

The text of CAR-1 in structure text — a formal pseudo code.

159

```
    MARK:= MARK + D (INTIME-LASTTM);
    LASTTM:= INTIME; read F;
  SECT3 end
  SECT4 seq
    MARK:= MARK + E (INTIME-LASTTM);
    DISPLAY CAR-ID, MARK; read F;
  SECT4 end
  close F;
CAR-1 end
```

This completes the function steps and also the complete specification.

11. Implementation of the Car Rally/Golden Handshake (1)

Scheduling Decision: schedule CAR-1 processes as soon as an input record is available.

Storage Decision: store state vectors (SVs) on a direct access file Transformations to achieve this:

1. Invert CAR-1 with respect to input stream F.

2. Separate state vectors of CAR-1 so that only a single text is used.

3. Write small special purpose SCHEDULER program.

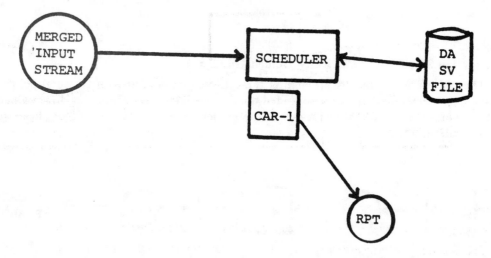

The following SCHEDULER ignores questions of creation, and deletion of processes or their state vectors.

```
    SCHEDULER seq
      open MIS; read MIS;
      SCHEDBDY iter while (not eof-MIS)
        get SV (CAR-ID);
        CALL CAR-1 (SV, MIS-REC);
        put SV (CAR-ID);
      SCHEDBDY end
      close MIS;
    SCHEDULER end
```

12. Implementation of the Car Rally/Dolgen Handshake (2)

The first implementation was an on-line system with immediate updating. This second implementation is a monthly batch system.

Scheduling Decision: schedule CAR-1 processes once per month, allowing them to consume all the input which has accumulated during the month.

Storage Decision: store state vectors in car-id order on a serial medium. Transformation to achieve this:

1. Invert the CAR-1 with respect to their input streams F.

2. Separate state vectors of CAR-1 so that only a single text is used.

3. Write special purpose scheduling program.

4. Implement scheduling program by dismembering it into pieces, part of which runs as program text, part by instructions to the operator.

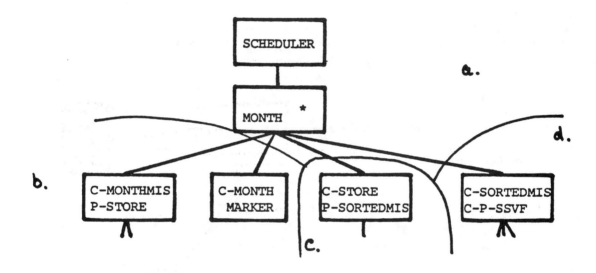

C- means Consume; P- means Produce, SSVF means serial state vector file.

The dismemberment here is in 4 parts. Possible implementations are:

a) By operator instructions: 'each month run b) until the month marker (2nd Thursday of month) and then run the SORT on the stored input. Take the sorted file and input it along with the Serial State Vector File (Car Master File) do d). Keep the new SSVF for next month's run.'

b) Either operator instructions — 'keep input cards on this tray' — or more likely nowadays a data entry program.

c) A standard SORT program.

d) A simple collate which calls CAR-1 to process matched records.

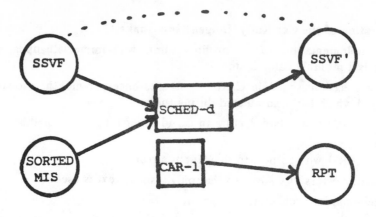

Creating and then dismembering special scheduling programs may seem a heavy handed way of making such simple scheduling schemes. But it is no more than a simple way of writing down and then implementing the decisions which have been made. Moreover, the same scheduling programs may be used for very different applications.

13. Imposed Functions — State Vector Inspection

So far, in the system, there is only one function, which was added to the model text. Other functions are better added by creating a new function process and allowing it to inspect the state vector of the model process. For example we may want to make ad hoc enquiries about the mark of a driver who is still on the course. The extended system specification diagram produced at the function step is:

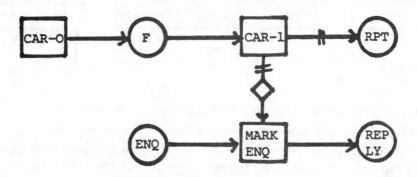

The diamond means that the process MARKENQ can examine (but not change) the state vector of the process CAR-1.

The implementation stage (not done here) must consider the scheduling of both the CAR-1 processes and the MARKENQ process.

14. Comparison between JSD modelling and data modelling.

Suppose that we make the Car Rally problem more complicated (and realistic) by acknowledging that not all cars complete the course, and that some may even follow the wrong route. Suppose that any car deviating from the correct route is disqualified and gets O marks, but that any car who completes the course correctly and passes some further checkpoints is not disqualified and keeps his marks. The new structure for a car is:

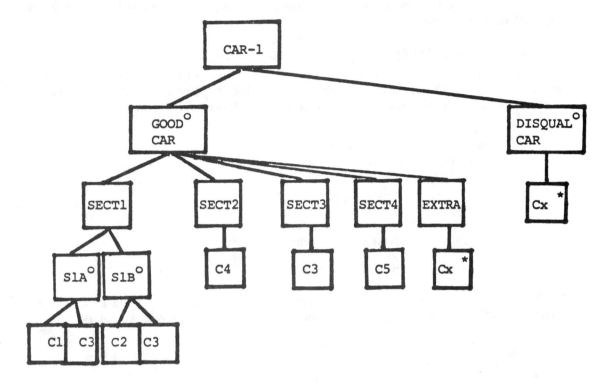

The state vector consists of the local variables of this process (after the embedded function has been added) plus the text pointer: three variable, QS, LASTTM and MARK. QS is the name conventionally given to the text pointer after an inversion.

A conventional solution would start by deciding what data needs to be stored for one car — by making a data model of a car. Perhaps:

MARK, LASTTM, LASTCHKPT, GOOD/DISQUAL FLAG, FINISHYETFLAG, CH3YETFLAG.

Note that:

- The latter 4 variables contain information equivalent to QS.

- There are obscure integrity constraints between these 4 variables.

- In the JSD model, evolution or updating is an integral part of the model; in the data model it is separate.

- The data model can only be constructed by intuitively making, but not writing down the update program.

- The FINISHYETFLAG variable is not needed if the meaning of LASTCHKPT is subtly changed.

- The reasoning used to make the data model is not always clear. Why, for example do we need the CH3YETFLAG?

(Note also that the JSD model has a backtracking problem soluble by ordinary JSP.)

15. Summary of the Car Rally and Golden Handshake problems.

This pair of problems illustrate the following points (at least): long running programs; basic JSD lifecycle of model-function-implementation; similarity of slow and fast real time system; a very simple embedded function, an imposed function, inversion, state vector separation and dismemberment as transformations used in implementation; building scheduling programs

163

during implementation; simple on-line and batch implementations; comparison of JSD modelling with data modelling.

16. An Order Processing System (1): Modelling steps.

The modelling steps are the first steps in building up a formal specification. In what follows, the reader is left to imagine the user dialogue which resulted in the decisions documented here, and also the wrong tracks which may have been followed some way.

Entities	Actions
Order	Place (an order)
Stock item	Amend "
	Delay "
	Allocate "
	Cancel "
	Introduce (a stock item)
	Issue (some qty of stock item)
	Receive "
	Write off "

The entity Customer, who places, amends and cancels orders and the entity Clerk who delays and allocated orders were both considered to be outside the model boundary.

Entity Structures

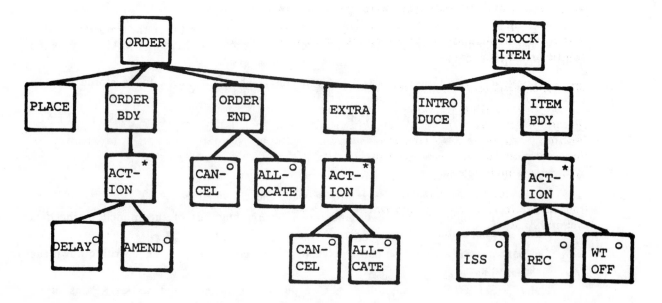

The extra actions in ORDER are there because it was possible for a customer to try to cancel an order after the clerk had allocated it, and vice versa.

Realizing the model

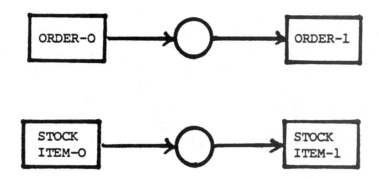

There is no problem creating input records for any of the actions. In the real world the allocation of an order is normally followed by the issue of a quantity of stock. But the connection is not certain; mistakes, strikes, fires can all happen. Such unreliable connections generally stay outside the model boundary and the level-1 processes remain unconnected. The level-1 model is a collection of processes with connections to the real world, but with few connections one to another.

Functions such as the following could be added to this model: ad-hoc enquiries about the state of particular orders; ad-hoc enquiries about the stock levels; apology notes to customers whose orders have been delayed; warnings about low stock levels; lists of allocated orders from which picking lists can be made; etc. The function steps are not considered further here. Nor is the implementation, except to remark that the system can be implemented as a batch, an on-line or a mixed system.

17. An order Processing System (2): Automation of Order Allocation

In this variation we want to replace the clerk by a computer program which will delay and allocate orders. Automation of this type is achieved by an interactive function, the 3rd type of function. An interactive function examines the state vector of a model process (like an imposed function) but also writes back a data stream, which directly or indirectly is consumed by the examined process.

As the following diagram indicates, we can regard this automation, this interactive function, as the formalization of a process (the clerk) and the movement of the process inside the system boundary.

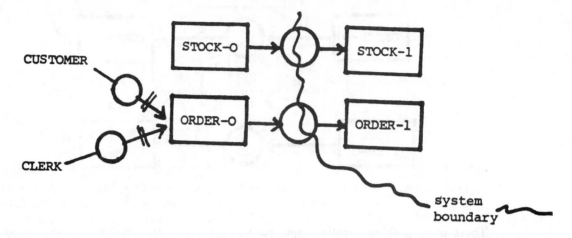

Order Processing System (1)

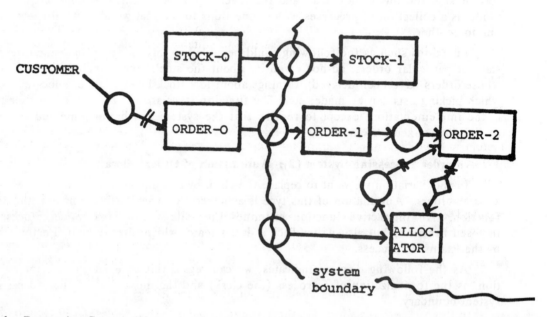

Order Processing System (2)

The ALLOCATOR is, like all the processes in the specification, a long running program, it does all the allocations in the system's life. Consumption of an input record triggers one allocation, in which some or all of the ORDER SVs are examined; ALLOCATOR sends some delay records and some allocate records back to ORDER-2. The structure and text of a suitable ALLOCATOR are not shown here.

CLERK and CUSTOMER are only shown in the above diagrams for clarification and motivation. The real world changes between System(1) and System(2); less happens in the real world of System(2). ORDER-O and ORDER-1 have the reduced structures shown here. ORDER-2 has the same structure in System(2) as ORDER-O and ORDER-1 in System (1).

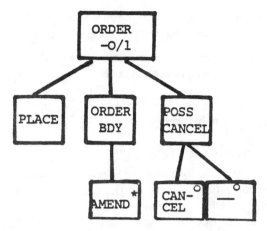

In many systems the extent of the automation is not clear from the start. The Interactive function step, which in JSD comes after the realization of the model but before considering the other functions, gives an opportunity to reconsider what happens externally in the real world, and perhaps as a results to redefine the model of the external real world.

Note that in Systems(1) the CLERK probably uses an imposed function (not shown here) to examine stock levels. Equivalent in System(2) there is probably a state vector connection (also not shown) from STOCK-1 to ALLOCATOR.

The functions mentioned at the end of section 16 can equally easily be added to System (2), except to remark that by the construction of suitable scheduling programs, the specification can be implemented as a batch system, as an on-line system or as a mixture of batch and on-line.

18. A Simple Lift System[†]

A single lift operates in a building which has 4 floors (0 = ground), 1, 2 and 3. The lift system is to be controlled by one or more microprocessors. The system has to switch the lift's motor on and off; set the motor polarity to up and down; it has to switch on and off lamps which give information to the users of the lift.

Input to the system comes from 2 main sources, sensors on the lift shaft and sensors attached to buttons which users press to request lift service. There is one sensor at each floor in the lift shaft; each sensor is connect to a bit which is accessible to the computer system. If the lift is within 6 inches of its home position at a floor the sensor causes the appropriate bit to be set to 1. Otherwise the sensor causes the bit to be set to 0. Thus all the bits are at 0 when the lift is between floors; all except one are at 0 when the lift is at a floor. By examining the bits the system has information about the position of the lift.

In this version, the lift is like those found in old department stores. There are only 4 buttons, all inside the lift. When a user presses the jth button, he want the lift to go to floor j; a device on the button causes a record to be sent into the computer system.

The microprocessor communicates with the motor and the lamps via an 8 bit output port. The meanings of the 8 bits area:

0	Set lamp for floor	0	(= ground)
1		1	
2	bit = 0 : lamp off	2	
3		3	
4	bit = 1 : lamp on		
5	not used		

---

† A lift is an elevator.

6   motor control. bit = 0/1 : motor off/on
7   motor polarity. bit = 0/1 : going up/down

These bits are set and reset directly by the program in the micro. A bit retains its value until it is reset. The hardware environment is such that setting these bits brings about the desired electronic and electric response. A lamp should be on when a user has an outstanding request for that floor. The motor should be switched on and off, up and down in such a way that user requests are serviced in a reasonable way.

19. A Simple Lift System — Modelling Steps

Even when we are given a fairly complete specification, we go through the steps, formalizing each aspect of the specification in turn. In the same way, if we were told that a certain system would certainly be run on-line, we would still start with the modelling steps and the function steps, deferring the use of this information until the implementation stage.

Entities   Actions
Lift   Leave floor (j)
Button   Arrive floor (j)
             Is Pressed

Entity Structures

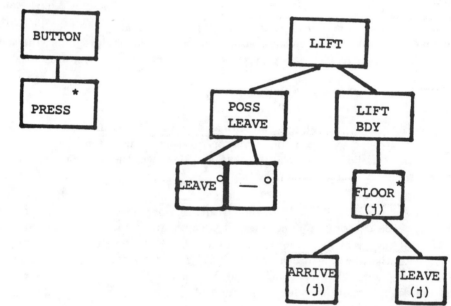

Model Realization

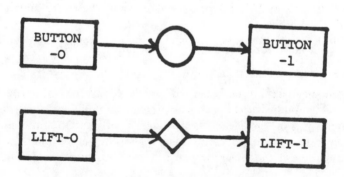

168

Notes.

1. Variable can be included in both LIFT-1 and LIFT-O which stores the last floor visited. The constraints on the lift shaft are reflected in this variable, which takes value O-3 and changes by at most 1 at a time.

2. Actions such as STOP, START and PASS FLOOR(j) might have appeared in a first attempt at an Action List. However they are not realizable in a level-1 model given only the sensors which are described. Either we must succeed in adding the required functions to a realizable model (which in fact we can here) or else we must seek extra means of collecting data.

3. The state connection between LIFT-O and LIFT-1 means that LIFT-1 must have a slightly more elaborate structure.

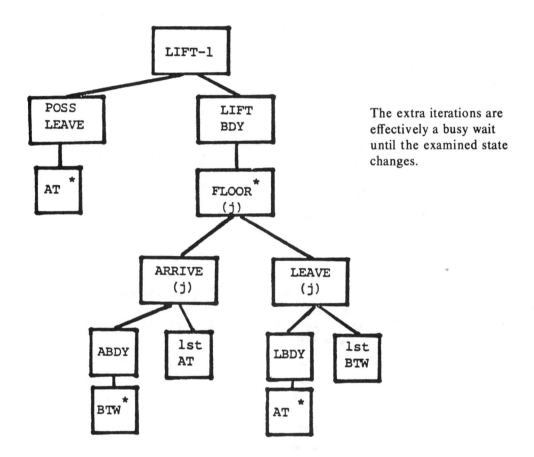

The extra iterations are effectively a busy wait until the examined state changes.

LIFT-1 continually examines the state of LIFT-O, sometimes finding it BeTWeen floors, sometimes finding it AT a floor.

4. The POSSible LEAVE is to take account of the variable starting position of the lift.

20. A Simple Lift System — Function Steps

To complete the specification we must add function processes of 2 types: a more elaborate button process, which embodies the idea of an outstanding request and which will switch on and off the lamp; and a LIFT CONTROL process which will output commands to the lift motor by following an appropriate algorithm and which gets information about outstanding requests from the new button process and information about the position and progress of the lift from LIFT-1.

The JSD system specification diagram for the system

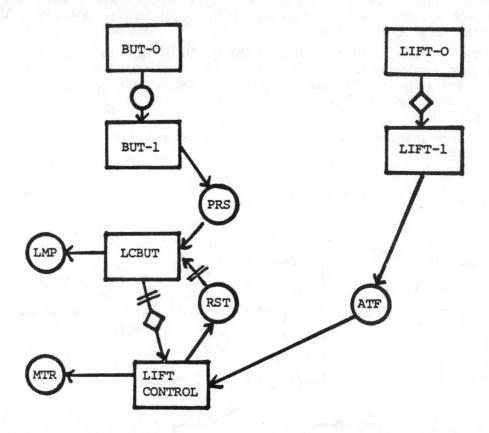

LCBUT is the more elaborate button process which groups the PRESSes of a BUTTON into groups delimited by a visit of the LIFT to that floor. LCBUT outputs lamp commands for one lamp (there are 4 LCBUTs), switching the lamp off when the lift visits the floor, and switching it off on the first press after a visit.

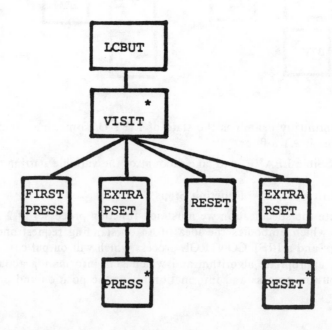

(An important point not considered in this paper: LCBUT is actually reading a merging of the PRS and RST data streams. There is a certain arbitrariness in this merging which cannot be avoided and which has a number of consequences. A fuller treatment would cover the different types of merging.)

The formal specification in section 18 said nothing of the algorithm which should be in LIFTCONTROL, except that it should be reasonable. The following LIFTCONTROL uses the simplest of algorithms: that the lift should wait only at the ground floor; that when there is any outstanding request at all the lift always travels to the top floor, stopping at any floors for which there is a request, and then travels down, also stopping at any requests.

Some important aspects are omitted from the process, so that it is easier to understand the main points: it is assumed the lift starts at the ground floor; no attention is paid to requests made for the ground floor while waiting.

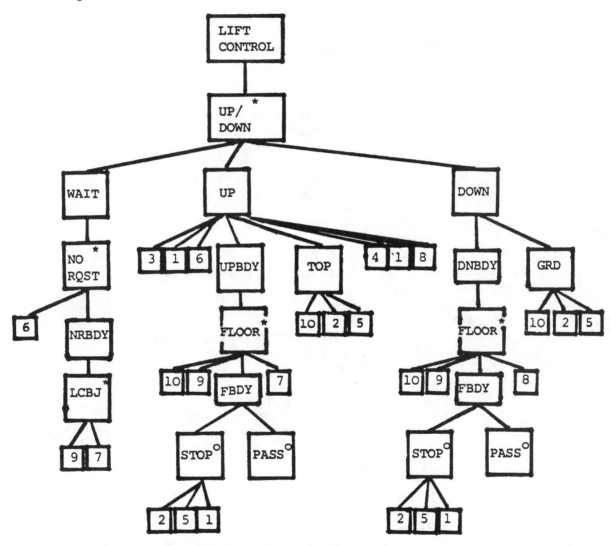

1.	MOTOR:= ON	
2.	MOTOR:= OFF	
3.	POLARITY:= UP	
4.	POLARITY:= DOWN	
5.	write RST(K)	
6.	K:= 1	
7.	K:= K+1	
8.	K:= K-1	
9.	get SV of LCBUT(K)	
10.	read ATF	

```
LIFTCONTROL iter
    UPDOWN seq
        WAIT iter
            NORQST seq
                K:= 1;
                NRBDY iter while (K LE 3)
                    get SV of LCBUT(K)
            WAIT quit (LCBUT(K) is PRESSed)
                    K:= K+1;
                NRBDY end
            NORQST end
        WAIT end
        UP seq
            POLARITY:= UP;
            MOTOR:= ON;
            K:= 1;
            UPBDY iter while (K LE 2)
                FLOOR seq
                    read ATF;
                    get SV of LCBUT(K)
                    FBDY select (LCBUT(K) IS PRESSed)
                        MOTOR:= OFF;
                        write RST(K);
                        MOTOR:= ON;
                    FBDY alt (LCBUT(K) NOT PRESSed)
                    FBDY end
                    K:= K+1;
                FLOOR end
            UPBDY end
            TOP seq
                read ATF; MOTOR:= OFF; write RST(K);
            TOP end
        UP end
        DOWN seq
            POLARITY:= DOWN; MOTOR:= ON; K:= K+1;
            DNBDY iter while (K GE 1)
                FLOOR seq
                    read ATF;
                    get SV of LCBUT (K);
                    FBDY select (LCBUT(K) is PRESSed)
                        MOTOR:= OFF; write RST(K); MOTOR:= ON;
                    FBDY alt (LCBUT(K) NOT PRESSed)
                    FBDY end
                    K:= K-1;
                FLOOR end
            DNBDY end
            GRD seq
                read ATF; MOTOR:= OFF; write RST(K);
            GRD end
        DOWN end
    UPDOWN end
LIFTCONTROL end
```

LIFT-1 outputs one ATF record when it arrives at a floor. When travelling, LIFTCON-
TROL is usually hung up waiting to read the next ATF record. When waiting, LIFTCONTROL

continually examines the SVs of LCBUT(K) for K==,2,3. As it stands, the lift only stops momentarily at a floor. We need to introduce a clock in the modelling steps to allow the timing of a stop.

21. Comparison of the Simple Lift System and the Order Processing System(2)

The patterns of processes in the system specification diagrams for these 2 systems are identical.

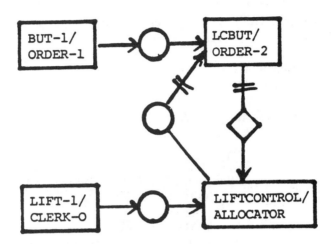

Of course, the detail of the structure and text of the various processes in different between the two systems, but the relationship between the processes is identical.

Note the LIFTCONTROL is an allocator of the single resource, the lift, between the competing claims of the outstanding requests. the LIFTCONTROL can b regarded as the replacement of the manual lift operator in the same way that the ALLOCATOR replaces the clerk, but in this problem there is no ambiguity about what the external real world is to be modelled. The change in the real world happened long before development work started on the Lift System.

The near identity of these problems throughout the modelling and function steps is a sign of our success at separating specification from implementation. Many approaches to system development, even some which claim the contrary, have specification decisions and implementation decision hopelessly entangled. Yet that entanglement is. in my view, one of the root causes of our software difficulties.

22. Comments on the Implementation of the Lift System.

1. In this specification, BUT-1 just copies its input to its output. There are 6 other processes, LIFT-1, LIFTCONTROL and 4 LCBTs. Each can be given its own microprocessor with n-bit communication areas to connect them. A data stream can be implemented as a single message buffer with one bit showing if the buffer is full; data streams of identical records such as PRS and RST only need this bit. SV connection can be implemented as one or more variable in the commarea, which are set in one process read by the other.

2. If a time slicing operating system is available, essentially this same implementation can be run on a single microprocessor.

3. Time slicing on uniprocessor DP systems is often implemented by operator instructions: 'run system A at 6 p.m. every evening and when it has finished run system B'.

4. Inversion is a transformation which introduces suspension points at certain data stream I/O operations. Another transformation introduces suspension point at busy waits which iterate around a SV inspection. With enough suspension points introduced into all 6 processes a general scheduler on a uniprocessor can invoke the processes round robin. More particular scheduling programs are possible for the lift, but oin this case the benefit is not so great.

5. Notice that a deadlock not present in the formal specification can be introduced at the implementation. If no suspension point is introduced within the WAIT iterations in LIFTCONTROL and a general scheduler on a uniprocessor invokes LIFTCONTROL then control will never pass on to the LCBUTs which must be run for there to be escape from the WAIT iteration.

6. One batch implementation of the Order Processing System would have a scheduling program similar to that described in section 12 for the Golden Handshake but with a 5th part to the sequence which runs the ALLOCATOR with immediate further updating of the ORDER processes. An on-line implementation might have a scheduling program which kept everything up to date.

23. Variations on the Simple Lift System

1. A different algorithm: the lift still only waits at the ground floor; when it is busy it only goes as high as the highest request, servicing requests on the way, and then only comes down as far as the lowest request servicing requests on the way. Changes to the specification. Thee are no changes at all in the modelling steps. The model and its realization remain the same. Only the structure of LIFTCONTROL changes, roughly to:

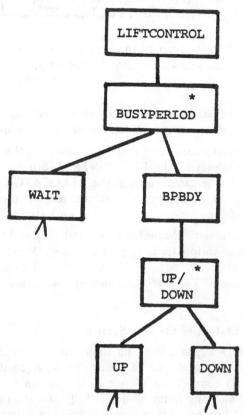

2. A more realistic set of buttons: 10 buttons in all; 4 as before inside the lift; 3 up request buttons on floor 0,1,2; 3 down request buttons on floors 1,2,3. Users press the buttons to operate the lift in the normal way.

Changes to the specification. Remarkably few changes are needed. LIFT-0 and LIFT-1 are unchanged. BUT-0, BUT-1 and LCBUT are also unchanged except of course now there are

10 of them. (Think about this; the buttons have different meanings, as the original 4 did, but they are still only PRESSed and in LCBUT RESET.) In fact the only real change is that the conditions in LIFTCONTROL are much more complex.

These two variations should give some idea of the power of the separation of model and function, the separation of those parts of the specification which describe the external reality and those which contain the information requirement and the invented algorithms. The reader is invited to consider other variations such as the introduction of doors, of a system clock, of safety features etc. None is very difficult. More complex is the introduction in a larger building of a second lift which must cooperate with the first one in some way. (For n floors there are 4n-2 BUT-1s, 2 LIFT-1s in the model; in the function part there are 4n-2 LCBUTs, 2 LIFTCONTROLs and some other invented processes to enforce the cooperation.) Even here some very simple solutions are possible.

24. Acknowledgments

Some of the most basic ideas of JSD are due to Michael Jackson. Other have been consciously or unconsciously derived from a number of sources which are hard to trace exactly and therefore also to acknowledge. JSD has been developed jointly by Michael Jackson and myself. Richard Beck of STL Ltd gave me the lift problem. The other problems and all the solutions are my own.

25. References

1. Jackson M A; Principles of Program Design; Academic Press, 1975.

2. JSP: A Practical Method of Program Design; Leif Ingevaldsson; Input Two-Nine, London 1979.

3. Information Systems: Modelling, Sequencing and Transformations; M A Jackson; in Proceedings of the 3rd International Conference on Software Engineering; ACM/IEEE.

INTRODUCING STRUCTURED SYSTEMS DESIGN

Kenneth T. Orr

INTRODUCTION

In the last few years, we have become used to hearing 'structured' used as an adjective in conjunction with nearly everything. First we had structured programming, then structured design and structured walk-throughs. We've also had structured testing, structured FORTRAN, structured COBOL, structured flowcharts and structured narratives. At this stage, no one would be very surprised if some enterprising intellect were to come up with a 'structured coffee-break' or 'structured exit interviews'. However, it does give you pause for thought when yet another entry in the structured sweepstakes appears. Immediately a number of questions come to mind. Why *structured systems design?* How does it differ from all the other systems design approaches which have been touted over the years? Do we really need another 'structured' anything?

Unfortunately, the structured revolution has been moving so fast that a great many quacks have jumped on the bandwagon. 'Structured' has been used so often as an adjective that it begins to have very little meaning; however, it is the best word that we have. At any rate structured systems design is a new concept; it is not simply just a warmed-over version of traditional systems design approaches. Structured systems design, like structured programming, is hierarchical, modular, and logically organized. In addition structured systems design is also output-oriented and data structured.

Let's discuss the need of structured systems design. For my own part, the degree to which a new systems approach was truly needed was not really clear until it became possible for me to bring the programming problem under control with structured techniques. For as we began to develop better and better programs, it became clear that we were in desperate need of structured systems. At first the shape that structured systems would take was not clear. In fact, we are only now beginning to see what it looks like.

EXPERIENCES WITH APPLYING STRUCTURED TECHNIQUES TO SYSTEMS DESIGN - A LITTLE HISTORY

At the time that structured programming was first beginning to be discussed seriously in the programming literature, some of us at my firm began to speculate about the possibility of applying some of the same techniques to systems documentation, specification and analysis as well. This was natural, since for the most part we were more involved in systems analysis and design than in programming. In 1973, based on a number of documentation experiments, we began to use and teach *structured systems design,* though we called it *top-down/structured programming.*

One of the first things that we discovered when we began to use structured techniques, was that some of these highly touted techniques did not seem to work as advertised. We experimented with top-down design and testing, for example, and we found serious problems with that approach as a systematic means of developing a logical systems framework. At that time we also experimented with the use of HIPO (IBM's Hierarchical Input-Process-Output Documentation Method). We even tried to use the Chief Programmer team organization. What we discovered both gratified and surprised us. Structured programming worked better than we have expected. However, top-down development did not.

About the same time, we discovered another train of research which seemed to fit perfectly with structured programming and structured systems design - the work of Jean-Dominique Warnier and his group at Honeywell-Bull in Paris. While the rest of the world was concerning itself with **gotos** and nested **ifs** and so on, Warnier was perfecting a method for developing logically correct program design structured from the basic data structure of the problem. Increasingly, we adopted Warnier's approach to fit with structured programming and found that our new methodology not only produced well-structured programs, it also fitted together almost perfectly with data base design. Our 'data structured' program even worked well with virtual memory!

Today, hundreds of organizations around the world are using the techniques pioneered by Warnier and by our firm to develop logically structured systems, data bases and programs. Our approach has been to take the best of Warnier's work and fit it together with structured programming and data base theory, along with our own ideas and experiences. The result is a totally 'structured' systems development methodology we call structured systems design. In the past four years, we have gone through at least three versions of structured systems design. Each of these new versions has been the result of learning more and more about the process of analyzing, designing and programming information systems.

THE IDEAS BEHIND STRUCTURED SYSTEMS DESIGN

First of all, structured systems design is a methodology for developing logically correct, hierarchical, structured systems. We started four or five years ago with the idea that what people wanted was a unified approach to building systems. Most data processing managers do not want any 'add-on' approaches. In most cases, they have already more complexity than they can handle. What they do want is an approach which encompasses problem definition, systems analysis, systems design, data base design, programming and project management in a unified package. Structured systems design, then, was built with those considerations in mind.

The second premise that we started with was that whatever approach we came up with, it would have to deal with the real world. We started with the assumption, therefore, that we needed an approach which would not only aid the analyst in designing a system once the problem was defined, but would help find out what the real problem was in the first place.

From our experience with other documentation schemes, we concluded that whatever we came up with would have to aid materially the analyst and/or programmer in doing his job better and easier. Systems methodologies which simply impose a high overhead by forcing the analyst or programmer to produce mounds of unused documentation never seem to have the enthusiastic support of the people who have to make the approach work.

The real test of any approach is to see how well it works in practice. Often when a new methodology is developed, people fail to follow up to see whether it is actually being used as designed. We have seen a great many approaches which, if you talked to the guy who had purchased or developed it, sounded super, only to find that in practice it was being ignored or worse yet actually making things worse. Therefore, we assumed that we would find out a great deal from actually trying these approaches. In fact, we found a great deal more than we bargained for. As a result of user feed-back we actually threw out our first series of structured design and documentation tools and went back to the drawing board. The result has been a new approach which incorporates a new design methodology, a set of systems documentation and design tools, a new set of training courses and approaches, and a new way of organizing and controlling projects.

Any strong systems approach requires a number of factors: a strong theory, simple easy-to-use tools, a straightforward management approach, and a means to perfect the approach as it grows. Structured systems design has all of these. In this section, we will talk directly about these features separately and as they fit together.

Theory

Structured programming is based on a deceptively simple theory, namely, all programs can be constructed from a very small set of logical constructs. On the face of it, this would appear to be a disadvantage rather than an advantage. In fact restricting oneself to a small subset of the possible ways of organization is a means of liberating the mind. What we have found since people began to use structured programming is that it is better to give people a small set of tools that are capable, if used in the right order, of constructing anything no matter how complicated, than it is to try to build large numbers of complicated tools which are good only for one or two tasks. Psychologically, we have found that people are simply not capable of using more than just a portion of the programming languages for operating systems that they already have. What happens is that they often fail to develop good simple solutions because they are confused or uncertain about which feature to use in which order. Freed of the necessity of making decisions about which tool to use in this case or that, the structured designer is in a position to spend more of his mental energies in understanding the problem as opposed to understanding his tools.

By underscoring the importance of correctness over efficiency or technique, structured programming has provided an important basis for the development of structured systems design. Indeed, we have to see that a system can be considered simply as a very large program in which segments (subsystems or programs) are executed at just the right time.

Structured programming provides only part of the theory which has resulted in the development of structured systems design. Another major element is data base management. During the last few years, a great deal has been learned about the importance of data management within a system. Much of this push for better data management has come from data base management systems. Clearly, we have learned just how powerful a logical, well-structured data base can be. The data base management system can provide a great deal of data independence and thereby reduce the cost of system maintenance. However, the major impact of data base theory on structured systems design has been to recognize that every system has a data base which has to be managed. In fact, the most startling discovery has been that only a small part of the data base is on the computer.

Every system, no matter how large or sophisticated, has a data base to maintain. That data base may be contained on a variety of files, some computerized, some manual. The key to data management is not minimizing redundancy, it is maximizing consistency. We have found that it is not nearly so important that a piece of data should only occur once, but that wherever it is used, it is updated consistently. Data base thinking, rather than data base management systems, is the real key to structured data base design.

Warnier's methodology provides a link between structured programming and data base thinking. We have called it 'data structured programming'. This marriage of data base design and programming design provides the framework for logical systems design. These factors allow the systems analyst and programmer a great deal of security in developing systems that work.

It is one thing to know how to develop a correct system given that you know what the inputs and outputs for the system are; it is something else altogether to develop a system from scratch. In the structured systems environment, the key is 'output-oriented' design. All of the major theories of systems design are agreed that the output is the place to start in defining a system. What we have done with structured systems design is systematically to exploit this idea. Structured systems design concentrates on the principal outputs of the system and works *backwards* to design the logical data base, the physical data base, and the inputs of the system. The principal difference between structured systems design and other forms of structured design is the systematic development of the logical and physical data bases.

Structured systems design, then, takes advantage of the theories of structured programming, data management and output oriented design. To make this approach work, these theories must be put together in a workable, manageable life-cycle. Structured systems design places an increased emphasis upon analysis and design over coding and testing. We have taken the ideas of logical structured design in conjunction with *systems teams* and *structured walk-throughs*. The new systems life-cycle is based on the actual management of logical information systems. Unlike many other approaches which have been advertised in recent years, structured systems design has followed up on the actual use of various techniques and management strategies. Increasingly, we have modified our approach to stress not only what to do, but how to do it as well.

Tools

One of the major contributions that structured programming has made to systems methodology has been in the area of design and documentation tools. The original efforts to eliminate **gotos** from programs was to improve the readability of programs. In fact, the first noticeable improvement that most programmers make is in the area of programs that are easier to understand. In short, structured coding makes it easier to comprehend the logic of a program.

With the rapid change over to structured programming and structured systems design, a wide variety of new documentation tools has been developed to aid in the process. Some of these tools are simply design aids, like Nassi-Shneiderman Charts or pseudo code. Others are documentation aids primarily, such as HIPO charts. Others still attempt to aid in both the design and documentation of systems, tools such as SofTech's SADT methodology, and the Yourdon-Constantine Structure Charts and Bubble Charts.

As we have progressed from one level of systems understanding to another, we have evolved a number of new documentation techniques, especially aimed at both the documentation of systems, programs and data. The principal means of documentation that we have arrived at is the Warnier-Orr Diagram. Through the systematic use of these tools, we have been able to make some major breakthroughs in understanding and representing complex, logical thoughts. We are finding it increasingly easier and easier to communicate, since we now have a major new tool for representing problems.

Some examples of Warnier-Orr Diagrams are shown in Figures 1, 2, 3, 4 and 5.

Warnier-Orr Diagrams have been used by ourselves and clients in a variety of different contexts. They have been used to define systems, to define outputs, to define data bases, to define procedures, and to plan projects. They are beginning to be used extensively to design programs in any number of languages. At present, we have clients programming from Warnier-Orr Diagrams in COBOL, FORTRAN, PL/1, Assembler, BASIC and, of all things, RPG 11. To date, the largest single program design I know of using Warnier Diagrams runs 110 pages and 8000 lines of code. Because of their clarity, these diagrams have been used to code as many as 400 to 500 lines of COBOL code per day. In an increasing number of cases programmers are telling us of large programs which run the first time.

One variation of Warnier-Orr Diagrams is the 'assembly line' diagram which we adapted from the works of the relational data base people as well as the Constantine-Yourdon 'bubble charts'. With these diagrams, we have been able to show how output-oriented designs can be understood and used to design complex logical structures. An example of an assembly line diagram is shown in Figure 6.

COMPARING STRUCTURED SYSTEMS DESIGN WITH OTHER STRUCTURED TECHNIQUES

There are so many techniques being used and promoted that it is often difficult to keep track of all the players without a scorecard. After all the variations are considered, the following are probably the most important:

- The Standard IBM/HIPO/Composite Design Method
- The Yourdon-Constantine Structured Design Method
- The Michael Jackson Method

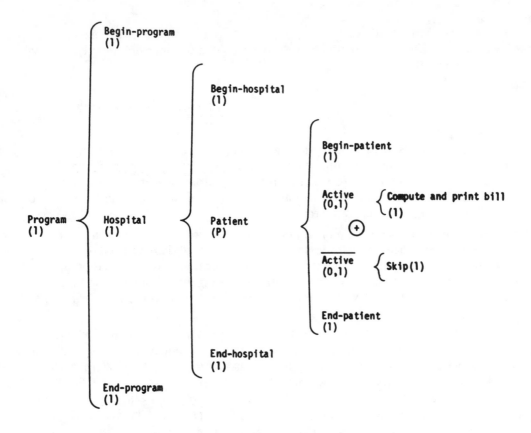

Figure 1: Diagram of a program

- The SofTech Structured Analysis and Design Technique (SADT)
- The Structured System Design Method (Warnier-Orr).

All of these techniques have a number of things in common; they are all hierarchical, they are all design oriented, and they all produce modular systems. However, each of these techniques differs somewhat in what they emphasize. For example, IBM's HIPO and SofTech's SADT are highly top-down, or level-of-abstraction, oriented. The Yourdon-Constantine approach is highly data flow oriented, while the Jackson approach and Structured Systems Design (Warnier-Orr) are data structured.

There are other differences as well. Some of the methods stress the ability to code as you go, an approach that we abandoned as inefficient and in many cases misleading. Other techniques stress modularity and the relations between modules as a principal design consideration. Others, in particular SADT, stress the need for a consistent means of blueprinting a design.

Why do we think that our approach is best? Well, for one thing, it is modeled around the problem. Moreover, it is easy to teach and easy to apply. Many of the techniques discussed above are difficult to teach, and somewhat arbitrary in the outcome. In general, the Jackson method and structured systems design are predictable and understandable. Because of the attention on simple tools which are used for everything, and upon systematic methods of coding from these designs, we have developed a strong track record. Increasingly, organizations previously using other methods have switched over, simply due to the ease of doing things that none of the other methods would allow them to do well.

We think that structured systems design is a far better technique than the others in that it builds in the concept of the logical and physical data base as a natural by-product. Of the other methods mentioned, only SADT gives anything more than lip service to the concept of data base design. In fact, only structured systems design and SADT are really interested in designing a program as opposed to designing programs. The problem, as you will recognize, is a major one.

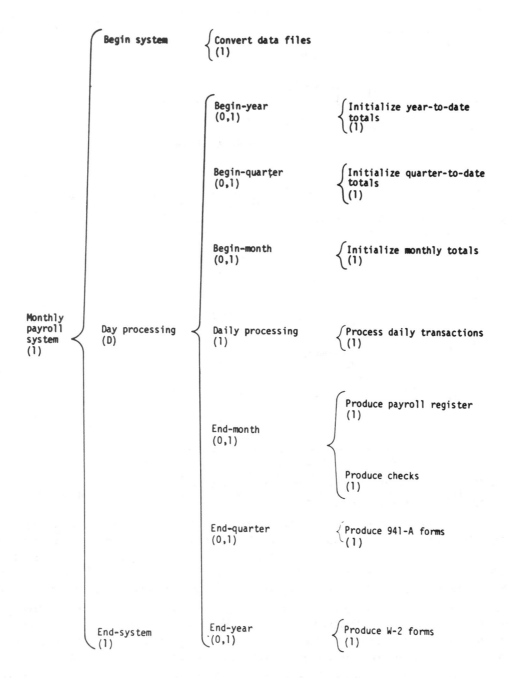

Figure 2: Diagram of a system

The final advantage for structured systems design is that it is a consistent approach. It is aimed at producing a workable manageable system on time. Moreover, we can now say that the programs and files that it produces will be efficient to build and operate. We are presently documenting the efficiency advantages of our designs in a virtual memory environment.

All of the techniques described above represent a major advantage over traditional design techniques. If applied intelligently, each of the approaches will provide you with significant gains. However, in general, the best approach is the one which will give you the best results with the least amount of effort and all things being equal the technique which is the easiest to teach and understand will also be the easiest to manage as well. We have a simple method of inducing people who are really serious to consider us. That approach is to talk to people who are actually using the approach. Unlike many

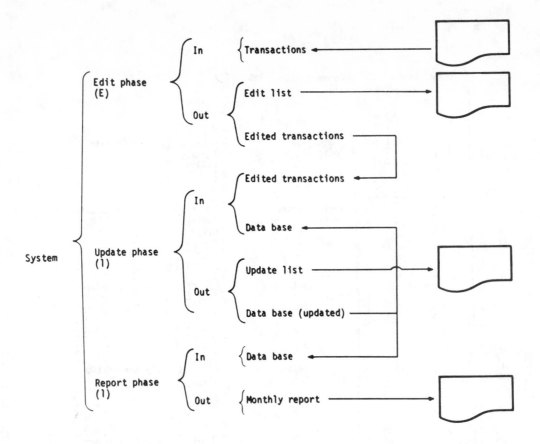

Figure 3: Data flow diagram of a system

approaches which are great to the guy who bought them and imposed them on the organization, we find our approaches being most widely accepted by the people who have to use them, the systems analysts, programmers, and users for whom the systems are actually intended. That, after all is where the action really is.

THE MANAGEMENT OF CHANGE

Those things we can do, we do; those things we cannot, we manage. Yesterday, we managed programming like a hawk because we were not really sure that our programmers could get the job done. Today, we have made some major headway in solving the 'programming problem'. We can now write programs that run the first or second time. Since we can *do programming* we can now turn our attention elsewhere. We can now begin to look at the big picture and begin to manage systems development.

The widespread use of canned systems approaches such as MBA's PRIDE is a signal of the recognition by managers that there must be some order brought into the system function. We are waking up, none too early, to the fact that good systems design can benefit from good management techniques just as well as anything else. Structured systems design makes this task easier by focusing upon doing just the right things in the right order.

The key to the use of all the new techniques is discipline. Like most new professions, systems development has had to evolve a methodology in which a basic systems discipline can be applied. Not surprisingly, the one that is beginning to emerge is remarkably like the engineering discipline which has evolved over the last two or three hundred years. We should not be overly apologetic about the fact that we have lacked a complete discipline. We have made great progress for a profession that is only twenty-five or thirty years old. What we must do is recognize that we are only now scratching the surface of the systems building technology. In five years, or ten at the outside, we will be *writing systems*

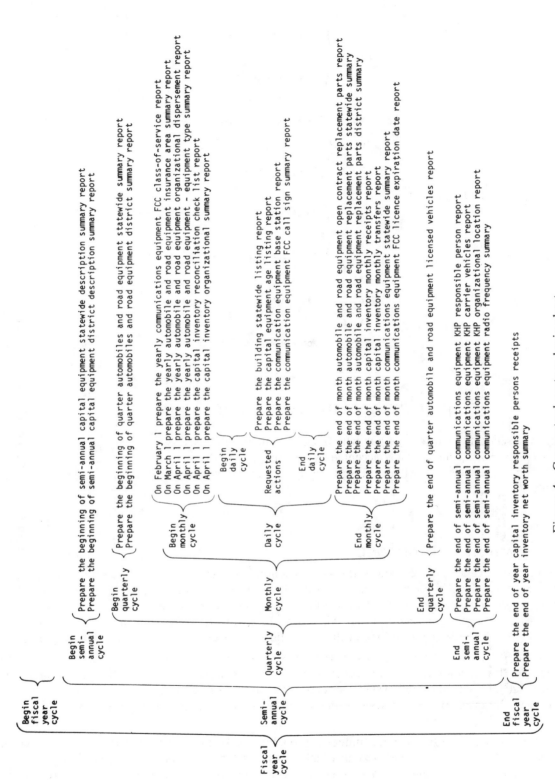

Figure 4: Conceptual system logic chart

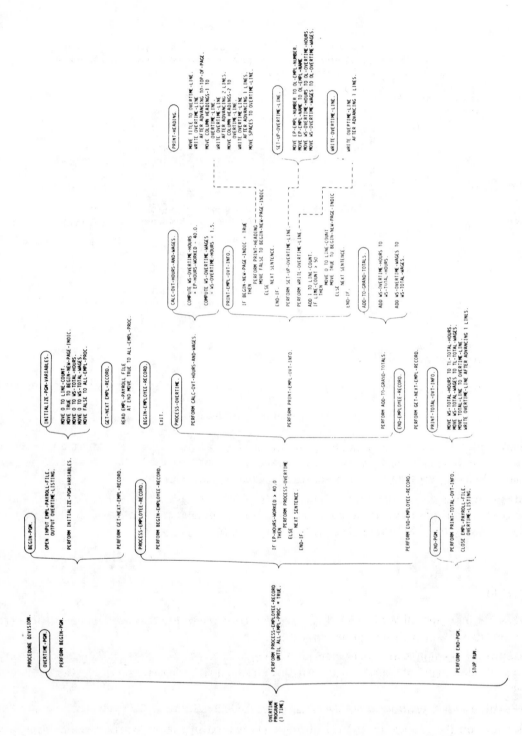

Figure 5: Diagrammatic version of program code

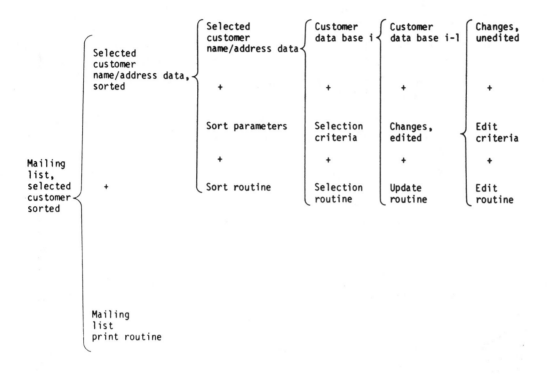

Figure 6: Assembly line diagram

not programs. In ten years, the computer will be 'designing' programs and data bases and even whole systems. In order to take advantage of that technology, we will have to develop a whole new set of professionals: analysts, programmers and, most especially, managers.

Structured systems design is a new way to look at old problems. As such it takes time to get used to. However, as we learn more and more about it, we come to understand how to apply it to solve problems that ten years ago we would not even have attempted. ■

REFERENCES

001 WARNIER J D and FLANAGAN B *Entrainment de la construction des programmes d'informatique* Vol 1 and II Editions d'Organization Paris (1972)

These two books represent a statement of Warnier's LCP Methodology. This methodology, relating the development of logical, data structured programs, is one keystone of structured systems design.

002 WARNER J D *L'Organization des donnees d'un systeme* Les Editions d'Organization Paris (1974)

This book, on the application of LCP to the construction of a systems data base, is a start toward the building of a systems science.

003 WARNER J D *Logical construction of programs* H F Stenfert Kroese B V - Leiden Holland (1974)

The only volume of Warnier's work in English. This book expounds Warnier's LCP Methodology in a very careful manner. While the book does not adopt structured programming directly, the programs developed are clearly well structured.

004 WARNER J D *La transformation des programmes Les Editions d'Organization Paris* (1975)

In this book, Warnier develops a method of modifying and maintaining 'well-structured' LCP programs.

005 ORR K T *Structured systems design* Student Handouts Langston Kitch and Associates Inc Merchants Towers Topeka Kansas (1975)

These handouts show the development of structured systems technology. Included are a variety of 'Warniers' Diagrams, HIPO/DB Charts, 'Structured' Narratives and 'Structured' COBOL.

006 ORR K T *Structured systems design - documentation guidelines* Langston Kitch and Associates Inc Merchants Towers Topeka Kansas (1975)

These guidelines were developed to describe the approach to documenting structured systems effort. Included are examples of the use of 'Warnier' Diagrams, HIPO/DB Charts and the Systems Design Language.

007 TAYLOR B and LLOYD S C *DUCHESS - a high level information system* Proc AFIPS vol 43 (1974)

One of the first articles on the development of a 'structured' data base management system. The paper describes the methodology of structured organization and utilization of data.

008 ORR K T *Structured systems design* Langston Kitch and Associates Inc 715 East 8th Topeka Kansas (1976)

009 TAYLOR B and LLOYD S C *Implementation of the DUCHESS data base structure* An unpublished paper Duke University Durham, NC (1975)

A further description of the use of structured data base methodology employed in the DUCHESS System.

010 BERTINI M-T and TALLINEAU Y *Le COBOL structure: un modele de programmation Editions d'Informatique Paris (1974)*

A description of coding LCP-designed solutions in a 'structured' COBOL.

011 NEELY P M *Fundamentals of programming* University of Kansas Computation Center (1973)

This was one of the first books to use Warnier's methodology in conjunction with structured programming.

012 NEELY P M and ORR K T *A home-handyman's guide to structured programming in COBOL* An unpublished paper Langston Kitch and Associates Topeka Kansas (1975)

013 CAINE S and GORDON E K *A tool for software design* Proc 1975 NCC ARIPS Press (1975)

A description of the use of a program design language (PDL) to aid in the systematic development of structured programs.

014 JACKSON M A *Principles of program design* Academic Press NY (1975)

A discussion of a programming methodology very similar in many respects to Warnier's LCP.

015 YOURDON E *How to manage structured programming* Yourdon Inc NY (1976)

A discussion of the management problems encountered in installing structured techniques in existing organizations. The book describes methods for getting started in a manner which is likely to prove successful.

016 ORR K T *et al* Proceedings of the 1st Annual Structured Systems Design Users Conference Langston Kitch and Associates Inc Topeka Kansas (1976)

USING STRUCTURED SYSTEMS DESIGN

Kenneth T. Orr

I was talking one day with a systems manager for one of our clients when the question arose of how good are Warnier Diagrams. He related this incident: It seems that during the course of a review session, the manager had asked to see the programmer's Warnier Diagram of the program in question. He made some criticisms, at which point the programmer replied angrily, "But you haven't even been to the structured systems design class!" To which the manager replied, "You're right, and I realize that I don't know how to make a good Warnier Diagram from scratch; however, the great advantage of these charts is that I can recognize a bad one when I see it!"

There is a moral to this story: Good communication is a two-edged sword. If you communicate more clearly, people can understand you better, but you also had better be prepared for more criticism. However, it is far better to have people criticize your intermediate thinking than your end product. We have found that it is more important to be clear than it is to be right, for if you are clearly wrong, someone will tell you. However, if you are absolutely right, you may never know it.

My manager friend was intelligent enough to recognize that he himself didn't have the training to prepare a good Warnier chart. Many people are not so observant. Because Warnier Diagrams are so easy to understand, many people imagine that constructing a good one is a simple task. With experience, they do become easier and easier to put together — but never simple.

We talk a great deal about the process of designing and discuss ways to appreciate its importance in systems building. Nowhere is the importance of design more evident than when you attempt to carefully describe a logical process using a Warnier Diagram.

How do you begin? Is there some sort of cookbook to use as a foolproof method? If not, is the process of design even teachable?

Some general rules about constructing a Warnier Diagram can be taught, but they certainly do not constitute a cookbook. Let's take a simple example similar to one seen before. Suppose a user calls me and says, "Look, I need a Project Status Report to keep track of all the work in the shop."

Step 1: Use the Warnier Diagram to sketch the overall problem.

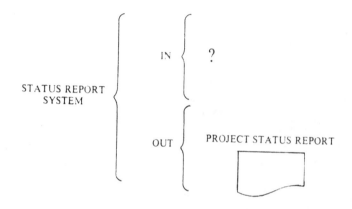

Figure 7.1. Warnier Diagram showing overall problem.

At this point, any good analyst will probe as deeply as he can without offending the user. As stated before, we want to get the user to think in terms of the outputs of the systems and especially of their uses. However, time after time, we find users developing what they think are the solutions to their problems. (I know of one organization that had actually designed and purchased the input forms before they had even talked with a systems analyst to determine the desired output.)

In the requirements stage, the analyst has to act much like a doctor in diagnosing an illness. He must take careful note of why the patient has come in, and he must see if the patient's conclusion is correct. Like the doctor, the analyst must start from where the user is. The analyst cannot browbeat, intimidate, or humiliate the user at the outset. The user has a problem and thinks the analyst can help him or he wouldn't be there. So *the analyst has to guide the user from where he is to where he ought to be to solve his problems.*

Returning to our original problem, you can probe the user with questions such as:

What are you going to use this report for?

What kind of status are you concerned with?

Then, when you are convinced that the user understands his problem,

Step 2: Identify the structure of the output of the system.

You can begin by producing a Warnier Diagram of the hierarchy of the desired output, sketching the overall format of what the user wants.

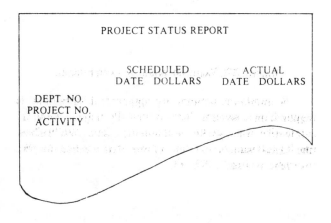

Figure 7.2. Sketch of overall format.

It is important to be very specific about the output, because most people have great difficulty with abstractions. This is one reason why systems work comes hard. At any rate, the next task in this step is to develop the logical data hierarchy for the report desired:

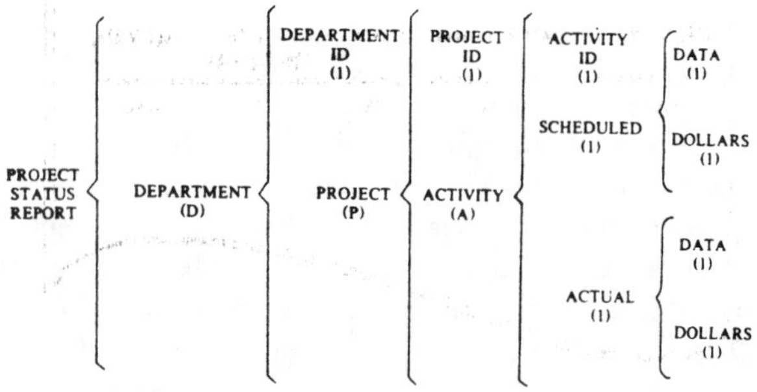

Figure 7.3. Warnier Diagram of logical data hierarchy.

Adding this further definition to our systems chart is usually not a good idea until the user is fairly certain he has what he wants. As you talk to the user, it becomes clear that he has omitted some things from this diagram. For one thing, he hasn't told you anything about the frequency of the output. Clearly, daily is too often for a report such as this; but, on the other hand, monthly may not be frequent enough to allow for corrective action. Suppose you determine that this report should be produced monthly, but that for project management purposes, a Trouble Report should be produced weekly. So you change your systems diagram as follows:

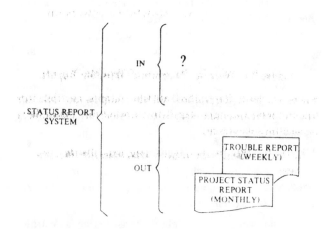

Figure 7.4. Revised systems diagram.

The Trouble Report has the following format:

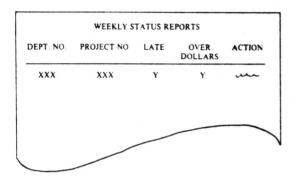

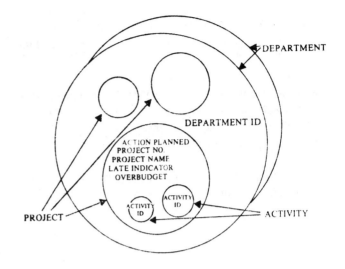

Figure 7.5. Trouble Report.

In discussing this report, we find that a list of projects is derived, with the most serious problems appearing first. The structure looks as follows:

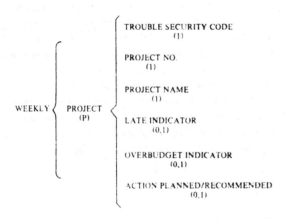

Figure 7.6. Warnier Diagram of Trouble Report.

Since we have determined all the outputs possible for the moment, the next step is to consider the logical data needed in this system.

Step 3: Identify the logical data base for the system.

Figure 7.7. Venn Diagram of system data.

A minimum amount of apparent information is required in a system. This is usually a good point to summarize what we know about that data. We'll show the logical sum or overlap of the data needed for the two reports already defined.

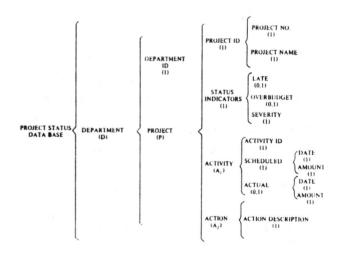

Figure 7.8. Warnier Diagram.

The data items appearing on the far right side of this diagram can be thought of as undefined elements that must be either further defined or captured as input. With the exception of the status indicators, we can

189

consider those data on the right to be input. However, the status indicators are a different story. Let's see how we might assign the status severity indicator. (See Figure 7.9 below.)

From this analysis, we see an interesting thing emerge: The STATUS SEVERITY CODE is a data item that is derived from other data (i.e., LATE and OVERBUDGET). We may find, therefore, that we do not want to store the severity code, but rather to generate it just before we produce the weekly report. In data base terminology, severity code is a "derived" or "virtual" data element.

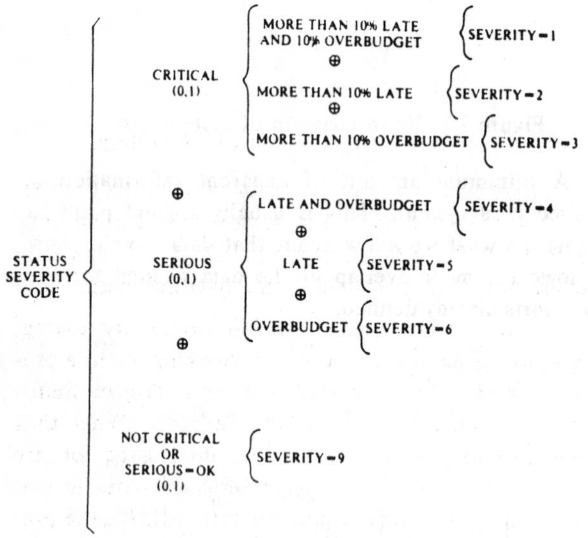

PROJECT OVERBUDGET
{
  TOTAL PROJECTED DOLLARS > TOTAL SCHEDULED DOLLARS { OVERBUDGET = TRUE
  ⊕
  TOTAL PROJECTED DOLLARS ≤ TOTAL SCHEDULED DOLLARS { OVERBUDGET = FALSE
}

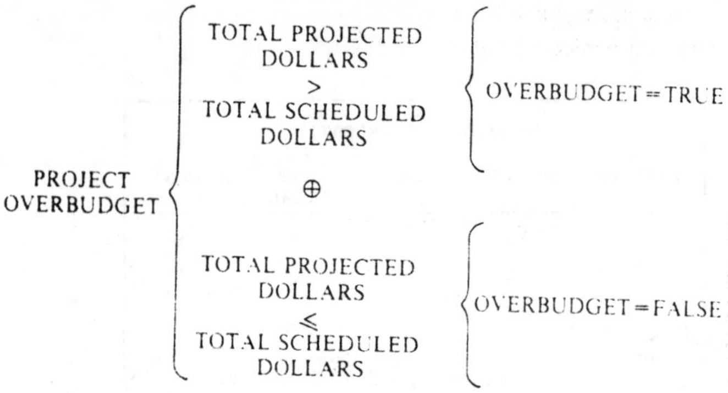

Figure 7.10. Data analysis of OVERBUDGET.

Now we need to go further.

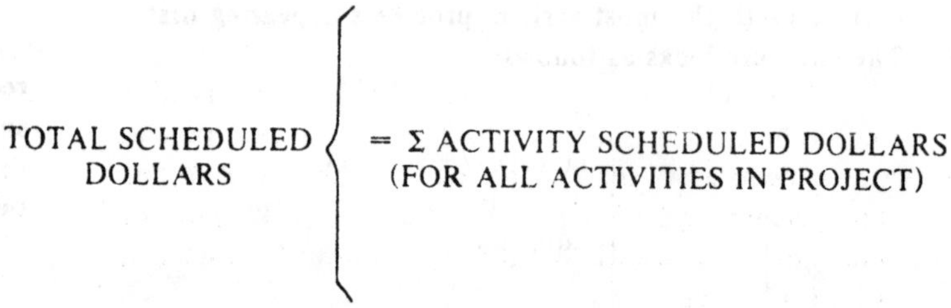

STATUS SEVERITY CODE
{
  CRITICAL (0,1)
  {
    MORE THAN 10% LATE AND 10% OVERBUDGET { SEVERITY = 1
    ⊕
    MORE THAN 10% LATE { SEVERITY = 2
    ⊕
    MORE THAN 10% OVERBUDGET { SEVERITY = 3
  }
  ⊕
  SERIOUS (0,1)
  {
    LATE AND OVERBUDGET { SEVERITY = 4
    ⊕
    LATE { SEVERITY = 5
    ⊕
    OVERBUDGET { SEVERITY = 6
  }
  ⊕
  NOT CRITICAL OR SERIOUS = OK (0,1) { SEVERITY = 9
}

Figure 7.9. Analysis of status severity indicator.

Now we begin to reach the heart of the analysis, the data elements LATE and OVERBUDGET. Let's take the easy one first.

TOTAL SCHEDULED DOLLARS { = Σ ACTIVITY SCHEDULED DOLLARS (FOR ALL ACTIVITIES IN PROJECT)

Figure 7.11. Further analysis of data item.

Again, we've reached a data item, ACTIVITY SCHEDULED DOLLARS, that we know to be input. But what about TOTAL PROJECTED DOLLARS?

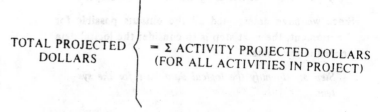

TOTAL PROJECTED DOLLARS { = Σ ACTIVITY PROJECTED DOLLARS (FOR ALL ACTIVITIES IN PROJECT)

Figure 7.12. Further analysis of data item.

How did we come up with the total projected dollars for the project? We began by considering actual dollars by activity and discovered that the method would reveal which projects were critical only after we were finished with the entire project — which is a little late!

In this case, we will have to return to our original report and add projected dates and dollars.

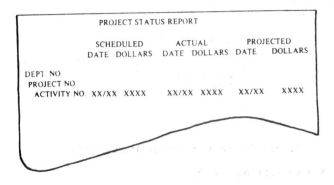

PROJECT STATUS REPORT

| | SCHEDULED | | ACTUAL | | PROJECTED | |
| | DATE | DOLLARS | DATE | DOLLARS | DATE | DOLLARS |

DEPT. NO.
PROJECT NO.
ACTIVITY NO. XX/XX XXXX   XX/XX XXXX   XX/XX   XXXX

Figure 7.13. Revised Project Status Report.

Thus, our analysis of exactly what data we needed led us to introduce data that are terribly important, but not anticipated. This is a normal occurrence. It is just the outcome we want. It is far better to discover an omission early, while we can still correct it. Now dealing with LATE, we have more problems:

LATE {
    EARLIEST PROJECTED
    COMPLETION DATE
    >
    PROJECT SCHEDULED DATE
    (0,1)
    { LATE = TRUE

    ⊕

    EARLIEST PROJECTED
    COMPLETION DATE
    ≤
    PROJECT SCHEDULED DATE
    (0,1)
    { LATE = FALSE
}

Figure 7.14. Data analysis of LATE.

We can see the origin of PROJECT SCHEDULED DATE, but what about the EARLIEST PROJECTED COMPLETION DATE (EPCD)? How do we determine it?

EARLIEST PROJECTED COMPLETION DATE (EPCD) {
    SET EPCD = PROJECT START DATE

    ACTIVITY (A) {
        CRITICAL PATH SEQ. (1)
        ON CRITICAL PATH (0,1) { ADD DURATION TO EPCD (1)

        ⊕

        ON CRITICAL PATH (0,1) { SKIP (1)
    }
}

Figure 7.15. Further analysis of data item.

This chart says that to know the EARLIEST PROJECTED COMPLETION DATE, sort the activities by the EARLIEST PROJECTED START DATE and sum the duration of those activities on any critical path.

At this point, many users probably are saying, "Hey, wait a minute! I didn't say anything about a project network; I just wanted a simple Project Status Report." Would they be right? Partially. What they would like and what they need to do a good job are often different things. Dollars differ from dates in that dollars can be summed to give the total cost for the project. The only dates for which this is true are those on one of the project's critical paths.

After this analysis, our logical data base has more information (see Figure 7.16). The actual placement of certain data structures has been rearranged, because it seems reasonable to put data elements following the data from which they are computed.

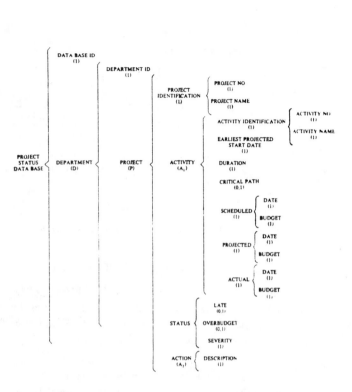

Figure 7.16. Logical data base with additional information.

By studying how the data can (or ought to) be organized from a logical standpoint, we begin to understand more clearly exactly what is required.

Step 4:   Place the systems requirements into a basic systems flow. (See Figure 7.17.)

Suppose we use one of our basic systems models to figure out how to capture the essence of the user's desires:

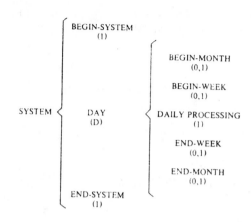

Figure 7.17. Basic systems flow.

We can clearly insert the correct output at the right time:

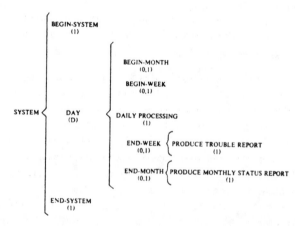

Figure 7.18. Systems flow with outputs specified.

That gives us a consistent place to put the principal output of the system. We know, though, that we will have to derive some of the data required for the Trouble Report and to sort it into sequence by severity.

192

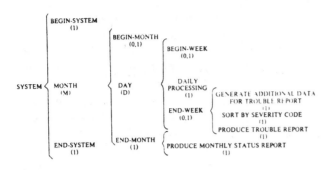

Figure 7.19. Sequenced data for the Trouble Report.

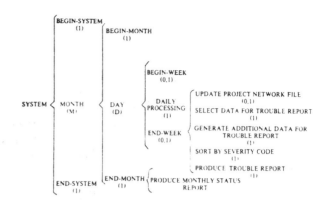

Figure 7.20. Diagram of a project network system.

If we could generate the data as specified in the logical data base, then we would produce the output required with little trouble. But that's a big "if." The next step, with a general picture of the system, is:

Step 5: Look to see if the data required already exists in the organization with the correct units and timing.

One of the reasons that so many fragmented systems exist today is that new applications were not carefully integrated with ongoing systems as they evolved. To make our little problem easier, assume that, after considerable research, we find the instance of a project network system that already maintains, on a weekly basis, the critical path, earliest start, and duration information by project and by activity. We decide to simply access this data rather than to recompute it. Because this needs to be done at the end of each week after updating the project network files, we reflect this in our systems flow. (See Figure 7.20.)

"Packaging" the system is the process of specifying which logical elements get grouped into programs or procedures, and so on. However, it is worth noting now that you don't need or want to make the commitment to packaging too early. All that is indicated in the chart in Figure 7.20 is that certain steps should be done in a certain sequence. In fact, it is possible to combine the various elements in END-WEEK processing in a number of ways. For example, at the extreme side, as in Figure 7.21, we could combine the bottom four elements into a single process.

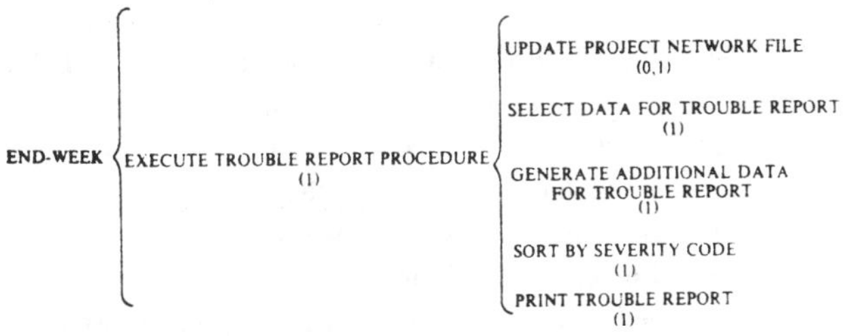

Figure 7.21. Process chart of END-WEEK.

As a matter of fact, the question of whether all this becomes one program or several programs depends upon a number of external factors, computer size, programming standards, and the like. The thing to emphasize is that logically the problem is the same, independent of the packaging. In design, we want to keep as many of our options open as possible. From a logical standpoint, however, doing things in a specific order makes a big difference. We cannot generate the additional data until we have obtained such information as the critical path indicator and duration. Neither can we sort until we have generated the severity code. We must become more like engineers and architects and develop logical, clean designs that flow simply.

After establishing a logical data base and a basic strategy for obtaining this information, what's the next step in structuring our system? It involves determining what will cause the logical data base to change:

Step 6: Attempt to identify what real world events will affect the logical data base and how.

We know from our previous analysis the minimum data needed to meet the user's output requirements. Now we need to consider exactly what things can affect that data. To start, consider the following chart:

EVENT	WHAT DATA	WHEN

Figure 7.22. Event analysis chart.

This chart indicates that we need to know all of the real world events that can affect our data base, including when each occurs and what data it affects. To reach this point, we work backwards from the logical data phase that tells just which sets of data we need to capture and maintain. For example, from our earlier chart, we know that we need data by department, by project, and by activity. Within the category "activity," we need data on scheduled, projected, and actual dates and dollars.

A word of warning at this point: One of our most common problems in getting users and analysis to strictly follow this approach is their desire to guess about the future. It is very hard to get people to settle for just the information that they know they need. Time after time, we hear experienced people saying, "Well, we might as well put X in there because we know we're going to need it someday." However, someday may never come; and if it does, the likelihood will be that we have collected the wrong information. Even if we haven't erred in collecting information, it won't be right if we haven't been using and maintaining the data, and data which are not used will not be correct.

Anyway, given that we have the strength of will to resist collecting a lot of data the system doesn't require, we then ask which events in the real world affect departments? projects? activities? Organizations do change, if only slowly, so we must provide for adding, modifying and deleting departments. We should not be allowed to delete a department unless all of their projects are either completed, terminated, or reassigned. On the other hand, we don't need to put a department on the file

unless they have at least one project.

How about projects? The same thing is true. Projects are added, modified, and deleted. Moreover, they have subsidiary activities, so the same general rules pertain to deleting projects as to departments, i.e., all of the activities should have terminated or been completed before we can delete a project. On the other hand, we may want to add a project without any activities, just for budgeting purposes. (However, would this make any sense from a project status standpoint?)

The same thinking applies to activities as well. We would need to identify all of the various events that can affect activities and how they would affect activities. We might never want to delete an activity after it had been placed on the file, so that even if its duration were set to zero, we would know that we had guessed wrong about the need for certain activities.

More of the events that affect our data base will occur in the area of modifications to activities, followed closely in frequency by modifications to projects. At this stage, we suggest that you think of all the things that can happen to the data base, including such events as completion, termination, reestimating, and rescheduling... *Rescheduling?* But we don't have any output that reflects rescheduling! Right! What do we do about it? We go back and see how to fit it in.

To avoid surprises, we must watch for potential errors in a systems design process. I remember seeing a classification of typical kinds of errors into four causes: clerical, consistency, communication, and completeness. Of the four, errors in communication and in completeness hurt the most. We can generally solve problems of clerical and consistency errors, *if we know what the problem actually is.* However, if we fail to obtain the right parameters, no amount of technical genius is apt to help us very much. By the real world changes, we can improve both the communication and the completeness of the systems design.

Step 7: Place logical updating actions into basic systems hierarchy.

We can suppose that our event analysis leads to a list of actions having to do with updating the various logical pieces of data in the data base. The next step, then, involves placing those logical updating actions in the correct location within the systems chart. For example, suppose that we decided to accept and edit all information immediately, but actually update project and activity data weekly before the production of the Trouble Report, and update department information only monthly before the Monthly Status Report.

For the moment, let's leave the design alone with the logical steps already specified. After considering where we are and how quickly we've reached this point, you must realize that we're doing all this on paper. As a matter of fact, this is about the point at which something unexpected usually happens. Typically, if the user for whom we've been working isn't reassigned, then somebody changes the definition, or we discover something rather important from just thinking about the problem in greater detail.

For our project, we have reached the point where the user, with our help, suddenly discovers that we're missing an important piece of information. "You know," he says, "we really need another set of dates and dollars in addition to scheduled, projected, and actual; we need revised dates and dollars!" Of course, he's right. To have a meaningful project status system, you must have the ability to change the schedule as you learn what the real system will look like. On the other hand, you need to remember what you originally projected, because that will help you see what was faulty in your original planning.

for in most cases we simply have to take their new requirements into account. Clearly, this is not always possible. Sometimes we must say to the user, "We can't make that change to this version of the system; however, we'll start working on it as soon as we get the current (first) version of the system installed." But in most cases, changing is not catastrophic, but failing to produce a correct system is.

Suppose we want to make a change to the systems design. How do we incorporate it into our current systems design? The answer is: *Start at the beginning of the systems procedure and go through the same steps with this new requirement as with the original specifications*, until we can stop.

First, we must reflect the additional information in the output. The addition of revised (scheduled) dates and dollars requires modifying the Monthly Project Status Report.

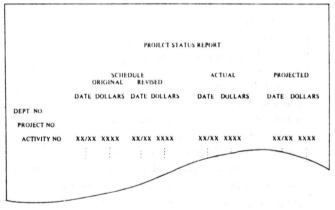

Figure 7.24. Revised Project Status Report.

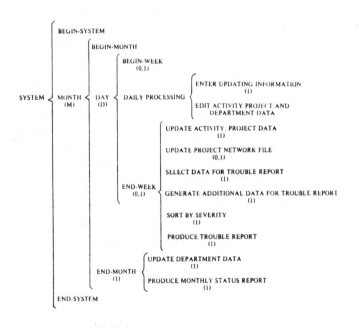

Figure 7.23. Systems chart with logical updating actions.

Now we see that we need to revise our system — and we haven't even gotten it into programming. As a matter of fact, maintenance of a systems design begins nearly as soon as you get the first design down on paper. Often people forget; sometimes they choose not to remember; sometimes things just change. No matter,

What about the data base? Clearly, we need to modify the data base as well. To keep it simple, we'll just show the data by activity. (See Figure 7.25.)

The process of applying structured systems design is a systematic one. It is a method of working from outputs to inputs, from the known to derive the unknown. One of the principal advantages of this approach over many others is that there are fewer points from which you must start over. As in the example below, you have to make changes or start over every time some new output is required, or the manner of deriving output is changed. But changes are *designed into* the system. This represents a significant advantage in the development of correct, rational systems. Too often in the past, we have simply added new features onto an existing system without thinking through what impact those changes are likely to have on the system as a whole. As a result, we have introduced a great deal of redundancy (and error) into our systems and, at the same time, have made them nearly unintelligible.

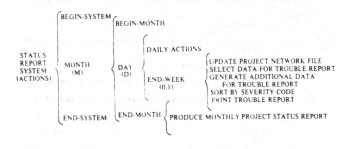

Figure 7.26. Systems description of actions and data elements

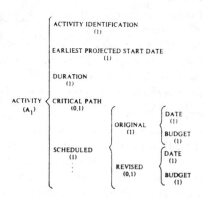

Figure 7.25. Data base diagram activity.

In a structured systems design, each action has its own place(s), as does each piece of data. Each change in the output, in the way output is derived, or in the events reflected in the output causes a well-defined change in the systems design and/or the systems data base. The systems design directly reflects the requirements of the system. If it doesn't, we have a complex system and we know we are going to have extreme difficulty in making complex systems work.

The process of producing a correct systems design, given a clear understanding of the user's requirements, is a kind of giant logical puzzle. But it does have a solution. Structured systems design, structured data base design, and data structured programming are methods of arriving at well-defined logical solutions to complex systems problems.

Our systems description, if it is to be comprehensive, must provide the complete and exhaustive statement of each action and data element.

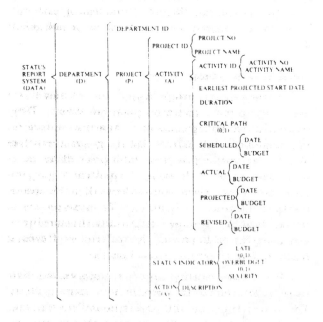

Figure 7.27. Complete systems description.

To restate the process of applying structured systems design, we can use a Warnier Diagram:

196

```
        ┌ USE WARNIER DIAGRAM TO STATE GENERAL PROBLEM
        │
        │ IDENTIFY THE STRUCTURE (AND FREQUENCY) OF THE SYSTEMS
        │    OUTPUTS
        │
        │ IDENTIFY THE LOGICAL DATA BASE OF THE SYSTEM
LOGICAL │
DESIGN ─┤ PLACE THE SYSTEMS REQUIREMENTS INTO A BASIC SYSTEMS FLOW
CYCLE   │    HIERARCHY
 (C)    │
        │ LOOK TO SEE IF DATA REQUIRED ALREADY EXISTS
        │
        │ IDENTIFY EVENTS IN REAL WORLD WHICH AFFECT THE DATA BASE
        │
        └ PLACE LOGICAL UPDATING ACTIONS INTO BASIC SYSTEMS HIERARCHY
```

Figure 7.28. Warnier Diagram of the logical design process.

As you can see, we don't assume that we can go through the design process only once. The design cycle should be repeated for each new output, going only as far as you have to. Indeed, many traditional systems approaches fail simply because management assumes, wrongly, that one pass through the design approach will work. In fact, it rarely does work, and we should admit it.

Correctness in systems design

A few years ago, people began asking whether there was a way to prove that a program was correct. They recognized that testing could only show that no failures had been discovered, but not that the program was free of error, no matter how much testing was done. So a whole new school of addressing the problem of program correctness arose. Since most of the work in this area is highly mathematical, it is difficult for many people to follow. However, Warnier's logical data structured programming has made proving the correctness of even a relatively large program a practical matter.

We are now entering an era in which we will have to be able to prove the correctness of entire systems. This is especially true with respect to on-line, real-time systems that handle such life-and-death situations as air-traffic control, patient monitoring, or electronic funds transfer. Clearly, the proof of correctness of large systems is a major undertaking, a subject impossible to address in this book. However, a number of insights allow us to consider for the first time the meaning of the correctness of systems and of the data within the system.

As stated earlier, correct systems design involves getting the right sets of actions done on the right sets of data at the right time. Thus, if we can prove that we have a systems framework in which this must happen, then we will have achieved our basic objective. But what does this mean? If we have a correct logical expression of our problem, we can ensure that that description is carried throughout the system itself using the same tools at the systems level as are employed at the program level.

The entire structured revolution began, in part, as an outgrowth of many people attempting to establish the correctness of program designs. Over the last ten years, this approach has produced many interesting results. Curiously, the area which first attracted attention, i.e., the proof of mathematical and scientific programs, is not the one in which the greatest gains have been made. For a variety of reasons, scientific and mathematical programming proofs of correctness are hard to come by. However, for the bulk of our work (the development of business and commercial programs), Warnier's methodology, built upon the mathematical foundations of set theory, represents a remarkable breakthrough.

A few years ago, the mere idea of establishing the correctness of an entire system would have been unthinkable. Indeed, until quite recently, we did not even have a reasonable idea of how a correct system might look. By recognizing that a correct system is one in which the right sets of actions are done on the right sets of data at the right time, we are now in a position to look more seriously at what it might be like to develop a correct system. Indeed, we can see now that developing a correct system is largely a matter of the proper grouping (structuring) of sets of actions (programs, procedures) and sets of data (data bases, files, records) in such a way that we can assure that all of the logical requirements of the system are met.

For example, in the system we have been developing to produce project status information, we have been continuously concerned to make sure that each set of data and each set of actions which we have defined had a logical placement within the systems or data base framework. This insistence on correct grouping and ordering provides the proof of correctness that the system will do exactly what is required, and nothing else.

The emphasis upon logical correctness, coupled with the appropriate tools, has begun to yield significant results. One is the growing awareness that most systems in business applications fall into predictable patterns, based on time. In case after case, we find systems whose basic chart looks like the one below:

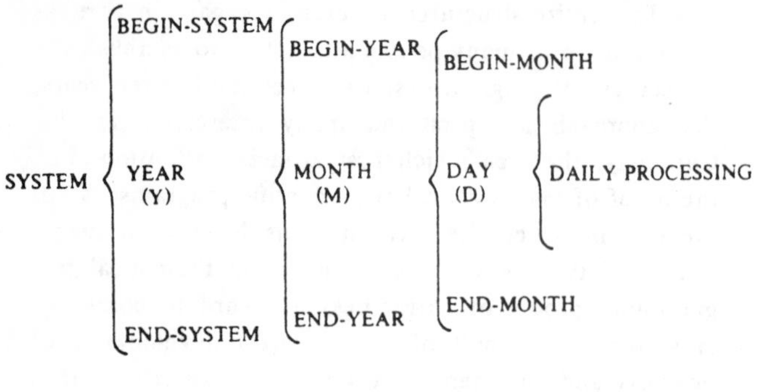

Figure 7.29. Basic systems chart.

Such a design, we find, is not accidental. Most business organizations manage a great many of their functions on a calendar basis. Moreover, even though the functions being managed may, in fact, be considerably different, they are often very similar in information systems operation.

Correctness, like so many other things, turns out to be quite simple to achieve, if you have designed it into the system. Moreover, solutions to other problems — such as how to logically fit a time frame that is not quite as nicely oriented as years, months, and weeks — also can be developed.

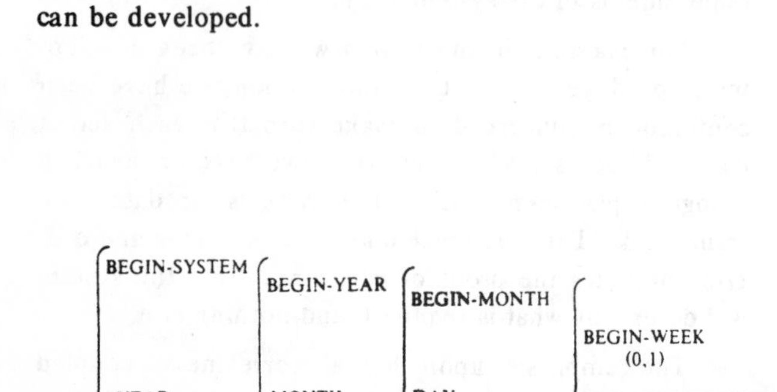

Figure 7.30. Systems functions organized on a calendar basis.

The logical placement of individual sets of actions, such as end-of-week and end-of-month operations, is an

extremely critical one. Historically, in part because of our lack of tools and training, we have failed to design systems that include only enough detail to insure that just the logical activities that we required were built into our systems in exactly the correct places. Structured systems design can now assure us that our systems will work as required before we put them on the machine.

It may seem that the approach we are describing here is an overly mechanical one. Often, systems analysts suggest that they do not want to be as specific as structured systems design requires, because they want to allow flexibility. Unfortunately, what they provide is flexibility to be wrong. Such flexibility is no great service to anyone, especially the user. Increasingly, structured systems designs are working better and more reliably because the analyst has carefully laid out each set of operations so that the correct ones must be done in the correct order. The impact of such a small change is enormous.

In building a structured system, we have not eliminated the necessity to do thorough analysis. Nor have we come up with any foolproof methodology. We are reaching the point, however, when it will be possible to deliver to our users exactly what they asked for. That alone represents a major break with the past. If the user asks for the wrong things, then we will unfortunately provide him with the wrong things. But at least we can defend what we did; and moreover, we can feel confident that if the right things can be specified, we can provide them in a reasonable time frame.

The correctness of a systems design, as we have said before, is the minimum that a systems analyst can deliver. If we cannot guarantee the validity of the results that our systems produce, then we have violated our professional ethics. Structured systems design will not provide miracle solutions. In fact, our solutions, in many cases, look remarkably like the good solutions of earlier eras. However, we are now in the position of being able to better understand and deal with our new solutions, and to maintain them at a far lower cost.

If we can show that the Warnier Diagram above (Figure 7.30) has been implemented (i.e., if we test the system logically), and if we can show that only the right sets of data are ever accessed, then we can be confident that the output produced by MONTH-END PROCESSING or QUARTER-END PROCESSING, and so fourth, will be correct. Moreover, this will be true of any set of information with which we are apt to deal.

Correctness in systems design is actually no more difficult (or no easier) to determine than is correctness of a complex or a simple program. The problem is fundamentally a logical, not a computer, one. Correct systems, then, depend upon correct programs and correct data. If we can show that the correct sets of actions always are done on the correct sets of data at the correct times within our systems designs, we also will know that our system is correct. We are only part way there. Correctness of output depends upon the correctness (or integrity) of the data base used; and that leads to a second major logical part to structuring systems, *the structuring of data*.

Considerations and techniques are proposed that reduce the complexity of programs by dividing them into functional modules. This can make it possible to create complex systems from simple, independent, reusable modules. Debugging and modifying programs, reconfiguring I/O devices, and managing large programming projects can all be greatly simplified. And, as the module library grows, increasingly sophisticated programs can be implemented using less and less new code.

Structured design

by W. P. Stevens, G. J. Myers, and L. L. Constantine

Structured design is a set of proposed general program design considerations and techniques for making coding, debugging, and modification easier, faster, and less expensive by reducing complexity.[1] The major ideas are the result of nearly ten years of research by Mr. Constantine.[2] His results are presented here, but the authors do not intend to present the theory and derivation of the results in this paper. These ideas have been called *composite design* by Mr. Myers.[3-5] The authors believe these *program design* techniques are compatible with, and enhance, the *documentation* techniques of HIPO[6] and the *coding* techniques of structured programming.[7]

These cost-saving techniques always need to be balanced with other constraints on the system. But the ability to produce simple, changeable programs will become increasingly important as the cost of the programmer's time continues to rise.

General considerations of structured design

Simplicity is the primary measurement recommended for evaluating alternative designs relative to reduced debugging and modification time. Simplicity can be enhanced by dividing the system into separate pieces in such a way that pieces can be considered, implemented, fixed, and changed with minimal consideration or effect on the other pieces of the system. Observability (the ability to easily perceive how and why actions occur) is another use-

Reprinted with permission from *IBM Systems Journal*, Volume 13, Number 2, 1974, pages 115-139. Copyright © 1974 by International Business Machines Corporation.

ful consideration that can help in designing programs that can be changed easily. Consideration of the effect of reasonable changes is also valuable for evaluating alternative designs.

Mr. Constantine has observed that programs that were the easiest to implement and change were those composed of simple, independent modules. The reason for this is that problem solving is faster and easier when the problem can be subdivided into pieces which can be considered separately. Problem solving is hardest when all aspects of the problem must be considered simultaneously.

The term *module* is used to refer to a set of one or more contiguous program statements having a name by which other parts of the system can invoke it and preferably having its own distinct set of variable names. Examples of modules are PL/I procedures, FORTRAN mainlines and subprograms, and, in general, subroutines of all types. Considerations are always with relation to the program statements *as coded*, since it is the programmer's ability to understand and change the *source* program that is under consideration.

While conceptually it is useful to discuss dividing whole programs into smaller pieces, the techniques presented here are for designing simple, independent modules originally. It turns out to be difficult to divide an existing program into separate pieces without increasing the complexity because of the amount of overlapped code and other interrelationships that usually exist.

Graphical notation is a useful tool for structured design. Figure 1 illustrates a notation called a *structure chart*,[8] in which:

1. There are two modules, A and B.
2. Module A *invokes* module B. B is *subordinate* to A.
3. B receives an input parameter X (its name in module A) and returns a parameter Y (its name in module A). (It is useful to distinguish which calling parameters represent data passed *to* the called program and which are for data to be *returned* to the caller.)

Coupling and communication

To evaluate alternatives for dividing programs into modules, it becomes useful to examine and evaluate types of "connections" between modules. A connection is a reference to some label or address defined (or also defined) elsewhere.

The fewer and simpler the connections between modules, the easier it is to understand each module without reference to other

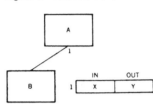

Figure 1   A structure chart

Table 1 Contributing factors

	Interface complexity	Type of connection	Type of communication
low	simple, obvious	to module by name	data
COUPLING			control
high	complicated, obscure	to internal elements	hybrid

modules. Minimizing connections between modules also minimizes the paths along which changes and errors can propagate into other parts of the system, thus eliminating disastrous "ripple" effects, where changes in one part cause errors in another, necessitating additional changes elsewhere, giving rise to new errors, etc. The widely used technique of using common data areas (or global variables or modules without their own distinct set of variable names) can result in an enormous number of connections between the modules of a program. The complexity of a system is affected not only by the number of connections but by the degree to which each connection couples (associates) two modules, making them interdependent rather than independent. Coupling is the measure of the strength of association established by a connection from one module to another. Strong coupling complicates a system since a module is harder to understand, change, or correct by itself if it is highly interrelated with other modules. Complexity can be reduced by designing systems with the weakest possible coupling between modules.

The degree of coupling established by a particular connection is a function of several factors, and thus it is difficult to establish a simple index of coupling. Coupling depends (1) on how complicated the connection is, (2) on whether the connection refers to the module itself or something inside it, and (3) on what is being sent or received.

Coupling increases with increasing complexity or obscurity of the interface. Coupling is lower when the connection is to the normal module interface than when the connection is an internal component. Coupling is lower with data connections than with control connections, which are in turn lower than hybrid connections (modification of one module's code by another module). The contribution of all these factors is summarized in Table 1.

When two or more modules interface with the same area of storage, data region, or device, they share a common environment. Examples of common environments are:

interface complexity

• A set of data elements with the EXTERNAL attribute that is copied into PL/I modules via an INCLUDE statement or that is found listed in each of a number of modules.

- Data elements defined in COMMON statements in FORTRAN modules.
- A centrally located "control block" or set of control blocks.
- A common overlay region of memory.
- Global variable names defined over an entire program or section.

The most important structural characteristic of a common environment is that it couples every module sharing it to every other such module without regard to their functional relationship or its absence. For example, only the two modules XVECTOR and VELOC might actually make use of data element X in an "included" common environment of PL/I, yet changing the length of X impacts *every* module making any use of the common environment, and thus necessitates recompilation.

Every element in the common environment, whether used by particular modules or not, constitutes a separate path along which errors and changes can propagate. Each element in the common environment adds to the complexity of the total system to be comprehended by an amount representing all possible pairs of modules sharing that environment. Changes to, and new uses of, the common area potentially impact all modules in unpredictable ways. Data references may become unplanned, uncontrolled, and even unknown.

A module interfacing with a common environment for some of its input or output data is, on the average, more difficult to use in varying contexts or from a variety of places or in different programs than is a module with communication restricted to parameters in calling sequences. It is somewhat clumsier to establish a new and unique data context on each call of a module when data passage is via a common environment. Without analysis of the entire set of sharing modules or careful saving and restoration of values, a new use is likely to interfere with other uses of the common environment and propagate errors into other modules. As to future growth of a given system, once the commitment is made to communication via a common environment, any new module will have to be plugged into the common environment, compounding the total complexity even more. On this point, Belady and Lehman,[9] observe that "a well-structured system, one in which communication is via passed parameters through defined interfaces, is likely to be more growable and require less effort to maintain than one making extensive use of global or shared variables."

The impact of common environments on system complexity may be quantified. Among M objects there are $M(M-1)$ ordered pairs of objects. (Ordered pairs are of interest because A and B sharing a common environment complicates both, A being coupled to B and B being coupled to A.) Thus a common environment of N elements shared by M modules results in NM $(M-1)$ first order (one level) relationships or paths along which changes and errors can propagate. This means 150 such paths in a FORTRAN program of only three modules sharing the COMMON area with just 25 variables in it.

It is possible to minimize these disadvantages of common environments by limiting access to the smallest possible subset of modules. If the total set of potentially shared elements is subdivided into groups, all of which are *required* by some subset of modules, then both the size of each common environment and the scope of modules among which it is shared is reduced. Using "named" rather than "blank" COMMON in FORTRAN is one means of accomplishing this end.

The complexity of an interface is a matter of how much information is needed to state or to understand the connection. Thus, obvious relationships result in lower coupling than obscure or inferred ones. The more syntactic units (such as parameters) in the statement of a connection, the higher the coupling. Thus, extraneous elements irrelevant to the programmer's and the modules' immediate task increase coupling unnecessarily.

Connections that address or refer to a module as a whole by its name (leaving its contents unknown and irrelevant) yield lower coupling than connections referring to the internal elements of another module. In the latter case, as for example the use of a variable by direct reference from within some other module, the entire content of that module may have to be taken into account to correct an error or make a change so that it does not make an impact in some unexpected way. Modules that can be used easily without knowing anything about their insides make for simpler systems.

Consider the case depicted in Figure 2. GETCOMM is a module whose function is getting the next command from a terminal. In performing this function, GETCOMM calls the module READT, whose function is to read a line from the terminal. READT requires the address of the terminal. It gets this via an externally declared data element in GETCOMM, called TERMADDR. READT passes the line back to GETCOMM as an argument called LINE. Note the arrow extending from *inside* GETCOMM to *inside* READT. An arrow of this type is the notation for references to internal data elements of another module.

Now, suppose we wish to add a module called GETDATA, whose function is to get the next data line (i.e., not a command) from a

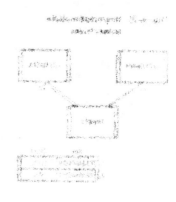

type of connection

Figure 2 Module connections

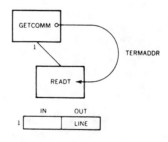

Figure 3 Improved module connections

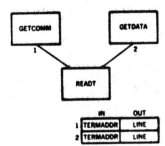

IN	OUT
1 TERMADDR	LINE
2 TERMADDR	LINE

type of communication

Figure 4 Control-coupled modules

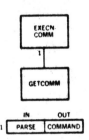

IN	OUT
1 PARSE	COMMAND

(possibly) different terminal. It would be desirable to use module READT as a subroutine of GETDATA. But if GETDATA modifies TERMADDR in GETCOMM before calling READT, it will cause GETCOMM to fail since it will "get" from the wrong terminal. Even if GETDATA restores TERMADDR after use, the error can still occur if GETDATA and GETCOMM can ever be invoked "simultaneously" in a multiprogramming environment. READT would have been more usable if TERMADDR had been made an input argument to READT instead of an externally declared data item as shown in Figure 3. This simple example shows how references to internal elements of other modules can have an adverse effect on program modification, both in terms of cost and potential bugs.

Modules must at least pass data or they cannot functionally be a part of a single system. Thus connections that pass data are a necessary minimum. (Not so the communication of control. In principle, the presence or absence of requisite input data is sufficient to define the circumstances under which a module should be activated, that is, receive control. Thus the explicit passing of control by one module to another constitutes an additional, theoretically inessential form of coupling. In practice, systems that are *purely* data-coupled require special language and operating system support but have numerous attractions, not the least of which is they can be fundamentally simpler than any equivalent system with control coupling.[10])

Beyond the practical, innocuous, minimum control coupling of normal subroutine calls is the practice of passing an "element of control" such as a switch, flag, or signal from one module to another. Such a connection affects the execution of another module and not merely the data it performs its task upon by involving one module in the internal processing of some other module. Control arguments are an additional complication to the essential data arguments required for performance of some task, and an alternative structure that eliminates the complication always exists.

Consider the modules in Figure 4 that are control-coupled by the switch PARSE through which EXECNCOMM instructs GETCOMM whether to return a parsed or unparsed command. Separating the two distinct functions of GETCOMM results in a structure that is simpler as shown in Figure 5.

The new EXECNCOMM is no more complicated; where once it set a switch and called, now it has two alternate calls. The sum of GETPCOMM and GETUCOMM is (functionally) less complicated than GETCOMM was (by the amount of the switch testing). And the two small modules are likely to be easier to comprehend than the one large one. Admittedly, the immediate gains here may appear marginal, but they rise with time and the number of alternatives in the switch and the number of levels over which it is passed. Control coupling, where a called module "tells" its caller what to do, is a more severe form of coupling.

Modification of one module's code by another module may be thought of as a hybrid of data and control elements since the code is dealt with as data by the modifying module, while it acts as control to the modified module. The target module is very dependent in its behavior on the modifying module, and the latter is intimately involved in the other's internal functioning.

Cohesiveness

Coupling is reduced when the relationships among elements *not* in the same module are minimized. There are two ways of achieving this—minimizing the relationships among modules and maximizing relationships among elements in the same module. In practice, both ways are used.

The second method is the subject of this section. "Element" in this sense means any form of a "piece" of the module, such as a statement, a segment, or a "subfunction". Binding is the measure of the cohesiveness of a module. The objective here is to reduce coupling by striving for high binding. The scale of cohesiveness, from lowest to highest, follows:

1. Coincidental.
2. Logical.
3. Temporal.
4. Communicational.
5. Sequential.
6. Functional.

The scale is not linear. Functional binding is much stronger than all the rest, and the first two are much weaker than all the rest. Also, higher-level binding classifications often include all the characteristics of one or more classifications below it *plus* additional relationships. The binding between two elements is the highest classification that applies. We will define each type of binding, give an example, and try to indicate why it is found at its particular position on the scale.

When there is no meaningful relationship among the elements in a module, we have coincidental binding. Coincidental binding might result from either of the following situations: (1) An existing program is "modularized" by splitting it apart into modules. (2) Modules are created to consolidate "duplicate coding" in other modules.

coincidental binding

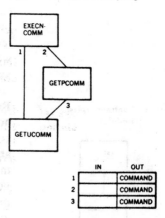

Figure 5 Simplified coupling

As an example of the difficulty that can result from coincidental binding, suppose the following sequence of instructions appeared several times in a module or in several modules and was put into a separate module called X:

A = B + C
GET CARD
PUT OUTPUT
IF B = 4, THEN E = 0

Module X would probably be coincidentally bound since these four instructions have no apparent relationships among one another. Suppose in the future we have a need in one of the modules originally containing these instructions to say GET TAPERE-CORD instead of GET CARD. We now have a problem. If we modify the instruction in module X, it is unusable to all of the other callers of X. It may even be difficult to *find* all of the other callers of X in order to make any other compatible change.

It is only fair to admit that, independent of a module's cohesiveness, there are instances when any module can be modified in such a fashion to make it unusable to all its callers. However, the *probability* of this happening is very high if the module is coincidentally bound.

logical binding   Logical binding, next on the scale, implies some logical relationship between the elements of a module. Examples are a module that performs all input and output operations for the program or a module that edits all data.

The logically bound, EDIT ALL DATA module is often implemented as follows. Assume the data elements to be edited are master file records, updates, deletions, and additions. Parameters passed to the module would include the data and a special parameter indicating the type of data. The first instruction in the module is probably a four-way branch, going to four sections of code—edit master record, edit update record, edit addition record, and edit deletion record.

Often, these four functions are also intertwined in some way in the module. If the deletion record changes and requires a change to the edit deletion record function, we will have a problem if this function is intertwined with the other three. If the edits are truly independent, then the system could be simplified by putting each edit in a separate module and eliminating the need to decide which edit to do for each execution. In short, logical binding usually results in tricky or shared code, which is difficult to modify, and in the passing of unnecessary parameters.

Temporal binding is the same as logical binding, except the elements are also related in time. That is, the temporally bound elements are executed in the same time period.

temporal binding

The best examples of modules in this class are the traditional "initialization", "termination", "housekeeping", and "clean-up" modules. Elements in an initialization module are logically bound because initialization represents a logical class of functions. In addition, these elements are related in time (i.e., at initialization time).

Modules with temporal binding tend to exhibit the disadvantages of logically bound modules. However, temporally bound modules are higher on the scale since they tend to be simpler for the reason that *all* of the elements are executable at one time (i.e., no parameters and logic to determine which element to execute).

A module with communicational binding has elements that are related by a reference to the same set of input and/or output data. For example, "print and punch the output file" is communicationally bound. Communicational binding is higher on the scale than temporal binding since the elements in a module with communicational binding have the stronger "bond" of referring to the same data.

communicational binding

When the output data from an element is the input for the next element, the module is sequentially bound. Sequential binding can result from flowcharting the problem to be solved and then defining modules to represent one or more blocks in the flowchart. For example, "read next transaction and update master file" is sequentially bound.

sequential binding

Sequential binding, although high on the scale because of a close relationship to the problem structure, is still far from the maximum—functional binding. The reason is that the procedural processes in a program are usually distinct from the *functions* in a program. Hence, a sequentially bound module can contain several functions or just part of a function. This usually results in higher coupling and modules that are less likely to be usable from other parts of the system.

Functional binding is the strongest type of binding. In a functionally bound module, all of the elements are related to the performance of a single function.

functional binding

A question that often arises at this point is what is a function? In mathematics, $Y = F(X)$ is read "Y is a function F of X." The function F defines a transformation or mapping of the independent (or input) variable X into the dependent (or return) variable Y. Hence, a function describes a transformation from some input data to some return data. In terms of programming, we broaden this definition to allow functions with no input data and functions with no return data.

In practice, the above definition does not clearly describe a functionally bound module. One hint is that if the elements of the module all contribute to accomplishing a single goal, then it is probably functionally bound. Examples of functionally bound modules are "Compute Square Root" (input and return parameters) "Obtain Random Number" (no input parameter), and "Write Record to Output File" (no return parameter).

A useful technique in determining whether a module is functionally bound is writing a sentence describing the function (purpose) of the module, and then examining the sentence. The following tests can be made:

1. If the sentence *has* to be a compound sentence, contain a comma, or contain more than one verb, the module is probably performing more than one function; therefore, it probably has sequential or communicational binding.

2. If the sentence contains words relating to time, such as "first", "next", "then", "after", "when", "start", etc., then the module probably has sequential or temporal binding.

3. If the predicate of the sentence doesn't contain a single specific object following the verb, the module is probably logically bound. For example, Edit All Data has logical binding; Edit Source Statement may have functional binding.

4. Words such as "initialize", "clean-up", etc. imply temporal binding.

Functionally bound modules *can* always be described by way of their elements using a compound sentence. But if the above language is unavoidable while still completely describing the module's function, then the module is probably not functionally bound.

One unresolved problem is deciding how far to divide functionally bound subfunctions. The division has probably gone far enough if each module contains no subset of elements that could be useful alone, and if each module is small enough that its entire implementation can be grasped all at once, i.e., seldom longer than one or two pages of source code.

Observe that a module can include more than one type of binding. The binding between two elements is the highest that can be applied. The binding of a module is lowered by every element pair that does not exhibit functional binding.

Predictable modules

A predictable, or well-behaved, module is one that, when given the identical inputs, operates identically each time it is called. Also, a well-behaved module operates independently of its environment.

To show that dependable (free from errors) modules can still be unpredictable, consider an oscillator module that returns zero and one alternately and dependably when it is called. It might be used to facilitate double buffering. Should it have multiple users, each would be required to call it an even number of times before relinquishing control. Should any of the users have an error that prevented an even number of calls, all other users will fail. The operation of the module given the same inputs is not constant, resulting in the module not being predictable even though error-free. Modules that keep track of their own state are usually not predictable, even when error-free.

This characteristic of predictability that can be designed into modules is what we might loosely call "black-boxness." That is, the user can understand what the module does and use it without knowing what is inside it. Module "black-boxness" can even be enhanced by merely adding comments that make the module's function and use clear. Also, a descriptive name and a well-defined and visible interface enhances a module's usability and thus makes it more of a black box.

Tradeoffs to structured design

The overhead involved in writing many simple modules is in the execution time and memory space used by a particular language to effect the call. The designer should realize the adverse effect on maintenance and debugging that may result from striving just for minimum execution time and/or memory. He should also remember that programmer cost, is, or is rapidly becoming, the major cost of a programming system and that much of the maintenance will be in the future when the trend will be even more prominent. However, depending on the actual overhead of the language being used, it is very possible that a structured design can result in less execution and/or memory overhead rather than more due to the following considerations:

For memory overhead

1. Optional (error) modules may never be called into memory.

Figure 6 Definitions of symbols used in structure charts

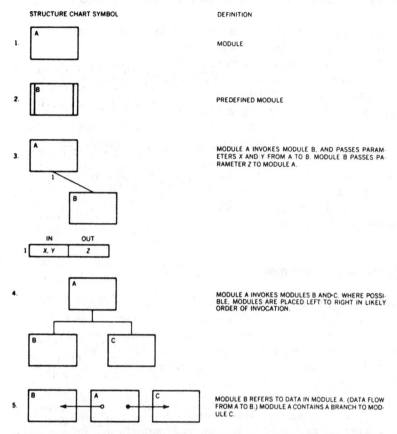

STRUCTURE CHART SYMBOL

DEFINITION

1.

MODULE

2.

PREDEFINED MODULE

3.

MODULE A INVOKES MODULE B, AND PASSES PARAM-
ETERS X AND Y FROM A TO B. MODULE B PASSES PA-
RAMETER Z TO MODULE A.

4.

MODULE A INVOKES MODULES B AND C. WHERE POSSI-
BLE, MODULES ARE PLACED LEFT TO RIGHT IN LIKELY
ORDER OF INVOCATION.

5.

MODULE B REFERS TO DATA IN MODULE A. (DATA FLOW
FROM A TO B.) MODULE A CONTAINS A BRANCH TO MOD-
ULE C.

THE MORE COMPREHENSIVE "PROPOSED STANDARD GRAPHICS FOR PROGRAM STRUCTURE," PREFERRED BY MR. CON-
STANTINE AND WIDELY USED OVER THE PAST SIX YEARS BY HIS CLASSES AND CLIENTS, USES SEPARATE ARROWS FOR
EACH CONNECTION, SUCH AS FOR THE CALLS FROM A TO B AND FROM A TO C, TO REFLECT STRUCTURAL PROPERTIES
OF THE PROGRAM. THE CHARTING SHOWN HERE WAS ADOPTED FOR COMPATIBILITY WITH THE HIERARCHY CHART OF HIPO.

2. Structured design reduces duplicate code and the coding necessary for implementing control switches, thus reducing the
amount of programmer-generated code.
3. Overlay structuring can be based on actual operating characteristics obtained by running and observing the program.
4. Having many single-function modules allows more flexible,
and precise, grouping, possibly resulting in less memory
needed at any one time under overlay or virtual storage constraints.

For execution overhead

1. Some modules may only execute a few times.
2. Optional (error) functions may never be called, resulting in
zero overhead.
3. Code for control switches is reduced or eliminated, reducing
the total amount of code to be executed.

4. Heavily used linkage can be recompiled and calls replaced by branches.

5. "Includes" or "performs" can be used in place of calls. (However, the complexity of the system will increase by at least the extra consideration necessary to prevent duplicating data names and by the difficulty of creating the equivalent of call parameters for a well-defined interface.)

6. One way to get fast execution is to determine which parts of the system will be most used so all optimizing time can be spent on those parts. Implementing an initially structured design allows the testing of a working program for those critical modules (and yields a working program prior to any time spent optimizing). Those modules can then be optimized separately and reintegrated without introducing multitudes of errors into the rest of the program.

Structured design techniques

It is possible to divide the design process into general program design and detailed design as follows. General program design is deciding *what* functions are needed for the program (or programming system). Detailed design is *how* to implement the functions. The considerations above and techniques that follow result in an identification of the functions, calling parameters, and the call relationships for a structure of functionally bound, simply connected modules. The information thus generated makes it easier for each module to then be separately designed, implemented, and tested.

The objective of general program design is to determine what functions, calling parameters, and call relationships are needed. Since flowcharts depict *when* (in what order and under what conditions) blocks are executed, flowcharts unnecessarily complicate the general program design phase. A more useful notation is the structure chart, as described earlier and as shown in Figure 6.

To contrast a structure chart and a flowchart, consider the following for the same three modules in Figure 7 — A which calls B which calls C (coding has been added to the structure chart to enable the proper flowchart to be determined; B's code will be executed first, then C's, then A's). To design A's interfaces properly, it is necessary to know that A is responsible for invoking B, but this is hard to determine from the flowchart. In addition, the structure chart can show the module connections and calling parameters that are central to the consideration and techniques being presented here.

The other major difference that drastically simplifies the nota-

structure
charts

Figure 7 Structure chart compared to flowchart

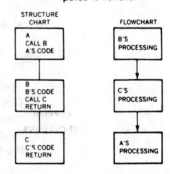

Figure 8 Basic form of low-cost implementation

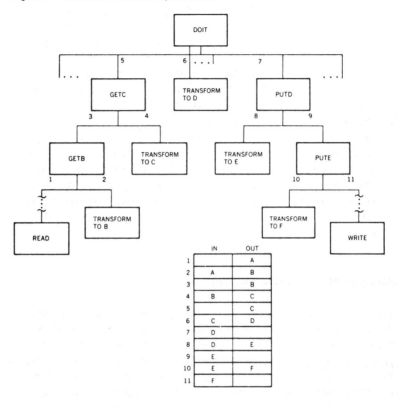

	IN	OUT
1		A
2	A	B
3		B
4	B	C
5		C
6	C	D
7	D	
8	D	E
9	E	
10	E	F
11	F	

Figure 9 Transaction structure

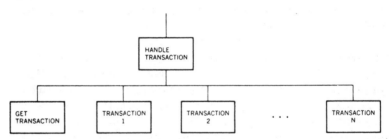

tion and analysis during general program design is the absence in structure charts of the decision block. Conditional calls can be so noted, but "decision designing" can be deferred until detailed module design. This is an example of where the *design* process is made simpler by having to consider only part of the design problem. Structure charts are also small enough to be worked on all at once by the designers, helping to prevent suboptimizing parts of the program at the expense of the entire problem.

common structures A shortcut for arriving at simple structures is to know the general form of the result. Mr. Constantine observed that programs of the general structure in Figure 8 resulted in the lowest-cost

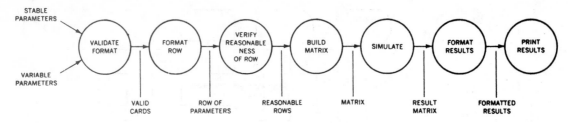

Figure 10   Rough structure of simulation system

implementations. It implements the input-process-output type of program, which applies to most programs, even if the "input" or "output" is to secondary storage or to memory.

In practice, the sink leg is often shorter than the source one. Also, source modules may produce output (e.g., error messages) and sink modules may request input (e.g., execution-time format commands.)

Another structure useful for implementing parts of a design is the transaction structure depicted in Figure 9. A "transaction" here is any event, record, or input, etc. for which various actions should result. For example, a command processor has this structure. The structure may occur alone or as one or more of the source (or even sink) modules of an input-process-output structure. Analysis of the transaction modules follows that of a transform module, which is explained later.

The following procedure can be used to arrive at the input-process-output general structure shown previously.

designing the structure

Step One. The first step is to sketch (or mentally consider) a functional picture of the problem. As an example, consider a simulation system. The rough structure of this problem is shown in Figure 10.

Step Two. Identify the external conceptual streams of data. An *external* stream of data is one that is external to the system. A *conceptual* stream of data is a stream of related data that is independent of any physical I/O device. For instance, we may have several conceptual streams coming from one I/O device or one stream coming from several I/O devices. In our simulation system, the external conceptual streams are the input parameters, and the formatted simulation the result.

Step Three. Identify the *major* external conceptual stream of data (both input and output) in the problem. Then, using the diagram of the problem structure, determine, for this stream, the points of "highest abstraction" as in Figure 11.

Figure 11 Determining points of highest abstraction

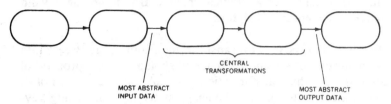

Figure 12 The top level

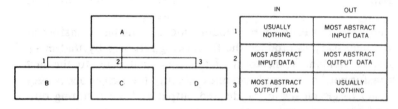

The "point of highest abstraction" for an input stream of data is the point in the problem structure where that data is farthest removed from its physical input form yet can still be viewed as coming in. Hence, in the simulation system, the most abstract form of the input transaction stream might be the built matrix. Similarly, identify the point where the data stream can first be viewed as going out—in the example, possibly the result matrix.

Admittedly, this is a subjective step. However, experience has shown that designers trained in the technique seldom differ by more than one or two blocks in their answers to the above.

Step Four. Design the structure in Figure 12 from the previous information with a source module for each conceptual input stream which exists at the point of most abstract input data: do sink modules similarly. Often only single source and sink branches are necessary. The parameters passed are dependent on the problem, but the general pattern is shown in Figure 12.

Describe the function of each module with a short, concise, and specific phrase. Describe what transformations occur when that module is called, not how the module is implemented. Evaluate the phrase relative to functional binding.

When module A is called, the program or system executes. Hence, the function of module A is equivalent to the problem being solved. If the problem is "write a FORTRAN compiler," then the function of module A is "compile FORTRAN program."

Module B's function involves obtaining the major stream of data. An example of a "typical module B" is "get next valid source statement in Polish form."

Module C's purpose is to transform the major input stream into the major output stream. Its function should be a nonprocedural description of this transformation. Examples are "convert Polish form statement to machine language statement" or "using keyword list, search abstract file for matching abstracts."

Module D's purpose is disposing of the major output stream. Examples are "produce report" or "display results of simulation."

Step Five. For each source module, identify the last transformation necessary to produce the form being returned by that module. Then identify the form of the input just prior to the last transformation. For sink modules, identify the first process necessary to get closer to the desired output and the resulting output form. This results in the portions of the structure shown in Figure 13.

Repeat Step Five on the new source and sink modules until the original source and final sink modules are reached. The modules may be analyzed in any order, but each module should be done completely before doing any of its subordinates. There are, unfortunately, no detailed guidelines available for dividing the transform modules. Use binding and coupling considerations, size (about one page of source), and usefulness (are there subfunctions that could be useful elsewhere now or in the future) as guidelines on how far to divide.

During this phase, err on the side of dividing too finely. It is always easy to recombine later in the design, but duplicate func-

Figure 13 Lower levels

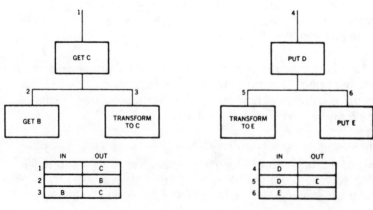

STRUCTURED DESIGN

Figure 14 Design form should follow function

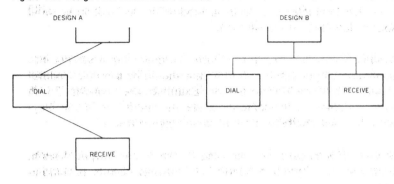

tions may not be identified if the dividing is too conservative at this point.

Design guidelines

The following concepts are useful for achieving simple designs and for improving the "first-pass" structures.

match program to problem

One of the most useful techniques for reducing the effect of changes on the program is to make the structure of the design match the structure of the problem, that is, form should follow function. For example, consider a module that dials a telephone and a module that receives data. If receiving immediately follows dialing, one might arrive at design A as shown in Figure 14. Consider, however, whether receiving is part of dialing. Since it is not (usually), have DIAL's caller invoke RECEIVE as in design B.

If, in this example, design A were used, consider the effect of a new requirement to transmit immediately after dialing. The DIAL module receives first and cannot be used, or a switch must be passed, or another DIAL module has to be added.

To the extent that the design structure does match the problem structure, changes to single parts of the problem result in changes to single modules.

Figure 15 Scope of control

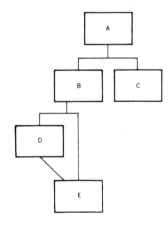

scopes of effect and control

The *scope of control* of a module is that module plus all modules that are ultimately subordinate to that module. In the example of Figure 15, the scope of control of B is B, D, and E. The *scope of effect* of a decision is the set of all modules that contain some code whose execution is based upon the outcome of the decision. The system is simpler when the scope of effect of a decision is in the scope of control of the module containing the decision. The following example illustrates why.

If the execution of some code in A is dependent on the outcome of decision X in module B, then either B will have to return a flag to A or the decision will have to be repeated in A. The former approach results in added coding to implement the flag, and the latter results in some of B's function (decision X) in module A. Duplicates of decision X result in difficulties coordinating changes to both copies whenever decision X must be changed.

The scope of effect can be brought within the scope of control either by moving the decision element "up" in the structure, or by taking those modules that are in the scope of effect but not in the scope of control and moving them so that they fall within the scope of control.

Size can be used as a signal to look for *potential* problems. Look carefully at modules with less than five or more than 100 executable source statements. Modules with a small number of statements may not perform an entire function, hence, may not have functional binding. Very small modules can be eliminated by placing their statements in the calling modules. Large modules may include more than one function. A second problem with large modules is understandability and readability. There is evidence to the fact that a group of about 30 statements is the upper limit of what can be mastered on the first reading of a module listing.[11]

module size

Often, part of a module's function is to notify its caller when it cannot perform its function. This is accomplished with a return error parameter (preferably binary only). A module that handles streams of data must be able to signal end-of-file (EOF), preferably also with a binary parameter. These parameters should not, however, tell the caller what to do about the error or EOF. Nevertheless, the system can be made simpler if modules can be designed without the need for error flags.

error and end-of-file

Similarly, many modules require some initialization to be done. An initialize module will suffer from low binding but sometimes is the simplest solution. It may, however, be possible to eliminate the need for initializing without compromising "black-boxness" (the same inputs *always* produce the same outputs). For example, a read module that detects a return error of file-not-opened from the access method and recovers by opening the file and rereading eliminates the need for initialization without maintaining an internal state.

intialization

Eliminate duplicate functions but not duplicate code. When a function changes, it is a great advantage to only have to change it in one place. But if a module's need for its own copy of a random collection of code changes slightly, it will not be necessary to change several other modules as well.

selecting modules

STRUCTURED DESIGN

Figure 16 Outline of problem structure

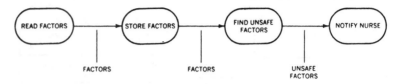

Figure 17 Points of highest abstraction

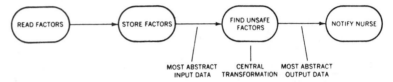

If a module seems almost, but not quite, useful from a second place in the system, try to identify and isolate the useful sub-function. The remainder of the module might be incorporated in its original caller.

Check modules that have many callers or that call many other modules. While not always a problem, it may indicate missing levels or modules.

isolate specifications Isolate all dependencies on a particular data-type, record-layout, index-structure, etc. in one or a minimum of modules. This minimizes the recoding necessary should that particular specification change.

reduce parameters Look for ways to reduce the number of parameters passed between modules. Count every item passed as a separate parameter for this objective (independent of how it will be implemented). Do not pass whole records from module to module, but pass only the field or fields necessary for each module to accomplish its function. Otherwise, all modules will have to change if one field expands, rather than only those which directly used that field. Passing only the data being processed by the program system with necessary error and EOF parameters is the ultimate objective. Check binary switches for indications of scope-of-effect/scope-of-control inversions.

Have the designers work together and with the complete structure chart. If branches of the chart are worked on separately, common modules may be missed and incompatibilities result from design decisions made while only considering one branch.

Figure 18   Structure of the top level

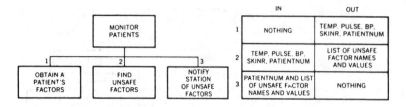

Figure 19   Structure of next level

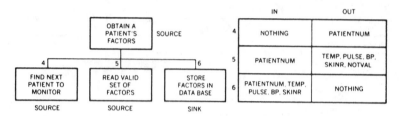

An example

The following example illustrates the use of structured design:

A patient-monitoring program is required for a hospital. Each patient is monitored by an analog device which measures factors such as pulse, temperature, blood pressure, and skin resistance. The program reads these factors on a periodic basis (specified for each patient) and stores these factors in a data base. For each patient, safe ranges for each factor are specified (e.g., patient X's valid temperature range is 98 to 99.5 degrees Fahrenheit). If a factor falls outside of a patient's safe range, or if an analog device fails, the nurse's station is notified.

In a real-life case, the problem statement would contain much more detail. However, this one is of sufficient detail to allow us to design the structure of the program.

The first step is to outline the structure of the problem as shown in Figure 16. In the second step, we identify the external conceptual streams of data. In this case, two streams are present, factors from the analog device and warnings to the nurse. These also represent the major input and output streams.

Figure 17 indicates the point of highest abstraction of the input stream, which is the point at which a patient's factors are in the form to store in the data base. The point of highest abstraction of the output stream is a list of unsafe factors (if any). We can now begin to design the program's structure as in Figure 18.

Figure 20 Complete structure chart

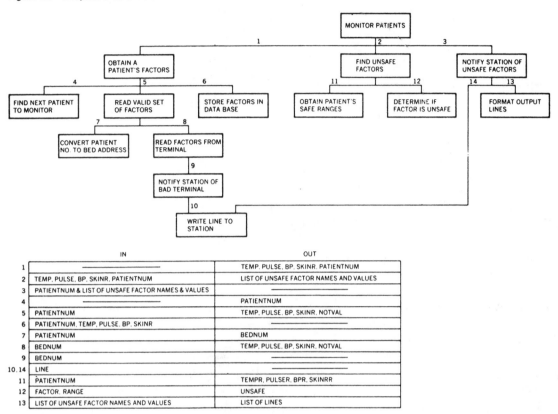

	IN	OUT
1	———————	TEMP, PULSE, BP, SKINR, PATIENTNUM
2	TEMP, PULSE, BP, SKINR, PATIENTNUM	LIST OF UNSAFE FACTOR NAMES AND VALUES
3	PATIENTNUM & LIST OF UNSAFE FACTOR NAMES & VALUES	———————
4	———————	PATIENTNUM
5	PATIENTNUM	TEMP, PULSE, BP, SKINR, NOTVAL
6	PATIENTNUM, TEMP, PULSE, BP, SKINR	———————
7	PATIENTNUM	BEDNUM
8	BEDNUM	TEMP, PULSE, BP, SKINR, NOTVAL
9	BEDNUM	———————
10, 14	LINE	———————
11	PATIENTNUM	TEMPR, PULSER, BPR, SKINRR
12	FACTOR, RANGE	UNSAFE
13	LIST OF UNSAFE FACTOR NAMES AND VALUES	LIST OF LINES

In analyzing the module "OBTAIN A PATIENT'S FACTORS," we can deduce from the problem statement that this function has three parts: (1) Determine which patient to monitor next (based on their specified periodic intervals). (2) Read the analog device. (3) Record the factors in the data base. Hence, we arrive at the structure in Figure 19. (NOTVAL is set if a valid set of factors was not available.)

Further analysis of "READ VALID SET OF FACTORS", "FIND UNSAFE FACTORS" and "NOTIFY STATION OF UNSAFE FACTORS" yields the results shown in the complete structure chart in Figure 20.

Note that the module "READ FACTORS FROM TERMINAL" contains a decision asking "did we successfully read from the terminal?" If the read was not successful, we have to notify the nurse's station and then find the next patient to process as depicted in Figure 21.

Modules in the scope of effect of this decision are marked with an X. Note that the scope of effect is *not* a subset of the scope

Figure 21 Structure as designed

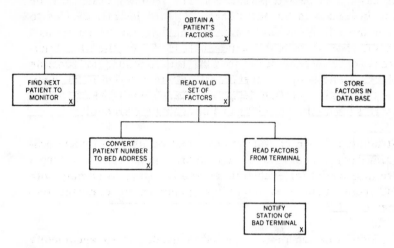

Figure 22 Scope of effect within scope of control

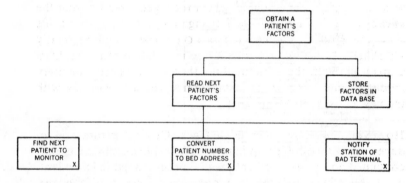

of control. To correct this problem, we have to take two steps. First, we will move the decision up to "READ VALID SET OF FACTORS." We do this by merging "READ FACTORS FROM TER-MINAL" into its calling module. We now make "FIND NEXT PA-TIENT TO MONITOR" a subordinate of "READ VALID SET OF FACTORS." Hence, we have the structure in Figure 22. Thus, by slightly altering the structure and the function of a few modules, we have completely eliminated the problem.

Concluding remarks

The HIPO Hierarchy chart is being used as an aid during general systems design. The considerations and techniques presented here are useful for evaluating alternatives for those portions of the system that will be programmed on a computer. The charting technique used here depicts more details about the interfaces than the HIPO Hierarchy chart. This facilitates consideration during general program design of each individual connection and its associated passed parameters. The resulting design can be documented with the HIPO charts. (If the designer decides to have more than one function in any module, the structure chart should show them in the same block. However, the HIPO Hierarchy chart would still show all the functions in separate blocks.) The output of the general program design is the input for the detailed module design. The HIPO input-process-output chart is useful for describing and designing each module.

Structured design considerations could be used to review program designs in a walk-through environment.[12] These concepts are also useful for evaluating alternative ways to comply with the requirement of structured programming for one-page segments.[7]

Structured design reduces the effort needed to fix and modify programs. If all programs were written in a form where there was one module, for example, which retrieved a record from the master file given the key, then changing operating systems, file access techniques, file blocking, or I/O devices would be greatly simplified. And if *all* programs in the installation retrieved from a given file with the same module, then one properly rewritten module would have *all* the installation's programs working with the new constraints for that file.

However, there are other advantages. Original errors are reduced when the problem at hand is simpler. Each module is self-contained and to some extent may be programmed independently of the others in location, programmer, time, and language. Modules can be tested before all programming is done by supplying simple "stub" modules that merely return preformatted results rather than calculating them. Modules critical to memory or execution overhead can be optimized separately and reintegrated with little or no impact. An entry or return trace-module becomes very feasible, yielding a very useful debugging tool.

Independent of all the advantages previously mentioned, structured design would *still* be valuable to solve the following problem alone. Programming can be considered as an art where each programmer usually starts with a blank canvas — techniques, yes, but still a blank canvas. Previous coding is often not used because previous modules usually contain, for example, *at least* GET and EDIT. If the EDIT is not the one needed, the GET will have to be recoded also.

Programming can be brought closer to a science where current work is built on the results of earlier work. Once a module is written to get a record from the master file given a key, it can be used by all users of the file and need not be rewritten into each succeeding program. Once a module has been written to do a table search, anyone can use it. And, as the module library grows, less and less new code needs to be written to implement increasingly sophisticated systems.

Structured design concepts are not new. The whole assembly-line idea is one of isolating simple functions in a way that still produces a complete, complex result. Circuits are designed by connecting isolatable, functional stages together, not by designing one big, interrelated circuit. Page numbering is being increasingly sectionalized (e.g., 4– 101) to minimize the "connections" between written sections, so that expanding one section does not require renumbering other sections. Automobile manufacturers, who have the most to gain from shared system elements, finally abandoned even the coupling of the windshield wipers to the engine vacuum due to effects of the engine load on the performance of the wiping function. Most other industries know well the advantage of isolating functions.

It is becoming increasingly important to the data-processing industry to be able to produce more programming systems and produce them with fewer errors, at a faster rate, and in a way that modifications can be accomplished easily and quickly. Structured design considerations can help achieve this goal.

CITED REFERENCES AND FOOTNOTES

1. This method has not been submitted to any formal IBM test. Potential users should evaluate its usefulness in their own environment prior to implementation.
2. L. L. Constantine, *Fundamentals of Program Design*, in preparation for publication by Prentice-Hall, Englewood Cliffs, New Jersey.
3. G. J. Myers, *Composite Design: The Design of Modular Programs*, Technical Report TR00.2406, IBM, Poughkeepsie, New York (January 29, 1973).
4. G. J. Myers, "Characteristics of composite design," *Datamation* 19, No. 9, 100– 102 (September 1973).
5. G. J. Myers, *Reliable Software through Composite Design*, to be published Fall of 1974 by Mason and Lipscomb Publishers, New York, New York.
6. HIPO– Hierarchical Input-Process-Output documentation technique. Audio education package, Form No. SR20-9413, available through any IBM Branch Office.
7. F. T. Baker, "Chief programmer team management of production programming," *IBM Systems Journal* 11, No. 1, 56– 73 (1972).
8. The use of the HIPO Hierarchy charting format is further illustrated in Figure 6, and its use in this paper was initiated by R. Ballow of the IBM Programming Productivity Techniques Department.
9. L. A. Belady and M. M. Lehman, *Programming System Dynamics or the Metadynamics of Systems in Maintenance and Growth*", RC 3546, IBM Thomas J. Watson Research Center, Yorktown Heights, New York (1971).
10. L. L. Constantine, "Control of sequence and parallelism in modular programs," *AFIPS Conference Proceedings, Spring Joint Computer Conference* 32, 409 (1968).
11. G. M. Weinberg, *PL/I Programming: A Manual of Style*, McGraw-Hill, New York, New York (1970).
12. *Improved Programming Technologies: Management Overview*, IBM Corporation, Data Processing Division, White Plains, New York (August 1973).

TRANSFORM ANALYSIS

Meilir Page-Jones

Transform analysis (or transform-centered design, as it is also known) is the major strategy for designing balanced systems, which — as we saw in Section 8.3 — are easier to develop and cheaper to maintain than physically input- or output-driven systems. The whole point of transform analysis is to convert the DFD of analysis to the structure chart of design.

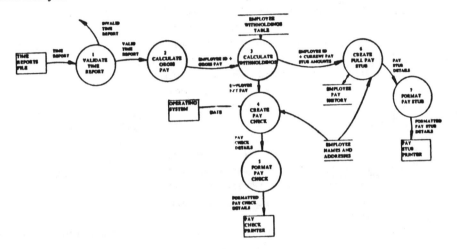

Figure 9.1

The application of transform analysis to the DFD shown above in Fig. 9.1, depicting an hourly workers payroll system that prints pay checks and pay stubs, would yield a balanced structure chart of the same payroll system as pictured in Fig. 9.2.

Notice that the top modules deal with refined, clean, and logical data while the bottom modules deal with unedited, format-dependent data. That, after all, is what a balanced system is. (I will return to this system in more detail later in this chapter.)

I have stated that transform analysis is a *strategy* — a plan of attack, a game plan. It is not an algorithm, for an algorithm provides a cookbook approach. If you follow the steps of an algorithm meticulously, you're assured of a correct result. If you follow the steps of a strategy, you will get within sight of a good result, but you will rarely attain perfection.

When you carry out transform analysis, remember that it is a strategy. You cannot unthinkingly follow its steps as you could those of an algorithm. From time to time, to stay on the right track, you must bring to bear your knowledge of what the system is supposed to accomplish. And, when you derive your first structure chart, you must use all the design criteria you have learned to improve it.

One day, transform analysis may become an algorithm. But if it does, the structure chart will disappear and the DFD will be implemented directly, for a machine can obey an algorithm much better than can a human being. At the moment, however, arbitrary DFDs cannot be implemented directly, because, in general, languages and operating systems are just not sophisticated enough.* By the year 2000, perhaps, we shall see DFDs being executed on a horde of

---

* However, the UNIX[†] operating system and the ADA programming language have made some dramatically successful advances in directly implementing simple DFDs. ([†]UNIX is a registered trademark of Bell

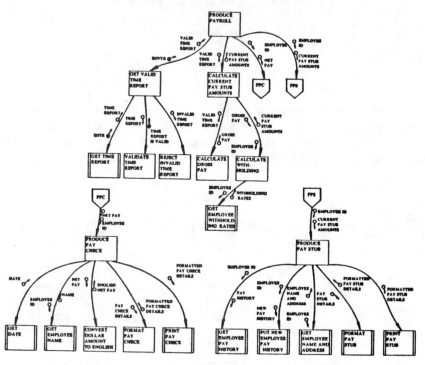

Figure 9.2

dynamically reconfigurable microprocessors. But until then, we must rely on transform analysis.

Transform analysis is composed of the following five steps: drawing a DFD for the problem, finding the central functions of the DFD, converting the DFD into a rough-cut structure chart, refining this structure chart by means of Structured Design criteria, and verifying that the final structure chart meets the requirements of the original DFD. I explain these step and their sub-topics below.

9.1 Step 1: Draw a DFD

If Structured Analysis has preceded Structured Design, then there will be a set of rigorous DFDs in the structured specification. If not, then it's worth the time it takes to sketch out some DFDs from the verbal outpourings of the functional specification.

Not only will the DFDs be the input to transform analysis, but drawing them will help to clarify the specification. Don't go to such a level of detail that you have more bubbles than you know what to do with. Stay at a level that has a few dozen bubbles at most. If you find you need more detail (or less detail) in a particular area, then go down (or up) a level in that area.

9.2 Step 2: Identify the central transform

The central transform is the portion of the DFD that contains the essential functions of the system and is independent of the particular implementation of the input and output. It can be found in either of two ways. The first way to identify the center of the DFD is just by looking at it. For example, study Fig. 9.3 on the next page.

The DFD in Fig. 9.3 is atrocious.* Its bubbles are named so bandly that we have only its shape

---

Laboratories.) For more information about ADA, see P. Wegner, *Programming with ADA* (Englewood Cliffs, N.J.: Prentice-Hall, 1980), especially Chapters 4 and 5.

* This DFD's author has been banished to Baffin Island with only a **COBOL ABEND** dump for companionship.

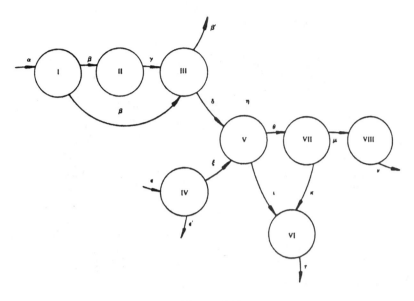

Figure 9.3

to help us to identify the central transform. Where is its center? V? VII? No one knows for sure, but it's reasonable to assume V, VI, and VII are in or near the central transform.

A second, better way to find the central transform is to identify the center of the DFD by pruning off its afferent and efferent branches. You do this by following three steps: First, trace each afferent stream from the outside of the DFD toward the middle. Mart the data flow that represents the input has been thoroughly refined, but has not yet been used for actual processing. Second, trace each efferent stream from the outside of the DFD toward the middle. Mark the data flow that represents the output at its most logical form. In other words, mark the stage at which the input has just been produced, but has not yet been formatted. Third, join all the marks in a closed curve.

Let's look at Fig. 9.3 to determine how we would use the second method to identify the DFD's central transform. First, however, we'd better put real names on it, as in Fig. 9.4.

A and B mark the beginnings of the two afferent streams, which we have to follow toward the center of the DFD. The data flow VALID TRANSACTION (at point E of Fig. 9.4) represents stream A at its most logical. A TRANSACTION, for instance, is not as refined as a VALID TRANSACTION. Conversely, we can't continue further toward the center in our search for more refined input because the bubble MATCH TRANSACTION WITH MASTER RECORD actually seems to be processing both afferent streams.

Similar reasoning tells us that VALID MASTER RECORD (at point F of Fig. 9.4) represents stream B at its most logical. So, we can now mark the most logical points of the afferent streams, as shown in the figure. C and D are the ends of the two efferent streams, which we have to follow back toward the center of the DFD. The data flow APPLIED TRANSACTION (at point G of Fig. 9.4) represents stream D at its most logical. (UPDATE MASTER RECORD, the next bubble inward, is doing the processing that generates APPLIED TRANSACTION.)

The efferent stream C is not so simple as D is. The shape of the DFD tells us to draw the line at NEW MASTER RECORD. However, there is a data flow that is more logical than is NEW MASTER RECORD. In fact, there are two of them! I would draw the line that marks stream C at its most logical across UNMATCHED MASTER RECORD and UPDATED MASTER RECORD (see points H and I on Fig. 9.4).

Now we connect the lines to make a closed curve (marked J on Fig. 9.4). The bubbles inside this curve comprise the central transform. As you can see, there is some subjectivity in choosing the central transform. Rarely, however, is there *much* disagreement about its boundary.

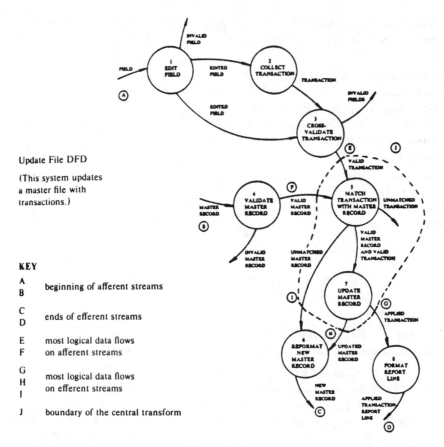

Update File DFD

(This system updates a master file with transactions.)

KEY

A
B   beginning of afferent streams

C
D   ends of efferent streams

E
F   most logical data flows
     on afferent streams

G
H
I   most logical data flows
     on efferent streams

J   boundary of the central transform

Figure 9.4

People typically will argue about a bubble here or there, but it generally turns out to make little difference in the final design whether a particular bubble is included in the central transform. The design criteria will eventually pull any divergences in the derived structure charts together. However, a dubious bubble usually does not belong in the central transform — if in doubt, leave it out.

People often use the "ideal-world" method to determine what bubbles are central to the DFD. To use this method, ask yourself: "If this were an ideal world, what bubbles in the DFD would just go away?" For example, if the input data never contained errors, there would be not need for validating processes. If the user didn't care about the format of his reports, there would be no need for formatting processes. What's left — the processes that would still have to be done even in an ideal world — comprises the central transform. It's interesting to note that in commercial systems, the central transform turns out to be a small proportion of the overall DFD, which often shows how far commercial EDP is from being an ideal world!

9.3 Step 3: Produce a first-cut structure chart

Remember that the purpose of transform analysis is to turn a DFD into a structure chart. The main difference between a DFD and a structure chart is that a structure chart depicts boss-hood.* In a DFD, there are no bosses. The bubbles are like happy workers in an idyllic commune, each one attending to its own work and sending its product to the next worker in line. But, the application of transform analysis introduces the shocking news that in the future the commune is to have bosses — and, in particular, one chief for the whole organization.

---

* The hierarchy of levels of a set of DFDs represents a hierarchy of detail; on a structure chart, the hierarchy of modules represents control as well as detail.

In the real world, we would have two choices about where to find this head honcho: We could promote someone from within the organization, or we could hire a new boss from outside the organization.

Transform analysis gives us the same two choices: A bubble in the central transform may stand out as a potential boss. One feature setting it apart from other bubbles may be that it does little processing but a lot of "traffic cop" activity, sending data hither and thither. That's equivalent to coordinating the work of other bubbles. Another feature setting it apart from other bubbles could be termed geometric: A bubble in the center of a spider's web of data flows is likely to have good coordinating abilities.

There may be two or three bubbles that each look worthy for promotion. If so, try each one in turn to see which gives the best initial design. However, it's very possible that there is *no* obvious candidate for boss, in which case you would have to choose a boss that is not presently in the DFD at all.

To sum up Step 3:

IF there is a good candidate for boss (in
the central transform)

THEN pick up the boss and let all the other bubble
hand down

OTHERWISE hire a new boss, consider the central
transform as one DFD bubble, and hand the central
transform and each afferent and efferent branch
from the new boss

Let's examine the promote-a-boss approach first. Picture the DFD as a set of ping-pong balls tied together with pieces of string.

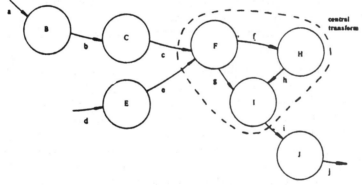

Figure 9.5

Choose one ping-pong ball from the central transform as boss. Now imagine that you pick up this boss ping-pong ball, and let the other ping-pong balls dangle. The DFD represented by our ping-pong balls is on its way to become a structure chart, as depicted in Fig. 9.6.

There's plenty of work still to do to complete this metamorphosis. Notice that I removed the arrowheads from the data flows. That's because DFD arrowheads won't necessarily correspond to structure chart arrowheads; direction of data flow isn't the same thing as direction of call. Next, the arrowheads for calls need to be added and the oval bubbles need to be redrawn as square modules. Names of modules won't necessarily correspond to names of bubbles, either; a module's name has to sum up the activities of its subordinates, while a bubble's name describes only its own activity.

229

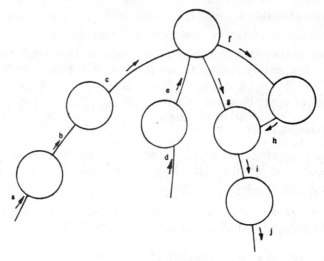

Figure 9.6

Adding read and write modules gives the diagram in Fig. 9.7, a first-cut structure chart.

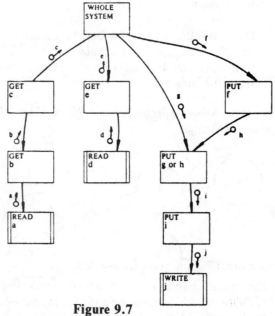

Figure 9.7

Let's follow the promote-a-boss method to Step 4.

Step 4: Revise the first-cut structure chart

The simple structure chart in Fig. 9.7 is good, but not great. It's a first cut that will benefit from the application of the design criteria — especially factoring and cohesion. In order to produce a better design, the following revision to the structure chart should be made:

Add read and write modules (with keys if necessary) for accessing sources, sinks, and files.

Factor and reorganize the afferent and efferent modules — but keep the system balanced.

Factor the central transform (if necessary) using the DFD as a guideline. The levels of the DFD are useful in this regard.

Add error-handling modules.

Add initialization and termination details (if required).

Ensure that all modules have names in keeping with their hierarchical roles.

Show all flags that are necessary on a structure chart but not on a DFD (for example, "end of stream" information).

Check all the design criteria and be prepared to improve the design in *keeping with those criteria*. Look first at system shape, factoring, cohesion, and decision-splitting.

Although an abstract example emphasizes the many mechanical aspects of transform analysis, it is also important to see the technique used in a real example. Let's repeat this process on a real example, the Update File DFD, as shown in Fig. 9.4. From the central transform, I've chosen MATCH TRANSACTION WITH MASTER RECORD as a potential boss, because that bubble makes a matching decision that coordinates the activities of the bubbles around it.

The next step in the strategy is to remove the data flow arrowheads and the names of the bubbles, and to lift the whole mass by MATCH TRANSACTION WITH MASTER RECORD. The result in Fig. 9.8.

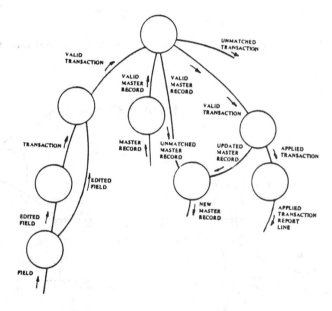

Figure 9.8

Adding some structure chart details gives us Fig. 9.9.

The module with the worst cohesion is UPDATE AND PUT MASTER RECORD AND REPORT TRANSACTION, which is communicational (to be precise, sequential and communicational in series). I'll try splitting this module and factoring out some of its functions (see Fig. 9.10).

Now, no module has less than sequential cohesion. The module FORMAT AND PUT NEW MASTER RECORD is sequentially cohesive and trivial (two simple lines of code). I would be tempted to place a hat on it, except that it is used by another module — UPDATE MASTER FILE — to output an UNMATCHED MASTER RECORD (see Fig. 9.9).

UPDATE AND PUT MASTER RECORD is also sequentially cohesive and trivial. But I *will* put a hat on this module. The only penalty I pay in getting rid of the module is the increased fan-out of the boss module, UPDATE MASTER FILE.

Now we have a second cut, shown in Fig. 9.11. My reason for not putting a hat on FORMAT AND PUT NEW MASTER RECORD (the reason being that it had fan-in) no longer holds true. Since I put a hat on UPDATE AND PUT MASTER RECORD, FORMAT AND PUT NEW MASTER RECORD is called only by UPDATE MASTER FILE. I could now put a hat

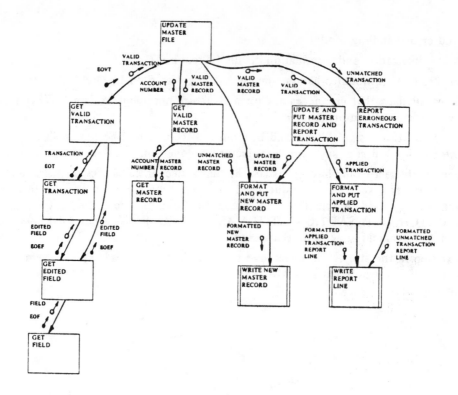

Figure 9.9

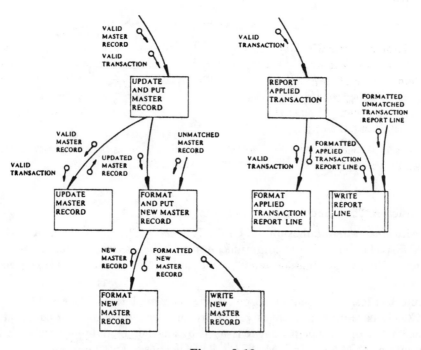

Figure 9.10

on this sequentially cohesive and trivial module. However, the fan-out from UPDATE MAS-TER FILE would then increase from six to seven. Worse, the whole system would become physically output-driven, for the boss would have to worry about the details of a FORMATTED NEW MASTER RECORD. So, FORMAT AND PUT NEW MASTER RECORD remains factored.

In the example above, we have accomplished Steps 3 and 4 of the transform analysis strategy: We have developed a rough structure chart, based upon the DFD of a problem (by

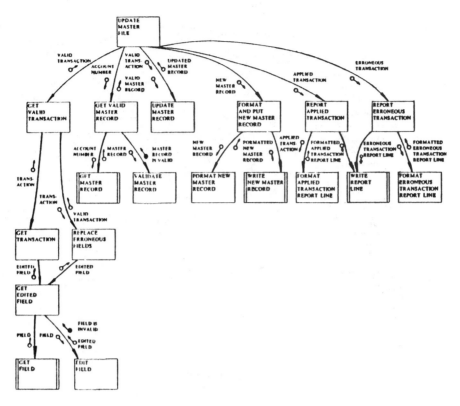

Figure 9.11

"promoting" a bubble), and we have revised that first, rough structure chart to develop an improved design. In our example for Step 3, we chose the THEN alternative (promoting a boss), rather than the OTHERWISE alternative (hiring a new boss). Hiring a new boss generally produces a better first-cut structure chart — although problems problems with both approaches will be resolved by an application of the design criteria. (Hiring a new boss also eliminates the need to choose one.)

So, let's backtrack and explore the OTHERWISE of Step 3, the hire-a-new-boss approach, and follow it through Steps 3 and 4. We start with the abstract DFD in Fig. 9.12.

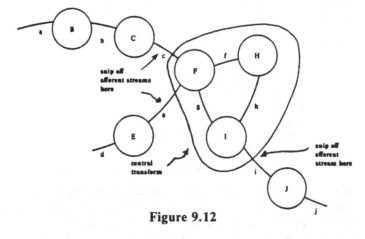

Figure 9.12

Find the central transform as before. Snip off all the afferent and efferent streams where they join the central transform. In this case, the DFD falls into four pieces. Tie each of these four pieces under the new, hired bubble, as shown in Fig. 9.13.

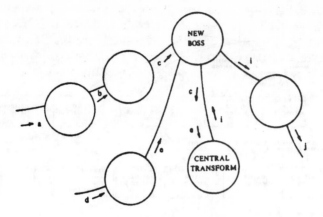

Figure 9.13

Once again, pick up the boss, and let the incipient structure chart dangle. The result is shown in Fig. 9.14 on the next page. Notice that in Fig. 9.14, I've taken an early opportunity to factor three modules from the central transform. These modules are the bubbles F, H, and I. It was easy for me to factor them out, since I knew that they were concealed in the central transform.

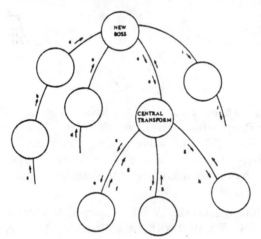

Figure 9.14

Figure 9.15 is the first-cut structure chart.

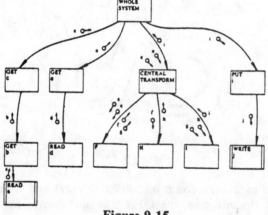

Figure 9.15

We've hired a new boss and — what do you know — the boss has brought its own lieutenant. The CENTRAL TRANSFORM module is needed on the structure chart merely to limit the fan-out from the boss. If we hadn't included it now, we'd probably have been obliged to do so later to reduce the fan-out from the boss. On the other hand, the boss module now may be so trivial that it acts as a mere messenger boy for c, e, and i. If that's so, we would put a hat on CENTRAL TRANSFORM and perhaps try factoring other subfunctions from the boss.

Let's try the hire-a-boss approach on a real example. We start, as before, by finding the central transform on our familiar Update File DFD, shown earlier in Fig. 9.4. Next we snip off the afferent and efferent streams and hand them with the whole central transform under the new boss (see Fig. 9.16).

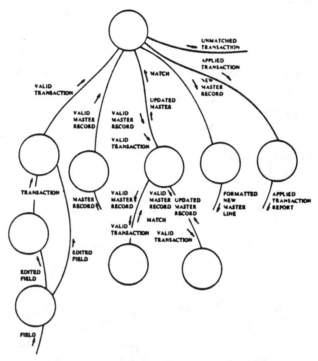

Figure 9.16

Figure 9.17 shows a first-cut structure chart that is much closer to the final design than was the first-cut produced by the promote-a-boss approach. The only real problem with this design is a decision-split. We could partially rectify this decision-split by putting a hat on the central transform module. I've called that module ?, because I can't think of a better name for it. That fact, together with the fact that it does almost nothing, makes it worth unfactoring. Once module ? has been removed, the decision-split is reduced to a single level. But neither UPDATE MASTER FILE nor MATCH MASTER WITH TRANSACTION has very complicated logic; indeed, MATCH MASTER WITH TRANSACTION is trivial. The decision-split can be eliminated entirely by unfactoring one step further and pushing MATCH MASTER WITH TRANSACTION into the boss module, to give Fig. 9.18. A beneficial result of this last step is that the fan-out from UPDATE MASTER FILE is reduced from seven to six.

Other areas worthy of factoring in both the promote-a-boss and the hire-a-boss approaches are the afferent and efferent branches, which often look very long and skinny. There's not much wrong with the afferent branch at the left, but it could be factored into the diagram at the right in Fig. 9.19.

Now that we've factored out two useful modules, EDIT FIELD and FORMAT FIELD, we have two very trivial modules named GET EDITED FIELD and GET FORMATTED FIELD. It's reasonable to put a hat on GET FORMATTED FIELD to give Fig. 9.20.

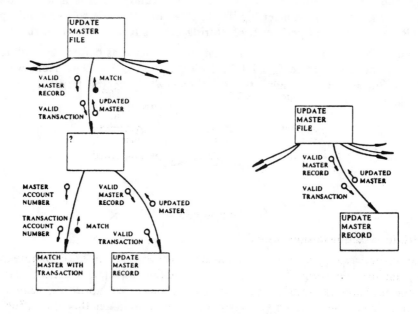

Figure 9.17   **Figure 9.18**

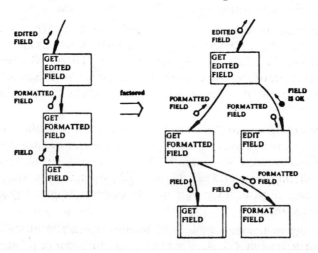

Figure 9.19

Don't carry out this process ad absurdum or you'll be left with a physically input-driven system that has some intolerable fan-outs. Already in this reasonable broadening of an afferent branch, we've lost a potentially useful module, GET FORMATTED FIELD. A good rule of thumb comes from our discussion of factoring in Section 8.1.6: When unfactoring the afferent or efferent branches of the structure chart, don't force a module to handle more than two different data structures. In this case, GET EDITED FIELD handles only one data structure, FIELD, although GET EDITED FIELD does encounter FIELD as a "raw" FIELD, as FORMATTED FIELD, and as EDITED FIELD.

Once the afferent and efferent modules are factored and slightly reorganized, the structure chart obtained by hiring a new boss looks very like that obtained by promoting a boss. Typically, the approach you take and the particular boss you choose become almost irrelevant once you've applied the design criteria.

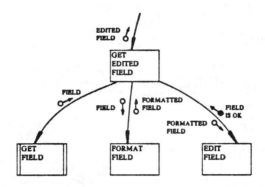

Figure 9.20

9.5 Step 5: Make sure the design works

The final step in the strategy is crucial: Make sure it works! The purpose of transform analysis is not to *do* transform analysis. The purpose is to attain quickly a structure chart that, first, implements the problem specification correctly and, second, lives up to the criteria for a maintainable system. People doing transform analysis sometimes forget this and, after having produced an excellent and correct structure chart, worry themselves silly about whether they drew the right boundary to the central transform or whether they chose the right boss.

The end is more important than the means. You can even discard transform analysis entirely if you can clearly see your way from the DFD to the final structure chart. Indeed, with a little practice, you should be able to do exactly that for many DFDs. But whatever approach you take to derive the structure chart, it's a good idea to have the author of the DFD review the structure chart derived from it to ensure that the structure chart correctly implements the requirements of the DFD.

Mechanically applying transform analysis is a good way to get a handle on any problem. But, if you don't look critically at the structure chart you produce and ensure that it makes sense, you can get some ludicrous results. For example, Fig. 9.21 is a DFD that updates a file with transactions. It's almost identical to the Update File DFD we've already been working with, except that during the updating of a record, errors may be discovered that require fresh, edited fields to replace the erroneous ones.

It is not obvious merely by looking at the DFD whether UPDATE MASTER RECORD should call GET EDITED FIELD or vice versa. The call could be either way (see Fig. 9.22).

However, common sense tells us that UPDATE AND PUT MASTER RECORD has to call GET EDITED FIELD since it is UPDATE MASTER RECORD that *wants* EDITED FIELD.

In more subtle cases, it might be necessary to look at the mini-specs for the bubbles to determine which module calls which.

9.6 Questions about transform analysis

So far in this chapter, in describing the basic transform analysis strategy, I have ignored several details and complications that may occur in practice. Below I cover these points in a question-and-answer format.

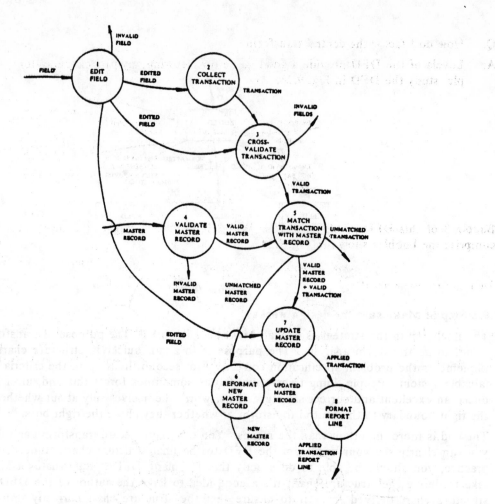

Figure 9.21

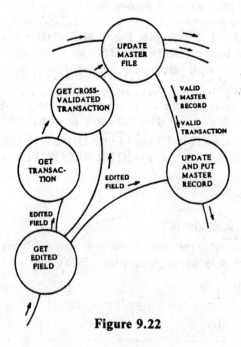

Figure 9.22

Q. How do I factor the central transform?

A. Levels of the DFD provide a good guide for factoring any part of the system. For example, study the DFD in Fig. 9.23.

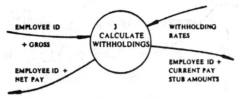

Figure 9.23

Bubble 3 of this DFD, CALCULATED WITHHOLDINGS, might at a lower level be seen to comprise the bubbles shown in Fig. 9.24.

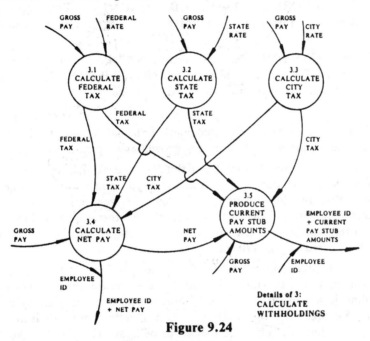

Figure 9.24

The factoring of the module CALCULATE WITHHOLDINGS is determined from the leveling of the bubble CALCULATE WITHHOLDINGS and is shown in Fig. 9.25.

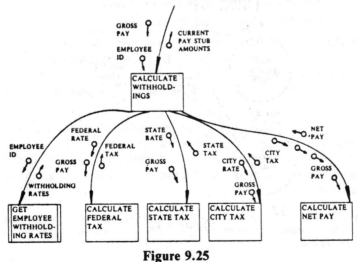

Figure 9.25

239

Four way in which my factoring of the structure chart differs from the leveling of the DFD are

I put a hat on PRODUCE CURRENT PAY STUB AMOUNTS, since in the DFD, it was just a dummy bubble drawn to bring together a number of data flows to form CURRENT PAY STUB AMOUNTS.

CALCULATE NET PAY involves a trivial piece of arithmetic which in COBOL would be:

$$\text{COMPUTE NET PAY} = \text{GROSS–PAY} - \text{FEDERAL–TAX}$$

$$- \text{STATE–TAX} - \text{CITY–TAX}$$

Since the module has only one boss and is unlikely to prove useful in the future, I can put a hat on it, too.

The DFD in Fig. 9.23 say I should have CALCULATE WITHHOLDINGS return EMPLOYEE ID with CURRENT PAY STUD AMOUNTS. I don't do that because the boss already knows the information in EMPLOYEE ID; he must, because he sent it down!

CALCULATE WITHHOLDINGS doesn't return NET PAY, although the DFD says it should. However, NET PAY is included in CURRENT PAY STUB AMOUNTS, a point that can be gleaned only from the data dictionary.*

Q.   What if I hire a new boss and then discover that the job he has to do is utterly trivial? Or, what if I decide on the promote-a-boss approach and I pick the wrong bubble?

A.   This question is an example of what I call the "Las Vegas" mentality exhibited by some designers. When you carry out transform analysis, you don't have to stake everything on a single throw. You should try out two or three different bosses. It takes only a few minutes to sketch the top of the structure chart. By the time you have completed the sketch, you can tell which approach will give you a design that is most easily improved by means of the Structured Design criteria.

However, I will answer the question as posed. The usual symptom of having chosen the wrong boss is a decision-split in which the rightful boss of the structure chart passes a flag up to the nominated boss telling it what to do. You can improve the decision-split by pushing the real boss up to "usurp" the pretender to the throne. But a better approach is to learn from the mistake and to try promoting the bubble that *wants* to be boss. (By the way, you'll never completely remove decision-splits from an average system. When you cure a decision-split, remember that cohesion, factoring, and balanced systems are more important criteria to follow than avoiding decision-splits: Don't jeopardize them.)

Q.   How can I apply transform analysis to large systems?

A.   It's unlikely that applying transform analysis alone will work on a large system, for you will find that seventy-five percent of the DFD seems to be central transform, and that there are dozens of afferent and efferent streams. The best way to tackle a complex DFD is to break it down by transactions. (I discuss this method in Chapter 10 on transaction analysis.)

Each transaction that a system accepts will use perhaps one or two afferent streams and two or three efferent streams. Treat the bubbles between the relevant afferent and efferent streams as a separate subsystem for the purpose of transform analysis. You can exploit any commonality among the subsystems as shared modules with fan-in when you put all the subsystems together into one structure chart.

---

* The data dictionary is an essential tool in creating a DFD (to check that Bubble 3 tallies with the detailed breakdown of Bubble 3, for example). A data dictionary is also essential is using a DFD because, without it, a complex DFD hardly makes sense.

Q. At which level of the DFD should I apply transform analysis?

A. Apply it at a fairly high level. If you try using it at a level of detail that forces you to deal with twenty or thirty bubbles per transaction, you'll soon get into a tangle. It's better to tackle at most ten to twenty higher-level bubbles first, and then to use the details from the lower levels as an aid in factoring.

9.7 Summary

In this chapter, we have seen how a DFD, the major product of Structured Analysis, can be used to derive a structure chart, the major product of Structured Design. That the transformation from DFD to structure chart is reasonably straightforward should not surprise you, for the aims of Structured Analysis and Structured Design are almost identical. Both disciplines seek to control the complexity of a system by partitioning the system in a top-down manner and with minimal interfaces between the components of the system, by striving for black-box functions whenever possible, by suppressing procedural details, and by minimizing redundancy.

However, there are some differences between the DFD and the structure chart: The DFD is intended to be a tool whose chief purpose is to tackle the problem — the requirements of the system — whereas the chief purpose of the structure chart is to tackle the solution to the problem — the design of a computer implementation of the system. The strategy of transform analysis enables us to bridge the gap between the network of processes that comprises a DFD and the hierarchy of modules that forms a structure chart, and hence to use Structured Analysis as a tremendous aid to quickly deriving a reasonable Structured Design.

TRANSACTION ANALYSIS

Meilir Page-Jones

Transform analysis, which we have just examined in Chapter 9, is the major strategy for converting a DFD into a structure chart. However, a supplementary technique called transaction analysis (or transaction-centered design) is extremely valuable in deriving the structure chart for a system that processes transactions.

Transaction analysis has two main uses: First, it can be used to cleave a large, complicated DFD into smaller DFDs — one for each transaction that the system processes. These smaller DFDs are then simple enough to be converted by transform analysis into a number of small structure charts. (This part of transaction analysis, which I call "route-mapping," is covered in Appendix E, the case study.) Second, transaction analysis can be used to combine the individual structure charts for the separate transactions into one larger structure chart that is very flexible under user changes.

I devote much of this chapter to the organization of the structure chart for maintainable transaction-processing systems. This is the most profound part of transaction analysis, for it marks a radical departure from traditional methods of handling transactions. If you understand how a well-organized transaction-centered structure chart should appear, then you will find the DFD representation of transactions and the transition from a transaction-centered DFD to a transaction-centered structure chart very straightforward. So in this chapter, I reverse the order of topics of the last chapter and cover the structure chart before I cover the DFD.

A transaction, in its broadest, most formal sense, is a stimulus to a system that triggers a set of activities within the system. Examples of transactions are a signal to a space vehicle to fire its retro engines, a coolant-temperature alarm in a fission reactor, or a clock interrupt in an operating system. The activities associated with these transactions would be, respectively, the firing of the space vehicle's retro engines, the shutting down of the reactor, and the starting of a new time slice.

The above definition of a transaction is broad enough to apply to real-time systems, such as process-control or operating systems. However, a definition that is valid for most other purposes is: A *transaction* is a single item or — more often — a collection of input data that can fall into one of a number of types. Each type of transaction if processed by a specific set of activities within the system.

Commercial data processing has thousands of examples of transactions. A transaction in a utility company system, for instance, might contain the information for adding a new customer, deleting an old customer, changing a customer's address, or billing a customer. Every customer transaction entering the system would carry a *tag* (alias *transaction code*) — for example, ADD, DELETE, BILL — to indicate its type. By referring to the tag, the system would determine what processing each respective transaction required and would make sure that the transaction was handled by the appropriate lines of code.

10.1 The difficulties with conventional transaction processing

Before the development of transaction analysis, the design of transaction-processing systems was notoriously ad hoc and haphazard. The systems that resulted were typically inflexible, error-prone, and difficult to understand. Theses problems arose because each type of transaction normally needs to be processed differently, and yet the processing for all types of transactions is often very similar. Consequently, programmers would use all manner of tricks to share common code between transactions.

For example, each of the transaction types described above would need to have its fields validated similarly and would need to access a customer master file. However, in other respects, the processing for each type of transaction would be quite different. So, traditionally, programmers would identify which lines of code could be shared among different types of transactions and which lines of code were peculiar to a specific type of transaction. Then they would set flags and switches — often in very obscure ways — to force each type of transaction to take the appropriate path through monolithic chunks of shared code. Thus, each transaction would meander through line after line of code until it hit a line that might be inapplicable to it. There, it would encounter a test something like the code example that follows:

> IF TRANSACTION IS A 'CHANGE,' 'CORRECT,' OR
> 'DELETE' TRANSACTION
> THEN GO TO CCD-12.

which would cause a skip over perhaps twenty lines of inapplicable code.

A system that has to process fifty, one hundred, or even two hundred transactions soon becomes a tangle of code if it is "designed" in this way; but the fact that all the different types of transactions are tied into a Gordian knot is not exposed until the user changes the way in which he handles one or two transactions. When modifications to those transactions are made, other transactions somehow develop mysterious bugs, since they no longer find their way through the correct lines of shared code. It takes a lot of effort for the maintainers of a system to restore it to completely correct operation for every type of transaction.

10.2 Transaction-analysis principles

Bell Telephone of Canada, in a response to the slapdash methods of conventional transaction processing, cut the Gordian knot by developing a new technique called SAPTAD (for "System, Analysis, Program, Transaction, Action, and Detail").* Transaction analysis, which is a refinement of SAPTAD, has this fundamental principle:

> Using the tag, separate the various transactions
> by *type* and not by any common processing
> requirements.

In other words, regardless of how similar or different the types of transaction might be, there should be a separate module responsible for the processing of each type. These modules are called *transaction* modules; there are, of course, as many of them as there are transaction types. There is another module that determines the type of each transaction entering the system (by inspecting its tag) and routes it to its appointed transaction module. This is called a *transaction-center* module.

Applied to our example of the utility company transaction, transaction analysis leads to the design shown in Fig. 10.1. The modules APPLY ADD-CUSTOMER TRANSACTION, APPLY DELETE-CUSTOMER TRANSACTION, and APPLY BILL-CUSTOMER TRANSACTION are the transaction modules. With their subordinates, they ensure that their respective transactions are processed. The module APPLY CUSTOMER TRANSACTION is the transaction-center module, which is responsible for discovering the type of each transaction and for sending it to its appropriate transaction module.

A diamond symbol at the bottom of a module signifies that the module calls *either* subordinate A *or* subordinate B *or* one of the other subordinates connected to the diamond, depending on the result of a test. (The test in APPLY CUSTOMER TRANSACTION would be the

---

* P. Vincent, "The System Structure Design Method," *Proceedings of the 1968 National Symposium on Modular Programming*, ed. by Tom O. Barnett (Cambridge, Mass.: Information & System Press, 1968 — out of print).

inspection of the transaction tag.) This construct is referred to as a *transaction center* and would be implemented by a case construct in the calling module (e.g., GOTO DEPENDING ON in COBOL, COMPUTED GOTO in FORTRAN, SELECT in PL/I, case in Pascal).*

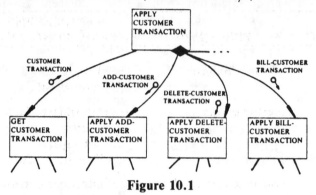

Figure 10.1

The advantage of this design over the shared-code approach is that the processing for all of the transaction types is cleanly partitioned, so that any change to the processing for one type of transaction will not affect that for any other type.

The penalty we've apparently paid for this cleanliness is having identical code in many different modules, since many transaction types require similar processing. Fear not, however. In the next section, we see how factoring comes to our rescue to eliminate this problem.

10.3 Factoring transaction modules

A less obvious example of a transaction than that in Fig. 10.1 — but one that nevertheless satisfies the definition of a transaction — is a field from a record. In Table 10.1, I show the processing (specifically validating and formatting) that each of seven types of fields requires.

The transaction-centered design for the piece of a system that validates and formats these fields is shown in Fig. 10.2. As the figure shows, there is one module to validate and format each type of field, plus one to report any field numbers that are out of range. Now, if the user should change the validating or formatting rules for the customer name, for example, then those changes could be addressed in the VALIDATE AND FORMAT CUSTOMER NAME module. The changes would have almost no chance of disturbing the correct operation of, say, VALIDATE AND FORMAT CUSTOMER CITY NAME.

So far, we've accounted for the differences in processing each type of field by having a separate module for validating and formatting each type of field. But, as Table 10.1 clearly shows, many of the processing details are identical from field type to field type. How can we make use of that fact? Simply by factoring out common functions into new modules at a lower level (this is the application of factoring discussed in Section 8.1.3 — the sharing of common functions).

In this example of validating and formating fields, we'll need the seven modules shown in Fig. 10.3.

These modules would be called as appropriate to validate and format each field. (Of course, in a high-level language, some of these modules could be single statements in the validating routines.) We've now gained a lot of flexibility, because if the validation criteria for a field change, we simply call on a different set of bottom-level modules. If a new field is introduced, all of the modules needed for its validation probably already exist.

To emphasize the value of transaction analysis, it's worthwhile contrasting the transaction-centered design of Figs. 10.2 and 10.3 with a more conventional approach to validating and formatting fields. A common way to organize the editing of a field is to have an EDIT ALL

---

* The case construct is an n-way test and can be thought of as an extension to the IF-THEN-ELSE construct, which is a two-way test.

Table 10.1

FIELD NUMBER (TAG)	FIELD TYPE	PROCESSING REQUIRED (VALIDATING AND FORMATTING)
02	account number	validate numeric check length of 6
02	customer name	validate alphabetic left-justify pad with spaces check length of 20
03	customer street address	validate alphanumeric left-justify pad with spaces check length of 30
04	customer city	validate alphabetic left-justify pad with spaces check length of 30
05	customer state	validate alphabetic check length of 2 ensure valid state
06	customer zip code	validate numeric check length of 5
07	customer balance	validate numeric right-justify pad with zeros

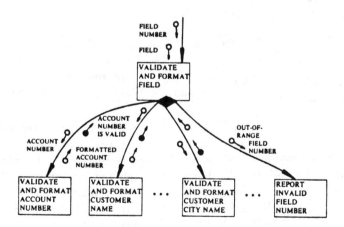

Figure 10.2

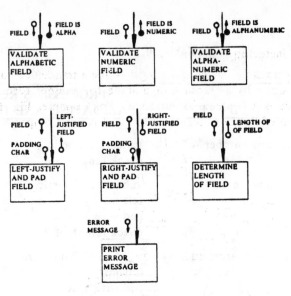

Figure 10.3

ALPHABETIC FIELDS module, the code for which might be

```
check field is alphabetic
if field number = 2 or field number = 4
then left justify field
          pad field with spaces
          if field number = 2
          then check number = 20
          else check length = 30
          endif
elseif field number = 5
then check length = 2
          check field against state table
elseif ...
...
endif
```

(or some even worse code containing GOTOS). Not only is this code difficult to understand but is would also be difficult to change if the user decided that, in the future, customer names would be alphanumeric. Implementing that change would require major internal surgery to both the EDIT ALL ALPHABETIC FIELDS and the EDIT ALL ALPHANUMERIC FIELDS modules.

The difference between the transaction-centered philosophy and the conventional transaction-handling philosophy should now be apparent. Transaction analysis assumes that each transaction will be processed totally differently and regards and similarities in function between transaction modules as pieces of good fortune that can be exploited by factoring. The conventional approach assumes that many transactions will be processed similarly and herds similar-looking transactions into the same module, leaving the code of the module to take care of the many differences that exist among the transactions. The transaction-centered approach leads to far more general and flexible systems than does the conventional approach because it avoids depending on similarities, which are susceptible to change.

Transaction analysis seems to violate the guideline of fan-out. For example, if the record in Fig. 10.2 contained 25 fields, then the VALIDATE AND FORMAT FIELD module would have had a fan-out of 26. Although 26 is well beyond human hrair (about 7), neither the original programmer nor the maintenance programmer should have any problem in understanding the module, for he will never have to think about all 26 subordinates at one time. Indeed, since a transaction center is essentially a case construct, he will have to consider only *one* subordinate at a time.

10.3.1 Another example of factoring modules

As a result of factoring, it is possible — and quite legal — for a transaction module for one type of transaction to be called upon by a transaction module for another type. Indeed, in many commercial applications, this is a frequent occurrence. For example, Fig. 10.4 shows part of the Customer Service System of the Consolidated Volts and Amps Company.

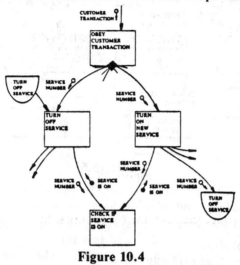

Figure 10.4

To turn on the electricity service for a new tenant, the company first may have to turn off the previous tenant's service. TURN ON NEW SERVICE checks whether service is already on. If it is, then the transaction module TURN ON NEW SERVICE call TURN OFF SERVICE, which is itself a transaction module.

10.4 Transaction centers in on-line systems

A kind of transaction center often found in on-line systems is one in which the user is given a menu of options from which to select one. An example would be in a system to direct a missile-bearing ship from a CRT.

Table 10.2

COMMAND TAG	COMMAND TYPE	PROCESSING REQUIRED
TURN	turn ship	turn ship from present angle by specified amount
SET	set ship course	set ship to absolute course
FIRE	fire missile	fire missile in specified direction
SCUTTLE	self-destruct	blow up ship after specified time

The transaction center to implement this system is shown in Fig. 10.5.

The interesting feature of the transaction center in Fig. 10.5 is that the top module calls each of the transaction modules with no data at all. This isn't a mistake; each transaction-processing subsystem is responsible for obtaining its own input and delivering its own output. Separating the respective inputs and outputs of each subsystem in this way leads to much greater flexibility

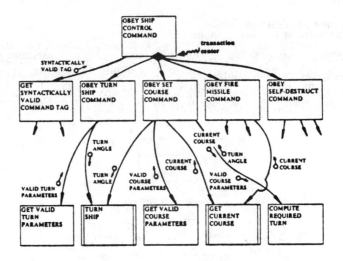

Figure 10.5

than was provided in Fig. 10.1, in which the top module collects the input, hands it to the appropriate transaction module, and accepts the transaction module's output. That method required the top module to be aware of the syntax of almost all of the information in the system. Since the top module doesn't need any of that information, we'd have a case of "tramp stamp" coupling! Worse, it would be difficult to modify the system to permit each subsystem to enter into its own conversation with the user or to obtain data from its own data base.

The ship system has fan-in to TURN SHIP from OBEY TURN SHIP COMMAND and OBEY SET COURSE COMMAND. The two subsystems for turning the ship and for setting a course are very similar: The main difference is that OBEY SET COURSE COMMAND must determine the ship's direction and how much it must turn the ship before it can call TURN SHIP. Almost certainly, there would be no fan-in between the OBEY SELF-DESTRUCT COMMAND subsystem and any other (except perhaps to some very low-level editing modules).

10.5 Cohesion of a transaction center

What is the cohesion of a transaction center? Well, it varies. Most transaction centers have high cohesion, but it's possible for a perfectly good transaction center to have coincidental cohesion. The cohesion of the top of a system is always at the mercy of the user. Imagine, for example, a system that does inventory, bullion-futures forecasting, and missile tracking: If the user insists, you will have to implement this system despite your abject cries of "coincidental cohesion!" But the application of transaction analysis would lead to a clean system, in which the strange bedfellows are separated at the top of the structure chart, as in Fig. 10.6.

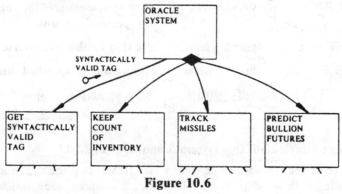

Figure 10.6

10.6 Identifying transactions on DFDs

Very often, it's extremely easy to recognize transactions, transaction centers, and transaction-processing bubbles on a DFD by the shape of the diagram alone. Wherever a data flow enters a bubble that determines its type, and routes it in one of several directions depending on its type, you can be sure that you've located a transaction entering a transaction center. The DFD for the editing field transaction center represented as a structure chart in Fig. 10.2 is shown in Fig. 10.7.

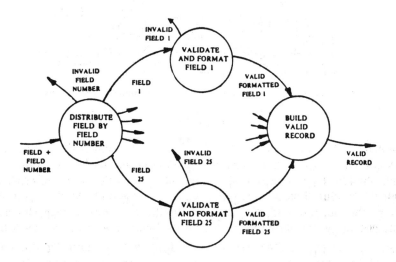

Figure 10.7

(I've assumed that all fields, having been validated and formatted, are collected into a single record.) The bubble DISTRIBUTE FILED BY FIELD NUMBER contains the transaction center, which, acting like a railroad switching yard, sends each field along its appropriate line to the bubble that validates and formats it. However, the manifestation of transactions on a DFD is often more subtle (see Fig. 10.8).

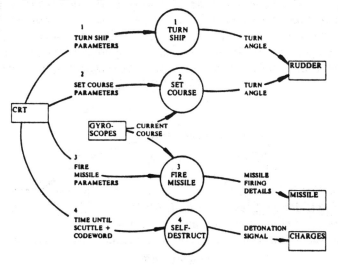

Figure 10.8

I've numbered the types of transactions entering this system 1, 2, 3, and 4. The bubbles that will become transaction modules on the DFD are also numbered 1, 2, 3, and 4. But where is

249

the transaction-center module to be found? Clearly, it is nowhere on the DFD.

Some people are tempted to insert a bubble that routes the input, as shown in Fig. 10.9.

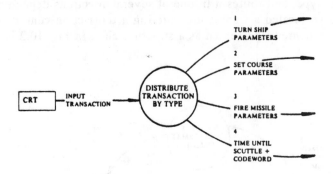

Figure 10.9

However, this violates the principle I laid down in Section 10.4 that no single module (or bubble) should need to be aware of every type of transaction in the system, for that would needlessly overcomplicate the module and would render the whole system inflexible. Instead, wherever possible, each transaction module should be responsible for obtaining its own input and dispatching its own output.

The best way to highlight a transaction center on a DFD is shown in Fig. 10.10.

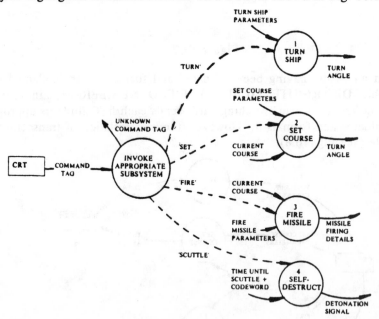

Figure 10.10

In the figure, I've shown dotted lines radiating from INVOKE APPROPRIATE SUBSYSTEM. They are, blatantly, lines of control that simply invoke the appropriate subsystem to handle the type of command the user has specified by the command tag. To show these as solid lines would be dishonest, for they bear no data. The transaction center of this DFD is clearly at INVOKE APPROPRIATE SUBSYSTEM. To transform the DFD into the structure chart of Fig. 10.5, you can simply pick up the bubble INVOKE APPROPRIATE SUBSYSTEM as if you were carrying out transform analysis.

250

Because of the graphic difficulties of showing a transaction center as explicitly as Fig. 10.10, most designers simply omit the bubble INVOKE APPROPRIATE SUBSYSTEM and work directly from Fig. 10.8, but with an image of Fig. 10.10 in their minds. That's what I have done in Appendix E (the case study), which shows how an apparently complicated system can be broken into subsystems, each of which handles the processing of a single type of transaction. (Appendix E also shows transform and transaction analysis being used in tandem.)

Partitioning a DFD into subsystems by transaction can go awry because of the temptation not only to route the input for every type of transaction through a single bubble, but also to combine bubbles that are similar or identical in function but belong to different transactions. Figure 10.11 illustrates the case in which a single process is being used to edit the customer name from two distinct types of transaction.

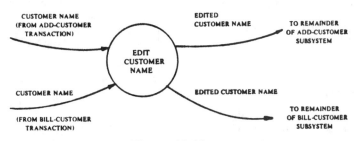

Figure 10.11

Resist the temptation to pull together data flows from afar simply because some of their processing is similar. If you do this, the DFD will soon look like a cat's cradle and will never yield to any strategy that attempts to convert it into a structure chart. Instead, keep the data flows separate and make a note of the similar features of any bubbles (possibly by a shared minispec). During design you can exploit any commonality of function by intelligent factoring and by the resultant fan-in to shared modules. Transaction analysis echoes once again the familiar theme of Structured Design: Divide and conquer.

An Illustration of Current Ideas on the Derivation of Correctness Proofs and Correct Programs

Reprinted from *IEEE Transactions on Software Engineering*, Volume SE-2, Number 4, December 1976, pages 238-244. Correction, *IEEE Transactions on Software Engineering*, Volume SE-3, Number 3, May 1977, page 262. Copyright © 1976, 1977 by The Institute of Electrical and Electronics Engineers, Inc.

DAVID GRIES

Abstract—The ideas behind correctness proofs for programs are outlined, and conventional definitions of assignment, etc., are given. The main part of this paper is the idealized development of a nontrivial program in a disciplined fashion. The use of Dijkstra's "calculus" for the formal development of programs as a guide to structuring program development is discussed in relation to the example presented.

Index Terms—Correctness proof, derivation of programs, programming methodology, programming language semantics.

I. CORRECTNESS PROOFS

A PROOF is an argument that convinces the reader (or listener) of the truth of some statement. The argument may be informal, or it may take the form of a proof as in logic—a finite sequence of statements (ending in the statement to be proved), each of which is an *axiom* or is derived from earlier statements by the application of an *inference rule*. A proof may indeed be faulty, as long as it convinces—until of course someone either finds a fault or discovers a counterexample to the statement "proved," in which case it is no longer convincing and hence no longer a proof.

Each programmer *tries* to prove his program correct, in that he argues to himself that it is so and writes documentation which hopefully will convince others. That the programmer has not really developed a proof is obvious, for even he himself is not convinced: he spends the majority of his time finding faults and attempting to cover them up. This is called "debugging." (Of course testing a program is necessary if it is to be executed to achieve some results, but if the program has been proved correct then the detection of a fault during testing would be the exception rather than the rule.)

The programmer cannot be blamed too much for this situation because by and large he has been given no tools or methods for proving programs correct. One of the more exciting developments in our field of programming was the development by Hoare [4], based on previous work by Floyd [3], of just such a logical system for proving programs correct. Hoare gave a definition of a programming language in the form of a logical system of axioms and inference rules, *without reference to how statements were to be executed*. That is, in his system, programs are regarded as mathematical objects in their own right, completely independent of the computer or of any "operational" definition which explains how to execute them. In the logical system, statements which have been

Manuscript received April 18, 1976; revised August 11, 1976. This work was partially supported by the National Science Foundation under Grant GJ-42512.

The author is with the Department of Computer Science, Cornell University, Ithaca, NY 14853.

proved true have the form $\{P\} \, S \, \{R\}$, where P and R can be interpreted as program assertions, and S as a program text. Under this interpretation, if execution of S is begun in a state in which P is true, then upon termination R will be true, provided of course that the implementation is consistent with the logical system.

Axiom schemes and inference rules for assignment, composition, alternation, and iteration are given below, using P and R for assertions, S for program statements, B for Boolean expressions, t for an integer function, and $t0$ for a constant.

Assignment: $\{P[e \rightarrow x]\} \, x := e \, \{P\}$

Composition: $\dfrac{\{P1\} \, S1 \, \{P2\}, \, \{P2\} \, S2 \, \{P3\}}{\{P1\} \, S1; S2 \, \{P3\}}$

Alternation: $\dfrac{B1 \textbf{ or } \cdots \textbf{ or } Bn, \quad \{P \wedge Bi\} \, Si \, \{R\} \text{ for } 1 \leqslant i \leqslant n}{\{P\} \textbf{ if } B1 \rightarrow S1 \, [] \, \cdots \, [] \, Bn \rightarrow Sn \textbf{ fi } \{R\}}$

Iteration: $\dfrac{\{P \textbf{ and } B\} \, S \, \{P\}, \quad \{P \textbf{ and } B \textbf{ and } t \leqslant t0 + 1\} \, S \, \{t \leqslant t0\}, \quad (P \textbf{ and } B) \Rightarrow t > 0}{\{P\} \textbf{ do } B \rightarrow S \textbf{ od } \{P \textbf{ and } \neg B\}}$

The assignment and composition rules are like those given by Hoare [4]. In the assignment rule, $P[e \rightarrow x]$ represents the assertion P, but with every occurrence of x replaced by e.

Alternation is expressed using Dijkstra's [1] nondeterministic guarded command structure. The rule may be interpreted as follows. The top line indicates that at least one of the expressions Bi must be true—otherwise abortion occurs. To execute the statement, one true "guard" Bi is nondeterministically chosen, and the corresponding command Si is executed. As an example, the following statement stores in z the maximum of x and y: if $x \geqslant y \rightarrow z := x \, [] \, y \geqslant x \rightarrow z := y$ fi.

For iteration, I have chosen to use a restricted form "do $B \rightarrow S$ od" of Dijkstra's [1] guarded command loop which is equivalent to the conventional loop "while B do S." In the definition of iteration, the relation P is called the (an) *invariant relation* of the loop. Modern programming methodology urges us to derive this relation P first, and to develop initialization, the terminating condition B, and the loop body S, all with the aid of P.

The iteration rule includes a termination requirement. Using t and $t0$ to denote an integer function and a constant, respectively, the second line of the rule can be interpreted to mean that execution of the loop body S must reduce t by at least 1. The third line then indicates that when t finally becomes nonpositive (which must happen after a finite number of iterations), B is false and the loop terminates.

252

Lack of time and space forces me to restrain myself to presenting this restricted form of Dijkstra's guarded command loop. I must limit myself to explaining only as much as I need in the subsequent program development. This is unfortunate, and I apologize for it, because the general nondeterministic guarded command loop is extremely useful and an important part of his theory.

I must also assume that the reader has seen and understands such axiomatic definitions somewhat. My purpose here is not to explain them, but to explain how they lend insight and can be used practically.

Now, such a logical system for proving programs correct can be used formally or informally. The purpose of the system is not just to introduce formalism for its own sake, but to lend insight into how to efficiently understand—and develop—programs.

When trying to apply the system, one quickly learns that it is difficult to prove an existing program correct. Instead, the correctness proof and the program itself should be developed hand in hand—with the former usually leading the latter! However, this is easier said than done. While the theory has helped us immensely in the past five years, and while some have developed considerable skill at using it, it has not been clear enough just how correctness ideas could be used to guide program development and to teach others how to develop programs.

Recently, displaying his characteristic insight, Dijkstra has provided us with some means for understanding program development better. In his paper [1] and his new book [2], he provides a "calculus"—a set of rules—for deriving programs. Successful application of these rules leads to a correct program. Of course, as with the integral calculus, we may not be able to apply it successfully. Success depends on the ability of the applier and the problem to which the rules are applied.

Besides introducing nondeterminism, Dijkstra's new twist is to view the definition of statements slightly differently. Reasoning that the definition of a statement type should reflect how the definition is to be used in *deriving* programs, Dijkstra defines a statement type S by giving the rule for deriving the weakest precondition $wp(S, R)$ for which execution of S will establish the desired postcondition R. For example, the definitions of assignment and composition are as follows (these should be compared with the earlier definitions):

$$wp(``x := e", P) = P[e \to x]$$
$$wp(``S1; S2", R) = wp(S1, wp(S2, R)).$$

A trivial change, you may say, but this new twist is enough to give us deeper insight into deriving programs. No longer are P, S, and R treated equally in the statement $\{P\} S \{R\}$. Instead, the definitions say that we must derive the precondition P from S and R. As such, S is a "predicate transformer" which transforms R into P. (And note that the definition still says nothing about execution of S.)

This is not the place for a full discussion of Dijkstra's ideas. Rather, I would like to give you a feel for their use by describing an idealized version of a program development. Hopefully, this will whet your appetite for more quality and quantity, which can be found in his book. While perhaps difficult to read (only because of the subject matter), it is a masterpiece. Of course, the subsequent program development is a mixture of my own experience and ideas, influenced by my interpretation of Dijkstra's ideas. I apologize for any misunderstandings that might arise because of this interpretation, and urge you to go back to the source—his new book.

II. DEVELOPMENT OF AN ALGORITHM

The problem I have chosen to discuss is a realistic one that occurs in any "text editor" or "format" program. At least initially, it does not seem very "mathematical," because it has to do with processing strings or words rather than integers. I do not remember solving it before, although I did give it as an "extra credit" part of a programming project many years ago, which few students actually completed. The development described below is an idealized version of the actual development that occurred when I tackled the problem in the spring of 1976. I did try to discipline my development, and indeed, the real development followed this idealized version quite closely, although it was naturally a bit rougher.

A *line justifier* inserts extra blanks between the words on a line so that the last character of the last word appears in the last column of the line. For example, the three lines

justifying ⊓ lines ⊓ by
inserting ⊓ extra ⊓ blanks ⊓ is
the ⊓ task ⊓ of ⊓ a ⊓ text ⊓ editor.   (1)

would appear right-justified on a 26-character line as

justifying ⊓⊓⊓⊓ lines ⊓⊓⊓⊓⊓ by
inserting ⊓⊓ extra ⊓ blanks ⊓ is
the ⊓ task ⊓ of ⊓ a ⊓ text ⊓ editor.   (2)

The number of blanks between different pairs of words on a line may differ by no more than 1. Secondly, in order to lessen the impact of extra blanks on the reader, the justifier uses an alternating technique for insertion: when necessary, for odd (even) lines more blanks are inserted toward the right (left) of the line. For example, in line 1 of (2) above, the number of blanks between successive pairs of words is 4 and 5; on line 2 it is 2, 1, and 1.

We want an algorithm for performing the more difficult part of justification. Given the column numbers where the words begin on the unjustified line, we want to determine the column numbers where they begin on the justified line. For line 1 of (1) above, the words begin in columns $(1, 12, 18)$; judging by line 1 of (2), this should be changed into $(1, 15, 25)$. For line 2, $(1, 11, 17, 24)$ should be changed to $(1, 12, 18, 25)$. For line 3, $(1, 5, 10, 13, 15, 20)$ remains unchanged.

The following would probably be typical of the kind of documentation produced by today's programmer for this problem (if any is written at all):

```
proc justify (n, z, s: integer;
        var b: array [*] of integer);
{Line z has n words on it. They begin in columns b[1],
    · · · , b[n]. Exactly one blank separates each pair. Param-
    eter s is the number of spaces which must be inserted be-
    tween words in order to justify the line.
```

Procedure determines new column numbers $b[1:n]$ so that the line will be justified in the conventional manner, alternating depending on the line number z.}

At this point, we ask the reader to attempt to develop a correct algorithm for the procedure, so that he can compare his development with the one presented subsequently.

Assuming our task is to develop the procedure body, where and how do we begin? Certainly the above specification is too vague (although five years ago I would not have thought so), and we must make it more precise. The proof method requires pre- and postconditions for the program. If we are to let the proof guide program development, then we have no choice but to write specifications as pre- and postconditions for the procedure body.

Using Bi to represent the initial value in $b[i]$, we write the input assertion

$$s \geqslant 0 \text{ and } (b[i] = Bi \text{ for } 1 \leqslant i \leqslant n) \qquad (3)$$

where the values Bi are the beginning column numbers of words $W1, \cdots, Wn$. We can infer that the line has the form

$$W1 \ [1] \ W2 \ [1] \ \cdots \ [1] \ Wn \ [s].$$

Here, an expression e in brackets denotes e blank columns. This is a rather informal description of the meaning of the $b[i]$. For example, we might have explicitly written $b[1] = 1$, $b[2] = b[1] + \text{length } (W1) + 1$, and so forth. However, we feel that this extra formalism will not help us understand the problem better.

We now need a characterization of possible output states. After some thought, we arrive at the following form:

$$W1 \ [p+1] \ W2 \ [p+1] \ \cdots \ [p+1] \ Wt \ [q+1] \ \cdots \ [q+1] \ Wn, \quad (4)$$

and from the informal specification we arrive at the following restrictions on p, q, and t:

$1 \leqslant t \leqslant n$ [Wt is one of the words $W1, \cdots, Wn$]

$p \geqslant 0, q \geqslant 0$,   [cannot insert a negative number of blanks]

$p \cdot (t - 1) + q \cdot (n - t) = s$,   [$s$ is the number of blanks inserted]

$(\text{odd}(z) \text{ and } q = p + 1) \text{ or } (\text{even}(z) \text{ and } p = q + 1)$ [formalizes the technique for inserting extra blanks].   (5)

Intuitively, we feel we should be able to determine p, q, and t from (5), and we shall see that, for the most part, this feeling is justified.

The purpose of the procedure is to change array b so that the line looks like (4). Noting the input assertion (3), we arrive at the following result assertion or postcondition

$$b[i] = Bi + p \cdot (i - 1) \text{ for } 1 \leqslant i \leqslant t,$$
$$b[i] = Bi + p \cdot (t - 1) + q \cdot (i - t) \text{ for } t < i \leqslant n. \qquad (6)$$

Assertion (6) with p, q, and t defined by (5) is indeed our postcondition. We have spent much time and effort developing it, but this time was well spent. We now have a precise postcondition, which is so clear and simple that we are immediately led to *try* the following algorithm:

$\{(3)\}$
Calculate p, q and t according to (5);
$\{(3) \text{ and } (5)\}$
Calculate new $b[1:t]$ according to (6);
$\left\{ \begin{array}{l} (5) \text{ and } (b[i] = Bi + p \cdot (i - 1) \text{ for } 1 \leqslant i \leqslant t) \\ \quad \text{and } (b[i] = Bi \text{ for } t < i \leqslant n) \end{array} \right\}$
Calculate new $b[t + 1:n]$ according to (6)
$\{(5) \text{ and } (6)\}$ (7)

Even these three statements seem easy to refine. In particular, the form of assertion (6) almost forces us to think of the second two statements in terms of iteration. We arbitrarily choose to first refine the statement to "calculate new $b[1:t]$."

It seems obvious that the loop to calculate $b[1:t]$ will have the form **do** $B \rightarrow S$ **od**, where for each iteration a "counter" k will be incremented (or decremented) and $b[k]$ will be calculated. We begin by determining the invariant relation $P1$ of the loop. Using a variable to contain the value $p \cdot (k - 1)$, we write:

$P1: \ 1 \leqslant k \leqslant t, \text{incr} = p \cdot (k - 1), \text{assertion (5)},$
$\quad b[i] = Bi + p \cdot (i - 1) \text{ for } 1 \leqslant i \leqslant k,$
$\quad b[i] = Bi \text{ for } k < i \leqslant n.$ (8)

We must derive loop initialization I, a loop body S, and a termination condition B. For loop initialization we choose the obvious: I: k, incr := 1, 0. [And indeed, if you calculate wp $(I, (8))$, you will arrive at the precondition of the statement under consideration in (7).]

The likely candidate for the loop body is

$$S: k, \text{incr} := k + 1, \text{incr} + p; b[k] := b[k] + \text{incr}$$

The terminating condition B must be chosen so that ($P1$ **and** $\neg B$) implies the postcondition of the second statement of (7), and secondly so that termination of the loop is ensured. An obvious choice for $\neg B$ is $k = t$, and so we can take $B \equiv k \neq t$.

However, the following efficiency considerations cause us to look for other candidates for B. We can expect p, the number of blanks to insert towards the left "half" of the line, to be 0 for many of the odd lines. If $p = 0$, then all values $p \cdot (i - 1)$ are also 0, and execution of the loop has no effect on the values $b[1:t]$. Hence, we would like the loop to terminate earlier in this case.

Deriving $\neg B$ from ($P1$ **and** $\neg B$) $\Rightarrow R$ (where R is the desired result) requires using information in $P1$. The only part of $P1$ not yet used is incr $= p \cdot (k - 1)$. Some thought leads us to conclude that $\neg B \equiv \text{incr} = p \cdot (t - 1)$ is a likely candidate. We have:

($P1$ **and** $\neg B$ **and** $p = 0$) $\Rightarrow R$ (since all values $p \cdot (i - 1)$ are zero),

($P1$ **and** $\neg B$ **and** $p \neq 0$) $\Rightarrow$ ($P1$ **and** $t = k$) $\Rightarrow R$.

Hence, $B \equiv \text{incr} \neq p \cdot (t - 1)$ is a suitable terminating condition, and with it, the loop terminates immediately if $p = 0$. Termination must be shown; we leave this to the reader using the integer function $p \cdot (t-1)\text{-incr}$.

We have finished development of the first loop—it is shown below in (9). The second loop is developed in a similar manner using the invariant

$P2$: $t \leqslant k \leqslant n$, $\text{incr} = p \cdot (t - 1) + q \cdot (k - t)$, assertion (5),
  $b[i] = Bi + p \cdot (i - 1)$ for $1 \leqslant i \leqslant t$,
  $b[i] = Bi + p \cdot (t - 1) + q \cdot (i - t)$ for $t < i \leqslant k$,
  $b[i] = Bi$ for $k < i \leqslant n$.

Putting both loops together yields

{Calculate $b[1:t]$ according to (6)}
  k, $\text{incr} := 1, 0$;
  do $\text{incr} \neq p \cdot (t - 1) \rightarrow k$, $\text{incr} := k + 1$, $\text{incr} + p$;
                $b[k] := b[k] + \text{incr}$
  od;
{Calculate $b[t + 1:n]$ according to (6)}
  $k := t$;
  do $k \neq n \rightarrow k$, $\text{incr} := k + 1$, $\text{incr} + q$;
              $b[k] := b[k] + \text{incr}$
od   (9)

Note carefully the initialization $k := t$ for the second loop. After the first loop terminates, we have $\text{incr} = p \cdot (t - 1)$ but not necessarily $k = t$, so that this initialization is needed. Secondly, we can not use the same trick for ending the second loop as we did for the first, because $P2$ **and** ($\text{incr} = p \cdot (t - 1) + q \cdot (n - t)$) does *not* imply the desired result (why not?).

We have completed the refinement of the calculation of the $b[i]$, and now turn our attention to determining p, q, and t according to (5). We begin by investigating the result assertion (5). We investigate the part $\text{even}(z)$. If z is even, we have $p = q + 1$, and the third line of (5) reduces to

$$(q + 1) \cdot (t - 1) + q \cdot (n - t) = s,$$

which simplifies to $q \cdot (n - 1) + (t - 1) = s$. If we restrict $t - 1$ to the range $0 \leqslant t - 1 < n - 1$, we see that we can satisfy the above equation by taking $q = s \text{ div } (n - 1)$, $t = s + 1 - q \cdot (n - 1)$, and of course $p = q + 1$. Hence, we are led to the sequence of assignments

$q := s \text{ div } (n - 1)$;
$p := q + 1$;
$t := s + 1 - q \cdot (n - 1)$.   (10)

Let us recapitulate what we have done here. We began investigating the *post*condition (5) of the statement we wanted to develop. Focusing our attention on one part of (5), we derived the assignment statement sequence (10), the execution of which under suitable conditions would establish (5). We must now derive these suitable conditions. That is, we want to derive $wp((10), (5))$—the weakest precondition such that

execution of (10) will establish (5). This weakest precondition, found quite simply using Dijkstra's rules $wp(S, R)$ where S is an assignment or composition, yields the precondition:

$$\text{even}(z) \textbf{ and } s \geqslant 0 \textbf{ and } (s \text{ div } (n - 1)) \geqslant 0.$$

Hence, execution of (10) yields the desired result only if the line number is even and if there are at least two words on it. The latter must hold, for if $n = 1$ the **div** operation is undefined, while $n \leqslant 0 \Rightarrow \neg(s \geqslant 0 \textbf{ and } (s \text{ div } (n - 1)) \geqslant 0)$. We come to the conclusion that a line with less than two words cannot be right-justified, and hence we have to change the procedure specifications.

Further analysis assuming $\text{odd}(z)$ leads us to rearrange the original algorithm (7) into the following one (11). Note that $n \leqslant 1$ is not assumed to be an error. Instead, execution of the algorithm with $n \leqslant 1$ simply leaves array b unchanged.

if $n \leqslant 1 \rightarrow$ **skip**
[] $n > 1 \rightarrow$ Determine p and q and t:
      if $\text{even}(z) \rightarrow q := s \text{ div } (n - 1)$;
              $p := q + 1$;
              $t := s + 1 - q \cdot (n - 1)$
      [] $\text{odd}(z) \rightarrow p := s \text{ div } (n - 1)$;
              $q := p + 1$;
              $t := p \cdot (n - 1) + n - s$
      fi;
      Calculate $b[1:t]$ (see (9));
      Calculate $b[t + 1:n]$ (see (9))
fi   (11)

III. Discussion

I do not suggest that this—or any—program must be developed precisely this way. That would be a ridiculous suggestion. My original development certainly did not proceed as smoothly as this idealized version, although it did follow the same pattern.

I do think, based on my own as-yet-limited experience, that forcing myself to think this way has improved my programming ability. Development proceeds more efficiently; there is less handwaving and arbitrary choosing of alternatives; I have sound reasons for proceeding in a particular manner; I feel that I am in control of the development instead of the development and my whims controlling me; the resulting programs seem clearer to me than they would be otherwise; and I have more confidence in their correctness.

Let me discuss some of the more important points about program development in light of this example.

1) The first step performed in the development was the determination of the input–output assertions in enough detail so as to create an understandable, precise specification, but not so much detail as to create chaos. Once these assertions were presented, the program itself was quite easy to develop. The hardest part was not programming, but the development of specifications for the program!

It is commonly agreed that problem specifications are too

often vague and ill-written. The programmer's *first* task must be to clarify the problem description and to rework it into a comprehensible form. If we are to prove programs correct, the specifications must be in the form of pre- and postconditions for the program.

Of course, in writing specifications it is difficult to know how much formalism is required. Formalism is our friend, but only if we first learn how to control him! Writing good specifications in the form of pre- and postconditions requires more mathematical ability than is usually expected from programmers.

2) When developing a loop, the importance of first clarifying the idea in terms of an invariant relation P cannot be overestimated. This is a clear case of "the proof leading the program." Once P is determined, the loop initialization, the loop body, and the terminating condition can usually be developed easily and systematically. And because of the way the terminating condition is derived, we *know* the loop terminates properly. (How often in the past have we all written a loop which required three "test runs" to determine the correct termination condition? There is no longer any excuse for this.)

Some contend that developing the invariant relation is too difficult and time-consuming. To this I have three answers. First, it is no more difficult and time-consuming than the debugging that takes place when one has not developed the invariant. Secondly, learning to program this way is just a matter of intelligence, education, and practice. Thirdly, most programmers subconsciously program in this fashion anyway. The method just forces them to make clear, precise, and explicit that which they have previously left vague, imprecise, and implicit.

3) This example again illustrates the importance of initially thinking in terms of the **while** loop (or preferably, Dijkstra's guarded command loop) instead of in terms of the "**for** $k :=$ $\cdots$" loop. Had we initially used "the obvious" form "**for** $k :=$ 1 **to** t **do** $\cdots$" for the loop with invariant (8), we would not have been able to explore different termination conditions as easily. The "**for** k" mentality does indeed limit the possibilities for algorithmic expression. I point out that out of 20 computer scientists and students that have written this program for me using their own conventional "methodology," not one has written the loop to terminate when $p = 0$, as I have.

4) The conventional programmer works "forwards:" given the precondition, he tries to write a program which transforms it into the postcondition. Dijkstra takes the opposite approach: start with the postcondition and work "backwards." The language is defined so that the weakest precondition is derived from the statement and postcondition. While this seems strange at first, with practice this begins to make more sense and to be more convenient. (In writing this, I am reminded of my early days playing golf. Although my swing *felt* good, I had a terrible slice. When I took lessons, the way the teacher wanted me to swing felt terrible. Reasoning that he knew more about the game than I did, I continued to prac-

tice his way of swinging. After a while I got used to it, and my slice disappeared! I still slice from time to time (the few rare times I play), for it is hard work to break a habit completely. I have sliced in this paper too, talking in terms of execution and going forward when I should not.)

We have used the "backward" approach to some extent in the program development, and it will be illuminating to discuss it.

We began the development of the segment to calculate p, q, and t by examining its postcondition (5), and isolating a part of it which we felt would be profitable to work with:

$$\text{even}(z) \text{ and } q \geq 0 \text{ and } s \geq 0 \text{ and } p = q + 1 \text{ and}$$
$$p \cdot (t - 1) + q \cdot (n - t) = s.$$

Manipulating these, we arrived at the relations $q = s \text{ div } (n - 1)$, $p = q + 1$, and $t = s + 1 - q \cdot (n - t)$. This led in an obvious manner to the sequence of assignments (10). We then determined the conditions under which execution of (10) would establish the *full* assertion (5)—the weakest precondition $wp((10), (5))$:

$$\text{even}(z) \text{ and } s \geq 0 \text{ and } n > 1.$$

We were able to arrive at the desired program segment by also considering, in a similar fashion, assertion (5) with $\text{odd}(z)$ instead of $\text{even}(z)$. Besides a small bit of insight into choosing the right part of the assertion to work with, in our case development consisted *solely* of manipulating expressions—something we know how to do well.

This development had another important advantage over conventional "forward" thinking: the singular cases $n \leq 1$ were detected automatically during the development. There is no way we could have missed them, unless of course we were not careful enough and had left out the part $q \geq 0$ in (5).

Many programs fail because such singular cases have not been taken into account. With haphazard, unguided program development, we cannot possibly hope to think of them all. A more systematic development guided by a good methodology has more chance of success in finding them.

5) To limit nesting of statements, one sometimes assigns special values to variables to take care of singular cases. For example, we could have written the program as follows, although in this case it is not warranted:

```
if n ⩽ 1 → Set p, q, t so that assigning
              to b[1 : n] later has no effect.
[] n > 1 and even(z) → · · ·
[] n > 1 and odd(z) → · · ·
fi;
Calculate b[1 : n].
```

While at times this might be advisable, it is dangerous unless properly documented. The program will be read and perhaps modified by others, and a correct proof must therefore accompany the program. This means that the postconditions of the alternative statement and "Calculate $b[1 : n]$" must be changed to describe the new relationships when $n \leq 1$. Should they not be changed, the proof will be faulty. A tenuous link will have been drawn between two parts of the program which will quite likely be overlooked by others.

6) The question of documenting a program which has been proved correct arises. Just what does the educated reader want to see? I give the complete justify procedure below in a Pascal-like notation, in order to illustrate my ideas on this matter. The reader is invited to revise the program so that the $b[i]$ are calculated in *descending* order of i. Which method is better, in descending or ascending order?

```
procedure justify (z, n, s: integer; var b: array [*] of integer);
{input:
    z: a line number;
    n: the number of words on the line;
    s ⩾ 0: the number of blanks at the end of the line;
    b[i] = Bi: the column number where word i begins on line, 1 ⩽ i ⩽ n.
    Using Wi to represent word i and [e] to represent e blanks, the
    line has the form
        W1 [1] W2 [1] · · · [1] Wn [s]
output: if n ⩽ 1, no change is made—b[i] = Bi for 1 ⩽ i ⩽ n.
    if n > 1, the column numbers b[i] are changed to right-justify the
    line. This means that the line will look like
        W1 [p + 1] W2 [p + 1] · · · [p + 1] Wt [q + 1] · · · [q + 1] Wn
    where p, q and t are defined by
        A1: p ⩾ 0, q ⩾ 0, 1 ⩽ t ⩽ n, s = p · (t − 1) + q · (n − t),
            (odd(z) and q = p + 1) or (even(z) and p = q + 1))
    Hence, upon exit we have
        A2: b[i] = Bi + p · (i − 1) for 1 ⩽ i ⩽ t,
            b[i] = Bi + p · (t − 1) + q · (i − t) for t < i ⩽ n.}
var p, q, t, k, incr, pt1: integer;
begin {Loops 1 and 2 below use the invariants P1 and P2, resp.:
    P1: 1 ⩽ k ⩽ t, incr = p · (k − 1), pt1 = p · (t − 1),
        b[i] = Bi + p · (i − 1) for 1 ⩽ i ⩽ k,
        b[i] = Bi for k < i ⩽ n.
    P2: t ⩽ k ⩽ n, incr = p · (t − 1) + q · (k − t),
        b[i] = Bi + p · (i − 1) for 1 ⩽ i ⩽ t,
        b[i] = Bi + p · (t − 1) + q · (i − t) for t < i ⩽ k,
        b[i] = Bi for k < i ⩽ n.}
    if n > 1 then
        begin {Determine p, q, t, thus establishing A1}
            if odd(z)
                then begin p := s div (n − 1); q := p + 1;
                    t := n + p (n − 1) − s end
                else begin q := s div (n − 1); p := q + 1;
                    t := s − q (n − 1) + 1 end;
        {Determine new b[1 : t], establishing first line of A2.
        The loop invariant is A1 and P1.}
            k := 1; incr := 0; pt1 := p + (t − 1);
            while incr ≠ pt1 do
                begin k := k + 1; incr := incr + p;
                    b[k] : = b[k] + incr end;
        {Determine new b[t + 1 : n], establishing A2.
        The loop invariant is A1 and P2.}
            k := t; {Note: last loop establishes incr = p · (t − 1)}
            while k ≠ n do
                begin k := k + 1; incr := incr + q;
                    b[k] := b[k] + incr end
        end
    end
```

REFERENCES

[1] E. W. Dijkstra, "Guarded commands, nondeterminacy and formal derivation of programs," *Commun. Ass. Comput. Mach.*, vol. 18, pp. 453–457, Aug. 1975.

[2] ——, *A Discipline of Programming*. Englewood Cliffs, NJ: Prentice-Hall, 1976.

[3] R. W. Floyd, "Assigning meanings to programs," in *Proc. Amer. Math. Soc. Symp. Applied Mathematics*, vol. 19, 1967, pp. 19–31.

[4] C. A. R. Hoare, "An axiomatic basis for computer programming," *Commun. Ass. Comput. Mach.*, vol. 12, pp. 576–583, Oct. 1969.

David Gries was born in Flushing, NY, on April 26, 1939. He received the B.S. degree from Queens College, New York, NY, in 1960, the M.S. degree from the University of Illinois, Urbana, in 1963, and the Dr. rer. nat. degree from the Technische Hochschule Munich, Munich, Germany, in 1966, all in mathematics.

He spent 1960 to 1962 as a Mathematician-Programmer at the U.S. Naval Weapons Laboratory, Dahlgren, VA. He was an Assistant Professor in Computer Science at Stanford University from 1966 to 1969, and has been an Associate Professor in Computer Science at Cornell University, Ithaca, NY, since 1969. Author of a well-known book on compiler construction, he recently coauthored *Introduction to (Structured) Programming*. His current research interests are in programming methodology and programming language design.

Dr. Gries is a member of the Association for Computing Machinery and SIGPLAN.

Programming
Languages

J.J. Horning
Editor

An Example of Hierarchical Design and Proof

Jay M. Spitzen, Karl N. Levitt, and
Lawrence Robinson
SRI International

Hierarchical programming is being increasingly recognized as helpful in the construction of large programs. Users of hierarchical techniques claim or predict substantial increases in productivity and in the reliability of the programs produced. In this paper we describe a formal method for hierarchical program specification, implementation, and proof. We apply this method to a significant list processing problem and also discuss a number of extensions to current programming languages that ease hierarchical program design and proof.

Key Words and Phrases: program verification, specification, data abstraction, software modules, hierarchical structures

CR Categories: 4.0, 4.6, 5.21, 5.24

1. Introduction

The use of structuring techniques in programming—for example, programming by successive refinement [5] (also called hierarchical programming)—has been recognized as increasingly helpful in the design and management of large system efforts. A number of such design techniques are now promoted for routine use in com-

mercial software development [33]. Some of these techniques are also alleged to permit the verification of large systems by reducing them to a collection of small programs, each easily verified.

Important questions about such hierarchical proofs are:

—Can systems be decomposed into subprograms that can be characterized by clear and natural assertions?
—Can proofs of the subprograms be combined to demonstrate the correctness of the system?
—Is it generally possible to formulate and prove significant implementation-independent properties of systems?

Several recent developments yield positive answers: the hierarchical design and module specification techniques of [24] and the data abstraction techniques of [9] and [26]. (The word "module" is very widely and imprecisely used and the reader should be wary of drawing inferences not based on our very specific use.) A module is the basic unit in a hierarchical decomposition—a collection of operations and data. The module permits the definition of complex abstract types. For example, a type "file" can be defined by a module with operations for creating a file, inserting a record into a file, reading a record, appending two files, etc., and data structures recording the file's contents.

To permit hierarchical proof, one must *formally specify* the modules of a hierarchical system. Styles of specification and their mathematical foundations differ (e.g. consult [8, 24, 27]; also, [15] and [13] are overviews), but the basic aim is to achieve abstract specification, i.e. specification that describes the input-output behavior of a module without recourse to an implementation of the module. This may be done in terms of the sequences of operations that have been performed on the module, or by abstracting from these sequences to a module *state*. In the first of these approaches, one may attempt to describe concisely the infinite class of possible histories by a small number of "algebraic specifications," as in [8]. In this paper, we will use the state approach. An important aspect of a good specification—in any method—is that, for a properly conceived module, it is a concise, intuitive, and precise characterization of the behavior of the module, successfully abstracting from the details of any implementation of the module. It is often possible to formulate and prove important properties of a module in terms of its specifications.

Similarly, both algebraic and state styles of specification lend themselves to two-stage implementations: First, the data structures of a module (other than the most primitive) are represented in terms of lower level data structures (as in [9] and [26]) and, second, *abstract programs* are written for each operation in terms of lower level operations. Each abstract program may then be proved to satisfy its specifications on the assumption that the more primitive modules it employs are correct, given the specific data representation used.

Should descriptions of hierarchical structure, formal

Research supported by the Office of Naval Research (Contract N00014-75-C-0816), the National Science Foundation (Grant DCR74-18661), and the Air Force Office of Scientific Research (Contract F44620-73-C-0068).

Authors' present addresses: J.M. Spitzen, Advanced Systems Department, Xerox Corporation, 3333 Coyote Hill Road, Palo Alto, CA 94304; K.W. Levitt and L. Robinson, SRI International, 333 Ravenswood Ave., Menlo Park, CA 94025.

© 1978 ACM 0001-0782/78/1200-1064 $00.75.

specifications of modules, and implementations all be written in a single language? We have chosen to separate these functions, and will describe a powerful specification language, SPECIAL, and a very simple implementation language ILPL. An alternative is to provide abstraction directly in the implementation language—the approach of [4, 11, 14, 31, 32]. A second language issue is what characteristics a language (or, in our view, set of languages) should have to enable the correct implementation of hierarchies of abstractions. For example, what protection principles are needed to ensure the data integrity of a module?

The primary contributions of this paper are a description of the design and proof of a nontrivial, useful program, and a demonstration of a technique that has promise of making proof and formal description possible for large programs. Our example is a program to maintain unique lists with an efficient underlying implementation. We have attempted to address three classes of readers: those who wish to learn about formal specification should be able to do so by following our specifications and the associated prose; those who wish to learn about so-called "functional program verification" will be introduced to this style of proof; and those who are unfamiliar with list processing may obtain an introduction to some relevant techniques.

In the next section, we introduce our design and proof method. Then in Section 3 and Section 4 we present formal specifications of the two modules that comprise the top-level machine of an illustrative hierarchy. Based on these specifications, we are able in Section 5 to prove several properties of this machine. The implementation of this machine and a proof of the correctness of this implementation are presented in Section 6 and Section 7. Section 8 outlines how the hierarchy described up to that point might be refined into an executable program. Finally, Section 9 presents some concluding remarks.

2. Design and Proof Method

Suppose a programming problem P and a machine M are given and it is required to construct a program C that executes on M to solve P. M may be either a physical machine or a virtual machine provided, for example, by the compiler for a particular programming language. We believe that the program construction should proceed as follows.

First, we design an abstract computer AM on which it is easy to solve P. AM is designed by describing its states and executable instructions. We deliberately leave vague the meaning of an "easy solution" of P—for some purposes this will be a solution by a program AC that is only a page or two long; for other purposes it will be a solution by a program that can be mechanically proved correct using state-of-the-art verification systems. Having designed AM, we implement a solution of P on AM,

and, in practice, usually alter the design of AM in the process. If AM is the same as M, then we have satisfied the original requirement if it can be demonstrated that the solution is correct. Otherwise, we have reduced the original requirement to the new one of realizing AM in terms of M. To do this, we design a new machine AM′ on which it is easy to realize AM. We represent the states of the first machine AM in terms of the states of AM′ and we implement the executable instructions of AM by means of a set of programs AC′ on AM′. The choice of *representation* or *implementation* may prove awkward; if so, we resort to altering the design of AM′ or even that of AM. (Unfortunately, we usually cannot alter the original requirement P, though requirements sometimes are changed when a problem is better understood.)

Next, the realization of AM on AM′ must be verified. This verification means that the (partial) solution of P obtained by executing AC on AM is equivalent to the (more complete) solution obtained by executing AC and AC′ together on AM′. In this latter solution, the execution of an instruction of AM by AC is viewed not as primitive but as a call on the subroutine in AC′ that realizes that instruction on AM′. Again, if AM′ is the same as M, we are done and otherwise we must continue to approach M by extending the sequence of machines AM, AM′, ... and programs AC, AC′, ... When we have extended this sequence to a program that executes on M, then the set of programs and subroutines AC, AC′, ... constitutes the required solution C on machine M.

This description of programming has been phrased in the top-down paradigm, but that is not what is important. To make the programming of large problems feasible, reliable, and controllable, they must be somehow divided into small parts. We have no special preference for top-down or bottom-up programming in arriving at this division, and suspect that a flexible mixture of both techniques is required in general. We do advocate the use of formal methods to describe the division, to validate the resulting design, and to prove the correctness of the final program.

The product of our endeavors will thus consist of:
—A hierarchy of abstract machines
—A formal specification of each machine
—A representation of the states of each machine (except the given machine) in terms of the states of the machine below it
—An implementation of the instructions of each machine (except the given machine) in terms of the instructions of the machine below it

We specify an abstract machine using a method originally proposed by Parnas [24] and subsequently extended by Robinson and Levitt [26]. (Our formal specification language, SPECIAL, is described in [28].) A machine has a state and an instruction set. We give the state by describing the initial values of a set of *V-functions*. We give the instructions, called *OV-functions*, by describing how each changes the state of the machine and what value it returns. (The return of a particular

260

Communications
of
the ACM

December 1978
Volume 21
Number 12

value may, for formal purposes, be thought of as part of the change of state.)

A V-function specification consists of a *header* that describes its arguments and result and an *initialization* that describes the values of the function in an initial machine state.

An OV-function specification consists of a *header* that describes its argument structure, an *assertion list* stating preconditions on the calls of the function, an *exception list* describing when its execution may have no effect other than signaling an error, and a set of *effects* that nonprocedurally describe the changed state due to an execution of the function by defining the resulting values of the V-functions of the machine. (These values are described in terms of the old values of the V-functions and the arguments to the OV-function.) The effects include, if appropriate, the designation of the value to be computed and may allow a nondeterministic choice of successor state.

It is usually possible to give additional structure to an abstract machine M by describing it as the "product" of modules M1, M2, ... , Mn. When we do this, we will refer to the Mi as submachines or modules of M; otherwise the terms machine and module are used as synonyms. To form such a product, we require that the functions of the Mi be renamed to avoid conflicts. M has as its V-functions each of the V-functions of the Mi with the same initial sections. M has as its OV-functions each of the OV-functions of the Mi, with augmented effects sections. Specifically, if I is an OV-function of Mi and V is a V-function of Mj, where $i \sim = j$, we add to the effects of I the assertion that V is not changed by the execution of I.

3. The ULIST Module

In this section and the next, we present an abstract machine consisting of two modules: one that maintains conventional list structures and one that maintains a class of *unique lists*—lists such that no two are structurally isomorphic. (Figure 1 illustrates the usual realization of conventional lists where distinct isomorphic lists are possible.) Thus the attempt to construct one of these unique lists yields an old list if there is already one with the right components.[1] Naturally, we want the check of existing cells to be efficient. We use a particularly effective method introduced by Deutsch in his verification system [6] to associate properties with arbitrary symbolic expressions.

We begin by presenting a formal specification of a machine providing unique lists, and explain our notation

---

[1] As an example of the utility of such a facility, suppose we save the property SIMPLIFIES-TO-ZERO in some table under—as key—the address of the list (SUBTRACT x x). If we subsequently independently create a conventional list of the same form, it will have a different address and the property will not be retrieved. But if both are unique then their addresses will be the same so that the property can be looked up successfully.

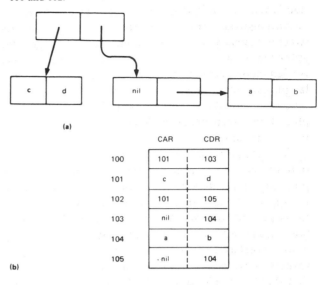

Fig. 1. Distinct isomorphic lists. (a)A picture of the list ((c.d) *nil* a.b). (b)Two distinct isomorphic versions of the list ((c.d) *nil* a.b) at 100 and 102.

by referring to this specification. The state of a ULIST machine is determined by what unique list cells exist. Hence we want a single V-function, UCELL(X1,X2) whose value is the cell with X1 and X2 as components—if there is any such cell—and the distinguished value "?" if there is no such cell. (All that will matter about "?" in this paper is that it does not satisfy the predicate ATOMP to be introduced in Section 3.) There are four instructions on the ULIST machine: UCONS to obtain a list with specified components, UCAR and UCDR to extract the components of a ULIST list, and ULISTP to test whether an arbitrary object is a ULIST list. The specification is given below.

```
module:  ULIST:
forall:  Z1,Z2
vfns:    UCELL(X1,X2)
            initial UCELL(X1,X2) = ?
define:  ISUCELL(X) = (exists X1,X2: UCELL(X1,X2)=X~=?)
ovfns:   UCONS(X1,X2) → X
            assert  ISUCELL(X1) or ATOMP(X1)
                    ISUCELL(X2) or ATOMP(X2)
            effects if UCELL(X1,X2) = ?
                    then UCELL(Z1,Z2)~=X and
                         'UCELL(X1,X2)=X and
                         X~=? and ~ATOMP(X) and
                         (X1~=Z1 or X2~=Z2)
                              ⇒ 'UCELL(Z1,Z2)
                              =UCELL(Z1,Z2))
                    else 'UCELL(Z1,Z2)=UCELL(Z1,Z2) and
                         X = UCELL(X1,X2)
         UCAR(X) → X1
            assert  ISUCELL(X)
            effects 'UCELL(Z1,Z2)=UCELL(Z1,Z2)
                    UCELL(Z1,Z2)=X ⇒ X1=Z1
         UCDR(X) → X2
            assert  ISUCELL(X)
            effects 'UCELL(Z1,Z2)=UCELL(Z1,Z2)
                    UCELL(Z1,Z2)=X ⇒ X2=Z2
         UCONSP(X) → B
            effects 'UCELL(Z1,Z2)=UCELL(Z1,Z2)
                    B = ISUCELL(X)
```

261

It will be common, in the specification of this module, to ask the question, "Is the object X a unique list cell?" Therefore we introduce the abbreviation ISUCELL, expressing this predicate in terms of the module's single V-function. Note also that in the specification we use the predicate ATOMP to distinguish the objects that may be the "leaves" of list structures from the objects that are list cells. Rather than implementing this predicate as we develop our hierarchy, we will simply assume that it is present in the most primitive machine of the hierarchy and is reflected upward, with the same meaning, in each nonprimitive machine. In Section 9, we will discuss the significance of this assumption.

In the initial ULIST state, there are to be no list cells. We specify this by requiring that $UCELL(Z1,Z2)$ be "?" initially. (We abbreviate slightly by listing at the head of each module symbols that should be read as universally quantified in all their uses in the module specification; for ULIST these are $Z1$ and $Z2$.)

Next, we specify the instruction $UCONS(X1,X2)$ to obtain a cell with components $X1$ and $X2$. This instruction has no exceptions: it is required to achieve its effects for any arguments and state; in particular, this requires that any implementation have an unlimited set of cells. (Although this requirement is idealistic, it simplifies our presentation; SPECIAL does provide for the description of *resource errors*.) We assert that the arguments to UCONS are either outputs of UCONS [ISUCELL(X)] or atoms [ATOMP(X)]. Its effects are stated with an "if-then-else" assertion. We need to refer to two sets of values of UCELL—those associated with the state before the UCONS instruction is executed and those reflecting the changed state due to the execution. We will do this by writing $UCELL(X1,X2)$ to refer to the old state and $'UCELL(X1,X2)$ to refer to the changed state. First, if the machine state is such that $UCELL(X1,X2)$ is "?", then a new cell must be created. We do not choose to specify how cells are represented (e.g. by their integer addresses on some machine), but say only that the new cell is a value X that is not a cell before the execution of this instruction (i.e. $UCELL(Z1,Z2)\sim=X$ for any $X1$, $X2$) and is the cell with the specified components afterwards [$'UCELL(X1,X2)=X$]. Besides constraining the value of the new cell, we must ensure that no other cells are affected by the instruction. Thus we say that if $(Z1,Z2)$ is any pair of cell components other than the $(X1,X2)$ given in the instruction call, then the new cell associated with $(Z1,Z2)$ is the same as the old [$'UCELL(Z1,Z2)=UCELL(Z1,Z2)$].

If $UCELL(X1,X2)$ is not "?", then the effects of the instruction are simpler. We constrain the result of UCONS to be the existing cell [$Z=UCELL(X1,X2)$] and require the new state to have exactly the same cells as the old [$'UCELL(Z1,Z2)=UCELL(Z1,Z2)$].

Next, we specify the UCAR and UCDR instructions. Our notion of the ULIST module is that it is not meaningful to ask for either of the components of an object other than a ULIST cell. Hence we assert that the arguments to UCAR and UCDR are ULIST cells using the predicate ISUCELL which requires that its argument be in the image, under UCELL, of the set of pairs $(Z1,Z2)$. The effects of UCAR and UCDR are similar. If $Z1$ and $Z2$ are such that $UCELL(Z1,Z2)$ is the argument to UCAR or UCDR, then the UCAR component of $UCELL(Z1,Z2)$ is $Z1$ and the UCDR component is $Z2$. (It is not obvious that such a specification is noncontradictory; this is a consequence of the theorem, proved below, that UCELL is single-valued: it maps distinct arguments to the same result only when that result is "?".) Besides giving the values of these functions, the specification asserts that they have no effect on UCELL [$'UCELL(Z1,Z2)=UCELL(Z1,Z2)$].

The last ULIST instruction is UCONSP. It is like UCAR and UCDR in that UCELL is unchanged. Its result B must be true or false, and true if and only if its argument is a ULIST list. But this is easily stated in terms of the UCELL V-function—it is equivalent to the existence of a pair $(Z1,Z2)$ such that $UCELL(Z1,Z2)$ is equal to the argument X [$B = $ exists $Z1,Z2$: $UCELL(Z1,Z2)=X$].

4. The List Module

Our goal is to design an abstract machine that provides its user with both unique and conventional list processing. This machine is the product of ULIST and a module LIST that we will specify next. The formal specification of LIST is given below.

```
module:   LIST:
forall:   Z1,Z2,Z
vfns:     CELL(X1,X2,X)
             initial CELL(X1,X2,X)=false
define:   ISCELL(X) = (exists X1,X2:CELL(X1,X2,X) and X~=?)
ovfns:    CONS(X1,X2) → X
             assert  ATOMP(X1) or ISCELL(X1)
                     ATOMP(X2) or ISCELL(X2)
             effects  'CELL(X1,X2,X)
                     not CELL(Z1,Z2,X)
                     X~=?
                     not ATOMP(X)
                     Z~=X ⇒ 'CELL(Z1,Z2,Z)=CELL(Z1,Z2,Z)
          CAR(X) → X1
             assert  ISCELL(X)
             effects  'CELL(Z1,Z2,Z)=CELL(Z1,Z2,Z)
                     exists Z2:CELL(X1,Z2,X)
          CDR(X) → X2
             assert  ISCELL(X)
             effects  'CELL(Z1,Z2,Z)=CELL(Z1,Z2,Z)
                     exists Z1:CELL(Z1,X2,X)
          CONSP(X) → B
             effects  'CELL(Z1,Z2,Z)=CELL(Z1,Z2,Z)
                     B = ISCELL(X)
```

The structure of this module is quite similar to ULIST: there is a single V-function CELL and four OV-functions CONS, CAR, CDR, and CONSP. However, there are important differences. First, whereas UCELL is a function from a UCAR/UCDR pair $(X1,X2)$ to the unique list cell X—if any—with $X1$ and $X2$ as UCAR and UCDR, CELL is a predicate on the triple $(X1,X2,X)$ that tests whether X is a conventional list cell with CAR X1 and CDR X2. This difference is necessary: because there may be more than one conventional list cell with a particular CAR and CDR, CELL cannot be a function. The second difference between the two modules is in the effects of UCONS and CONS. UCONS does not always change the ULIST state, but CONS always changes the LIST state. Even if there are already X1, X2, and X~=? such that CELL(X1,X2,X), an execution of CONS(X1,X2) will create a new cell with this CAR and CDR.

5. Properties of ULIST and LIST

Even though we have not yet implemented ULIST × LIST, we can prove properties of this machine just on the basis of its specifications. We illustrate this point by proving three results: that UCELL is one-to-one, that two structurally isomorphic unique lists are identical, and that if two conventional lists are structurally isomorphic, then certain corresponding unique lists are identical.

Consider the claim that the specification of ULIST is consistent, that is, implementable. For example, if UCELL is not one-to-one on that part of its domain that does not map to "?", then the specifications for UCAR and UCDR are not realizable. For suppose X=UCELL(Z1,Z2)=UCELL(Z3,Z4)~=?. If Z1 is not equal to Z3, then UCAR(X) is required to return both Z1 and Z3, an impossibility. Similarly, if Z2 is different from Z4, then UCDR(X) is required to return two different values.

This result is not, by itself, sufficient to show that ULIST can be implemented. On the other hand, a provably correct implementation of ULIST—given below—implies this result. However, the result is easy to state and has interesting consequences. Moreover, its proof illustrates a general proof technique applicable to abstract machines.

THEOREM 1. forall Z1,Z2,Z3,Z4:
$$UCELL(Z1,Z2)=$$
$$UCELL(Z3,Z4)\sim=?$$
$$\Rightarrow Z1=Z3 \text{ and } Z2=Z4.$$

PROOF. The theorem will be proved by induction on sequences of states of ULIST. This method of proving properties of abstract machines, which we call *generator induction*, is discussed in [3, 9, 30]. We must prove the theorem for any initial state of ULIST and for any state S' such that the theorem holds in a state S and S' is a state resulting from executing a ULIST instruction in S.

The basis of the induction is immediate, since UCELL is always "?" in an initial machine state. Thus it suffices to assume the theorem holds in some state S and to deduce its validity in a successor state S' that results from the operation UCONS(X1,X2) (since UCONS is the only operation that changes UCELL's re-

sults). Suppose that this execution of UCONS returns X and that, in the resulting state, there are Z1, Z2, Z3, and Z4 such that 'UCELL(Z1,Z2)='UCELL(Z3,Z4)~=?. If there has been no state change—the "else clause" of the effects—or if 'UCELL(Z1,Z2)=UCELL(Z1,Z2) and 'UCELL(Z3,Z4)=UCELL(Z3,Z4), then the inductive assumption gives the desired result. Suppose that there has been a state change—the "then clause" and that 'UCELL(Z1,Z2)~=UCELL(Z1,Z2). Thus Z1=X1 and Z2=X2. If Z3=X1 and Z4=X2, we are done. If Z3~=X1 or Z4~=X2, then the second equation of the else clause implies that 'UCELL(Z3,Z4)=UCELL(Z3,Z4) which is not equal to X by the first equation of the else clause, a contradiction. This completes the proof.

Next, we extend this result to show that structural equality implies identity for ULIST lists. Let us write UCAR*, UCDR*, and UCONSP* to refer to the values returned by these instructions in some state. (We introduce this notation to emphasize the careful distinction between these values, useful in stating static mathematical properties of a specification, and the instructions that might be executed to obtain them in some implementation.) Theorem 1 implies that, in any state, UCAR* and UCDR* are functions mapping the set of X such that UCONSP*(X) to a range not containing "?". It is a simple matter, using Theorem 1, to show that the conclusion X=Y follows from the hypotheses UCONSP*(X), UCONSP*(Y), UCAR*(X)= UCAR*(Y), and UCDR*(X)=UCDR*(Y); we leave the details to the reader. Using this corollary, we can prove that structural isomorphism implies identity for the lists of the ULIST machine. We define structural isomorphism of unique lists recursively by:

$$UISO(X,Y) \Leftarrow \text{if } UCONSP*(X) \text{ and } UCONSP*(Y)$$
$$\text{then } UISO(UCAR*(X), UCAR*(Y))$$
$$\text{and } UISO(UCDR*(X),UCDR*(Y))$$
$$\text{else } X=Y,$$

and can then prove:

THEOREM 2. forall X,Y:UISO(X,Y) $\Rightarrow$ X=Y.

Discussion. We wish to prove this theorem by structural induction on unique lists. (Structural induction is described by Burstall in [3]; the theorem can also be proved, less easily, by generator induction.) We will prove the theorem for the atoms that form the leaves of a unique list and we will prove that if the theorem holds for the proper sublists of a unique list, then it holds for the entire list. For such an induction to be sound, it is essential that there be no circular lists. Fortunately, the ULIST machine instructions provide no way to create circular lists. Since there are no lists in an initial ULIST state, since each instruction creates at most one new list, and since we are only interested in machine states achievable by the execution of finitely many instructions, this induction is well-founded. (This same argument demonstrates that UISO is total.)

PROOF. The basis of the induction is the case that

263

~UCONSP*(X) or ~UCONSP*(Y), and it is an immediate consequence of the definition of UISO. We make the inductive assumptions UCONSP*(X), UCONSP*(Y), UISO(UCAR*(X),UCAR*(Y)) ⟹ UCAR*(X)=UCAR*(Y), and UISO(UCDR*(X), UCDR*(Y)) ⟹ UCDR*(X)=UCDR*(Y), and must prove that UISO(X,Y) ⟹ X=Y. Expanding the definition of UISO(X,Y), we conclude that UISO (UCAR*(X),UCAR*(Y)) and UISO(UCDR*(X), UCDR*(Y)); hence by the inductive assumptions, UCAR*(X)=UCAR*(Y) and UCDR*(X)=UCDR*(Y). The corollary of Theorem 1 now yields the desired result.

Next we prove a theorem about a program that might be run by a top-level user of the ULIST × LIST machine to translate conventional lists to unique lists. (Because of the overhead associated with the maintenance of unique lists, it is common to do some computations with the corresponding conventional lists, and convert only the final result to a unique list.) We claim that this may be done by the program UCOPY defined as follows:

UCOPY(X) ⟸ if CONSP(X)
        then UCONS(UCOPY(CAR(X)),
                UCOPY(CDR(X)))
        else X.

The major result about UCOPY is that if two conventional lists are isomorphic, then their U-copies are identical. Isomorphism of conventional lists is defined by:

ISO(X,Y) ⟸ if CONSP*(X) and CONSP*(Y)
        then ISO(CAR*(X),CAR*(Y))
        and ISO(CDR*(X),CDR*(Y))
        else X=Y.

Let UCP(XA,XB) be an abbreviation for ISO(XA,XB) ⟹ UCOPY(XA)=UCOPY(XB). We will then prove:

THEOREM 3. forall XA,XB : UCP(XA,XB)

Discussion. The meaning of this formula is subtle, since the effects and result of UCOPY are contingent upon the machine state in which it is executed. A more precise statement would be as follows. Suppose ISO(XA,XB). Suppose that UCOPY is applied to XA, beginning in some state S1. This application terminates (since our lists are acyclic) yielding a value XA′ and a state S2. Suppose, moreover, that S3 is any successor of S2, resulting from a series of state transitions, starting at S2. Finally, suppose that UCOPY, applied to XB from state S3, yields value XB′ and state S4. Then XA′=XB′.

We are going to prove this result by induction. An inductive assumption of this rather lengthy form would be very cumbersome. Fortunately, the machine specifications imply that if UCONSP*(X) holds in some state S, then it holds in every successor state. Also, if UCAR*(X) and UCDR*(X) are defined in a state S, then they remain defined and retain the same value in all successor states. In view of these facts, sometimes called *frame axioms*, we can safely omit further refer-

ences to changing states and use the simple statement of the theorem. (It is very interesting to consider whether this kind of problem reduction might be done mechanically.)

PROOF. First, suppose ~CONSP*(XA). Then ISO(XA,XB) implies that XA=XB. Also, UCOPY(XA)=XA and UCOPY(XB)=XB so that the desired result is immediate. Next suppose CONSP*(XA). Then ISO(XA,XB) implies that CONSP*(XB). We proceed by simultaneous structural induction on XA and XB. That is, we assume

I1.   forall X : UCP(s(XA),X)
I2.   forall X : UCP(X,s(XB))

where s is either CAR* or CDR*. (Clearly, UCP is symmetric in its two arguments.) From ISO(XA,XB) it follows that

I3.   ISO(Car*(XA),CAR*(XB)), and
I4.   ISO(CDR*(XA),CDR*(XB)).

Combining these results with I1 and I2 we obtain

I6.   UCOPY(CDR*(XA))=UCOPY(CDR*(XB)).

We must prove that UCOPY(XA)=UCOPY(XB). This is done as follows:

UCOPY(XA) = UCONS*(UCOPY(CAR*(XA)),
                   UCOPY(CDR*(XA)))
       {by the definition of UCOPY}
   = UCONS*(UCOPY(CAR*(XB)),
                  UCOPY(CDR*(XB)))
       {by I5, I6}
   = UCOPY(XB)
       {by the definition of UCOPY}.

6. Implementation of ULIST × LIST

We now wish to implement the machine specified above in terms of more primitive facilities. Specifically, we will consider a machine, LIST × SEARCH, that has conventional list processing capabilities and an associative search capability. Since we retain the LIST facilities in this second level machine, the main problem is to describe ULIST in terms of associative search and conventional list processing.

Our SEARCH machine is formally specified below.

```
module:   SEARCH:
forall:   K,T
vfns:     PRIMARYTABLE( )
            initial PRIMARYTABLE( )~=?
          GET(KEY,TABLE)
            initial GET(KEY,TABLE)=?
          TABLEP(TABLE)
            initial TABLEP(TABLE) =
              (TABLE=PRIMARY-TABLE( ))
ovfns:    NEWTABLE( ) → TABLE
            effects 'PRIMARYTABLE( )=PRIMARYTABLE( )
              'GET(K,T) = GET(K,T)
              'TABLEP(T) = (TABLEP(T) or T=TABLE)
              not TABLEP(TABLE)
              TABLE~=?
```

Communications
of
the ACM

December 1978
Volume 21
Number 12

```
SAVE(VALUE,KEY,TABLE)
    assert   TABLEP(TABLE) and VALUE~=? and
                KEY~=?
    effects 'PRIMARYTABLE( )=PRIMARYTABLE( )
            'GET(K,T) =   if K=KEY and T=TABLE
                            then VALUE
                            else GET(K,T)
            'TABLEP(T)=TABLEP(T)
GETOP(KEY,TABLE) → VALUE
    assert   TABLEP(TABLE) and KEY~=?
    except NOTTHERE: GET(KEY,TABLE)=?
    effects 'PRIMARYTABLE( )=PRIMARYTABLE( )
            'GET(K,T)=GET(K,T)
            'TABLEP(T)=TABLEP(T)
            VALUE=GET(KEY,TABLE)
PRIMARYTABLEOP( ) → TABLE
    effects TABLE='PRIMARYTABLE( )=
                PRIMARY-TABLE( )
            'GET(K,T)=GET(K,T)
            'TABLEP(T)=TABLEP(T)
```

Fig. 2. Implementation of ULIST.

1. (c)
2. (b c)
3. (a b c)
4. (d b c)
5. (e c)
6. ((b c) c)
7. (a (b c) c)

(a)   A SET OF SEVEN LIST STRUCTURES

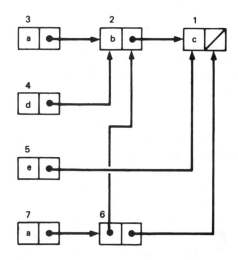

(b) THE SAME LIST STRUCTURES IMPLEMENTED WITH SHARING OF COMMON CELLS

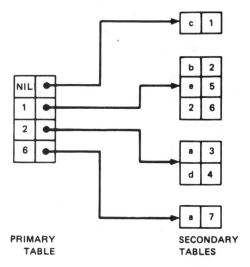

(c)   THE SEARCH TABLES FOR THESE LISTS

The basic idea is that there are a number of "search tables"—a special table called PRIMARYTABLE that exists initially, and as many secondary tables as the user wishes to create using the NEWTABLE instruction. In each table one can save a value under a key, writing over any previously saved value, or look up the value saved under a key. (We could simplify the argument structure and specifications of the instructions of this module by using only a single table and a GETOP instruction whose single argument combined the information in the two arguments of the present GETOP. But we believe that the version given yields a clearer implementation and it is also more suggestive of the implementation used by Deutsch [6].)

Note that the specification of GETOP uses an exception if there is no entry in the table under the key that is sought. It is worthwhile to contrast the use of exceptions and assertions in this specification. We assert that TABLEP(TABLE), indicating that a compilation or verification assert that TABLEP(TABLE), indicating that a compilation or verification may assume this fact in processing the implementation of GETOP but must verify it for uses of GETOP. The assertion describes a condition that must be guaranteed to hold at calls of the function. The exception, on the other hand, describes a condition—the presence of a particular entry in the table—that may or may not hold. Implementation programs are simplified by the possibility of structuring them to consider the "normal" and "exceptional" cases separately.

Any scheme for implementing unique lists requires determining whether a given pair of arguments to UCONS are the UCAR and UCDR of a previously UCONSed cell. In the specification of ULIST, the V-function UCELL serves to map from arguments pairs to cells; however, because of a quirk of Interlisp (the possibility of basing a hash probe on a single pointer but not on a pair of pointers), UCELL is not directly implementable in Interlisp. Instead, Deutsch employed—and we formally describe—a scheme based on two levels of search. This scheme is illustrated in Figure 2(c). The lists

in Figure 2(a) are shown as they might be uniquely represented in Figure 2(b). Each list cell is shown with a numeric cell identifier corresponding to the list number. The primary table of Figure 2(c) represents the association between UCDRs of cells and secondary tables. A secondary table, corresponding to a particular UCDR X2, then associates UCARs of cells with the cell, if any, having that UCAR and UCDR X2.

Implementation of ULIST × LIST by LIST × SEARCH is now possible. The implementation has three parts: a representation of states, an initialization program, and programs realizing each of the OV-functions of the upper level. First, the state representation is described by two formulas:

UCELL(X1,X2) ⇐ GET(X1,GET(X2,PRIMARYTABLE( )))
CELL(X1,X2,X) ⇐ CELL(X1,X2,X)
and GET(X1,GET(X2,
PRIMARY-TABLE( )))~=X

In these formulas, the left-hand sides refer to V-functions of the upper machine and the right-hand sides to V-functions of the lower machine. The first of these formulas describes the state correspondence needed to implement the two level search procedure: it provides that an upper state where UCELL(X1,X2) is not "?" will be represented by a lower state where the double search with X1 and X2 yields a result other than "?". Also, it requires that if UCELL(X1,X2) is "?", then the double search in the lower level state must yield "?" too.

The second formula describes how the upper level conventional lists are represented. The answer is, they are represented by lower level lists. We state this by using CELL on both sides of the definition, to be read as describing the upper level CELL in terms of the lower level CELL. However, there is a subtlety: some of the lower level lists will be used in the implementation to represent upper level unique lists and these, so far as the upper level is concerned, do not exist as lists. Thus, we add the second conjunct to this formula to exclude these lists from the set of upper level cells.

The initialization program must start from an initial state of LIST × SEARCH and arrive at a state of that machine that represents an initial state of ULIST × LIST. However, all that is required of an initial state of ULIST × LIST is that UCELL(X1,X2) is "?" and CELL(X1,X2,X) is "false" and, in view of the representation just given, this is represented by an initial state of LIST × SEARCH. Hence, the empty program suffices for initialization.

Finally, we must realize the upper level OV-functions UCONS, UCAR, UCDR, UCONSP, CONS, CAR, CDR, and CONSP by lower level programs. These are given below.

```
UCONS(X1,X2) : begin locals TABLE, C;
    execute TABLE ← GETOP(X2,PRIMARYTABLEOP( )) then
      on normal: execute C ← GETOP(X1, TABLE) then
        on normal: return(C);
        on NOTTHERE: C ← CONS(X1,X2);
                     SAVE(C,X1,TABLE);
                     return(C) end;
      on NOTTHERE: TABLE ← NEWTABLE( );
        C ← CONS(X1,X2);
        SAVE(C,X1,TABLE);
        SAVE(TABLE,X2,PRIMARYTABLEOP( )) end end;
UCAR(X)     : CAR(X);
UCDR(X)     : CDR(X);
UCONSP(X)   : begin locals TABLE, C;
    if CONSP(X)
      then execute
              TABLE ← GETOP(CDR(X),PRIMARYTABLEOP( ))
              then
         on normal:
            execute C ← GETOP(CAR(X),TABLE);
            then
```

```
          on normal:     return(C=X);
          on NOTTHERE: return(false) end;
        on NOTTHERE: return(false) end
      else return(false) end;
CONS(X1,X2)  : CONS(X1,X2);
CAR(X)       : CAR(X);
CDR(X)       : CDR(X);
CONSP(X)     : CONSP(X) and ~UCONSP(X);
```

First, note that occurrences of CONS, CAR, CDR, and CONSP in the defining programs denote these instructions on the lower level machine. Next, note that the defining programs for the top level functions CONS, CAR, and CDR are trivial because exactly the right instruction exists at the lower level. The defining programs for UCAR and UCDR are also single instructions; this is a consequence of the decision we made to represent upper level unique lists by lower level conventional lists. The nontrivial implementations are those for UCONS, UCONSP, and CONSP.

The implementation for UCONSP is a block that introduces two local variables: TABLE and C. If the argument X does not satisfy the lower level CONSP predicate, it cannot—in view of the representation—satisfy UCONSP. However, if it is a list cell, the UCONSP program uses the "execute" statement, a special feature of our implementation language. We use this statement to call an OV-function that may have exceptions and then deal with the normal exit and the exceptional exits in turn. Thus the UCONSP program first searches in the primary table with CDR(X) as key. If there is no exception, then the TABLE that results is searched with CAR(X) as key. A normal exit from this second search with result C indicates that C is a unique list with the same components as X and therefore is the only such unique list. Hence X is a unique list if and only if it is C. If either search has an exceptional exit, this means that there is no unique list with CAR(X) and CDR(X) as components. Thus UCONSP returns "false."

The implementation of UCONS has a similar structure. If both searches have normal exits and result C, then UCONS just returns C. If the first search encounters the NOTTHERE exception, this means that there are no existing unique lists with UCDR X2. Hence we create a new search table to record such unique lists, enter it in the primary table under key X2, create the new (representation of a) unique list CONS(X1,X2), and enter it in the new secondary table under key X1. The new list is then the answer returned by UCONS.

If the first search has a normal exit, but the second search has a NOTTHERE exception, this indicates that there is already a secondary search table TABLE for unique lists with UCDR X2, but that there is no entry in TABLE with X1 as UCAR. Hence we again create a new unique list representation CONS(X1,X2), enter it in TABLE under Key X1, and return it as the answer of UCONS.

Finally, the implementation of CONSP introduces some difficulty. Although there is a CONSP instruction at the lower level, it does not suffice: the lower level

CONSP is satisfied by the lower level cells that represent upper level unique lists but these are not conventional lists in the abstraction provided by the upper level machine. We have given an implementation that makes an additional test [~UCONSP(X)] to avoid this problem, a correct but unpleasantly inefficient implementation of what ought to be a low-overhead type checking operation. For present purposes, the correct but inefficient implementation suffices; Section 9 discusses some alternatives.

7. Correctness of the Implementation

The proof that an implementation is correct with respect to a pair of machine specifications and a state representation has two parts. First, we must prove that the initialization program for the lower level—in this case the empty program—can be executed from any initial state of the lower level machine to yield a lower level state that represents an initial state of the upper level machine. Second, we must prove that this representation is preserved by the execution of the implementations of OV-functions in the lower machine. That is, suppose S and S′ are states of the upper machine and T and T′ are states of the lower machine. Suppose that S′ is a state that results from the execution of an OV-function call "F(X)" according to the specification of the upper machine. Also, suppose that T′ is a state that results from the execution of the implementation of "F(X)" in the lower machine. Then, we must prove that T′ is a representation of S′. (This may be thought as a proof that the diagram of Figure 3 commutes.)

In doing these proofs, it is important to note that the execution of the implementations of the upper machine instructions does not fully exercise the facilities of the lower machine. For example, in our LIST × SEARCH machine there are states such that, for some X, the result of "GETOP(X,PRIMARYTABLEOP( ))" is neither an exception nor a secondary table but, instead, a list cell. Since we never store anything other than secondary tables in the primary table, we know that this can never occur and would like to use this knowledge to help the proof. We can do this by formulating an invariant predicate I(T) on the states T of the lower machine. We then prove that I holds for states resulting from the initialization of the lower machine. We also prove that if I(T) holds, and P is the implementation of an upper machine OV-function, then I(T′) holds where T′ results from T when P is executed in the lower machine. Having proved such an invariant property, we may assume that I holds for all states that arise in the proofs described in the previous paragraph.

We will illustrate the proof of correctness of implementations in this methodology (Figure 3) by proving the correctness of the implementation given in the preceding section. The necessary invariant assertion has two parts. First, if a fetch from the primary table yields a

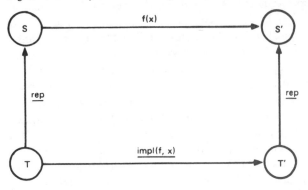

Fig. 3. A necessary condition for implementation correctness.

result, not "?", then that result is a (secondary) table. Second, if a fetch from the secondary table yields a result, not "?", then that result is a list cell whose components are the keys of the two fetches. Stating this formally, we have

$$I(T) = GET(Z2,PRIMARYTABLE( ))=TABLE{\sim}=?$$
$$\text{implies (TABLEP(TABLE) and}$$
$$(GET(Z1,TABLE)=Z{\sim}=?$$
$$\text{implies (CONSP(Z) and CAR(Z)=Z1}$$
$$\text{and CDR(Z)=Z2))).}$$

(Note that the notation is such that the state T does not appear explicitly in the right-hand side of this definition; note also the implicit universal quantification of Z1, Z2, Z, and TABLE.) It is easy to show that I is an invariant of the lower machine states that arise in the implementation. It is true of the initial state because its antecedent is always false in this initial state. If it is true of a state T, then the execution of the implementations of UCAR, UCDR, UCONSP, CONS, CAR, CDR, and CONSP involve no calls of SAVE and therefore no changes in GET. The remaining case is the implementation of UCONS(X1,X2). This implementation can affect the truth of I because it does call SAVE. However, it calls SAVE only with C, which has the proper CAR and CDR and is stored under the appropriate keys, and with TABLE which does satisfy TABLEP (in view of the effects of NEWTABLE) and is also saved in the primary table under the proper key. Thus I is indeed invariant.

We have already shown that an initial state of the lower machine, followed by an empty initialization, represents an initial state of the upper machine. We must now prove that the representation of the upper machine state by the lower machine state is preserved by the execution of the implementations. It should be clear, in each case, that the result returned satisfies the corresponding specification. Except for UCONS and CONS, the instructions of the upper machine are implemented by programs whose only effect is the return of a result; thus these implementations all preserve the representation of the specified upper state by the resulting lower state.

The upper machine's CONS instruction is implemented by the CONS of the lower machine. Since the execution of the lower machine CONS affects only the V-function CELL, and only in a way consistent with the representation, this implementation also preserves the representation. The remaining upper machine construction is UCONS; consider its implementation. If both execute statements are "normal," there is no state change; that the result returned is correct is immediate from the invariant. If the outer execute statement has a normal exit and the inner a "NOTTHERE" exception, then the implementation creates exactly one new cell, and saves it in the proper table, thus preserving the representation of UCELL. Moreover, since the first conjunct of the representation of CELL becomes true exactly where the second conjunct becomes false, the specification that the representation of the upper level CELL be unaffected by execution of UCONS is satisfied.

Finally, if both execute statements have "NOTTHERE" exceptions, then a new secondary table is created and saved under the proper key in the primary table. This does not affect the representation, and the remainder of code in this case preserves the representation by the argument just made for the case of a single exception.

This completes the proof of the ULIST implementation.

8. Further Implementations

The preceding sections have described how properties of an unimplemented machine can be proved from its formal specifications, how such a machine can be realized in terms of a more primitive machine, and how such a realization can be proved with respect to the two machines. To save space, we will in this section sketch rather than fully presenting the further refinement of the LIST × SEARCH machine.

If Interlisp is an acceptable primitive machine, then the programs described so far solve the original problem, since it provides the LIST and SEARCH facilities to which we have reduced the problem. This would raise an interesting problem for the proof of the LIST × SEARCH specifications. The most complete extant specification of Interlisp, [19], is not written in SPECIAL; this proof would thus require a different theory from that discussed here.

A more primitive Lisp than Interlisp can also be used as the basis of our hierarchy. For example, one can easily implement the facilities of SEARCH, except for the PRIMARYTABLEOP instruction, in terms of Lisp lists; the implementation is just the usual Lisp "association list." The implementation of PRIMARYTABLEOP can be accomplished by using a single variable to remember which association list represents the primary search table. That is, LIST × SEARCH can be implemented in terms of VARIABLE × LIST. (VARIABLE is a very simple module: its state is the value saved in the variable and it has two instructions, one to read the value and one to save a new value.) The machines of this hierarchy, and their component modules, are shown in Figure 4.

Alternatively, one can distinguish two kinds of search

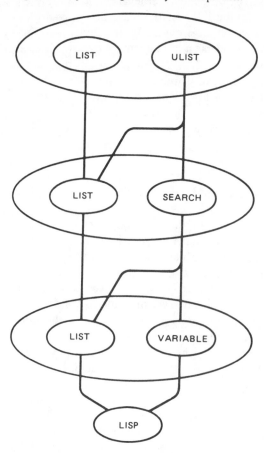

Fig. 4. An implementing hierarchy for unique lists.

operations in the implementation of ULIST—those that start from the primary table and those that start from one of the secondary tables. Actual use of ULIST suggests that it is reasonable to use a hashtable for the primary search table and association lists for the secondary tables. Since Interlisp provides named hashtables, this means that LIST × SEARCH could be realized by HASHTABLE × LIST and, in turn, HASHTABLE × LIST could be realized by Interlisp. (We will not provide an implementation of HASHTABLE here. The interested reader should consult [30]; in that paper, HASHTABLE is implemented in terms of arrays and a "hash probe" function and it is proved that the implementation is correct.)

9. Concluding Remarks

In Section 6, we implemented some specifications in an Algol-like language called ILPL, which is described in Appendix C of [22]. However, the use of this language, while convenient, is not essential to the use of our methodology. On the contrary, we believe that enough structure is given to even a large system by its decomposition and precise specification in SPECIAL to permit implementation in many languages. The critical points in the design and implementation of systems tend to be

Communications of the ACM

December 1978
Volume 21
Number 12

global issues such as a decision on how to decompose a system into modules or how to describe the implementation of a module by a hierarchy of abstractions—exactly the areas in which SPECIAL is expressive. By contrast, the details of any particular programming language usually address very local issues in programming, e.g. whether to use a case or conditional statement to describe a choice, whether to use a "while-do" or a "repeat-until" statement to describe a particular iteration. While such local decisions certainly have an impact on the clarity of the programs that can be written, we believe that this impact is negligible by comparison with the impact of well or poorly done overall design and specification. If the latter is precise, so that a large system is implementable by a large number of loosely coupled small parts, then many different languages may be equally good for implementing the parts.

This is not to deny that care should be taken in the choice of an implementation language. Certainly one ought to use a language with lucid syntax and a flexible set of control structures. Since we advocate the decomposition of a program into many parts, it follows that we recommend choosing a language that can be compiled into a form in which linkage between the parts is economical. Since we seek to implement systems, we are interested in the ultimate efficiency of implementations and therefore require a language in which machine-level representations can be described for the use of the most primitive levels of a hierarchy.

A related issue is the provision of data structures by the base language. For example, we assumed above that our base machine provided a set of objects satisfying the predicate ATOMP and disjoint sets of objects to represent abstractions such as cells and tables. If an adequate facility for defining concrete data types is present in the base, then it need not be provided by the hierarchy and—if the base language is carefully implemented—the cost of soundly manipulating objects of different types will be kept to a minimum. (Such a base should permit an efficient implementation of the upper level CONSP instruction in Section 6; by contrast, [6] is not intended as a hierarchical solution to the unique list problem, does not distinguish the list cells of the different levels of abstraction, and uses the same selectors CAR and CDR for all of them.) If the base does not have a sufficient facility, for example because it is a bare machine, then a type system must be synthesized as part of the hierarchy of machines. This can be quite hard, but it is possible [22].

Some base languages will provide not only concrete but also abstract data structures; these include CLU [15], a modification of Simula [23], Modula [31], and Alphard [32]. Some of these facilities are clearly redundant if our methodology is used with a tool that statically confirms that implementation programs are compatible with specifications, e.g. in what functions they call or what objects they refer to. On the other hand, the use of such a base language can ease the proof that implemen-

tation programs have the protection semantics implicit in the methodology.

Boyer and Moore have developed a formal semantics and a verification condition generator for our methodology [1], using the underlying theory of their Lisp Theorem Prover [2]. This makes it possible to produce precise machineable versions of the theorems given in Section 7 and preliminary experiments encourage us in the hope that these theorems may be mechanically proved. This will be a major theme in our future work.

There are certainly many other ways to specify programs formally. We think that the method of algebraic specifications [8] is very promising. It is similar to our method in its precision and compatibility with formal proof. It appears, in some published examples, to produce specifications that are quite concise but may require of readers greater mathematical sophistication than do ours; we are not aware of its use on examples as large as [22]. It would be premature to draw firm conclusions about the relative merits of the two methods and we look forward to the further development of both.

Acknowledgments. We thank B. Elspas, R. Boyer, and the referees for their helpful suggestions; R. Boyer and J Moore for their work on formalizing SPECIAL; and S. German for the idea of trying to prove Theorem 3.

Received January 1976; revised August 1977

References
1. Boyer, R.S., and Moore, JS. Private communication, June 1977.
2. Boyer, R.S., and Moore, JS. A lemma driven automatic theorem prover for recursive function theory. Proc. Int. Joint Conf. Artificial Intelligence, Cambridge, Mass., Aug. 1977.
3. Burstall, R.M. Proving properties of programs by structural induction. *Comptr. J. 12*, 1 (Jan. 1969), 41–48.
4. Dahl, O.J., Myhrhaug, B., and Nygaard, K. Common base language, S-22. Norwegian Comptng. Ctr., Oslo, Norway, Oct. 1970.
5. Dahl, O.J., Dijkstra, E.W., and Hoare, C.A.R. *Structured Programming*. Academic Press, New York, 1972.
6. Deutsch, L.P. An interactive program verifier. Ph.D. Th., Dept. of Comptr. Sci., U. of California, Berkeley, 1973.
7. Good, D.I. Provable programming. Proc. Int. Conf. Reliable Software, SIGPLAN Notices (ACM) *10*, 6 (June 1975), 411–419.
8. Guttag, J. Abstract data types and the development of data structures. *Comm. ACM 20*, 6 (June 1977), 396–404.
9. Hoare, C.A.R. Proof of correctness of data representations. *Acta Informatica 1*, 4 (1972), 271–281.
10. Hoare, C.A.R., and Wirth, N. An axiomatic definition of the programming language PASCAL. *Acta Informatica 2*, 4 (1973), 335–355.
11. Ichbiah, J.D., et al. The system implementation language LIS. Tech. Rep. 4549, E/EN, Compagnie Internationale pour l'Informatique, Louveciennes, France, Dec. 1974.
12. Igarashi, S., London, R.L., and Luckham, D.C. Automatic program verification I: A logical basis and its implementation. *Acta Informatica 1*, 4 (1975), 145–182.
13. An appraisal of program specifications. Computation Structures. Group Memo 141-1, Lab. for Comptr. Sci., M.I.T., Cambridge, Mass., April 1977.
14. Liskov, B., and Zilles, S. Programming with abstract data types. Proc. ACM SIGPLAN Conf. Very High Level Languages, SIGPLAN Notices (ACM) *9*, 4 (April 1974), 50–59.
15. Liskov, B., and Zilles, S. Specification techniques for data abstraction. *IEEE Trans. Software Eng. SE-1*, 1 (March 1975), 7–19.
16. McCarthy, J. A basis for a mathematical theory of computation.

In *Computer Programming and Formal Systems*, Braffort and Hirschberg, Eds., North-Holland, Amsterdam, 1963, pp. 33–70.

17. McCarthy, J., et al. *LISP 1.5 Programmer's Manual.* M.I.T. Press, Cambridge, Mass., 1962.

18. Manna, Z., Ness, S., and Vuillemin, J. Inductive methods for proving properties of programs. *Comm. ACM 16,* 8 (Aug. 1973), 491–502.

19. Moore, JS. The Interlisp virtual machine specification. Rep. CSL 76-5, Xerox Palo Alto Res. Ctr., Palo Alto, Calif., Sept. 1976.

20. Morris, J. Protection in programming languages. *Comm. ACM 16,* 1 (Jan. 1973), 15–21.

21. Morris, J.M. Types are not sets. Proc. ACM Symposium on Principles of Programming Languages, Boston, Mass., Oct. 1973, pp. 120–124.

22. Neumann, P.G., et al. A provably secure operating system: The system, its applications, and proofs. Final Rep., SRI Proj. 4332, SRI Int., Menlo Park, Calif., Feb. 1977.

23. Palme, J. Protected program modules in Simula 67. Res. Inst. of Nat. Defense, Stockholm, Sweden, July 1973.

24. Parnas, D.L. A technique for software module specification with examples. *Comm. ACM 15,* 5 (May 1972), 330–336.

25. Parnas, D.L. On the criteria to be used in decomposing systems into modules. *Comm. ACM 15,* 12 (Dec. 1972), 1053–1058.

26. Robinson, L., and Levitt, K.N. Proof techniques for hierarchically structured programs. *Comm. ACM 20,* 4 (April 1977), 271–283.

27. Robinson, L., et al. On attaining reliable software for a secure operating system. Proc. Int. Conf. Reliable Software, SIGPLAN Notices (ACM) *10,* 6 (June 1975), 267–284.

28. Roubine, O., and Robinson, L. SPECIAL Reference Manual. Tech. Rep. CSL-45, SRI Project 4828, SRI Int., Menlo Park, Calif., 3rd ed., Jan. 1977.

29. Wegbreit, B. The treatment of data types in EL1. *Comm. ACM 17,* 5 (May 1974), 251–264.

30. Wegbreit, B., and Spitzen, J. M. Proving properties of complex data structures. *J. ACM 23,* 2 (April 1976), 389–396.

31. Wirth, N. Modula: A language for modular multiprogramming. *Software—Practice and Experience 7* (1977), 3–35.

32. Wulf, W.A. ALPHARD: Toward a language to support structured programs. Comptr. Sci. Dept., Carnegie-Mellon U., Pittsburgh, Pa., April 1974.

33. Yourdon, E., and Constantine, L.L. *Structured Design.* Yourdon Press, New York, 1975.

270

Communications
of
the ACM

December 1978
Volume 21
Number 12

COROUTINES AND NETWORKS OF PARALLEL PROCESSES

GILLES KAHN
Iria-Laboria
Rocquencourt, France

DAVID B. MacQUEEN
University of Edinburgh
Edinburgh, Scotland, U.K.

Reprinted with permission from *Information Processing 77*, 1977, page 993-998. Copyright © 1977 by IFIP, Elsevier/North Holland Publishing Company.

The concept of *coroutine* or *process* is useful in a large class of applications, usually involving incremental generation or transformation of data. We present a language based on a clear semantics of process interaction, which facilitates well-structured programming of dynamically evolving networks of processes. These networks exhibit the same input/output behavior whether they are executed sequentially or in parallel. Sample program proofs are used to illustrate the benefits of the language's simple denotational semantics. The language serves also to clarify the relationships between coroutines, call-by-need, dynamic data structures and parallel computation.

1. INTRODUCTION

Many algorithms are naturally organized as systems of independent processes which coexist and interact with one another. In this paper, we present a structured approach to the programming of such systems. This approach is embodied in a programming language which subordinates control to structure, relieving the programmer of the burden of control management and permitting process systems to be executed either sequentially or concurrently with the same result. The language was designed to reflect the clear semantic conception of process interaction presented in [1], with the result that programs are relatively easy to verify.

1.1 Coroutines, multipass algorithms, and pipelines

Our notion of a *process* is derived from Conway's original concept of coroutines, [2] which he introduced as an improved way of executing multipass algorithms. In his words, "... *a coroutine is an autonomous program which communicates with adjacent modules as if they were input and output subroutines*." The coroutines represent successive passes each of which *incrementally* transforms a stream of data, so that their execution can be interleaved in time according to a "demand-driven" scheduling strategy. This mode of execution was described succinctly : "*When coroutines A and B are connected so that A sends items to B, B runs for a while until it encounters a read command, which means it needs something from A. The control is then transferred to A until it wants to write, whereupon control is returned to B at the point where it left off*."

Conway went on to note that coroutines can be executed *simultaneously* if parallel hardware is available. This is possible without time-dependent side effects because the coroutines communicate with each other only via input/output instructions, and this in turn follows from the fact that the coroutines are modelling separate passes of a multipass algorithm. When executed in parallel, such a system is called a "pipeline." Many studies of parallel program schemata have been concerned with generalizing this simple linear organization.[3-5]

The classic illustration of coroutines is the cooperation between the lexical analyzer and the parser in a compiler. However, algorithms structured as a set of interacting coroutines occur in many applications besides compiling, such as input/output handling, [6] text manipulation, [7] algebraic manipulations, [8] sorting, [9] numerical computation, [10] and artificial intelligence. [11] The UNIX operating system [12] provides a "pipelining combinator" in its command language which is used to connect programs together in linear pipelines for quasi-parallel execution.

1.2 Alternative approaches to coroutines

A different approach to coroutines, typified by the SIMULA control primitives *call*, *detach* and *resume*, is fairly widespread. [13-14] The SIMULA primitives can be used to *implement* Conway's style of coroutines, where control transfers are hidden in the input/output commands, but they also allow many other types of interaction which often result in intricate control relationships. Use of the *resume* command in particular leads to obscure control structures, because it resembles a *go to* command with a moving target. For the sake of program reliability and verification one needs to impose discipline on the use of these primitives, and when this is done [16-18] it leads to the structuring of process interaction along the lines of Conway's original proposal.

1.3 Related ideas

The evaluation mechanism used in our system has its origins in theoretical work [19-20] on "call-by-need" parameter passing. The same work has inspired "lazy evaluators" for LISP [21,22] which in some respects behave like our process networks and can execute slightly modified versions of some of our examples. These systems, however, do not have any analogue of our cyclic network structures.

Communication channels are related to the *streams* of Landin, [23] who foresaw their connection with coroutines. In fact, our language can be viewed as a powerful stream processing language. A simplified version of streams already exists in POP-2 [24] in the form of *dynamic lists*, but their usefulness is limited because the lack of processes in POP-2 makes it awkward to define stream transformations.

2. THE PROGRAMMING LANGUAGE

2.1 Introduction

The language presented here provides concise and flexible means for creating complex networks of processes which may evolve during execution. The key concepts are *processes* and structures called *channels* which interconnect processes and buffer their communications. Channels carry information in one direction only from a *producer process* to one or more *consumer processes*, and they behave like unbounded FIFO queues.

In this section we explain how processes are declared, how they communicate via channels, and how networks of processes are created and transformed. Then we introduce a more powerful functional notation and discuss iterative versus recursive reconfiguration of processes.

271

The language has been implemented in Edinburgh as an extension of POP-2. [20] Although its concrete syntax follows the style of POP-2 (e.g., the Algol assignment "A:=B" is written B → A in POP-2), no feature of POP-2 that departs significantly from PASCAL or ALGOL is used.

2.2 Processes

Each process is specified in a *process declaration*, patterned after a procedure/function declaration in POP-2 :

> *Process* <name> <parameter-list> ;
> <process body>
> *Endprocess*

The parameter list is partitioned into two sublists : the *ordinary* parameters and the *port* parameters. Parameters in the first group are evaluated according to the rules of POP-2. Port parameters [25] will be bound to communication channels so that a process may communicate with its neighbors in the network. In the declaration of TRANSDUCER (see fig.1) A is an ordinary parameter, called by value, while QI and QO are respectively input and output ports. In a typed language, say PASCAL, the process heading would appear like this :
Process TRANSDUCER (A: *integer*; QI: *in integer*;
       QO: *out integer*);

The body of a process declaration is similar to the body of a procedure in POP-2 : variables and functions may be declared local to the process (thus no restriction is placed on the amount of memory available to a process). Conceptually, each process is thought of as executing on a separate machine so that it cannot communicate with any other process except through interconnecting channels. Hence :

(1) No global variable may be *updated* by a process
(2) Arrays, but *not* references to arrays, may be sent along communications lines
(3) More generally, if a reference to the dynamic storage area is sent by a process, the area that may be reached through this reference must become read-only.

(Note that (3) is automatically satisfied in purely applicative languages). The constraints above do not mean that two processes cannot access a common file or table, but a process should be responsible for the management of all accesses to such a shared object, in the manner advocated in [26]. This is the way, for example, in which we deal with input/output in our system.
All constructs of POP-2 may occur in the body of a process. Two *primitive functions* are provided to transmit information between processes, and a *reconfiguration instruction* allows the redefinition of the network.

2.3 Transmission primitives

A process is connected to its neighbours via one-way communication channels. The function GET is used to obtain data : if A is an input port, the evaluation of the *expression* GET(A) yields the next item arriving via port A. If no value ever arrives, this evaluation does not terminate. Consecutive evaluations of GET(A) yield consecutive items, as if A was a sequential input file. The *procedure call* PUT(<expression>,B) sends the result of evaluation of the first argument along the channel bound to output port B.

Availability of an item at an input port *cannot* be tested. This is not an oversight but a deliberate decision to exclude time-dependent input/output behavior. Certain sections of an operating system *demand* a primitive of this kind, but the absence of time-dependencies gives a distinct flavour to pipelining as opposed to other kinds of parallel processing and permits the simulation of a pipeline by a set of coroutines. Note also that including such a primitive changes drastically the mathematical semantics of the language. [27]

2.4 Reconfiguration

While a process program is running, it may be visualised as a directed graph where nodes represent processes and edges stand for communication channels. During computation, this graph may evolve in a top-down fashion : a node may be replaced by a subgraph, provided this subgraph can be appropriately *spliced* into the incoming/outgoing edges (i.e., channels) of the original node. A *reconfiguration instruction* has the form :

> *doco* <body> *closeco*

and its body specifies a transformation of this sort. The keyword *doco* stands for "do concurrently" or "do coroutines." *Closeco* is just the matching closing bracket. The body of the instruction has two parts :

(i) the declaration of new communication's lines (edges in the new subgraph)
(ii) a list of *process calls*. Port parameters in these calls may be bound either to channels that have just been declared or to ports of the *parent* process, i.e., the process in which this reconfiguration instruction occurs.

In fig.1, the process GO contains a reconfiguration instruction. Its evaluation provokes the graph transformation displayed on fig.2.
The two calls to TRANSDUCER set up two *distinct* instances of this process. As a reconfiguration instruction merely *specifies* a new setup, the order in which process calls occur is, for the moment, irrelevant.*

```
Process PRODUCER out QO;
    vars N; 0 → N;
    repeat INCREMENT N;  PUT(N,QO) forever
Endprocess;
Process TRANSDUCER A in QI out QO;
    repeat PUT(A + GET(QI),QO) forever
Endprocess;
Process  CONSUMER in QI;
    repeat 20 times  PRINT(GET(QI)) close
Endprocess;
Process GO;
    doco channels Q1 Q2 Q3;
    PRODUCER (Q1);  TRANSDUCER(1,Q1,Q2);
    TRANSDUCER(-1,Q2,Q3);  CONSUMER(Q3);
    closeco
Endprocess;

Start doco GO( ) closeco;
```

1 2 3 4 5 6 7 8 9 10 11 12 13 14 15 16 17 18 19 20 :

Fig.1. First example.

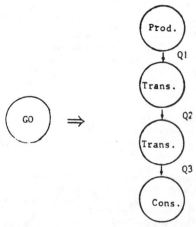

Fig.2. Reconfiguration.

* As the reader realizes by now, the program of fig.1 does not achieve very much. It just serves to illustrate the first features of the language.

Remark : In Algol, a procedure call lumps together three distinct operations : the creation of new procedures, the binding of formal to actual parameters and control transfer. In ISWIM [28] or SL5[29] some of these actions may be performed separately. Here, processes are bound to their arguments as soon as they are created, but control is transferred in an entirely separate manner.

Conway's original coroutine scheme requires the coroutine network to be acyclic. The theory tells us that this restriction is unnecessary. From a pragmatic point of view, the extra cost incurred at execution time is minimal and feedback loops in coroutine programs are *in fact* quite useful. Another constraint, implicit in Conway's paper, is essential. Call a process a *producer* (resp. *consumer*) for Q if it is bound to channel Q via an output port (resp. input port). The sequence of items that will be sent on Q during execution of the program is the *history* of Q. If the history of every communication variable is determined by the value of the program's parameters, a parallel program is called *determinate*. A simple rule guarantees determinacy of process programs : at any given time during execution, a channel must be bound to a single producer, and to a single output port of that producer. Note that several consumers may share the same input line : in this case all consumers get the same input sequence.

2.5 Activation

Within a POP-2 program, an activation instruction of the form :

  start <reconfiguration instruction>

may be issued to request execution of a process program. This instruction terminates when the process program terminates. Once an initial network has been set up by the reconfiguration instruction, it is set in motion and from then on control transfer is automatic. In the simple program of fig.1, an activation instruction is issued at top-level. The occurrence of the POP-2 prompt character (':') after the results shows that the program did terminate.

The program of fig.3 is more interesting. This form of the sieve of Eratosthenes appears, to the best of the authors' knowledge, for the first time in [30]. For each newly discovered prime, a FILTER process is created by SIFT, whose task it is to remove all multiples of that prime from the integers to be considered. A proof of the correctness of this program is sketched in section 4.

```
Process INTEGERS out QO;
    Vars N; 1 → N;
    repeat INCREMENT N; PUT(N,QO) forever
Endprocess;

Process FILTER PRIME in QI out QO;
    Vars N;
    repeat GET(QI) → N;
        if (N MOD PRIME)≠ 0 then PUT(N,QO) close
    forever
Endprocess;

Process SIFT in QI out QO;
    Vars PRIME; GET(QI) → PRIME;
    PUT (PRIME,QO); comment emit a discovered prime;
    doco channels Q;
     FILTER(PRIME,QI,Q); SIFT(Q,QO)
    closeco
Endprocess;

Process OUTPUT in QI; Comment this is a library process;
    repeat PRINT(GET(QI)) forever
Endprocess;

Start doco channels Q1 Q2;
    INTEGERS(Q1); SIFT(Q1,Q2); OUTPUT(Q2);
    closeco
```

    Fig.3. Sieve of Eratosthenes.

2.6 Functional notation

The constructs explained so far are sufficient for all programming. However, we can write much more elegant programs in a functional notation. Most processes have a single output line so that they are functions from streams to streams. [23] Thus in the way that ALGOL 60 permits functions along with procedures, processes may be declared functional and used to build stream expressions. In process calls occurring in reconfiguration instructions, such expressions may be provided as arguments where input channels are expected. For example, the program in fig.3 will now look like :

    Process INTEGERS => QO;
    ...
    Process FILTER PRIME *in* QI => QO;
    ...
    Process SIFT *in* QI => QO;
    ...
    Process OUTPUT *in* QI;
    ...
    start doco OUTPUT(SIFT(INTEGERS())) *closeco*;

This new notation is very convenient because many channels are created implicitly. But stream expressions denote only acyclic subnets. A simple construct (akin to Landin's WHEREREC) allows networks to be built with cycles. In a reconfiguration instruction, we allow now a list of *elementary reconfigurations* where, in the familiar BNF notation :

<elem.reconf>::=<process call>
  |<elem.reconf>WHERE<chan-list>$\{^{IS}_{ARE}\}$<stream-exp-list>

In the program of fig.4, a reconfiguration written in this style can be found in the activation. Since X occurs both in the channel list and within the stream expression on the right of IS, a network with a cycle is being specified. Note also that X is shared as input by the three instances of TIMES and the process OUTPUTF.

Finally, a difficulty crops up when, as a consequence of a reconfiguration, the newly created network has to output values on a channel previously bound to an output port of the parent process, as happens in SIFT for example (see fig.3). Another kind of elementary reconfiguration, called *splicing* must be included :

<list of stream expressions> => <list of output ports>

This specifies that the stream expressions on the left are to provide data to the channels bound to the ports on the right. So the reconfiguration in SIFT is now :

    doco SIFT(FILTER(PRIME,QI)) => QO *closeco*

Note that this device offers a simple way to have a network shrink rather than expand. For example the process QCONS :

    Process QCONS A *in* QI => QO;
       PUT(A,QO);
       doco QI => QO *closeco*
    Endprocess

first emits A and then ties its input to its output channel and vanishes.

2.7 Optimizing recursion

The situation of the process SIFT is a common one. This process reconfigures into a subgraph containing a new instance of SIFT and disappears. Instead, SIFT could merely create in front of itself new FILTERs upon receiving new inputs and thus be iterative rather than recursive. To indicate that the parent process is to be included in a new configuration, the dummy process call *CONTINUE* is used. Usually the bindings of the parent process have to change. An assignment permits switching inputs, splicing is needed to reconnect outputs. The transformed version of SIFT is :

```
Process SIFT in QI => QO;
  Vars PRIME;
  repeat
    GET(QI) → PRIME; PUT(PRIME,QO)
    doco FILTER(PRIME,QI)→QI; CONTINUE closeco
  forever
Endprocess;
```

In our implementation, significant time and space savings result from this transform.

2.8 An example

The programming style is now much less imperative. To illustrate this, consider a problem treated by Dijkstra. [31] One is requested to generate the first N elements of the sequence of integers of the form $2^a3^b5^c$(a,b,c≥0) in increasing order, without omission or repetition. The idea of the solution is to think of that sequence as a single object and to notice that if we multiply it by 2, 3 or 5, we obtain sub-sequences. The program of fig.4 embodies the idea that the solution sequence is the least sequence containing 1 and satisfying that property. The process MERGE assumes two increasing sequences of integers as input and merges them, eliminating duplications on the fly. The process TIMES multiplies all elements of its input channel by the scalar A. The process OUTPUTF is a library process. Notice that control considerations do not intervene in the design of this program.

Remarks : (1) What is an implicit quantity in other coroutine systems, the history of a communication's variable ("mytical" variable in [16]), is now explicit and subject to calculations. The style of programming also recalls LUCID, [34] which has a similar semantics. The pay-off will be in easier correctness proofs. Note also that this programming language is just what is needed to compute over real numbers with unlimited accuracy. [35]

```
Process MERGE in QI1 QI2 => QO;
  Vars I1, I2; comment local buffers;
  GET(QI1)→I1; GET(QI2)→I2; Comment initialisation;
  loopif I1<I2 then PUT(I1,QO); GET(QI1)→I1
  elseif I1>I2 then PUT(I2,QO); GET(QI2)→I2
  else comment I1 = I2. Remove duplications;
    PUT(I1,QO);GET(QI1)→I1; GET(QI2)→I2
  close
Endprocess;

Process TIMES A in QI => QO
  repeat PUT(A*GET(QI),QO) forever
Endprocess;

Start doco
  OUTPUTF(20,X)
  where channels X is
    QCONS(1,MERGE(TIMES(2,X),
                  MERGE(TIMES(3,X),
                        TIMES(5,X))))
  closeco

1 2 3 4 5 6 8 9 10 12 15 16 18 20 24 25 27 30 32 36
:
```

Fig.4. An example from Dijkstra.

(2) Returning to the particular program of fig.4, it can be made much more efficient if we eliminate redundant number generation, calling it with :

```
start doco OUTPUTF(20,X)
  where channels X,Y,Z are
    QCONS(1,MERGE(TIMES(2,X),Y)),
    QCONS(3,MERGE(TIMES(3,Y),Z)),
    QCONS(5,TIMES(5,Z))
  closeco
```

3. EXECUTION

3.1 Outline

From an operational point of view, a process network is a collection of independent machines which interact by making demands upon or sending data along communication channels. Processes are represented by data structures containing local access environments and control continuations. A channel is represented by a linear list containing items stored in the channel and terminating with a reference to the current producer for the channel. Consumers have pointers into this list which are updated by the GET operation, while the producer inserts new items at the end of the list via the PUT operation. A reconfiguration instruction results in :
(1) creation of new processes and channels,
(2) initializing or updating input channel pointers,
(3) initializing or updating channel producer information.

A single constraint regulates the activity of processes : if a process requests input data from an empty channel, it must stop and wait until that data is provided by the channel's producer, which must be activated if possible. Given this constraint, a range of scheduling strategies are possible, from *pure coroutine* execution where a single process is active at any time to *full parallelism* where all processes run except when they are waiting for input. These scheduling strategies all yield the same input/output behavior, because the exclusive use of channels for interprocess communication and the careful choice of data transmission primitives serve to insulate processes from scheduling-dependent information.

3.2 Coroutine mode of execution

In this mode, activation of processes is strictly *demand driven*. Since the demand must originate somewhere, a process is selected to drive the whole network, and the demands of this driving process propagate through the network via the execution of transmission primitives and reconfiguration instructions.
(i) Selection of the driving process

The last process created in the execution of the activation instruction is designated as the initial driving process and is the first process activated. Normally, it is that process which is responsible for producing (e.g. printing) the ultimate outcome.*
(ii) Transmission primitives

Both GET and PUT may involve transfer of control. Applying GET to an empty input channel C causes suspension of the running process and activation of the producer for C. The channel C is made *hungry* to indicate that there is a consumer waiting on it. Applying PUT to a hungry output channel causes suspension of the running process and resumption of the waiting consumer, whereupon the interrupted GET operation is completed.

Remarks : (1) There is no transfer of control when GET is applied to a nonempty input channel or PUT is applied to a nonhungry output channel.
(2) If as a result of a GET operation the scheduler attempts to activate a producer which is itself waiting, further computation is impossible and deadlock has been detected.
(iii) Reconfiguration

Except for the driving process, any process which is active is trying to satisfy some hungry output channel. After such a process reconfigures, the scheduler gives control to the (possibly new) producer for that hungry channel.
When the driving process reconfigures it may survive (i.e., remain in the new configuration) in which case it retains control, or it may disappear, in which case the last process created is chosen as the new driving process and is activated.

3.3 Parallel mode of execution

After a PUT instruction sends an item on a hungry channel, the waiting consumer must be reactivated. But if additional processors are available there is

---

* The last process created in a reconfiguration is the outermost one in the last elementary reconfiguration.

274

no need to deactivate the producer process ; it may continue to run in *anticipation* of further demands for its output. In this way, computations that were interleaved in time can be made to overlap, and some process switching overhead is saved as well, without increasing the programmer's burden. The one drawback is that the process which was not deactivated *may* carry out *nonessential* computation, i.e., computation that is not needed to produce the final outcome of the program. This nonessential computation may even involve the recursive creation of superfluous processes.

We have developed a method of restraining such over-anticipation and verified its effectiveness in quasi-parallel simulations. The idea is to associate with each channel C a non-negative integer $A(C)$, called the anticipation coefficient. Once activated, the producer for C will not be deactivated by PUT until C contains at least $A(C)$ many unconsumed items. Note that the coroutine mode of execution results when $A(C) = 0$ for all channels C. The anticipation coefficient can only be accessed by the primitives GET and PUT. It is set by a special primitive $ANT(n,C)$. Normally, the anticipation coefficient should be set as the channel is passed as an input parameter to a new process. In any case, the specifications for anticipation will not affect the semantics of the program, nor will they require alterations to its basic design.

4. PROGRAM PROOFS

For a detailed presentation of the mathematical semantics of the programming language, the reader is referred to [1]. Roughly, to any program one associates a set of recursive equations. Standard proof techniques can then be used. [19,32] A form of *structural induction* is used repeatedly. Suppose one wishes to prove that a sequence X has property P :

(1) First one proves, usually by induction, that P holds for a sufficiently rich set of *finite* initial segments of X.
(2) Second one proves that P *admits induction*, that is that if it holds for sufficiently many finite initial segments of some sequence, it must hold for the whole sequence as well.

Formal proofs are too long to be given here in detail, so we present only the articulating lemmas.

4.1 Program of fig.4

Lemma 1 (Properties of MERGE) : If L_1 and L_2 are strictly increasing sequences of integers then
(1) $MERGE(L_1,L_2)$ is strictly increasing

(2) As sets, $MERGE(L_1,L_2) \subseteq L_1 \cup L_2$ and if L_1 and L_2 are infinite, equality holds.
(3) length $(MERGE(L_1,L_2)) \geq \min(length(L_1),length(L_2))$

Lemma 2 (Properties of TIMES) : if A is a positive integer, L a strictly increasing sequence of integers then :
(1) $TIMES(A,L)$ is a strictly increasing sequence of integers.
(2) Each element of $TIMES(A,L)$ is the product of A by some element of L.
(3) $length(TIMES(A,L)) = length(L)$

Lemma 3 : The variable X denotes a sequence of infinite length.
Lemma 4 : The solution sequence satisfies the recursive equation defining X.
A special case of McCarthy's recursion induction [33] is applicable here and so we conclude from lemmas 3 and 4 that X is the solution sequence. (The proof of the improved version presents no difficulty.)

4.2 Sieve of Eratosthenes (recursive form)

Lemma 1 : INTEGERS() is exactly the increasing sequence of all integers starting with 2.
Lemma 2 : For any integer p and sequence L, the sequence FILTER(p,L) is a subsequence of L that contains :
(1) no multiples of p
(2) all members of L that aren't multiples of p.

Lemma 3 : For any sequence L, SIFT(L) is a subsequence of L.
Lemma 4 : If L is an increasing sequence and p occurs in SIFT(L) no other multiple of p occurs in SIFT(L).
Lemma 5 : If every element of L is greater than 1 and if p is a prime occurring in L, then p occurs in SIFT(L).

By lemmas 1 and 5, the output of the program must contain all primes. By lemma 4, composite numbers cannot occur. Hence the program generates exactly the primes, in increasing order by lemma 3.

Remark : Notice that in contrast to [21-22] our semantics involves recursively defined data as well as recursively defined functions.

CONCLUSION

In the course of developing this language we have written a considerable number of applications programs, including four types of sorting, a formal power series package with 17 series operations, and a pipeline version of the discrete Fourier transform. This experience has confirmed most of our expectations, indicated limitations, and suggested generalizations.
We have found the language conducive to clear, well-structured programming. Programs are conceived *functionnally* and operational concerns such as process scheduling do not enter into their design. The reconfiguration statement encourages top-down development, and the functional notation provides a concise way of expressing the relationships between processes. Program proofs can be carried out at a level of abstraction which avoids the intricacies of dynamic behavior -i.e., in terms of operations on abstract data rather that machine state transitions.
As our ideas about process networks evolved, channels, considered as data structures, assumed a more central role. A channel is an example of a *dynamic data structure*, i.e., a structure which is gradually generated by processes embedded within itself. To a consumer, these structures behave *as though they were already fully defined*, because as soon as one accesses a new part of the structure it *becomes defined*. Our experience, together with theoretical work by Kahn and Plotkin, suggests that process networks should be generalized by broadening the class of dynamic data structures used for process communication - from linear lists to trees, tableaux, etc. For example, in a compiler the abstract syntax tree might be a dynamic tree generated from the input text by a number of parser processes operating in parallel, while several consumer processes work from the top down generating code.
As a final comment, this study seems to provide further evidence for developing the model theory of programming languages. [36] As the level of expression in programming languages increases, their interpreters will also become increasingly sophisticated. In the design and proof of programs, a firm grip on the model theory of the language will prove more useful than the knowledge of a delicate (and mythical) interpretive mechanism.

ACKNOWLEDGMENT

We owe thanks to Rod Burstall, Gordon Plotkin, and Jerry Schwarz for many helpful discussions. The authors gratefully acknowledge support from (respectively) the Compagnie Internationale des Services en Informatique and the U.K. Science Research Council.

REFERENCES

[1] Gilles Kahn, The semantics of a simple language for parallel programming, Proceedings of IFIP CONGRESS 74, North-Holland Publ. Co, 1974.

[2] Melvin E. Conway, Design of a separable transition-diagram compiler, Communications of the ACM, vol. 6, no 7, July 1963, 396-408.

[3] Richard M. Karp and Raymond E. Miller, Parallel program schemata, Journal of Computer and System Sciences, vol. 3, no 1, 1969, 147-195.

[4] Duane Adams, A computation model with data flow sequencing, Ph.D. Dissertation, Stanford University, Computer Science Dept., December 1969.

[5] Jack B. Dennis, On the design and specification of a common base language, in Computers and Automata, Brooklyn Polytechnic Institute, 1971.

[6] Donald E. Knuth, The art of computer programming, Fundamental Algorithms, vol. 1, Addison-Wesley, Reading, Mass. 1968.

[7] Brian W. Kernighan and P.J. Plauger, Software Tools, Addison-Wesley, Reading, Mass. 1976.

[8] D. Barton, I.M. Willers and R.V.M. Zahar, An implementation of the Taylor series method for ordinary differential equations, The Computer Journal vol. 14, no.3, 243-248.

[9] Donald E. Knuth, The art of computer programming Sorting and searching, vol. 3, Addison-Wesley, Reading, Mass. 1973.

[10] W.K. Pratt, J. Kane and H. Andrews, Hadamard transform image coding, Proceedings of the IEEE, vol. 57, no.1, 58-67.

[11] J.L. Stansfield, Programming a dialogue teaching situation, Ph.D. Thesis, Dept. of Artificial Intelligence, University of Edinburgh, 1974.

[12] Dennis M. Ritchie and K. Thompson, The UNIX operating system, Communications of the ACM, vol. 17, no. 7, July 1974.

[13] Ole-Johan Dahl and C.A.R. Hoare, Hierarchical program structures, in Structured Programming, Academic Press, 1972.

[14] W. Morven Gentleman, A portable coroutine system, Proceedings of the IFIP CONGRESS 1971, North-Holland, 1971.

[15] G. Lindstrom, Control extension in a recursive language, BIT, vol. 13, no.1, 1973, 50-70.

[16] Maurice Clint, Program proving : coroutines, Acta Informatica, vol. 2, no.1, 1973, 50-63.

[17] P.A. Pritchard, A proof rule for multiple coroutine systems, Information Processing Letters, vol. 4, no.6, March 1976.

[18] Ole-Johan Dahl, An approach to correctness proofs of semi-coroutines, Symposium on Mathematical Foundations of Computer Science, A. Blikle Ed., Springer Verlag, 1976, 157-174.

[19] Jean E. Vuillemin, Proof techniques for recursive programs, Ph.D. Thesis, Stanford University 1973.

[20] Christopher P. Wadsworth, Semantics and pragmatics of the lambda-calculus, Ph.D. Thesis, University of Oxford, September 1971.

[21] James H. Morris and P. Henderson, A lazy evaluator, Proceedings of the Third ACM Conference on Principles of Programming Languages, January 1976.

[22] D.P. Friedman and D.S. Wise, CONS should not evaluate its arguments, Third International Colloquium on Automata, Languages and Programming, Edinburgh University Press, 1976.

[23] Peter J. Landin, The correspondence between ALGOL 60 and Church's lambda notation : Part 1, Communications of the ACM, vol. 8, no.2, February 1965, 89-101.

[24] R.M. Burstall, J.S. Collins and R.J. Popplestone, Programming in POP-2, Edinburgh University Press, 1971.

[25] Robert M. Balzer, An overview of the ISPL computer system design, Communications of the ACM, vol. 16, no.2, February 1973, 117-122.

[26] Carl Hewitt, et al. Behavioral semantics of nonrecursive control structures, Colloque sur la Programmation, Springer Verlag, 1976.

[27] Gordon Plotkin, A powerdomain construction, to appear in SIAM Journal on Computing.

[28] Peter J. Landin, A lambda-calculus approach, in Advances in Programming and Non-numerical Computation, Pergamon Press, 1966.

[29] D.E. Britton, F.C. Druseikis, R.E. Griswold, D.R. Hanson and R.A. Holmes, Procedure referencing environments in SL5, Third ACM Symposium on Principles of Programming Languages, January 1976.

[30] M. Douglas McIlroy, Coroutines, Internal report, Bell Telephone Laboratories, Murray Hill, New Jersey, May 1968.

[31] Edsger W. Dijkstra, A discipline of programming, Prentice Hall, New Jersey, 1976.

[32] Robin Milner, Implementation and applications of Scott's logic for computable functions, ACM Conference on Proving Assertions about Programs, January 1972.

[33] John McCarthy, A basis of a mathematical theory of computation, in Computer Programming and Formal Systems, Braffort and Hirschberg, Ed., North-Holland, Amsterdam, 1963.

[34] Edward A. Ashcroft, William Wadge, Proving programs without tears, Symposium on Proving and Improving programs, IRIA, Rocquencourt, G. Huet and G. Kahn Ed., 1975.

[35] Edwin Wiedmer, Exaktes rechnen mit rellen Zahlen, Eidgenössische Technische Hochschule, Zürich, Bericht no. 20, July 1976.

[36] Dana Scott, Outline of a mathematical theory of computation, Proceedings of the Fourth annual Princeton Conference on Information Sciences and Systems, 1970, 169-176.

Programming
Techniques

S. L. Graham, R. L. Rivest
Editors

Communicating Sequential Processes

C.A.R. Hoare
The Queen's University
Belfast, Northern Ireland

This paper suggests that input and output are basic primitives of programming and that parallel composition of communicating sequential processes is a fundamental program structuring method. When combined with a development of Dijkstra's guarded command, these concepts are surprisingly versatile. Their use is illustrated by sample solutions of a variety of familiar programming exercises.

Key Words and Phrases: programming, programming languages, programming primitives, program structures, parallel programming, concurrency, input, output, guarded commands, nondeterminacy, coroutines, procedures, multiple entries, multiple exits, classes, data representations, recursion, conditional critical regions, monitors, iterative arrays

CR Categories: 4.20, 4.22, 4.32

1. Introduction

Among the primitive concepts of computer programming, and of the high level languages in which programs are expressed, the action of assignment is familiar and well understood. In fact, any change of the internal state of a machine executing a program can be modeled as an assignment of a new value to some variable part of that machine. However, the operations of input and output, which affect the external environment of a machine, are not nearly so well understood. They are often added to a programming language only as an afterthought.

Among the structuring methods for computer pro-

grams, three basic constructs have received widespread recognition and use: A repetitive construct (e.g. the **while** loop), an alternative construct (e.g. the conditional **if..then..else**), and normal sequential program composition (often denoted by a semicolon). Less agreement has been reached about the design of other important program structures, and many suggestions have been made: Subroutines (Fortran), procedures (Algol 60 [15]), entries (PL/I), coroutines (UNIX [17]), classes (SIMULA 67 [5]), processes and monitors (Concurrent Pascal [2]), clusters (CLU [13]), forms (ALPHARD [19]), actors (Hewitt [1]).

The traditional stored program digital computer has been designed primarily for deterministic execution of a single sequential program. Where the desire for greater speed has led to the introduction of parallelism, every attempt has been made to disguise this fact from the programmer, either by hardware itself (as in the multiple function units of the CDC 6600) or by the software (as in an I/O control package, or a multiprogrammed operating system). However, developments of processor technology suggest that a multiprocessor machine, constructed from a number of similar self-contained processors (each with its own store), may become more powerful, capacious, reliable, and economical than a machine which is disguised as a monoprocessor.

In order to use such a machine effectively on a single task, the component processors must be able to communicate and to synchronize with each other. Many methods of achieving this have been proposed. A widely adopted method of communication is by inspection and updating of a common store (as in Algol 68 [18], PL/I, and many machine codes). However, this can create severe problems in the construction of correct programs and it may lead to expense (e.g. crossbar switches) and unreliability (e.g. glitches) in some technologies of hardware implementation. A greater variety of methods has been proposed for synchronization: semaphores [6], events (PL/I), conditional critical regions [10], monitors and queues (Concurrent Pascal [2]), and path expressions [3]. Most of these are demonstrably adequate for their purpose, but there is no widely recognized criterion for choosing between them.

This paper makes an ambitious attempt to find a single simple solution to all these problems. The essential proposals are:

(1) Dijkstra's guarded commands [8] are adopted (with a slight change of notation) as sequential control structures, and as the sole means of introducing and controlling nondeterminism.

(2) A parallel command, based on Dijkstra's *parbegin* [6], specifies concurrent execution of its constituent sequential commands (processes). All the processes start simultaneously, and the parallel command ends only when they are all finished. They may not communicate with each other by updating global variables.

(3) Simple forms of input and output command are introduced. They are used for communication between concurrent processes.

(4) Such communication occurs when one process names another as destination for output *and* the second process names the first as source for input. In this case, the value to be output is copied from the first process to the second. There is *no* automatic buffering: In general, an input or output command is delayed until the other process is ready with the corresponding output or input. Such delay is invisible to the delayed process.

(5) Input commands may appear in guards. A guarded command with an input guard is selected for execution only if and when the source named in the input command is ready to execute the corresponding output command. If several input guards of a set of alternatives have ready destinations, only one is selected and the others have *no* effect; but the choice between them is arbitrary. In an efficient implementation, an output command which has been ready for a long time should be favored; but the definition of a language cannot specify this since the relative speed of execution of the processes is undefined.

(6) A repetitive command may have input guards. If all the sources named by them have terminated, then the repetitive command also terminates.

(7) A simple pattern-matching feature, similar to that of [16], is used to discriminate the structure of an input message, and to access its components in a secure fashion. This feature is used to inhibit input of messages that do not match the specified pattern.

The programs expressed in the proposed language are intended to be implementable both by a conventional machine with a single main store, and by a fixed network of processors connected by input/output channels (although very different optimizations are appropriate in the different cases). It is consequently a rather static language: The text of a program determines a fixed upper bound on the number of processes operating concurrently; there is no recursion and no facility for process-valued variables. In other respects also, the language has been stripped to the barest minimum necessary for explanation of its more novel features.

The concept of a communicating sequential process is shown in Sections 3–5 to provide a method of expressing solutions to many simple programming exercises which have previously been employed to illustrate the use of various proposed programming language features. This suggests that the process may constitute a synthesis of a number of familiar and new programming ideas. The reader is invited to skip the examples which do not interest him.

However, this paper also ignores many serious problems. The most serious is that it fails to suggest any proof method to assist in the development and verification of correct programs. Secondly, it pays no attention to the problems of efficient implementation, which may be particularly serious on a traditional sequential computer. It is probable that a solution to these problems will require (1) imposition of restrictions in the use of the proposed features; (2) reintroduction of distinctive no-

tations for the most common and useful special cases; (3) development of automatic optimization techniques; and (4) the design of appropriate hardware.

Thus the concepts and notations introduced in this paper (although described in the next section in the form of a programming language fragment) should not be regarded as suitable for use as a programming language, either for abstract or for concrete programming. They are at best only a partial solution to the problems tackled. Further discussion of these and other points will be found in Section 7.

2. Concepts and Notations

The style of the following description is borrowed from Algol 60 [15]. Types, declarations, and expressions have not been treated; in the examples, a Pascal-like notation [20] has usually been adopted. The curly braces { } have been introduced into BNF to denote none or more repetitions of the enclosed material. (Sentences in parentheses refer to an implementation: they are not strictly part of a language definition.)

```
<command> ::= <simple command>|<structured command>
<simple command> ::= <null command>|<assignment command>
    |<input command>|<output command>
<structured command> ::= <alternative command>
    |<repetitive command>|<parallel command>
<null command> ::= skip
<command list> ::= {<declaration>; |<command>;} <command>
```

A command specifies the behavior of a device executing the command. It may succeed or fail. Execution of a simple command, if successful, may have an effect on the internal state of the executing device (in the case of assignment), or on its external environment (in the case of output), or on both (in the case of input). Execution of a structured command involves execution of some or all of its constituent commands, and if any of these fail, so does the structured command. (In this case, whenever possible, an implementation should provide some kind of comprehensible error diagnostic message.)

A null command has no effect and never fails.

A command list specifies sequential execution of its constituent commands in the order written. Each declaration introduces a fresh variable with a scope which extends from its declaration to the end of the command list.

2.1 Parallel Commands

```
<parallel command> ::= [<process>{||<process>}]
<process> ::= <process label> <command list>
<process label> ::= <empty>|<identifier> ::
    |<identifier>(<label subscript>{,<label subscript>}) ::
<label subscript> ::= <integer constant>|<range>
<integer constant> ::= <numeral>|<bound variable>
<bound variable> ::= <identifier>
<range> ::= <bound variable>:<lower bound>..<upper bound>
<lower bound> ::= <integer constant>
<upper bound> ::= <integer constant>
```

Each process of a parallel command must be *disjoint* from every other process of the command, in the sense that it does not mention any variable which occurs as a target variable (see Sections 2.2 and 2.3) in any other process.

A process label without subscripts, or one whose label subscripts are all integer constants, serves as a name for the command list to which it is prefixed; its scope extends over the whole of the parallel command. A process whose label subscripts include one or more ranges stands for a series of processes, each with the same label and command list, except that each has a different combination of values substituted for the bound variables. These values range between the lower bound and the upper bound inclusive. For example, $X(i:1..n) :: CL$ stands for

$$X(1) :: CL_1 || X(2) :: CL_2 ||...|| X(n) :: CL_n$$

where each CL_j is formed from CL by replacing every occurrence of the bound variable i by the numeral j. After all such expansions, each process label in a parallel command must occur only once and the processes must be well formed and disjoint.

A parallel command specifies concurrent execution of its constituent processes. They all start simultaneously and the parallel command terminates successfully only if and when they have all successfully terminated. The relative speed with which they are executed is arbitrary.
Examples:

(1) [cardreader?cardimage||lineprinter!lineimage]

Performs the two constituent commands in parallel, and terminates only when both operations are complete. The time taken may be as low as the longer of the times taken by each constituent process, i.e. the sum of its computing, waiting, and transfer times.

(2) [west :: DISASSEMBLE||X :: SQUASH||east :: ASSEMBLE]

The three processes have the names "west," "X," and "east." The capitalized words stand for command lists which will be defined in later examples.

(3) [room :: ROOM||fork(i:0..4) :: FORK||phil(i:0..4) :: PHIL]

There are eleven processes. The behavior of "room" is specified by the command list ROOM. The behavior of the five processes fork(0), fork(1), fork(2), fork(3), fork(4), is specified by the command list FORK, within which the bound variable i indicates the identity of the particular fork. Similar remarks apply to the five processes PHIL.

2.2 Assignment Commands

```
<assignment command> ::= <target variable> := <expression>
<expression> ::= <simple expression>|<structured expression>
<structured expression> ::= <constructor>(<expression list>)
<constructor> ::= <identifier>|<empty>
<expression list> ::= <empty>|<expression>{,<expression>}
<target variable> ::= <simple variable>|<structured target>
<structured target> ::= <constructor>(<target variable list>)
<target variable list> ::= <empty>|<target variable>
    {,<target variable>}
```

An expression denotes a value which is computed by an executing device by application of its constituent operators to the specified operands. The value of an expression is undefined if any of these operations are undefined. The value denoted by a simple expression may be simple or structured. The value denoted by a structured expression is structured; its constructor is that of the expression, and its components are the list of values denoted by the constituent expressions of the expression list.

An assignment command specifies evaluation of its expression, and assignment of the denoted value to the target variable. A simple target variable may have assigned to it a simple or a structured value. A structured target variable may have assigned to it a structured value, with the same constructor. The effect of such assignment is to assign to each constituent simpler variable of the structured target the value of the corresponding component of the structured value. Consequently, the value denoted by the target variable, if evaluated *after* a successful assignment, is the same as the value denoted by the expression, as evaluated *before* the assignment.

An assignment fails if the value of its expression is undefined, or if that value does not *match* the target variable, in the following sense: A *simple* target variable matches any value of its type. A *structured* target variable matches a structured value, provided that: (1) they have the same constructor, (2) the target variable list is the same length as the list of components of the value, (3) each target variable of the list matches the corresponding component of the value list. A structured value with no components is known as a "signal."

Examples:

(1) $x := x + 1$	the value of x after the assignment is the same as the value of $x + 1$ before.
(2) $(x, y) := (y, x)$	exchanges the values of x and y.
(3) $x := cons(left, right)$	constructs a structured value and assigns it to x.
(4) $cons(left, right) := x$	fails if x does not have the form $cons(y, z)$; but if it does, then y is assigned to left, and z is assigned to right.
(5) $insert(n) := insert(2*x + 1)$	equivalent to $n := 2*x + 1$.
(6) $c := P()$	assigns to c a "signal" with constructor P, and no components.
(7) $P() := c$	fails if the value of c is not P(); otherwise has no effect.
(8) $insert(n) := has(n)$	fails, due to mismatch.

Note: Successful execution of both (3) and (4) ensures the truth of the postcondition $x = cons(left, right)$; but (3) does so by changing x and (4) does so by changing left and right. Example (4) will fail if there is *no* value of left and right which satisfies the postcondition.

2.3 Input and Output Commands

```
<input command> ::= <source>?<target variable>
<output command> ::= <destination>!<expression>
<source> ::= <process name>
```

<destination> := <process name>
<process name> := <identifier>|<identifier>(<subscripts>)
<subscripts> := <integer expression>{,<integer expression>}

Input and output commands specify communication between two concurrently operating sequential processes. Such a process may be implemented in hardware as a special-purpose device (e.g. cardreader or lineprinter), or its behavior may be specified by one of the constituent processes of a parallel command. Communication occurs between two processes of a parallel command whenever (1) an input command in one process specifies as its source the process name of the other process; (2) an output command in the other process specifies as its destination the process name of the first process; and (3) the target variable of the input command matches the value denoted by the expression of the output command. On these conditions, the input and output commands are said to *correspond*. Commands which correspond are executed simultaneously, and their combined effect is to assign the value of the expression of the output command to the target variable of the input command.

An input command fails if its source is terminated. An output command fails if its destination is terminated or if its expression is undefined.

(The requirement of synchronization of input and output commands means that an implementation will have to delay whichever of the two commands happens to be ready first. The delay is ended when the corresponding command in the other process is also ready, or when the other process terminates. In the latter case the first command fails. It is also possible that the delay will never be ended, for example, if a group of processes are attempting communication but none of their input and output commands correspond with each other. This form of failure is known as a deadlock.)

Examples:

(1) cardreader?cardimage — from cardreader, read a card and assign its value (an array of characters) to the variable cardimage

(2) lineprinter!lineimage — to lineprinter, send the value of lineimage for printing

(3) $X?(x, y)$ — from process named X, input a pair of values and assign them to x and y

(4) DIV!(3*a + b, 13) — to process DIV, output the two specified values.

Note: If a process named DIV issues command (3), and a process named X issues command (4), these are executed simultaneously, and have the same effect as the assignment: $(x, y) := (3*a + b, 13)$ ($\equiv x := 3*a + b; y := 13$).

(5) console(i)?c — from the ith element of an array of consoles, input a value and assign it to c

(6) console($j - 1$)!"A" — to the $(j - 1)$th console, output character "A"

(7) $X(i)?V( )$ — from the ith of an array of processes X, input a signal $V( )$; refuse to input any other signal

(8) sem!P( ) — to sem output a signal P( )

2.4 Alternative and Repetitive Commands

<repetitive command> :=*<alternative command>
<alternative command> := [<guarded command>
     {☐<guarded command>}]
<guarded command> := <guard> → <command list>
     |(<range>{,<range>})<guard> → <command list>
<guard> := <guard list>|<guard list>;<input command>
     |<input command>
          <guard list> := <guard element>{;<guard element>}
<guard element> := <boolean expression>|<declaration>

A guarded command with one or more ranges stands for a series of guarded commands, each with the same guard and command list, except that each has a different combination of values substituted for the bound variables. The values range between the lower bound and upper bound inclusive. For example, $(i:1..n)G \to CL$ stands for

$$G_1 \to CL_1 \| G_2 \to CL_2 \| ... \| G_n \to CL_n$$

where each $G_j \to CL_j$ is formed from $G \to CL$ by replacing every occurrence of the bound variable i by the numeral j.

A guarded command is executed only if and when the execution of its guard does not fail. First its guard is executed and then its command list. A guard is executed by execution of its constituent elements from left to right. A Boolean expression is evaluated: If it denotes false, the guard fails; but an expression that denotes true has no effect. A declaration introduces a fresh variable with a scope that extends from the declaration to the end of the guarded command. An input command at the end of a guard is executed only if and when a corresponding output command is executed. (An implementation may test whether a guard fails simply by trying to execute it, and discontinuing execution if and when it fails. This is valid because such a discontinued execution has no effect on the state of the executing device.)

An alternative command specifies execution of exactly one of its constituent guarded commands. Consequently, if all guards fail, the alternative command fails. Otherwise an arbitrary one with successfully executable guard is selected and executed. (An implementation should take advantage of its freedom of selection to ensure efficient execution and good response. For example, when input commands appear as guards, the command which corresponds to the earliest ready and matching output command should in general be preferred; and certainly, no executable and ready output command should be passed over unreasonably often.)

A repetitive command specifies as many iterations as possible of its constituent alternative command. Consequently, when all guards fail, the repetitive command terminates with no effect. Otherwise, the alternative command is executed once and then the whole repetitive command is executed again. (Consider a repetitive command when all its true guard lists end in an input guard. Such a command may have to be delayed until either (1) an output command corresponding to one of the input guards becomes ready, or (2) all the sources named by the input guards have terminated. In case (2), the repetitive command terminates. If neither event ever occurs, the process fails (in deadlock.)

Examples:

(1) $[x \geq y \to m := x \, [] \, y \geq x \to m := y]$

If $x \geq y$, assign x to m; if $y \geq x$ assign y to m; if both $x \geq y$ and $y \geq x$, either assignment can be executed.

(2) $i := 0; *[i < \text{size}; \text{content}(i) \neq n \to i := i + 1]$

The repetitive command scans the elements content(i), for $i = 0, 1, \ldots$, until either $i \geq$ size, or a value equal to n is found.

(3) $*[c:\text{character}; \text{west}?c \to \text{east}!c]$

This reads all the characters output by west, and outputs them one by one to east. The repetition terminates when the process west terminates.

(4) $*[(i:1..10)\text{continue}(i); \text{console}(i)?c \to X!(i, c); \text{console}(i)!\text{ack}();$
$\quad \text{continue}(i) := (c \neq \text{sign off})]$

This command inputs repeatedly from any of ten consoles, provided that the corresponding element of the Boolean array continue is true. The bound variable i identifies the originating console. Its value, together with the character just input, is output to X, and an acknowledgment signal is sent back to the originating console. If the character indicated "sign off," continue(i) is set false, to prevent further input from that console. The repetitive command terminates when all ten elements of continue are false. (An implementation should ensure that no console which is ready to provide input will be ignored unreasonably often.)

(5) $*[n:\text{integer}; X?\text{insert}(n) \to \text{INSERT}$
$\quad []n:\text{integer}; X?\text{has}(n) \to \text{SEARCH}; X!(i < \text{size})$
$\quad]$

(Here, and elsewhere, capitalized words INSERT and SEARCH stand as abbreviations for program text defined separately.)

On each iteration this command accepts from X either (a) a request to "insert(n)," (followed by INSERT) *or* (b) a question "has(n)," to which it outputs an answer back to X. The choice between (a) and (b) is made by the next output command in X. The repetitive command terminates when X does. If X sends a nonmatching message, deadlock will result.

(6) $*[X?V() \to \text{val} := \text{val} + 1$
$\quad []\text{val} > 0; Y?P() \to \text{val} := \text{val} - 1$
$\quad]$

On each iteration, accept *either* a V() signal from X and increment val, *or* a P() signal from Y, and decrement val. But the second alternative cannot be selected unless val is positive (after which val will remain invariantly nonnegative). (When val > 0, the choice depends on the relative speeds of X and Y, and is not determined.) The repetitive command will terminate when both X and Y are terminated, or when X is terminated and val ≤ 0.

3. Coroutines

In parallel programming coroutines appear as a more fundamental program structure than subroutines, which can be regarded as a special case (treated in the next section).

3.1 COPY

Problem: Write a process X to copy characters output by process west to process east.

Solution:

$X :: *[c:\text{character}; \text{west}?c \to \text{east}!c]$

Notes: (1) When west terminates, the input "west?c" will fail, causing termination of the repetitive command, and of process X. Any subsequent input command from east will fail. (2) Process X acts as a single-character buffer between west and east. It permits west to work on production of the next character, before east is ready to input the previous one.

3.2 SQUASH

Problem: Adapt the previous program to replace every pair of consecutive asterisks "**" by an upward arrow "↑". Assume that the final character input is not an asterisk.

Solution:

$X :: *[c:\text{character}; \text{west}?c \to$
$\quad [c \neq \text{asterisk} \to \text{east}!c$
$\quad []c = \text{asterisk} \to \text{west}?c;$
$\quad\quad [c \neq \text{asterisk} \to \text{east}!\text{asterisk}; \text{east}!c$
$\quad\quad []c = \text{asterisk} \to \text{east}!\text{upward arrow}$
$\quad]] \quad]$

Notes: (1) Since west does not end with asterisk, the second "west?c" will not fail. (2) As an exercise, adapt this process to deal sensibly with input which ends with an odd number of asterisks.

3.3 DISASSEMBLE

Problem: to read cards from a cardfile and output to process X the stream of characters they contain. An extra space should be inserted at the end of each card.

Solution:

$*[\text{cardimage}:(1..80)\text{character}; \text{cardfile}?\text{cardimage} \to$
$\quad i:\text{integer}; i := 1;$
$\quad\quad *[i \leq 80 \to X!\text{cardimage}(i); i := i + 1]$
$\quad X!\text{space}$
$]$

Notes: (1) "(1..80)character" declares an array of 80 characters, with subscripts ranging between 1 and 80. (2) The repetitive command terminates when the cardfile process terminates.

3.4 ASSEMBLE

Problem: To read a stream of characters from process X and print them in lines of 125 characters on a lineprinter. The last line should be completed with spaces if necessary.

281

Solution:

```
lineimage:(1..125)character;
i:integer; i := 1;
*[c:character; X?c →
    lineimage(i) := c;
    [i ≤ 124 → i := i + 1
    []i = 125 → lineprinter!lineimage; i := 1
]   ];
[i = 1 → skip
[]i > 1 → *[i ≤ 125 → lineimage(i) := space; i := i + 1];
    lineprinter!lineimage
]
```

Note: (1) When X terminates, so will the first repetitive command of this process. The last line will then be printed, if it has any characters.

3.5 Reformat
Problem: Read a sequence of cards of 80 characters each, and print the characters on a lineprinter at 125 characters per line. Every card should be followed by an extra space, and the last line should be completed with spaces if necessary.
Solution:

```
[west::DISASSEMBLE||X::COPY||east::ASSEMBLE]
```

Notes: (1) The capitalized names stand for program text defined in previous sections. (2) The parallel command is designed to terminate after the cardfile has terminated. (3) This elementary problem is difficult to solve elegantly without coroutines.

3.6 Conway's Problem [4]
Problem: Adapt the above program to replace every pair of consecutive asterisks by an upward arrow.
Solution:

```
[west::DISASSEMBLE||X::SQUASH||east::ASSEMBLE]
```

4. Subroutines and Data Representations

A conventional nonrecursive subroutine can be readily implemented as a coroutine, provided that (1) its parameters are called "by value" and "by result," and (2) it is disjoint from its calling program. Like a Fortran subroutine, a coroutine may retain the values of local variables (*own* variables, in Algol terms) and it may use input commands to achieve the effect of "multiple entry points" in a safer way than PL/I. Thus a coroutine can be used like a SIMULA class instance as a concrete representation for abstract data.

A coroutine acting as a subroutine is a process operating concurrently with its user process in a parallel command: [subr::SUBROUTINE||X::USER]. The SUBROUTINE will contain (or consist of) a repetitive command: *[X?(value params) → ... ; X!(result params)], where ... computes the results from the values input. The subroutine will terminate when its user does. The USER will call the subroutine by a pair of commands: subr!(arguments);

... ; subr?(results). Any commands between these two will be executed concurrently with the subroutine.

A multiple-entry subroutine, acting as a representation for data [11], will also contain a repetitive command which represents each entry by an alternative input to a structured target with the entry name as constructor. For example,

```
*[X?entry1(value params) → ...
[]X?entry2(value params) → ...
]
```

The calling process X will determine which of the alternatives is activated on each repetition. When X terminates, so does this repetitive command. A similar technique in the user program can achieve the effect of multiple exits.

A recursive subroutine can be simulated by an array of processes, one for each level of recursion. The user process is level zero. Each activation communicates its parameters and results with its predecessor and calls its successor if necessary:

```
[recsub(0)::USER||recsub(i:1..reclimit)::RECSUB].
```

The user will call the first element of

```
recsub: recsub(1)!(arguments); ... ; recsub(1)?(results);.
```

The imposition of a fixed upper bound on recursion depth is necessitated by the "static" design of the language.

This clumsy simulation of recursion would be even more clumsy for a mutually recursive algorithm. It would not be recommended for conventional programming; it may be more suitable for an array of microprocessors for which the fixed upper bound is also realistic.

In this section, we assume each subroutine is used only by a *single* user process (which may, of course, itself contain parallel commands).

4.1 Function: Division With Remainder
Problem: Construct a process to represent a function-type subroutine, which accepts a positive dividend and divisor, and returns their integer quotient and remainder. Efficiency is of no concern.
Solution:

```
[DIV::*[x,y:integer; X?(x,y) →
    quot,rem:integer; quot := 0; rem := x;
    *[rem ≥ y → rem := rem − y; quot := quot + 1];
    X!(quot,rem)
    ]
||X::USER
]
```

4.2 Recursion: Factorial
Problem: Compute a factorial by the recursive method, to a given limit.
Solution:

```
[fac(i:1..limit)::
*[n:integer;fac(i − 1)?n →
    [n = 0 → fac(i − 1)!1
```

282

```
  []n > 0 → fac(i + 1)!n - 1;
    r:integer;fac(i + 1)?r;fac(i - 1)!(n * r)
  ]]
||fac(0)::USER
]
```

Note: This unrealistic example introduces the technique of the "iterative array" which will be used to a better effect in later examples.

4.3 Data Representation: Small Set of Integers [11]
Problem: To represent a set of not more than 100 integers as a process, S, which accepts two kinds of instruction from its calling process X: (1) S!insert(n), insert the integer n in the set, and (2) S!has(n); ... ; S?b, b is set true if n is in the set, and false otherwise. The initial value of the set is empty.

Solution:

```
S::
content:(0..99)integer; size:integer; size := 0;
*[n:integer;X?has(n) → SEARCH;X!(i < size)
[]n:integer; X?insert(n) → SEARCH;
    [i < size → skip
    []i = size; size < 100 →
        content (size) := n; size := size + 1
]   ]
```

where SEARCH is an abbreviation for:

```
i:integer; i := 0;
*[i < size; content(i) ≠ n → i := i + 1]
```

Notes: (1) The alternative command with guard "size < 100" will fail if an attempt is made to insert more than 100 elements. (2) The activity of insertion will in general take place concurrently with the calling process. However, any subsequent instruction to S will be delayed until the previous insertion is complete.

4.4 Scanning a Set
Problem: Extend the solution to 4.3 by providing a fast method for scanning all members of the set without changing the value of the set. The user program will contain a repetitive command of the form:

```
S!scan( ); more:boolean; more := true;
*[more;x:integer; S?next(x) → ... deal with x ....
[]more; S?noneleft( ) → more := false
]
```

where S!scan( ) sets the representation into a scanning mode. The repetitive command serves as a **for** statement, inputting the successive members of x from the set and inspecting them until finally the representation sends a signal that there are no members left. The body of the repetitive command is *not* permitted to communicate with S in any way.

Solution: Add a third guarded command to the outer repetitive command of S:

```
... []X?scan( ) → i:integer; i := 0;
              *[i < size → X!next(content(i)); i := i + 1];
              X!noneleft( )
```

4.5 Recursive Data Representation: Small Set of Integers
Problem: Same as above, but an array of processes is to be used to achieve a high degree of parallelism. Each process should contain at most one number. When it contains no number, it should answer "false" to all inquiries about membership. On the first insertion, it changes to a second phase of behavior, in which it deals with instructions from its predecessor, passing some of them on to its successor. The calling process will be named S(0). For efficiency, the set should be sorted, i.e. the ith process should contain the ith largest number.

Solution:

```
S(i:1..100)::

*[n:integer; S(i - 1)?has(n) → S(0)!false
[]n:integer; S(i - 1)?insert(n) →
    *[m:integer; S(i - 1)?has(m) →
        [m ≤ n → S(0)!(m = n)
        []m > n → S(i + 1)!has(m)
        ]
    []m:integer; S(i - 1)?insert(m) →
        [m < n → S(i + 1)!insert(n); n := m
        []m = n → skip
        []m > n → S(i + 1)!insert(m)
]  ]  ]
```

Notes: (1) The user process S(0) inquires whether n is a member by the commands S(1)!has(n); ... ; [(i:1..100)S(i)? b → skip]. The appropriate process will respond to the input command by the output command in line 2 or line 5. This trick avoids passing the answer back "up the chain." (2) Many insertion operations can proceed in parallel, yet any subsequent "has" operation will be performed correctly. (3) All repetitive commands and all processes of the array will terminate after the user process S(0) terminates.

4.6 Multiple Exits: Remove the Least Member
Exercise: Extend the above solution to respond to a command to yield the least member of the set and to remove it from the set. The user program will invoke the facility by a pair of commands:

```
S(1)!least( ); [x:integer;S(1)? x → ... deal with x ...
              []S(1)?noneleft( ) → ...
              ]
```

or, if he wishes to scan and empty the set, he may write:

```
S(1)!least( );more:boolean; more := true;
          *[more; x:integer; S(1)?x → ... deal with x ... ; S(1)!least( )
          []more; S(1)?noneleft( ) → more := false
          ]
```

Hint: Introduce a Boolean variable, b, initialized to true, and prefix this to all the guards of the inner loop. After responding to a !least( ) command from its predecessor, each process returns its contained value n, asks its successor for its least, and stores the response in n. But if the successor returns "noneleft( )," b is set false and the inner loop terminates. The process therefore returns to its initial state (solution due to David Gries).

283

5. Monitors and Scheduling

This section shows how a monitor can be regarded as a single process which communicates with more than one user process. However, each user process must have a different name (e.g. producer, consumer) or a different subscript (e.g. $X(i)$) and each communication with a user must identify its source or destination uniquely.

Consequently, when a monitor is prepared to communicate with *any* of its user processes (i.e. whichever of them calls first) it will use a guarded command with a range. For example: $*[(i:1..100)X(i)?(\text{value parameters}) \rightarrow ... ; X(i)!(\text{results})]$. Here, the bound variable i is used to send the results back to the calling process. If the monitor is not prepared to accept input from some particular user (e.g. $X(j)$) on a given occasion, the input command may be preceded by a Boolean guard. For example, two successive inputs from the same process are inhibited by $j = 0$; $*[(i:1..100)i \neq j; X(i)?(\text{values}) \rightarrow ... ; j := i]$. Any attempted output from $X(j)$ will be delayed until a subsequent iteration, after the output of some other process $X(i)$ has been accepted and dealt with.

Similarly, conditions can be used to delay acceptance of inputs which would violate scheduling constraints—postponing them until some later occasion when some other process has brought the monitor into a state in which the input can validly be accepted. This technique is similar to a conditional critical region [10] and it obviates the need for special synchronizing variables such as events, queues, or conditions. However, the absence of these special facilities certainly makes it more difficult or less efficient to solve problems involving priorities—for example, the scheduling of head movement on a disk.

5.1 Bounded Buffer
Problem: Construct a buffering process X to smooth variations in the speed of output of portions by a producer process and input by a consumer process. The consumer contains pairs of commands $X!\text{more}( )$; $X?p$, and the producer contains commands of the form $X!p$. The buffer should contain up to ten portions.
Solution:

```
X::
buffer:(0..9) portion;
in,out:integer; in := 0; out := 0;
comment 0 ≤ out ≤ in ≤ out + 10;
    *[in < out + 10; producer?buffer(in mod 10) → in := in + 1
    []out < in; consumer?more( ) → consumer!buffer(out mod 10);
        out := out + 1
    ]
```

Notes: (1) When out < in < out + 10, the selection of the alternative in the repetitive command will depend on whether the producer produces before the consumer consumes, or vice versa. (2) When out = in, the buffer is empty and the second alternative cannot be selected even if the consumer is ready with its command $X!\text{more}( )$.

However, after the producer has produced its next portion, the consumer's request can be granted on the next iteration. (3) Similar remarks apply to the producer, when in = out + 10. (4) X is designed to terminate when out = in and the producer has terminated.

5.2 Integer Semaphore
Problem: To implement an integer semaphore, S, shared among an array $X(i:1..100)$ of client processes. Each process may increment the semaphore by $S!V( )$ or decrement it by $S!P( )$, but the latter command must be delayed if the value of the semaphore is not positive.
Solution:

```
S::val:integer; val := 0;
    *[(i:1..100)X(i)?V( ) → val := val + 1
    [](i:1..100)val > 0; X(i)?P( ) → val := val − 1
    ]
```

Notes: (1) In this process, no use is made of knowledge of the subscript i of the calling process. (2) The semaphore terminates only when all hundred processes of the process array X have terminated.

5.3 Dining Philosophers (Problem due to E.W. Dijkstra)
Problem: Five philosophers spend their lives thinking and eating. The philosophers share a common dining room where there is a circular table surrounded by five chairs, each belonging to one philosopher. In the center of the table there is a large bowl of spaghetti, and the table is laid with five forks (see Figure 1). On feeling hungry, a philosopher enters the dining room, sits in his own chair, and picks up the fork on the left of his place. Unfortunately, the spaghetti is so tangled that he needs to pick up and use the fork on his right as well. When he has finished, he puts down both forks, and leaves the room. The room should keep a count of the number of philosophers in it.

Fig. 1.

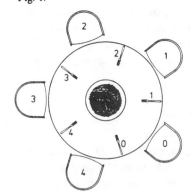

Solution: The behavior of the ith philosopher may be described as follows:

```
PHIL = *[... during ith lifetime ... →
        THINK;
        room!enter( );
        fork(i)!pickup( ); fork((i + 1) mod 5)!pickup( );
        EAT;
        fork(i)!putdown( ); fork((i + 1) mod 5)!putdown( );
        room!exit( )
        ]
```

The fate of the *i*th fork is to be picked up and put down by a philosopher sitting on either side of it

```
FORK =
  *[phil(i)?pickup( ) → phil(i)?putdown( )
  []phil((i − 1)mod 5)?pickup( ) → phil((i − 1) mod 5)?putdown( )
  ]
```

The story of the room may be simply told:

```
ROOM = occupancy:integer; occupancy := 0;
  *[(i:0..4)phil(i)?enter( ) → occupancy := occupancy + 1
  [](i:0..4)phil(i)?exit( ) → occupancy := occupancy − 1
  ]
```

All these components operate in parallel:

[room::ROOM||fork(*i*:0..4)::FORK||phil(*i*:0..4)::PHIL].

Notes: (1) The solution given above does not prevent all five philosophers from entering the room, each picking up his left fork, and starving to death because he cannot pick up his right fork. (2) Exercise: Adapt the above program to avert this sad possibility. Hint: Prevent more than four philosophers from entering the room. (Solution due to E. W. Dijkstra).

6. Miscellaneous

This section contains further examples of the use of communicating sequential processes for the solution of some less familiar problems; a parallel version of the sieve of Eratosthenes, and the design of an iterative array. The proposed solutions are even more speculative than those of the previous sections, and in the second example, even the question of termination is ignored.

6.1 Prime Numbers: The Sieve of Eratosthenes [14]
Problem: To print in ascending order all primes less than 10000. Use an array of processes, SIEVE, in which each process inputs a prime from its predecessor and prints it. The process then inputs an ascending stream of numbers from its predecessor and passes them on to its successor, suppressing any that are multiples of the original prime. Solution:

```
[SIEVE(i:1..100)::
  p,mp:integer;
  SIEVE(i − 1)?p;
  print!p;
  mp := p; comment mp is a multiple of p;
*[m:integer; SIEVE(i − 1)?m →
    *[m > mp → mp := mp + p];
    [m = mp → skip
    []m < mp → SIEVE(i + 1)!m
  ] ]
||SIEVE(0)::print!2; n:integer; n := 3;
    *[n < 10000 → SIEVE(1)!n; n := n + 2]
||SIEVE(101)::*[n:integer;SIEVE(100)?n → print!n]
||print::*[(i:0..101) n:integer; SIEVE(i)?n → ...]
]
```

Note: (1) This beautiful solution was contributed by David Gries. (2) It is algorithmically similar to the program developed in [7, pp. 27–32].

6.2 An Iterative Array: Matrix Multiplication
Problem: A square matrix *A* of order 3 is given. Three streams are to be input, each stream representing a column of an array IN. Three streams are to be output, each representing a column of the product matrix IN × *A*. After an initial delay, the results are to be produced at the same rate as the input is consumed. Consequently, a high degree of parallelism is required. The solution should take the form shown in Figure 2. Each of the nine nonborder nodes inputs a vector component from the west and a partial sum from the north. Each node outputs the vector component to its east, and an updated partial sum to the south. The input data is produced by the west border nodes, and the desired results are consumed by south border nodes. The north border is a constant source of zeros and the east border is just a sink. No provision need be made for termination nor for changing the values of the array *A*.

Fig. 2.

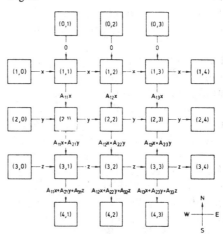

Solution: There are twenty-one nodes, in five groups, comprising the central square and the four borders:

```
[M(i:1..3,0)::WEST
||M(0,j:1..3)::NORTH
||M(i:1..3,4)::EAST
||M(4,j:1..3)::SOUTH
||M(i:1..3,j:1..3)::CENTER
]
```

The WEST and SOUTH borders are processes of the user program; the remaining processes are:

```
NORTH = *[true → M(1,j)!0]
EAST = *[x:real; M(i,3)?x → skip]
CENTER = *[x:real; M(i,j − 1)?x →
    M(i, j + 1)!x; sum:real;
    M(i − 1, j)?sum; M(i + 1,j)!(A(i, j)•x + sum)
  ]
```

7. Discussion

A design for a programming language must necessarily involve a number of decisions which seem to be

285

fairly arbitrary. The discussion of this section is intended to explain some of the underlying motivation and to mention some unresolved questions.

7.1 Notations

I have chosen single-character notations (e.g. !,?) to express the primitive concepts, rather than the more traditional boldface or underlined English words. As a result, the examples have an APL-like brevity, which some readers find distasteful. My excuse is that (in contrast to APL) there are only a very few primitive concepts and that it is standard practice of mathematics (and also good coding practice) to denote common primitive concepts by brief notations (e.g. $+,\times$). When read aloud, these are replaced by words (e.g. plus, times).

Some readers have suggested the use of assignment notation for input and output:

<target variable> := <source>
<destination> := <expression>

I find this suggestion misleading: it is better to regard input and output as distinct primitives, justifying distinct notations.

I have used the same pair of brackets ([...]) to bracket all program structures, instead of the more familiar variety of brackets (**if**..**fi**, **begin**..**end**, **case**...**esac**, etc.). In this I follow normal mathematical practice, but I must also confess to a distaste for the pronunciation of words like **fi**, **od**, or **esac**.

I am dissatisfied with the fact that my notation gives the same syntax for a structured expression and a subscripted variable. Perhaps tags should be distinguished from other identifiers by a special symbol (say #).

I was tempted to introduce an abbreviation for combined declaration and input, e.g. $X?(n:integer)$ for n:integer; $X?n$.

7.2 Explicit Naming

My design insists that every input or output command must name its source or destination explicitly. This makes it inconvenient to write a library of processes which can be included in subsequent programs, independent of the process names used in that program. A partial solution to this problem is to allow one process (the *main* process) of a parallel command to have an empty label, and to allow the other processes in the command to use the empty process name as source or destination of input or output.

For construction of large programs, some more general technique will also be necessary. This should at least permit substitution of program text for names defined elsewhere—a technique which has been used informally throughout this paper. The Cobol COPY verb also permits a substitution for formal parameters within the copied text. But whatever facility is introduced, I would recommend the following principle: Every program, after assembly with its library routines, should be printable as a text expressed wholly in the language, and it is this printed text which should describe the execution of the program, independent of which parts were drawn from a library.

Since I did not intend to design a complete language, I have ignored the problem of libraries in order to concentrate on the essential semantic concepts of the program which is actually executed.

7.3 Port Names

An alternative to explicit naming of source and destination would be to name a *port* through which communication is to take place. The port names would be local to the processes, and the manner in which pairs of ports are to be connected by channels could be declared in the head of a parallel command.

This is an attractive alternative which could be designed to introduce a useful degree of syntactically checkable redundancy. But it is semantically equivalent to the present proposal, provided that each port is connected to exactly one other port in another process. In this case each channel can be identified with a tag, together with the name of the process at the other end. Since I wish to concentrate on semantics, I preferred in this paper to use the simplest and most direct notation, and to avoid raising questions about the possibility of connecting more than two ports by a single channel.

7.4 Automatic Buffering

As an alternative to synchronization of input and output, it is often proposed that an outputting process should be allowed to proceed even when the inputting process is not yet ready to accept the output. An implementation would be expected automatically to interpose a chain of buffers to hold output messages that have not yet been input.

I have deliberately rejected this alternative, for two reasons: (1) It is less realistic to implement in multiple disjoint processors, and (2) when buffering is required on a particular channel, it can readily be specified using the given primitives. Of course, it could be argued equally well that synchronization can be specified when required by using a pair of buffered input and output commands.

7.5 Unbounded Process Activation

The notation for an array of processes permits the same program text (like an Algol recursive procedure) to have many simultaneous "activations"; however, the exact number must be specified in advance. In a conventional single-processor implementation, this can lead to inconvenience and wastefulness, similar to the fixed-length array of Fortran. It would therefore be attractive to allow a process array with no a priori bound on the number of elements; and to specify that the exact number of elements required for a particular execution of the program should be determined dynamically, like the maximum depth of recursion of an Algol procedure or the number of iterations of a repetitive command.

However, it is a good principle that every actual run of a program with unbounded arrays should be identical to the run of some program with all its arrays bounded in advance. Thus the unbounded program should be defined as the "limit" (in some sense) of a series of bounded programs with increasing bounds. I have chosen to concentrate on the semantics of the bounded case—which is necessary anyway and which is more realistic for implementation on multiple microprocessors.

7.6 Fairness

Consider the parallel command:

```
[X :: Y!stop( )|| Y :: continue:boolean; continue := true;
    *[continue; X?stop( ) → continue := false
    []continue → n := n + 1
    ]
]
```

If the implementation always prefers the second alternative in the repetitive command of Y, it is said to be *unfair*, because although the output command in X could have been executed on an infinite number of occasions, it is in fact always passed over.

The question arises: Should a programming language definition specify that an implementation must be *fair*? Here, I am fairly sure that the answer is NO. Otherwise, the implementation would be obliged to successfully complete the example program shown above, in spite of the fact that its nondeterminism is unbounded. I would therefore suggest that it is the programmer's responsibility to prove that his program terminates correctly—without relying on the assumption of fairness in the implementation. Thus the program shown above is incorrect, since its termination cannot be proved.

Nevertheless, I suggest that an efficient implementation should try to be reasonably fair and should ensure that an output command is not delayed unreasonably often after it first becomes executable. But a proof of correctness must not rely on this property of an efficient implementation. Consider the following analogy with a sequential program: An efficient implementation of an alternative command will tend to favor the alternative which can be most efficiently executed, but the programmer must ensure that the logical correctness of his program does not depend on this property of his implementation.

This method of avoiding the problem of fairness does not apply to programs such as operating systems which are intended to run forever because in this case termination proofs are not relevant. But I wonder whether it is ever advisable to write or to execute such programs Even an operating system should be designed to bring itself to an orderly conclusion reasonably soon after it inputs a message instructing it to do so. Otherwise, the *only* way to stop it is to "crash" it.

7.7 Functional Coroutines

It is interesting to compare the processes described here with those proposed in [12]; the differences are most striking. There, coroutines are strictly deterministic: No choice is given between alternative sources of input. The output commands are automatically buffered to any required degree. The output of one process can be automatically fanned out to any number of processes (including itself!) which can consume it at differing rates. Finally, the processes there are designed to run forever, whereas my proposed parallel command is normally intended to terminate. The design in [12] is based on an elegant theory which permits proof of the properties of programs. These differences are not accidental—they seem to be natural consequences of the difference between the more abstract applicative (or functional) approach to programming and the more machine-oriented imperative (or procedural) approach, which is taken by communicating sequential processes.

7.8 Output Guards

Since input commands may appear in guards, it seems more symmetric to permit output commands as well. This would allow an obvious and useful simplification in some of the example programs, for example, in the bounded buffer (5.1). Perhaps a more convincing reason would be to ensure that the externally visible effect and behavior of every parallel command can be modeled by some sequential command. In order to model the parallel command

$Z :: [X!2||Y!3]$

we need to be able to write the sequential alternative command:

$Z :: [X!2 → Y!3[]Y!3 → X!2]$

Note that this *cannot* be done by the command

$Z :: [true → X!2; Y!3[]true → Y!3; X!2]$

which can fail if the process Z happens to choose the first alternative, but the processes Y and X are synchronized with each other in such a way that Y must input from Z before X does, e.g.

$Y :: Z?y; X!go( )$
$||X :: Y?go( ); Z?x$

7.9 Restriction: Repetitive Command With Input Guard

In proposing an unfamiliar programming language feature, it seems wiser at first to specify a highly restrictive version rather than to propose extensions—especially when the language feature claims to be primitive. For example, it is clear that the multidimensional process array is not primitive, since it can readily be constructed in a language which permits only single-dimensional arrays. But I have a rather more serious misgiving about the repetitive command with input guards.

The automatic termination of a repetitive command on termination of the sources of all its input guards is an extremely powerful and convenient feature but it also involves some subtlety of specification to ensure that it is implementable; and it is certainly not primitive, since the required effect can be achieved (with considerable inconvenience) by explicit exchange of "end()" signals. For example, the subroutine DIV(4.1) could be rewritten:

```
[DIV :: continue:boolean; continue := true;
 *[continue; X?end() → continue := false
 []continue; x,y:integer; X?(x,y) → ... ; X!(quot,rem)
||X :: USER PROG; DIV!end()
 ]
```

Other examples would be even more inconvenient.

But the dangers of convenient facilities are notorious. For example, the repetitive commands with input guards may tempt the programmer to write them without making adequate plans for their termination; and if it turns out that the automatic termination is unsatisfactory, reprogramming for explicit termination will involve severe changes, affecting even the interfaces between the processes.

8. Conclusion

This paper has suggested that input, output, and concurrency should be regarded as primitives of programming, which underlie many familiar and less familiar programming concepts. However, it would be unjustified to conclude that these primitives can wholly replace the other concepts in a programming language. Where a more elaborate construction (such as a procedure or a monitor) is frequently useful, has properties which are more simply provable, and can also be implemented more efficiently than the general case, there is a strong reason for including in a programming language a special notation for that construction. The fact that the construction can be defined in terms of simpler underlying primitives is a useful guarantee that its inclusion is logically consistent with the remainder of the language.

Acknowledgments. The research reported in this paper has been encouraged and supported by a Senior Fellowship of the Science Research Council of Great Britain. The technical inspiration was due to Edsger W. Dijkstra [9], and the paper has been improved in presentation and content by valuable and painstaking advice from D. Gries, D. Q. M. Fay, Edsger W. Dijkstra, N. Wirth, Robert Milne, M. K. Harper, and its referees. The role of IFIP W.G.2.3 as a forum for presentation and discussion is acknowledged with pleasure and gratitude.

Received March 1977; revised August 1977

References
1. Atkinson, R., and Hewitt, C. Synchronisation in actor systems. Working Paper 83, M.I.T., Cambridge, Mass., Nov. 1976.
2. Brinch Hansen, P. The programming language Concurrent Pascal. *IEEE Trans. Software Eng. 1,* 2 (June 1975), 199–207.
3. Campbell, R.H., and Habermann, A.N. The specification of process synchronisation by path expressions. *Lecture Notes in Computer Science 16,* Springer, 1974, pp. 89–102.
4. Conway, M.E. Design of a separable transition-diagram compiler. *Comm. ACM 6,* 7 (July 1963), 396–408.
5. Dahl, O-J., et al. SIMULA 67, common base language. Norwegian Computing Centre, Forskningveien, Oslo, 1967.
6. Dijkstra, E.W. Co-operating sequential processes. In *Programming Languages,* F. Genuys, Ed., Academic Press, New York, 1968, pp. 43–112.
7. Dijkstra, E.W. Notes on structured programming. In *Structured Programming,* Academic Press, New York 1972, pp. 1–82.
8. Dijkstra, E.W. Guarded commands, nondeterminacy, and formal derivation of programs. *Comm. ACM 18,* 8 (Aug. 1975), 453–457.
9. Dijkstra, E.W. Verbal communication, Marktoberdorf, Aug. 1975.
10. Hoare, C.A.R. Towards a theory of parallel programming. In *Operating Systems Techniques,* Academic Press, New York, 1972, pp. 61–71.
11. Hoare, C.A.R. Proof of correctness of data representations. *Acta Informatica 1,* 4 (1972), 271–281.
12. Kahn, G. The semantics of a simple language for parallel programming. In *Proc. IFIP Congress 74,* North Holland, 1974.
13. Liskov, B.H. A note on CLU. Computation Structures Group Memo. 112, M.I.T., Cambridge, Mass, 1974.
14. McIlroy, M.D. Coroutines. Bell Laboratories, Murray Hill, N.J., 1968.
15. Naur, P., Ed. Report on the algorithmic language ALGOL 60. *Comm. ACM 3,* 5 (May 1960), 299–314.
16. Reynolds, J.C. COGENT. ANL-7022, Argonne Nat. Lab., Argonne, Ill., 1965.
17. Thompson, K. The UNIX command language. In *Structured Programming,* Infotech, Nicholson House, Maidenhead, England, 1976, pp. 375–384.
18. van Wijngaarden, A. Ed. Report on the algorithmic language ALGOL 68. *Numer. Math. 14* (1969), 79–218.
19. Wulf, W.A., London, R.L., and Shaw, M. Abstraction and verification in ALPHARD. Dept. of Comptr. Sci., Carnegie-Mellon U., Pittsburgh, Pa., June 1976.
20. Wirth, N. The programming language PASCAL. *Acta Informatica 1,* 1 (1971), 35–63.

Programming
Languages

J.J. Horning
Editor

Distributed Processes: A Concurrent Programming Concept

Per Brinch Hansen
University of Southern California

A language concept for concurrent processes without common variables is introduced. These processes communicate and synchronize by means of procedure calls and guarded regions. This concept is proposed for real-time applications controlled by microcomputer networks with distributed storage. The paper gives several examples of distributed processes and shows that they include procedures, coroutines, classes, monitors, processes, semaphores, buffers, path expressions, and input/output as special cases.

Key Words and Phrases: concurrent programming, distributed processes, microprocessor networks, nondeterminism, guarded regions, programming languages, process communication and scheduling, sorting arrays, coroutines, classes, monitors, processes, semaphores, buffers, path expressions, input/output

CR Categories: 3.8, 4.2, 4.22, 4.32, 5.24

1. Introduction

This paper introduces *distributed processes*—a new language concept for concurrent programming. It is proposed for real-time applications controlled by microcomputer networks with distributed storage. The paper gives several examples of distributed processes and shows that they include procedures, coroutines, classes, monitors, processes, semaphores, buffers, path expressions and input/output as special cases.

Real-time applications push computer and program-

ming technology to its limits (and sometimes beyond). A real-time system is expected to monitor simultaneous activities with critical timing constraints continuously and reliably. The consequences of system failure can be serious.

Real-time programs must achieve the ultimate in simplicity, reliability, and efficiency. Otherwise one can neither understand them, depend on them, nor expect them to keep pace with their environments. To make real-time programs manageable it is essential to write them in an abstract programming language that hides irrelevant machine detail and makes extensive compilation checks possible. To make real-time programs efficient at the same time will probably require the design of computer architectures tailored to abstract languages (or even to particular applications).

From a language designer's point of view, real-time programs have these characteristics:

(1) A real-time program interacts with an environment in which many things happen simultaneously at high speeds.

(2) A real-time program must respond to a variety of *nondeterministic requests* from its environment. The program cannot predict the order in which these requests will be made but must respond to them within certain time limits. Otherwise, input data may be lost or output data may lose their significance.

(3) A real-time program controls a computer with a fixed configuration of processors and peripherals and performs (in most cases) a fixed number of concurrent tasks in its environment.

(4) A real-time program never terminates but continues to serve its environment as long as the computer works. (The occasional need to stop a real-time program, say at the end of an experiment, can be handled by ad hoc mechanisms, such as turning the machine off or loading another program into it.)

What is needed then for real-time applications is the ability to specify a fixed number of concurrent tasks that can respond fast to nondeterministic requests. The programming languages *Concurrent Pascal* and *Modula* come close to satisfying the requirements for abstract concurrent programming [1, 2, 10]. Both of them are based on the *monitor* concept [3, 7]. Modula, however, is primarily oriented towards multiprogramming on a single processor. And a straightforward implementation of Concurrent Pascal requires a single processor or a multiprocessor with a common store. In their present form, these languages are not ideal for a microcomputer network with distributed storage only.

It may well be possible to modify Concurrent Pascal to satisfy the constraints of distributed storage. The ideas proposed here are more attractive, however, because they unify the monitor and process concepts and result in more elegant programs. The new language concepts for real-time applications have the following properties:

(1) A real-time program consists of a fixed number of concurrent processes that are started simultaneously

and exist forever. Each process can access its *own variables* only. There are no common variables.

(2) A process can call *common procedures* defined within other processes. These procedures are executed when the other processes are waiting for some conditions to become true. This is the only form of process communication.

(3) Processes are synchronized by means of nondeterministic statements called *guarded regions* [4, 8].

These processes can be used as program modules in a multiprocessor system with common or distributed storage. To satisfy the real-time constraints each processor will be dedicated to a single process. When a process is waiting for some condition to become true then its processor is also waiting until an external procedure call makes the condition true. This does not represent a waste of resources but rather a temporary lack of useful work for that processor. Parameter passing between processes can be implemented either by copying within a common store or by input/output between separate stores.

The problems of designing verification rules and computer architectures for distributed processes are currently being studied and are not discussed. This paper also ignores the serious problems of performance evaluation and fault tolerance.

2. Language Concepts

A concurrent program consists of a fixed number of sequential processes that are executed simultaneously. A *process* defines its own variables, some common procedures, and an initial statement

process name
own variables
common procedures
initial statement

A process may only access its *own variables*. There are no common variables. But a process may call *common procedures* defined either within itself or within other processes. A procedure call from one process to another is called an *external request*.

A process performs two kinds of *operations* then: the *initial statement* and the *external requests* made by other processes. These operations are executed one at a time by *interleaving*. A process begins by executing its initial statement. This continues until the statement either terminates or waits for a condition to become true. Then another operation is started (as the result of an external request). When this operation in turn terminates or waits the process will either begin yet another operation (requested by another process) or it will resume an earlier operation (as the result of a condition becoming true). This interleaving of the initial statement and the external requests continues forever. If the initial statement terminates, the process continues to exist and will still accept external requests.

So the interleaving is controlled by the program (and *not* by clock signals at the machine level). A process switches from one operation to another only when an operation terminates or waits for a condition within a guarded region (introduced later).

A process continues to execute operations except when all its current operations are delayed within guarded regions or when it makes a request to another process. In the first case, the process is idle until another process calls it. In the second case, the process is idle until the other process has completed the operation requested by it. Apart from this nothing is assumed about the order in which a process performs its operations.

A process guarantees only that it will perform *some* operations as long as there are any unfinished operations that can proceed. But only the programmer can ensure that *every* operation is performed within a finite time.

A *procedure* defines its input and output parameters, some local variables perhaps, and a statement that is executed when it is called.

proc name (input param#output param)
local variables
statement

A process *P* can call a procedure *R* defined within another process *Q* as follows:

call $Q.R$ (expressions, variables)

Before the operation *R* is performed the expression values of the call are assigned to the *input* parameters. When the operation is finished the values of the *output* parameters are assigned to the variables of the call. Parameter passing between processes can therefore be implemented either by copying within a common store or by input/output between processors that have no common store.

In this, paper processes can call procedures within one another without any restrictions. In a complete programming language additional notation would be added to limit the access rights of individual processes. It may also be necessary to eliminate recursion to simplify verification and implementation. But these are issues that will not concern us here.

Nondeterminism will be controlled by two kinds of statements called *guarded commands* and *guarded regions*. A guarded region can delay an operation, but a guarded command cannot.

A guarded command [6] enables a process to make an arbitrary choice among several statements by inspecting the current state of its variables. If none of the alternatives are possible in the current state the guarded command cannot be executed and will either be skipped or cause a program exception.

The guarded commands have the following syntax and meaning:

if $B1:S1|B2:S2|$ ... **end**
do $B1:S1|B2:S2|$ ... **end**

If statement: If some of the conditions $B1$, $B2$, ..., are true then select one of the true conditions Bi and execute the statement Si that follows it; otherwise, stop the program.

(If the language includes a mechanism whereby one process can detect the failure of another process, it is reasonable to let an exception in a process stop that process only. But, if recovery from programming errors is not possible then it is more consistent to stop the whole program. This paper does not address this important issue.)

Do statement: While some of the conditions are true select one of them arbitrarily and execute the corresponding statement.

A guarded region [4, 8] enables a process to wait until the state of its variables makes it possible to make an arbitrary choice among several statements. If none of the alternatives are possible in the current state the process postpones the execution of the guarded region.

The guarded regions have the following syntax and meaning:

when $B1:S1|B2:S2|$ ... **end**
cycle $B1:S1|B2:S2|$ ... **end**

When statement: Wait until one of the conditions is true and execute the corresponding statement.

Cycle statement: Endless repetition of a when statement.

If several conditions are true within a guarded command or region it is unpredictable which one of the corresponding statements the machine will select. This uncertainty reflects the nondeterministic nature of real-time applications.

The *data types* used are either integers, Booleans, or characters, or they are finite sets, sequences, and arrays with at most n elements of some type T:

int   bool   char
set[n]T seq[n]T array[n]T

The following statement enumerates all the elements in a data structure:

for x **in** $y:S$ **end**

For statement: For each element x in the set or array y execute the statement S. A **for** statement can access and change the values of array elements but can only read the values of set elements.

Finally, it should be mentioned that the empty statement is denoted *skip* and the use of semicolons is optional.

3. Process Communication

The following presents several examples of the use of these language concepts in concurrent programming. We will first consider communication between processes by means of procedure calls.

Example: *Semaphore*

A general semaphore initialized to zero can be implemented as a process *sem* that defines *wait* and *signal* operations.

process sem; s: int
proc wait **when** $s > 0$: $s := s - 1$ **end**
proc signal; $s := s + 1$
$s := 0$

The initial statement assigns the value zero to the semaphore and terminates. The process, however, continues to exist and can now be called by other processes

call sem.wait   **call** sem.signal

Example: *Message Buffer*

A buffer process stores a sequence of characters transmitted between processes by means of *send* and *receive* operations.

process buffer; s: **seq**[n]char
proc send(c: char) **when not** s.full: s.put(c) **end**
proc rec($\neq v$: char) **when not** s.empty: s.get(v) **end**
$s := [\,]$

The initial statement makes the buffer empty to begin with. The buffer operations are called as follows:

call buffer.send(x)   **call** buffer.rec(y)

The semaphore and buffer processes are similar to *monitors*: They define the representation of a shared data structure and the meaningful operations on it. These operations take place one at a time. After initialization, a monitor is idle between external calls.

Example: *Character Stream*

A process inputs punched cards from a card reader and outputs them as a sequence of characters through a buffer process. The process deletes *spaces* at the end of each card and terminates it by a *newline* character.

```
process stream
b: array[80]char; n, i: int
do true:
    call cardreader.input(b)
    if b = blankline: skip|
       b ≠ blankline: i := 1; n := 80
          do b[n] = space: n := n - 1 end
          do i ≤ n: call buffer.send(b[i]); i := i + 1 end
    end
    call buffer.send(newline)
end
```

This use of a process is similar to the traditional *process* concept: the process executes an initial statement only. It calls common procedures within other processes, but does not define any within itself. Such a process does not contain guarded regions because other processes are unable to call it and make the conditions within it true.

The example also illustrates how *peripheral devices* can be controlled by distributed processes. A device (such as the card reader) is associated with a single process. Other processes can access the device only through common procedures. So a peripheral device is just another process.

While a process is waiting for input/output, no other operations take place within it. This is a special case of a more general rule: When a process *P* calls a procedure *R* within another process *Q* then *R* is considered an indivisible operation within process *P*, and *P* will not execute any other operation until *R* is finished (see Section 2).

Notice, that there is no need for *interrupts* even in a real-time language. Fast response to external requests is achieved by dedicating a processor to each critical event in the environment and by making sure that these processors interact with a small number of neighboring processors only (to prevent them from being overloaded with too many requests at a time).

Exercise: Write a process that receives a sequence of characters from a buffer process and outputs them line by line to a printer. The process should output a *formfeed* after every 60 lines.

4. Resource Scheduling

We will now look at a variety of scheduling problems solved by means of guarded regions. It should perhaps be mentioned that resource schedulers are by nature *bottlenecks*. It would therefore be wise in a real-time program to make sure that each resource either is used frequently by a small number of processes or very infrequently by a larger number of processes. In many applications it is possible to avoid resource scheduling altogether and dedicate a resource to a single process (as in the card reader and line printer examples).

Example: Resource Scheduler
A set of user processes can obtain exclusive access to an abstract resource by calling request and release operations within a scheduling process.

```
process resource; free: bool
proc request when free: free := false end
proc release if not free: free := true end
free := true
```

```
call resource.request ... call resource.release
```

The use of the Boolean *free* forces a strict alternation of request and release operations. The program stops if an attempt is made to release a resource that already is free.

In this example, the scheduler does not know the identity of individual user processes. This is ideal when it does not matter in which order the users are served. But, if a scheduler must enforce a particular scheduling policy (such as *shortest job next*) then it must know the identity of its users to be able to grant the resource to a specific user. The following example shows how this can be done.

Example: Shortest Job Next Scheduler

A scheduler allocates a resource among *n* user processes in shortest-job-next order. A request enters the identity and service time of a user process in a queue and waits until that user is selected by the scheduler. A release makes the resource available again.

The scheduler waits until one of two situations arise:

(1) A process enters or leaves the queue: the scheduler will scan the queue and select the next user (but will not grant the resource to it yet).

(2) The resource is not being used and the next user has been selected: the scheduler will grant the resource to that user and remove it from the queue.

User processes identify themselves by unique indices 1, 2, ... , *n*. The constant *nil* denotes an undefined process index.

The scheduler uses the following variables:

queue	the indices of waiting processes
rank	the service times of waiting processes
user	the index of the current user (if any)
next	the index of the next user (if any)

```
process sjn
queue: set[n] int; rank: array[n]int
user, next, min: int
proc request(who, time: int)
begin queue.include(who); rank[who] := time
    next := nil; when user = who: next := nil end
end
proc release; user := nil

begin queue := [ ]; user := nil; next := nil
    cycle
        not queue.empty & (next=nil):
            min := maxinteger
            for i in queue:
                if rank[i] > min: skip|
                    rank[i] ≤ min: next := i; min := rank[i]
                end
            end|
        (user=nil) & (next≠nil):
            user := next; queue.exclude(user)
    end
end
```

In a microprocessor network where each processor is dedicated to a single process it is an attractive possibility to let a process carry out computations *between* external calls of its procedures. The above scheduler takes advantage of this capability by selecting the next user while the resource is still being used by the present user. It would be simpler (but less efficient) to delay the selection of the next user until the previous one has released the resource.

The scheduling of individual processes is handled completely by means of guarded regions without the use of synchronizing variables, such as semaphores or event queues.

The periodic evaluation of a synchronizing condition, such as "user = who," might be a serious load on a *common* store shared by other processors. But it is quite acceptable when it only involves the *local* store of a single processor that has nothing else to do. This is a good example of the influence of hardware technology on abstract algorithms.

Exercise: Write a first-come, first-served scheduler.

Example: Readers and Writers

Two kinds of processes, called readers and writers, share a single resource. The readers can use the resource simultaneously, but each writer must have exclusive access to it. The readers and writers behave as follows:

```
call resource.startread          call resource.startwrite
read                             write
call resource.endread            call resource.endwrite
```

A variable *s* defines the current resource *state* as one of the following:

$s = 0$ 1 writer uses the resource
$s = 1$ 0 processes use the resource
$s = 2$ 1 reader uses the resource
$s = 3$ 2 readers use the resource
...   ...

This leads to the following solution [4]:

```
process resource; s: int
proc startread when s ≥ 1: s := s + 1 end
proc endread if s > 1: s := s − 1 end
proc startwrite when s = 1: s := 0 end
proc endwrite if s = 0: s := 1 end
s := 1
```

Exercise: Solve the same problem with the additional constraint that further reader requests should be delayed as long as some writers are either waiting for or are using the resource.

Example: Alarm Clock

An alarm clock process enables user processes to wait for different time intervals. The alarm clock receives a signal from a timer process after each time unit. (The problems of representing a clock with a finite integer are ignored here.)

```
process alarm; time: int
proc wait(interval: int)
due: int
begin due := time + interval
    when time = due: skip end
end
proc tick; time := time + 1
time := 0
```

5. Process Arrays

So far we have only used one instance of each process. The next example uses an array of *n* identical processes [9]

```
process name[n]
```

A standard function *this* defines the identity of an individual process within the array ($1 \leq$ this $\leq n$).

Example: Dining Philosophers

Five philosophers alternate between thinking and eating. When a philosopher gets hungry, he joins a round table and picks up two forks next to his plate and starts eating. There are, however, only five forks on the table. So a philosopher can eat only when none of his neighbors are eating. When a philosopher has finished eating he puts down his two forks and leaves the table again.

```
process philosopher[5]
do true: think
    call table.join(this); eat; call table.leave(this)
end

process table; eating: set[5]int
proc join(i: int)
when ([i⊖1, i⊕1] & eating) = []: eating.include(i) end
proc leave(i: int); eating.exclude(i)
eating := []
```

This solution does not prevent two philosophers from starving a philosopher between them to death by eating alternately.

Exercise: Solve the same problem without starvation.

Example: Sorting Array

A process array sorts *m* data items in time $O(m)$. The items are input through sort process 1 that stores the smallest item input so far and passes the rest to its successor sort process 2. The latter keeps the second smallest item and passes the rest to its successor sort process 3, and so on. When the *m* items have been input they will be stored in their natural order in sort processes 1, 2, ... , *m*. They can now be output in increasing order through sort process 1. After each output the processes receive the remaining items from their successors.

A user process behaves as follows:

```
A: array[m] int
for x in A: call sort[1].put(x) end
for x in A: call sort[1].get(x) end
```

The sorting array can sort *n* elements or less ($m \leq n$). A sorting process is in equilibrium when it holds one item only. When the equilibrium is disturbed by its predecessor, a process takes the following action:

(1) If the process holds two items, it will keep the smallest one and pass the largest one to its successor.

(2) If the process holds no items, but its successor does, then the process will fetch the smallest item from its successor.

A sorting process uses the following variables:

here   the items stored in this process ($0 \leq$ here.length ≤ 2)
rest   the number of items stored in its successors

A standard function *succ* defines the index of the successor process (succ = this + 1).

```
process sort[n]
here: seq[2]int; rest, temp: int
proc put(c: int) when here.length < 2: here.put(c) end
proc get(#v: int) when here.length = 1: here.get(v) end
```

```
begin here := [ ]; rest := 0
  cycle
    here.length = 2:
      if here[1] ≤ here[2]: temp := here[2]; here := [here[1]] |
        here[1] > here[2]: temp := here[1]; here := [here[2]]
      end
      call sort[succ].put(temp); rest := rest + 1 |
    (here.length = 0) & (rest > 0):
      call sort[succ].get(temp); rest := rest − 1
      here := [temp]
  end
end
```

A hardware implementation of such a sorting array could be used as a very efficient form of a priority scheduling queue.

Exercise: Program a process array that contains $N = 2^n$ numbers to begin with and which will add them in time $O(\log_2 N)$.

Since a process can define a common procedure it obviously includes the *procedure* case as a special case. In [9] Hoare shows that a process array also can simulate a *recursive* procedure with a fixed maximum depth of recursion.

Exercise: Write a process array that computes a Fibonacci number by recursion.

6. Abstract Data Types

A process combines a data structure and all the possible operations on it into a single program module. Since other processes can perform these operations only on the data structure, but do not have direct access to it, it is called an *abstract* data structure.

We have already seen that a process can function as a *monitor*—an abstract data type that is shared by several processes. The next example shows that a process also can simulate a *class* - an abstract data type that is used by a single process only.

Example: Vending Machine

A vending machine accepts one coin at a time. When a button is pushed the machine returns an item with change provided there is at least one item left and the coins cover the cost of it; otherwise, all the coins are returned.

```
process vending_machine
items, paid, cash: int
proc insert(coin: int) paid := paid + coin
proc push(#change, goods: int)
if (items > 0) & (paid ≥ price):
    change := paid − price; cash := cash + price
    goods := 1; items := items − 1; paid := 0 |
  (items = 0) or (paid < price):
    change := paid; goods := 0; paid := 0
end
begin items := 50; paid := 0; cash := 0 end
```

7. Coroutines

Distributed processes can also function as coroutines. In a coroutine relationship between two processes P and Q only one of them is running at a time. A resume operation transfers control from one process to the other. When a process is resumed it continues at the point where it has transferred control to another process.

```
process P; go: bool
proc resume; go := true

begin go := false
  ...
  call Q.resume
  when go: go := false end
  ...
end
```

Process Q is very similar.

8. Path Expressions

Path expressions define meaningful *sequences* of operations P, Q, ... , [5]. A path expression can be implemented by a scheduling process that defines the operations P, Q, ... , as procedures and uses a state variable s to enforce the sequence in which other processes may invoke these procedures.

Suppose, for example, that the operation P only can be followed by the operation Q as shown by the graph below:

$$\rightarrow P \rightarrow Q \rightarrow$$

To implement this path expression one associates a distinct state a, b, and c with each arrow in the graph and programs the operations as follows:

```
proc P if s = a: ... s := b end
proc Q if s = b: ... s := c end
```

If P is called in the state $s = a$ it will change the state to $s = b$ and make Q possible. Q, in turn, changes the state from b to c. An attempt to perform P or Q in a state where they are illegal will cause a program exception (or a delay if a *when* statement is used within the operation).

The next path expression specifies that either P or Q can be performed. This is enforced by means of two states a and b.

```
proc P if s = a: ... s := b end

proc Q if s = a: ... s := b end
```

If an operation P can be performed zero or more times then the execution of P leaves the state $s = a$ unchanged as shown below.

```
proc P if s = a: ... end
```

The simple resource scheduler in Section 4 implements a composite path expression in which the sequence *request ... release* is repeated zero or more times.

The readers and writers problem illustrates the use of a state variable to permit some operations to take place *simultaneously* while other operations are temporarily *excluded* (in this case, simultaneous reading by several processes excludes writing). Each simultaneous operation P is surrounded by a pair of scheduling operations, *startP* and *endP*. The state variable counts the number of P operations in progress.

9. Implementation Hints

The following outlines the general nature of an implementation of distributed processes but ignores the details which are currently being studied.

In a well-designed concurrent program one may assume that each process communicates with a small number of neighboring processes only. For if the interactions are not strongly localized one cannot expect to gain much from concurrency. (A few resource schedulers may be an exception to this rule.)

Each processor will contain a distributed process P and a small, fixed number of anonymous processes which are the *representatives* of those distributed processes that can call process P. Additional notation in the language should make it possible for a compiler to determine the number of processes which call a particular process.

Whenever a processor is idle it activates a local representative which then waits until it receives a request with input data from another processor. The representative now calls the local procedure requested with the available input. When the procedure terminates, its output data are returned to the other processor and the representative becomes passive again. The switching from one *quasiconcurrent* process to another within a processor takes place as described in Section 2.

Since processes are permanent and procedures are nonrecursive, a compiler can determine the maximum storage required by a distributed process and the local representatives of its environment. So the storage allocation is *static* within each processor.

The parameter passing between two processors requires a single *input* operation before a procedure is executed and a single *output* operation when it terminates.

The speed of process switching within a single processor will probably be crucial for its real-time response.

The technique of representing the environment of a processor by local processes synchronized with external processes seems conceptually attractive. Although these processes are anonymous in this proposal one could design a language in which the store of a single processor is shared by local quasiconcurrent processes which communicate with nonlocal processes by input/output only.

10. Final Remarks

It would certainly be feasible to adapt the processes and monitors of Concurrent Pascal to multiprocessor networks with distributed storage by restricting the parameter passing mechanism as proposed here. All the examples discussed here could then be programmed in that language—but not nearly as elegantly!

What then are the merits of distributed processes? Primarily, that they are a combination of *well-known* programming concepts (processes, procedures, and conditional critical regions) which *unify* the class, monitor, and process concepts. They include a surprising number of basic programming concepts as special cases:

procedures
coroutines
classes
monitors
processes
semaphores
buffers
path expressions
input/output

Since there is a common denominator for all these concepts, it may well be possible to develop common proof rules for them. The use of a single concept will certainly simplify the language implementation considerably.

The Concurrent Pascal machine distinguishes between 15 virtual instructions for classes, monitors, and processes. This number would be reduced by a factor of three for distributed processes. In addition, numerous special cases would disappear in the compiler.

It is also encouraging that distributed processes can be used to write elegant algorithms both for the more well-known concurrent problems and for some new ones that are non-trivial.

A recent proposal by Hoare has the same pleasant properties [9]. Both proposals attack the problem of concurrency without shared variables and recognize the need for nondeterminacy within a single process.

Hoare's *communicating sequential processes* can be created and terminated dynamically. A single data transfer from one process to another is the communication mechanism. A process synchronizes itself with its environment by guarded input commands which are executed when a Boolean expression is true *and* input is available from another process. The relationship between two communicating processes is symmetrical and requires both of them to name the other. The brief and nonredundant notation does not require declarations of communication channels but depends (conceptually) on dynamic type checking to recognize matching input and output commands in two processes.

In their present form communicating sequential processes seem well-suited to a theoretical investigation of concurrency and as a concise specification language that suppresses minor details. However, as Hoare points out, the language concepts and the notation would have to

295

be modified to make them practical for program implementation.

The proposal for *distributed processes* is intended as a first step toward a practical language for networks. The proposal recognizes that the exchange of input and output in one operation is a frequent case, particularly for peripheral devices which return a result after each operation. The notation is redundant and enables a compiler to determine the number of processes and their storage requirements. The relationship between two communicating processes is asymmetrical and requires only that the caller of an operation name the process that performs it. This asymmetry is useful in hierarchical systems in which servants should be unaware of the identities of their masters.

Distributed processes derive much of their power from the ability to delay process interactions by means of Boolean expressions which may involve both the global variables of a process *and* the input parameters from other processes (as illustrated by the *sjn* scheduler and the alarm clock). The price for this flexibility is the need for quasiconcurrent processes in the implementation. A more restricted form of Hoare's proposal might be able to implement process synchronization by the simpler method of polling a number of data channels until one of them transmits data.

But more work remains to be done on verification rules and network architectures for these new concepts. And then the ideas must be tested in *practice* before a final judgment can be made.

Acknowledgments. I am grateful to Nissim Francez, Wolfgang Franzen, Susan Gerhart, Charles Hayden, John Hennessy, Tony Hoare, David Lomet, David MacQueen, Johannes Madsen, David Musser, Michel Sintzoff, Jørgen Staunstrup and the referees for their constructive comments.

Received September 1977; revised December 1977

References
1. Brinch Hansen, P. The programming language Concurrent Pascal. *IEEE Trans. Software Eng. 1*, 2 (June 1975), 199–207.
2. Brinch Hansen, P. *The Architecture of Concurrent Programs.* Prentice-Hall, Englewood Cliffs, N.J., 1977.
3. Brinch Hansen, P. *Operating System Principles.* Prentice-Hall, Englewood Cliffs, N.J., 1973.
4. Brinch Hansen, P., and Staunstrup, J. Specification and implementation of mutual exclusion. Comptr. Sci. Dept., U. of Southern California, Los Angeles, Sept. 1977.
5. Campbell, R.H., and Habermann, A.N. The specification of process synchronization by path expressions. *Lecture Notes in Computer Science 16*, Springer-Verlag, 1974, pp. 89–102.
6. Dijkstra, E.W. Guarded commands, nondeterminacy, and formal derivation of programs. *Comm. ACM 18*, 8 (Aug. 1975), 453–57.
7. Hoare, C.A.R. Monitors: an operating system structuring concept. *Comm. ACM 17*, 10 (Oct. 1974), 549–57.
8. Hoare, C.A.R. Towards a theory of parallel programming. In *Operating Systems Techniques*, Academic Press, New York, 1972.
9. Hoare, C.A.R. Communicating sequential processes. Comptr. Sci. Dept., Queen's U., Belfast, N. Ireland, March 1977.
10. Wirth, N. Modula: A programming language for modular multiprogramming. *Software—Practice & Experience 7*, 1 (Jan. 1977), 3–35.

STRUCTURED DESIGN METHODOLOGIES

G. D. Bergland

Bell Telephone Laboratories, Inc.
Information Processing Research Department
Murray Hill, New Jersey 07974

Reprinted from *15th Annual Design Automation Conference
Proceedings*, June 1978, pages 475-493. Copyright © 1978 by
The Institute of Electrical and Electronics Engineers, Inc.

ABSTRACT

This tutorial considers the structure and construction of
reliable software (see Figure 1).

Figure 1. A Good Design Implies a Good Structure.

By way of introduction, several of the structured programming and software engineering techniques are classified into
three groups; those which impact primarily on the program
structure, the development process, and the development support tools.

Structural Analysis Concepts are described which have their
major impact at the code level, the module level, and the system
level.

Finally, three of the major structured design methodologies
which have been reported in the literature are developed and
compared. Functional Decomposition, the Data Flow Design
Method, and the Data Structure Design Method are described,
characterized, and applied to a specific example.

While no one design methodology can be shown to be
"correct" for all types of problems, it is felt that these three can
cover a variety of applications. An "interim" approach for large
software design problems is suggested which may be useful until
an accepted "correct" methodology comes along.

INTRODUCTION

Motivation

The major motivation for looking at Programming Productivity Techniques, Software Engineering Techniques, and finally
Structured Design Methodologies centers around a desire to
reduce the cost of producing and maintaining software. In some
cases there is the secondary motivation of developing reliable
enough programs to support nonstop computer systems, but
these applications seem to be in the minority. All but one of the
claims in Figure 2 were taken out of technical journals,
conference proceedings, or short course advertisements which
heralded the virtues of new design methodologies.

If one were to take these claims at face value, it would
seem that the problems of producing inexpensive, reliable
software were solved. Unfortunately, to many people the
benefits of Structured Programming, Software Engineering Techniques or whatever, have remained either nebulous or illusive.

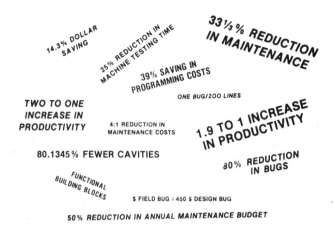

Figure 2. Motivation for New Methodologies.

Techniques Hierarchy

Software Engineering has been defined by Parnas as multi-
person construction of multi-version programs. As such, there
is a lot of emphasis on the development process and its atten-
dant support tools as well as on the basic structure of a program.
In Figure 3 a representative sampling of some of the more
fashionable Software Engineering Techniques is given. While
many of the techniques may impact more than one area, they
are listed under the category where their impact is the greatest.

STRUCTURE
- TOP DOWN DESIGN
- VIRTUAL MACHINES
- HIERARCHICAL MODULAR PROGRAMMING
- INFORMATION HIDING
- DATA ABSTRACTIONS
- BOTTOM UP DESIGN
- STRUCTURED CODE

PROCESS
- TEAMS
- WALKTHRUS
- REVIEWS
- TOP DOWN IMPLEMENTATION
- CONTINUOUS INTEGRATION
- PHASED BUILDS

TOOLS
- HIGH LEVEL LANGUAGE
- DEVELOPMENT SUPPORT LIBRARY
- PROGRAMMERS WORK BENCH
- PROGRAM LIBRARIANS
- AUTOMATIC TEST GENERATION
- CAUSE-EFFECT CHARTS

Figure 3. Fashionable Software Engineering Techniques.

While concepts like teams, design reviews, program librarians, etc. can be implemented quite quickly, their major benefits can only be realized in the context of a well structured program. In my view, those techniques dealing with program structure form the foundation on which the other techniques should be applied. This view is represented pictorially in Figure 4.

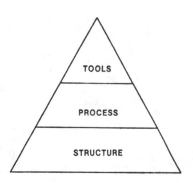

Figure 4. Software Engineering Techniques Hierarchy.

Program structure is the single most important determinant of the life-cycle cost of a software system. Thus it seems worth discussing in detail some of the concepts which play a role in analyzing the structure of a program.

STRUCTURAL ANALYSIS CONCEPTS

While most structural analysis concepts apply at more than one level of a software system, it is convenient in this discussion to separate them into three categories. Concepts are discussed which have their major impact at the code level, the module level, and the software system level.

Code Level Concepts

Abstraction. The concept of abstraction ranks as one of the most important advances in programming which has occurred in the last 20 years. It is the basis for high level languages, virtual machines, virtual I/O devices, data abstractions, and a host of other concepts. A few of the software engineering terms which are built on the concept of abstraction are shown in Figure 5 below.

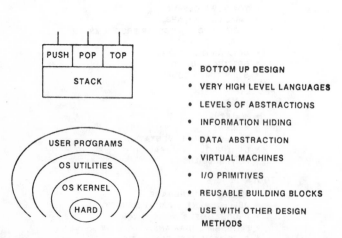

Figure 5. Applications of Abstraction.

The whole concept of bottom up design consists of building up layers of abstract machines which get more and more powerful until only one instruction is needed to solve the problem. In most cases people stop far short of defining that one super-powerful instruction, but they do significantly enhance the environment in which they have to program. Device drivers, operating system primitives, I/O routines and user-defined macros all are built on the concept of abstraction and all raise the level at which the programmer thinks and programs.

In many cases the objective is to abstract out many of the complicated interactions which can occur when many users or user programs are sharing the same machine. In other cases a virtual machine is created to hide the ideosyncracies of a particular machine from the user so that the resulting program will be more portable.

When the Modular Programming era began in the 1960's, many people had the hope that hundreds of reusable building-block programs would become available in their programming library and that they could finally begin to "build on the work of others." Unfortunately, as Weinberg noted, program libraries are unique; everyone wants to put something in but no one wants to take anything out.

Communication. A program communicates with both people and machines. The comments in Figure 6 were taken from real listings. They clearly were intended to communicate with people and not the machine.

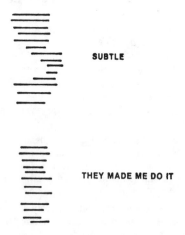

Figure 6. Programs Communicate with People and Machines.

The effect of some comments can be profound. The program with the comment "subtle" is left alone at all costs. The person who wrote the program is long gone and has left a legacy of problems which will last as long as the program.

The "They made me do it!" comment is an apology for corrupting the structure of the program to provide an expedient fix to a pressing problem. I'm sure you've never been in that situation. Clearly the program is a little harder to understand, modify and change now. This type of change is not unusual; it's the apology that's unusual.

These changes in the long run tend to obscure the structure of the program and thus make the processes of error correction and feature addition difficult and dangerous. A program is meant to communicate its structure to the programmer as well as to give instructions to the machine. The life-cycle cost of operating a program in most cases depends far more on how well it communicates with people than on how much it was optimized.

Clarity. It has been said that a person who writes English clearly can write a program clearly. In studying English we are first taught to read and then taught to write. In programming we are usually only taught to write. In fact one language which is famous for its "one liners" has been affectionately called a "write-only language."

The structure of a good article, paper, or book is very important for clearly communicating ideas. The structure of a program is equally important for communicating both the algorithm and the context of a problem solution.

In Figure 7, clarity of program structure was obviously not the primary concern.

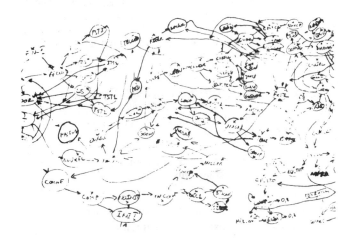

Figure 7. A Clearly Presented Program Structure?

This program has been running reliably for more than 10 years. Fortunately very few changes or feature enhancements have been required. This diagram was drawn by the last person who had to change it in an attempt to understand what was happening.

The concept of "data hygiene" has been around for quite a while now. That is, you should leave data as you would like to find it. The concept of "program structure hygiene" has never quite caught on. Every new change seems likely to increase the unstructuredness of a program.

The "structuredness" of a program, of course, is not very well defined. There is still no generally accepted metric for measuring the goodness or badness of a program structure. The unavailability of such a metric leads to some very strange happenings. For example, do you know someone who writes complicated, unintelligible code, and spends long hours and late nights finally getting it "done" just before the deadline all the while letting everyone know how difficult his task is and what a hero he is for having gotten it done just in time?

Contrast this with a neat, well organized programmer who takes care to plan ahead, to do a proper design, document her work and get done well ahead of the deadline with no one even aware that she was involved. How often have you thought, "Boy, John has certainly earned his wings with that difficult program while Jane still hasn't had a chance to prove herself."

In the best of all worlds the criterion of clarity could be applied quantitatively. Lacking that, we'll have to stick with peer pressure applied in design reviews and code walkthroughs.

Control Flow Constructs. The concept of limiting the number and type of control flow constructs is now pretty generally accepted. The forms recommended by Michael Jackson (Reference 1) are shown in Figure 8.

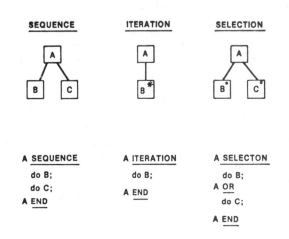

Figure 8. The Three Basic Control Flow Constructs.

The sequence and selection constructs shown in Figure 8 can be generalized in the obvious way to a sequence or selection of N items where N can be arbitrarily large. The iteration stands for "zero or more" program executions. The advantage of these constructs is that they tend to provide a map of the program structure instead of an itinerary of tasks.

The transformation of a program using these constructs to schematic logic (as also shown in Figure 8) is remarkably straightforward, as is the subsequent transformation to a specific programming language.

Module Level Concepts

Cohesion. Cohesion is the "glue" that holds a module together (Reference 2). It can also be thought of as the association between the component elements of a module. Generally one wants the highest level of cohesion possible. While no quantitative measure of cohesion exists, a qualitative set of levels of cohesion has been suggested by Constantine and proposed in modified form by Myers (References 2 and 3). The levels proposed by Constantine are shown in Figure 9 below.

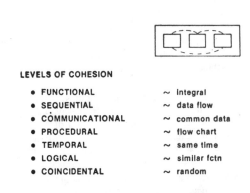

LEVELS OF COHESION

● FUNCTIONAL	~ Integral
● SEQUENTIAL	~ data flow
● COMMUNICATIONAL	~ common data
● PROCEDURAL	~ flow chart
● TEMPORAL	~ same time
● LOGICAL	~ similar fctn
● COINCIDENTAL	~ random

Figure 9. Levels of Cohesion.

The lowest level of cohesion is called coincidental cohesion. In this case the component parts of a module are just there by coincidence. There is no meaningful relationship among them.

Logical cohesion is present when a module performs one of a set of logically related functions. An example might be a module composed of ten different types of print routines. The routines do not work together or pass work to each other but logically perform the same function of printing.

Temporal cohesion is present when a module performs a set of functions that are related in time. An INITIALIZATION module performs a set of operations at the beginning of a program. The only connection between these operations is that they are all performed at essentially the same point in time.

Procedural cohesion occurs when a module consists of functions that are related to the procedural processes in a program. Functions which can be represented together well on a flowchart are often grouped together in a module with procedural strength. Conversely when a module is designed by using a flowchart, the resulting module often has procedural strength.

Communicational cohesion results when functions which operate on common data are grouped together. A data abstraction or Data Cluster (see Reference 4), is a good example of a module with communicational strength.

Sequential cohesion often results when a module represents a partition of a data flow diagram. Typically the modules so formed accept data from one module, modify or transform it, and then pass it on to another module.

Functional cohesion results when every function within the module contributes directly to performing one single function. The module often transforms a single input into a single output. An example often used is SQUARE ROOT. This is the highest level of cohesion in the hierarchy and as such is desirable whenever it can be achieved.

A program of any reasonable size will usually contain modules of several different levels of cohesion. In fact many modules exhibit characteristics of a multiplicity of levels simultaneously. Where possible, functional, sequential, and communicational strength modules should be given preference over modules with lower levels of cohesion. On a scale of 1 to 10, coincidental, logical and temporal cohesion would score approximately 1, 2, and 3, respectively. Procedural cohesion would score 5. Communicational, sequential and functional cohesion would score 8, 9, and 10 respectively.

While levels of cohesion can be useful guides in evaluating the structure of a program, they don't provide a clear cut methodology for attaining high levels of cohesion. Also, levels of cohesion do not allow us to say that program A is right and program B is wrong. They do, however, represent a definite step forward. Before levels of cohesion were introduced there was no recognized basis for comparison. Now one can say in some inexact way that structure A is probably better than structure B.

Coupling. Coupling is a measure of the strength of interconnection between modules. In Figure 10 two program structures are represented which would result in significantly different degrees of coupling.

High coupling among program modules results when a problem is partitioned in a relatively arbitrary way such as cutting off sections of a flowchart. Often, this method of chopping up a large program complicates the total job because of the resultant tight coupling between the pieces. This latter type of partitioning has been called "mosaic" modularity (see Reference 18).

The other extreme in structuring a program is to consider only pure tree structures. These structures give rise to the concept of hierarchical modularity and provide many advantages for abstraction, testing and subsequent modification. Jackson would accuse you of "Arboricide" (the killing of trees) whenever you deviate from a pure hierarchical tree structure.

Brooks (Reference 5) said that,

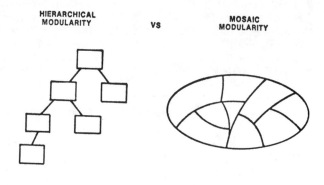

Figure 10. Partitioning Method Affects Level of Coupling.

"I am persuaded that top down design (incorporating hierarchy, modularity, and stepwise refinement) is the most important new programming formalization of the decade."

Dijkstra (Reference 6) said that,

"The sooner we learn to limit ourselves to hierarchical program constructs the faster we will progress."

Hierarchical modular programs can be characterized as:

(1) Implementing a single independent function.

(2) Performing a single logical task.

(3) Having a single entry and exit point.

(4) Being separately testable.

(5) Satisfying a number of other rules which have been listed at length in the literature (see Reference 7).

When these rules are followed, the result is a set of nested modules which can be connected together in a hierarchy to form very large programs.

When modularity is used without hierarchy, one is only able to implement independent functions which can be executed in sequence. This corresponds to drawing circles around portions of a flowchart. This approach tends to work on small programs but can seldom be applied to complex programs without seriously compromising module independence, connectivity, and testability. Only when the concepts of modular programming are combined with the concepts of hierarchical program structure can one preserve the capability for both implementing arbitrarily complex functions and maintaining module integrity.

Modularity can be applied without hierarchy in cases which lend themselves very naturally to the efficient use of a very high level language. Very high level language statements are examples of functions which can be implemented relatively independent of each other but can still be strung together sequentially in a useful form. Unfortunately for most real-time control applications, the design of an efficient very high level language is very difficult.

Hierarchical modularity forms an extremely attractive foundation for most of the other Software Engineering Techniques. While some of these techniques can be used without having a hierarchical program structure, the primary benefit can only be gained when the techniques are all used as a unit and build upon each other. Specifically, a hierarchical modular program structure enhances top-down development, programming teams, modular programming, design walkthroughs, and other techniques which deal with improving the development process.

Complexity. The control of program complexity is perhaps the underlying objective of most of the Software Engineering Techniques. The concept of divide and conquer as an answer to complexity is very important provided it is done correctly. When a program can be divided into two independent parts, complexity is reduced dramatically as shown in Figure 11.

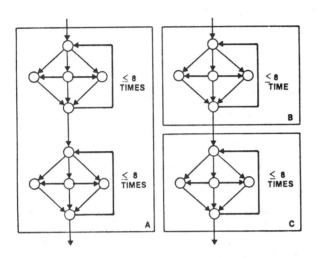

Figure 11. Control of Complexity.

Consider program A where you have access to only the input and the output. (see Reference 3). A noble goal would be to "completely" test this program by executing each unique path. In the example shown there are approximately 250 billion unique paths through this module. If you were capable of performing one test each millisecond, it would take you 8 years to completely test all of the unique paths. If, however, you had knowledge of what was inside the program, and recognized that it could be partitioned into two independent modules B and C which have very low connectivity and coupling, your testing job could be reduced. To test both of these modules separately requires that you only test the one million unique paths through each module. At one millisecond per test, these tests would take a total of only 17 minutes.

In this particular example, from a testing viewpoint, it is clearly worth trying to partition the problem so that small, independently testable modules can be dealt with instead of just the input and output of a large program. Unfortunately, partitioning most programs into independently testable modules requires much more work than simply drawing small circles around portions of the flowchart shown here.

It should also be clear from this example that the testing problem is best solved during the design stage. It is impossible to exhaustively test any program of meaningful size. Testing is experimental evidence (Reference 1). It does not verify correctness. It raises your confidence and may in fact increase reliability, but not very much.

Correctness. A "correct program" is one which accurately implements the specification. In many cases a "correct program" is of limited value since the specifications are in error. As shown in Figure 12, in many cases the specification is either excessive, incomplete, or inconsistent.

As discussed previously, correctness cannot be verified by testing. Its like searching for mermaids. Just because you haven't seen one doesn't mean they don't exist.

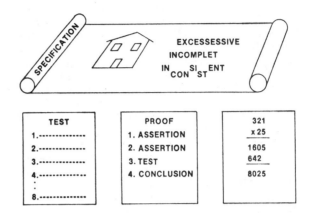

Figure 12. The Problem of Verifying Correctness.

It is also unfortunate that for most problems mathematical proofs of correctness are as difficult to produce as a correct program. They have the additional disadvantage that a program must be reproven each time it is modified. Apparently some people can write and prove their programs quickly and easily. For most of us, however, the day to day proving of programs is still a long ways off.

The most promising approach for the near future may lie in finding a constructive proof of correctness. We will really have something if a design methodology can be found which leads one through the design process step by step and guarantees the correctness of the final program if each of the steps has been done correctly. While I don't remember that 321 x 25 is 8025, I do remember that 5 x 1 = 5, 5 x 2 = 10, 5 x 3 = 15, etc. Knowing these values and the steps of multiplication, I can rest assured that 8025 is indeed the correct answer. If only a design process existed which was as foolproof and easy to apply.

Without such a process we must live with a limitless capacity for producing errors (Weinberg pointed out that errors can be produced in arbitrarily large numbers for an arbitrarily low cost).

Correspondence. In Jackson's view, perhaps the most critical factor in determining the life-cycle cost of a program is the degree to which it faithfully models the problem environment (see Reference 1). That is, the degree to which the program model corresponds to the real world (see Figure 13). All too often we are faced with a situation in which a small local change in the problem environment results in a large diffuse change in the program which purports to model that environment.

The world is always bigger than the program specification says it is, but the specification can always be extended if it corresponds to reality.

Since users tend to be gradualists, the changes in a realistic problem model will tend to be gradual. If the program is built around the static versus the dynamic properties of the problem, it can prove to be resilient to changes which occur over many years.

While the program's model of the world cannot be complete, it must as a minimum be useful and true. If these criteria are met, many future maintenance and feature enhancement problems are avoided.

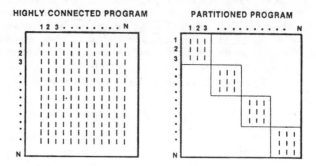

Figure 15. Low Connectivity Implies Low Maintenance Costs.

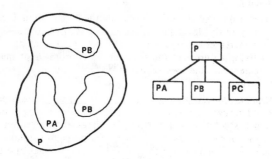

Figure 13. The Concept of Correspondence.

System Level Concepts

Consistency. One important objective of a good design methodology should be that of producing a consistent program structure independent of who is applying it (see Figure 14). Given the same problem environment, three different programs which model that environment using the same design methodology should essentially be the same.

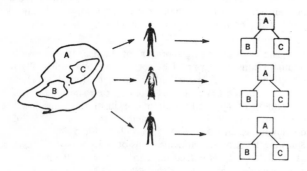

Figure 14. Different People Should Produce Similar Designs.

Unless consistent designs can be achieved by different people, there can never be a true right or a wrong structure for a given problem.

One of the problems with design methodologies like Functional Decomposition is that there is no one preferred, consistently obtainable solution. Instead, each designer seems to pull his own unique solution out of the air. There can never be a discussion of it being right or wrong, there can only be a discussion of my style versus your style.

Connectivity. The harmful effects of high connectivity on system modifiability can best be illustrated by using an analogy (see Figure 15 and Reference 8).

Consider a system composed of 100 light bulbs. Each light in the system can either be on or off. Connections are made between light bulbs such that if the light is on, it has a 50-percent chance of going off in the next second; if the light bulb is off, it has a 50-percent chance of going on in the next second provided one of the lights it is connected to is on. If none of the lights connected to it is on, the light stays off. Sooner or later this system of light bulbs will reach an equilibrium state in which all of the lights go off and stay off.

The average length of time required for this system to reach equilibrium is solely a function of the interconnection pattern of the lights. The most trivial interconnection pattern is one in which all of the lights operate independently. None of them is connected to any of it's neighbors. In this case, the average time for the system to reach equilibrium is approximately the time required for any given lamp to go off. The time for this to occur is approximately 2 seconds; and thus, the system can be expected to reach equilibrium in a matter of seconds.

At the other extreme, consider a case in which each light in the array is fully connected to all of the other lights in the array; that is, in Figure 15, consider a value of N equal to 100. The array on the left side of the figure then describes the connectivity matrix of the lights and shows that every light is connected to every other light. In this case the length of time required for the system to reach equilibrium is 10^{22} years. It is clear that this is a very long time when you consider that the current age of the universe is only 10^{10} years.

Now consider one final interconnection pattern in which the set of 100 lights is partitioned into ten sets of ten lights each, with no connections between the sets, but full interconnection within each set. In this case, the time required for the complete system of lights to reach equilibrium is approximately 17 minutes. This dramatically shows the effect of connectivity. In terms of the concepts described earlier, this example represents very high cohesion within each module and very low coupling between modules.

Much as proper physical partitioning can dramatically reduce the time required for the system of lights to reach equilibrium, proper functional partitioning can dramatically reduce the time required for a program which must be changed to reach stability. It has been said that errors are like criminals; if they just killed each other law enforcement would be a breeze. Unfortunately they go off killing other people too.

Concurrency. At the system level, different programs often model concurrent asynchronous processes. Thus a proper model of the system would include implementing concurrent asynchronous programs. The initial partitioning of such a system often comes from a high level system flow diagram or data flow diagram. As shown in Figure 16, there is often a producer-consumer relationship between process A and process B. For example, process A could produce data which process B consumes.

Continuity/Change/Chaos. As noted by Belady and Lehman (Reference 9), a large program often appears to live a life of its own, independent of the noble intentions of those trying to control it. Two important observations are summarized in the Law of Continuing Change, and the Law of Increasing Entropy which are shown in Figure 17.

302

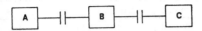

Figure 16. Cooperating Concurrent Processes.

Figure 17. Continuity/Change/Chaos.

These laws dramatize the key role played by the program structure during the life-cycle of software systems. The natural order of things is to produce disorder. If the program structure is unclear from the beginning, things will only get worse later. It is these two laws coupled with a poor program structure that have produced the maintenance cost horror stories.

Costs. Representative development cost trends were described by Boehm (see Reference 10) in the form of Figure 18.

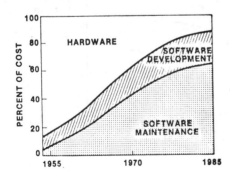

Figure 18. Development Cost Trends.

Some people have attributed this trend to the fact that thinking 10 times more efficiently is harder than getting 1000 times more speed from hardware. Michael Slavin has proposed that there is a fundamental truth of programmer arithmetic coming into play. That is, if it takes one programmer one year to do a job it will take two programmers two years to do the same job.

The magnitude of the problem is hitting people right where it hurts; in the pocketbook. Approximately $25 billion is now spent annually in the United States on software. People are gaining a life-cycle awareness which says that:

(1) Software is a much bigger problem than hardware.

(2) Maintenance costs often greatly exceed the cost of the initial development.

(3) Design and Analysis is a much more difficult problem than coding.

This says that a good design methodology should catch errors early in the development cycle. The relative cost of fixing an error increases dramatically as one gets further along. The cost of fixing an error in the field can be two orders of magnitude greater than the cost of fixing the error during a requirements review.

Optimization/Packaging. All too often people confuse packaging and design. Design is the process of partitioning a problem and it's solution into meaningful pieces. Optimization and Packaging consist of clustering pieces of a problem solution into computer load modules which run within system space and time requirements without unduly compromising the integrity of the original design.

There are at least three different types of modules which must be considered in programming. They are functional modules, data modules, and physical modules. Packaging is concerned with placing functional modules and data modules into physical modules. In packaging a program, several of these pieces of the program may be put together as one load module or even written together as one program. As shown in Figure 19, independent program functions can be lexically included in the calling module to save time and memory, or to improve understandability.

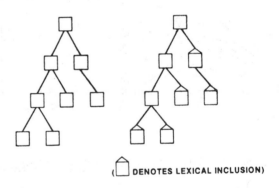

(⌂ DENOTES LEXICAL INCLUSION)

Figure 19. Packaging and Design are Separate Problems.

It is in the packaging phase of a design where optimization should be considered for the first time. This phase is done at the very end and great care should be taken to preserve the program structure which you have worked so hard to create. In Jackson's words it is very easy to make a program that is right, faster. It is very difficult to make a program that is fast, right. Once an optimization has been cast in code it is like concrete. It's very difficult to undo.

Summary

The concepts described in this section are listed in Figure 20.

In the next section, some of these concepts will be used to characterize and evaluate each of the different design methodologies.

CODE

- ABSTRACTION
- COMMUNICATION
- CLARITY
- CONTROL

MODULE

- COHESION
- COUPLING
- COMPLEXITY
- CORRECTNESS
- CORRESPONDENCE

SYSTEM

- CONSISTENCY
- CONNECTIVITY
- CONCURRENCY
- CONTINUITY
- CHANGE
- CHAOS
- COST
- PACKAGING

Figure 20. Structural Analysis Concepts.

STRUCTURED DESIGN METHODOLOGIES

Design has been defined as "the process of making dreams come true" (see Reference 11). Unfortunately, many of these dreams get so large and complex that they become nightmares.

In this section we will deal with the problem of reducing program size and complexity by examining different methods of partitioning the problem and it's solution. We want an approach which untangles independent parts of the problem so that we can achieve a "separation of concerns."

While there are a lot of design methodologies around, only a few of them have been extensively tested. Three types of methodologies which have been used more than most are:

(1) Functional Decomposition.

(2) Data Flow Design Method.

(3) Data Structure Design Method.

In this section, each method will be reviewed and in the next section an example will be worked through using all three methodologies.

Functional Decomposition

Design Strategy. Functional Decomposition is simply the divide and conquer technique applied to programming (see Figure 21).

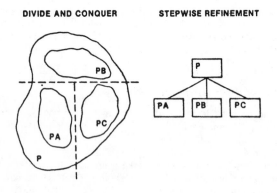

Figure 21. Functional Decomposition.

When applied in stages or levels it is sometimes achieved by a process called stepwise refinement. It has been popularized by a host of people including: Dijkstra, Wirth, Parnas, Liskov, Mills, Baker, and McHenry (see References 12-17). The general concept involves pretending that you are programming on a machine which has a language powerful enough to solve your problem in only a handful of commands. In your level 1 decomposition, you simply write down that handful of commands and you have a complete program.

In your level 2 decomposition you try to refine each of your level 1 instructions into a set of less powerful instructions. By continuing to successively refine each instruction, one level at a time, you eventually get to a program which can be executed on your own real computer. In carrying out this process you will have decomposed the problem into its constituent functions by "stepwise refinement."

There are several problems involved in applying this technique. First, the method specifies that a functional decomposition be performed but does not say what you are decomposing with respect to. If you decompose with respect to time you get modules like Initialize, Process, and Terminate and have a structure with temporal cohesion. If you cluster functions which access a shared data base you have made a start toward defining abstract data types and will get communicational cohesion. If you decompose using a data flow diagram you may end up with sequential cohesion. If you decompose around a flowchart you will often end up with logical cohesion.

The problems faced in doing a Functional Decomposition are similar to those faced by a manager trying to reorganize an organization. The organization could be divided into project organizations or it could be divided along functional lines. Neither choice is correct in all situations. It depends upon the circumstances and goals which apply at that point in time.

Experience. Functional Decomposition has been around for more than a decade, so there have been many well documented success stories and even a few well documented failures. One success story which I have seen was summarized quite well by the designers using the diagrams in Figure 22.

USED WITH: HIERARCHICAL STRUCTURE, STEPWISE REFINEMENT, HIGH LEVEL LANGUAGE, TEAMS, WALKTHRUS, CAUSE EFFECT CHARTS, ETC.

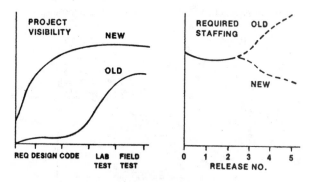

Figure 22. Functional Decomposition Experience.

Note that project visibility was dramatically improved by the application of Functional Decomposition with the other techniques noted. Note also that project staffing was reduced over that which would normally have been required. In this particular example, there was a lot of personnel turnover during the life of the project. This was taken in stride, partly due to the effects of the new techniques.

Comments. In surveying several projects and talking to a number of people, it seems that Functional Decomposition can lead to a "good" hierarchical program structure if carefully applied. It sometimes leads toward logical cohesion, and occasionally leads toward telescoping. (i.e. toward defining smaller and smaller modules which are not independent but in fact have strong coupling with each other. See Reference 18.) Applying Functional Decomposition to mathematical functions (e.g. SQUARE ROOT) is relatively easy. Unfortunately, SQUARE ROOT is the exception rather than the rule.

The disadvantages of Functional Decomposition are numerous. For any given problem, the number of potential decompositions can seem to be almost infinite. This makes applying the technique much more of an art than a science. I know that Dijkstra can do beautiful Functional Decompositions. Unfortunately, programmers like Dijkstra are hard to find.

In Johnson's words Functional Decomposition seems to be a triumph of individual intellect over lack of an orderly strategy (see Reference 18). The question of "Decomposition with respect to what?" is always a point to ponder. The measures of "goodness" are very difficult to apply consistently. Finally, this method requires that the intellectual tasks of problem modeling and program construction be addressed simultaneously. Ideally, these two tasks would be separated.

Data Flow Design Method.

The data flow design method was first proposed by Larry Constantine (Reference 2) and has since been propogated and extended by Ed Yourdon and Glen Myers (References 2,3). It has been called by several different names including Transform Centered Design, and Composite Design. In it's simplest form it is nothing more than the functional decomposition of a problem obtained by successive application of the engineering definition of a black box. When given a function, one considers the inputs, the outputs, and the transform in between. Each of these functions is then considered to be a new black box and the process is repeated.

Design Strategy. The first step in using the Data Flow Design Method is that of drawing a Data Flow Diagram (see Figure 23). In some sense this diagram is a model of the problem environment which is later transformed into a program structure.

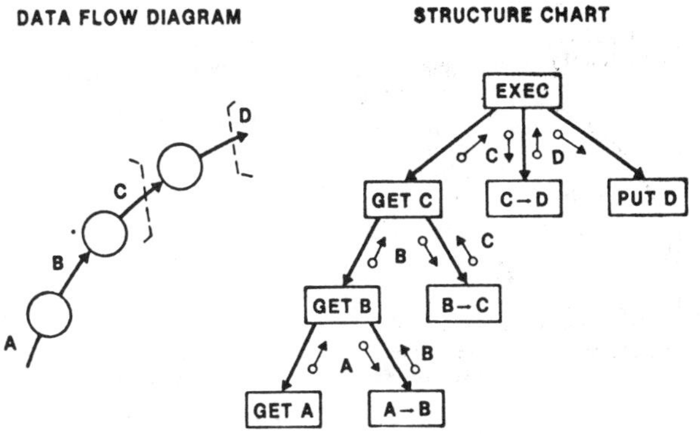

DATA FLOW DIAGRAM   STRUCTURE CHART

Figure 23. Data Flow Design Method.

Where the modules in Functional Decomposition tend to be attached by a "Uses" relationship, the bubbles in a Data Flow Diagram could be labeled "Becomes". That is data input A becomes data output B. Data B becomes C, C becomes D, etc.

Once the Data Flow Diagram is drawn, the program structure chart is derived in a relatively mechanical way. Given the Data Flow Diagram of Figure 23, the modules of the structure chart are defined as GET A, GET B, and GET C. Also defined are the modules which transform A into B, B into C, C into D, and so on. The outputting module is illustrated by the PUT D

module. The GET modules are called Afferent modules and the PUT modules are called Efferent modules (Reference 2). The TRANSFORM C TO D module is known as the "central transform."

Note that a lot of data is passed between modules in the structure in an assembly line fashion. This results in sequential cohesion and by Constantine's measure of goodness, the Data Flow Design Method produces a very good program structure.

It should be noted that concentrating the I/O functions in the afferent and efferent "ears" of the program structure may or may not model the problem environment accurately. In many cases this seems very artificial to me and seems to violate the principle of correspondence.

Note that the central transform in this case is shown as being quite simple, but in many cases it requires a sophisticated Functional Decomposition in its own right. That is, except for the "ears" which come from the data flow diagram, one is forced right back to the art of Functional Decomposition. A better approach may be to look at implementing bubbles on the data flow diagram as concurrent asynchronous processes which pass messages.

Experience. The concept of Data Flow Design came later than pure Functional Decomposition and therefore has not been tested as extensively. Apparently several projects within IBM are using the "Composite design" version of Data Flow Design with varying degrees of success. I have seen several success stories which praise the ease of doing Data Flow Design but they have also pointed out the high overhead associated with passing all that data from one "ear" to the other "ear" of their structure diagrams.

The concepts of Coupling and Cohesion which accompanied the introduction of the Data Flow Design method (Reference 2) have been found to be at least thought provoking and on some occasions have even been very revealing. They have given people a language to express previously unverbalized thoughts.

Comments. The Data Flow Design Method can be used to produce a hierarchical program structure with all of it's intrinsic advantages. The tendency is strongly toward modules with sequential cohesion at the system level, although within the central transform anything can happen.

The partitioning of a program into afferent and efferent branches seems to be artificial at best. In more involved programs this separation is difficult to enforce.

I feel that the concepts of cohesion and coupling represent a real step forward from straight Functional Decomposition. A qualitative measure of goodness is not as good as a quantitative measure, but it is better than nothing. Likewise I feel that the Data Flow Diagram in some sense models the problem before one must worry about the detailed structure of the program. Unfortunately, deriving the correct Data Flow Diagram (or "bubble chart") is still very much an art for large systems.

Data Structure Design Method

The Data Structure Design Method was developed in slightly different forms by Michael Jackson in England and Warnier in France (see References 1 and 19). (In this paper Jackson's formulation and notation will be used).

In both cases the premise is that a program sees the world through it's data structures and therefore a correct model of the data structures can be transformed into a correct model of the world. This view was stated earlier as the principle of correspondence and is largely due to Michael Jackson who states that,

> "A program that doesn't directly correspond to the problem environment is not poor, is not bad, but is wrong!"

Design Strategy. The Data Structure Design Method is built on the premise that simple programs are hard to write. Complex programs are impossible. The trick then is to partition complex problems into simple programs.

The first step involves drawing a system flow diagram as shown schematically in Figure 24.

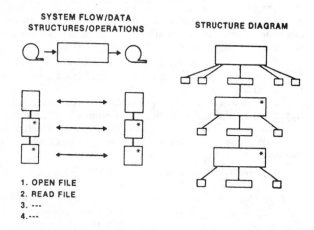

Figure 24. **Data Structure Design Method.**

Given a system flow diagram, the data structure of each file is represented via data structure diagrams. If the data structures correspond well (i.e. have no structure clashes) then a program structure can be drawn which encompasses both data structures. Since the program structure models the data structures, and most operations are performed on data elements, it becomes a relatively simple task to appropriately "allocate" elementary operations to a component of the program structure. These elementary operations are shown by the small squares in the structure diagram and are shown to be listed in the lower left hand corner of Figure 24.

Since the data structures for a given problem specification are usually reasonably well defined, and the problem structure mirrors the data structures, most of the people using this method will come up with remarkably similar program structures. (Thus this method to a large degree satisfies the principle of consistency).

The major problem with the Data Structure Design Method is, in Jackson's words, that it is being developed bottom up. That is, it is clear how to apply it to relatively small problems but a methodology for applying it to large problems has yet to be developed.

Experience. Neither the Jackson nor the Warnier methodologies were widely used in this country until quite recently. They have, however, been used for a number of years in Europe. In my opinion, Jackson's method is closer to a true methodology than any of the other design methodologies currently available. In most cases it is repeatable, teachable, reliable, and results in a program structure which is an excellent model of reality.

Comments. The Data Structure Design Method results in a hierarchical program structure if the data structure is hierarchical. It produces multiple, independent hierarchies if they are present in the problem environment. It is difficult to determine the level of cohesion of the modules within the resulting program structure. In some cases it tends to be functional, in other cases communicational. By modeling the data structures and therefore the problem environment first, the problem modeling task is done before the program construction task.

While there is still no clear methodology for large systems and deriving the "correct" data structures can be quite difficult, it still seems that this method is a big step forward. Being able to ask whether a structure is right or wrong is somehow much more satisfying than trying to decide whether it is good, better or best.

Summary

Summary of Claims. As shown in Figure 25, many claims have been made about the different strategies for designing software.

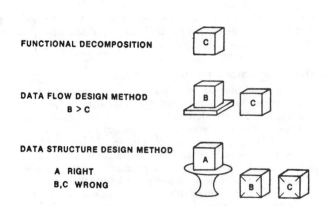

Figure 25. **Summary of Program Design Methodology Claims.**

In the case of Functional Decomposition, the proponents have largely said, "This is a good design, believe me." In the case of Data Flow Design Methods, people have said, "Program B is better than program C. Let me tell you why." In the case of Data Structure Design Methods, the claim is that, "A is right, B and C are wrong." In the words of Michael Jackson,

"A program that works isn't necessarily right."

The Data Structure Design Method will tell you why program B and C are wrong and why program A is right. It will also show you how to construct program A.

State of the Art. In my view there is still a lot of room for innovation in the area of program design methodologies. the current state of the art was represented schematically by Johnson (Reference 18) in the form of Figure 26.

Clearly we need to get a better handle on the "magic" part.

McDONALD'S FROZEN FOOD WAREHOUSE PROBLEM

The McDonald's example and it's Data Structure Design solution are patterned after Jackson's treatment of the "stores movement" problem (see reference 1).

Problem Specification

McDonald's Frozen Food Warehouse receives and distributes food items. Each shipment received or distributed is recorded on a punched card which contains the name of the item, the type of shipment (R for received, D for distributed) and the quantity of each item affected. These transaction cards are sorted by another program and appear grouped in alphabetical order by item name. A management report showing the net-change in inventory of each item is to be produced once a week.

The input file and output report formats are shown in Figure 27.

306

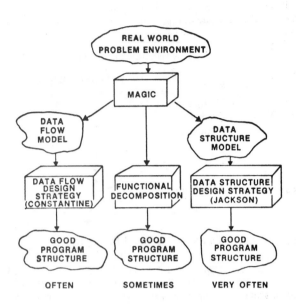

Figure 26. Current State of the Art.

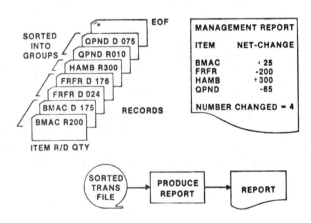

Figure 27. McDonald's Warehouse I/O Formats.

Functional Decomposition

The hero who originally designed this program just happened to be named Ivan Norbert Competent, or I. N. Competent for short. Ivan is a very "with it" fellow. He swore off GO TOs years ago. His code is structured like the Eiffel Tower. He can whip out a neatly indented structured program in nothing flat.

The Design Phase. In this particular case, Ivan was in a bit of a hurry, but he did of course take the time to do volume testing. After all you can't be too careful. In doing his design, Ivan was very careful to do the five level, hierarchical, functional decomposition shown in Figure 28.

Clearly recognizing the first card from each item group is the key. Once this card is found, everything else falls into place.

At this point, it may be worth examining the structure of Ivan's program. The obvious question is, "Is this a good decomposition?" The obvious reply is "Good with respect to what?"

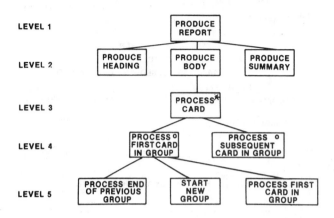

Figure 28. A Five Level Functional Decomposition.

If we apply the concept of cohesion to this structure, it might seem that the level 1 module (PRODUCE REPORT) has temporal cohesion since the PRODUCE HEADING module is something like an INITIALIZATION module and the PRODUCE SUMMARY module is something like a TERMINATE module. On the other hand one could argue that the HEADING, BODY and SUMMARY are such integral parts of the report that this is really functional cohesion.

Likewise the PROCESS CARD module seems to have been partitioned along temporal lines as well. On the other hand, PROCESS CARD seems to be an integral part of the PRODUCE BODY module so maybe PRODUCE BODY is also functionally cohesive.

As you can tell by the preceding dialogue, while levels of cohesion may be an advance from having no basis for comparison, they are still difficult to apply consistently. In cases where more than one type of cohesion seems to be present, the rule (Reference 2) is to assume it is really the higher of the two levels.

It should be noted that Figure 28 represents but one of many possible Functional Decompositions of this problem.

Just to show that he believed in following the steps of Stepwise Refinement faithfully, Ivan wrote the level 1, 2, and 3 programs shown in Figure 29.

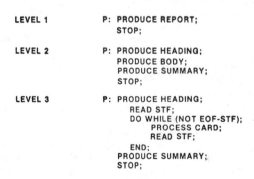

Figure 29. Steps in Functional Decomposition.

The level 4 decomposition, shown in Figure 30, started to look like a finished product.

```
P: PRODUCE HEADING;

    READ STF;
    DO WHILE (NOT EOF—STF);
        IF FIRST CARD IN GROUP THEN
            PROCESS FIRST CARD IN GROUP;
            ELSE PROCESS  SUBSEQUENT CARD IN GROUP;
            READ STF;
    END;

    PRODUCE SUMMARY;
    STOP;
```

Figure 30. Level 4 Functional Decomposition.

The level 5 decomposition shown in Figure 31 was the finished product.

```
P: PRODUCE HEADING;

    READSTF;
    DO WHILE (NOT EOF—STF);
    IF FIRST CARD IN GROUP THEN
        DO;
                    PROCESS END OF PREVIOUS GROUP;

                    PROCESS START OF NEW GROUP
                    PROCESS CARD;

        END;
        ELSE DO; PROCESS CARD;
            END;
        READ STF;
    END;

    PRODUCE SUMMARY;
    STOP;
```

Figure 31. The Final Functional Decomposition.

In his normal thorough manner, Ivan volume tested his program and turned it over to the user. It was perfect except for one very small glitch. You see the systems programmers were still playing with the compiler and obviously hadn't fixed all of the errors. The result was that the program worked fine but some garbage appeared on the first line of the output immediately after the headings. This of course would disappear as soon as they fixed that %&"**?> compiler.

The Friendly User Phase. Now Ronald McUser was a friendly sort of person. He had been in a hurry to use the program so he had not complained about the small glitch which would of course disappear very soon. Ronald's boss Big Mac, however, failed to see the humor of it all. The compiler had been fixed for three months now and the Management Report that went to the Board of Directors still had that garbage in it.

Finally, one day, Ronald could stand it no more. The program had to be fixed. When Ronald came down, Ivan was in his cubicle listening to an audio cassette of Dijkstra's Turing lecture. He of course didn't learn anything; that's the way he had always done things. Ronald showed Ivan the printout shown in Figure 32.

COMPILER ERROR?

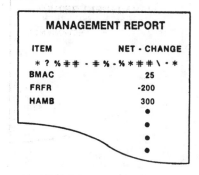

Figure 32. A Small Problem.

After a few MMMs and AAAHHHHs and AAAHHHAAAs he saw the problem. The first time through the program there was no previous group. Thus the output was just random noise. The solution to any first time through problem is of course obvious. Add a first time switch (see Figure 33).

```
P: PRODUCE HEADING;
    SW1:=0;
        READSTF;
        DO WHILE (NOT EOF—STF);
            IF FIRST CARD IN GROUP THEN
                DO;IF SW1=1 THEN
                    DO;  PROCESS END OF PREVIOUS GROUP;
                    END; SW1: = 1;
                            PROCESS START OF NEW GROUP
                            PROCESS CARD;

            END;
            ELSE DO; PROCESS CARD;
                END;
            READ STF;
        END;

        PRODUCE SUMMARY;
        STOP;
```

Figure 33. Quick Fix No. 1.

The Maintenance Phase. Six months later our hero was in the McDonald's "think room" contemplating possible job opportunities, when Ronald McUser came in and said, "I put 80 transactions in last week and nothing came out!" Our hero looked at the printout (see Figure 34) and saw that indeed, nothing had come out.

Ivan knew what the problem was immediately. It must be a hardware problem. After all, his program had been running nearly a year now with only one small complaint.

Well I. N. spent most of the night running hardware diagnostics until Steve Saintly (a keypunch operator) wandered by and said, "With that nation-wide special on Big Macs last week, that's all we handled. Everything else had to wait."

BIG MAC ATTACK!

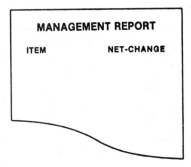

Figure 34. Another Small Problem.

A little later, Sally Saintly came by and said, "Isn't it about time you included those new Zebra Sodas in the Management Report?"

By this time, Ivan was very discouraged with his diagnostics so he followed last weeks inputs through the code. "HORRORS! There was only one item group processed last week, Big Macs!"

As Ivan soon discovered, the last item group was never processed. Since only one item group was processed all week (Big Macs) nothing was output. Up until this time only Zebra Sodas had been skipped. Since they were not a big winner, it seems that no one had even cared that they had been left off. In fact everyone assumed they were being left off on purpose. Ivan's solution is shown in Figure 35.

```
P: PRODUCE HEADING;
   SW1:=0;
      READSTF;
      DO WHILE (NOT EOF—STF);
         IF FIRST CARD IN GROUP THEN
            DO;IF SW1=1 THEN
               DO;  PROCESS END OF PREVIOUS GROUP;
               END; SW1: = 1;
                     PROCESS START OF NEW GROUP
                     PROCESS CARD;

            END;
         ELSE DO; PROCESS CARD;
            END;
         READ STF;
      END;
            PROCESS END OF LAST GROUP;

   PRODUCE SUMMARY;
   STOP;
```

Figure 35. Quick Fix No. 2.

Meanwhile Sally Saintly asked, "Why didn't you see that during all that volume testing you did? You tied up the machine for most of a day."

The answer again is obvious. In volume testing you put in thousands of inputs but don't look at the output.

Passing the Baton. Six months later Ivan was feeling pretty pleased with himself. He had just turned the program over to a new hire. There would still be some training, but everything should go well. After all hadn't the program run for nearly a year and one-half with only a couple of small problems. Suddenly Ronald burst in, "I thought you fixed this problem and here it is again." (See Figure 36.)

TRUCKERS STRIKE!

Figure 36. Yet Another Small Problem.

Ivan knew immediately what the problem was. That new program librarian that they had forced him to use, had put in an old version of the program which didn't have his first patch in it.

After many heated comments plus a core dump, I. N. was baffled. Finally in desperation he sat down to look at the input data and found out there wasn't any. Last week a trucker's strike had shut down the warehouse. Nothing came in; Nothing went out. They ran the program anyway. Good grief, who would have thought they would run the program with no inputs!

The problem, as it turns out, was that the new PROCESS END OF LAST GROUP module needed protection just like the PROCESS END OF PREVIOUS GROUP module had before. Since that first time switch worked so nicely before, it's clearly the solution to apply again (see Figure 37).

```
P: PRODUCE HEADING;
   SW1:=0;   SW2=0;
      READSTF;
      DO WHILE (NOT EOF—STF);
         IF FIRST CARD IN GROUP THEN
            DO;IF SW1=1 THEN
               DO;  PROCESS END OF PREVIOUS GROUP;
               END; SW1: = 1;
                     PROCESS START OF NEW GROUP
                     PROCESS CARD;

            END;
         ELSE DO; PROCESS CARD; SW2: = 1;
            END;
         READ STF;
      END; IF SW2:=1  THEN
            DO;  PROCESS END OF LAST GROUP;
            END;
   PRODUCE SUMMARY;
   STOP;
```

Figure 37. Quick Fix No. 3.

We all know now that Ivan's troubles are all over. Or are

they? Two months later Sally Saintly came in and said, "Where are the Zippo sandwiches?" They were in for two months but now they've suddenly disappeared from the report.

After much complaining that the new hire was supposed to maintain that program now, Ivan looked at the input data and noticed that only one order per item was issued during the whole run.

"What Happened?" he exclaimed.

It seems that a new manager, Mary Starr, had started a new policy to try and get things better organized. She had asked each of the stores to place only one order a day instead of placing orders at random. In addition she had said that it would be nice if they could schedule things so that each day the warehouse only had to be concerned with receiving one particular item, and the next day with distributing that item. In addition she wanted the Management Report Program run once a day from now on.

The effect on Ivan's program was to drop Zippo sandwiches (see Figure 38).

LET'S GET ORGANIZED!

MANAGEMENT REPORT

ITEM	NET-CHANGE
BMAC	+25
FRFR	-200
●	●
●	●
●	●
ZEBRA SODAS	+100

Figure 38. Would You Believe Yet Another Small Problem?

Instead of moving the set for S2 the safest thing to do, according to the principles of defensive programming, is to add an extra set. Since you don't know what you're doing you never touch a previous fix, just add a new one (see Figure 39).

Now we can all rest assured that Ivan's program works, right?

The effect of all of these changes on the program structure is shown in Figure 40.

What was Ivan Norbert's major sin? It was simply that the program structure didn't correspond to the problem structure. In the original data there existed something called an item group. There is no single component in Ivan's program structure which corresponds to an item group. Thus the actions which should be performed once per group, before a group, or after a group, have no natural home. They are spread all over the program and have to rely on first time switches and the like to control them. Instead of components which start a new group, process a group, or process the end of a group, we have a mess.

In Jackson's words, when this correspondence is not present, the program is not poor, suboptimal, inefficient, or tricky. It's WRONG. The problems we have seen are in reality nothing but self inflicted wounds stemming from an incorrect program structure.

Data Flow Design Method

The heroine who designed this program was Ivan's sister, Ivy. Ivy Nadine to be more specific. Ivy is a child of the late 60's. When modular programming came she jumped right on the

```
P: PRODUCE HEADING;
   SW1: = 0;   SW2 = 0;
      READSTF;
      DO WHILE (NOT EOF—STF);
         IF FIRST CARD IN GROUP THEN
            DO; IF SW1=1 THEN
               DO;  PROCESS END OF PREVIOUS GROUP;
               END; SW1: = 1;
                  PROCESS START OF NEW GROUP
                  PROCESS CARD;
                  SW2: = 1;
            END;
         ELSE DO; PROCESS CARD;  SW2: = 1;
            END;
         READ STF;
      END; IF SW2: = 1  THEN
            DO;  PROCESS END OF LAST GROUP;
            END;
   PRODUCE SUMMARY;
   STOP;
```

Figure 39. Quick Fix No. 4.

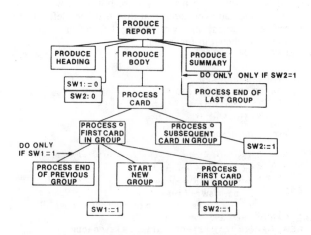

Figure 40. Functional Decomposition with Quick Fixes.

bandwagon. Her modules had only one entrance and one exit. She passed all of her parameters in each call statement. Each of her modules performs only a single logical task, is independent, and can be separately tested. She remembers nearly every error that she has ever made. She remembers the day she designed this program quite well.

The Design Phase. Ivy has learned to make good use of a program librarian. In designing this program, she wrote the program, gave the coding sheets to the librarian, and went on to read the gospel according to Harlan Mills.

Her program structure is shown in Figure 41.

Note that the concept of a card group emerges somewhat naturally out of the data flow diagram and leads to a reasonably straightforward program structure. Note that the TRANSFORM CARD IMAGES TO CARD GROUP module is shown with a roof (denoting lexical inclusion). That is, while TRANSFORM CARD IMAGES TO CARD GROUP is a functional module it is not necessarily a physical module. In this example it will be packaged together with the GET CARD GROUP module.

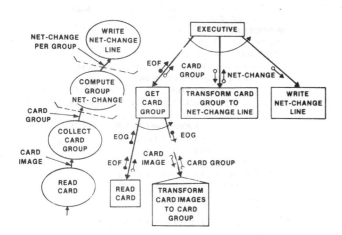

Figure 41. Data Flow Design Structure.

The curved arrows in Figure 26 denote iteration. That is, the GET CARD GROUP module calls its two subtending modules once per card image. The EXECUTIVE module calls it's three subtending modules once per card group. Note that the READ CARD module is assumed to pass an End of File flag up the chain when it is detected. Ivy's program listing is shown in Figure 42.

```
EXECUTIVE:  EOF: = FALSE;

    DO WHILE(EOF = FALSE);
        GET_CARD_GROUP(CG,EOF          );
        TRANSFORM_CG_TO_NC_LINE(CG,NC);
        WRITE_NC_LINE (NC,EOF);
    END;                    STOP;

GET_CARD_GROUP(CG,EOF         ): EOG:=FALSE; I: = 0;
    DO WHILE (EOG =FALSE); I: = I +1;
        READ_CARD (CI,EOG,EOF      );CG(I) = CI;
    END;              RETURN;

READ_CARD(CI,EOG,EOF        ):
    NEW_CARD: = READ  STF;
    IF NEW_CARD_ITEM ≠ CRITEM THEN
        DO; EOG: = TRUE; CRITEM=NEW_CARD_ITEM;
                    END;
    ELSE      CI: =NEW_CARD;
    IF CI=EOF _ STF THEN EOF:=TRUE;  RETURN;
```

Figure 42. Data Flow Design Program.

Only three of the six modules are shown. The TRANSFORM CARD IMAGES TO CARD GROUP module was lexically included in the GET CARD GROUP module. The other two modules are not necessary for this particular discussion. Note for starters that the READ CARD module leaves much to be desired.

The program librarian faithfully executed his duties and brought Ivy back the printout shown in Figure 43.

It seems that Ivy had forgotten to make sure all of her variables had been initialized. Oh well, this should be easy. How about setting CRITEM:=XXXX at the beginning of the GET CARD GROUP module. That would be before CRITEM was used the first time and sort of has a symmetry about it with the

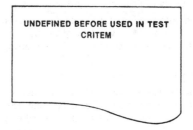

Figure 43. A Small Problem.

way EOG (End of Group) is initialized.

Unfortunately, something just didn't seem right about it. GET CARD GROUP gets executed many times during the program and CRITEM only needs to be initialized once.

Ivy decided to initialize CRITEM at the very beginning instead. Of course that does mean passing it as a parameter up two levels just for being initalized, but that certainly sounds better than a bunch of first time switches (see Figure 44).

```
EXECUTIVE:  EOF: = FALSE;
    CRITEM: = XXXX;
    DO WHILE(EOF = FALSE);
        GET_CARD_GROUP(CG,EOF,CRITEM      );
        TRANSFORM_CG_TO_NC_LINE(CG,NC);
        WRITE_NC_LINE (NC,EOF);
    END;                STOP;

GET_CARD_GROUP(CG,EOF,CRITEM      ): EOG:=FALSE; I: = 0;
    DO WHILE (EOG=FALSE); I: = I +1;
        READ_CARD (CI,EOG,EOF,CRITEM      );CG(I) = CI;
    END;              RETURN;

READ_CARD(CI,EOG,EOF,CRITEM      ):
    NEW_CARD: = READ  STF;
    IF NEW_CARD_ITEM ≠ CRITEM THEN
        DO; EOG: = TRUE; CRITEM=NEW_CARD_ITEM;
                    END;
    ELSE      CI: =NEW_CARD;
    IF CI=EOF _ STF THEN EOF:=TRUE;  RETURN;
```

Figure 44. Quick Fix No. 1.

On the next run, Ivy's efforts were rewarded with some output. Nothing fancy but still some output (see Figure 45).

"What happened to the heading?" exclaimed Ivy. "That data link must be dropping bits again."

"Where did you write out the heading?" asked the program librarian. Enter Quick Fix no. 2.

"Wait, what about that garbage in the front?"

The problem, of course, is that the program has no way of knowing when it's through with a group until it's already started processing the next group. Thus the first card of a new group serves as a key to tell the rest of the program to send on the previous group. It can't do this, however, without distorting the structure.

"I think it's time to call out my secret weapon," said Ivy, "my UNREAD command." Enter quick fix No. 3. (See Figure 46.)

Field Debugging. This fix apparently worked fine for about two months. It was not exactly speedy, but it did work. Then

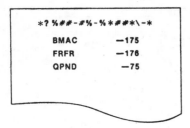

```
*? %##-#%-%###\-*
BMAC        -175
FRFR        -176
QPND        -75
```

Figure 45. Another Small Problem.

```
EXECUTIVE:  EOF: = FALSE;  WRITE HEADING;

    CRITEM: = XXXX;
    DO WHILE(EOF = FALSE);
        GET_CARD_GROUP(CG,EOF ,CRITEM    );
        TRANSFORM_CG_TO_NC_LINE(CG,NC);
        WRITE_NC_LINE (NC,EOF);
    END;                STOP;


GET_CARD_GROUP(CG,EOF ,CRITEM    ): EOG:=FALSE; I: = 0;
    DO WHILE (EOG=FALSE); I: = I +1;
        READ_CARD (CI,EOG,EOF ,CRITEM    );CG(I) = CI;
    END;            RETURN;


READ_CARD(CI,EOG,EOF ,CRITEM    ):
    NEW_CARD: = READ  STF;
        IF NEW_CARD_ITEM ≠ CRITEM THEN
            DO; EOG: = TRUE; CRITEM = NEW_CARD_ITEM;
            UNREAD STF;  END;
        ELSE    CI: = NEW_CARD;
        IF CI = EOF _ STF THEN EOF: = TRUE; RETURN;
```

Figure 46. Quick Fixes No. 2 and No. 3.

all of the sudden a visit from on high. Big Mac himself came down and said, "Our people in Provo, Utah have been trying to bring up your program and it just doesn't work."

It turns out that in Provo they never did find it necessary to buy a tape reader. Ivy's UNREAD operation didn't work on cards. This meant that Ivy had to find another way of UNREADing.

In this Data Flow Design, the equivalent of an UNREAD is very messy at best. It corrupts the structure badly no matter how it's done. Modules end up storing internal states or values, and first time switches abound.

In Ivy's case, she chose to read ahead by one, passing state information by SW1 and storing the NEW CARD value within module READ CARD. Other solutions are possible, of course, but it isn't clear that they are a whole lot better (see Figure 47).

The effect of these changes on the program stucture is shown dramatically in Figure 48.

In Jackson's words, Ivy has committed arboricide (the killing of trees). What was a nice clean tree structure now has two programs calling the same READ CARD module. In my mind, I think that READ and WRITE operations should be thought of as general purpose I/O routines which are callable from anywhere within the program structure. To hope to constrain them to the "ears" of a structure diagram seems unwise at best.

In this simple program, of course, things look much better if we simply package the whole thing as one module. (See Figure 49).

```
EXECUTIVE:  EOF:=FALSE;  WRITE HEADING;  SW1:=FALSE;
    CRITEM: = XXXX;  CI:=READ STF;
    DO WHILE(CI NOT EOF-STF);
        EOG: = FALSE  I:=0;
        DO WHILE (EOG=FALSE);  I=I+1;
            IF SW1 = FALSE THEN NEW_CARD: = READ STF;
            IF NEW_CARD_ITEM≠CRITEM  THEN
                DO; EOG:=TRUE; CRITEM:=NEW_CARD_ITEM;
                SW1: = TRUE;
                END;
                ELSE DO; CI:=NEW_CARD  SW1:=FALSE;
                    END;
                CG(I) = CI;
        END;
        SW1:=TRUE
        TRANSFORM_CG_TO_NC_LINE (CG,NC);
        WRITE_NC_LINE (NC,EOF);
    END;
STOP;
```

Figure 47. Quick Fix No. 4.

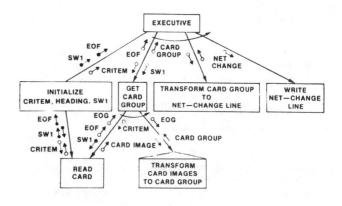

Figure 48. Data Flow Design With Fixes.

```
EXECUTIVE: EOF:=FALSE;  WRITE HEADING;  SW1:=FALSE;
    CRITEM:= XXXX;  CI:=READ STF;
    DO WHILE(CI NOT EOF-STF);
        EOG: = FALSE  I:=0;
        DO WHILE (EOG=FALSE);  I=I+1;
            IF SW1 = FALSE THEN NEW_CARD: = READ STF;
            IF NEW_CARD_ITEM≠CRITEM  THEN
                DO; EOG:=TRUE; CRITEM:=NEW_CARD_ITEM;
                SW1: = TRUE;
                END;
                ELSE DO; CI:=NEW_CARD  SW1:=FALSE;
                    END;
                CG(I) = CI;
        END;
        SW1:=TRUE
        TRANSFORM_CG_TO_NC_LINE (CG,NC);
        WRITE_NC_LINE (NC,EOF);
    END;
    STOP;
```

Figure 49. Data Flow Design Packaged in One Module.

The point, however, is that the problems Ivy had were representative of larger problems in larger programs when the Data Flow Design Method is applied.

Data Structure Design Method

Ida Marie Greatness is a Data Stucture Designer from way back. She went to London to study the Jackson Design Method. She learned French just so she could read Warnier's six paperbacks. (She says they lose a lot in translation). For the McDonald's problem she is certain that a Data Structure Design is the only way to go. After all it fit's into one of Jackson's canonical forms (i.e. the stores movement problem format.)

The Design Phase. The first thing Ida did was to draw the input and output data structures. From these structures she constructed the program structure which encompased all of the parts in each data structure. Where there were one to one correspondences, the modules took the form of "Produce ... From ..." or "Process ... to Produce ...." Where there were modules corresponding to only the input data structure, the form was "Process ...." Where there were modules corresponding to only the output data structure she formed modules of the form "Produce ...." These are all shown in Figure 50.

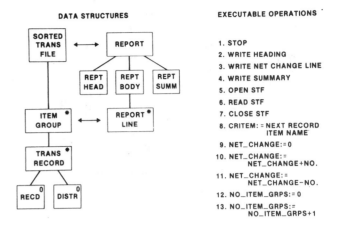

Figure 51. Listing Executable Operations.

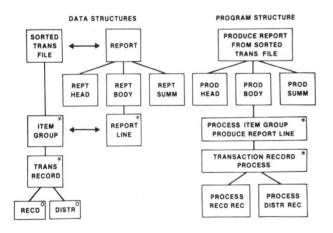

Figure 50. Data and Program Structures.

Executable operations are identified by working back from the output data structure to the input data structure (see Figure 51). If necessary the equivalent of a data flow diagram can be drawn with nodes being used to represent intermediate varibles.

One other operation is required for completeness. This is shown as operation number 8. This operation denotes the key which will be used in determining item group boundaries.

The last· design task involves allocating the executable operations to the program structure (see Figure 52).

In each case the questions to ask are "How often should this operation be executed?" and "Should this operation occur before or after ...?" The answer to the first question in this example could be once per report, once per sorted transaction file, once per heading, once per summary, once per item group, once per report line, once per transaction record, once per item received record or once per item distributed record.

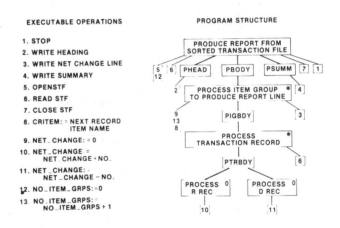

Figure 52. Allocating Executable Operations.

Clearly you open the STF (Sorted Transaction File) before you read it, you close the STF before you stop, etc.

Although the structure of the program is now secure, Jackson recommends one final step before coding. That is to translate the structure diagram into schematic logic as shown in Figure 53.

Schematic logic is very straight forward and easy to understand as long as your program labels are short. With long program labels it becomes a mess. (See Figure 54.)

This implies that both the data structure diagram and the schematic logic should be kept as a permanent part of the documentation. This seems unreasonable unless an automated structure chart drawer is available which will store the structure chart with the code in a convenient form so that it can be updated when the code is changed. At this point, available machine aids are far from adequate.

Ida's final program looked something like Figure 55.

It should be noted that this program implements the complete specification. (Although the functional decomposition solution said PRINT SUMMARY it included none of the logic to compile the summary data. The Data Flow Design Method solution ignored the problem of printing the summary altogether.)

```
PREPT SEQ                                    SCHEMATIC LOGIC
      OPEN STF;
      NO_ITEM_GRPS:=0;
      READ STF;
      WRITE HEADING;
      PBODY ITER UNTIL EOF - STF
            PIGRP SEQ
                  NET_CHANGE:=0;
                  NO_ITEM_GRPS:=NO_ITEM_GRPS+1;
                  CRITEM:=NEXT RECORD ITEM NAME
                  PIGBDY ITER UNTIL ITEM-NO OF NEXT TRANS ≠ CRITEM
                         P TRANS SEQ
                                 PTRBDY SEL CODE = R
                                        NET_CHANGE:=NET_CHANGE+NO;
                                 PTRBDY OR CODE = D
                                        NET_CHANGE:=NET_CHANGE-NO;
                                 PTRBDY END
                                        READ STF;
                                 PTRANS END
                         PIGBDY END
                         WRITE NET CHANGE LIN;
                  PIGRP END
      PBODY END
      WRITE SUMMARY;
      CLOSE STF;
      STOP;
PREPT END
```

Figure 53. Schematic Logic.

```
PRODUCE_REPORT SEQ
               OPEN STF;
               NO_ITEM_GRPS:=0;
               READ STF;
               WRITE HEADING;
   PRODUCE_REPORT_BODY ITER UNTIL EOF-STF

      PROCESS_ITEM_GROUP SEQ
                         NET_CHANGE:=0;
                         NO_ITEM_GRPS:=NO_ITEM_GRPS+1
                         CRITEM:=NEXT RECORD ITEM NAME
         PROCESS_ITEM_GROUP_BODY ITER UNTIL ITEM-NO OF NEXT TRANS ≠ CRITEM
         PROCESS_TRANSACTION_RECORD SEQ
            PROCESS_TRANSACTION_RECORD_BODY SEL CODE=R
                                            NET_CHANGE:=NET_CHANGE+NO;
            PROCESS_TRANSACTION_RECORD_BODY OR CODE=D
                                            NET_CHANGE:=NET_CHANGE-NO;
            PROCESS_TRANSACTION_RECORD_BODY END
                                            READ STF;
         PROCESS_TRANSACTION_RECORD END
         PROCESS_ITEM_GROUP_BODY END
                                 WRITE NET CHANGE LINE;
      PROCESS_ITEM_GROUP END
   PROCESS_REPORT_BODY END
               WRITE SUMMARY;
               CLOSE STF;
               STOP;
PRRODUCE_REPORT END
```

Figure 54. Schematic Logic With Long Labels.

```
PREPT        OPEN STF; READ STF; NO_ITEM_GRPS:=O;
             WRITE HEADING;
PBODY        DO WHILE (NOT EOF-STF);
PIGRP        NET_CHANGE:O;
             NO_ITEM_GRPS:=NO_ITEM_GRPS + 1;
             CRITEM:=NEXT RECORD ITEM NAME;
PIGBDY       DO WHILE (ITEM NO OF NEXT TRANS.=CRITEM)
PTRANS           IF (CODE=R) THEN
                     NET_CHANGE:=NET_CHANGE + NO;
                 ELSE IF (CODE=D) THEN
                     NET_CHANGE:=NET_CHANGE-NO;
                 ELSE PRINT "ERROR";
PTRANS END       READ STF;
PIGBDY END   END;
PIGRP END    WRITE NET CHANGE LINE
PBODY END    END;
             WRITE SUMMARY; CLOSE STF;
PREPT END    STOP;
```

Figure 55. Final Data Structure Design Program.

Did you notice any other errors? (e.g. was CI initialized in the Data Flow Design Method Example).

CONCLUSIONS

There are a number of different design methodologies available. Most of them have yet to be tested on a project of any size. The three methodologies discussed in this tutorial have all been used quite extensively and to a large measure successfully.

Each of the methods has certain characteristics and tends to be most useful for a certain class of problems. For problems of the McDonald's class it would seem that the Data Structure Design Method has distinct advantages. For other classes of problems the answer may be different. Clearly there is still a lot of good work that can be done.

The results I would like to see from the work yet to come are listed below:

(1) A complete methodology for partitioning "Big" problems.

(2) Both the shortcomings and attributes of existing methodologies better documented.

(3) Guidelines for combining methods when appropriate.

(4) A generally accepted metric for quantifying program complexity (or entropy).

(5) Help for the 4 out of 5 programmers maintaining and enhancing old programs.

(6) More published examples of real-time applications.

Some possible requirements on a "complete" methodology might include:

(1) It must include a rational procedure for partitioning and modeling the problem.

(2) It must result in consistant designs when applied by different people.

(3) It must systematically scale upward to very large problems while interacting consistently with a model of the real world.

(4) It must partition the design process as well as the problem solution.

(5) The correctness of individual design steps must guarantee the correctness of the final combination.

(6) It should minimize the need for innovation during the design process. The innovation should occur in the algorithm specification phase.

Until we know the "Right" method for designing the structure of a large program, I would propose the following "Interim" procedure.

(1) Define the high level language and operating system macros bottom up using the principle of abstraction to hide the peculiarities of the hardware and to create a desirable virtual machine environment.

(2) Map the system flow diagram into your virtual machine environment.

(3) Construct a data flow model of the "Big" problem.

(4) Construct data structure diagrams which correspond to each data flow path.

(5) Cluster and combine bubbles which can be treated by one of Jackson's "simple" programs.

(6) Use the Jackson Design Method to combine simple programs and reduce the number of intermediate files.

(7) Implement each cluster as concurrent, asynchronous processes if you are operating under a UNIX-like operating system.

(8) Work through the inversion process or construct some other kluge if a decent operating system is not available.

These "Interim" suggestions do not fit together well enough to call them a method, but they may form an approach to follow until a true methodology for large problems is found.

Note that for small problems, the method's described here can usually be made to work in quite a reasonable fashion.

ACKNOWLEDGMENTS

The discussion of the McDonald's functional decomposition solution is patterned (with permission) after a story called "Getting it Wrong" which has been related by Michael Jackson on numberous occasions in his short courses and seminars. "Getting it Wrong" will appear in print in an article currently being written by Michael, which will be published in the near future.

Much of the material presented here has been developed and discussed over the years with J. W. Johnson. His inputs and support are gratefully acknowledged.

REFERENCES

1. Jackson, M. A., *Principles of Program Design.* Academic Press, New York, 1975.

2. Yourdon, E., and Constantine, L. L., *Structured Design.* Yourdon, Inc., New York, 1975.

3. Myers, G. J., *Reliable Software Through Composite Design.* Petrocelli/Charter, New York, 1975.

4. Liskov, B., and Zilles, S, "Programming with Abstract Data Types," Proc. ACM Conference on Very High-Level Languages, SIGPLAN Notices, April, 1974, Vol. 9.

5. Brooks, F. P., Jr., *The Mythical Man-Month.* Addison-Wesley Publishing Company, Reading, Massachusetts, 1975.

6. Dijkstra, E. W., "The Humble Programmer," Communications of the ACM 15, October 10, 1972, pp. 859-66.

7. *Implications of Using Modular Programming,* Central Computer Agency, London: Her Majesty's Stationery Office, 1973.

8. Alexander, C., *Notes on Synthesis of Form.* Cambridge, Massachusetts, Harvard University Press, 1964.

9. Belady, L. A., and Lehman, M. M., "Characteristics of Large Systems," Research Directions in Software Technology Proceedings, Brown University, October, 1977.

10. Boehm, B., "Software Engineering: R&D Trends and Defense Needs," Research Directions in Software Technology Proceedings, Brown University, October, 1977.

11. Koberg, D., and Bagnall, J., *The Universal Traveler.* William Kaufmann, Inc., Los Altos, California, 1976.

12. Dijkstra, E. W., *A Discipline of Programming.* Prentice-Hall Inc., Englewood Cliffs, N.J., 1976.

13. Wirth, N., *Systematic Programming.* Prentice-Hall, Englewood Cliffs, N.J., 1973.

14. Parnas, D. L., "Some Software Engineering Principles," (to be published), 1978.

15. Liskov, B. H., "A Design Mehodology for Reliable Software Systems." FJCC 72, 1972, pp. 191-99.

16. Cammack, W. B., and Rodgers, H. J., Jr., "Improving the Programming Process." IBM, Poughkeepsie, New York, TR 00.2483, October 19, 1973.

17. Baker, F. T., "Structured Programming in a Production Programming Environment," IEEE Transactions on Software Engineering, June, 1975, Vol. SE-1, No. 2, pp. 241-252.

18. Johnson, J. W., "Software Design Techniques," National Electronics Conference Proceedings, Chicago, Illinois, Oct. 12, 1977.

19. Warnier, J. D., *Logical Construction of Programs.* Van Nostrand Reinhold Company, New York, 1974.

Comparing Software Design Methodologies

by Lawrence J. Peters and Leonard L. Tripp

Software design has evolved to the stage where methodologies for handling classes of problems are proliferating. But just how helpful are they?

In progressing from infancy to adulthood, a human's approach to problem solving shifts dramatically. In infancy, a challenge such as locomotion is treated as new and different each time it is faced. After a while, it is recognized that a certain class of challenges can be met using the same approach. Similarly in software we have grown from treating each new development effort as unique to recognizing certain classes can be met by a specific approach. This type of evolutionary process quite evidently has already occurred in other professions such as architecture and engineering.

The last ten years in the software industry have been marked by a procession of new approaches to software design problems. The cause of this influx of software design methods is uncertain. Perhaps it is part of evolution or it may be due to the increasing complexity of the problems being addressed. In any event, the availability of so many approaches has left many wondering which—if any—they should adopt, which ones fit which classes of problems.

We've asked ourselves that question. We've studied several of the more promising or more popular approaches. And we think we can provide at least a partial answer.

Where do I begin? Now that I have begun, how do I measure my progress? How will I know when I am done? These questions have always tormented designers. Designers are also vexed by having to think intuitively, rationally, and procedurally at the same time during a design effort. As the effort progresses, the emphasis shifts, but all three modes often are involved simultaneously. At the outset, the designer initiates some idea or "spark" which sets a design into motion. He has an intuitive feel for the solution to the problem but suspects he may be wrong. So he scrutinizes his idea and then documents the conclusions. This process has been characterized as divergence, transformation, and convergence, in that order. The big problem is broken down into smaller problems,

they are solved, and then reassembled into *the* solution. Simple isn't it?

Not so, say those who have attempted to develop non-trivial designs. Some even conjecture that software designing is somewhat diabolical. On examining the process of design, it becomes apparent that there is no agreement on how to describe that process and/or its products. The following definition may be a helpful start; at least it works for several individual methods in the latest procession: *A software design method is a collection of techniques based upon a concept.*

Many forms of this notion are being championed. A representative list includes:

- Structured Design
- The Jackson Methodology
- Logical Construction of Programs
- METAStepwise Refinement (MSR)
- Higher Order Software (HOS)

The author of each such software design method has structured his solution to address the design issue(s) he views as germane. Quite understandably, each holds a different opinion. Those that advocate "Structured Design" declare that the key to a successful software design is the identification of the data flow through the system and the transformation(s) that the input data undergo in the process of becoming output.

A view held by those who advocate either the "Jackson Methodology" or the "Logical Construction of Programs" (the "Warnier Methodology") is that the identification of the inherent data structure is vital, and the structure of the data (input and output) can be used to derive the structure (and some details) of the program.

Advocates of META Stepwise Refinement (MSR) state that success is assured if the problem is solved several times, each solution being more detailed and complete than its predecessor.

Last, supporters for Higher Order Software (HOS) provide a set of axioms which must be used to attain success.

In addition to making certain as-

sumptions, each of the representative methods also prescribes a set of activities and techniques intended to ensure successful software design.

Structured design

Structured Design is based on concepts originated by Larry L. Constantine and later published by him while working with Ed Yourdon, and by Glenford J. Myers. (See Bibliography for exact references.)

The method consists of concepts, measures, analysis techniques, guidelines, rules-of-thumb, notation, and terminology. Reliance is placed upon following the flow of data through the system to formulate program design. The data flow is depicted through a special notational scheme which identifies each data transformation, transforming process, and the order of their occurrence.

The interpretation of the system specification is used to produce the data flow diagram, the diagram used to develop the structure chart, the structure chart to develop the data structure, and all of the results used to reinterpret the system specification. While the design process is iterative, the order of iteration is not rigid.

The process seems deceptively simple; but when attempts are made to use it, difficulties are encountered. For example, consistently identifying transformations of data is not easy to do. It is possible to be overly detailed in one part of the data flow and much less so in another. No formula is available to detect this condition.

Also, identifying afferent (incoming) and efferent (outgoing) flow boundaries plays an important role in the definition of the modules and their relationships. However, the boundaries of the modules can be moved *almost* arbitrarily, leading to different system structures. Again, no formal guide is provided.

Use of the structured design method does aid in the rapid definition and refinement of the data flows. The verification of the consistency of one data flow with its less detailed predecessor is crucial to this, but how to do the verif cation is not satisfactorily addressed. Admittedly, this activity has been addressed for a military command and control application we learned of, but the technique used there is not an integral part of the structured design method. We find that this method and particularly its graphics do reveal previously unknown properties of some systems, though, such as the generation of information already contained elsewhere in the system.

This method turns out to be well suited to design problems where a well-defined data flow can be derived from the problem specifications. We found that some of the characteristics that make a data flow "well-defined" are that input and output are clearly distinguished from each other, and that transformations of data are done in incremental steps—that is, single transformations do not produce major changes in the character of the data.

Jackson methodology

The Jackson Methodology views data structure as a driving force to successful software design. The method was popularized in England through the efforts of Michael Jackson, hence its name, and more recently through efforts of Infotech Information Ltd.

In this methodology a program is viewed as the means by which input data are transformed into output data. An explicit assumption is that paralleling the structure of the input (data) and output (report) will ensure a quality design. One *implicit* assumption is that the resulting data structure will be compatible with rational program structure. Other implicit assumptions include that only serial files will be involved and that the user of the method knows how to structure data.

Some claimed characteristics of this method include:

- It is not dependent on an analyst's experience or creativity.
- It is based on principles by which each design step can be verified.

- It is not difficult to learn and use correctly. (So if given the same problem, two designers working independently would arrive at very nearly the same design.)
- It results in designs which are easy and practical to implement.

Again, the process seems simple. But when we attempted to employ this technique, several difficulties were encountered. One was with the supporting documentation (Jackson's book) which is laden with examples and too few explanatory notes. We also encountered problems with the practicality of the method and began to question its basic premises. To illustrate, error processing had to be "wedged in" as erroneous data do not exist in a structural sense. Also, various file accessing and manipulation schemes took their toll. For instance, much data structuring is dictated by the data base management system employed. Thus, whether the data are tree-structured or not, we still may end up with an unimplementable program because there

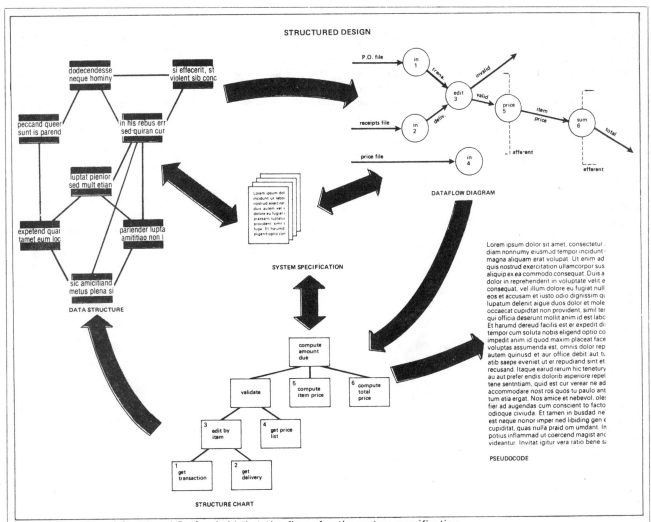

Fig. 1. Advocates of Structured Design hold that the flow of data through a system is the key to program design. The system specification is used to produce the data flow diagram, the diagram to develop the data structure chart, the chart to develop the data structure, and all of the pieces to reinterpret the system specification.

As might be expected, the methodology works best where input data are transformed into output in incremental, easy to follow steps.

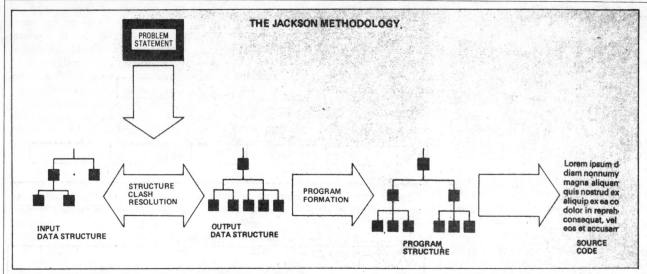

Fig. 2. The Jackson Methodology assumes that making the output data structure parallel to the structure of the input data will lead to a "good" design. (Some of the other methodologies share this assumption, too.) Unfortunately, the method may be practically limited to serial files. Also unfortunately, there may be no causal link between data structure and program quality.

does not appear to be a casual link between data structure and program quality; the basic assumption is invalid.

Logical construction of programs

LCP is a method similar in nature to Jackson's design methodology in that it also assumes data structure is the key to successful software design. However, this method is more proceduralized in its approach to program design than the Jackson method. Originated by Jean-Dominique Warnier in France, it has become popular outside the United States. It will now have its opportunity to become popular with English-speaking designers as English translations of the original French text are now available and the method has been incorporated into training offered by Infotech.

The LCP method is as follows:

1. Identify all input data to the software and organize in a hierarchical manner (files, records, entries, items). The exact format is not of concern here, but rather how the various parts of the input file are related to one another.

2. Define and note the number of times each element of the input file occurs, using variable names to relate the ratio of occurrences (such as: one active customer file, N customer records, each customer record has four entries: address, most recent payment, current balance, new charges).

3. Do step 1 and step 2 above for the desired output.

4. Obtain the details of the program by identifying the types of instructions contained in the design in a specific order: read instructions, preparation and execution of branches, calculations, outputs, and subroutine calls.

5. In flowchart-like fashion, depict the logical sequence of instructions using "Begin Process," "End Process," "Branch," and "Nesting" indicators.

6. Number the elements of the logical sequence and expand each

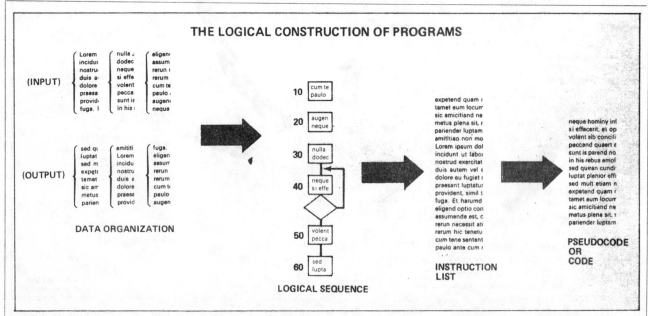

Fig. 3. The "Logical Construction of Programs" has become more popular outside of the U.S. than within its borders, possibly due to the lack of good English language documentation. The method again involves structuring the input and output data, using its own graphic conventions (Warnier diagrams), but adds a set of sequencing procedures and instruction types to translate the logical arrangement into pseudocode.

COMPARING

through the instructions identified in Step 4. (There exist several other guidelines regarding how data structure conflicts are involved, but they are not pertinent to our discussion.)

Many of the difficulties associated with the use of this method are similar to those encountered in using the Jackson Methodology. For instance, some problems force us to contrive a hierarchical data structure where none was previously apparent. Also, this method is somewhat misnamed in that it deals with program design issues and not construction issues (such as packaging, run environment, file access methods, etc.). Although for a problem with a readily apparent hierarchical data structure we get to a pseudocode statement of the program very rapidly, closer inspection often reveals that the resulting program is not what we would have chosen.

This method appears to be well suited to problems involving one module or only a few modules, and where the data are tree-structured. The latter leaves it susceptible to the same kind of problems as the Jackson Methodology.

Meta stepwise refinement

MSR is based on the premise that the more times you do something, the better the final results. It allows the designer to assume a simple solution to a problem and gradually build in more and more detail until the complete, detailed solution is derived. Several refinements, all at the same level of detail, are conjured up by the designer each time additional detail is desired. The "best" of these is selected, more detailed versions proposed, the best of these selected, and so on. Only the *best* solution is refined at each level of detail. Specific attributes of this method include:

1. It requires an exact, fixed problem definition.
2. It is programming language independent in early stages.
3. Design is by levels.
4. Details are postponed to lower levels.
5. Correctness is ensured at each level.
6. The design is successively refined.

MSR was authored by Henry Ledgard and later given this name by Ben Schneiderman. It is a synergism of Mill's top-down notions, Wirth's stepwise refinement, and Dijkstra's level structuring. It produces a level-structured, tree-structured program.

It is well known that by proper program organization it is possible to separate functionally independent levels

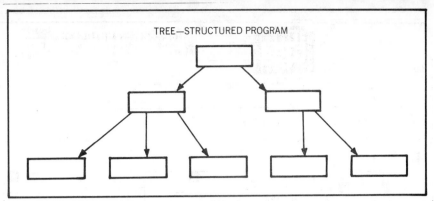

Fig. 4a. In a tree-structured program, the "root" module contains an outline or general image of the program, while the lower levels contain increased amounts of implementation detail.

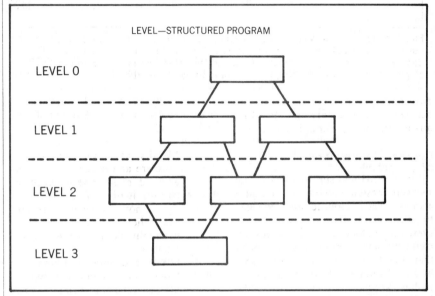

Fig. 4b. The basic rule of organization in a level-structured program is that modules at one specific level invoke only modules at the next lower level and never the reverse.

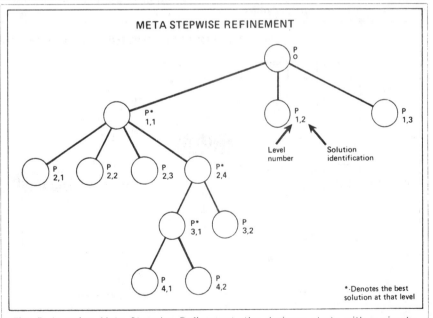

Fig. 5. In using Meta Stepwise Refinement, the designer starts with a simple, general solution and builds in increasing amounts of detail at lower levels in the design. MSR requires that the designer actually develop several potential solutions at each level, discarding all but the best of these. It may take a special kind of person to do this.

319

METHOD	Requirements Analysis and Specification			Design			Implementation	
	Problem Definition	Value System Design	Systems Analysis	Architecture Design	Data Design	Module Design	Code Construction	Testing
STRUCTURED DESIGN				1	2	2		
THE JACKSON METHODOLOGY				1-2	2	1	1	
LOGICAL CONSTRUCTION OF PROGRAMS					2	1	1	
META-STEPWISE REFINEMENT				2		1	1	
HIGHER ORDER SOFTWARE	2			3		1	1	

1 = addressed directly   2 = covered but no substantive guidelines offered   3 = supported by automated processor(s)   blank = does not cover

or layers in programs (as is illustrated in Figs. 4a and 4b). The higher levels reflect the problem statement while the lower ones have increasing amounts of implementation detail. The basic rule is that modules at a specific level invoke only modules at the next lower level, and never the reverse. This is how MSR works.

Although the method's theory sounds good, the practice leaves a lot to be desired. For example, in real life, non-trivial problems undergo constant reinterpretation, reevaluation, and modification. They are not stable. If they were, this method would not be needed. Since the solution at any one level depends on prior (higher) levels, and since any change in the problem statement affects prior levels, our ability to produce a solution at any level is undermined until the changes are made.

One approach is to refuse changes until the design is complete. This results in the solution and the requirements being unsynchronized. The production of multiple solutions is another difficulty. Coming up with fundamentally different solutions to a problem is not a likely occurrence for an individ-

ual. Also, how to decide which solution is "best" is not addressed by this method.

Due to the number of times the problem is going to be solved, this approach works best on small problems, perhaps those involving only a single module. It is particularly useful where the problem specifications are fixed and an elegant solution is required, as in developing an executive for an operating system.

Higher order software

HOS initially was developed and promoted by Margaret Hamilton and Saydean Zeldin while working on NASA projects at MIT. The method was invented in response to the need for a formal means of defining reliable, large scale, multiprogrammed, multiprocessor systems. Its basic elements include:

1. a set of formal laws
2. a specification language
3. an automated analysis of the system interfaces
4. layers of system architecture produced from the analyzer output
5. transparent hardware

This design method is based on axioms

which explicitly define a hierarchy of software control, wherein control is a formally specified effect of one software object on another:

Axiom 1: A given module controls the invocation of the set of valid functions on its immediate, and only its immediate, lower level.

Axiom 2: A given module is responsible for elements of only its own output space.

Axiom 3: A given module controls the access rights to each set of variables whose values define the elements of the output space for each immediate, and only each immediate, lower level function.

Axiom 4: A given module controls the access rights to each set of variables whose values define the elements of the input space for each immediate, and only each immediate, lower level function.

Axiom 5: A given module can reject invalid elements of its own, and only its own, input set.

Axiom 6: A given module controls the ordering of each tree for the immediate, and only the immediate, lower levels.

In practice, HOS has been used with an automated analyzer program which checks the solution design as expressed in HOS' own metalanguage. The need for the analyzer is not inherent in the methodology, however, and in fact we used pseudocode in examining the method since the analyzer was not available to us.

Our evaluation is that HOS is an asset in applications where the accuracy and particularly auditability of the algorithm are the primary concerns, applications such as scientific problems and detailed financial computations.

Our exposure to this methodology is limited, due in part to its very nature, its scale. We did use it enough to find some of its characteristics, however. For example, one objective of HOS seems to be to ensure correctness and consistency by interface definition and attention to detail. It was this emphasis on the details of system execution which first focused our attention on a

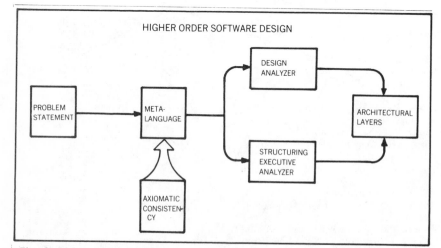

Fig. 6. Higher Order Software Design involves the use of a set of axioms to explicitly define the hierarchy of software control. It has been used with analyzer programs which check the design solution as expressed in HOS' own metalanguage. Developed for large scale NASA projects, the methodology may be well suited for such things as operating system design, but it does not address the structure of the data base very well.

METHOD	ATTRIBUTE								
	Specialized Graphics	Defined Procedure(s)	Training Support	Tutorial Documents	Requirements Traceability	Known Experience Base	Compatibility With Other Techniques/ Schemes	Area of Application	Evaluation (Quality) Criteria
STRUCTURED DESIGN	use structure charts for system architecture	an iterative framework which guides the solution development	two courses offered by Yourdon, Inc.	book by Yourdon & Constantine; book by G. J. Myers	designer's responsibility	up to 5 years experience within firms like IBM & Hughes	usable with any module design strategy	systems whose data flow can be communicated graphically	a well-defined set of design heuristics
THE JACKSON METHODOLOGY	tree-like charts for data structures	loosely defined guidelines to address various problems	two-week course offered through Infotech	book by Jackson (challenge to read) presented via examples	designer's responsibility	early versions available since 1972 with emphasis on business application	usable with other data structuring methods	business & other systems with well-understood data structure(s)	verify compliance with basic assumptions
LOGICAL CONSTRUCTION OF PROGRAMS	use Warnier chart for data structure	well-defined set of procedures at all levels of detail	incorporated in a course offered by Infotech	book by J.-D. Warnier	designer's responsibility	extensive use throughout Europe & other foreign countries	procedural nature would limit compatibility	business & other systems with well-understood data structure(s)	verify compliance with basic assumptions
META-STEPWISE REFINEMENT	use a tree diagram for program structure	high-level guidelines for the basic steps	no formal offerings	book by H. F. Ledgard	designer's responsibility	primarily limited to theoretical developments	would benefit from design evaluation criteria	applications with well-understood, stable requirements	no specific guidelines
HIGHER ORDER SOFTWARE	structured flowcharts for control structure	mostly theoretical discussion(s) with limited operational details	by arrangement with Higher Order Software	no formal text, several papers in journals	potentially available through an analyzer	proposed application on NASA Space Shuttle program	would benefit from design guidelines	applications with high reliability requirements	primarily automated analysis of design

fraction of the software design problem: we found that the issue of data base design was, at best, addressed implicitly, with the structure of the code appearing to be the primary problem. Our experience with large systems has taught us that the design of code and data base must be synchronous.

Now what do we know?

Now that we've gone through all the experimentation, what have we learned?

The preceding remarks are based on our experiences and reflect personal biases, but four observations should be apparent by now. The first is that no single method exists which would be an asset in every design problem. That's no surprise. The second observation is that the assumptions made by each method are just that—things taken for granted and not provable. The third is that methods can only contribute so much to the design effort. Designers produce designs, methods do not. A design problem, although well suited to a particular technique, will always have some quirk which makes it unique. Software design methods merely assist in solving routine aspects of a problem. Using a methodology only reveals the critical issues in a design effort and gives us more time to address them.

The final observation is that designing is problem solving—a fundamental, personal issue. To many, design methods are something of an affront and are resisted if imposed. Adoption of a method or methods requires a behavioral change, an alteration in how problems (of a certain class) are solved. And accomplishing the desired behavioral change can be a very difficult undertaking.

Methods are important but their successful application occurs only in supportive environments. Specifically, the necessary management elements (planning, scheduling, control systems, etc.) must all be present and effective. The larger the system, the more important these "non-technical" factors. The balance between methods and environments is a delicate one. The merging of these may very well be the next evolutionary step. ✿

Bibliography

Bazjanac, V. "Architectural Design Theory: Models of the Design Process," in *Basic Questions of Design Theory*, W.R. Spillers, editor. (New York: American Elsevier Publishing Co., Inc., 1974).

Hamilton, M., and Zeldin, S. "Higher Order Software—A Methodology for Defining Software," *IEEE Transactions on Software Engineering*, Vol. SE-2, No. 1, March 1976, pp. 9-31.

Jackson, M.A. *Principles of Program Design* (New York: Academic Press, 1975).

Jensen, E.P. *1975 IR & D Structural Design Methodology—Volume II* (Hughes Aircraft Co., December, 1975).

Jones, J.C. *Design Methods* (New York: Wiley-Interscience, 1970).

Ledgard, H.F. "The Case for Structured Programming, *Bit*, Vol. 13, 1973, pp. 45-57.

Myers, Glenford J. *Reliable Software Through Composite Design* (New York: Petrocelli Charter, 1975).

Peters, L.J., and Tripp, L.L. "Is Software Design Wicked?," *Datamation*, Vol. 22, No. 6, June 1976.

Rittel, H.W.J., and Webber, M.M. "Dilemmas in a General Theory of Planning, Working Paper No. 194," (Berkeley: Institute of Regional Development, University of California, Nov., 1972).

Schneiderman, Ben. "A Review of Design Techniques for Programs and Data," *Software—Practice and Experience*, Vol. 6, pp. 555-567, Chichester, England, 1976.

Stevens, W.P., Myers, G.J., and Constantine, L.L. *Structural Design* (New York: Yourdon, Inc, 1975).

Warnier, J.-D. *Logical Construction of Programs* (Leiden: H.E. Stenfert Kroese B.V., 1974).

Yourdon, E., and Constantine, L.L., *Structured Design* (New York: Yourdon, Inc., 1975).

Mr. Peters is a software engineering consultant with Boeing Computer Services Inc. His ten years of dp experience include periods spent on commercial, scientific, and real-time applications while working at Aerojet Electrosystems, Bell-Northern Research (in Canada), and BCS. Since 1973 he has been involved in the development and promotion of modern programming practices within BCS.

Mr. Tripp started as a software engineer (although the title wasn't yet invented) at the Boeing Company in 1966, working on large matrix structural analysis systems and on non-linear differential solving. He too has been working on the programming practices project at BCS since 1973, lately in his capacity as manager of software methods development and implementation within the Advanced Techniques and Applications Div.

DESIGN METHODOLOGIES—A COMPARISON

S. N. Griffiths

INTRODUCTION

This paper addresses itself to providing some manner of answer to the question "Of all the major techniques in the public domain, which describe themselves or may legitimately be described as 'design methodologies', which is/are the best?" It is impossible to provide an authoritatively complete answer; indeed, it is not easy even to be objective and equitable. The questions foreshadows a profounder one, which may well be put in the future—"Is there a 'right' design methodology?"

This second question presupposes the possibility that sufficient insight will be gained into the basic structural properties of systems for all instances of system design to be made obedient to one invariant set of principles. Whether this is a short-term or a long-term prospect, the methodologies considered in this paper most certainly hint at the possibility, and this is one reason for the importance to be attached to an evaluation of them, however qualified the conclusions have to be. The second reason looks to the past and present rather than the future: of all the major elements which go (or should go) into the commitment of a system—choice of hardware, choice of software, interfacing with corporate data management, decentralization of processing and so forth—the design methodology to be used has nearly always, until very recently, been accorded relatively little importance. This was so despite the fact that, if there are to be any guarantees of reliability, maintainability and extensibility of the developed system, it is only from the design methodology (assuming that the associated project management assures its effectiveness) that they can come.

In comparing major methodologies (seven have been selected for comparison) there is a problem of scale. To explore fully all details of all the methodologies and to make a comparison of all aspects amenable to direct comparison is not practicable. The approach adopted here assumes an outline acquaintance with at least some of the methodologies so that much can be taken as read. The comparison is then made at two levels:

- Firstly in terms of those properties (principally those which conduce to accurate and effective project management) of the methodologies which would properly influence a corporate decision to adopt any one of them now (the '1977' comparison)

- Secondly in more fundamental terms of structural approach and presumed long-term prospects (the 'predictive' comparison).

The reason why this separation has been made is that none of the methodologies yet claims to be comprehensive, that is, 'packaged'. It may well be that the real value of a given methodology lies in its potential rather than in the benefits it may bring to the user now. In any case, the major benefits claimed for the methodologies are, for the most part, long-term, since they have to do with the cutting of maintenance costs and the preservation of investment by making large systems enhanceable and adaptable.

The majority of writings on design methodologies in the last two or three years have been, necessarily, greatly concerned to win the sceptical reader over to the view that design in the narrow sense is vital to success and to overcome his antipathy to sometimes seemingly revolutionary methods. The present paper is not a piece of apologetic; it assumes that the case for formal, methodological design is already sufficiently made and therefore can confine itself to the making of comparisons, even though the comparisons are made against a set of necessarily subjective ideals.

WHAT IS A DESIGN METHODOLOGY?

The term 'design methodology' is not readily defined. A serviceable definition may be arrived at by considering these questions:

- Is design a synthetic (creative) or an analytic (perceptive) activity?
- What distinguishes a methodology from a method or technique?
- Where is the dividing line to be drawn between the nucleus of a methodology—the essential part—and those peripheral techniques which perhaps greatly increase its effectiveness but properly belong under the heads of documentation and project control?
- What does a design methodology demand as its starting-point?
- What is the relationship between design and modularity?
- What is the relationship between design and implementation?
- What is the relationship between design and software engineering?
- What is the relationship between design and corporate data management?

Synthesis or analysis?

The answer to the synthetic/analytic question must be that it partakes of both qualities. The issue is much confused, however, by the lack of a proper definition of systems design on the one hand and program design on the other.

The designer of a system, in a sense that includes that of computer system but is not confined to it, has to decide what information is required for what purposes, with what events the information is to be associated, what the ordering in time of each train of events (if any) is to be and precisely in what way each event-train will interact with and pass information to what others. In this situation the designer's task is wholly synthetic; he is creating an information system from nothing. However, the creative freedom is seldom so untrammelled as this: there are massive constraints which limit it—constraints of hardware resources, processing speeds and existing systems to be interfaced with. Above all, there is the constraint of physical time: events take place in a particular order which has to be accepted no matter how 'inconvenient' it is to process.

These constraints limit the system designer's creative function and compel him to perceive entities, orderings, relationships and attributes (data) that he must accept as the starting-point of his work. And in this work, whatever techniques or methodology he may use, he makes commitments to the existence and interfaces of certain objects which comprise his solution to the system design problem. These objects are files (conceptual or real), programs or processes (conceptual or real) and 'language elements' (data structures or types and common procedures or subroutines). It is this material which constitutes the starting point of program design, and because the commitments to data organization and the ordering of events (an event, so far as a program is concerned, is the presentation to it of an input record or its creation of an output record) have already been made, the designer's task is to all intents and purposes wholly analytic. This being so, the door is opened to the possibility of determinate, automatable design of programs, given only a design methodology possessed of the appropriate analysis tools to deduce the transformations needed to convert inputs to outputs. A consequence of this will be to conform system design to the requirements of program design, resulting in a partitioning of systems into components radically different from that which is now customary.

Method or methodology

The distinction between methodology and method has never been made explicit. The word *methodology* itself is claimed as a neologism by the Cincinnati pioneer of integrated system planning and control strategies, Milt Bryce. It seems to have acquired the connotation of dependence on basic principles rather than mere rules of thumb found to work in practice. That is to say, a methodology provides, in some measure, reasons for all the steps in the design process and reasons furthermore which may be understood completely without reference to the particular application or to any broad classification, such as real-time, transaction processing or batch update. Because it meets this definition 'Modular Programming' is included in the comparison, even though it may seem now a poor thing in relation to the later methodologies derived from it or intended to supplant it.

Essential and peripheral features

The next question, relating to the dividing line between the essential and the merely peripheral parts of a design methodology, is the most difficult of all these questions to address squarely. It is undoubtedly true that the kernel of a methodology should uncompromisingly deal with the truly structural aspects—what programming is really all about—but it cannot be sold in those terms. What makes or mars a methodology in the market-place is how close it comes to satisfying the principal project management requirements:

- Truly quantifiable assessment of progress
- Early warning of major errors before they become entrenched
- Predictable and uniform consumption of resources
- Testing reduced to the role of being confirmatory of system correctiveness
- High programmer productivity and so forth.

Such factors as these must fundamentally depend on how good the kernel of the methodology is, but they also depend on the accidents of how its practitioners see it—the associated diagrams and notations—representation of compilable code, manual procedures, checkpoints and reviews etc. This calls for some caution. It is perfectly possible for a very sound methodology to be presented with a poor practitioner interface. Conversely, a poor methodology may be 'dressed up' with an impressive and effective one. Indeed, the methodology may be so interleaved with these peripheral techniques for it to be impossible to assess it on its merits as a methodology. This phenomenon, to be observed to some extent in all the methodologies considered, is another reason why the comparisons are made both in '1977' terms and 'predictive' terms.

The starting-point

The starting-point required by a designer using one of the new methodologies is as intractable a matter as the answer to any of these questions. So long as design is seen only as program design the issue can be disguised beneath the platitude that the program specification should be complete and consistent, setting aside how these attributes are to be assured, and even in what form the specification is to be expressed. Moreover, completeness and consistency are perhaps all that it is legitimate to ask for when the program's existence and function have been decided on in a way to which the program designer is largely indifferent. As soon as program and system design are taken to be a single discipline the problem of 'specification' has to be solved—there is nowhere else to pass the buck to as it were. This point is returned to later.

The relationship between design and modularity

A possible solution to the relationship of design and modularity is suggested later, but the central issue affects the design methodology question so largely that it should be stated here. It is whether the modules of a system are separated one from another according to criteria which have to do with the way the data processing problem is solved, or whether by criteria having to do with the actual trains of events.

The relationship between design and implementation

The question of where design stops and implementation begins is one which the new methodologies have made easier to answer—design proceeds so far as to make implementation, in principle, a mechanical task concerned solely with transcribing the complete solution from some diagrammatic or textual form to another which is compilable and thus executable. This clear-cut situation, wherein design and implementation form a true sequence without iterative interaction, is often not perceived for what it is because of the use of design/coding overlap as part of a general system implementation strategy. Needless to say, such a strategy will not work if there are not built-in guarantees that continuing design work in one area will not invalidate development work already completed in another. The importance attached to completeness in design as a pre-requisite to implementation is one of the characteristics of the newer design methodologies which most obviously demark them from their more primitive predecessors.

Software engineering and corporate data management

The last two questions, concerning software engineering and corporate data management, may be dealt with together for, in somewhat different senses, they place design in a wider context. The earlier questions have, tacitly, treated 'the system' as the designer's universe, within which he is required to create a unified model of a set of related entities, any relationships that lie outside being by definition so trivial as not to affect his work. In an environment with well-developed software engineering techniques and/or committed corporate data management, the designer is not only bound to some extent by the constraints they impose but is expected to serve interests which are wider than that of his system. One of the objectives of software engineering, as part of its overall plan to make the production of large-scale software amenable to the sort of standard practices which characterize civil, electrical and electronic engineering, is the creation of general purpose, multi-use components for the benefit of future development work. It has to be recognised that this objective and the basic objective of system design, namely the faithful modelling of event-trains and their data in executable code, are in conflict.

Furthermore, the better a design methodology becomes at modelling the specific aspects of a system (with the consequent advantages of certainty in specification, ease of understanding and precision in maintenance), the less easy it becomes to create standard components as by-products without compromising the overall integrity of the system. There is no resolution, because the two objectives are utterly different. Either one sets out to design a particular system knowing in advance in what language its structure will be represented, or one sets out to develop components which will in effect increase the power of the language to be used to represent all future systems' structures.

So it is necessary that a design methodology should not trespass outside its own boundary. Of course, within a system, the requirement for general purpose components exists too and with this the design methodology must deal. This point is taken up as an aspect of modularity.

A definition

The definition of the term design methodology assumed in this paper is an austere one:

- A set of principles which enables an exact model to be built of the trains of events
- Their associated data and the information to be derived from them—expressed in a procedural form capable of being executed by a computer or other reliable means.

The definition may seem obvious but if a methodology which meets the definition rather than merely pays lip-service to it can be found, then a revolution is at hand that will irreversibly alter both management and practitioner attitudes to programming, redefine the personnel roles in the programming profession, and raise the ceiling of feasibility.

Design and requirements analysis

In a nutshell, *requirements analysis* is the examination of the information to be output by a system (on the assumption that this has been decided on) to ascertain what data, input to the whole system, recorded in association with what entities, are necessary for the input-to-output transformation which defines the system. Requirements analysis must not trespass on design; that is, it must not make assumptions about the process-and-file constitution of the system because it is the task of system design to deduce these from the specification which is the result of the requirements analysis. In a similar fashion it must deal with events and their information content not the records and data which the design process may deem necessary to represent them.

It would be ungenerous to detract from the work of those who have striven hard to reduce to order the task of specifying exactly what a system should and should not do by formalizing requirements analysis, particularly those who have laboured for several years on the many facets of ISDOS, but the fact is that no simple means is yet available for specifying a system without making some commitment to its structure. Until this means becomes available, design methodologies will have to complete a specification as well as generate a structure. Doing these two things in parallel compels the design methodology to be, to some extent, iterative and certainly prevents, even if it were otherwise possible, the automation of the design process.

Design and modularity

That there are two basic types of modularity, problem-oriented and solution-oriented, has already been alluded to. For example, a basic premise of Modular Programming is that a large piece of work can be divided into separate compilation units so as to limit flow-of-control complexity, permit parallel development by several programmers and cut recompilation costs. This premise generates wholly solution-oriented modules and relies on (almost) wholly solution-oriented criteria of modular division. At the other extreme a program which responds to stimuli in a process-control application, lies dormant between stimuli, has no means of termination, and is wholly problem-oriented because it is structured so as to reflect the time-ordering of its input. Again, the situation where two programs, separated by a sort mechanism, are required is illustrative of the obligatory separation of two modules brought about by a situation—the non-matching ordering criteria of the two programs' input files—which is inherent in the problem. One last example (of a cautionary nature): the familiar weekly update of a master file. This is usually solution-oriented modularity. The transactions are grouped in weekly batches for operational convenience even though the events which require the updating of the entities represented by the master file records need not themselves be scheduled on a weekly basis.

The distinction between a sub-routine and a program has to be made clear. For present purposes a sub-routine may be defined as a means of processing a single input datum in one invocation; a program as a means of processing a succession of related input datums (*sic*) in one activation. For the basis of modularity to be problem-oriented it is obvious that some unit other than the sub-routine is needed. It has to be some generalization of the concept of 'program' which corresponds to the largest aggregation of data whose parts are related in some way. But the type of program exemplified by the weekly update above is as solution-oriented as the sub-routine. The type of program that is required is one in which the succession of input data which drives it is derived from a chain of events in the real world. In the case of the weekly update the 'real' programs are the models of the *life-histories* of every individual entity represented by a master-file record. Each of these has the essential requirement of a program— serial input—but is not invoked or run independently. Indeed it is 'invoked' repeatedly by some other program or programs which give data to it or take data from it. When this happens the real files which link programs in a batch environment are replaced by some form of intermediate record buffering. Such programs as these may be termed processes. Two processes in the simple case where they cooperate synchronously are conventional co-routines.

The type of modularity just outlined may conveniently be called *vertical modularity* adapting a term of Theodore A. Linden (007). The term vertical is appropriate in that it suggests a type of modularity 'at right angles to' the type of modularity arising from successive breakdowns of modules in top-down working. This latter, because it is always so diagrammatized, may be termed horizontal modularity.

The third type is common modularity. Common modules in effect extend the language to be used in writing the procedure around a structure determined by vertical and horizontal considerations, or their role is sometimes enlarged to provide generalized functions in the manner of software engineering in a wider context than any one system.

In either case they are not significant in the *structure* of the system containing them. Their significance lies in the maintainability of the system because it is possible to use them so as to localize or 'hide' certain types of information or structure in a way that generates freedom from side-effects under amendment. It must be emphasised, however, that common modularity, for all its importance, must play second fiddle to vertical and horizontal modularity. It has to do with providing an enhanced language for the expression of a solution to a problem and with the independence and isolation of a system's components. It has not to do with solving the problem.

In addition to the foregoing one may also define *pragmatic modularity* as that which is neither problem nor solution oriented but which is determined by such factors as programmer availability and skill, economics of compilation etc.

Alternative design emphases

So long as no methodology presents more than a partial picture of how to determine system structure it is inevitable that competing methodologies will stress some aspects at the expense of others. Their advocates, with complete intellectual honesty, derive as much mileage as they can out of stressing the benefits which their particular emphasis confers. It is this situation which causes puzzlement to many who, while they realize that all the protagonists cannot be 'right' to the exclusion of the others, cannot make any assessment of the methodologies' merits because the different emphases obscure the criteria of comparison. Matters are made worse by the fact that most serious users of these methodologies can claim large increases in controllability and maintainability of their systems in comparison with their former methods. It is easy for a user to be led into attributing the improvements to the methodology's emphasis when it should in fact be attributed to the associated project management techniques or the increased sense of purpose, cooperation and achievement experienced by designers and implementors.

Briefly, the principal emphases to have appeared so far are:

- *The procedural emphasis* Epitomized by the flowchart, now discredited.

- *The control-flow-limitation emphasis* This is structured Programming in its narrow sense: the restriction of control flow figures to those of sequence, selection and iteration (with variants), all of which are single-entry and single-exit. It is merely a refinement of the procedural emphasis.

- *The invocation emphasis* Epitomized by Modular Programming and tainted by association with the bottom-up implementation strategy. Now discredited.

- *The decomposition emphasis* The driving force behind top-down. A procedural unit (a 'function', in the looser sense) is divisible into subordinate functions which are in turn sub-divisible. In its ideal form the modular structure derived is literally a hierarchy (each module knows only its single parent module and its immediate descendants).

- *The change-of-state emphasis* Sees a system as a set of independent entities each of which goes through its own succession of self-contained transformations from input form to output.

- *The independence emphasis* Makes the objective of design the attainment of maximum change-independence in the way a system is modularized. The ideal is that when a system is enhanced one or more modules are altered, without affecting their interfaces with other modules, so that when replaced, the unaltered part of the system is in no way affected.

- *The data-structure emphasis* Sees the expression of time-ordered data relationships in the form of tree-structures as the central requirement of design and builds programs or processes around these structures.

The procedural and control-flow-limitation emphases have no modularity connotations. The invocation emphasis ignores vertical modularity and scarcely distinguishes horizontal from common modularity. The decomposition emphasis has a limited view of vertical modularity (programs not processes) and exploits horizontal modularity to the detriment of common. The change-of-state emphasis is again without modular implications. The independence emphasis exploits common modularity. The data-structure emphasis exploits vertical modularity, accommodates horizontal modularity and largely ignores common modularity.

The independence and data-structure emphases are by far the most important. The independence emphasis represents the software engineering approach at its most refined with by-products which help avoid bad solutions to problems. The data-structure emphasis, while not denying the relevance of independence, makes a start at establishing the principle that the solution of a problem is implicit in its statement.

A BASIS OF COMPARISON

One common way of approaching the task of comparing the members of a set of intractably incomparable things is to choose the most comparable and measurable properties exhibited by all the members to serve as the basis of comparison and then by great scrupulousness in performing the comparison, hope to conceal the arbitrary, unrepresentative nature of the original choice. In comparison at least this extreme bias is avoided by dividing the comparison into two parts. The first part (the 1977 comparison) looks at what each methodology offers in terms relevant to computing practice in 1977. This comparison takes the methodologies (numbers 3 to 7 in the list) as they are published or practised now. The second part of the comparison attempts to discover what their fundamental merits are and what potential there is for extension, particularly to become integrated system design tools, whether by their present developers or by the incorporation of the basic concepts in other, more comprehensive, methodologies. In one particular sense is it prudent to split the comparison in this way. Very broadly, the monetary benefits to be gained lie either in short-term project development savings or in long-term maintenance and enhancement economies. The latter are probably more significant than the former but none of the methodologies has yet been used on a large enough scale for long enough, for any long-term assessment of benefits to have been published. Thus it is only on the project development side that usable evidence exists.

THE METHODOLOGIES

Which methodologies are worth comparing?

A reasonable answer seems to be—those with an established following, subject to the proviso that there be not so many as to make the comparison unwieldy. Those selected are:

1. Modular Programming
2. Top-down design based on Functional Decomposition
3. Composite Design, developed by Glenford J. Myers
4. Structured Design, developed by Larry L. Constantine
5. Structured Analysis Design Technique (SADT) developed by Douglas Ross of SofTech
6. Logical Construction of Programs (LCP) and its sister methodology Logical Construction of Systems (LCS), developed by Jean-Dominique Warnier
7. The Jackson Design Method, developed by Michael Jackson.

Modular Programming is included not as a viable candidate (no-one would now dignify it as a design methodology), but to provide a datum line and in recognition of the fact that it was the first technique developed, which attempted to solve some of the problems of design, that succeeded in attracting a large following. Unlike most of the others in the list it is not the product of one person or one organization, but is rather a consensus view of what had to be done to remedy the evils of the monolithic program.

Top-down design based on Functional Decomposition is a contrived name to denote the family of methods based on the IBM strategy of top-down development. Since it is an antecedent to both the Myers and the Constantine methodologies, it, as well as Modular Programming, is accorded a briefer treatment than the other five.

The remaining methodologies need no definition as they are the productions of known individuals or organizations.

For the sake of brevity the seven are abbreviated to MP, TDD, CD, SD, SADT, LCP/LCS, MJSD hereafter.

Their affinities and common origins

Modular Programming

Modular Programming arose as a crude device for containing a situation which had got out of hand— the intolerable complexity and opacity of the unconstrained control logic of large programs. MP is basically the divide-and-conquer rule applied unhappily in a situation where the sum of the parts is less than the whole. As the technique was refined certain rules of thumb were found to be useful and two of them were the germs of concepts to be more fully exploited in later methodologies. One was the idea of 'functional separateness' for constituent modules (as an ideal to be striven for more than a rule to be obeyed). This concept is refined and extended by both Myers and Constantine. The second was the notion of a central 'control module' directing the processing carried out by all subordinate modules.

Here lies the germ of the top-down approach to implementation and functional decomposition in design.

Top-down Design

Top-down design based on Functional Decomposition was first popularized as part of IBM's IPT (Improved Programming Techniques) approach to structured team programming. The basic idea is simple—that of horizontal modularity. Its appeal, however, springs from the orderly, progressive implementation strategy that goes with it.

Structured/Composite Design

The two very similar methodologies of Myers and Constantine have been separately developed from the joint work of Myers, Constantine and others under the aegis of IBM and represent an attempt to remedy an obvious weakness in the functional decomposition approach, namely the absence of any means of telling whether a proposed functional decomposition into modules is good or bad. This is done by establishing measures of the interdependence of the parts of a module and the independence of one module from another, both properties being considered conducive to sound design. These methodologies may be considered the two most advanced of the functional decomposition school which is characterized by the 'independence' emphasis. The other main school, which has the 'data-structure' emphasis, is represented by the methodologies of Warnier and Jackson.

SADT

SADT stands somewhat apart. It is undoubtedly closer to functional decomposition than data-structure in its emphasis but it differs from the Myers/Constantine approach in two important respects. Firstly it is pure design; it is the problem which is analysed, broken down and the parts analysed again until a complete self-consistent picture is obtained, with the mapping onto programs and modules left undefined. Secondly, it is, of all the methodologies here reviewed, the most inextricably bound up with project control techniques, principally documentation and review. Indeed much of the appeal of the methodology lies in the way that a thorough understanding of a whole system can be gained without the need to consider more than the outline of the manner of its implementation.

Warnier and Jackson

The two methodologies of the data-structure school, although they develop the idea in different ways, do not first address themselves to what has to be done, but instead consider the structure of the data to be input and output, both in its physical form and in the light of the necessary abstractions. This data is the whole of the input of a program, i.e., one stream of data that has to be processed serially and one or more output streams. Both take the fundamental theorem of Structured Programming that all forms of procedural control constructs (anything that can be built from a combination of IF and GO TO statements) may be reduced to the set of three single-entry, single-exit constructs of sequence, selection and iteration, and apply it instead to the data streams or files. Each file is represented as a tree-structure of sequences, selections and iterations reflecting not only the physical nature of the data but also the interpretations (or abstractions) of it imposed by the problem to be solved. From this starting-point, well-defined stages in the program design activity lead to a program capable of being translated straightforwardly into compilable code.

Conclusions

The difference in approach between the functional decomposition and data-structured schools is enormous. The former is solution-oriented and dominated by the 'independence' emphasis whereas the latter is problem-oriented and seeks to ascertain all the relationships pertinent to the problem to be solved across the whole body of data to be processed before lower levels of modularity or the procedural steps in the final program are considered.

Without pre-judging the issue—and the issue is, in its simplest terms, which of the two schools is likely to supplant the other as the mainstream of design ideology—it can be discerned that the functional decomposition school makes no major break with the modular programming tradition of which it forms a continuation. It refines the pre-existing concepts of modularity, including some that are patently solution-oriented, and formalizes design by first recognising and classifying difficulties and dangers and then giving guidance on their solution and mitigation. The data-structure school, contrastingly, does make a break with the modular programming tradition. It states, or at least allows one to infer, that functional decomposition is wrong simply because function is implicit in data and data relationships. Data-structures must be the starting-point, must be recognisably preserved through the stages of design, must be supported by vertical modularity so that whole data-structures are not broken up into pieces and must be detailed enough for the executable operations needed to turn the structural framework into a runnable program to be expressed in a suitable language of conventional type; all of this by-passes the concept of function and makes the incorporation of the procedural part only the final step in a well-defined design process.

THE COMPARISON IN 1978 TERMS

The factors

The difficulties attending an objective evaluation have already been alluded to. It is not the purpose of this paper to penetrate so far into the methodologies that a comparison of like with like can be made. Instead a number of factors which are individually meaningful have been chosen. These factors overlap to a large extent because they are the external manifestations of combinations of the underlying factors, but by presenting the methodologies in terms of them a general picture can be discerned.

The factors are divided into two groups, structural and peripheral, those in the structured category being treated in greater detail that the peripheral ones. For many factors an ideal is suggested, taking the factor in its own right, with account not necessarily being taken of its probable dependencies on others. A summary of the attributes of the methodologies in relation to the ideal is then given. Not all factors are relevant to all methodologies so the analysis is, in general selective.

The criteria adopted

The structural factors are classified as:

1. Basis—the fundamental tenets of the methodology.
2. Complexity—the means whereby complexity is recognised and its effect on design contained.
3. Modularity—the types of modularity recognised and the criteria of modular separation.
4. Scale—the provision made for program design and system design and the way they are integrated.
5. Scope—the range of problems which can successfully be solved.
6. Structural integrity—those attributes of the design methodology which ease maintenance and enhancement and conversely the demands made by the methodology on the way any kind of alteration to the system is made so as to preserve its structured integrity.

The peripheral factors are grouped as:

1. The design stages and their documentation
2. Project control
3. Testing
4. Portability and external compatibility.

Structural factor 1—the basis of the methodologies

The basis of a methodology is the principle or principles on which its more detailed aspects depend. These principles are seldom stated so they have to be inferred. They determine the static view of the design-object in which correctly to bridge the gap from a statement of requirement to a completed design is all that matters, the possibility of future changes in the statement of requirement being disregarded.

If it is taken that a system is a set of cooperating sequential processes, each process representing the computation of desired attributes for a succession of entities from attributes already possessing values, then the ideal basis of system design is the determination of the processes and the data interfaces through which they cooperate. Similarly, program design is the derivation of the structure of each process from the interfaces already determined expressed in a procedural language, itself extended from some arbitrary base language by the addition of special functions. The approximation to this of the seven methodologies is outlined below.

Modular Programming (MP)

MP divides a task, which is always less than a full system and often no more than a conventional program, into modules whose reasons for existence are largely pragmatic, with two exceptions. These are the control module, which represents the skeleton structure of the only or main process, and those common modules which are devised to replace what would otherwise be procedural code repeated inline in many places.

MP has no governing principle—it is a primitive implementation strategy which capitalizes on those few structural properties which its imperfect view of modularity allows it to perceive. The modules of MP are all functionally or pragmatically derived. All but the two types mentioned above represent some state or states of one or more processes. Accordingly, most are variable state sub-routines which require access to global data and data computed by their own earlier invocations. Because of this the structural distinctions pertinent to complete processes are represented only, and obscurely, as switches of one sort or another.

Top-down Design (TDD)

TDD is MP to which is added a rationale of functional decomposition. The constituent modules are determined by a combination of pragmatic criteria and the top-down principle. The top-down principle, roughly, is that the procedural code of a module may be written in a high-level form including invocation references to hypothetical lower-level modules. As with MP the constituent processes are obscured, but the fact that all modules are in some sense parts of others avoids the worst excesses of arbitrary module demarcation which can so disfigure MP. The modules tend to be small (for pragmatic, project-control reasons) and the requirement for references from one module to a lower-level module to be by invocation satisfies the single-entry, single exit requirement of Structured Programming. TDD thus gains the benefits of Structured Programming in a way which MP seldom can.

Composite Design (CD)

CD has one major and one minor principle—major and minor, that is, as a measure of the importance attached to them. The major principle is that all modules should be each strongly bound internally and weakly coupled to each other. Strength and coupling, which are really alternative ways of expressing the same thing, are not easily defined. In fact, CD does not define them but it does provide a scale going from worst to best for each and each level of strength and coupling is given a name. Rules are given whereby the strength of any module or the level of coupling between any two may be determined. The strength rules are curious, however, in that they rely largely on the verbal expression of the module's function—its clause structure, presence of conjunctions, certain key words and so forth—to determine the strength. The rules of coupling are more readily intelligible in that they are based on the way non-local data are referenced.

The 'best' level of coupling (called data coupling) is that in which all data required by a module is explicitly passed to it via parameters and all data computed by it are passed back in the same way to the point of invocation. The 'best' level of module strength (called functional strength) is that for which the module's task is expressible by a simple subject-predicate statement e.g., 'Remove redundant blanks from input record').

The strength and coupling scales do not recognise vertical modularity as such. A module representing some internal states of a process, although it might earn top marks for module strength (if it performs one well-defined transformation in the process) cannot earn top marks for coupling because of the 'impure' nature of its external data references. This limitation is evident not only in the coupling of distinct modules but more importantly, in the design of individual modules. When a module is variable-state, its execution forming part of an unacknowledged 'process', it is natural and necessary that it should be 'control-coupled' to itself from one invocation to the next. CD enjoins *data* coupling, with the result that data truly local to the process ('own' variables, in ALGOL terminology) are passed backwards and forwards as parameters. The effect of this is serious: the designer is falsely persuaded that his objective is the demarcation of a set of data-coupled modules of functional strength, when in most cases this is impossible, it being necessary first to distinguish the constituent processes for each of which separately the objective is obtainable.

Two further aspects of the strength/coupling principle are striking. First the justification of the principle is made in terms of system maintainability—the better are the strength and coupling the more readily an amendment or extension can be made without precipitating an error elsewhere than in the part amended. This is to elevate maintainability above structural correctness when in fact structural correctness is one of the prerequisites of maintainability. Secondly the strength and coupling rules are applied *a posteriori*. The designer has to make a tentative modular division before he can measure the strengths. Worse, he may have to go some way towards implementing a module before he can measure its coupling (because of coupling's dependence on data references). CD's second principle is that of 'levels of abstraction' applied to the principal input and output streams. By tracing through the successive transformations required to reduce the various input streams to a form in which the input is no longer discernible as such and similarly tracing backward from the various output streams through successive transformations a source-process-sink model is built up for a single instance of an entity. By adding the extra dimension required by the fact that there are multiple instances of the entity, each transformation becomes a program or process. This procedure provides some formalism in the demarcation of programs but is highly intuitive because the separate transformations are not deduced *a priori* but instead result from a pre-conception of the procedural steps needed to transform an entity in its input form to its output form.

Structured design

SD is best described by comparing it with CD. Its two basic principles are similar but it is characterized by a greater degree of formalization (as well as much implementation strategy, which is of no concern here) and innovative terminology than CD. The differences in the two approaches to the two principles is interesting because their relative prominences are reversed. Strength (called *cohesion)* and coupling are treated more or less as in CD except that, for coupling, the factors contributing to bad coupling are used to provide better module division rather than to calibrate a scale.

The concept of progressive abstraction from source through process to sink reappears as *afferent* and *efferent* transformations and the whole concept of data flow is made more explicit. The process of demarking the constituent programs on the basis of data flow is called 'transform analysis' and roughly parallels the approach of CD. However, an alternative approach, called *transaction analysis* is made an integral part of the methodology. When using transform analysis, one transformation forms the kernal of each program and the seriality characteristic of a program is provided by the multiplicity of entities to be processed. However, when transaction analysis is used the seriality in each program comes from the succession of states through which one entity passes in its passage from afferent to efferent. Transform and transaction analysis are alternative, one might say orthogonal, ways of looking at the same structural reality. It is a manifest weakness of SD that it offers the two types of analysis as alternatives with little guidance on which to use in a given case.

Structured Analysis and Design Technique (SADT)

SADT appears to have three basic principles but they are not dominant in its presentation. They are simply the axioms around which the impressive documentation and control techniques of the methodology are built.

The first is the top-down principle in a very pragmatic form—so pragmatic in fact that it is enjoined that any function (or data aggregate) be decomposed into no fewer than three, no more than six at the next level, because to decompose into fewer generates too many levels and to decompose into more causes 'span of control' problems. Since SADT's levels of decomposition do not map directly onto physical modules no problems ensue, but it must be understood that such an approach is essentially a convenience not an elucidation of structure.

The second, and pivotal, principle is represented by the rectangular transformation box with its four symmetrically disposed arrows. If the box represents an *activity* the left arrow describes the input data (which is destroyed by the transformation), the right arrow the output data (which is created by the transformation), the upper arrow the control data (data influencing the transformation but not itself altered) and the lower arrow the means used to effect the transformation (not data at all). This is a formalization of the change-of-state emphasis, but decoupled entirely from any computer representation.

The third principle is that the system, as an alternative to its representation as a connected set of activity boxes, may be represented equally by a connected set of *data* boxes. The activity boxes are connected by links representing data (roughly) while the data boxes are connected by links representing activities. The methodology acknowledges that the activity and data representations are symmetric and equally valid, but since a system has to be implemented (i.e., coded) from its constituent activities the activity-based approach is the dominant one. In fact the drawing of the corresponding data-based diagrams is recommended mainly as a means of checking consistency and completeness. There is an interesting parallel here between the activity/data ambivalence of SADT and the transform/transaction ambivalence of SD. The two ambivalences, although occupying different places in the methodologies' respective basic principles, have in common that they expose the possibility of taking two different though equivalent views of the same thing. Both methodologies are honest enough not to conceal the ambivalence: neither, however, knows how to penetrate beneath it to the structural verity which would remove it.

Logical Construction of Programs/Systems (LCP/LCS)

LCP/LCS takes as its starting-point the statement that it is possible and necessary both to base the existence of programs on pre-existent hierarchical structures of data and to determine the structures of programs from them. The procedural approach, underlying all traditional programming as well as that of the functional decomposition school, is rejected since such an approach compels the designer to consider not only what operations are required to build a problem solution in terms of the input and output data but at the same time to deal with all the procedural work necessitated by the method of implementation and the computing environment. This dependence of both system and program structure on hierarchies of data is the only principle of the methodology: the rest is a development of it in detail and the provision of sufficient rules to take (in the case of LCP) a design from the data tree-structure (represented diagrammatically as a horizontal set of interconnected vertical braces) to a 'structured' flow-chart with references to a list of executable operations.

The LCS part may be summarised as an insistence on establishing the total information content of a proposed system as a set of static relationships between a finite number of hierarchies. This is seen as a prerequisite to the determination of the dynamic relationships necessitated by seriality of processing and the time-succession of events in the real world. This dynamic modelling (called LCE) of the static relationships, in which files are defined, forms a bridge between LCS and LCP and claimedly ensures that the whole gamut of system and program design is covered.

Michael Jackson structured design (MJSD)

In many ways MJSD is similar. It, too, takes a hierarchic view of the data structures as totally determining program structures and suggests (MJSD in its published form does not deal in such great detail with the problem of total system design as LCP/LCS) a similar formalism in defining the major components of a system. To compensate for this it undoubtedly provides the designer with greater insight into the real causes of complexity in program logic. There are two major achievements.

The first, a standard solution to the *backtracking* problem, enables the correspondence of data structures and program structure to be maintained in those cases where the serial nature of reading an input stream prohibits the making decisions at the points where they are required. A simple illustration may be provided by considering a program to validate batches of data records. The records from batches found to be erroneous are to be written to an error file but there is no means in general of classifying the batch as erroneous until the whole of it has been read—by which time it is too late to redirect the earlier records. MJSD enables the essential distinction between a good batch and a bad batch to be preserved in the structure of the program when in all other methodologies the difficulty is not even recognised for what it is. In such cases *ad hoc* solutions, such as multiple passes of the file, multiple buffering to permit look-ahead and so forth, are resorted to by the methodologies, so design and implementation become hopelessly entangled. MJSD does not provide and cannot provide a panacea for this problem but it does give the designer the means to recognise and resolve it.

The second major achievement of MJSD is the recognition of *structure clashes*. Where LCP largely confines itself to designing programs from a single data structure or a set of structures which do not differ significantly from one another, MJSD provides the means to recognise cases whose constituent data structures are for example interleaved or wrongly ordered, decouple the clashing structures, design simple programs around each and link them at implementation time by standard coded interfaces. As with backtracking the designer is able to apply standard, simple solutions to what would otherwise have been problems of seemingly great, though in truth spurious, complexity.

One structure clash in particular holds the key to the value of MJSD. This is the *boundary clash*. Again, an illustration is necessary. Consider a file of statistics, presented as records each relating to one of a set of consecutive arbitrary periods defined by a start date and an end date, which have to be edited for output for a wholly different set of periods, also consecutive and spanning the same calendar interval overall, but bearing no relation whatever to the input periods. Whereas a conventional program designer, even one proficient in structured programming, might devise a solution which yielded a working program, he would naturally concern himself, in testing the program, with a large number of special cases; for example, that of an input period covering the same time-span as a number of output periods or vice versa. Using MJSD the designer would not even consider such manifestations of the interaction between the input structure and the output structure. He would build a simple program structured as an iteration of input periods each structured as an iteration of calendar days and a similar, quite separate program based on an iteration of output periods each structured as an iteration of calendar days. The two programs would be designed largely in isolation, retain their separate simplicities and communicate in operation by the one writing and the other reading an intermediate 'file' of entities called calendar dates, the data entity common to both program structures. Moreover, the structures of the two programs would be wholly unaffected by the mechanism of communication between the two.

One important effect is that the execution of the programs could be distinct in time, with a real intermediate file being output by one for later reading by the other, or they could operate synchronously in a co-routine relationship or even, if circumstances so required, execute asynchronously with a varying-size buffer of common items (the calendar date entities) continuously bridging the gap between them. This aspect of MJSD, which in large measure is a full recognition of vertical modularity, is vitally important for two reasons. Firstly, it separates the problem-solving part of the task (which is what design solely is) from the mechanism needed to realize it and makes those mechanisms like those beloved of software engineering—standard, reproducible and reusable. Secondly, the recognition of structure clashes, particularly the boundary clash, opens the way to a more satisfactory basis for system design, although MJSD does not fully exploit this yet. MJSD perceives the need for separate programs in many more cases than any other methodology. The effect of this is a larger number of cooperating sequential processes or programs all of which are necessarily simple in structure even though the mechanisms for linking them may be awkward to realize with present high-level languages. Because each program or process is built round its own local, serial data structure, a system comprised of such programs automatically evidences optimal coupling (data coupling as defined by CD). However, the components of a MJSD system are not sub-routines of defined function and high module strength/cohesion; they are serial processes. Only in this way can the impossibility of attaining optimum coupling in CD and SD because of variable state sub-routines be overcome.

In MJSD we meet an interesting parallel with the transaction analysis 'option' of SD. One of the consequences of decoupling clashing structures, especially in the case of the boundary clash, is that it becomes possible to design processes which have the same sort of structural integrity as a conventional program but whose execution is suspended from time to time, perhaps for long periods. A conventional program executes in one burst from start to finish but this aspect of its behaviour is not structurally significant; what matters is the total relationship of the entities to be processed and the associated computations, regardless of any 'interruptions'. Consider, for example, the task of keeping up to date, in a banking application, the current accounts of numerous depositors. Conventional systems analysis will see the necessity here for a master accounts file, keyed probably by account number and a daily update program to apply the transactions for the day, pre-sorted into account number order. So will CD and the transform analysis 'option' of SD. MJSD, on the other hand, will perceive instead a large number of parallel processes (one for each account) which model the time-series of events in each account. It is this single process (the multiple accounts do not necessitate the creation of multiple processes, merely multiple instantiations of the one process) that more truly reflects the problem to be solved. How else than by having a process to model the 'life-history' of an account can it be shown, for instance, in the process structure, that the first transaction in the account must be a deposit not a withdrawal or that there exists an entity called 'overdrawn period' which either exceeds or stays within the limits agreed for duration or average overdrawn balance in an overdraft arrangement? In the conventional or 'transform analysis' view it is the mechanism of the daily update and the keying of the account records which dominate the design. The account history is left, as it were, to fend for itself in the form of data items stored in each account record. MJSD will generate a similar solution eventually but it will see the problem as modelling the possible transactions on the account first and only then will it proceed to deal with the mechanism required to save the internal state of each instantiation of the account process during each daily 'interruption'. It will do this, of course, in a file to be called, in the usual way, the accounts master file.

Thus MJSD solves at least one dilemma of SD, whether to use transform or transaction analysis. Uncompromisingly, the decision is always for transaction analysis.

Structural factor 2: complexity — its recognition and effect

The ideal for complexity is easily stated — simplicity! But it is much less easy to define. The definition adopted here is that complexity in a system or program is the presence of anything which cannot be traced back, as a whole, to a corresponding factor in the problem or one of the implementation constraints which modify it. By this is excluded the complexity which may be inherent in a problem and which of course must appear in the solution. If it does not, it is false or spurious simplicity that is bound, in the long run, to impair the system's maintainability. The key to containment of complexity by a design methodology is its ability to perceive simple patterns of relationships and capitalize on them.

MP has no defences against complexity at all. TDD has little more in fact, but introduces sometimes a spurious simplicity (and the complacent feeling of well-being that goes with it) because its design process of breaking down a program or system into small, manageable pieces with well-defined interfaces seems so eminently reasonable. But it does so in ignorance of whether the pieces resulting from the breakdown can be deemed truly independent. CD and SD improve greatly on this by providing a measure of the independence of modules but are nonetheless unable to prevent the complexity that comes from being unable to recognise all types of process. SADT is a step backwards; it can only moderate the effects of complexity by providing an extremely effective means of portraying solutions. The complexity of the design still depends on the skill of the designer at the procedural level. LCP/LCS enforces non-complex solutions but its capacity to do this is limited. It certainly prevents the introduction of spurious complexity when it is possible to design the information base of a system in the hierarchical way it requires, but it is not competent to handle the type of complexity — the 'structure clashes' of MJDS — which arises from the external constraints of physical data representation and ordering, for example. MJSD is competent to handle much of this complexity and in consequence is best able to keep spurious complexity at bay.

However, it may be wondered, especially since the mechanisms used to resolve the structure clashes are themselves complex, whether the LCP/LCS emphasis on simple data structures at the system level — in MJSD terms the design of the system with the fewest possible structure clashes — is not more profitable than the MJSD approach which, by concentrating on program design is willing to accept a situation where many clashes have to be resolved.

Structural factor 3: modularity

Modularity is of course inseparable from the structural basis of the methodologies already outlined, but it has to be considered in its own right because there are two quite separate ideals for modularity. They are that the modules of the solutions should correspond one-to-one with the major structural components of the data base of the problem system and that the physical modules should exhibit the minimum possible interdependence. The one-to-one correspondence rule, when broken, leads to spurious complexity as defined above. The minimum interdependence rule is essential if maintenance and enhancement of the system are not either to destroy structural integrity, or else to be economically burdensome because the effects of changes are spread over many modules. Moreover, the two ideals conflict. The conflict is only to be avoided if the one-to-one correspondence rule takes precedence. That is, the vertical modularity of the system—its constituent programs and processes, however interconnected—must be established first.

Once this is done, and the constituent processes and their computational requirements have also been designed, it becomes possible to determine what functional commonality exists and where, so that common modules (and sometimes common processes) may be defined and designed. Only by taking this system-wide view can the system's process structure and common function structure be kept separate through the life of the system. It can be seen that horizontal modularity, one of the mainstays of TDD, is in fact only a form of pragmatic modularity. That is to say, it does not greatly matter, structurally, how large processes (or large common functions) are broken down. The pragmatic criteria of breakdown—size, parallel allocation of work, high likelihood of change, efficient re-compilation, etc.—are as vitally important as they have always been but they must not conflict with the breakdowns reflecting vertical and common modularity. The ideal process of modularization may thus be summarised as:

- Firstly ascertain the vertical modularity (define the processes)
- Secondly ascertain the common modularity (define the functional extensions to the base language)
- Lastly divide the modules already defined for practical reasons, if necessary.

MP, in common with most of the others, finds little difficulty in defining the 'obvious' processes—programs to be separated by a sort, for instance. Indeed, the scale of MP is usually thought of only as the predetermined program. Within this scope, MP relies mainly on pragmatic criteria as the basis of modularity. Common modularity is recognised but provision for it is always made ad hoc.

TDD goes little further than MP in vertical modularity. Its scale too, is more properly that of the single program. Nearly all modular breakdowns are done on the horizontal principle and this may lead to a very poor detection of common modularity needs, if top-down implementation is used, unless the centralized control of, for example, a chief programmer (in the Chief Programmer Team sense) who can take a global view is present. CD deals well with common modularity (by emphasising the merit of data coupling). Its approach to vertical modularity is an improvement in that it does at least recognise the need for formal criteria to divide one process from another.

SD recognises, by including transaction analysis, that there is more to vertical modularity than the recognition of transformations on large sets of data, but fails to exploit it.

Modularity is scarcely relevant to SADT.

LCS does not have a transform/transaction option but does provide comprehensive analytical tools to define the data structures corresponding to programs. Common modularity is not emphasised.

MJSD recognises, as an integral part of its approach, the need to resolve systems into processes, even cooperating and synchronous processes. It places no emphasis on horizontal modularity, largely because it ceases to be a difficulty. Common modularity, however, it does not address itself to at all.

Structural factor 4: scale

It has to be accepted that system design and program design are really distinct sciences. The history of large-scale programming bears out this presumption of distinctness but has seldom dared to define it. The definition that system design is essentially to recognise and demark processes and define the data content of their interfaces while program design is to deduce the flow-of-control structure which is implicit in those interfaces, can be put forward with confidence. If it is accepted then the ideal capability of a methodology is that the system design tools should enable the processes of a system to be fixed in a way that subsequent program design cannot invalidate.

Whether a methodology must provide equally for both types of design is less sure. It would seem that if it has the ideal capability in system design then it is not to be criticised for omitting program design. The converse is not true; a program design technique, whatever its merits, is of limited use if its programs are wrongly defined.

On this view MP comes out very badly indeed for it neither concerns itself with system design as just defined nor provides a means to structure internally the modules it creates. TDD fares almost as badly.

CD and SD rate quite well, however, for they do at least try to ensure, by their strength/cohesion and coupling approach, that the internal design of modules will not have an iterative effect on the system design, even though that system design does not necessarily demark all the processes.

SADT, although not divisible into system and program design components, and partly because of this, imposes no restriction of scale.

LCP/LCS (with its intermediate technique, LCE) does cover both system and program design very fully. Indeed it approaches the ideal capability, defined above, but, because of its inadequate treatment of complex cases, only for systems whose processes are inherently simple.

MJSD, by defining programs and processes in a way which guarantees for each a structural independence of all the others, makes program design more nearly an automatic procedure than is the case with any of the other methodologies. By so doing it provides one of the prerequisites of the ideal capability, but it has not yet capitalized on this in its system design techniques.

Structural factor 5: scope

So far as scope is concerned, there is no point in formulating an ideal. What can be usefully said is that there is no way of even beginning to define 'the range of problems' that a methodology can handle except in terms of their structural principles—there is no external definition, except perhaps in terms such as batch, on-line, real-time and TP. What distinguishes these categories are not differences of structure or principles of design but mechanisms, principally the mechanisms of invocation, synchronization, data access, initiation etc., all of which have to do with the transfer of data between processes rather than their existence or internal structure.

Tacitly, all the methodologies recognise this by not making special provision for these distinctions. So far as defining the range of soluble problems in terms of structural principles is concerned, it proves impossible to make any statement at all for MP, TDD, CD, SD and SADT, simply because all these are solution-oriented. Given a well-defined problem any of these will produce a solution, however particular characteristics of the problem are defined. With LCP/LCS and MJSD at least a relative statement is possible. MJSD offers backtracking and the mechanical decoupling of clashing structures as already described. LCP has no conception of the former and only a vestigial treatment of the latter; what MJSD makes so central to the understand of program structure LCP dismisses (under the name of 'processing phases') in a few paragraphs with trivial illustrations; what in MJSD is obviously a basis for future system design is merely, in LCP, the obligatory mention of a universal difficulty which the methodology otherwise takes no account of.

Both methodologies also deal with the problem of multiple input files where items in different files have to be collated. LCP has a cumbersome approach based on the selection, arbitrarily, one of the files as a 'guide' file. MJSD correctly perceives that the essence of the collation problem is the physical disjunction (the separateness of the files) of what is essentially a single iteration of entities and therefore forces a similar program structure that 'reads' each entity from all the files in a way that does not falsely attribute structural importance to any one of them. But in one way LCP does go further than

MJSD. It contains an extensive coverage of the logical basis for making multiple selections, roughly the province of decision table theory; MJSD confines itself to simple selections and those amenable to backtracking; it does not deal with the optimal combination of selections as LCP does.

In a more general sense MJSD is more competent than LCP. LCP deals only with what may be termed, deprecatingly, 'commercial file-processing problems'. In such problems the data which make up the entities represented by the files may well require considerable computation to produce the required output but the entities are self-identifying themselves, clearly delimited—keys are present and iterations are either of known extent (each X is known to consist of N instances of Y, for example, and the value of N does not have to be discovered by the program) or else are represented by the familiar control-break structure. MJSD is capable of dealing with cases in which both the classification and extent of the principal entities in the files have to be computed.

Structural factor 6: integrity

Structural integrity is the most important single attribute that a system should possess. One half of it is 'correctness'. The structure of a system—its partition into processes and their internal structures—may be said to be correct if it corresponds directly to the data structures it models and the existent orderings of the entities composing them. Furthermore, this correspondence must be visible; in whatever form the design, or its derivative code, is represented, that which is present for reasons of language, optimization and physical input/output must be in some sense separable from what is the realization of the problem structure. But 'correctness' so defined is a static term. Structural integrity connotes the possession of correctness by a system at every stage in its evolution. In other words, a system has complete structural integrity if an outsider ignorant of its development history can deduce the problem it solves by inspection of the design notations or compilable code and, further, cannot tell whether it has ever been amended.

For the reason that they are solution-oriented, none of MP, TDD, CD, SD and SADT can reveal structural correctness by inspection. CD and SD, however, do meet the evolutionary requirement because if the strength/cohesion and coupling rules are kept wherever the system is amended the patches do not show. What this means is that a system designed by CD or SD may not have the best possible structure but it is possible to ensure that the structural quality does not deteriorate under repeated alteration.

The two data-structured methodologies do permit the preservation of structural integrity in a fuller sense. LCP/LCS with its straightforward problems and MJSD with its more taxing ones both provide sufficient insight for the full effects of any proposed amendment to be worked out and the necessitated structural changes made at both system and program levels.

These changes are, of course, sometimes much more extensive than those of a 'patch' with the same immediate functional effect but this trade-off of operational expedience against long-term economics lies outside the evaluation of methodologies as such. In any case, it is always possible, by means of properly organized project control, to phase enhancements so that re-structuring costs are contained and not to use 'patched' versions of the system for enhancement.

Peripheral factors 1: design states and their documentation

The requirements are simply stated as:

- The stages needed should be a strict succession, invariable for all types of problem
- Each stage should have a documented record without which progress to the next should be impossible and which should include everything requisite for that next stage
- The documentation of any stage should be a total statement of the problem/solution (depending on the stage)

It is worth pointing out that the design stages are nothing to do with the functional decomposition and amplification of detail implicit in the top-down principle.

MP has no significant design stages after the initial modular division and no de facto standards of documentation.

TDD recognises the documentation problem and attempts to overcome it by having small modules easily understood at the source code level. Often used with TDD are HIPO charts or their equivalent. Each HIPO chart shows all inputs and outputs of a module, including those which act as controls, summarises the functional content of the module and connects each constituent function to those inputs, outputs and controls which relate to it. HIPO charts provide a module specification and a sketch of its anticipated functional breakdown. The HIPO charts are themselves related by a Visual Table of Contents which gives a hierarchical picture of the system's modules. Thus the design stages are three, as determined by the documented output—hierarchy chart, HIPO chart, structured source code. The three requirements laid down above are largely satisfied, given the imprecision of the design principles.

CD uses only the hierarchical diagram but supplements it with special symbols in an attempt to convey the dynamic relationship of modules (e.g., in what order and how often they are invoked). These symbols correspond, in a very disguised form, to the explicit statements of sequence and iteration employed by LCP/LCS and MJSD. They totally fail to convey precise information because they are notational addenda to a static module hierarchy chart which in itself only expresses the relative subordination of modules.

SD has similar notations to CD but also has a bubble chart showing the major transformations (or programs) and data flow lines between them. Here, too, there are supplementary symbols. In particular there are symbols for disjunction and conjunction of files (for example to show that the output of a transformation on one transaction entity will be routed to one of file A or file B but not both). Again, the symbols are an *ad hoc* and partial attempt to represent some special cases of selection in the wrong sort of diagram. In SD the data flow diagram is the predecessor stage to the module hierarchy chart stage. Neither satisfies the requirement of being a sufficient record to support the design stage which follows it.

SADT has design stages in only a limited sense. The multi-level breakdown is followed by the detailed procedural structuring of the 'modules' according to a very precise and comprehensive set of rules. As *procedural* documentation it has no peer for clarity and immediacy. So complete and self-explanatory is the documentation equally detailed review procedures are based on written communication between reviewer and reviewee. This is insisted on to ensure that a documented structure does reveal not only the designer's broad intentions but also any mistakes he has made, and of course to guarantee completeness. SADT comes very close to satisfying the requirement that the final design documentation is a total solution, alone sufficient for transcription to source code, subject to the proviso concerning modularity.

LCP's design stages are firstly an hierarchic description of the program's output data structure, the various levels being represented as sequences (in the sense given by structured programming; LCP itself uses the term sequence differently). Iteration factors and special symbols to denote, for example, mutual exclusion of pairs of elements in the sequence complete the diagram. Taken together these represent the selection and iteration constructs of structured programming. By so compounding selection and iteration LCP manages to produce a tree-structured diagram of data in which the connections of elements (or sub-trees) to the sub-tree node above (in LCP to the left) are all of the same type. The derivation of these diagrams can require the drawing of truth tables, the drawing of Karnaugh maps and extensive manipulations in Boolean algebra, but these are not to be considered as part of the documentary record of the design process. The completed structure diagram is such that a structured flowchart using the conventional box-shapes can be drawn from it without faultless design work. It is only at this stage that the executable operations are considered.

There is no means of ensuring that the designer includes all the necessary operations (apart from a check-list including such designations as inputs, branches, preparations of branches, sub-routine calls, etc.) but there is a built-in protection against incorrect structure for if the structure is incorrect some required operations will be found not to be allocatable. The design is completed by merging the operation list and the flowchart derived from the structure diagram. The operations are written in pseudo code. Because the derived structure is represented as a flowchart the selections and iterations implicit in the data structure diagram are not carried down to the final pseudo code, ordinary branch operations taking their place. For the same reason the pseudo code is not written in indented form and readability suffers as a result. LCP's design stages have a greater value that the above outline suggests, however, for there is an abundance of precise rules to cover every situation LCP is competent to deal with. It is a great misfortune that the published material in English is so invariably pedestrian and often obscure as to conceal the comprehensiveness of these rules.

MJSD's design stages are very similar. The data structure diagram is clearer than LCP's because it embodies explicit notations to distinguish sequences, selections and iterations and because it is set out vertically. The crucial difference from LCP is the extra design stage in which the separate data structures (at least one for input and at least one for output) are combined into program structure(s). Correspondences (boxes in two data structures are said to correspond if the number and ordering of all the instances of the datum represented by the box are the same) are established and rules given to determine whether both (or all) the data structures can be combined into one program structure. If they cannot, a structure clash exists and more than one program structure is required. LCP has no equivalent of this. Once the program structure is derived, as with LCP's derivation of the flowchart, it is a more or less mechanical task to transform it to a form of indented pseudo code called schematic logic. In this pseudo code selections and iterations are represented as select-end and iter-end statement pairs, with Boolean expressions appended to the selection and iteration keywords. Further, to maintain one-to-one correspondence with the program structure diagram sequence-end statement pairs are written, although no executable code is derived from them. The derived schematic logic is basically structured code, with only important exception: when backtracking is needed the select-end statement pair is augmented with quit statements, which are GOTOs with implied targets.

Much as with LCP, operations are listed, numbered and appended to the program structure diagram by means of their reference numbers and are then written into the schematic logic to complete the design documentation. The process of ascertaining the necessary operations and then allocating them to the right places in the structure has precisely the same weakness and strength as in LCP.

MJSD has the best-defined design stages of all the methodologies (in the program design area) and comes closest of all to satisfying the three requirements stated as the ideal. What principally is lacking, and the same goes for all the others, is an unequivocal statement of how input data and output data are related—a problem statement language in fact. So long as this is missing and until the definition of the problem in terms of such a language is seen as a prerequisite to program design one of the functions of the design process must be to purge the written specification of omissions and inconsistences. Putting this extra burden on to the design activity prevents the design stages from being a true succession.

Peripheral factors 2: project control

The only thing that Project Control wants from a design methodology is the means to quantify real progress in development—either the initial development or a subsequent enhancement, because without this accurate quantification the planning, resource-scheduling and time-tabling functions of project control are made nugatory.

Quantification of progress may be reduced to three factors:

- As many design stages as possible, all of them 'non-iterative'
- Design stage documentation that is self-contained so that review is straightforward and error detection very likely
- An intrinsic measure of completion for each design stage: that is to say, independently of the problem to be solved, and taking a hypothetical case, a standard set of cumulative percentages such as that of data structures represent 35% of the total work, program structures 50%, allocated operations 65%, source code 80%, and so forth.

All the methodologies make exhortations about factor number 2 and SADT goes far actually toward satisfying it. Only MJSD offers any prospect of satisfying factor number 3. Although the ascription of cumulative percentage completion value to its various design stages has not been made, its capability to recognise complexity at the beginning of program design and create multiple, simple, components in consequence, does suggest that it could be.

Both LCP and MJSD answer all to the requirement of factor number 1, the latter especially. CD and SD do not, in the program design area, because of their built-in approach which can be summarised as 'divide, measure the quality which results, and try again'. Both LCS and CD/SD have very formal system design stages.

Peripheral factors 3: testing

Testing, whether at the system, program, or lower level, is always of two kinds: the first kind seeks to ascertain whether the components (test-objects) function reliably in their operational contexts. It is indifferent to the structures of the components. It is always·necessary, always a sequel to the second kind, establishes its criteria of reliability independently of the methodology used to produce the code and its only relevance to a comparison of design methodologies is the possibility that a design methodology might be so bad as to make a great deal of it necessary. The second kind seeks to show that a component's behaviour is correct, in relation to its specification (or, if that is not definitive, to its documented design), in all the cases its coded structure reveals as being distinct.

It is intuitively obvious that the second kind is more important than the first, if only because its effectiveness (assuming it to be necessary at all) governs how much of the first kind, which is much more costly, will required. So the testing aspects of the methodologies reduce to a consideration of the second kind only.

There are two important questions to ask: what approximation to exhaustiveness is possible? and, more profoundly, how necessary is internal testing? After all, testing is not the obligatory first kind of testing to be gone through before a system or one of its components becomes operational.

The question of exhaustiveness is a vexed one. Testing is exhaustive (though it does not necessarily prove correctness) if all the truly distinct cases are exercised, given that there is a definition of what a case is. The obstacle to the achievement of exhaustiveness is not the labour of test-case definition, preparation and execution; it is rather the difficulty of establishing an applicable set of criteria which can be applied to any component so as to make testing nondiscretionary. The functional decomposition school cannot hope to do this because it trades in variable-state sub-routines, the possible control paths through which are only deducible by laborious inspection. MJSD does make all the control paths in a program or process enumerable but fails to insist on the absolute independence of data items in data structures at the beginning of design which would be the only way of guaranteeing that all the apparent paths were operationally possible. Nonetheless this refinement could be made.

It would seem scarcely worthwhile, however, for MJSD questions the need for extensive internal testing. It argues that since the testing of the millions of 'cases' arising from the combination of possible paths in many components is impossible, it is money better spent to ensure that the components are structurally separated so that the combinations become meaningless as independent sources of malfunction. This it does by its recognition of structure clashes. Evidence from the use of MJSD cannot directly substantiate the claim that 'exhaustive' testing is a waste of time—obviously, the designer's proficiency is still a large factor in creating reliable programs—but the ample circumstantial evidence of drastically reduced numbers of test shots per component and of impressive levels of operational reliability, is very compelling.

Peripheral factors 4: portability and external compatibility

There is little to be said concerning portability for all the methodologies ensure it in their own ways, either by not descending to a level of detail where it matters or else by causing code to be generated in a language-independent form—as pseudo code.

With external compatibility there is the irony that the more a methodology differs from conventional modularity in the systems it creates the more difficult it is to interface with existing systems or subsystems. MJSD suffers in this way as a system design tool, although not as a program design tool. MJSD should only be used for designing systems if the systems are to be designed from scratch.

THE COMPARISON IN PREDICTIVE TERMS

In being bold enough to make predictions in a field as quixotic as system design, it is essential to ensure that the evaluation should not depend only on factors which owe their importance, or even their relevance, to the present state of technology as applied to computing. It is not easy to do this as computing has so preoccupied Itself with mechanisms, procedures and tools in its thirty years that the principles underlying it all have only recently received their fair share of attention. As a consequence of this imbalance it is difficult to exclude the possibility of being wrongly influenced by *de facto* technological assumptions in drawing up the evaluation factors. A good example of this is seriality in program execution. A program seems to be an intrinsically serial thing. Control is acquired once, the operations forming the program text redirect control to different places in the text until eventually it is relinquished. Yet the very fact that this statement can be made, without any reference to the transformations of data effected by the program, shows that the concept of control has not necessarily anything to do with any problem to be solved; it is merely a mechanism made necessary by the fact that computers' CPUs are built in a particular way. The lesson is that seriality in execution must not be assumed as an axiom when evaluating methodologies to generate programs.

Thus five factors (perhaps talking-points would be a better term) have been selected to cover those aspects seemingly independent of technological change. They are:

- The extent to which implementation (and, of course, optimization) can be separated from the process of design

- The extent to which full information systems, not just computer systems, can be designed

- The properties ensuring the preservation of structural integrity throughout the life-cycle of the system

- The extent to which every component, every structural element, every fact indeed is explicitly ascribable to a defined requirement in the specification

- Whether the completeness and consistency of the specification are assumed by the design process, in contradistinction to its being dependent on them.

These are now considered individually.

Separation of design and implementation

All the methodologies avoid the more obvious sorts of implementation constraint, either by expressing the end product of the design in some pseudo code or by not dealing with the internal structure of modules/programs at all. But this is merely a limited view of implementation independence. A more satisfactory separation must treat as implementation some things which are now thought of as part of design. Consider again the imposed seriality mentioned above in the context of a very small program whose sole function is to list the decimal equivalents of a set of hexadecimal numbers, input one per record. The majority of the logic in this case is to do with handling the iteration of records—opening and closing files, any initialization needed, the reading of successive records and the recognition of end of file in some way. All this is properly a mechanism common to all instances of iteration. Therefore it should be taken out of the province of design because mechanisms are always capable of being incorporated automatically after the design has been done.

This one example shows that the methodologies of the functional decomposition school can never be extended to achieve a high level of implementation independence. The sort of trivial process just described, if it were represented as variable-state sub-routines, could not have its serial mechanism automatically included by any conceivable means since the modularity, which is not vertical, totally conceals the existence of the process.

With the data-structured school the prospects are better. Neither LCP nor MJSD goes so far as to express the design without reference to seriality but both could be easily modified to do so, because LCP is potentially and MJSD is actually able to distinguish independent data structures to base process structures on. Then the designer would be able to model the real world accurately; when the seriality was real (a train of events in real time) he would be compelled to incorporate it in his data model; when the seriality was imposed by the processor he would be compelled to build a data model reflecting the unordered nature of its parts, knowing that for implementation a serial iteration mechanism was in some form available for incorporation. The separation of design from implementation in fact reduces to the recognition and temporary setting aside of standard mechanisms so that they do not interfere with design. MJSD does not, it is true, explicitly deal with all the necessary mechanisms, but it does enormously clarify design by recognising some of the important ones. It already has the power to produce exactly the same correct design for two cooperating processes whether they execute synchronously, asynchronously or even interruptedly, over a long period of time. It could be extended so that a single design would serve for a program to execute in two modes, one conventional serial and the other using an array of parallel processors.

It is difficult to draw a hard and fast line between implementation and optimization. Strictly speaking there can be none for both are concerned to take cognisance of computing environment constraints when mapping a design into executable form. But if implementation is taken to be that part of the mapping which is necessary to have the program or system run at all and optimization that part required to make it run faster or consume fewer resources in general, then it can be seen that the relation of optimization to implementation is precisely that of implementation to design: optimization must follow implementation and be separable from it so that changing operational circumstances will allow new optimization of an unchanging implementation representation.

Most of the methodologies do not make much of this important point. MJSD, rightly, goes so far as to emphasise the point and suggest a few optimization techniques that do not mask or invalidate the basic program structure but unfortunately it is not entirely consistent. Some of its techniques require data structures to be drawn which suppress relevant data relationships (relevant, that is, to understanding and accuracy, not to the program's execution) in the interests of economy and efficiency. Nonetheless, MJSD has in its program design stages a basis which could incorporate an extra stage to show structural abstractions occasioned by the need to optimize.

Information systems and computer systems

None of the methodologies professes to be other than a tool for designing computer systems though LCS comes close to it in its treatment of the information content of major data structures. A system is a family of cooperating but structurally independent processes or programs. Sometimes the overall unity of a system is difficult to see because the processes carried out by the computer form only a part of the full set of processes. The others are performed by human beings and interact with the computer processes in a co-routine relationship by communicating data in both directions across the interface. Strictly, whether to run a process on a computer or 'on' a person is an implementation decision: if the logical structure of the process is simple, if it is formally expressible, if it is not too much subject to external change, if the physical data are available and machine-readable, or if the computations are tedious to perform, a computer should be used; otherwise a person is more suitable.

The point is that the processes themselves have to be determined before this 'implementation' decision can sensibly be made. And it has to be stressed that actions performed by people are not closed sub-routines any more than their computer counterparts. The decisions they make (and thus the nature of the data returned to computer processes) are based not only on the current data output by the computer processes but on the data content of earlier interactions. Any full information system must treat computer and human processes alike, and a prerequisite of this is the recognition of the processes themselves. Only the data-structure school is positioned to do this.

Preserved structural integrity

To preserve structural integrity throughout the life of a system it is necessary to be prepared to do two things—incorporate as much generalization as possible in the initial design so as to minimize the later effects of quantitative change and, since no steps can be taken initially to provide for unforeseen qualitative change, accept that the system has to be re-structured whenever it is to be enhanced. With luck a given enhancement will cause only a partial and local re-structuring. With ill luck the whole system will have to be structurally 'demolished' and re-structured to reflect its new specification, re-using whatever fragments of structure are unaffected by the change. For this to be feasible not only must the components of the system be isolable, but the separate design stages of each must be recoverable so that the obligatory re-working is reduced to a minimum. Again it is vertical modularity which gives the best division into components and the preserve of discrete design stages with definitive associated documentation which ensure the needed flexibility in re-design.

It has to be said in this connection that full compliance with these stated requirements of structural integrity is so onerous as to be economically impossible for the foreseeable future. It is not just a matter of a supportive methodology (MJSD in particular goes some small way to provide the support) but the fact that software support is so very crude. High-level languages do not provide support above the sub-routine level by and large; none of the widely used ones even recognises the fundamental importance of processes and their inter-communication; none of them provides more than a few of the standard 'mechanisms' for implementation; none is integrated with a compatible set of specification and design notations or languages. So overwhelming are these present obstacles to re-structuring that the second-best approach of CD and SD, whereby a change is made and its effects are suitability measured by the known coupling of modules, will remain attractive for a very long time.

Structural ascribability

Structural ascribability is the property of a design methodology which permits the outside reader of the defining documentation of a system to learn the reason for every detail of its structure. It is not enough to know that A precedes B: one must also know why; it is not enough that C, D and E should form a three-element sequence: it is required also to know why they do not form a three-element iteration.

Briefly put, structural ascribability comes down to the total exclusion of arbitrariness from specification, design and implementation. It is the only absolute guarantee there is that the effects of making a change to a system can all be deduced and provision made for them—estimations of inter-module coupling are very hopeful in modularizing a system so that changes are localized in effect but they do not relate a set of perhaps scattered structural manifestations to a single cause which, if affected by a change of specification, will certainly require all its manifestations to be changed too. What is needed is a cause-to-manifestation mapping in the design documentation. CD and SD, by their coupling rules, attempt to reduce the number of manifestations, but when they only partially succeed, they do not ease the task of certainly tracing all those that remain. Nor does any other of the methodologies. The point is made here because the concept of Abstract Data Types would provide the ascribability. So far, this important structural principle has not been incorporated formally by any of them.

Design and specification

It is a moot point whether design (meaning system design) depends on an unequivocal specification or is a means of arriving at it. It raises the question of whether specification and design are truly distinct activities. They have seemed so in the past. Specification has concerned itself with relationships between input and output data and design with the modular, procedural and serial implications. By reducing these to the status of ready-made mechanisms, as the data-structure school promises, the design task becomes the specification task. It is therefore the design methodology that shows some prospect of being able to take account of and make patent in its documentation everything traditionally relevant to specification that holds the key to the future. What is needed is a way of devoting a structure in terms of data entities, their dependences, relative orderings and associated data attributes which is such that internal consistency and completeness are subject to verification by inspection, as well as being such that the mechanisms of implementation and optimization may be successively applied to it to transform it to executable form. It reduces to the need for a single document per program to 'tell the truth' about the physical data of its external interface and the abstractions superimposed on that physical view as well as allowing 'automatic' generation of code.

It is a pity that MJSD, which in many respects meets these requirements, does not go further towards enabling this level of automation.

The upshot of the foregoing is that MJSD has the best long-term prospect of survival. SADT may well become more popular because it so successfully addresses the problems of documentation, communication and review which underpin the effectiveness of project control. CD and particularly SD no doubt will flourish too, because they do contain remedies for so many familiar difficulties encountered in building systems on a functional/procedural basis and because they do attempt to solve the 'bottom-up' problem of establishing common and multiple-use components. But only MJSD even hits at the long-term goal—a system defined as a set of static, invariant expressions of relationships—the program specifications—to which may be applied a series of standard engineering-like transformations to produce a correct operational system.

DESIGN METHODOLOGIES AND ADVANCING TECHNOLOGY

The dichotomy of practice and theory in computing is a familiar one, so familiar as to be almost a truism. Moreover, in the last few years it seems to have become more pronounced.

On the computer science side much useful work resulting in real progress in the understanding of the nature of computing has been done in the areas of relevance to this paper. Relational data bases, the formalization of the concept of abstract data type, the establishment of a rigorous basis for structured programming, modest advances in proving programs correct in their textual form, and languages like SIMULA, PASCAL and ALPHARD may be cited.

On the manufacturers'/users' side the pursuit of operational flexibility and sheer computing power coupled with an ever-increasing effort to maintain backward compatibility (which must, ultimately, be a disservice to the end user) have dominated the scene. Even where this pattern has been broken, as it increasingly is being, with the use of minis and micros, there has been a technological regression manifested by limited support software and programming languages.

In between have sat the standardization committees, rightly praised for their work in standardizing and normalizing, rightly reviled for preserving and increasing the momentum of high-level languages devised twenty years ago when data base management was scarcely understood.

But there was no effective bridge between large-scale data processing and computer science (and not only to the detriment of DP) until structured programming was first applied in DP, and that only a flimsy one. The new design methodologies promise to make a bridge permanent. No longer can DP plead preoccupation with problems of size, compatibility, people and 'efficiency' as an excuse for ignoring its primary task of analysing problems rigorously and solving them determinately, because the means to discharge this task are now well enough established for it to be obvious that an adequately comprehensive approach is only a few years away.

Some large organizations have been prepared to invest the large sums required for re-training, re-orientation and re-definition of personnel roles and successfully gone over to one or other of the new methodologies. But there is good reason to think that the future usage of formal design in DP will not be an extension of this practice once all the major corporations are won over. One reason is the size of the investment needed. The use of even Structured Programming, which is relatively non-disruptive when introduced, is still very small nearly ten years after its inception. It is difficult to believe that small organizations are going to adopt a full-blown design methodology when they do not or cannot take up a modest improvement like Structured Programming.

Secondly, there is the obviously transient nature of the situation today. No-one expects any of the methodologies to survive in their present forms for more than a couple of years. This engenders a wait-and-see attitude among prospective users.

The third reason is the weightiest. The methodologies of the data-structure school promise automation of the design process and vastly improved techniques in the engineering of the mechanisms required to translate design into executable code. If this promise is fulfilled, it can only mean the creation of the necessary software tools and in particular the development of a new generation of very high-level languages to supplant those of the late 1950s. The reader who doubts that this will happen is urged to count the structured dialects of FORTRAN and COBOL and the independent structured pre-processors for these languages.

The end result of the automation of design must be the use of wholly non-procedural 'problem statement languages'. It is not to be thought that the design methodologies will be alone responsible for this major shift of emphasis; they will act merely as vectors or as catalysts of the theoretical work already done. But they (or at least the data-structure methodologies) do show that the change can be made. To date, even the most successful commercial non-procedural languages (such as Mark IV) have been limited in the range of problems amenable to solution. That limitation is likely to be removed. ■

REFERENCES

001 MYERS G J *Reliable software through composite design* Petrocelli/Charter (1975)

002 DELTAK *Structured design reference guide* Deltak Inc (1977)

003 SOFTECH *Structured analysis reader guide* The Software Technology Company (SofTech) (1975)

004 WARNIER J-D *Logical construction of programs* H E Stenfert Kroese B V (1974)

005 WARNIER J-D *L'organisation des données d'un système* Les Editions d'Organisation (1974)

006 JACKSON M A *Principles of program design* Academic Press (1975)

007 LINDEN T A *Operating system structures to support security and reliable software* U S Department of Commerce (1976)

SOFTWARE DEVELOPMENT ENVIRONMENTS

Software development spans many different types of activities, from system requirements analysis through the production, maintenance, and administration of the system itself. When these activities can be organized into a design methodology and a development process that works, the next logical step is to automate those things that are routine so that more time can be spent on the most creative parts of the design. Design is essentially a problem-solving procedure, and problem solving is by nature a trial-and-error process. By automating the routine parts of the design process, more trials can be made with fewer errors.

Too often the tools are the first thing developed, without a proper understanding of what design strategies and development processes they are intended to support. *This is wrong!* Tools should support and enforce the design and development process but after a conscious decision is made about what that process is. If the tools come first, too often the design and development methods end up accommodating the tools instead of vice versa. The power of tools in determining what and how things get done was recognized early by Eli Whitney:

"I will form the tools such that the tools themselves shall fashion the work."

Tools will fashion good work and good procedures; or they will cause you grief. The approach we take in this tutorial is to emphasize proper design strategies first and then note the requirements that they place on your development support environment.

DEVELOPMENT SUPPORT LIBRARY

The concept of a development support library[1] was a major step toward moving programming from a private art to a public science (see Figure 1). It has the advantage of relieving the programmers from the clerical duties associated with programming, yet keeps the progress, quality, and interfaces visible to team members and supervisors throughout the development cycle.

A successful development support library is based largely on following a set of logical, orderly procedures during the development process. These procedures are often aided and enforced by automated support tools for

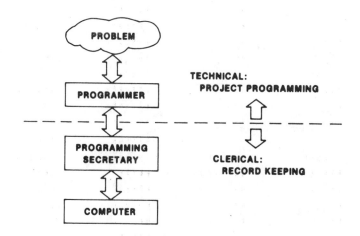

Figure 1. Development Support Library Interface.

controlling and manipulating the text and code associated with the software system. The intent is to keep the programmer working on the problem to be solved and to automate or at least standardize the procedure for integrating each program into its environment. In many cases, a programming secretary who interfaces the programmer is involved with the development support library.

In more sophisticated computer-aided design systems such as the PSL/PSA system developed by the University of Michigan, many of the clerical, bookkeeping, and documentation functions are performed automatically by the computer. This tool is described in detail by D. Teichroew and E. B. Hershey, III in their paper, **"PSL/PSA: A Computer-Aided Technique for Structured Documentation and Analysis of Information Processing Systems."**[27]

The collection, analysis, and reporting of information needed to prepare realistic proposals for information processing systems can be aided by the use of such a system. In addition, this tool can assist in checking the completeness and consistency of information specifying

347

the system, and it aids in the production of textual and graphic reports defining system elements and the system's expected behavior.

Manual preparation of software systems proposals and design documentation using natural languages suffers from several deficiencies. For one thing, natural languages are not sufficiently precise, and thus, it is difficult to ensure the consistency of the documentation. As well, there is often insufficient time and resources to determine what information is missing, let alone to assemble available information into useful reports describing the various aspects of the proposed system. The computer-aided technique described in this paper assists the systems analyst in preparing accurate, up to date, and complete system definitions.

The computer-aided design system uses a software package called the Problem Statement Analyzer (PSA) to maintain, modify, analyze, and produce reports from a machine-readable data base containing all the information about the proposed system. This information is entered, and commands are issued to PSA using the Problem Statement Language (PSL).

The language supports a model of information systems composed of named objects. Objects have properties or characteristics that distinguish them from other objects. Properties are named and, considered as objects, are also distinguished by having properties. At the lowest level of description are property values that define the most basic properties. Objects may be interrelated in various ways, and these connections are known to the system by means of relationships. Processes specify: what information objects are used, their derivation, the procedure employed to derive new objects, and the events leading to and resulting from the process activity.

PSL is capable of expressing, in machine-analyzable form, much of the information that constitutes a system definition report. From this information, PSA is used to produce reports showing the dynamic behavior of the system described; definitions, properties, and relationships among objects; analysis reports detailing inconsistencies, omissions, or unreferenced objects; and summaries based on properties and relationships detailed for the proposed system. Textual, tabular, and graphical reports may be generated also.

Experience to date indicates that this computer-based tool can be used to significantly aid in system development during the requirements definition phase. As a result, PSL/PSA is currently being used by a number of organizations for documenting systems and by academic institutions for education and research.

We have progressed to the point that the most pressing language problems seem to be in the area of requirements specification languages. PSL/PSA is, of course, one such attempt. The ultimate objective is to specify a problem in an easy-to-use, problem-oriented language that is written at a very high level but which is still machine executable. This is both a noble and a difficult task.

The Software Requirements Engineering Methodology (SREM) is another technique that was developed specifically for the management and technical aspects of generating software requirements for real-time systems. An excellent background paper on this technique is "A Requirements Engineering Methodology for Real-Time Processing Requirements."[6] SREM has progressed and has been successfully used on a number of very large projects. The current state of the SREM technology is described by Mack W. Alford in "**Software Requirements Engineering Methodology (SREM) at the Age of Four**."[26]

SREM consists of a formal requirements description language called the Requirements Specification Language (RSL) and a set of automated tools that operate on the RSL description to check for completeness and consistency and to generate simulations for validation of the correctness of the requirements. These are applied following guidelines that provide a set of step by step procedures to prepare the description of the system's function in RSL and to generate and validate the requirements.

SREM is based on a simple observation that real-time software is ultimately tested by entering a message into the system and by studying the resulting output messages. Thus, the requirements specification language is used to describe relationships between the input messages (or stimuli) and the resulting output messages, processing steps, and the data utilized and produced.

Processing is documented using a graphical diagram that shows the relationship between input and output messages and the steps of the computation. These diagrams are called PATH's. Performance requirements, appearing as a test specified in terms of variables measured along the PATH, are also indicated using PATH diagrams.

Several PATHS are required to describe all of the processing that may occur for a given type of input message. A requirements network, R-net, is simply an integration of several PATHS that treat the same input message type. The R-net is annotated with selector variables at node branches, so that the branch through the network for a specific condition is visible.

Another development support system that is finding wide use in the Bell System is called "Programmer's Workbench." This is a UNIX[TM] based, interactive, source-control system that automates much of the administrative part of producing a large software system.

Developing a large software system is complicated. Several software designers and programmers are involved, and many software development tools are required. These tools include support for program code as well as for program documentation. A computer system environment that can effectively support the needs of the development activity is often very much different than that needed for the efficient execution of the final application code.

In the past, one would try for a compromise that would permit software development on the same system intended for the application. While such a decision eliminates the need for a separate development facility, the resulting environment may be very ineffective. By tying both the development and application systems to the same computer facilities, it becomes much more disruptive to change equipment as the requirements of the development effort or application evolve. Moving to a different processor or operating system, for example, requires not only the reworking of the application code, but also the recreation of the software development tools.

The Programmer's Workbench concept addresses this conflict between development and support activities and the application environment. In the paper by Evan L. Ivie, **"The Programmer's Workbench—A Machine for Software Development,"**[25] a production-level collection of simple (but effective) tools that support the production, testing, and multi-version tracking of software is described. These tools also make it much easier to prepare specification, documentation, and user manuals as well as to prepare trouble reports and modification requests.

Workbench tools execute on a computer system that is separate from the application host. It runs a time-sharing operating system and supports many concurrent users. Code developed on the workbench is down-loaded for execution on the application's host machine.

Several advantages result when a separate development system is used. The development system and tools need not change as the application system evolves. Thus, we may invest more time and effort in the construction of the development tools themselves. The Workbench may provide the development support for a number of applications. Since the tools remain constant, and little time is wasted on retraining, the efficiency of the development effort is increased.

The development of a Programmer's Workbench brings us closer to a more professional and stable approach for software development. No longer must we

fashion tools only to be "left on the job" when the application system is completed and we move on to another task. The paper by Evan Ivie motivates the use of the Workbench concept, identifies those situations in which it is most useful, and discusses possible drawbacks.

HIGH-LEVEL LANGUAGES

High-level languages have long been recognized as aids to improving the quantity and quality of a programmer's output. It seems that errors are directly correlated with the number of pencil strokes, and with a high-level language you use less strokes.

A noble long-term objective for the use of a high-level language continues to be to prevent writing bad programs. Unfortunately, many people share the view voiced by Lawrence Flon:

> "There does not now, nor will there ever exist a programming language in which it is the least bit hard to write bad programs."

A practical near-term objective might be that programming languages should at least allow you to write good programs. Any higher-level language should provide control and data constructs that support structured programming (see Figure 2). Proponents of higher-level languages state that the increase in understandability that results allows the programmer to optimize in the large, rather than in the small. Thus, there is the hope of gaining back any reduction in code efficiency that results from the use of a higher-level language.

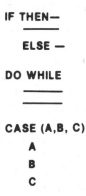

Figure 2. High-Level Language Constructs.

Other advantages claimed include the conjecture that even though the best assembly-language programmers can often write significantly more efficient code than the best high-level-language programmers, the programs written by average assembly-language programmers; and average high-level-language programmers do not vary greatly.

A recent high-level language developed for business data processing is called JSP Cobol (Jackson Structured Programming Cobol). It is well suited to the data structure design strategy described earlier and eliminates some of the well-defined but messy steps in the procedure.[2] Among other things, it automates the process called program inversion.

The program-design language that is presented by P. Van Leer in "Top-Down Development Using a Program Design Language,"[30] is a tool for designing programs in detail prior to coding. The syntax of the design language supports the structured coding constructs SEQUENCE, IF-THEN-ELSE, DO-WHILE, PERFORM-UNTIL, and CASE. Designs can be readily modified and quickly converted to a programming language. The use of the program design language encourages top-down program development, stepwise refinement, and levels of abstraction. Although it is similar to a programming language, it is more informal and cannot be directly compiled.

The simplicity and informality of applying the program design language allows the designer (who is usually the programmer) to concentrate on developing the detailed logic of a program. It also reduces the impact of correcting errors discovered before the code has been produced. The design process follows three distinct phases: (1) determining requirements, (2) abstracting functions, and (3) function detailing.

In phase one, determining program requirements, the system specifications for the program are studied, and a complete list of functions is compiled. Abstracting the functions involves organizing the identified operations into a hierarchy and creating major abstract functions as needed to encompass subordinate functions.

Generally, one cannot code the program from the hierarchically organized function lists produced at this stage. Functions are therefore expanded until all operations can be easily coded. Expansion is applied in turn to the highest-level, most important function that is yet undeveloped. This function is analyzed to determine what must be accomplished. Supportive subfunctions may be defined, And the relationships between subfunctions are specified using appropriate conditions and control structures. At this point, new variables are introduced (as required) to evaluate the conditions specified. Verification is the last stage of function expansion. The program designer reviews the detailed function, lists the various inputs required to test the function's operation, and verifies its completeness.

Encouraging the top-down development of structured code, the application of a program design language has resulted in programs that were ultimately more easily changed. Ease of implementation and a reduction in errors have been observed for programs designed in this manner.

TOPD is a program development system that is most useful after problem analysis, system specification, and major software design have been completed. It is described by R. A. Snowdon and P. Henderson in the reprint "The TOPD System for Computer-Aided System Development."[31] Program development proceeds through the design of classes that define data objects within the system. Properties associated with classes include operations, states, and state transitions.

Operations are represented by a procedure, identifying the name of the operation, its arguments, and an executable body that provides an algorithm-realizing operation.

The states of a class describe the expected behavior of a program and enumerate the condition in which objects of the class may be found.

State transitions specify how the conditions of objects may change when manipulated by operations.

Classes may be specified with varying degrees of completeness as the program is developed. The textual fragments that have been entered and the relationships among them are recorded in a data base. Access to this data is through a collection of separate program tools that can retrieve, modify, and store information in the data base. Tools are available to carry out exhaustive symbolic execution of pieces of abstract code according to the finite-state descriptions provided, to verify the behavior of an operator algorithm against the valid state transitions specified, and to produce COBOL source code from the completed hierarchy of classes.

TOPD is aimed at reducing the complexity of program development by providing a language and structuring discipline in which large, partially developed programs may be represented, mechanically verified, and more easily modified.

DOCUMENTATION

There are almost as many documentation techniques as there are design methodologies. For discussion, they can be sorted into general categories depending on whether they are primarily text oriented or graphical, on-line or off-line, mechanized or manual, etc.

Text-oriented documentation strategies (e.g., cause-effect charts) have the advantage that they can be easily stored and updated on a computer using only a simple text editor. The documentation is also easy to adapt to automatic test generation schemes or for program consistency checking. Structured English and pseudo code have the advantage of being able to be stored conveniently and compactly in the same file as the code itself. In cases where the pseudo code is itself a very high-level language that is executable, one can substantially reduce, if not eliminate, the age old problem of having the documentation and the code out of phase. Unfortunately, however, the closer the documentation format comes to a programming language, the worse it becomes at providing a clear view of the overall program structure. The completeness required by an executable language seems to be at odds with the clarity that a good documentation technique should provide.

Anymore, there is nearly universal agreement that flowcharts represent an inferior method of documenting a program. This consensus very nearly coincided with the time that automatic flowchart-drawing programs became widely available. An improved form of telescoping sets of hierarchical flow graphs is described by Douglas T. Ross in the reprint "**Structured Analysis (SA): A Language for Communicating Ideas.**"[28] While flow graphs appear to involve a lot of detailed artwork, much of the effort can be automated. Structured analysis has found application in both business data processing and in real-time control applications.

Structured Analysis (SA) is a communication tool that combines a graphic language with the nouns and verbs of written language to provide a hierarchic model that Ross hopes will be well suited for documentation of ideas. The goal of structured analysis is to provide a framework through which ideas can be precisely represented and communicated in an efficient manner.

Both objects (data) and events (activities) are documented using a basic building block. Arrows represent input, output, control, and mechanism relationships among the blocks in the structured analysis model. Approximately 40 features of this tool are presented, together with the rationale for understanding and communicating ideas to the structured collection of diagrams and notation that constitute SA models.

The human mind can understand and work with concepts of almost unlimited complexity when presented as a collection of hierarchically structured components, each of limited complexity. Hence, an SA model consists of an organized structure of separate diagrams, each diagram exposing only a limited portion of the subject. Constraints based on the purpose and viewpoint of the model motivate the specific hierarchy that results.

Bounded pieces of subject matter are diagramed using a box representing a transformation of an object or an activity. Arrows interconnecting these boxes go from the output face of one to the input or control face of another box. Input activity to an object box *creates* the object; output activity *references* such an object. For an activity, the input *causes* the activity; the output is

the transformed input object. The control constrains the transformation to ensure that it applies only under the appropriate circumstances. Further, the control constraints for activity boxes define and impose the structural decomposition of the model. An arrow terminating on the fourth face of the box specifies the mechanism for affecting the transformation diagramed.

These interconnecting arrows allow one to express how the component pieces go together to constitute the complete object. The SA model represents both the objects and activities of the system being described, and using the same box notation, thus emphasizes the duality of activities and data. The graphical syntax provides a framework upon which all of the aspects and relationships between concepts can be effectively organized.

The SA language also includes non-graphic notation. This provides a convenient means of referencing the diagrams and component boxes and special graphical conventions used to simplify the illustrations.

Structured analysis is a rigorous documentation and communication tool that forms the basis of SofTech's Structured Analysis and Design Technique (SADT[TM]). By structuring language, the medium that we use to think and communicate, SA allows ideas to be more effectively developed, understood, and communicated.

Structured Analysis and Design Technique, the proprietary methodology of SofTech, Inc. describes systems based on the structured analysis language. It is described by M. E. Dickover, C. L. McGowan, and D. T. Ross in the reprint "**Software Design Using SADT.**"[29] The application of SADT results in multiple models that describe the system from different viewpoints. Such models can be explicitly interrelated, thus identifying shared common detail and providing the opportunity to verify the consistency of the models.

The system models produced include activity and data models from the viewpoints of the designer, manufacturer, user, etc. An important model also produced is a mechanism model. Encapsulating and insulating their design and implementation details from other models of the system, and isolated for reasons of shareability and changeability, mechanisms are well suited as representations for abstract data types, monitors, and abstract machines. By using "call" notation, support for transformations diagramed in one model can be explicitly interconnected with a mechanism model.

Activation rules augment the graphically documented information by specifying sequencing constraints. Normally, a transformation box is considered to be activated only when all inputs to the box are available, at that time all outputs are produced. Thus, a high degree of parallelism can be displayed. Activation rules can be used to detail the production of some outputs, based on the availability of a subset of inputs or the sequencing of transformations that would otherwise appear to be executable in parallel. If appropriate, the graphical illustrations can also be detailed to show such constraints.

SADT combines a notation for communicating one's ideas and understanding with a technique for the production of clear and accurate documentation of these ideas and perceptions of a system. It is compatible with the contemporary design methodologies proposed by Yourdon and Constantine (Structured Design), Jackson (The Jackson Design Methodology), and Parnas (Information Hiding). SADT offers a conceptual and notational vehicle for expressing, evaluating, and comparing design alternatives.

Even though graphical techniques usually provide a clearer view of the program, they usually suffer from requiring manual updating. This leads to a "documentation lag" that can cause trouble. The graphical technique that we recommend for use with any of the structured design strategies discussed in the previous section is the "structure chart." Its basic elements are shown in Figure 3. This particular version of the structure chart is described in detail by Jackson,[3] and a similar version is discussed by Yourdon and Constantine.[4]

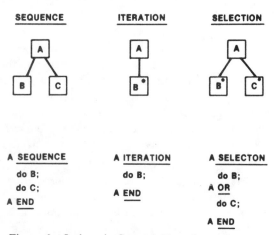

Figure 3. Jackson's Control-Flow Constructs.

Ultimately, we would like to see an automated structure-chart-drawing program that can be viewed at several levels of detail and, in fact, is automatically derived from a structured text source for the program. Ideally, the source program could be easily displayed and even modified in either the form of a CRT-displayed graph or the equivalent structured text. This technique would have the clarity intrinsic in a graphical representation and the correctness implied by letting the documentation itself be the source. By changing the level of detail presented on a CRT screen, the programmer has some control over the clarity and completeness of the presentation. Unfortunately, a documentation tool with these characteristics is currently not generally available.

STRUCTURED TESTING AIDS

Structured design and development imply a testing effort that proceeds, step-by-step, in parallel with the application program development effort. This function may or may not be performed by a separate organization. A library of tests that can be applied repeatedly for regression testing, and a library of stubs that stand in for program modules that have yet to be developed, are crucial at each stage of the top-down development process.

When testing is considered as an integral part of the development process, the possibility—indeed, the probability—of finding errors early is increased. In this case, the testing philosophy and programs are carried through the specification, design, and coding walk-throughs concurrently with the application programs (see Figure 4).

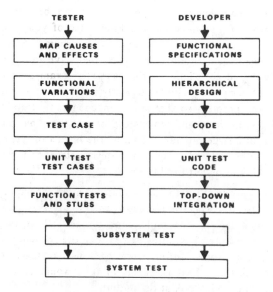

Figure 4. Structured Testing.

Automated testing has progressed to the point that a "cover set" of tests can be generated automatically. These will guarantee that every "leg" of code is executed at least once. This is, of course, much different than testing every combination of paths that could be taken through the program (which would be necessary for "exhaustive" testing). Exhaustive testing is just not feasible for many problems of interest. Even the simple program shown in part A of Figure 5 has 250 billion unique paths through it.[5] If you were capable of performing one test each millisecond, it would take eight years to completely test all of these unique paths!

WANT SEPARATION OF CONCERNS — SMALL INDEPENDENT PIECES

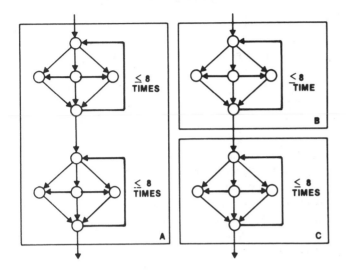

Figure 5. Exhaustive Testing is Impractical.

The completeness of your testing can be helped somewhat if you have enough knowledge of your program structure to permit you to partition program A into two independent modules B and C that have low connectivity and coupling. In this particular example, and from a testing viewpoint, it is clearly worth trying to partition the problem so that small, independently testable modules can be dealt with instead of just the input and output of a large program. That is, the impact of testing must be considered early in the design stage; it is not something to be left until the end.

In our example, to test modules B and C separately you must test *only* one million unique paths through each module. At one millisecond per test, these tests would take only 17 minutes. Even with the reduction in paths, this would suffer from the disadvantages of volume testing. That is, reams of tests would be run, but no one would look at the output.

At this point, it should be clear that tests can be written and automated that will give you some degree of confidence in the program if the initial design is done properly. It should also be clear that, in most cases, there is no way that the correctness of the program can be verified by testing. Exhaustive testing is usually impractical; and without exhaustive testing, the correctness of the program cannot be guaranteed. Just because you haven't seen any errors doesn't mean they don't exist. Can you prove that mermaids don't exist?

REFERENCES

1. Luppino, F. M., and Smith, R. L., "Programming Support Library (PSL) Functional Requirements," IBM Corporation, Gaithersburg, Maryland. Final report prepared under Contact F 30602-74-C-0186 with the U. S. Air Force Rome Air Development Center. Griffiss Air Force Base, Rome, New York, July 1974.

2. Jackson, Michael A., "JSP Cobol User's Manual," Michael Jackson Systems, Limited, 1979.

3. Jackson, Michael A., *Principles of Program Design.* Academic Press, New York, 1975.

4. Yourdon, Edward, and Constantine, L. L., *Structured Design.* Yourdon, Inc., New York, 1975.

5. Myers, G. J., *Reliable Software Through Composite Design.* Petrocelli/Charter, New York, 1975.

6. Alford, Mack W., "A Requirements Engineering Methodology for Real-Time Processing Requirements," *IEEE Transactions on Software Engineering,* Volume SE-3, Number 1 (January 1977), pp. 60-69.

Reprinted with permission from *Communications of the ACM*, Volume 20, Number 10, October 1977, pages 746-753. Copyright © 1977 by the Association for Computing Machinery.

Computer Systems

G. Bell, D. Siewiorek, and S.H. Fuller

The Programmer's Workbench— A Machine for Software Development

Evan L. Ivie
Bell Telephone Laboratories, Murray Hill

On almost all software development projects the assumption is made that the program development function will be done on the same machine on which the eventual system will run. It is only when this production machine is unavailable or when its programming environment is totally inadequate that alternatives are considered. In this paper it is suggested that there are many other situations where it would be advantageous to separate the program development and maintenance function onto a specialized computer which is dedicated to that purpose. Such a computer is here called a Programmer's Workbench. The four basic sections of the paper introduce the subject, outline the general concept, discuss areas where such an approach may prove beneficial, and describe an operational system utilizing this concept.

Key Words and Phrases: computer configurations, computer networks, software development, software engineering, software maintenance, UNIX

CR Categories: 3.2, 3.5, 3.7, 3.8, 4.0

Author's address: Bell Telephone Laboratories, Inc., 600 Mountain Ave., Murray Hill, NJ 07974.

354

1. Introduction

Although the computer industry now has some 30 years of experience, the programming of computer-based systems persists in being a very difficult and costly job. This is particularly true of large and complex systems where schedule slips, cost overruns, high bug rates, insufficient throughput, maintenance difficulties, etc., all seem to be the rule instead of the exception. Part of the problem stems from the fact that programming is as yet very much a trial and error process. There are at this point only the beginnings of a methodology or discipline for designing, building, and testing software. The situation is further aggravated by the rapidly changing hardware industry and by the continuing evolution of operating systems which continues to nullify much of the progress that is made in the development of programming tools.

What can be done to move the programming industry toward a more professional and stable approach to software development? Certainly education (courses, books, conferences, etc.) will play a part in the long run [1]. And, of course, the development of new techniques in programming and program management will contribute as these techniques are accepted and put into use. More compatibility and standardization of hardware, operating systems, languages, and programming procedures will be of great value. Also, an increased investment in the development of programming tools and procedures must occur, but much of this will continue to be lost as computer hardware and operating systems evolve.

2. The Programmer's Workbench Concept

In this paper a very different approach to improving the development process is proposed. It is suggested that the programming community develop a program development "facility" (or facilities) much like those that have been developed for other professions (e.g. carpenter's workbench, dentist's office, engineer's laboratory).

Such an approach would help focus attention on the need for adequate tools and procedures; it would serve as a mechanism for integrating tools into a coordinated set; and it would tend to add stability to the programming environment by separating the tools from the product (the current approach is equivalent to carpenters leaving their tools in each house they build).

Figure 1 shows the separation between the Workbench, which performs the development and maintenance function, and the host or target computer on which the production system will run. The link shown between the two machines represents a physical connection which is used to transfer data, run tests, etc.

The idea of splitting off a well-defined and cohesive function onto a separate dedicated computer is certainly not a new idea. Front-end computers for message

Fig. 1. Division of functions between workbench and host.

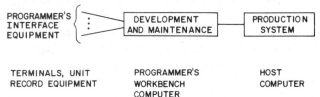

TERMINALS, UNIT
RECORD EQUIPMENT

PROGRAMMER'S
WORKBENCH
COMPUTER

HOST
COMPUTER

concentration and line discipline control are in wide use, having proved to be not only economical, but beneficial for other reasons also [4]. Back-end computers for database management are just beginning to impact the database management field [2, 3]. Specialized computers for the control of peripherals (disks, terminals, photocomposers, etc.) have become commonplace. Indeed the availability of inexpensive microprocessors is certainly going to increase the pressure to go to networks of interacting computers with each processor performing certain specialized functions. The proposal that there should be computers which have been designed and configured to perform just the program development function is merely a further step in this direction.

2.1. Workbench Capabilities

The term "Programmer," in Programmer's Workbench, should be taken in its most general sense and should not be restricted to the coding function. To emphasize this, the steps which go into the development and maintenance of a computer-based system will be briefly outlined:

Step 1. Define what the application system is to do (e.g. system specification, functional description).

Step 2. Design the system. This is normally done at numerous levels of detail (e.g. system, subsystem, program, subroutine) and for various components of the system (e.g. the software, the hardware configuration, the user interface, the operating procedures, etc.).

Step 3. Implement the system through installation of the hardware, coding of the software, writing of users' manuals, etc.

Step 4. Test and evaluate the system. This occurs at numerous levels and for various components as in step 2 and includes the integration of all of the pieces of the system into a working whole.

Step 5. Convert to the system and cut it over to live operation. This is generally a much neglected but significant part of the total job.

Step 6. Operate, support, and maintain the live system. This involves machine operation, user consultation, software bug fixing and enhancement, hardware maintenance and change, etc.

Some of the capabilities that the ultimate Programmer's Workbench might contain to perform these steps are as follows:

(1) Generation, modification, and production of specifications, manuals, catalogs, reports, and documents in general.
(2) Creation, editing, and control of programs and test data.
(3) Compilation, execution, and debugging of programs (either directly or through the host computer).
(4) System generation, integration, and installation.
(5) Regression testing and load testing of subsystems and of the total system.
(6) Analysis and reduction of test results.
(7) Tracking of changes to the system (e.g. trouble reports, enhancement requests).
(8) Evaluation and monitoring of system performance. Also, system modeling and simulation.
(9) Conversion of data files and the loading of the database into the host for live operation.
(10) Production of lists, reports, and statistics for use by management in the control of each phase in the development and maintenance process.

The implementation of the Workbench concept described in Section 4 currently includes only capabilities (1), (2), (3), (5), and (7). The full list is presented here to convey the possible scope of the Workbench concept.

3. Areas of Applicability of Workbench Concept

Four situations will now be described where a dedicated machine for program development would be of particular merit. Some arguments relating to why the Workbench might or might not be a good approach in general will then be presented.

3.1. Multi-Vendor Installations

Many companies operate a variety of different computers. This diversity might occur across several manufacturers or it might be across several different models of a given manufacturer. For example, in the Business Informations Systems Programs (BISP) area of Bell Laboratories, where the Workbench is in use, there is an IBM 370/158 and 168, a Univac 1108 and 1110, two Xerox sigma 5's, plus a number of minicomputers.

Initial efforts in BISP concentrated on development of a programming environment for each vendor line (IBM, Univac, Xerox). Programming tools were implemented on two and sometimes three machines so that the tools would be available to all of the projects. An attempt was also made to keep these tools fully compatible across machines, but this met with only partial success.

Part of the motivation which led to the implementation of the Workbench was based on the realization that a much better set of tools could be provided for less money by concentrating efforts on building and enhancing a single set of development tools. As a specific example, Figure 2 compares the approximate costs for developing and maintaining a specific programming tool on the Workbench versus doing it directly on two host machines. Development and maintenance costs for the Workbench version actually turned out to be less than half that of the dual

355

Fig. 2. Comparison of development and maintenance costs for a specific programming tool (includes both staff and computer time).

	WORKBENCH IMPLEMENTATION	IMPLEMENTATIONS ON IBM AND UNIVAC
DEVELOPMENT (NOT INCLUDING DESIGN)	$50,000	$120,000
MAINTENANCE (PER YEAR)	$22,000	$56,000

implementation, owing perhaps to the better programming environment. The savings would be even more significant if more than two hosts were included, or if more than one tool were considered.

A second benefit of the Workbench approach is the more nearly uniform programming environment that is possible, even across projects which run on different computers and under different operating systems. Such a standard environment offers the following advantages:

(1) *Training* — It has been found that many of the same training courses on programming tools can be offered to programmers on, for example, both IBM and UNIVAC projects.

(2) *Documentation* — Only one set of users' manuals is needed for describing the common programming tools.

(3) *Standards* — The development of standard policies, procedures, and methods relating to program development and maintenance are greatly simplified because one no longer has to take account of a multitude of environments every time a standards decision is made. The enforcement of standards is also simplified.

(4) *Programmer mobility and retraining* — Programmers can become productive much more quickly when they are transferred from one project to another.

It should be quickly noted that while the Workbench system currently in operation (Section 4) has in general achieved host machine independence for those tools that have been implemented, there is still much about the host machine that the programmer must be painfully aware of. Take, for example, the job control language. Eventually it may be possible to develop a universal job control language (jcl) for use of the Workbench which can be translated into the appropriate jcl for each host. Until then the best the Workbench can do is to provide various facilities for generating, concatenating, and modifying host-specific jcl.

In addition to the advantages offered to existing projects, the Workbench approach also offers substantial benefits to new projects. If a particular Workbench system has been accepted as the standard approach at an installation and if all the programmers there are trained in its use, then a new project can bypass much of that lengthy "getting started" period during which tools and standards are developed, adopted, and learned. This should save not only money but also provide a quicker start, and thereby shorten schedules.

It would, of course, be necessary to develop a Workbench interface to the new host and to expand any host-dependent tools to handle the new machine. (However, the only parts of the current implementation that are host dependent are certain aspects of the job submission module.)

3.2. Installations in Transition

Even companies that make it a policy to use only one type of hardware find it necessary to periodically upgrade their equipment or to change operating systems. The transition to the new equipment or to the new operating system is usually a very painful period. If the installation were using the Workbench approach, it could make the transition a less painful process in several ways.

First, a change in the program development environment is no longer inextricably tied to a change in the production equipment. That is, changes in the two machines can be scheduled independently. Indeed, one would probably want to avoid a change in the Workbench at the time the production machine is changing so that all of the programmers' attention could be concentrated on the new equipment and so that they would not have to simultaneously worry about changes in their tools. This should shorten the transition period in bringing up the new equipment significantly. It should also eliminate that difficult "uncovered" period on a new machine when adequate tools are not available, and one has to make do with whatever happens to be provided by the vendor. Then, after the new production equipment is installed and operational, one could consider upgrading the Workbench equipment and/or software.

In addition to being able to stagger changes in the production equipment with upheavals in the program development environment, the Workbench approach also allows one to independently decide upon the frequency with which changes in these two areas will occur. Indeed, if one has a good development environment on a Workbench, it might be well to decide to adopt a much less frequent change cycle, thereby providing more stability to standards, less retraining, smaller tool development costs, etc.

One also has more flexibility in upgrading the host (production) machine when it becomes obvious that such a move is advantageous. This is true since such a decision is no longer clouded by considerations of what it will do to the programmer's ability to develop a code.

3.3. Projects Where Needs of Developer and User Conflict

One of the most critical decisions in the development of a computer-based application is the selection of the computer on which it is to run. In many cases a formal selection procedure is not undertaken because the decision is based on machine availability or other compelling factors. In those cases where an actual choice can be made, there is generally a conflict between the needs of the developer and the user.

If the selection is based strictly on the ability of the computer to perform the eventual application, then software developers may have to survive in an environment that is poorly suited to their needs. If the selection is based entirely on the needs of the developer then the target system may perform its functions expensively if at all. The third possibility is that both the developer and the user compromise their needs in the machine selection process. This may, of course, leave neither very happy.

The development programmer is looking for a machine that has a powerful command language, sophisticated editing tools, flexible and easy to use file structure, terminal access (time-shared), quality document production facilities, and good human engineering in general. The end user is, on the other hand, more concerned with sufficient throughput and size, appropriate peripherals and equipment to support the application, hardware, and software options to optimize certain features (e.g. access methods, block sizes, physical placement), special needs in the areas of availability and reliability, and quality maintenance.

In addition to these potential functional conflicts, opposing needs can also manifest themselves because of a desire to utilize existing equipment or because of the experience and background of the programmers, the operators, or the terminal users.

All of these conflicts are based on the assumption that the development of the software for a project will be done on the same machine as the one on which the project will finally run. The Workbench approach helps to eliminate these built-in conflicts by providing an independent choice of the computer for the developer and for the user. No compromises are necessary and each can choose the machine best suited to their needs and experience. Here again not only the initial choice but the frequency with which a change is to be made is decoupled. This also eliminates possible downstream conflicts and compromises.

3.4. Terminal-Oriented Systems

One of the most time consuming and critical parts of software development is testing, especially total system testing. If the application being developed services terminals, the testing is additionally complicated. It is very unsatisfactory to perform such testing by stationing people at terminals and having them type in data and examine output. Aside from the cost and frustration, it also is a nonrepeatable and error-prone approach. A reasonable solution to this dilemma is to provide a canned scenario of user interactions that can be fed into the system in a timed manner. However, if the insertion of the input messages and the capturing of the output messages is done in the internal queues, then the total system is not really being tested (e.g. terminals, lines, controllers, line servicing software, etc.). To help circumvent this problem, various "loop

back" devices can be developed which allow one program operating within the computer to send out data which is returned as though it came from a terminal.

Such an approach provides more complete testing but still suffers from certain side effects. For example, it may be difficult to isolate whether a failure occurred because of an error in the test driver or in the application being tested. This is because of the various possible interactions that can occur between two systems operating simultaneously within the same computer. Also if the application operates on a dedicated computer, it is impossible to effectively load test it to determine its total capacity since the test driver is consuming a portion of the resources. Thus there are special reasons why a system test facility needs to be on a separate computer such as a Workbench.

3.5. General Advantages

It's probably safe to assume that every installation will periodically upgrade to a new computer. It is also fair to say that user and developer needs always conflict to some extent. Thus, to a greater or lesser extent, the advantages ascribed to the Workbench approach in the preceding paragraphs apply to all installations.

Additionally there are potential economies which may accrue to the Workbench because of specialization. Applications computers are typically large general purpose computers with complex operating systems having many options and features. The Workbench consists of a specialized set of functions running on a dedicated system. The hardware configuration for the Workbench should be much simpler, the operating system should be less cumbersome, and the actual tools should therefore be smaller and faster. Front-end and back-end computers have been found to be economically attractive for the same reasons.

Another general advantage to the Workbench is the fact that it encourages the development of machine independent programming tools. Each tool must now function for programmers developing code for a number of different vendor machines. There is no room for shortcuts which are dependent on the idiosyncrasies of a given machine (or a given project). One is thus forced into a more stable and generalized software development approach which should be more applicable to new machines.

It has already been noted that a separate program development facility will help focus attention on the importance of the programming environment in the software development process. It should also provide some stimulus for the integration of the programming tools operating on the Workbench into a coordinated set of interconnected functions.

3.6. Potential Disadvantages

Thus far a number of arguments favoring the Workbench concept have been presented. The other side of the ledger will now be examined. One disadvantage to

357

the Workbench approach is that another machine is needed which costs money and which is one more link in the system that can fail. The cost may be counterbalanced by the fact that the host computer(s) may not have to be available quite as early in the development cycle, they may not have to be as big, and fewer may be needed. Having an extra link that can fail is a problem if the components cannot do useful work on a stand-alone basis (e.g. program editing and document production on the Workbench when the host is down) or if there is insufficient redundancy (e.g. other Workbenches to shift the load to when one fails).

In addition to the question of the actual purchase or rental cost, there may be other "costs" in having a second (Workbench) machine. For example, the. Workbench machine may be manufactured by a vendor which is different from the host machine vendor. This will duplicate all the problems associated with contracts, maintenance procedures, operator training, system programming support, etc. It will also force the programmer to be aware of two machines and not just one. However, if the Workbench has a good user interface, it may actually be easier for the programmer to keep track of it and the operational aspects of the host than to use the host tools.

A second general problem relates to the fact that data and functions are now split between two machines. This may manifest itself in slower response to some requests for data and cpu processing because of transmission and queueing delays. It may also result in some duplication of data to avoid these delays. The best solution to this problem is a judicious choice of what data is stored on each machine and what processing is done on each machine. Also, the use of a high speed link will minimize the delays.

A third problem is the fact that machines use different character sets, number representations, etc. Thus there is a conversion cost in shipping data back and forth between machines. (However, in the current implementation this amounts to a very small fraction of the total Workbench cpu load).

A final problem may occur because a fixed part of one's computational power is dedicated to a given function (i.e. program development). Some flexibility is thereby lost in being able to balance the computational load. Potential imbalances can occur in any of the available resources: cpu, disk, printers, etc. Imbalances may also develop at certain points in the development cycle. For example, one may find that the host is being underutilized during the initial phases of the project. How serious this problem is depends a great deal on the relative costs and sizes of Workbench and host machines. If the Workbench machines are small and constitute a small fraction of the total computational budget, then adding or deleting a Workbench machine to match the total Workbench load may be adequate. Also, because of the link, some functions such as printing and disk storage can be shifted from one machine to the other to help balance the load.

4. Description of Current Workbench Implementation

When the potential benefits of, and the possible difficulties with, the Workbench were first considered, a number of questions arose. For example, were there unforeseen problems in the implementation or in the use of a Workbench system which would outweigh all of the projected advantages? Could such a system be implemented in a reasonable amount of time and with a modest expenditure of resources? Would programmers be willing to try something new and give the approach an honest trial? Could such a system be assimilated into an ongoing software development organization? How many of the benefits would turn out to be real? How serious would the potential problems be?

The idea of the Workbench was first conceived in April 1973. The Business Information Systems Programs (BISP) area in Bell Laboratories appeared to be an ideal environment in which to try the idea because all of the conditions described in Section 3, for which the Workbench approach would be beneficial, were present. Thus the decision was made to try out the approach on an experimental basis. The first Workbench machine was installed in October 1973. Three additional machines have since been installed with two more due to be installed in 1976.

The machines currently being used as the Workbench machine are the Digital Equipment Corporation PDP 11's. Initially 11/45's were used; more recently 11/70's have been used. The decision to use PDP 11's was based mainly on the fact that the UNIX [6] timesharing system operated on the PDP 11. UNIX was developed at Bell Laboratories by Ken Thompson and Dennis Ritchie. It is an outgrowth of the MULTICS [5] system, but much simplified and streamlined. It has offered an ideal base on which to build program development tools which have been developed thus far.

One of the current Workbench configurations is shown in Figure 3. Monthly rental for such a system is in the neighborhood of $6,000. Such a system can provide good response to 24–30 users simultaneously logged in. If one assumes that the average user is logged in about two hours a day, then one PDP 11/45 could handle a project of about 100 people. A PDP 11/70 can handle 45–50 users simultaneously or about double the 11/45 load.

Before discussing the components of the Workbench that are in operation, a brief comment on implementation philosophy is in order. The idea of designing and building a complete and fully integrated Workbench system was rejected for a number of reasons, not the least of which is the fact that no one in the programming field knows what that system should look like at this point in time. Instead, every effort was made to identify some of the immediate needs of potential users and to develop pieces of the Workbench that could satisfy those needs quickly. This approach provided the Workbench designers with much valuable

358

Fig. 3. Configuration of one of the workbench computers.

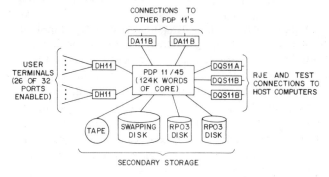

Fig. 4. Example of a workbench job submission network.

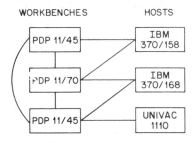

user feedback quickly, and it allowed the projects to start picking up pieces of the Workbench to satisfy their most critical needs immediately and thus to start a phased transition to the complete Workbench.

4.1. Basic Components

It is not the purpose of this paper to fully describe the current Workbench implementation. Other papers are planned which will describe in detail each of the Workbench subsystems. However, a brief description of each of the five Workbench components currently in operation will be presented here to establish the fact that the basic Workbench concept has in fact been given a live shakedown with a useful subset of functions. The five basic components of the Workbench which were selected for initial implementation are job submission, module control, change management, document production, and test drivers.

1. **Job submission.** The whole Workbench concept depends on having the capability to transfer data easily and quickly between the workbench and the host machines. Each Bell Labs Workbench system currently provides this capability by operating as a remote job entry (RJE) station to one or more host computers. Take, for example, the three Workbench machines currently located in Piscataway, New Jersey. Figure 4 shows the job submission network for these three machines. Inter-Workbench links provide access to a host not directly connected to a given Workbench. There are also links for test drivers which are not shown in Figure 4.

The RJE facility can be broken into four components:

(1) *Job preparation* – this step performs file concatenation (e.g. combining the job control language (jcl) file with the data file(s)), character conversion (ASCII to EBCDIC), and queueing.

(2) *Transmission* – this component empties the transmission queue, monitors the status of the communication line, and receives results from the hosts.

(3) *Status reporting* – facilities are provided so that Workbench users can determine the overall load on the host machine and the progress of each individual job. Each user can select what status is to be sent automatically. The user can also initiate requests for status information.

(4) *Post processing* – the output from each run can be returned to the Workbench or selectively routed to a host printer or elsewhere. That which is returned to the Workbench is placed in the appropriate file for examination. Various scanning programs have been developed to help determine such things as the success of the run, etc. The RJE link does not, of course, provide direct interaction with a program executing on the host. This capability is part of the test driver.

2. **Module control.** In the development of a software system, particularly a large system, each program goes through a number of revisions (releases, versions). In fact, at any one point in time there will probably be several revisions of a program in use simultaneously. The revision in use in the field may be different from the one in trial, which in turn may be different from the one in system test, which finally may be different from the one the programmer is working on. Also, there may be differences caused by different operating systems, data management systems, and user needs. Keeping track of all of these revisions is a major task. An even larger task is to make sure that the right modifications are applied to the right revisions and not to the others. The module control system developed for the Workbench provides:

(1) Creation of any revision of a program from any previous point in time.
(2) Protection against accidental tampering and change.
(3) Selective propagation of each change to a module to each of its revisions which should contain that change.
(4) Identification of object and source (revision number, date created, etc.).

In addition to programs, all sorts of other documentation on a project also go through many revisions. The Workbench module control system was generalized to handle not only source but any type of text. In fact, it is currently being used heavily for keeping track of the evolution of user manuals, test plans, error lists, etc. The module control system is also called the Source Code Control System (SCCS) and is described in [7].

3. **Change management.** When a software system goes into production, it becomes necessary to formalize

359

the way changes are made to it. For a large software system, some type of formal change control is necessary fairly early in the development cycle and increases in importance as time progresses. The mechanism for change control is usually some type of trouble reporting form describing the reason why a change (in programs, hardware, or documents) is needed. To this form is added information as to who will make the change, what it consists of, and when it will be made. The Bell Labs Workbench currently provides a facility for entering trouble reports into a project database and of subsequently editing and updating them. Facilities for generating summary, status, and other reports have also been developed.

4. **Documentation production.** Having accurate, up to date, and understandable documentation (e.g. design specs, test plans, user manuals) is vital to the success of a project. On a large software project it is generally a larger and more difficult job to produce such documentation than it is to produce the source programs.

A wide variety of document production tools have been built for the UNIX time sharing system on which the Workbench operates: text editors, formatters, typographical error finders, etc. [7]. A phototypesetter which provides multiple character fonts and point sizes has also been connected to the system. A document writer has the option of having text printed on a terminal, routed to a host machine for high speed printing, or sent to the phototypesetter for high quality output.

Over the past year a number of "macro packages" have been developed for the UNIX documentation tools. These packages automate the production of many of the standard document formats used by the BISP projects by producing headings, footings, labels, tables of contents, etc. Users can thus produce highly structured documents with minimal input effort. Typing pools, document production centers, programmers, and managers are all heavy users of this UNIX/Workbench facility.

5. **Test drivers.** Two test drivers have been implemented on the Workbench thus far. The IBM test driver simulates IBM 3271 cluster controllers, each with several 3277 terminals. It serves as a driver to projects which use the data management systems operating on IBM/360 and IBM/370 computers. The IBM test driver is used for both load testing and regression testing. The UNIVAC test driver simulates a teletype cluster controller with up to four terminals and is used for regression testing.

4.2. Possible Extensions

All of the above components are under continuing revision and improvement. In addition, efforts are now underway to integrate the current components into a more closely cooperating set of tools. For example, each change made to a module should be related to the trouble report(s) that initiated that change. This will allow one to supply a list of all the trouble reports that are to be resolved by a given release of a system and to have the Workbench automatically select which revisions of each program are needed in that release. Besides integration, several of the other functions noted in Section 2.1 are in various stages of planning. The system generation and configuration control area is one example. Also, consideration is now being given to connecting the Workbench to other types of host computers.

In addition to these short term efforts, some long term objectives are being studied. For example, an attempt may be made to develop a uniform job control language (jcl) which can be translated into each of the host jcl's. Also, a standard programming language might be designed which has code generators for each of the host machines. The value of this would be enhanced considerably if a set of Workbench system calls were devised that could be mapped into system calls to each of the host operating systems. These steps toward software portability are obviously very difficult but might well be eventually achieved in an environment like that offered on the Workbench.

4.3. Workbench Usage

As of February 1976 there were three Workbench machines in operation at the Bell Labs facility in Piscataway, N.J. and one in use at Murray Hill, N.J. Workbench facilities are also beginning to be used at two other Bell Labs locations. The four New Jersey machines were providing about 2600 hours of connect time per week to some 300 users, and they were maintaining disk files containing about 250 million characters. Both of these figures are expected to double by mid 1977 (with the addition of two more 11/70's). All of the Business Information Systems Projects in Bell Labs are using at least some parts of the system.

4.4. Example of Use

Perhaps the most effective way to describe the current operation of the Workbench is to give a very simple example of how it might be used. Assume a trouble report has been written describing a bug in the "sum" program. After the programmer responsible for the maintenance of the program dials in, the following interaction might take place. (The characters typed by the programmer are in bold type. The UNIX prompt symbol is the "%.")

login **Jones** | *The programmer enters the appropriate identification code and is told that there is mail.*
You have mail. |

% **mail** | *The programmer uses the UNIX mail command to print the mail and finds that a trouble report has been assigned.*
From smith Fri Mar 14 12:48 1975 |
tr number: a-75-83-3 |
originated by: R.H. Johnson |
description: The value printed by the sum program is incorrect. |

Communications
of
the ACM

October 1977
Volume 20
Number 10

SOFTWARE REQUIREMENTS ENGINEERING METHODOLOGY (SREM)

AT THE AGE OF FOUR

M. W. Alford

TRW Defense and Space Systems Group
Huntsville, Alabama

1.0 INTRODUCTION

The Software Requirements Engineering Methodology (SREM) was presented to the Software Engineering community four years ago at the Second International Software Engineering Conference[1]; the SREM support software, the Requirements Engineering and Validation System (REVS), was also presented then[2]. SREM was developed for the Ballistic Missile Defense Advanced Technology Center (BMDATC) to address the generation and validation of software requirements for Ballistic Missile Defense Weapons Systems -- the motivation and environment for this research has been previously described[3]. At that time, REVS was operational only on the Texas Instruments Advanced Scientific Computer (TI ASC), and the methodology had been applied to one moderate sized "proof of principle" demonstration problem.

Since then, SREM has been successfully applied to both the generation and independent validation of software requirements for several systems. REVS has been transported to a number of other host computers, and its performance has been improved. The methodology has been successfully transferred to a number of other organizations, and applied to a wider class of problems. The purpose of this paper is to provide a status report of the SREM requirements development procedures, requirements language, support software, and transfer of this technology to other organizations, and to provide an overview of plans for extensions and improvements. The first such status report was presented two years ago[4].

The remainder of this section provides an overview of SREM. Section 2.0 presents a comparison of SREM to other requirements techniques. Section 3.0 contains a summary of the transfer of SREM technology to other organizations, the availability and cost of REVS, and the results of and assessment by other organizations of the utility of SREM. Section 4.0 contains an overview of the extensions which are being made to SREM and REVS. Section 5.0 presents a summary of our status and plans.

1.1 SREM OVERVIEW

The objectives of the research leading to SREM were to reduce the ambiguity and errors in software requirements, to make the software requirements development process more manageable, and to provide more automation in validating the software requirements. More details can be found in references 1, 2, and 3.

The SREM requirements development procedures identify the steps and objective completion criteria necessary to define software requirements using the Requirement Statement Language (RSL) and the Requirements Engineering and Validation System (REVS). SREM thus provides a road map of the sequence of activities necessary for the definition of software requirements and the manner in which REVS can be used to ensure that an activity is complete -- thereby providing a high degree of management visibility of the requirements development process.

SREM is based on a Graph Model of Software Requirements[5] which is an extension of the Graph Model of Computation[6]. The basic concept underlying SREM is that design-free functional software requirements should specify the required processing in terms of all possible responses (and the conditions for each type of response) to each input message across each interface. Thus, functional requirements identify the required stimulus/response relationships, and autonomously generated outputs. These required actions of the software are expressible in terms of Requirements Networks (R-Nets) of processing steps. Each processing step is defined in terms of input data, output data, and the associated transformation. Figure 1 presents an R-Net for a Hospital Patient Monitoring System[7] which accepts a measurement of the blood pressure, temperature, skin resistance, etc., for a patient, and tests it for validity, and attempts to correlate the message with a patient. If the message is bad or no correlation is made, a diagnostic message is sent to the Nurses Station. If valid, the data processor is then required to record it, request the next measurement, and test the measurement against pre-specified upper and lower limits. Note that six paths of processing are identified which combine into four possible stimulus/response requirements -- the paths to request the next measurement and record the current measurement occur regardless of whether the measurement violates the constraints.

The concepts of the Graph Model of Software Requirements are embodied in the design of the Requirements Statement Language (RSL), a machine-processible language for the unambiguous statement of software requirements. RSL is composed of elements (e.g., R-Nets, Alpha to represent a Processing Step, Data, Messages, Input Interfaces -- the "nouns" of the language), their attributes (e.g., units of data, required response times of processing paths, descriptions -- the "adjectives" of the language), their

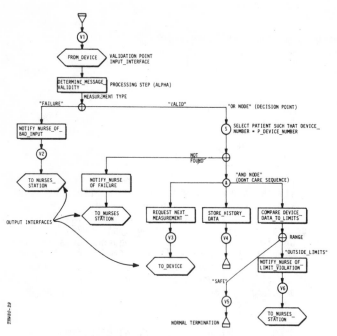

TRW80-29

Figure 1 Example R-Net

relationships (e.g., data is input to an Alpha, a message is passed by an output interface -- the "verbs" of the language), and structures (used to define the conditions and sequences of processing steps which comprise the required stimulus/response relationships to be satisfied by the software). Table 1 presents a subset of the requirements for the Patient Monitoring System expressed in RSL. In addition to nouns, verbs,

Table 1 Examples RSL Definitions

```
MESSAGE: DEVICE_REPORT.

    PASSED THROUGH: INPUT_INTERFACE FROM_DEVICE.

    MADE BY: DATA DEVICE_NUMBER
             DATA TYPE_MESSAGE
             DATA DEVICE_DATA.

DATA: DEVICE_DATA.

    INCLUDES: DATA PULSE
              DATA TEMPERATURE
              DATA BLOOD_PRESSURE
              DATA SKIN_RESISTANCE.

FILE: FACTOR_HISTORY.

    CONTAINS: DATA MEASUREMENT_TIME
              DATA HPULSE
              DATA TEMPERATURE
              DATA HBLOOD_PRESSURE
              DATA HSKIN_RESISTANCE.

    TRACED FROM: SENTENCE_2
                 SENTENCE_3.

    ASSOCIATED WITH: ENTITY_CLASS PATIENT.

ALPHA: STORE_HISTORY_DATA.

    INPUTS: DEVICE_DATA.

    OUTPUTS: FACTOR_HISTORY.

    DESCRIPTION: "THE DATA PROCESSOR SHALL RECORD EACH VALID
                 MEASUREMENT FOR EACH PATIENT".

VALIDATION_PATH: MEASUREMENT_OUT_OF_LIMITS.

    PATH: VALIDATION_POINT V1, VALIDATION_POINT V6.

MAXIMUM TIME: 1.

    UNITS: SECONDS.
```

TRW80-74

and adjectives for stating requirements, RSL also contains elements, attributes, and relationships that express management concepts (e.g., traceability, completeness, authorship, and version). In all, RSL is composed of 21 elements, 21 attributes, 23 relationships, and three types of structures. It is the structures (R-Nets, Subnets, and Paths) and their formal mathematical foundations, and the stimulus-response orientation which distinguish RSL from the traditional techniques for stating software requirements (e.g., the PSL[8] approach, or standard DoD Military Specifications[9]).

REVS is a large software tool that handles a potentially large data base of requirements, therefore requiring a host computer with a large effective memory space and a moderately fast instruction rate (See Section 3.0).

REVS accepts RSL as input, translates it into an automated requirements data base, and provides a set of capabilities for analyzing and manipulating this data base. Specific capabilities include the following:

● Translation of an RSL expression of requirements into a central requirements data base.

● Extraction, under user control, of information from the requirements data base for analysis and documentation.

● Identification, under user control, of subsets of the data base for automatic consistency, completeness, and traceability analyses.

● Automated checking of the requirements data base for specific properties of data flow consistency (made possible only because of the underlying formal foundations).

● Graphical representation of the requirements structures, both on-line and off-line.

● Automated generation and execution of simulations directly traceable to the requirements definition.

The REVS program itself consists of over 40,000 executable PASCAL statements, making it the largest PASCAL program known to us. (In comparison, the PASCAL compiler consists of approximately 6,000 PASCAL statements). An additional 10,000 FORTRAN statements perform data base management functions. The RSL Translator is produced from the Backus-Naur Form (BNF) definition of RSL using the Lecarme-Bochmann Compiler Writing System from the University of Montreal, plus additional code for the definition of the semantic actions.

The SREM requirements development procedures identify in detail how RSL and REVS are used to generate and validate the processing requirements. The approach is to define functional requirements in terms of paths of processing, then to attach performance requirements to the paths, summarized below.

First, all interfaces of the data processor are identified, together with the messages that cross interfaces and the message contents. The entity classes of the system are identified (i.e., objects about which data is required to be maintained by the data processor), entity types are identified (i.e., the states of the entity class in which a specified subset of data is maintained in the data processor), and then messages are categorized by entity class and type. This allows the problem of specifying input/output transforms for hundreds of input messages to be decomposed into a number of smaller problems of associating a few inputs (for a given entity state) with a few outputs legal for an object in that entity state. R-Nets are then developed to specify stimulus/response relationships required of the software. This top-level information is then checked to assure that each output message is output in at least one way. The methodology continues by identifying data to be maintained by the software, the data flow between processing elements, and a series of consistency and completeness checks identify errors and holes in the data specification. After these functional requirements are identified and checked for static consistency, functional simulations are generated to verify the dynamic consistency of the requirements, and to derive required processing rates for interactive software systems. When all processing paths have been identified, performance requirements are derived and expressed with respect to these functional requirements. The functional requirements represent the "what" of the processing, while the performance requirements represent the "how well" attributes. Analytical simulations can then be used to demonstrate the non-real-time feasibility of the processing requirements, i.e., that algorithms exist which can meet the processing accuracy requirements -- only a real-time software design will demonstrate the real-time feasibility of the processing requirements.

At the time of our presentations four years ago, SREM, RSL, and REVS had been applied to one moderately sized BMD problem to demonstrate capability and to illustrate the sequence of steps and associated outputs of the methodology. At that time, it was concluded that the research objectives had been achieved, but that SREM's applicability to other environments and utility in realistic software development environments had yet to be determined.

At the time of our presentations two years ago, REVS had been installed on four host machines, and SREM had been applied to about a dozen projects. The results of these applications, and a number of planned extensions and improvements were discussed.

The remainder of this paper presents an overview of progress made since then, and our current activities and plans to achieve a complete automated comprehensive software requirements and design methodology.

2.0 COMPARISON TO OTHER TECHNIQUES

It is impossible in a few short pages to adequately describe the many requirements and specification techniques and compare and contrast them with SREM. Over 30 techniques were discussed in[10], and new ones are being reported all of the time. In spite of this, comparison of techniques is worthwhile to highlight some unique features of SREM. For this purpose, the following techniques were selected for comparison: the Michael Jackson Program Design Method[11], PSL/PSA[8], HOS[12], SADT[13], and IORL[14]. The comparison is summarized in Table 2.

Table 2 A Comparison of Some Requirements Techniques

CONTENT	SREM/REVS	JACKSON	PSL/PSA	HOS	SADT	IORL
PROCESSING FUNCTIONS DATA I/O	E	E	E	E	E	E
SEQUENCES OF FUNCTIONS FOR ONE INPUT	E		E			E
SEQUENCE OF I/O	P	E				
FUNCTION HIERARCHY (STRUCTURE)	P	E	E	E	E	E
TRACEABILITY	E		P			
PERFORMANCE REQUIREMENTS	E					
AUTOMATED TOOLS						
- LANGUAGE	E	M	E	D	D	E
- CONSISTENCY CHECKING	E	M	P	M	D	E
- DATA FLOW ANALYSIS	P	M				
- SIMULATION GENERATION	E		D			
- USER EXTENSIBLE	E					

TRW80-73

E EXPLICITLY ADDRESSED M MANUAL
P PARTIALLY ADDRESSED D IN DEVELOPMENT

All techniques define processing in terms of "functions" with inputs and outputs. It is interesting to note that SREM, HOS, and IORL attempt to define a stimulus/response relationship of inputs to outputs, while Jackson, PSL/PSA, and SADT express data flow but not precedence or control flow. All techniques except SREM explicitly define processing in terms of a "hierarchy of functions", whereas SREM is based on a "flat" graph model which can be expressed in terms of a hierarchy of subnets, a subtle but important difference. Current concepts of decomposition are discussed in Section 4.0.

Sequences of inputs and outputs are explicitly defined by Jackson's technique, partially defined by SREM but not defined by other techniques. The comparison with Jackson's technique is interesting: Jackson emphasizes definition of a life cycle of inputs about an object, and describes the life cycle of processing those sequences, and thus derives the information (state) which must be kept in the data base about the object. SREM requires the identification of ENTITY_CLASSes (i.e., objects about which data is maintained in the data processor), and the ENTITY_TYPEs which compose them (i.e., states of the entity which require maintenance of unique subsets of data), and the DATA which is ASSOCIATED with the entity CLASS and TYPEs. Input and output messages are identified with the ENTITY_TYPE, stimulus/response requirements are expressed in terms of graphs of functions, and these are then merged together to form the R_NETs. Thus the sequences of I/O messages are partially defined by the transitions between ENTITY_TYPEs (See Section 4.0).

SREM explicitly provides for the expression and analysis of traceability between a set of originating requirements and the final processing requirements. Versions of PSL/PSA have incorporated this capability.

SREM is the only technique which addresses the explicit definition of performance requirements, i.e., response times and accuracy of the processing from input to output. This is done in four steps:

(1) Paths of processing are specified in terms of Validation points on the R-Nets (e.g., in Figure 1, one could define a PATH with name ALERT_NURSE by the sequence V1 - V5).

(2) The paths are matched with the originating requirements which are applicable.

(3) The originating requirements performance numbers are decomposed and allocated to the paths of processing in a series of tradeoff studies.

(4) A PERFORMANCE REQUIREMENT is defined which CONSTRAINS the path, and is given as an attribute TEST which inputs specific data from the validation points, and outputs either "PASS" or "FAIL".

The result is a set of performance requirements with pre-conditions and decision points of the R-Net (i.e., input data is valid but with an out-of-range measurement), functional post-conditions (i.e., specific data accessed, specific data updated, specific message output), and performance post-conditions (i.e., response time and testable I/O accuracy requirement). The R-Net thus provides the mechanism for graphically presenting similarities and differences of conditions for path expressions.

When we compare automated tools, we find that SREM has an automated language RSL with tools to check static data consistency, the dynamic data consistency processing a single message, limited consistency checking for sequences of messages (i.e., data is initialized when a new Entity-type is set) and tools to support simulation generation. The language and report generation facilities are truely user extensible, allowing a user to add new elements, attributes, and relationships, input instances of the new elements and relationships, and retrieve it on the same run.

Both Jackson and HOS techniques are (at the time of this writing) currently manual, but tools are currently being developed to support SADT. IORL has automated tools on a mini-computer for defining information in a text-file and diagram data base, and limited consistency analysis is available via comparison of parameter tables.

The relationship of RSL/PSL is worth special attention. PSL defines processing requirements in terms of elements, attributes, and relationships by defining a hierarchy of functions, data, etc. R-Nets were defined as a mechanism for defining sequences of processing requirements before RSL was defined[5]. In seeking an approach for defining a language expressing these concepts, TRW noted the PSL work, and decided to

express RSL in terms of elements, attributes, relationships, and structures (i.e., R-Nets, Subnets, paths) to define the stimulus/response conditions. REVS was then developed using the FORTRAN Data Base Management System used by PSA. In turn, later versions of PSA incorporated data consistency checking techniques first developed for REVS, and techniques for automated simulator generation first developed for REVS are under development for PSA. Thus PSL/PSA and RSL/REVS have had a substantial interactive effect on one another.

3.0 WHERE WE ARE TODAY

The decision to use SREM technology on a software development project is dependent on several factors: the availability of SREM expertise; availability and cost of REVS to support the use of SREM; and the utility of SREM as perceived by the software engineering community. The progress made in these areas in the last two years is discussed below.

3.1 TECHNOLOGY TRANSFER

The transfer of SREM technology involves transfer of the basic concepts (which requires a shift in point of view of people already experienced with writing requirements), a working knowledge of the SREM procedures and RSL, and hands-on experience with REVS. The preferred mode of transfer is a workshop, alternating lectures and exercises, which is a variation of the three week training course discussed in reference 4.

In the past two years, versions of this training course have been presented several times, ranging in duration from three days (an in-depth overview without exercises) to three weeks. We are still experimenting with the format to balance cost and time spent with the amount of knowledge transferred, and use of alternate dissemination techniques is being explored.

3.2 REVS AVAILABILITY AND COST

Availability

A critical element for using SREM is the availability of REVS to support its application. Table 3 summarizes the current installations of REVS. The only new installation in the past two years is at the Naval Air Development Center (NADC) at Warminster, PA. At NADC, REVS is accessible via a CDC User 200 equivalent terminal over telephone lines.

The dissemination of REVS has not occurred as rapidly as originally expected due to the overall lack of production level PASCAL compilers for the more popular host machines. As mentioned previously, REVS consists of over 40,000 lines of PASCAL in over 1100 procedures; the RSL translator is a 500 line procedure; and another 200 FORTRAN routines to perform the management of the relational data base. Thus, REVS requires a production level PASCAL Compiler with a working NEW and DISPOSE, and the ability to interleave PASCAL and FORTRAN I/O statements. This level of sophistication of PASCAL Compilers is just now being reached.

To disseminate REVS more widely, two different strategies are possible:

Table 3 Current REVS Installations

LOCATION	HOST	ON-LINE GRAPHICS	REMOTE BATCH	TELETYPE	OFF-LINE GRAPHICS
		I/O CAPABILITIES			
ADVANCED RESEARCH CENTER, HUNTSVILLE, ALABAMA	CDC 7600	X	X		X
NAVAL RESEARCH LABS, WASHINGTON, D. C.	TI-ASC			X	X
MDAC, HUNTINGTON BEACH, CALIFORNIA	CDC 7600	X			X
TRW, REDONDO BEACH, CALIFORNIA	CDC CYBER 74/174 TSS	X	X		X
NAVAL AIR DEVELOPMENT CENTER, WARMINSTER, PENNSYLVANIA	CDC CYBER 174 / 175	X / X			X / X

THW8G-72

- Wait for production-level PASCAL compilers to become available for popular mainframe machines (e.g., IBM, UNIVAC), and invest effort to re-host, optimize, and maintain REVS.

- Re-host REVS on a capable, affordable mini-computer so that a project can have its own "requirements machine".

In other words, do we bring the software to a potential user's machine, or do we provide a user an affordable hardware/software package for requirements engineering? After some consideration, the latter strategy has been adopted. REVS is currently being hosted on a DEC VAX 11/780, selected for its capability, cost, and popularity. This should provide widespread dissemination of REVS for a modest cost.

Cost

The second critical element for using SREM is the cost of using REVS. As previously stated, REVS was originally developed in a research atmosphere to demonstrate feasibility of using computer-aided techniques to verify requirements consistency and completeness. It was first developed on the TI ASC and transferred to the CDC 7600 (both large, fast machines), so little effort was devoted to the optimization of the software for production use. When REVS was transferred to the TRW TSS, initial application of REVS to large projects proved to be economically impractical. As a result of this, and recognition of the projected benefits of using such a tool, TRW sponsored a program to reduce CPU time and cost required to use REVS. The result was a decrease in CPU time, wall-clock time, and cost for the most used REVS functions by factors of 10 to 100; Table 3 summarizes the results. The data contained in this table is a comparison of benchmark test cases run on the original REVS installation (Release 0) and the current installation (Release 2). The RSL inputs used to generate the information are the Track Loop System (TLS) and an Information Evaluation System (IES). The TLS is a small data base from the first SREM demonstration problem. The IES, a large and realistic case, was one of the first applications of REVS on TSS that signalled the need for reducing the cost of using REVS.

The measure of performance improvements in Table 4 is given in terms of an improvement factor which is the ratio of original cost to the current cost of using REVS. The RSL translator is the most used function of REVS, and cost reductions here range from a factor of 10 to 28 (note that the factors grow with data base size). The list capabilities are the second most used function, and the most expensive for Release 0. For Release 2, cost is reduced by factors of 22 to 110. (Again, the reduction grows with size). Other function costs are reduced by factors of four to ten. The current cost entries indicate that REVS has become a practical engineering tool.

Table 4 Summary of Cost and CPU Time Improvements for Cyber 174

CASE	CPU TIME COMPARISONS (SECONDS)			COST COMPARISONS ($)		
	RELEASE 0	RELEASE 2	IMPROVEMENT FACTOR	RELEASE 0	RELEASE 2	IMPROVEMENT FACTOR
RSL TRANSLATION						
TLS	899	111	8.1	567	39	14.5
IES-1	1710	170	10.0	695	65	10.7
IES-2	463	44	10.5	364	17	21.4
IES-3	1029	78	13.2	895	32	28.0
LIST OPERATIONS						
LIST ALL TLS	1511	35	43.2	785	16	49.1
LIST ALL IES-1	4446	69	64.4	2083	27	77.1
LIST ALL IES-2	5716	83	68.8	2889	32	90.3
LIST ALL IES-3	8129	110	73.9	4551	41	110.0
LIST TLS BY HIERARCHY	3815	348	11.0	2110	94	22.4
ANALYSIS						
SET ANALYSIS TLS	820	76	10.8	448	42	10.7
SIMULATE TLS	478	94	5.1	267	57	4.7
DATA-FLOW/SIMULATE TLS	917	139	6.6	533	84	6.3
TOTAL	29,933	1,357	22.1	16,187	546	29.6

SRE78-142.1

TLS - TRACK LOOP SYSTEM
IES - INFORMATION EVALUATION SYSTEM

Memory Usage

One of the functions in the first installation of REVS had a restriction of operating on data bases with a limited number of elements. This restriction occurred because central memory was used to store pointers to the elements in a data base. By using an external file to store these pointers, Release 2 can now function independent of the number of elements in a data base and the capability of REVS to operate with large data bases has been significantly enhanced.

Certain REVS capabilities, such as Simulation Generation and RADX static analysis, use dynamic memory (called heap storage in PASCAL terminology) to perform a task. Generally, the amount of heap used by REVS increases as the size of the data bases increase. To allow REVS to perform these tasks on larger data bases, the data structures that are allocated to the heap were packed and, in some instances, reconfigured. Certain changes to the data structures required modifications to the procedures which use the structures. These changes have reduced the amount of required heap storage more than 50 percent and will allow these operations to be performed on larger data bases. Table 5 provides a summary of the amount and percentage of heap memory that has been saved by Release 2 as compared to Release 0. The units for the heap memory are decimal words.

3.3 USER COMMUNITY EVALUATION

The transfer of the SREM research results into the software engineering community has been observed to take place in the following way:

Table 5 Memory Savings Summary

CASE	RELEASE 0 HEAP USED	RELEASE 2 HEAP USED	AMOUNT SAVED BY RELEASE 2	% SAVED BY RELEASE 2
SET ANALYSIS	11242	5247	5995	53.3%
TLS SIMULATION	10515	4448	6067	57.7%
SAMPLE SIMULATION	5404	2056	3348	62.0%
DATA FLOW TEST	9356	4339	5017	53.6%
SET ANALYSIS & BETA SIMULATION	11935	5694	6241	52.3%
SET ANALYSIS & GAMMA SIMULATION	11703	5055	6648	56.8%

STATIC ANALYSIS AND SIMULATION CAN NOW BE APPLIED TO LARGER DATA BASES

(1) The developers disseminate information about the technique (e.g., conferences[1]).

(2) The developers perform demonstrations on modest problems[4].

(3) Other researchers perform demonstrations and evaluate the results, and disseminate the evaluation[15, 16, 17].

(4) Project managers evaluate the results of the demonstrations, and apply the technique to real projects, and assess the results.

In reference 4, the status of some demonstrations and real projects were discussed. Since that time, three evaluations of SREM have been published[15, 16, 17]. These are briefly summarized below.

● In reference 15, Dr. Salwin at Johns Hopkins University, Applied Physics Laboratory compared RSL/REVS and PSL/PSA in detail on small problems, and concluded that: (1) any automated tool is better than none; and (2) RSL/REVS provides significant capabilities over PSL/PSA.

● In reference 16, Mr. Slegel reported on a demonstration conducted by APL and CORADCOM for verification of requirements for maintenance and diagnostic software in a real-time command and control system. It was concluded that SREM was applicable for this type of problem, and that "there is much to be gained from this type of tool".

● In reference 17, Mr. Furia at Grumman Aerospace compared RSL/REVS and PSL/PSA. He concluded in part, "RSL/REVS has far more developed features over PSL/PSA" and "Grumman Aerospace is now working with the University of Michigan on an advanced version of PSL/PSA which incorporates real-time simulation".

Thus, the published literature so far is providing positive feedback. Additional demonstrations for realistic projects are currently in procurement by the U. S. Army and Air Force.

On the management level, two recent actions are of interest: portions of TRW are incorporating use of SREM into its standard practices; and BMDATC will require use of SREM to write requirements for upcoming experimental software.

4.0 SREM EXTENSIONS

In reference 4, plans for a number of potential extensions of SREM were identified. These plans addressed the issues of reducing REVS cost (discussed above), providing a smoother transition from system engineering to SREM, providing smoother transitions from SREM to DDP design, process design, and Software V&V, and application to Business Data Processing. Research on these topics is continuing, but the systems engineering/SREM interface research is beginning to produce concrete results. In reference 18, the graph model of functions is presented and used to formally define the concept of decomposition and allocation of requirements to subsystems. This graph model is used to identify how requirements for Distributed Data Processors are defined in a manner consistent with SREM.

Figure 2 illustrates the functional requirements aspects of the decomposition procedure -- for a rigorous treatment, see reference 18. The steps of decomposition, and the correspondence to the elements of RSL, are briefly discussed below.

(1) If a system deals with inputs from a number of objects, the functions of the system can be decomposed in terms of system functions which handle individual objects, and coordination/resource management functions (See Figure 2a). [Note: this corresponds to the RSL identification of ENTITY_CLASS].

(2) The interaction between one of the objects and the system can be described in terms of a graph representing sequences of actions (See Figure 2b). [Note: the actions or states correspond to the RSL identification of the ENTITY_TYPEs which compose an ENTITY_CLASS].

(3) The actions can be decomposed into potentially concurrent functions which can be assigned to the data processor or other subsystems (See Figure 2c). In general, these functions input time series and output time series. [Note: the inputs to the DP and outputs from the DP correspond to the RSL definition of the MESSAGEs and associated contents].

(4) The DP functions can be further decomposed into iterated subfunctions which deal with single messages and the data which must be saved from processing one message in order to process the next message (See Figure 2d). [Note: this data corresponds to the RSL definition of DATA which is ASSOCIATED with an ENTITY_TYPE].

(5) The subfunctions can then be further decomposed into a stimulus/response graph of processing steps (i.e., ALPHA of RSL) to define all of the conditions under which a message might be processed, the resulting responses in terms of data input/output, and messages output for each condition (See

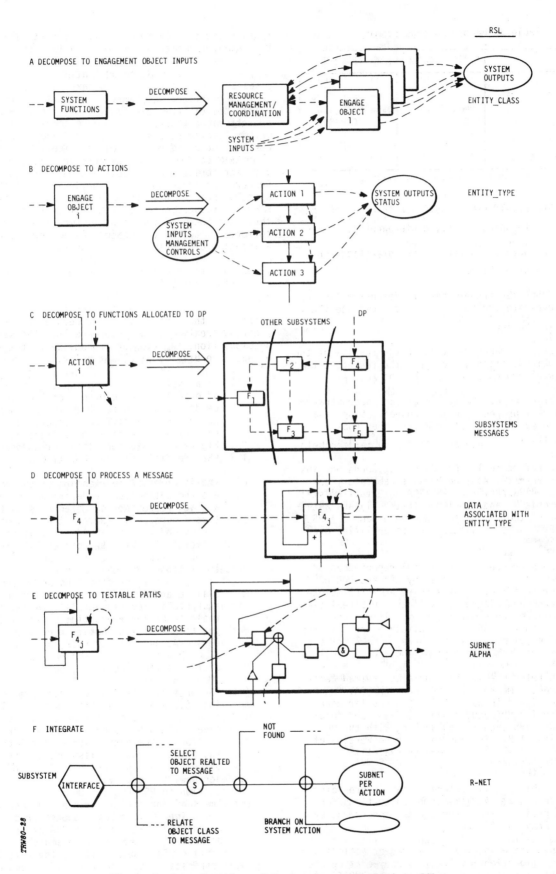

Figure 2 Decomposition of System Requirements into RSL

Figure 2e). [Note: these can be described as SUBNETs of processing and associated ALPHAS, INPUTS, OUTPUTS, and MESSAGES in RSL].

(6) The logical interface design between DP and other subsystems, establishes the logical interface links. The paths of processing for messages crossing those interfaces for all objects are combined into an R-Net. The generic form of that R-Net appears in Figure 2f. At the back end are the subnets which express processing for specific system actions. A branch on the ENTITY_TYPE of an object performs integration across all system actions. A branch using criteria for associating a message with a specific object provides integration across all objects. Criteria for associating a message with a specific object class provides integration necessary to address all messages across an interface for all classes of objects in all phases of engagement. Thus, the R-Nets represent the explicit integration by projection of all paths starting with the same interface.

The concept linking the graph model of functions to the R-Nets is simple: when the nodes of the graph input data sets (not data streams), the graph model of functions collapses into a graph model of computation, the foundation for the R-Nets.

This is viewed as a significant breakthrough in several ways:

- It provides a formally based integrated approach for the front-end system design and software requirements development activities.

- It provides formal justification for some of the RSL elements (Entity_class, Entity_type), and the steps of the SREM procedures.

- Since any system can be so represented, it provides a rationale for the applicability of SREM to the definition of software requirements for any type of system.

- It provides a formal context for addressing man/machine interface problems (e.g., the user can be considered as a subsystem), as well as others (e.g., resource management, hierarchical fault detection and recovery).

Research is on-going to extend RSL to provide a formal language to state these concepts, and to extend REVS to translate them into an automated data base, check them for consistency and completeness, and to aid generation of systems level simulators traceable to these requirements.

5.0 CONCLUSIONS

At the age of two, SREM technology had been demonstrated, transferred to others, and the REVS software had been made available, and a number of possible extensions had been addressed. As SREM

approaches the age of four, dissemination of the technology is continuing, REVS availability will be considerably enhanced by hosting it on the VAX 11/780, the results of demonstrations are being assessed, and steps are being taken to use SREM on large software development projects within the year. Meanwhile, research is continuing: a significant milestone has been reached on the systems engineering/SREM interface, and these results are being reduced to practice, thereby extending the scope of SREM to address all front-end activities.

Thus, at the age of four, it appears that SREM is making the transition from a research result into a practical engineering tool for defining and validating software requirements.

REFERENCES

1. M. W. Alford, "A Requirements Engineering Methodology for Real-Time Processing Requirements", IEEE Transactions on Software Engineering, Vol. SE-3, No. 1, January 1977, pp. 60-69.

2. T. E. Bell, D. C. Bixler, and M. E. Dyer, "An Extendable Approach to Computer-Aided Software Requirements Engineering", IEEE Transactions on Software Engineering, Vol. SE-3, No. 1, January 1977, pp. 69-84.

3. C. G. Davis and C. R. Vick, "The Software Development System", IEEE Transactions on Software Engineering, Vol. SE-3, No. 1, January 1977, pp. 69-84.

4. M. W. Alford, "Software Requirements Engineering Methodology (SREM) at the Age of Two", COMSAC 78 Proceedings, pp. 332-339.

5. M. W. Alford and I. F. Burns, "An Approach to Stating Real-Time Processing Requirements", presented at the Conference on Petri Nets and Related Methods, Massachusetts Institute of Technology, Cambridge, MA, 1-3 July 1975.

6. V. C. Cerf, "Multi-Processors, Semaphores, and a Graph Model of Computation", Department of Computer Science, University of California, Los Angeles, CA, Report UCLA-ENG-7233, April 1972.

7. W. P. Stevens, G. F. Myers, and L. C. Constantine, "Structured Design", IBM Systems Journal, Vol. 13, No. 2, 1974, pp. 115-139.

8. D. Teichroew, E. Hershey, and M. Bastauche, "An Introduction to PSL/PSA", ISDOS Working Paper 86, Department of Industrial and Operations Engineering, University of Michigan, Ann Arbor, MI, March 1974.

9. Department of Defense, "Military Standard Specification Practices", Report MIL-STD-490, October 1968.

10. C. V. Ramamoorthy and H. H. So, Software Require-
    ments and Specifications: Status and Perspec-
    tives, Memorandum No. VCB/ERL M78/44, Electronics
    Research Laboratory, University of California,
    Berkely, June 1978.

11. M. A. Jackson, Principles of Program Design,
    Academic Press, New York, 1975.

12. M. Hamilton and S. Zeldin, "Higher Order Software
    - A Methodology for Defining Software", IEEE
    Transactions on Software Engineering, Vol. SE-2,
    No. 1, pp. 9-32, March 1976.

13. D. Ross, "Structured Analysis (SA): A Language
    for Communicating Ideas", IEEE Transactions on
    Software Engineering, Volume SE-3, No. 1,
    January 1977.

14. C. R. Everhart, "User Experience with a Formally
    Defined Requirements Language IORL", Proceedings
    Second U. S. Army Software Symposium, U. S.
    Computer System Command, 25-27, Oct. 1978,
    pp. 211-219.

15. A. E. Salwin, "A Test Case Comparison of URL/URA
    and RSL/REVS", Fleet Systems Department - The
    Johns Hopkins University, July 1977.

16. R. C. Slegel, "Applying SREM to the Verification
    and Validation of an Existing Software Require-
    ments Specification", Presented at COMSAC 78.

17. M. J. Furia, "A Comparative Evaluation of RSL/
    REVS and PSL/PSA Applied to Digital Flight
    Control System", Proceedings AIAA 2nd Computers
    in Aerospace Conference, 22-24 Oct. 1979, Los
    Angeles, pp. 330-337.

18. M. W. Alford, "Requirements for Distributed Data
    Processing," Proceedings 1st International Con-
    ference on Distributed Computing Systems,
    Huntsville, AL, 1-5 October 1979, IEEE Catalog
    No. 79 CH 1445-6C.

PSL/PSA: A Computer-Aided Technique for Structured Documentation and Analysis of Information Processing Systems

DANIEL TEICHROEW AND ERNEST A. HERSHEY, III

Abstract—PSL/PSA is a computer-aided structured documentation and analysis technique that was developed for, and is being used for, analysis and documentation of requirements and preparation of functional specifications for information processing systems. The present status of requirements definition is outlined as the basis for describing the problem which PSL/PSA is intended to solve. The basic concepts of the Problem Statement Language are introduced and the content and use of a number of standard reports that can be produced by the Problem Statement Analyzer are briefly described.

The experience to date indicates that computer-aided methods can be used to aid system development during the requirements definition stage and that the main factors holding back such use are not so much related to the particular characteristics and capabilities of PSL/PSA as they are to organizational considerations involved in any change in methodology and procedure.

Index Terms—Computer-aided documentation, problem statement analysis, PSL/PSA, requirements analysis.

I. INTRODUCTION

ORGANIZATIONS now depend on computer-based information processing systems for many of the tasks involving data (recording, storing, retrieving, processing, etc.). Such systems are man-made, the process consists of a number of activities: perceiving a need for a system, determining what it should do for the organization, designing it, constructing and assembling the components, and finally testing the system prior to installing it. The process requires a great deal of effort, usually over a considerable period of time.

Throughout the life of a system it exists in several different "forms." Initially, the system exists as a concept or a proposal at a very high level of abstraction. At the point where it becomes operational it exists as a collection of rules and executable object programs in a particular computing environment. This environment consists of hardware and hard software such as the operating system, plus other components such as procedures which are carried out manually. In between the system exists in various intermediary forms.

The process by which the initial concept evolves into an operational system consists of a number of activities each of which makes the concept more concrete. Each activity takes the results of some of the previous activities and produces new results so that the progression eventually results in an operational system. Most of the activities are data processing activities, in that they use data and information to produce other data and information. Each activity can be regarded as receiving specifications or requirements from preceding activities and producing data which are regarded as specifications or requirements by one or more succeeding activities.

Since many individuals may be involved in the system development process over considerable periods of time and these or other individuals have to maintain the system once it is operating, it is necessary to record descriptions of the system as it evolves. This is usually referred to as "documentation."

In practice, the emphasis in documentation is on describing the system in the final form so that it can be maintained. Ideally, however, each activity should be documented so that the results it produces become the specification for succeeding activities. This does not happen in practice because the communications from one activity to succeeding activities is accomplished either by having the same person carrying out the activities, by oral communication among individuals in a project, or by notes which are discarded after their initial use.

This results in projects which proceed without any real possibility for management review and control. The systems are not ready when promised, do not perform the function the users expected, and cost more than budgeted.

Most organizations, therefore, mandate that the system development process be divided into phases and that certain documentation be produced by the end of each phase so that progress can be monitored and corrections made when necessary. These attempts, however, leave much to be desired and most organizations are attempting to improve the methods by which they manage their system development [20], [6].

This paper is concerned with one approach to improving systems development. The approach is based on three premises. The first is that more effort and attention should be devoted to the front end of the process where a proposed system is being described from the user's point of view [2], [14], [3]. The second premise is that the computer should be used in the development process since systems development involves large amounts of information processing. The third premise is that a computer-aided approach to systems development must start with "documentation."

This paper describes a computer-aided technique for documentation which consists of the following:

1) The results of each of the activities in the system development process are recorded in computer processible form as they are produced.

2) A computerized data base is used to maintain all the basic data about the system.

3) The computer is used to produce hard copy documentation when required.

Manuscript received June 29, 1976; revised September 20, 1976.

The authors are with the Department of Industrial and Operations Engineering, University of Michigan, Ann Arbor, MI 48109.

Reprinted from *IEEE Transactions on Software Engineering*, Volume SE-3, Number 1, January 1977, pages 41-48. Copyright © 1977 by the Institute of Electrical and Electronics Engineers, Inc.

The part of the technique which is now operational is known as PSL/PSA. Section II is devoted to a brief description of system development as a framework in which to compare manual and computer-aided documentation methods. The Problem Statement Language (PSL) is described in Section III. The reports which can be produced by the Problem Statement Analyzer (PSA) are described in Section IV. The status of the system, results of experience to date, and planned developments are outlined in Section V.

II. LOGICAL SYSTEMS DESIGN

The computer-aided documentation system described in Sections III and IV of this paper is designed to play an integral role during the initial stages in the system development process. A generalized model of the whole system development process is given in Section II-A. The final result of the initial stages is a document which here will be called the System Definition Report. The desired contents of this document are discussed in Section II-B. The activities required to produce this document manually are described in Section II-C and the changes possible through the use of computer-aided methods are outlined in Section II-D.

A. A Model of the System Development Process

The basic steps in the life cycle of information systems (initiation, analysis, design, construction, test, installation, operation, and termination) appeared in the earliest applications of computers to organizational problems (see for example, [17], [1], [4], and [7]). The need for more formal and comprehensive procedures for carrying out the life cycle was recognized; early examples are the IBM SOP publications [5], the Philips ARDI method [8], and the SDC method [23]. In the last few years, a large number of books and papers on this subject have been published [11], [19].

Examination of these and many other publications indicate that there is no general agreement on what phases the development process should be divided into, what documentation should be produced at each phase, what it should contain, or what form it should be presented in. Each organization develops its own methods and standards.

In this section a generalized system development process will be described as it might be conducted in an organization which has a Systems Department responsible for developing, operating, and maintaining computer based information processing systems. The System Department belongs to some higher unit in the organization and itself has some subunits, each with certain functions (see for example, [24]). The System Department has a system development standard procedure which includes a project management system and documentation standards.

A request for a new system is initiated by some unit in the organization or the system may be proposed by the System Department. An initial document is prepared which contains information about why a new system is needed and outlines its major functions. This document is reviewed and, if approved, a senior analyst is assigned to prepare a more detailed document. The analyst collects data by interviewing users

and studying the present system. He then produces a report describing his proposed system and showing how it will satisfy the requirements. The report will also contain the implementation plan, benefit/cost analysis, and his recommendations. The report is reviewed by the various organizational units involved. If it passes this review it is then included with other requests for the resources of the System Department and given a priority. Up to this point the investment in the proposed system is relatively small.

At some point a project team is formed, a project leader and team members are assigned, and given authority to proceed with the development of the system. A steering group may also be formed. The project is assigned a schedule in accordance with the project management system and given a budget. The schedule will include one or more target dates. The final target date will be the date the system (or its first part if it is being done in parts) is to be operational. There may also be additional target dates such as beginning of system test, beginning of programming, etc.

B. Logical System Design Documentation

In this paper, it is assumed that the system development procedure requires that the proposed system be reviewed before a major investment is made in system construction. There will therefore be another target date at which the "logical" design of the proposed system is reviewed. On the basis of this review the decision may be to proceed with the physical design and construction, to revise the proposed system, or to terminate the project.

The review is usually based on a document prepared by the project team. Sometimes it may consist of more than one separate document; for example, in the systems development methodology used by the U. S. Department of Defense [21] for non-weapons systems, development of the life cycle is divided into phases. Two documents are produced at the end of the Definition subphase of the Development phase: a Functional Description, and a Data Requirements Document.

Examination of these and many documentation requirements show that a Systems Definition Report contains five major types of information:

1) a description of the organization and where the proposed system will fit; showing how the proposed system will improve the functioning of the organization or otherwise meet the needs which lead to the project;

2) a description of the operation of the proposed system in sufficient detail to allow the users to verify that it will in fact accomplish its objectives, and to serve as the specification for the design and construction of the proposed system if the project continuation is authorized;

3) a description of its proposed system implementation in sufficient detail to estimate the time and cost required;

4) the implementation plan in sufficient detail to estimate the cost of the proposed system and the time it will be available;

5) a benefit/cost analysis and recommendations.

In addition, the report usually also contains other miscellaneous information such as glossaries, etc.

C. Current Logical System Design Process

During the initial stages of the project the efforts of the team are directed towards producing the Systems Definition Report. Since the major item this report contains is the description of the proposed system from the user or logical point of view, the activities required to produce the report are called the logical system design process. The project team will start with the information already available and then perform a set of activities. These may be grouped into five major categories.

1) Data collection. Information about the information flow in the present system, user desires for new information, potential new system organization, etc., is collected and recorded.

2) Analysis. The data that have been collected are summarized and analyzed. Errors, omissions, and ambiguities are identified and corrected. Redundancies are identified. The results are prepared for review by appropriate groups.

3) Logical Design. Functions to be performed by the system are selected. Alternatives for a new system or modification of the present system are developed and examined. The "new" system is described.

4) Evaluation. The benefits and costs of the proposed system are determined to a suitable level of accuracy. The operational and functional feasibility of the system are examined and evaluated.

5) Improvements. Usually as a result of the evaluation a number of deficiencies in the proposed system will be discovered. Alternatives for improvement are identified and evaluated until further possible improvements are not judged to be worth additional effort. If major changes are made, the evaluation step may be repeated; further data collection and analysis may also be necessary.

In practice the type of activities outlined above may not be clearly distinguished and may be carried out in parallel or iteratively with increasing level of detail. Throughout the process, however it is carried out, results are recorded and documented.

It is widely accepted that documentation is a weak link in system development in general and in logical system design in particular. The representation in the documentation that is produced with present manual methods is limited to:

1) text in a natural language;

2) lists, tables, arrays, cross references;

3) graphical representation, figures, flowcharts.

Analysis of two reports showed the following number of pages for each type of information.

Form	Report A	Report B
text	90	117
lists and tables	207	165
charts and figures	28	54
total	335	336

The systems being documented are very complex and these methods of representation are not capable of adequately describing all the necessary aspects of a system for all those who must, or should, use the documentation. Consequently, documentation is

1) ambiguous: natural languages are not precise enough to describe systems and different readers may interpret a sentence in different ways;

2) inconsistent: since systems are large the documentation is large and it is very difficult to ensure that the documentation is consistent;

3) incomplete: there is usually not a sufficient amount of time to devote to documentation and with a large complex system it is difficult to determine what information is missing.

The deficiencies of manual documentation are compounded by the fact that systems are continually changing and it is very difficult to keep the documentation up-to-date.

Recently there have been attempts to improve manual documentation by developing more formal methodologies [16], [12], [13], [22], [15], [25]. These methods, even though they are designed to be used manually, have a formal language or representation scheme that is designed to alleviate the difficulties listed above. To make the documentation more useful for human beings, many of these methods use a graphical language.

D. Computer-Aided Logical System Design Process

In computer-aided logical system design the objective, as in the manual process, is to produce the System Definition Report and the process followed is essentially similar to that described above. The computer-aided design system has the following capabilities:

1) capability to describe information systems, whether manual or computerized, whether existing or proposed, regardless of application area;

2) ability to record such description in a computerized data base;

3) ability to incrementally add to, modify, or delete from the description in the data base;

4) ability to produce "hard copy" documentation for use by the analyst or the other users.

The capability to describe systems in computer processible form results from the use of the system description language called PSL. The ability to record such description in a data base, incrementally modify it, and on demand perform analysis and produce reports comes from the software package called the Problem Statement Analyzer (PSA). The Analyzer is controlled by a Command Language which is described in detail in [9] (Fig. 1).

The Problem Statement Language is outlined in Section III and described in detail in [10]. The use of PSL/PSA in computer-aided logical system design is described in detail in [18].

The use of PSL/PSA does not depend on any particular structure of the system development process or any standards on the format and content of hard copy documentation. It is therefore fully compatible with current procedures in most organizations that are developing and maintaining systems.

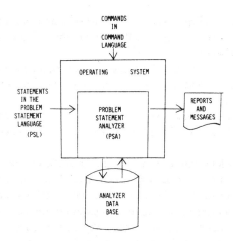

Fig. 1. The Problem Statement Analyzer.

Using this system, the data collected or developed during all five of the activities are recorded in machine-readable form and entered into the computer as it is collected. A data base is built during the process. These data can be analyzed by computer programs and intermediate documentation prepared on request. The Systems Definition Report then includes a large amount of material produced automatically from the data base.

The activities in logical system design are modified when PSL/PSA is used as follows:

1) Data collection: since most of the data must be obtained through personal contact, interviews will still be required. The data collected are recorded in machine-readable form. The intermediate outputs of PSA also provide convenient checklists for deciding what additional information is needed and for recording it for input.

2) Analysis: a number of different kinds of analysis can be performed on demand by PSA, and therefore need no longer be done manually.

3) Design: design is essentially a creative process and cannot be automated. However, PSA can make more data available to the designer and allow him to manipulate it more extensively. The results of his decisions are also entered into the data base.

4) Evaluation: PSA provides some rudimentary facilities for computing volume or work measures from the data in the problem statement.

5) Improvements: identification of areas for possible improvements is also a creative task; however, PSA output, particularly from the evaluation phase, may be useful to the analyst.

The System Definition Report will contain the same material as that described since the documentation must serve the same purpose. Furthermore, the same general format and representation is desirable.

1) Narrative information is necessary for human readability. This is stored as part of the data but is not analyzed by the computer program. However, the fact that it is displayed next to, or in conjunction with, the final description improves the ability of the analyst to detect discrepancies and inconsistencies.

2) Lists, tables, arrays, matrices. These representations are prepared from the data base. They are up-to-date and can be more easily rearranged in any desired order.

3) Diagrams and charts. The information from the data base can be represented in various graphical forms to display the relationships between objects.

III. PSL, A PROBLEM STATEMENT LANGUAGE

PSL is a language for describing systems. Since it is intended to be used to describe "proposed" systems it was called a Problem Statement Language because the description of a proposed system can be considered a "problem" to be solved by the system designers and implementors.

PSL is intended to be used in situations in which analysts now describe systems. The descriptions of systems produced using PSL are used for the same purpose as that produced manually. PSL may be used both in batch and interactive environments, and therefore only "basic" information about the system need to be stated in PSL. All "derived" information can be produced in hard copy form as required.

The model on which PSL is based is described in Section III-A. A general description of the system and semantics of PSL is then given in Section III-B to illustrate the broad scope of system aspects that can be described using PSL. The detailed syntax of PSL is given in [10].

A. Model of Information Systems

The Problem Statement Language is based first on a model of a general system, and secondly on the specialization of the model to a particular class of systems, namely information systems.

The model of a general system is relatively simple. It merely states that a system consists of things which are called OBJECTS. These objects may have PROPERTIES and each of these PROPERTIES may have PROPERTY VALUES. The objects may be connected or interrelated in various ways. These connections are called RELATIONSHIPS.

The general model is specialized for an information system by allowing the use of only a limited number of predefined objects, properties, and relationships.

B. An Overview of the Problem Statement Language Syntax and Semantics

The objective of PSL is to be able to express in syntatically analyzable form as much of the information which commonly appears in System Definition Reports as possible.

System Descriptions may be divided into eight major aspects:
1) System Input/Output Flow,
2) System Structure,
3) Data Structure,
4) Data Derivation,
5) System Size and Volume,
6) System Dynamics,
7) System Properties,
8) Project Management.

PSL contains a number of types of objects and relationships which permit these different aspects to be described.

```
Parameters:  DB=-EXRDB  NAME=hourly-employee-processing  NOINDEX  NOPUNCHED-NAMES  PRINT  EMPTY
NOPUNCH  SMARG=5  NMARG=20  AMARG=10  BMARG=25  RMARG=70  CMARG=1  HMARG=60  NODESIGNATE
SEVERAL-PER-LINE  DEFINE  COMMENT  NONEW-PAGE  NONEW-LINE  NOALL-STATEMENTS
COMPLEMENTARY-STATEMENTS  LINE-NUMBERS  PRINTEOF  DLC-COMMENT

 1  PROCESS                                          hourly-employee-processing;
 2      /*  DATE OF LAST CHANGE - JUN 26, 1976, 13:56:44 */
 3    DESCRIPTION;
 4          this process performs those actions needed to interpret
 5          time cards to produce a pay statement for each hourly
 6          employee.;
 7    KEYWORDS:    independent;
 8    ATTRIBUTES ARE:
 9          complexity-level
10                         high;
11    GENERATES:    pay-statement, error-listing,
12                  hourly-employee-report;
13    RECEIVES:     time-card;
14    SUBPARTS ARE: hourly-paycheck-validation, hourly-emp-update,
15                  h-report-entry-generation,
16                  hourly-paycheck-production;
17    PART OF:      payroll-processing;
18    DERIVES:      pay-statement
19       USING:     time-card, hourly-employee-record;
20    DERIVES:      hourly-employee-report
21       USING:     time-card, hourly-employee-record;
22    DERIVES:      error-listing
23       USING:     time-card, hourly-employee-record;
24    PROCEDURE;
25          1. compute gross pay from time card data.
26          2. compute tax from gross pay.
27          3. subtract tax from gross pay to obtain net pay.
28          4. update hourly employee record accordingly.
29          5. update department record accordingly.
30          6. generate paycheck.
31          note: if status code specifies that the employee did not work
32            this week, no processing will be done for this employee.;
33    HAPPENS:
34          number-of-payments TIMES-PER pay-period;
35    TRIGGERED BY:  hourly-emp-processing-event;
36    TERMINATION-CAUSES:
37                   new-employee-processing-event;
38    SECURITY IS:   company-only;
39
40  EOF EOF EOF EOF EOF
```

Fig. 2 Example of a FORMATTED PROBLEM STATEMENT for one PROCESS.

The System Input/Output Flow aspect of the system deals with the interaction between the target system and its environment.

System Structure is concerned with the hierarchies among objects in a system. Structures may also be introduced to facilitate a particular design approach such as "top down." All information may initially be grouped together and called by one name at the highest level, and then successively subdivided. System structures can represent high-level hierarchies which may not actually exist in the system, as well as those that do.

The *Data Structure* aspect of system description includes all the relationships which exist among data used and/or manipulated by the system as seen by the "users" of the system.

The *Data Derivation* aspect of the system description specifies which data objects are involved in particular PROCESSES in the system. It is concerned with what information is used, updated, and/or derived, how this is done, and by which processes.

Data Derivation relationships are internal in the system, while System Input/Output Flow relationships describe the system boundaries. As with other PSL facilities System Input/Output Flow need not be used. A system can be considered as having no boundary.

The *System Size and Volume* aspect is concerned with the size of the system and those factors which influence the volume of processing which will be required.

The *System Dynamics* aspect of system description presents the manner in which the target system "behaves" over time.

All objects (of a particular type) used to describe the target system have characteristics which distinguish them from other objects of the same type. Therefore, the PROPERTIES of particular objects in the system must be described. The PROPERTIES themselves are objects and given unique names.

The *Project Management* aspect requires that, in addition to the description of the target system being designed, documentation of the project designing (or documenting) the target system be given. This involves identification of people involved and their responsibilities. schedules, etc.

IV. REPORTS

As information about a particular system is obtained, it is expressed in PSL and entered into a data base using the Problem Statement Analyzer. At any time standard outputs or reports may be produced on request. The various reports can be classified on the basis of the purposes which they serve.

1) *Data Base Modification Reports:* These constitute a record of changes that have been made, together with diagnostics and warnings. They constitute a record of changes for error correction and recovery.

2) *Reference Reports:* These present the information in the data base in various formats. For example, the Name List Report presents all the objects in the data base with their type and date of last change. The Formatted Problem Statement Report shows all properties and relationships for a particular object (Fig. 2). The Dictionary Report gives only data dictionary type information.

3) *Summary Reports:* These present collections of information in summary from, or gathered from several different relationships. For example, the Data Base Summary Report provides project management information by showing the totals of various types of objects and how much has been said about them. The Structure Report shows complete or partial hierarchies. The Extended Picture Report shows the data flows in a graphical form.

4) *Analysis Reports:* These provide various types of analysis of the information in the data base. For example, the Contents Comparision Report analyzes similarity of Inputs and Outputs. The Data Process Interaction Report (Fig. 3) can be used to detect gaps in the information flow, or unused data objects. The Process Chain Report shows the dynamic behavior of the system (Fig. 4).

```
                    1111111111222222222333
               1234567890123456789012345 6789012
               +----+----+----+----+----+----+--+
           1 :D    :    :    :    :    :   : :
           2 : FDF FR   :    :    :    :   : :
           3 :    : D   :    :    :    :   : :
           4 :    : R   :    :    :    :   : :
           5 +----+--R-+----+----+----+----+--+
           6 :    : R   :    :    :    :   : :
           7 :    : :DR R :   :    :    :   : :
           8 :    : :D   :    :    :    :   : :
           9 :    : F : D:    :    :    :   : :
          10 +----+----F--+----+----+----+--+
          11 :    :  :    R    :    :    :   : :
          12 :    :    : DR   :    :    :   : :
          13 :    :    : : DR :    :    :   : :
          14 :    D   :    : R F:    :   : :
          15 +R--+----+----+----+----+----+--+
          16 : FFR    :    : D    :    :   : :
          17 :D   :    :    :    :    :   : :
          18 :    : F  :    :    : FDF FR   : :
          19 :    :    :    : RD:    :    : :
          20 +----+--F-+----+----+----F DR--+--+
          21 :  FD    :    : P:    :    :   : :
          22 : FR :    :    :    : F   F:D : :
          23 :    : :R F :   :    :    : D : :
          24 :    :    : F:   :    :    : D : :
          25 :    :    :    :    :    : FF  : :
               +----+----+----+----+----+----+--+
```

Fig. 3. Example of part of a Data Process Interaction Report.

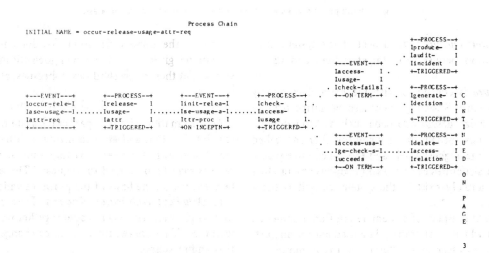

Fig. 4. Example of a Process Chain Report.

After the requirements have been completed, the final documentation required by the organization can be produced semiautomatically to a presented format, e.g., the format required for the Functional Description and Data Requirements in [21].

V. CONCLUDING REMARKS

The current status of PSL/PSA is described briefly in Section V-A. The benefits that should accrue to users of PSL/PSA are discussed in Section V-B. The information on benefits actually obtained by users is given in Section V-C. Planned extensions are outlined in Section V-D. Some conclusions reached as a result of the developments to date are given in Section V-E.

A. Current Status

The PSL/PSA system described in this paper is operational on most larger computing environments which support interactive use, including IBM 370 series (OS/VS/TSO/CMS), Univac 1100 series (EXEC-8), CDC 6000/7000 series (SCOPE, TSS), Honeywell 600/6000 series (MULTICS, GCOS), AMDAHL 470/VS (MTS), and PDP-10 (TOPS 10). Portability is achieved at a relatively high level; almost all of the system is written in ANSI Fortran.

PSL/PSA is currently being used by a number of organizations including AT&T Long Lines, Chase Manhattan Bank, Mobil Oil, British Railways, Petroleos Mexicanos, TRW Inc., the U.S. Air Force and others for documenting systems. It is also being used by academic institutions for education and research.

B. Benefit/Cost Analysis of Computer-Aided Documentation

The major benefits claimed for computer-aided documentation are that the "quality" of the documentation is improved and that the cost of design, implementation, and maintenance will be reduced. The "quality" of the documentation, measured in terms of preciseness, consistency, and completeness is increased because the analysts must be more precise, the software performs checking, and the output reports can be reviewed for remaining ambiguities, inconsistencies, and omissions. While completeness can never be fully guaranteed, one important feature of the computer-aided method is that all the documentation that "exists" is the data base, and therefore the gaps and omissions are more obvious. Consequently, the organization knows what data it has, and does not have to depend on individuals who may not be available when a specific item of data about a system is needed. Any analysis performed and reports produced are up-to-date as of the time it is performed. The coordination among analysts is greatly simplified since each can work in his own area and still have the system specifications be consistent.

Development will take less time and cost less because errors, which usually are not discovered until programming or testing, have been minimized. It is recognized that one reason for the high cost of systems development is the fact that errors, inconsistencies, and omissions in specifications are frequently not detected until later stages of development: in design, programming, systems tests, or even operation. The use of PSL/PSA during the specification stage reduces the number of errors which will have to be corrected later. Maintenance costs are considerably reduced because the effect of a proposed change can easily be isolated, thereby reducing the probability that one correction will cause other errors.

The cost of using a computer-aided method during logical system design must be compared with the cost of performing the operations manually. In practice the cost of the various analyst functions of interviewing, recording, analyzing, etc., are not recorded separately. However, it can be argued that direct cost of documenting specifications for a proposed system using PSL/PSA should be approximately equal to the cost of producing the documentation manually. The cost of typing manual documentation is roughly equal to the cost of entering PSL statements into the computer. The computer cost of using PSA should not be more than the cost of analyst time in carrying out the analyses manually. (Computer costs, however, are much more visible than analysts costs.) Even though the total cost of logical system design is not reduced by using computer-aided methods, the elapsed time should be reduced because the computer can perform clerical tasks in a shorter time than analysts require.

C. Benefits/Costs Evaluation in Practice

Ideally the adoption of a new methodology such as that represented by PSL/PSA should be based on quantitative evaluation of the benefits and costs. In practice this is seldom possible; PSL/PSA is no exception.

Very little quantitative information about the experience in using PSL/PSA, especially concerning manpower requirements and system development costs, is available. One reason for this lack of data is that the project has been concerned with developing the methodology and has not felt it necessary or worthwhile to invest resources in carrying out controlled experiments which would attempt to quantify the benefits. Furthermore, commercial and government organizations which have investigated PSL/PSA have, in some cases, started to use it without a formal evaluation; in other cases, they have started with an evaluation project. However, once the evaluation proj-

ect is completed and the decision is made to use the PSL/PSA, there is little time or motivation to document the reasons in detail.

Organizations carrying out evaluations normally do not have the comparable data for present methods available and so far none have felt it necessary to run controlled experiments with both methods being used in parallel. Even when evaluations are made, the results have not been made available to the project, because the organizations regard the data as proprietary.

The evidence that the PSL/PSA is worthwhile is that almost without exception the organizations which have seriously considered using it have decided to adopt it either with or without an evaluation. Furthermore, practically all organizations which started to use PSL/PSA are continuing their use (the exceptions have been caused by factors other than PSL/PSA itself) and in organizations which have adopted it, usage has increased.

D. Planned Developments

PSL as a system description language was intended to be "complete" in that the logical view of a proposed information system could be described, i.e., all the information necessary for functional requirements and specifications could be stated. On the other hand, the language should not be so complicated that it would be difficult for analysts to use. Also, deliberately omitted from the language was any ability to provide procedural "code" so that analysts would be encouraged to concentrate on the requirements rather than on low-level flow charts. It is clear, however, that PSL must be extended to include more precise statements about logical and procedural information.

Probably the most important improvement in PSA is to make it easier to use. This includes providing more effective and simple data entry and modification commands and providing more help to the users. A second major consideration is performance. As the data base grows in size and the number of users increases, performance becomes more important. Performance is very heavily influenced by factors in the computing environment which are outside the control of PSA development. Nevertheless, there are improvements that can be made.

PSL/PSA is clearly only one step in using computer-aided methods in developing, operating, and maintaining information processing systems. The results achieved to date support the premise that the same general approach can successfully be applied to the rest of the system life cycle and that the data base concept can be used to document the results of the other activities in the system life cycle. The resulting data bases can be the basis for development of methodology, generalized systems, education, and research.

E. Conclusions

The conclusions reached from the development of PSL/PSA to date and from the effort in having it used operationally may be grouped into five major categories.

1) The determination and documentation of requirements and functional specifications can be improved by making use

of the computer for recording and analyzing the collected data and statements about the proposed system.

2) Computer-aided documentation is itself a system of which the software is only a part. If the system is to be used, adequate attention must be given to the whole methodology, including: user documentation, logistics and mechanics of use, training, methodological support, and management encouragement.

3) The basic structure of PSL and PSA is correct. A system description language should be of the relational type in which a description consists of identifying and naming objects and relationships among them. The software system should be data-base oriented, i.e., the data entry and modification procedures should be separated from the output report and analysis facilities.

4) The approach followed in the ISDOS project has succeeded in bringing PSL/PSA into operational use. The same approach can be applied to the rest of the system life cycle. A particularly important part of this approach is to concentrate first on the documentation and then on the methodology.

5) The decision to use a computer-aided documentation method is only partly influenced by the capabilities of the system. Much more important are factors relating to the organization itself and system development procedures. Therefore, even though computer-aided documentation is operational in some organizations, that does not mean that all organizations are ready to immediately adopt it as part of their system life cycle methodology.

REFERENCES

[1] T. Aiken, "Initiating an electronics program," in *Proc. 7th Annu. Meeting, Systems and Procedures Assoc.*, 1954.
[2] B. W. Boehm, "Software and its impact: A quantitative assessment," *Datamation*, pp. 48–59, May 1973.
[3] ——, "Some steps toward formal and automated aids to software requirements analysis and design," *Inform. Process.*, pp. 192–197, 1974.
[4] R. G. Canning, *Electronic Data Processing for Business and Industry*. New York: Wiley, 1956.
[5] T. B. Glans, B. Grad, D. Holstein, W. E. Meyers, and R. N. Schmidt, *Management Systems*. New York: Holt, Rinehart, and Winston, 1968, 340 pp. (Based on IBM's study Organization Plan, 1961.)
[6] J. Goldberg, Ed., "The high cost of software," in the proceedings of a symposium held in Monterey, CA, Sept. 17–19, 1973, sponsored by the U.S. Air Force Office of Scientific Research, U.S. Army Research Office, Office of Naval Research. Menlo Park, CA: Stanford Research Institute, 1973.
[7] R. H. Gregory and R. L. Van Horn, *Automatic Data Processing Systems*. Belmont, CA: Wadsworth Publishing Co., 1960.
[8] W. Hartman, H. Matthes, and A. Proeme, *Management Information Systems Handbook*, (ARDI). New York: McGraw-Hill, 1968.
[9] E. A. Hershey and M. Bastarache, "PSA—Command Descriptions," ISDOS Working Paper no. 91, 1975.
[10] E. A. Hershey, E. W. Winters, D. L. Berg, A. F. Dickey, and B. L. Kahn, *Problem Statement Language—Language Reference Manual*, ISDOS Working Paper no. 68, 1975.
[11] G. F. Hice, W. S. Turner, and L. F. Cashwell, *System Development Methodology*. Amsterdam, The Netherlands: North-Holland Publishing Co., 1974, 370 pp.
[12] IBM Corporation, Data Processing Division, White Plains, NY, "Hipo—A design aid and documentation technique," Order no. GC-20-1851, 1974.
[13] M. N. Jones, "HIPO for developing specifications," *Datamation*, pp. 112–125, Mar. 1976.
[14] G. H. Larsen, "Software: Man in the middle," *Datamation*, pp. 61–66, Nov. 1973.
[15] G. J. Meyers, *Reliable Software Through Composite Design*. New York: Mason Charter Publishers, Inc., 1975.
[16] D. T. Ross and K. E. Schoman, Jr., "Structured analysis for requirements definition," in *Proc. 2nd Int. Conf. Software Eng.*, San Francisco, CA, Oct. 13–15, 1976.
[17] H. W. Schrimpf and C. W. Compton, "The first business feasibility study in the computer field," *Computers and Automation*, Jan. 1969.
[18] D. Teichroew and M. Bastarache, *PSL User's Manual*, ISDOS Working Paper no. 98, 1975.
[19] TRW Systems Group, *Software Development and Configuration Management Manual*, TRW-55-73-07, Dec. 1973.
[20] U.S. Air Force, "Support of Air Force automatic data processing requirements through the 1980's," Electronics Systems Division, L. G. Hanscom Field, Rep. SADPR-85, June 1974.
[21] U.S. Department of Defense, *Automated Data Systems Documentation Standards Manual*, Manual 4120.17M, Dec. 1972.
[22] J. D. Warnier and B. Flanagan, *Entrainment de la Construction des Programs D'Informatique*, vol. I and II. Paris: Editions d'Organization, 1972.
[23] N. E. Willworth, Ed., *System Programming Management*, System Development Corporation, TM 1578/000/00, Mar, 13, 1964.
[24] F. G. Withington, *The Organization of the Data Processing Function*, Wiley Business Data Processing Library, 1972.
[25] E. Yourdon and L. Constantine, *Structured Design*. New York: Yourdon, Inc., 1975.

Daniel Teichroew was born in Canada in 1925. He received the B.S. and M.A. degrees in mathematics from the University of Toronto, Toronto, Ont., Canada, in 1948 and 1949, respectively, and the Ph.D. degree in experimental statistics from the Institute of Statistics, North Carolina State College, Raleigh, NC.

From 1952 to 1955 he worked for the National Bureau of Standards, Washington, DC. In 1955 he was the Senior Electronics Application Specialist for the National Cash Register Company. From 1955 to 1956 he was Special Representative of Product Development and from 1956 to 1957 was Head of Business Systems Analysis for the National Cash Register Company. He was Associate Professor of Management and Professor of Management at the Stanford University Graduate School of Business from 1957 to 1962 and from 1962 to 1964, respectively. From 1964 to 1968 he was Professor and Head of the Division of Organizational Sciences at Case Institute of Technology. Since 1968 he has been Professor of Industrial and Operations Engineering, University of Michigan, Ann Arbor, and served as Chairman of that department from 1968 to 1973. He is also Director of the ISDOS Project.

Dr. Teichroew is President of the Society for Management Information Systems.

Ernest A. Hershey, III was born in Indiana in 1949. He received the B.S. degree in computer and communications science in 1971 and the M.S. degree in industrial and operations engineering in 1973 from the University of Michigan, Ann Arbor. He is presently working on the Ph.D. degree in industrial and operations engineering at the University of Michigan.

From 1969 to 1970 he worked for the IBM Corporation, New York, on their Internal Teleprocessing System Operations. From 1971 to 1973 he did counseling at the University of Michigan Computer Center. From 1971 to the present he has been a Research Associate on the ISDOS Project, University of Michigan.

Structured Analysis (SA): A Language for Communicating Ideas

DOUGLAS T. ROSS

Reprinted from *IEEE Transactions on Software Engineering*, Volume SE-3, Number 1, January 1977, pages 16-34. Copyright © 1977 by the Institute of Electrical and Electronics Engineers. Inc.

Abstract—Structured analysis (SA) combines blueprint-like graphic language with the nouns and verbs of any other language to provide a hierarchic, top-down, gradual exposition of detail in the form of an SA model. The things and happenings of a subject are expressed in a data decomposition and an activity decomposition, both of which employ the same graphic building block, the SA box, to represent a part of a whole. SA arrows, representing input, output, control, and mechanism, express the relation of each part to the whole. The paper describes the rationalization behind some 40 features of the SA language, and shows how they enable rigorous communication which results from disciplined, recursive application of the SA maxim: "Everything worth saying about anything worth saying something about must be expressed in six or fewer pieces."

Index Terms—Graphic language, hierarchic, requirements analysis, requirements definition, structured analysis (SA), structured programming, system analysis, system design, top-down.

I. BLUEPRINT LANGUAGE

NEITHER Watt's steam engine nor Whitney's standardized parts really started the Industrial Revolution, although each has been awarded that claim, in the past. The real start was the awakening of scientific and technological thoughts during the Renaissance, with the idea that the lawful behavior of nature can be understood, analyzed, and manipulated to accomplish useful ends. That idea itself, alone, was not enough, however, for not until the creation and evolution of blueprints was it possible to express exactly how power and parts were to be combined for each specific task at hand.

Mechanical drawings and blueprints are not mere pictures, but a complete and rich language. In blueprint language, scientific, mathematical, and geometric formulations, notations, mensurations, and naming do not merely describe an object or process, they actually model it. Because of broad differences in subject, purpose, roles, and the needs of the people who use them, many forms of blueprint have evolved, but all rigorously present well structured information in understandable form.

Failure to develop such a communication capability for data processing is due not merely to the diversity and complexity of the problems we tackle, but to the newness of our field. It has naturally taken time for us to escape from naive "programming by priesthood" to the more mature approaches, such as structured programming, language and database design, and software production methods. Still missing from this expanding repertoire of evidence of maturity, however, is the common thread that will allow all of the pieces to be tied together into a predictable and dependable approach.

Manuscript received June 21, 1976; revised September 16, 1976.
The author is with SofTech, Inc., Waltham, MA 02154.

II. STRUCTURED ANALYSIS (SA) LANGUAGE

It is the thesis of this paper that the language of structured analysis (SA), a new disciplined way of putting together old ideas, provides the evolutionary natural language appropriate to the needs of the computer field. SA is deceptively simple in its mechanics, which are few in number and have high mnemonic value, making the language easy and natural to use. Anybody can learn to read SA language with very little practice and will be able to understand the actual information content being conveyed by the graphical notation and the words of the language with ease and precision. But being a language with rigorously defined semantics, SA is a tough taskmaster. Not only do well conceived and well phrased thoughts come across concisely and with precision, but poorly conceived and poorly expressed thoughts also are recognized as such. This simply *has* to be a fact for any language whose primary accomplishment is valid communication of understanding. If both the bad and the good were *not* equally recognizable, the understanding itself would be incomplete.

SA does the same for any problem chosen for analysis, for every natural language and every formal language are, by definition, included in SA. *The only function of SA is to bind up, structure, and communicate units of thought expressed in any other chosen language.* Synthesis is composition, analysis is decomposition. *SA is structured decomposition, to enable structured synthesis to achieve a given end.* The actual building-block elements of analysis or synthesis may be of any sort whatsoever. Pictures, words, expressions of any sort may be incorporated into and made a part of the structure.

The facts about Structured Analysis are as follows.

1) It incorporates any other language; its scope is universal and unrestricted.

2) It is concerned only with the orderly and well-structured decomposition of the subject matter.

3) The decomposed units are sized to suit the modes of thinking and understanding of the intended audience.

4) Those units of understanding are expressed in a way that rigorously and precisely represents their interrelation.

5) This structured decomposition may be carried out to any required degree of depth, breadth, and scope while still maintaining all of the above properties.

6) Therefore, SA greatly increases both the quantity and quality of understanding that can be effectively and precisely communicated well beyond the limitations inherently imposed by the imbedded natural or formal language used to address the chosen subject matter.

The universality and precision of SA makes it particularly effective for requirements definition for arbitrary systems problems, a subject treated in some detail in a companion paper (see [5]). Requirements definition encompasses all aspects of system development prior to actual system design, and hence is concerned with the discovery of real user needs and communicating those requirements to those who must produce an effective system solution. Structured Analysis and Design Technique (SADT (TM)) is the name of SofTech's proprietary methodology based on SA. The method has been applied to a wide range of planning, analysis, and design problems involving men, machines, software, hardware, database, communications procedures, and finances over the last two years, and several are cited in that paper. It is recommended that that paper (see [5]) be read prior to this paper to provide motivation and insight into the features of SA language described here.

SA is not limited to requirements definition nor even problems that are easily recognized as system problems. The end product of an SA analysis is a working model of a well-structured understanding, and that can be beneficial even on a uniquely personal level—just to "think things through." Social, artistic, scientific, legal, societal, political, and even philosophic subjects, all are subject to analysis, and the resulting models can effectively communicate the ideas to others. The same methods, approach, and discipline can be used to model the problem environment, requirements, and proposed solution, as well as the project organization, operation, budget, schedule, and action plan. Man thinks with language. Man communicates with language. SA structures language for communicating ideas more effectively. *The human mind can accommodate any amount of complexity as long as it is presented in easy-to-grasp chunks that are structured together to make the whole.*

III. OUTLINE OF THE DEMONSTRATION

Five years ago I said in an editorial regarding software [1]: "Tell me *why* it works, not *that* it works." That is the approach taken in this paper. This paper does not present a formal grammar for the SA language—that will come later, elsewhere. This paper also is not a user manual for either authors or readers of the language—a simple "how to" exposition. Instead, we concentrate here on the motivation *behind* the features of SA in an attempt to convey directly an appreciation for its features and power even beyond that acquired through use by most SA practitioners. SA has been heavily developed, applied, taught, and used for almost three years already, but the design rationale behind it is first set down here.

SA (both the language and the discipline of thought) derives from the way our minds work, and from the way we understand real-world situations and problems. Therefore, we start out with a summary of principles of exposition—good storytelling. This turns out to yield the familiar top-down decomposition, a key component of SA. But more than that results, for consideration of how we view our space-time world shows that we always understand anything and everything in terms of *both* things *and* happenings. This is why all of our languages have *both* nouns *and* verbs—and this, in turn, yields the means

(TM)Trademark of SofTech, Inc.

by which SA language is universal, and can absorb any other language as a component part.

SA supplies rigorous structural connections to any language whose nouns and verbs it absorbs in order to talk about things and happenings, and we will spend some time covering the basics carefully, so that the fundamentals are solid. We do this by presenting, in tabular form, some 40 basic features, and then analyzing them bit by bit, using SA diagrams as figures to guide and illustrate the discussion.

Once the basics have thus been introduced, certain important topics that would have been obscure earlier are covered in some depth because their combinations are at the heart of SA's effectiveness. These topics concern constraints, boundaries, necessity, and dominance between modular portions of subject matter being analyzed. It turns out that constraints based on purpose and viewpoint actually *make* the structure. The depth of treatment gives insight into how we understand things.

The actual output of SA is a hierarchically organized structure of separate diagrams, each of which exposes only a limited part of the subject to view, so that even very complex subjects can be understood. The structured collection of diagrams is called an *SA model*. The demonstration here concludes with several special notations to clarify presentation and facilitate the orderly organization of the material. Since actual SA diagrams (some good, some illustrating poor style) are used, as figure illustrations, the reader is exposed here to the style of SA even though the SA model represented by the collection of figures is not complete enough to be understandable by itself. Later papers will treat more advanced topics and present complete examples of SA use and practice in a wide variety of applications.

IV. PRINCIPLES OF GOOD STORYTELLING

There are certain basic, known principles about how people's minds go about the business of understanding, and communicating understanding by means of language, which have been known and used for many centuries. No matter how these principles are addressed, they always end up with hierarchic decomposition as being the heart of good storytelling. Perhaps the most relevant formulation is the familiar: "Tell 'em whatcha gonna tell 'em. Tell 'em. Tell 'em whatcha told 'em." This is a pattern of communication almost as universal and well-entrenched as Newton's laws of motion. It is the pattern found in all effective forms of communication and in all analyses of why such communication is effective. Artistic and scientific fields, in addition to journalism, all follow the same sequence, for that is the way our minds work.

Only something so obvious as not to be worth saying can be conveyed in a single stage of the communication process, however. In any worthwhile subject matter, Stage Two ("Tell 'em") requires the parallel introduction of several more instances of the same pattern starting again with Stage One. Usually a story establishes several such levels of telling, and weaves back and forth between them as the need arises, to convey understanding, staying clear of excesses in either detail (boredom) or abstraction (confusion).

V. The SA Maxim

This weaving together of parts with whole is the heart of SA. The natural law of good communications takes the following, quite different, form in SA:

"Everything worth saying
about anything worth saying something about
must be expressed in six or fewer pieces."

Let us analyze this maxim and see how and why it, too, yields hierarchically structured storytelling.

First of all, there must be something (anything) that is "worth saying something about." We must have some subject matter that has some value to us. We must have an interest in some aspect of it. This is called establishing the *viewpoint* for the model, in SA terminology. Then we must have in mind some audience we want to communicate with. That audience will determine what is (and is not) "worth saying" about the subject from that viewpoint. This is called establishing the *purpose* for the model, in SA terminology. As we will see, every subject has many aspects of interest to many audiences, so that there can be many viewpoints and purposes. But each SA model must have only one of each, to bound and structure its subject matter. We also will see that each model also has an established *vantage point* within the purpose-structured context of some other model's viewpoint, and this is how multiple models are interrelated so that they collectively cover the whole subject matter. But a single SA model considers only worthy thoughts about a single worthy subject.

The clincher, however, is that *every* worthy thought about that worthy subject must be included. The first word of the maxim is *everything*, and that means exactly that—absolutely nothing that fits the purpose and viewpoint can be left out. The reason is simple. By definition everything is the subject itself, for otherwise it would not *be* that subject—it would be a *lesser* subject. Then, if the subject is to be broken into six or fewer pieces, every single thing must go into exactly one of those (nonoverlapping) pieces. Only in this way can we ensure that the subject stays the same, and does not degenerate into some lesser subject as we decompose it. Also, if overlapping pieces were allowed, conflicts and confusions might arise.

A "piece" can be anything we choose it to be—the maxim merely requires that the single piece of thought about the subject be broken into several (not too few, and not too many[1]) pieces. Now, certainly if the original single piece of thought about the subject is worthy, it is very unlikely that the mere breaking of it into six-or-fewer pieces exhausts that worth. The maxim still applies so that every one of them must similarly be expressed in six-or-fewer *more* pieces—again and again—until the number of pieces has grown to suit the

[1] Many people have urged me to relate the magic number "six" to various psychological studies about the characteristics of the human mind. I won't. It's neither scientific nor "magic." It is simply the *right* number. (Readers who doubt my judgement are invited to read for themselves the primary source [6].) The only proper reference would be to the little bear in the Goldilocks story. His portions always were "just right," too!

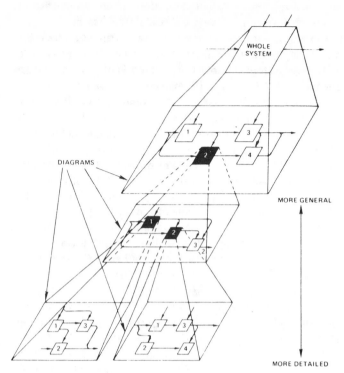

Fig. 1. Structured decomposition.

total worthiness. At a fine enough level of decomposition, it is not worth continuing. No further decomposition is required for completely clear understanding. Thus we see that the SA maxim must be interpreted *recursively*, and yields top-down hierarchic decomposition. The SA language allows this hierarchic structure to be expressed (see Fig. 1).

VI. Expression

In the maxim, the word "express" covers both the rigorous grammar of SA language itself, as well as the grammar (however well or ill formed) of the natural language chosen to address the subject matter. By definition, SA language includes all other languages, and regardless of what language is embedded, the decomposition discipline (expressed by the SA language component of the combined language) ensures that at each stage, the natural language (whatever it may be) is used to address and express only every worthy thought about a more and more restricted piece of the worthy subject matter. Because of this orderly zeroing-in, SA certainly cannot decrease the effectiveness of that chosen language. In effect, the SA maxim is valid by definition, for whenever the subject matter has already been broken down to such a fine level that the SA decomposition would add nothing to what already would be done (as, for example, in jokes or some poetry) the chosen language stands by itself, not decreased in effectiveness.

Most of the time the conscious practice of Structured Analysis and its thought discipline improves people's ability to think clearly and find solutions. In the cases where this does not happen, however, Structured Analysis still "works," in the sense that the bad portions stand out more clearly and are understood to be bad and needing further attention. For the next step in our demonstration we consider thoughts, and the expression of thoughts in language.

VII. THINGS AND HAPPENINGS

We live in a space-time world. Numerous philosophical and scientific studies, as well as the innate experience of every person, shows that we never have any understanding of any subject matter except in terms of our own mental constructs of "things" and "happenings" of that subject matter. It seems to be impossible for us to think about anything without having that subject automatically be bounded in our minds by a population of parts or pieces (concrete or abstract—but in any case "nominal" things, i.e., literally things to which we give names or nouns) which provide the basis for our even conceiving of the subject matter as a separate subject. Immediately, however, once we are aware of the things, we are aware of the happenings—the relationships, changes, and transformations which take place between and among those things and make the subject matter meaningful or interesting (the "verbial" things, to which we give action words or verbs).

The universality of things and happenings provides the next basic step of decomposition (after the still more fundamental decomposition of recognizing and isolating the purpose and viewpoint which established the "worth" of possible things to say about the "worth" of the subject matter). Every one of our languages, whether natural or artificial, formal or informal, has those two complementary aspects—nouns and verbs, operators and operands, etc.—to permit the expression of thoughts about the subject matter. Thus the means is provided to incorporate any other language into SA. The incorporation of other languages into SA is not forced, nor awkward.

SA language provides the same graphic notation for both the things and the happenings aspects of any subject. Every SA model has two dual aspects—a *thing* aspect, called the *data decomposition*, and a *happening* aspect, called the *activity decomposition*. The model is incomplete without both decompositions.

VIII. BOUNDED SUBJECT MATTER

So we have now established the starting premises. The SA maxim forces gradual, top-down decomposition, leaving nothing out at any stage, and matching good storytelling exposition. The things and happenings (*data* and *activities*, in SA technical terms) match the nominal and verbial construction of any chosen language for directly addressing the subject, so we will never be "at a loss for words." Now we are ready to address the specifics—how SA language (mostly graphical, using boxes and arrows) actually allows well structured expression of well structured thought. We do this in stages: 1) we dump the entire body of the subject matter all at once into a table of some 40 separate items of notation and conventions—just to bound the subject itself; 2) we then start to pick our way through these topics, starting with those that define the basics of boxes and arrows; and 3) then we will use those basic expository capabilities to complete the consideration of the list.

In a prior, companion paper [2], which had its roots in the same background that led to the development of SA, we described and illustrated a univeral, standard pattern or process which appears to permeate all of software engineering and problem-solving in general. Since that pattern is so close to the natural phenomena of understanding which we are discussing here with respect to SA itself, we will use it to motivate, clarify, and structure the presentation. The idea of the pattern is captured in five words: 1) purpose; 2) concept; 3) mechanism; 4) notation; and 5) usage. Any systematic approach to a problem requires a concise purpose or objective that specifies which aspect of the problem is of concern. Within that purpose we formulate a valid conceptual structure (both things and happenings) in terms of which the problem can be analyzed and approached. We then seek out (or work out) the designs (mechanisms—concrete or abstract. but always including both data and activity aspects) which are capable of implementing the relevant concepts and of working together to achieve the stated purpose. (This combines three of the five words together.) Now, purpose, concepts, and mechanism, being a systematic approach to a *class* of problems, require a notation for expressing the capabilities of the mechanism and invoking its use for a particular problem in the class. Finally, usage rules are spelled out, explicitly or by example, to guide the use of the notation to invoke the implementation to realize the concept to achieve the specified purpose for the problem. The cited paper [2] gives numerous carefully drawn examples showing how the pattern arises over and over again throughout systematic problem solving, at both abstract and concrete levels, and with numerous hierarchic and cross-linked interconnections.

IX. THE FEATURES OF SA LANGUAGE

Fig. 2 is a tabulation of some 40 features or aspects of SA which constitute the basic core of the language for communication. For each feature, the purpose, concept, mechanism, and notation are shown. Usages (for the purposes of this paper) are covered only informally by the examples which follow. The reader should scan down the "purpose" column of Fig. 2 at this time, because the collection of entries there set the objectives for the bounded subject matter which we are about to consider. Note also the heavy use of pictures in the "notation" column. These are components of graphic language. But notice that most entries mix *both* English *and* graphic language into a "phrase" of SA notation. Clearly, any other spoken language such as French, German, or Sanskrit could be translated and substituted for the English terms, for they merely aid the understanding the syntax and semantics of SA language itself.

In Fig. 2, the *name* and *label* portions of the "notation" column for rows 1 and 2, and the corresponding *noun* and *verb* indications in rows 6 and 7, are precisely the places where SA language absorbs other natural or formal languages in the sense of the preceding discussion. As the preceding sections have tried to make clear, *any* language, whether informal and natural or formal and artificial, has things and happenings aspects in the nominal and verbial components of its vocabulary. These are to be related to the *names of boxes* and *labels on arrows* in order to absorb those "foreign" languages into SA language.

Notice that it is not merely the nouns and verbs which are absorbed. Whatever richness the "foreign" language may possess, the full richness of the nominal and verbial expressions, including modifiers, is available in the naming and labeling por-

Fig. 2. SA language features.

Left table (features 1–21):

	PURPOSE	CONCEPT	MECHANISM	NOTATION	NODE
1	BOUND CONTEXT	INSIDE/OUTSIDE	SA BOX	NAME	A11
2	RELATE/CONNECT	FROM/TO	SA ARROW	LABEL	A12
3	SHOW TRANSFORMATION	INPUT-OUTPUT	SA INTERFACE	INPUT --- OUTPUT	A13
4	SHOW CIRCUMSTANCE	CONTROL	SA INTERFACE	CONTROL	A14
5	SHOW MEANS	SUPPORT	SA MECHANISM	MECHANISM	A15
6	NAME APTLY	ACTIVITY (HAPPENINGS) / DATA (THINGS)	SA NAMES	ACTIVITY [VERB] DATA [NOUN]	A211
7	LABEL APTLY	THINGS / HAPPENINGS	SA LABELS	NOUN VERB	A212
8	SHOW NECESSITY	I-O / C-O	PATH		A213
9	SHOW DOMINANCE	C / I	CONSTRAINT		A214
10	SHOW RELEVANCE	ICO / ICO	ALL INTERFACES		A215
11	OMIT OBVIOUS	C-O / I-O	OMITTED ARROW		A216
12	BE EXPLICIT WITHOUT CLUTTER	PIPELINES, CONDUITS, WIRES	BRANCH		A221
13			JOIN		A221
14	BE CONCISE AND CLEAR	CABLES, MULTI-WIRES	BUNDLE	C (=A∪B)	A222
15			SPREAD	C=(A∪B)	A222
16	SHOW EXCLUSIVES	EXPLICIT ALTERNATIVES	OR BRANCH	A OR B	A223
17			OR JOIN	A OR B	A223
18	SHOW INTERFACES TO PARENT DIAGRAM	ARROWS PENETRATE	SA BOUNDARY ARROWS (ON CHILD)	PARENT / NO BOX SHOWN	A231
19	SHOW EXPLICIT PARENT CONNECTION	NUMBER CONVENTION FOR PARENT, WRITE ICOM CODE ON CHILD BOUNDARY ARROWS		(ON CHILD)	A232
20	SHOW UNIQUE DECOMPOSITION	DETAIL REFERENCE EXPRESSION (DRE)	C-NUMBER OR PAGE NUMBER OF DETAIL DIAGRAM	BOX — DRE	A233
21	SHOW SHARED OR VARIABLE DECOMPOSITION	DRE WITH (MODEL NAME)	SA CALL ON SUPPORT	BOX / STUB — DRE	A234

Right table (features 22–40):

	PURPOSE	CONCEPT	MECHANISM	NOTATION	NODE
22	SHOW COOPERATION	INTERCHANGE OF SHARED RESPONSIBILITY	SA 2-WAY ARROWS		A311
23	SUPPRESS INTERCHANGE DETAILS	ALLOW 2-WAY WITHIN 1-WAY PIPELINES	2-WAY TO 1-WAY BUTTING ARROWS		A312
24	SUPPRESS "PASS-THROUGH" CLUTTER	ALLOW ARROWS TO GO OUTSIDE DIAGRAMS	SA "TUNNELING" (WITH REFERENCES)	PARENT OFFSPRING	A313
25	SUPPRESS NEEDED-ARROW CLUTTER	ALLOW TAGGED JUMPS WITHIN DIAGRAM	TO ALL or FROM ALL	TO ALL (A)	A314
26	SHOW NEEDED ANNOTATION	ALLOW WORDS IN DIAGRAM	SA NOTE	NOTE:	A32
27	OVERCOME CRAMPED SPACE	ALLOW REMOTE LOCATION OF WORDS IN DIAGRAM	SA FOOTNOTE	$(n=integer)$ n words	A32
28	SHOW COMMENTS ABOUT DIAGRAM	ALLOW WORDS ON (NOT IN) DIAGRAM	SA META-NOTE	$(n=integer)$	A32
29	ENSURE PROPER ASSOCIATION OF WORDS	TIE WORDS TO INTENDED SUBJECT	SA "SQUIGGLE"	(TOUCH REFERENT)	A32
30	UNIQUE SHEET REFERENCE	CHRONOLOGICAL CREATION	SA C-NUMBER	AUTHOR INITS INTEGER	A41
31	UNIQUE BOX REFERENCE	PATH DOWN TREE FROM BOX NUMBERS	SA NODE NUMBER (BOX NUMBERS)	A, D, OR M ε PARENT # ε BOX #	A42
32	SAME FOR MULTI-MODELS	PRECEDE BY MODEL NAME	SA MODEL NAME	MODEL NAME/NODE#	A42
33	UNIQUE INTERFACE REFERENCE	ICOM WITH BOX NUMBER	SA BOX ICOM	BOX# ICOM CODE	A43
34	UNIQUE ARROW REFERENCE	FROM - TO	PAIR OF BOX ICOMs	BOX ICOM$_1$ BOX ICOM$_2$	A44
35	SHOW CONTEXT REFERENCE	SPECIFY A REFERENCE POINT	SA REF.EXP. "DOT"	A122.411 "WHICH SEE"	A45
36	ASSIST CORRECT INTERPRETATION	SHOW DOMINANCE GEOMETRICALLY (ASSIST PARSE)	STAIRCASE LAYOUT	DOMINANCE	A5
37	ASSIST UNDERSTANDING	PROSE SUMMARY OF MESSAGE	SA TEXT	NODE# ε T ε INTEGER	A5
38	HIGHLIGHT FEATURES	SPECIAL EFFECTS FOR EXPOSITION ONLY	SA FEOs	NODE# ε F ε INTEGER	A5
39	DEFINE TERMS	GLOSSARY WITH WORDS & PICTURES	SA GLOSSARY	MODEL NAME ε G ε INTEGER	A5
40	ORGANIZE PAGES	PROVIDE TABLE OF CONTENTS	SA NODE INDEX	NODE# ORDER	A5

Fig. 2. SA language features.

tions of SA language. As we shall see, however, normally these capabilities for richness are purposely suppressed, for simplicity and immediacy of understanding normally require brevity and conciseness.

Fig. 2 has introduced our subject and has served to point out the precise way in which SA absorbs other languages, but this mode of discourse would make a long and rambling story. I therefore proceed to use SA itself to communicate the intended understanding of Fig. 2. This will not, however, be a perfect, or even a good example of SA communication in action, for the intent of this paper is to guide the reader to an understanding of SA, not to teach how to fully exploit SA diagrams and modeling. The SA diagrams presented here only as figures are incomplete and exhibit both good *and* bad examples of SA expressiveness, as well as showing all the language constructs. Our subject is too complex to treat in a small model, but the figures at least present the reader with some measure of the flexibility of the language.

The reader is forewarned that there is more information in the diagrams than is actually referenced here in text which uses them as "figures." After the paper has been read, the total model can be studied for review and for additional understanding. Everything said here about the SA language and notations applies to each diagram, and most features are illustrated more than once, frequently before they are described in the text. Therefore, on first reading, please ignore any features and notations not explicitly referenced. Non-SA "first-reading" aids are isolated by a bold outline, in the diagrams.

In practical use of SofTech's SADT, a "reader/author cycle" is rigorously adhered to in which (similar to the code-reading phase of egoless structured programming) authors, experts, and management-level personnel read and critique the efforts of each individual SADT author to achieve a fully-acceptable quality of result. (It is in fact this rigorous adherence to quality control which enables production SA models to be relied upon. So far as possible *everything* worthy has been done to make sure that *everything* worthy has been expressed to the level required by the intended readership.)

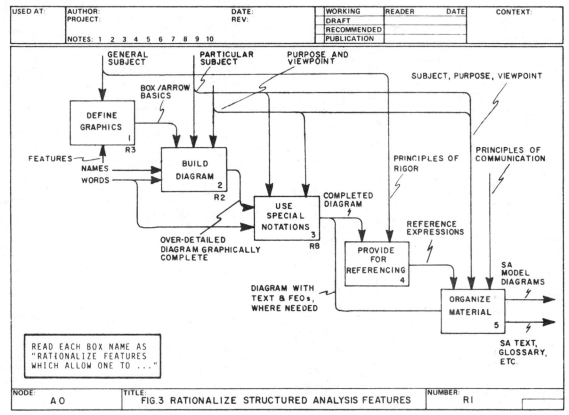

Fig. 3. Rationalize SA features.

X. PURPOSE AND VIEWPOINT

Fig. 3 is an SA diagram[2] and, by definition, it is a meaningful expression in SA language. It consists of box and arrow graphical notation mixed with words and numbers. Consonant with the tutorial purpose of this paper, I will not, here, try to teach how to *read* a diagram. My tutorial approach aims only to lead to an understanding of what is *in* a diagram.

So we will just begin to examine Fig. 3. Start with the title, "Rationalize structured analysis features"—an adequate match to our understanding of the purpose and viewpoint of this whole paper. We seek to make rational the reasons behind those features. Next read the content of each of the boxes: "Define graphics; build diagram; use special notations; provide for referencing; organize material." These must be the six-or-fewer "parts" into which the titled subject matter is being broken. In this case there are five of them, and sure enough this aspect of SA follows exactly the time-tested outline approach to subject matter. Because our purpose is to have a graphics-based language (like blueprints), once we have decided upon some basics of graphic definition we will use that to build a diagram for some particular subject, adding special notations (presumably to improve clarity), and then because (as with blueprints) we know that a whole collection will be required

to convey complex understanding in easy-to-understand pieces, we must provide for a way of referencing the various pieces and organizing the resulting material into what we see as an understandable whole.

Now, I have tried to compose the preceding long sentence about Fig. 3 using natural language constructs which, if not an exact match, are very close to terms which appear directly in Fig. 3. In fact, the reader should be able to find an exact correspondence between things which show in the figure and every important syntactic and semantic point in each part of the last sentence of the preceding paragraph, although the diagram has more to it than the sentence. Please reread that sentence now and check out this correspondence for yourself. In the process you will notice that considerable (though not exhaustive) use is made of information which is not *inside* the boxes, but instead is associated with the word-and-arrow structure of the diagram *outside* the boxes. This begins to show why, although SA in its basic backbone does follow the standard outline pattern of presentation, the box-and-arrow structure conveys a great deal more information than a simple topic outline (only the box *contents*) could possibly convey.

XI. THE FIRST DETAIL VIEW

Fig. 4 is another SA diagram. Simpler in structure than the diagram of Fig. 3, but nonetheless with much the same "look."

---

[2] The SADT diagram form itself is © 1975, SofTech, Inc., and has various fields used in the practice of SADT methodology.

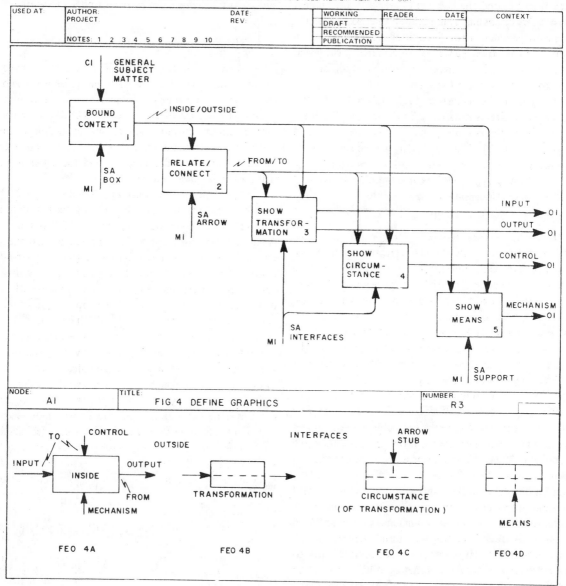

SADT⊕ DIAGRAM FORM ST098 9 75
Form © 1975 SofTech Inc 460 Totten Pond Road. Waltham Mass 02154 USA

USED AT	AUTHOR: PROJECT:		DATE: REV:	WORKING DRAFT RECOMMENDED PUBLICATION	READER	DATE	CONTEXT
	NOTES: 1 2 3 4 5 6 7 8 9 10						

CI GENERAL SUBJECT MATTER

BOUND CONTEXT 1

INSIDE/OUTSIDE

SA BOX

MI

RELATE/ CONNECT 2

FROM/TO

SA ARROW

MI

SHOW TRANSFOR- MATION 3

INPUT OI

OUTPUT OI

SHOW CIRCUM- STANCE 4

CONTROL OI

SA INTERFACES

MI

SHOW MEANS 5

MECHANISM OI

MI SA SUPPORT

NODE: A1	TITLE: FIG 4 DEFINE GRAPHICS	NUMBER R3

TO CONTROL

INPUT

INSIDE

OUTSIDE

OUTPUT

FROM

MECHANISM

FEO 4A

INTERFACES

TRANSFORMATION

FEO 4B

ARROW STUB

CIRCUMSTANCE (OF TRANSFORMATION)

FEO 4C

MEANS

FEO 4D

Fig. 4. Define graphics.

The title, "Define graphics," is identical to the name inside the first box of Fig. 3, which is here being broken into five component worthy pieces, called the *nested factors* in SA terminology. Again the words written inside the boxes are legible, but are they understandable? How can "Bound context; relate/connect; show transformation; show circumstance; show means," be considered parts of "Define graphics?" It is not very clear, is it? It would seem that something must be wrong with SA for the touted understandability turns out to be, in fact, quite obscure!

Look at Fig. 4 again and see if you don't agree that we have a problem—and see if you can supply the answer to the problem.

The problem is not with SA at all, but with our too-glib approach to it. SA is a rigorous language and thereby is unforgiving in many ways. In order for the communication of un-

derstanding to take place we ourselves must understand and conform to the rules of that rigor. The apparent obscurity should disappear in a twinkling once the following factor is pointed out: namely, *always be sure to do your understanding in the proper context*. In this case, the proper context was established by the title of Fig. 3, "Rationalize structured analysis features," and the purpose, to define graphical concepts and notations for the purpose of representing and conveying understanding of subject matters. Now, if we have all of that firmly implanted in our mind, then surely the name in Box 1 of Fig. 4 should be amply clear. Read, now, Box 4. 1[3] for yourself, and see if that clarity and communication of intended understanding does not take place.

[3] To shorten references to figures, "Box 4. 1" will mean "Box 1 of Fig. 4," etc. in the following discussion.

You see, according to the diagram, the first feature of defining graphics is to "Bound the context"–precisely the subject we have just been discussing and precisely the source of the apparent obscurity which made SA initially appear to be on shaky ground. To aid first reading of the figures, a suggested paraphrasing of the intended context is given in a bold box on each of the other diagrams (see Fig. 3).

As we can see from the section of Fig. 4 labeled FEO 4A[4] the general subject matter is isolated from the rest of all subject matter by means of the SA box which has an inside and an outside (look at the box). The only thing we are supposed to consider is the portion of that subject matter which is *inside* the box–so the boundary of the box does bound the context in which we are to consider the subject.

XII. THE SA BOX AS BUILDING BLOCK

We lack the background (at this point) to continue an actual reading of Fig. 4, because it itself defines the basic graphic notations used in it. Instead, consider only the sequence of illustrations (4A-4D) labeled FEO. FEO 4A shows that the fundamental building block of SA language notation is a box with four sides called INPUT, CONTROL, OUTPUT, and MECHANISM. As we have seen above, the bounded piece of subject matter is *inside* the box, and, as we will see, the actual boundary of the box is made by the collection of *arrow stubs* entering and leaving the box. The bounded pieces are related and connected (Box 4.2) by SA arrows which go *from* an OUTPUT of one box *to* the INPUT or CONTROL of another box, i.e., such arrow connections make the *interfaces* between subjects. The names INPUT and OUTPUT are chosen to convey the idea that (see FEO 4B and Box 4.3) the box represents a *transformation* from a "before" to an "after" state of affairs. The CONTROL interface (see FEO 4C and Box 4.4) interacts and constrains the transformation to ensure that it applies only under the appropriate circumstances. The combination of INPUT, OUTPUT, and CONTROL fully specifies the bounded piece of subject, and the interfaces relate it to the other pieces. Finally, the MECHANISM *support* (not interface, see FEO 4D and Box 4.5) provide means for realizing the complete piece represented by the box.

We will see shortly why Fig. 4 contains no INPUT arrows at all, but except for that anomaly, this description should make Fig. 4 itself reasonably understandable. (Remember the context–"Rationalize the features of SA language which allow one to define graphic notation for....") The diagram (with FEO's and discussion) is the desired rationalization. It fits quite well with the idea of following the maxim. We don't mind breaking *everything* about a bounded piece of subject matter into pieces as long as we are sure we can express completely how all those pieces go back together to constitute the whole. Input, output, control, and mechanism provide that capability. As long as the right mechanism is provided, and the right control is applied, whatever is inside the box can be a valid transformation of input to output. We now must see

how to use the "foreign" language names and labels of boxes and arrows. Then we can start putting SA to work.

XIII. USING THE BASICS FOR UNDERSTANDING

Fig. 4, and especially FEO 4A, now that we have digested the meaning of the diagram itself, has presented the basic box-and-arrow-stubs-making-useful-interfaces-for-a-bounded-piece-of-subject-matter building block of SA. We now can start to use the input, output, control, and mechanism concepts to further our understanding. Knowing even this much, the power of expression of SA diagrams beyond that of simple outlining will start to become evident.

Fig. 5, entitled "Build diagram," details Box 3.2. Referring back to Fig. 3 and recalling the opening discussion of its meaning (which we should do in order to establish in our mind the proper context for reading Fig. 5) we recall that the story line of Fig. 3 said that after Box 3.1 had defined the arrow and box basics, then we would build an actual diagram with words and names for a particular subject in accordance with a purpose and viewpoint chosen to convey the appropriate understanding. Looking at Box 3.2 in the light of what we have just learned about the box/arrow basics in Fig. 4, we can see that indeed the inputs are words and names, which will be transformed into a diagram (an over-detailed, but graphically complete diagram, evidently). Even though the mechanism is not specified, it is shown that this diagramming process will be controlled by (i.e., constrained by) the graphic conventions, subject, and viewpoint. Now refer to Fig. 5 with this established context and consider its three boxes:–"Build box structure; build arrow structure; build diagram structure." That matches our understanding that a diagram is a structure of boxes and arrows (with appropriate names and labels, of course). Study Fig. 5 yourself briefly keeping in mind the points we have discussed so far. You should find little difficulty, and you will find that a number of the technical terms that were pure jargon in the tabulated form in Fig. 2 now start to take on some useful meaning. (Remember to ignore terms such as "ICOM" and "DRE," to be described later.)

If you have taken a moment or so to study Fig. 5 on your own, you probably have the impression things are working all right, but you are still not really sure that you are acquiring the intended level of understanding of Fig. 5. It seems to have too many loose ends semantically, even though it makes partial sense. If this is your reaction, you are quite right. For more detail and information is needed to make all the words and relationships take on full meaning. Fig 5 does indeed tell *everything* about "Build diagram" in its three boxes, which are themselves reasonably understandable. But we need more information for many of the labels to really snap into place. This we will find in the further detailing of the three boxes. Context *orients* for understanding (*only* orients!); details *enable* understanding (and strengthen context).

Fig. 6 provides the detailing for Box 5.1. Especially for this diagram, it is important to keep in mind the appropriate context for reading. It is not "*Draw* an SA diagram," but to motivate the *features* of SA. Thus, when we read the title, "Build

---

[4]This notation refers to the sequence of imbedded illustrations in Fig. 4 which are "For exposition only" (FEO).

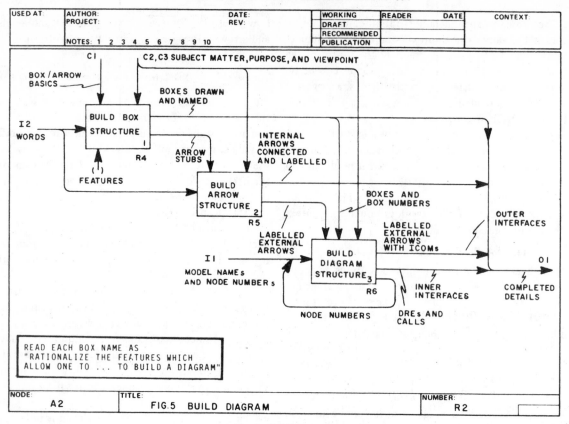

Fig. 5. Build diagram.

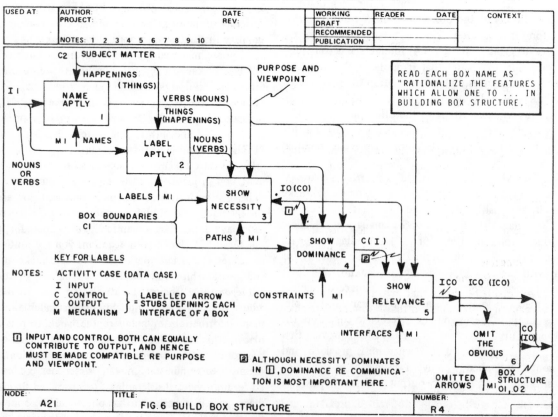

Fig. 6. Build box structure

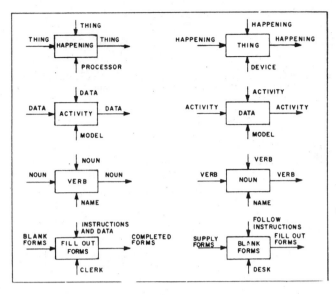

Fig. 7. Duality of activities and data.

box structure," of Fig. 6, we must keep in mind that the worthy piece of subject matter is not *how* to build box structure, nor even the features which *create* box structure, but motivation for *explanation* of the features which allow box structure to represent the bounded context subject matter. This actually is a very sophisticated subject and normally we would only be diagramming it after we had already prepared rather complete models of the "how to" of SA so that many of the terms and ideas would already be familiar. In this paper, however, the opening discussion must serve instead. The next four sections discuss Fig. 6.

XIV. DUALITY OF DATA AND ACTIVITIES

Recall that a complete SA model has to consider both the things and happenings of the subject being modeled. Happenings are represented by an activity decomposition consisting of activity diagrams and things are represented by data decomposition consisting of data diagrams. The neat thing about SA language is that both of these complementary but radically different aspects are diagrammed using exactly the same four-sided box notation. Fig. 7 illustrates this fact. The happening/activity and thing/data domains are completely dual in SA. (Think of an INPUT activity on a data box as one that creates the data thing, and of OUTPUT as one that uses or references it.) Notice that mechanism is different in interpretation, but the role is the same. For a happening it is the *processor*, machine, computer, person, etc., which makes the happening happen. For a thing it is the *device*, for storage, representation, implementation, etc. (of the thing).

A quick check of Fig. 4 shows that mechanism's purpose is to show the means of realization, and that it is *not an interface* but is instead something called "support" in SA (described later in Section XXIII). For either activity or data modeling, a support mechanism is *a complete model*, with both data and activity aspects. As Fig. 7 shows, that complete "real thing" is *known by its name*, whereas things and happenings are identified by nouns and verbs (really nominal expressions and verbial expressions). With this in mind, we can see that the first two boxes in Fig. 6 motivate the naming and labeling

features of SA to do or permit what Fig. 7 requires—boxes are named, and arrows are labeled, with either nouns or verbs as appropriate to the aspect of the model, and of course, in accordance with the intended purpose and viewpoint of the subject matter.

XV. CONSTRAINTS

We will consider next Boxes 6.3 and 6.4 together, and with some care, for this is one of the more subtle aspects of SA—the concept of a *constraint*—the key to well structured thought and well structured diagrams. The word *constraint* conjures up visions of opposing forces at play. *Something can be constrained only if there is something stronger upon which the constraining force can be based.* It might seem that from the ideas of SA presented so far, that that strong base will be provided by the rigorously defined bounded context of a box. Given a strong boundary, it is easy to envision forces saying either to stay inside the boundary or to stay outside the boundary. It is a pleasing thought indeed, and would certainly make strong structure in both our thinking and our diagrams. The only trouble is it does not work that way (or at least not immediately), but in fact it is just the opposite! In SA thinking *it is the constraints that make the boundaries, not the other way around.* This is a tricky point so we will approach it slowly. It is still true that a constraint, to be a constraint, has to have something to push against. If it is not the bounded-context boundary, then what is it?

The subtle answer is that *the purpose and viewpoint of the model provide the basis for all constraints* which in turn provide the strength and rigidity for all the boundaries which in turn create the inescapable structure which forces correct understanding to be communicated. This comes about through the concepts of *necessity* and *dominance*, which are the subjects of Boxes 6.3 and 6.4. Dominance sounds much like constraint, and we will not be surprised to find it being the purveyor of constraint. But "necessity" has its own subtle twist in this, the very heart of SA. Therefore we must approach it, too, with some deliberation.

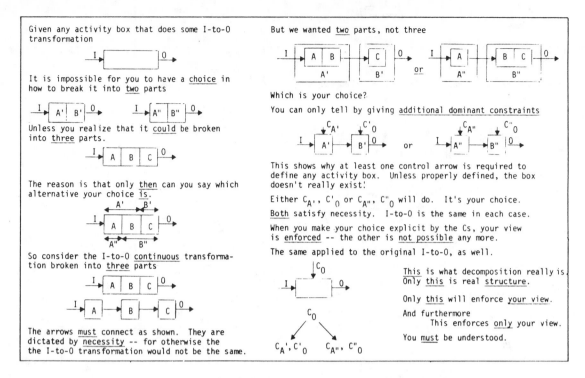

Fig. 8. Dominance and necessity.

Fig. 8 tells the story in concise form. Please read it now. Then please read it again, for all experience with SA shows that this simple argument seems to be very subtle and difficult for most people to grasp correctly. The reason is that the *everything* of the SA maxim makes the I-to-O *necessity* chain the *weakest possible structure*—akin to *no structure at all!*. It merely states a fact that *must be true* for every SA box, because of the maxim. Therefore *dominant constraints*, expressed by the control arrows for activity boxes are, in fact, the *only* way possible, to impose structure. Furthermore, that enforcement of structure is unique and compelling—no other structure can be (mis-) understood in place of that intended by the SA author. This is, of course, all mediated by the effectiveness with which the SA author wields the chosen non-SA language used for names of boxes and labels on arrows, but the argument presented in this paper holds, nonetheless. This is because whenever the imprecision of the non-SA language intrudes, more SA modeling (perhaps even with new purpose and viewpoint for greater refinement, still, of objectives) is forced by the reader/author cycle of the SADT discipline.

XVI. THE RULE OF OMISSION

Now consider Boxes 6.5 and 6.6 "Show relevance" and "Omit the obvious." These two ideas follow right along with the above discussion. Namely, in the case of activity diagramming, *if inputs are relevant* (i.e., if they make a strong contribution to understandability) *then they are drawn*. But on the other hand, since the important thing is the structure imposed by the control dominance and output necessity, and inputs *must* be supplied in any case for those outputs to result, *obvious inputs can and should be omitted from* the box struc-

ture of SA *activity diagramming*. In other words, whenever an obvious input is omitted in an activity diagram, the reader knows that (because of the SA maxim) whatever is needed will be supplied in order that the control and output which *are* drawn can happen correctly. Omitting the obvious makes the understandability and meaning of the diagram much stronger, because inputs when they *are* drawn are known to be important and nonobvious. Remember that SA diagrams are not wiring diagrams, they are vehicles for communicating understanding.

Although activity and data are dual in SA and use the same four-sided box notation, they are not quite the same, for the concept of dominance and constraint in the *data* aspect centers on *input* rather than control. In the data case, the weak chain of necessity is C-O-C-O-··· not I-O-I-O-··· as it is in the activity case. The reason comes from a deep difference between space and time (i.e., between things and happenings). In the case of the happening, the dominant feature is the control which says when to cut the transformation to yield a desired intermediate result, because the "freedom" of happenings is in time. In the case of things, however, the "freedom" which must be constrained and dominated concerns which version of the thing (i.e., which part of the data box) is the one that is to exist, regardless of time. The input activity for a data box "creates" that thing in that form and therefore it is the dominant constraint to be specified for a data box. An unimportant control activity will happen whenever needed, and may be omitted from the diagram.

Therefore, the rule regarding the obvious in SA is that *controls may never be omitted from activity diagrams and inputs may never be omitted from data diagrams*. Fig. 6 summarizes all of this discussion.

388

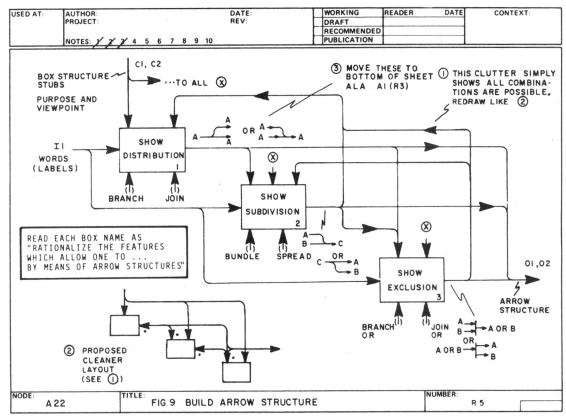

SADT⊖DIAGRAM FORM ST098 9/75
Form © 1975 SofTech, Inc., 460 Totten Pond Road, Waltham, Mass. 02154, USA

Fig. 9. Build arrow structure.

XVII. STRENGTHENING OF BOUNDARIES

Recall that a constraint does need something to push on. What is that? The answer is the one originally proposed, but rejected. *Constraints are based on the boundary of a bounded context—but of the single box of the parent diagram which the current diagram details.* (A parenthesized hint that this would turn out to be the case *does* appear in the original rejection of the view that boundaries provide the base for constraints, above.) In other words, the constraints represented by the arrows on a diagram are *not* formed by the several boundaries of the boxes of *that* diagram, but all are based on the single boundary of the corresponding box in the *parent* diagram. As was stated above in Section XV, the constraints form the box boundary interfaces and define the boxes, not the other way around. The strength of those constraints comes from the corresponding "push" passed through from the parent. As the last "C_O" portion of Fig. 8 indicates, this hierarchic cascading of constraints is based entirely on the *purpose* of the model as a whole (further constrained in spread by the limited *viewpoint* of the model) as it is successively decomposed in the hierarchic layering forced by the six-or-fewer rule of the SA maxim.

All of this is a direct consequence of the *everything* of the SA maxim, and may be inferred by considering Fig. 8 recursively. The boundary of the top-most box of the analysis is determined entirely by the subject matter, purpose, and viewpoint of the agreed-upon outset understanding. ("Tell 'em whatcha gonna tell 'em.") Then each of the subsequent constraints derives its footing only insofar as it continues to reflect that subject, purpose, and viewpoint. And, each, in turn, provides the same basis for the next subdivision, etc. Inconsistencies in an original high-level interpretation are ironed out and are replaced by greater and greater precision of specific meaning.

Even though the basis for all of the constraint structure is the (perhaps ill-conceived, ambiguous, ill-defined) *outer* boundary, that boundary and the *innermost* boundary, composed of the collective class of all the boundaries of the finest subdivision taken together, are merely two representations of the *same* boundary—so that *strengthening of the inner boundary through extensive decomposition automatically strengthens the outer boundary.* It is as though the structured analyst (and each of his readers as well) were saying continually "My outermost understanding of the problem as a whole can only make sense, now that I see all this detail, if I refine my interpretation of it in this, this, and this precise way." This is the hidden power of SA at work. This is how SA greatly amplifies the precision and understandability of any natural or formal language whose nouns and verbs are imbedded in its box and arrow structure.

XVIII. ARROW CONNECTIONS

Fig. 6, which led to this discussion, detailed Box 5.1 "Build box structure"; Fig. 9 decomposes Box 5.2, "Build arrow

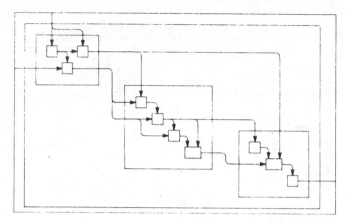

Fig. 10. Nested factors.

structure." From Fig. 5 we see that the controlling constraints that dominate Box 5.2 are the subject matter, purpose, and viewpoint, as we would expect, along with the "arrow stubs" which resulted from building each box separately. The outputs are to be internal arrows connected and labeled, as well as labeled external arrows. A relevant (i.e., nonobvious) input is the collection of words—nouns or verbs—for making those labels.

With this context in mind, we are now ready to look at Fig. 9, "Build arrow structure." Here is an example of the use of non-English language to label arrows. Small graphical phrases show the intended meaning of "branch" and "join" for distribution, and "bundle" and "spread" with respect to subdivision, as well as two forms of logical OR for exclusion. We have seen many examples of these in use in the diagrams already considered, so that the ideas should be quite transparent.

The little pictures as labels show how the labels attach to arrows to convey the appropriate meaning. In most good SA diagramming the OR's are used very sparingly--only when they materially assist understanding. In most circumstances, the fact that arrows represent constraints either of dominance or necessity supplies the required understanding in clearer form merely by topological connection. This also is the reason why there is no graphical provision for the other logical functions such as AND, for they are really out of place at the level of communication of basic SA language. In order for them to have an appropriate role, the total context of interpretation of an SA model must have been drawn down very precisely to some mathematical or logical domain at which point a language more appropriate to that domain should be chosen. Then logical terms in the nominal and verbial expressions in labels can convey the conditions. This is preferable to distorting the SA language into a detailed communication role it was not designed or intended to fulfill.

XIX. BOUNDARIES

Fig. 12, "Build diagram structure," will provide detailing for the third and last box of Fig. 5. It is needed as a separate consideration of this motivation model because the building of box structure (Box 5.1, detailed in Fig. 6) and arrow structure (Box 5.2, detailed in Fig. 9) only cover arrows between boxes in a single diagram—the *internal* arrows. Box 4.2 requires that

every arrow which relates or connects bounded contexts must participate in both a *from* and a *to* interface. Every *external* arrow (shown as the second output of Box 5.2) will be missing either its source (from) or its destination (to) because the relevant boxes do not appear on this diagram. As the relationship between Boxes 5.2 and 5.3 in Fig. 5 shows, these labeled arrows are indeed a dominant constraint controlling Box 3, "Build diagram structure."

Fig. 10 helps to explain the story. This is a partial view of three levels of nesting of SA boxes, one within the other, in some model (not an SA diagram). Except for three arrows, every arrow drawn is a complete from/to connection. The middle, second-level box has four fine-level boxes within it, and it in turn is contained within the largest box drawn in the figure. If we consider the arrows in the middle, second-level box, we note that only two of them are internal arrows, all of the others being external. But notice also that every one of those external arrows (with respect to that middle-level box) are in fact *internal* with respect to the model as a whole. Each of those arrows does go from one box to another box— a lowest-level box in each case. In completing the connection, *the arrows penetrate the boundaries of the middle-level boxes* as though those boundaries were not there at all. In fact, there are only two real boundaries in all of Fig. 10—the two boundaries characteristic of every SA decomposition. These are 1) the *outer boundary* which is the outermost edge of Fig. 10, itself, and 2) the *inner boundary* which is the entire set of edges of all of the lowest-level boxes drawn in Fig. 10, considered as a single boundary. As was stated above, the SA maxim requires that the outer boundary and the inner boundary must be understood to be *exactly the same* so that the subject is merely decomposed, not altered in any way.

XX. PARENTS AND CHILDREN

To understand how the structuring of Fig. 10 is expressed in SA terms we must be clear about the relationship between boundaries and interfaces, boxes and diagrams, and the parent/child relationship. Fig. 11 lays all of this out. In the upper right appears the diagram for the largest box drawn in Fig. 10, and in the lower left appears the diagram for the central middle-level box which we were discussing. The first thing to notice is that the diagrams are here drawn as though they were

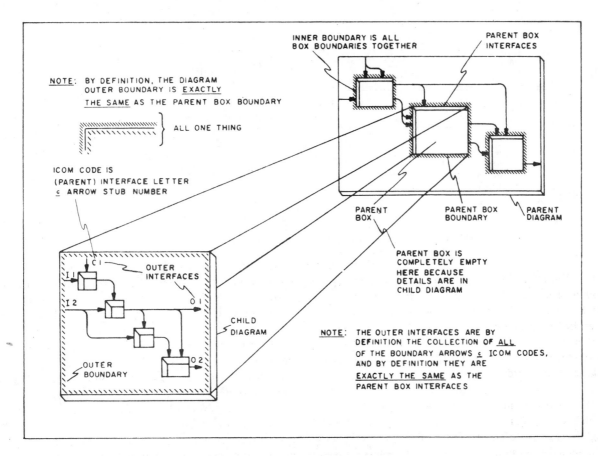

Fig. 11. Boundaries and interfaces.

punched out of Fig. 10, (like cutting cookies from a sheet of cookie dough). Although the dimensions are distorted, the note in the upper left points out that, by definition, *the diagram outer boundary is actually the same as the parent box boundary* (i. e., the current child diagram is the "cookie" removed from the sheet of dough and placed to one side).

Fig. 11 also points out that, just as for the hierarchic decomposition as a whole, the *inner boundary of the parent diagram is the collection of all its child box boundaries considered as a single entity.* Notice the terminology—with respect to the current child diagram, one of the boxes in the parent diagram is called the *parent box* of the child diagram. By definition of Fig. 4, that *parent box boundary* is the collection of *parent box interfaces and support* which compose it. Since we have just established that the outer boundary of the current diagram is the same as the corresponding parent box boundary, the parent box edges (interfaces *or* support) which compose the parent box boundary must somehow match the outer edges of the child diagram. This is the connection which we seek to establish rigorously.

By Fig. 10 we know that the external arrows of the child diagram penetrate through the outer boundary and are, in fact, the *same* arrows as are the stubs of the interfaces and support which compose the parent box boundary. Therefore, the connection which has to be made is clear from the definition. But for flexibility of graphic representation, *the external arrows of the current diagram need not have the same geometric layout, relationship, or labeling* as the corresponding stubs on the par-

ent diagram, which are drawn on a completely different (parent) diagram.

In order to allow this flexibility, we construct a special code-naming scheme called *ICOM codes* as follows: An ICOM code begins with one of the letters I-C-O-M (standing for INPUT, CONTROL, OUTPUT, MECHANISM) concatenated with an integer which is obtained by considering that the stubs of the corresponding parent box edge are numbered consecutively from top to bottom or from left to right, as the case may be. With the corresponding ICOM code written beside the unattached end of the arrow in the current diagram, that arrow is no longer called "external," but is called a *boundary arrow.* Then *the four outer edges of the child diagram are, by definition, the four collections of ICOM boundary arrows* which are, by definition, exactly the same as the corresponding parent box edges, as defined by Fig. 4 and shown in Fig. 11. Thus even though the geometric layout may be radically different, the rigor of interconnection of child and parent diagrams is complete, and the arrows are continuous and unbroken, as required. Every diagram in this paper has ICOM codes properly assigned.

The above presentation is summarized in the first two boxes of Fig. 12 and should be clear without further discussion. Boxes 12.3 and 12.4 concern the SA language notations for establishing the relationships between the child and parent diagram cookies by means of a *detail reference expression* (DRE) or an SA *call.* We will consider these shortly. For now it is sufficient to note that the topics we have considered here

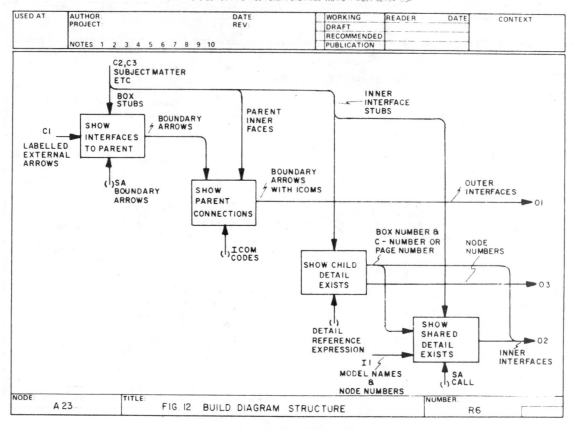

SADT DIAGRAM FORM ST098 9 75
Form 1975 SofTech Inc 460 Totten Pond Road Waltham Mass 02154 USA

Fig. 12. Build diagram structure.

complete the detailing of Fig. 5, "Build diagram"—how the box structure and arrow structure for individual diagrams are built, and then how the whole collection of diagrams is linked together in a single whole so that *everything* of the top-most cookie (treated as a cookie sheet from which other cookies are cut with zero width cuts) is completely understandable. Each individual diagram itself is only a portion of the cookie dough with an outer boundary and an inner boundary formed by the decomposition operation. Nothing is either gained or lost in the process—so that the SA maxim is rigorously realized. Everything can indeed be covered for the stated purpose and viewpoint. We now complete our presentation of the remaining items in the 40 features of Fig. 2, which exploit further refinements of notation and provide orderly organization for the mass of information in a complete SA model.

XXI. Word Notes

In SA language, not everything is said in graphical terms. Both words and pictures are also used. If the diagram construction notations we have considered so far were to be used exclusively and exhaustively, very cluttered and nonunderstandable diagrams would result. Therefore SA language includes further simplifying graphic notations (which also increase the expressive power of the language), as well as allowing nongraphic additional information to be incorporated into SA diagrams. This is the function of Fig. 13 which details Box 3.3 Fig. 13 points out that the (potentially) cluttered diagram is only graphically complete so that special *word* notations are needed. Furthermore, special arrow notations can supply more clarity, to result in a complete *and* understandable diagram.

We will not further detail Box 13.2. We merely point out that its output consists of three forms of verbal additions to the diagram. The first two—NOTES and [n] footnotes—are actual parts of the diagram. The diagrams we have been examining have examples of each. The third category, (n) metanotes, are *not* parts of the diagram themselves, but are instead notes *about* the diagram. The (n) metanotes have only an observational or referential relation to the actual information content of these diagrams and therefore they do not in any way alter or affect the actual representational function of the SA language, either graphical or verbal. There is no way that information in (n) metanotes can participate in the information content of the diagrams, and therefore they should not be used in an attempt to affect the interpretation of the diagrams themselves, but only for mechanical operations regarding the diagram's physical format or expression. Examples are comments from a reader to an author of a diagram suggesting an improved layout for greater understandability. A few examples are included on the diagrams in this paper. The [n] footnotes are used exclusively for allowing large verbal expressions to be concisely located with respect to tight geometric layout, in addition to the normal footnoting function commonly found in textual information.

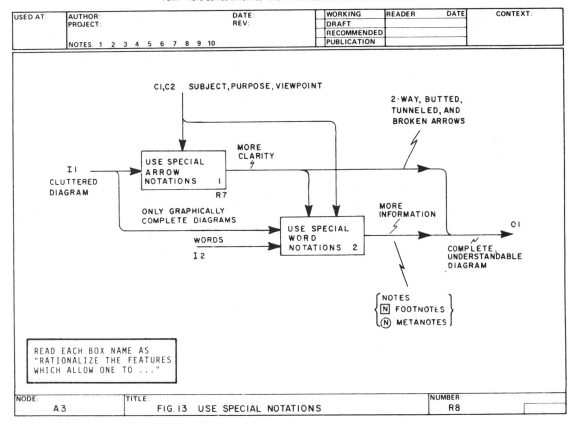

USED AT:	AUTHOR: PROJECT: NOTES: 1 2 3 4 5 6 7 8 9 10	DATE: REV:	WORKING DRAFT RECOMMENDED PUBLICATION	READER	DATE	CONTEXT:

CI,C2   SUBJECT, PURPOSE, VIEWPOINT

2-WAY, BUTTED, TUNNELED, AND BROKEN ARROWS

MORE CLARITY

I1 CLUTTERED DIAGRAM

USE SPECIAL ARROW NOTATIONS   1   R7

ONLY GRAPHICALLY COMPLETE DIAGRAMS

WORDS
I 2

USE SPECIAL WORD NOTATIONS   2

MORE INFORMATION

O1

COMPLETE UNDERSTANDABLE DIAGRAM

NOTES
N FOOTNOTES
(N) METANOTES

READ EACH BOX NAME AS "RATIONALIZE THE FEATURES WHICH ALLOW ONE TO ..."

NODE: A 3	TITLE: FIG. 13 USE SPECIAL NOTATIONS	NUMBER: R8

Fig. 13. Use special notations.

XXII. SPECIAL GRAPHIC NOTATIONS

Fig. 14 provides the motivation for four very simple additions to the graphic notation to improve the understandability of diagrams. With respect to a specific aspect of the subject matter, two boxes sometimes really act as one box inasmuch as each of them shares one portion of a well-defined aspect of the subject matter. In this case, arrowheads with dots above, below, or to the right of the arrowhead are added instead of drawing two separate arrows as shown in FEO 14A. Two-way arrows are a form of bundling, however, *not* a mere shorthand notation for the two separate arrows. If the subject matters represented by the two separate arrows are not sufficiently similar, they should *not* be bundled into a two-way arrow, but should be drawn separately. Many times, however, the two-way arrow *is* the appropriate semantics for the relationship between two boxes. Notice that if other considerations of diagrams are sufficiently strong, the awkward, nonstandard two-way arrow notations shown also may be used to still indicate dominance in the two-way interaction.

SA arrows should always be thought of as conduits or pipelines containing multistranded cables, each strand of which is another pipeline. Then the branching and joining is like the cabling of a telephone exchange, including trunk lines. Box 14.2 is related to both two-way arrows and pipelines, and points out that a one-way pipeline stub at the parent level may be shown as a two-way boundary arrow in the child. This is

appropriate since, with respect to the communication of understanding at the parent level, the relationship between boxes is one-way, whereas when details are examined, two-way cooperation between the two sets of detailing boxes may be required. An example is the boss-worker relation. The boss (at parent level) provides one-way command, but (at the child diagram level) a two-way interchange between worker and boss may be needed to clarify details.

Box 14.3 motivates an additional and very useful version of Box 6.6 ("Omit the obvious"). In this case, instead of omitting the obvious, we only postpone consideration of necessary detail until the appropriate level is reached. This is done by putting parentheses around the unattached end of an external arrow, or at the interface end of a parent box stub. The notation is intended to convey the image of an arrow "tunneling" out of view as it crosses a parent box inner boundary only to emerge later, some number of levels deeper in a child's outer interface, when that information is actually required. These are known as "tunneled" or "parenthesized" boundary arrows when the sources or destinations are somewhere within the SA model, and as (proper) *external* arrows when the missing source or destination is unspecified (i.e., when the model would need to be imbedded in some context larger than the total model for the appropriate connection to be made).

Finally, Box 14.4 is a seldom-used notation which allows internal arrows themselves to be broken by an ad hoc labeling scheme merely to suppress clutter. Its use is discouraged be-

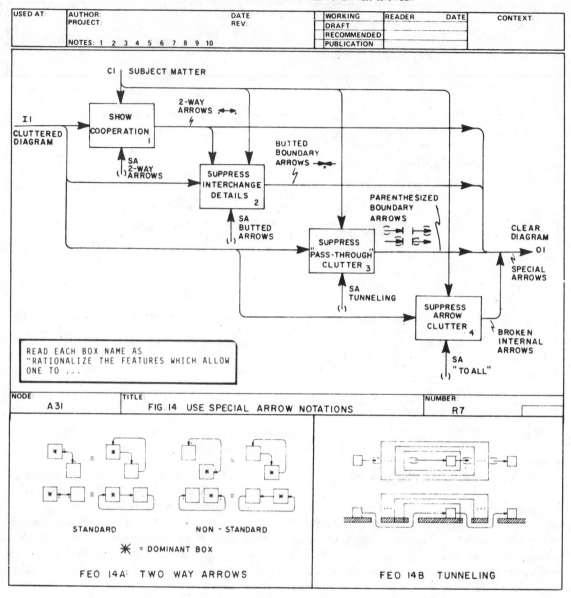

Fig. 14. Use special arrow notations.

cause of its lack of geometric continuity and because its use is forced only by a diagram containing so much information already that it is likely not be be clearly understood and should be redrawn. Examples occur in Fig. 9 just for illustration.

XXIII. The Reference Language

Returning to Fig. 3, we now have considered all of the aspects of basic SA language which go into the creation of diagrams themselves, with the single exception of the detail reference expressions and SA call notation of Fig. 12, which were saved until this point since they relate so closely to Box 3.4, "Provide for referencing."

A complete and unique SA reference language derives very nicely from the hierarchically nested factors imposed by the SA maxim. Diagrams, boxes, interfaces, arrows, and complete contexts can be referenced by a combination of model names,

node numbers (starting with A for activity or D for data, and derived directly from the box numbers), and ICOM codes. The insertion of a dot, meaning "which see" (i. e. "find the diagram and look at it"), can specify exactly which diagram is to be kept particularly in mind to provide the context for interpreting the SA language. Thus "A122. 4I1" means "in diagram A122, the first input of box 4"; "A1224. I1" means "in diagram A1224, the boundary arrow I4"; "A1224I1" means "the first input interface of node A1224." The SA language rules also allow such reference expressions to degenerate naturally to the minimum needed to be understandable. Thus, for example, the mechanism for showing that the child detailing exists is merely to write the corresponding chronological creation number (called a *C-number*) under the lower right-hand corner of a box on the diagram, as a DRE. (A C-number is the author's intials, concatenated with a sequential integer—

assigned as the first step whenever a new diagram sheet is begun.) When a model is formally published, the corresponding detail reference expression is normally converted into the page number of the appropriate detail diagram. The omission of a detail reference expression indicates that the box is not further detailed in this model. (For all the diagrams considered in this paper, the DRE's have been left in C-number form.)

The *SA call* notation consists of a detail reference expression preceded by a downward pointing arrow stub, and allows sharing of details among diagrams. It will not be covered in this paper beyond the illustration in Fig. 15, which is included here more to illustrate why mechanism support is not an interface (as has repeatedly been pointed out) than to adequately describe the SA call scheme. That will be the subject of a future paper, and is merely cited here for completeness. The SA call mechanism (see also [2]) corresponds very closely to the subroutine call concept of programming languages, and is a key concept in combining multiple purposes and viewpoints into a single model of models.

XXIV. ORGANIZING THE MODEL

The final box of Fig. 3, Box 3.5, "Organize material," is not detailed in this model. Instead, we refer the reader back to the tabulation of Fig. 2 where the corresponding items are listed. In final publication form each diagram is normally accompanied by brief, carefully-structured *SA text* which, according to the reading rules, is intended to be read *after* the diagram itself has been read and understood. The SA text supplements but does not replace the information content of the diagram. Its purpose is to "tell 'em whatcha told 'em" by giving a walk-through through the salient features of the diagram, pointing out, by using the reference language, how the story line may be seen in the diagram. Published models also include glossaries of terms used, and are preceded by a *node index*, which consists of the node-numbered box names in indented form in node number sequence. Fig. 16 is the node index for the model presented in this paper, and normally would be published at the beginning to act as a table of contents.

XXV. CONCLUSION

The principle of good storytelling style (see Section IV) has been followed repeatedly in this paper. We have provided motivations for each of the 40 SA language features of structured analysis by relating each one to a need for clear and explicit exposition with no loss from an original bounded context. (The "node" column of Fig. 2 maps each feature to a diagram box in the other figures.) In the process, we have seen how the successive levels of refinement strengthen the original statement of purpose and viewpoint, to enforce unambiguous understanding. The best "tell 'em whatcha told 'em" for the paper as a whole is to restudy the SA model in the figures. (Space precludes even sketching the corresponding data decomposition.) The diagrams not only summarize and integrate the ideas covered in the paper, but provide further information, as well.

There are more advanced features of the SA language which will be covered in subsequent papers in the context of applications. In practice, SA turns out to depend heavily on the

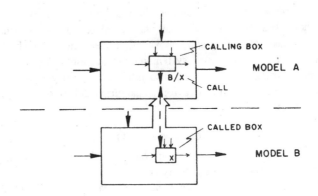

Fig. 15. SA "call" for detailing.

```
RATIONALIZE SA FEATURES
A1  DEFINE GRAPHICS
      A11   Bound Context
      A12   Relate/Connect
      A13   Show Transformation
      A14   Show Circumstance
      A15   Show Means

A2  BUILD DIAGRAM
    A21   Build Box Structure
            A211   Name Aptly
            A212   Label Aptly
            A213   Show Necessity
            A214   Show Dominance
            A215   Show Relevance
            A216   Omit the Obvious

    A22   Build Arrow Structure
            A221   Show Distribution
            A222   Show Subdivision
            A223   Show Exclusion

    A23   Build Diagram Structure
            A231   Show Interfaces to Parent
            A232   Show Parent Connections
            A233   Show Child Detail Exists
            A234   Show Shared Detail Exists

A3  USE SPECIAL NOTATIONS
    A31   Use Special Arrow Notations
            A311   Show Cooperation
            A312   Supress Interchange Details
            A313   Supress "Pass-Through" Clutter
            A314   Supress Arrow Clutter

    A32   Use Special Word Notations

A4  PROVIDE FOR (UNIQUE) REFERENCING
    ( A41   Sheet Reference)
    ( A42   Box Reference)
    ( A43   Interface Reference)
    ( A44   Arrow Reference)
    ( A45   Context Reference)

A5  ORGANIZE MATERIAL
```

Fig. 16. Node index.

disciplined thought processes that lead to well-structured analyses expressed in well-structured diagrams. Additional rules and supporting methodology organize the work flow, support the mechanics of the methods, and permit teams of people to work and interact as one mind attacking complex problems. These are covered in SofTech's SADT methodology. The fact that SA incorporates by definition any and all languages within its framework permits a wide variety of natural and artificial languages to be used to accomplish specific goals with respect to understanding the requirements for solution. Then those requirements can be translated, in a rigorous, organized, efficient, and, above all, understandable fashion, into actual system design, system implementation, maintenance, and training. These topics also must of necessity appear in later papers, as well as a formal language definition for the ideas unfolded here.

ACKNOWLEDGMENT

The four-sided box notation was originally inspired by the match between Hori's activity cell [3] and my own notions of Plex [4]. I have, of course, benefitted greatly from interaction with my colleagues at SofTech. J. W. Brackett, J. E. Rodriguez, and particularly J. B. Goodenough gave helpful suggestions for this paper, and C. G. Feldmann worked closely with me on early developments. Some of these ideas have earlier been presented at meetings of the IFIP Work Group 2. 3 on Programming Methodology.

REFERENCES

[1] D. T. Ross, "It's time to ask why?" *Software Practise Experience*, vol. 1, pp. 103-104, Jan.–Mar. 1971.
[2] D. T. Ross, J. B. Goodenough, C. A. Irvine, "Software engineering: Process, principles, and goals," *Computer*, pp. 17–27, May 1975.
[3] S. Hori, "Human-directed activity cell model," in *CAM-J* long-range planning final rep., CAM-I, Inc., 1972.
[4] D. T. Ross, "A generalized technique for symbol manipulation and numerical calculation," *Commun. Ass. Comput. Mach.*, vol. 4, pp. 147–150, Mar. 1961.
[5] D. T. Ross and K. E. Schoman, Jr., "Structured analysis for requirements definition," this issue, pp. 6–15.
[6] G. A. Miller, "The magical number seven, plus or minus two: Some limits on our capacity for processing information," *Psychol. Rev.*, vol. 63, pp. 81-97, Mar. 1956.

Douglas T. Ross, for a photograph and biography, see this issue, p. 5.

SOFTWARE DESIGN USING SADT

M. E. Dickover
C. L. McGowan
D. T. Ross

Reprinted with permission from *Structured Analysis and
Design*, Volume II, 1978, pages 101-114. Copyright © 1978 by
Infotech International Limited.

INTRODUCTION

SADT* (Structured Analysis and Design Technique) is a graphical language for describing systems together with a methodology for producing such descriptions. Here a 'system' may be defined as any combination of machinery (hardware), data and people working together to perform a useful function. More generally a system can be viewed as consisting of things (objects, documents or data), happenings (activities performed by people, machines, software, etc.) and their interrelationships. This fundamental starting-point accounts for SADT's broad applicability. For example, the definition of requirements (without necessarily specifying whether they are to be achieved by people, by software, by machines), a structured software design, and even a P^3 organization (people, papers and procedures) are 'systems' and thus amenable to a precise SADT description. The use of SADT for the definition of requirements has been described previously (001, 002). This paper focuses on the features of the graphic language that provide a powerful design vocabulary. SADT also includes steps for ensuring adequate design review and effective use of design walk-throughs; these methods are similar to those described for use during analysis (002).

SADT has been further developed and refined at SofTech as a result of extensive use dating from 1973. It has thus far been successfully applied to a variety of complex system problems ranging from real-time telephonic communications design (004) and computer-aided manufacturing (005) to military policy planning (006). The largest software system designed with SADT has been a microprocessor-based PABX telephonic system developed by International Telephone and Telegraph (007).

THE SADT NOTATION

A SADT system description is a set of diagrams each depicting only a limited amount of detail. The diagrams expose a system structure a piece at a time from the top down. Quite literally SADT espouses the principle that 'to divide is to conquer', *provided* we know how the divided pieces are combined to constitute the whole. This proviso applies to the diagram contents as well as to the relationships among diagrams. The rules of language usage encourage and even enforce unfolding a system description in intellectually manageable information units. At all times the system structure and hence the relationship of any part to the whole remains graphically visible.

As a language SADT has a syntax, a semantics and, of course, an associated pragmatics of use. Its syntactic notation has an elegant simplicity that has been described in detail elsewhere (008). Diagrams consist principally of boxes (representing parts of a whole) interconnected by arrows (representing interfaces between the parts), each suitably labelled with nouns (for things) or verbs phrases (for happenings).

Each box on a diagram (representing, say, a system activity) can be further detailed on a separate diagram with more interconnected boxes and arrows. The notation requires that a box and the corresponding diagram detailing it represent exactly the same part of a system. In particular, the

---

* SADT is a trademark of SofTech Inc.

external interfaces in the form of inputs, outputs, and controls must match ('the geometry goes together'). Thus, the diagrams in a SADT system description can be placed directly into a tree-like hierarchy, This information is encoded by an indexing scheme in a natural fashion so that the appropriate context for any diagram can be immediately determined. Figure 1 depicts two diagrams. A box on the first diagram is detailed by the second diagram.

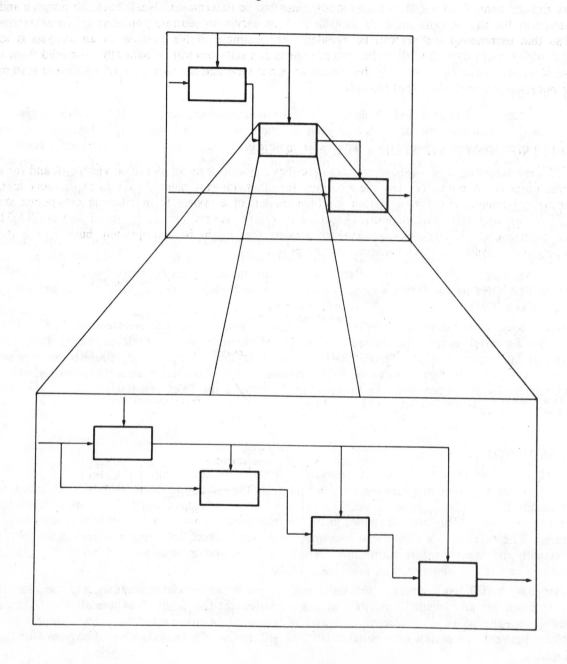

Figure 1: A diagram detailing the box of another

Bertrand Russell has written that 'a good notation has subtlety and suggestiveness which at times makes it seem almost like a live teacher ... a perfect notation would be a substitute for thought'. SADT as a language and as a methodology directs and disciplines the analysis and design of systems. Crucial concepts are naturally expressible and thus are more easily discerned and then communicated. For instance, system feedback and control can be concisely and clearly captured. It is indeed 'a good notation'.

As with any language, ease of expression encourages certain patterns of thought. Within SADT one is naturally led by the notation to bound the context of consideration initially. That is, the inputs, the outputs and the controls of a system under study must first be determined. Next, both the purpose and the viewpoint for the analysis must be identified. This serves to separate concerns by focusing the effort so that extraneous matters can be avoided. For example, if the purpose of an analysis is to obtain a management overview, then the system objects and activities will be naturally examined from a suitable level of abstraction. Similarly the system designer view and the user view of a software system are, of necessity, quite distinct (but related).

MODELLING FROM A VIEWPOINT FOR A PURPOSE

A SADT *model* contains a set of diagrams that describes a system from an identified viewpoint and for a particular purpose. A model can provide a context for other relevant material such as explanatory text, supporting documents, and forms. Often multiple models of a system from differing viewpoints are required for an adequate understanding. Figure 2 represents several hierarchic, multi-diagram SADT models by triangles. It suggests the range of models that might be appropriately built during the development of a system involving computers and people.

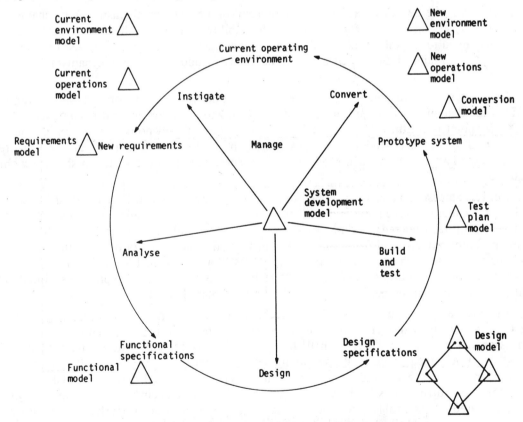

Figure 2: Models appropriate to system development cycle stages

The range extends from conception through installation and even includes the management of this process. The scope of certain key models should be mentioned:

- A Requirements Model crystallizes criteria the new system must meet in order to satisfy the requestor's need (along with those of the manager, users, etc)

- A Functional Model expresses what functions the new system must perform and their implications.

- A Design Model depicts a particular design that meets the requirement by performing the specified functions.

Actually the design model in Figure 2 is shown as an interconnected group of models. This represents SADT's capability of isolating important design decisions for separate treatment as models.

Figure 3 shows two models (i.e., system descriptions with different viewpoints) sharing common detail. Consistency can be checked by 'tying' the different models for a system together, i.e., by making explicit their interrelationships.

REPRESENTING A DESIGN WITH SADT

The SADT graphic notation provides a powerful design vocabulary in which a designer can concisely and unambiguously express his design. SADT does not assume the designer is using one particular design methodology; the relationship of SADT to several widely used design methodologies is briefly discussed later in this paper.

Mechanisms

An important aspect of the design vocabulary is the concept of a SADT mechanism. A mechanism is a distinct model that has been isolated for reasons of shareability and changeability. As such, mechanisms are naturally suited to the information hiding approaches such as abstract data types, monitors, and levels of abstraction. Major design decisions can be encapsulated within a mechanism for greater modifiability.

The SADT call notation corresponds very closely to the subroutine call concept of programming language. The notation shown in Figure 4a on a diagram in Model X means that decomposition from the Model X viewpoint is continued in Model Y from the Model Y viewpoint at the box identified by C. Model Y is said to 'support' Model X and this can be shown graphically as in Figure 4b. Figure 4c shows a box in Model X calling a box in Model Y, which corresponds to the situation shown schematically in Figure 3.

The call reference expression may, in fact, be conditional, giving several different called boxes, each one flagged with a condition specifying the particular box to be called to supply detailing. Therefore, depending upon the parameterized conditions, such a box is changeable. Similarly, a mechanism may support many different models, and from any one of those models an ordinary or a conditional call may be made. Thus that node is shared among many models as represented in Figure 5. These provisions allow precise representation within a single overall design of alternative design approaches. In addition, commonalities of any sort can be modeled once and applied in many places.

The example in Figure 6 illustrates the use of a mechanism which models a monitor (009), a system structuring concept that provides safe access to a resource. The example is a real-time pair of concurrent processes, drawn from Brinch Hansen(010). 'Record' measures a parameter and periodically, as controlled by 'Clock A', updates a cumulative 'total'. 'Output' periodically, as controlled by 'Clock B', reads the 'total', resets it to zero, and prints the 'sum' which is computed based on 'total'. The relationship between the two functions is shown in Figure 6a. As can be seen by the splitting and joining arrow 'total', a shared access problem to 'total' exists, and if not handled properly, the two processes will not work together accurately. A monitor for 'total' is introduced to solve the problem as shown in Figure 6b. 'Total' is now internal data to the monitor and therefore, the representation of 'total' is known only to the monitor. The monitor is represented by a separate SADT model; the top-level diagram in the monitor model is shown in Figure 6c. Decomposition of 'Record' and 'Output' which make calls to the monitor are shown in Figures 6d and 6e. Figure 6d shows that the 'tally' operation of the Record function is realized by the monitor operation 'update total' specified by the downward 'call' arrow. To perform tally the monitor must:

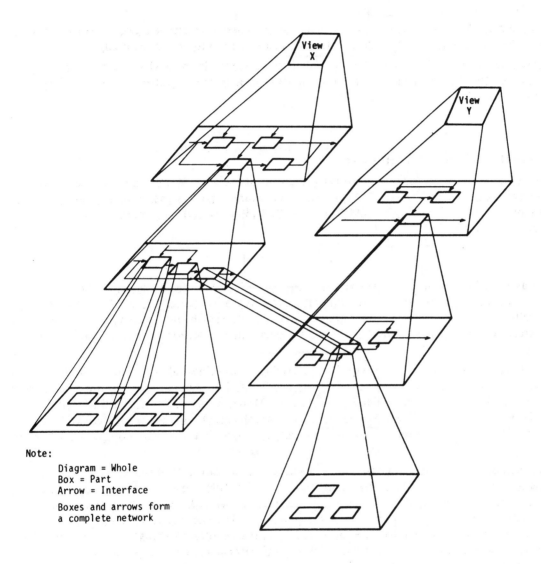

Note:

```
Diagram = Whole
Box = Part
Arrow = Interface

Boxes and arrows form
a complete network
```

Figure 3: Two interconnected models of a system from different viewpoints

- Activate 'get total' to supply 'total' to 'update total'
- Activate 'update total' to yield the new total value
- Activate 'store new total' to store the updated total.

In reviewing the figures, note that:

- Some arrow labels on diagram MON/AO do not match those on diagrams A1 and A2. This is allowed because in SADT, interface-matching is based on 'ICOM' codes, not on spelling.

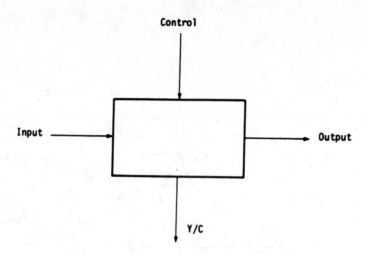

Figure 4a: Decomposition continues in model Y at box C

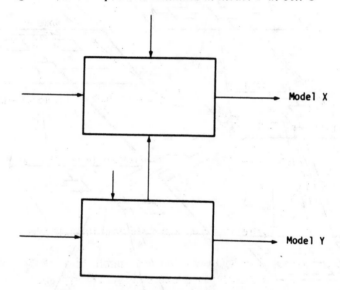

Figure 4b: Model Y supports model X

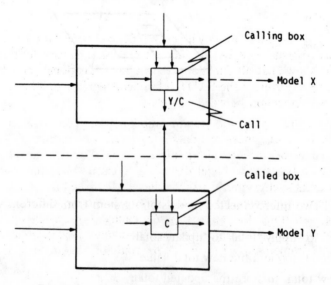

Figure 4c. A model X box calling a box in model Y

Figure 4: SADT call notation

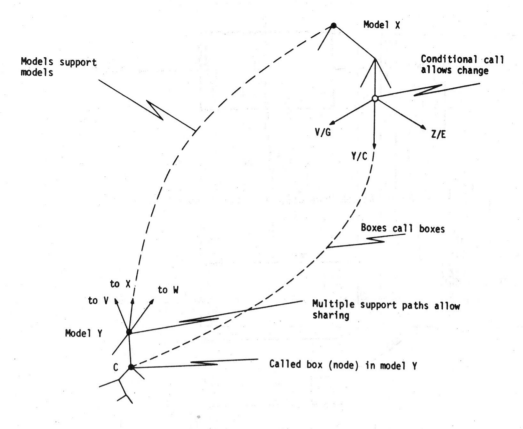

Figure 5: Change and sharing through calls

- Similarly the activity names in MON/AO do not match those of the calling activities in diagrams A1 and A2. The SADT call reference expression written beside the call arrow (↓ MON/A2) uniquely identifies the called activity in the mechanism model.

Traceability between models

The SADT models shown in Figure 2 are not independent but represent different viewpoints that must be demonstrated to be consistent. The SADT 'model tie' process is used to document the relationships between models, i.e., to show that all functions shown in a functional model are carried out by the design model. The tie process utilizes the SADT reference language (008) and concept of mechanisms to show explicitly the interconnection between models.

Each model (e.g., design) is built from the previous model (e.g., functional) and must be 'tied back' to its predecessor to ensure the correctness of the step that created the model (011). Requirements traceability follows immediately because requirements definition initiates the process. That is, requirements definition produces a functional model depicting precisely what the system must do along with the system design constraints such as performance criteria, the need for robustness and recovery, target machine(s) and implementation language(s). Analysis discovers what functions must be performed; design structures these functions for optimal understandability, modifiability and maintainability; specification then selects algorithms to realize the key functions. Hence, an algorithm in a specification model ties back (realizes, implements) into a design module that, in turn, ties to a function in the requirements model.

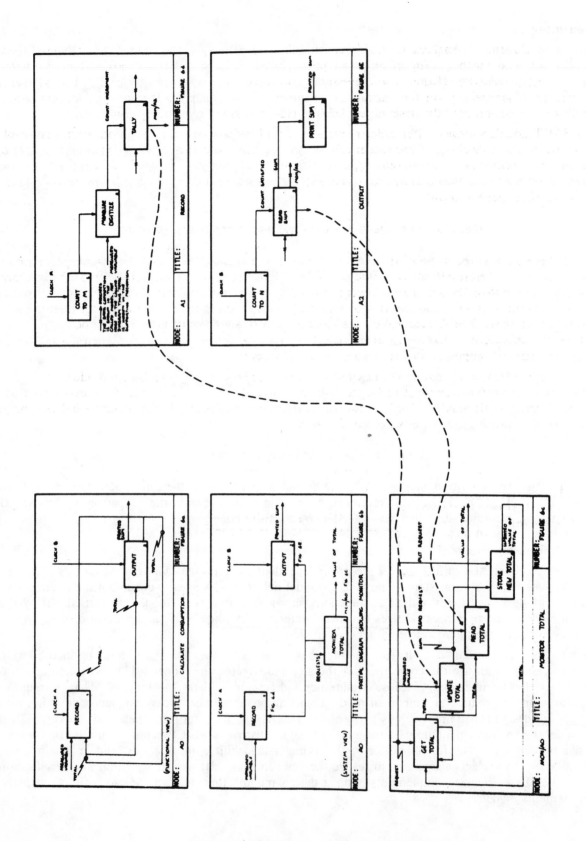

Figure 6: Modeling a mechanism monitor

404

Sequencing

Arrows in Structured Analysis represent constraining relationships, not control flow. Nonetheless, because a box at the beginning of an arrow must precede in some sense the box at the end of the arrow, these precedence relations (not necessarily sequential, but implying many potential parallelisms) do impose a 'sequencing' on the diagrams of a model. SADT diagrams represent all the parallelism implicit in the design until the designer explicitly decides to impose sequencing constraints.

The SADT notation for activation rules provides a way of communicating both information that would be shown by more detailing of the model and sequencing constraints that the designer wishes to add to the model. Activation rules employ logic and finite state machine notation, superimposed on the diagrams, in order to indicate in human readable form the sequencing information known to a designer. They are of the general form:

$$<\text{box-i.d.}>/<\text{rule-}\#>:<\text{pre-conditions}>\rightarrow<\text{post-conditions}>$$

where $<\text{box-i.d}>$ is the name of the box to which the rule applies, $<\text{rule-}\#>$ is a sequential numbering of the rules, $<\text{pre-conditions}>$ is the set of conditions necessary for this activation of the box, and $<\text{post-conditions}>$ is the set of conditions produced by this activation. Activation rules can be used to provide the information to the reader who would otherwise assume the standard rule for interpreting a SADT activity box. The standard rule states that an activity box is constrained from producing its outputs by the absence of the contents of *any one* of its input or control arrows; only when all are present does it produce its outputs, and then it produces *all* of its outputs.

The situation often arises that some subset of the inputs and controls is sufficient to produce some subset of the outputs; for example if in Figure 7 the presence of I1 and C1 is sufficient to produce 02, and I1 and C2 produce 01 and 03. This is information about the insides of A3, and therefore belongs in the detailing of it, which might be as shown in Figure 8.

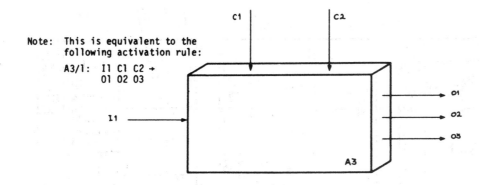

Figure 7: Activity box and activation rule

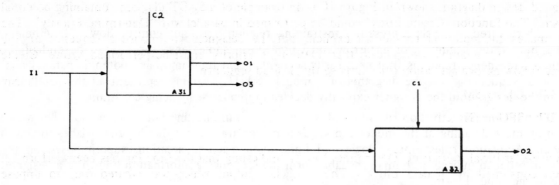

Figure 8: Detailing of activity box A3

In the absence of this detailing, the following activation rules can be used to relate the outputs to the inputs and controls:

$$3/1 : I1\ C1 \rightarrow 02$$

$$3/2 : I1\ C2 \rightarrow 01\ 03$$

The *pre-conditions* list for a rule may specify the absence of an input or control rather than its presence. This negation is indicated by a bar over the appropriate *pre-* or *post-condition*.

$$3/1 : I1\ \overline{C1}\ \overline{C2} \rightarrow 02$$

$$3/2 : I1\ \overline{C1}\ C2 \rightarrow 01\ 03$$

Activation of a box may result in the cancellation of one of the *pre-conditions;* that is, part of the *post-condition* is that one of the *pre-conditions* has been negated. This is indicated by putting the appropriate term in the *post-conditions* with a negation bar:

$$3/2 : I1\ \overline{C1}\ C2 \rightarrow 01\ 03\ \overline{I1}$$

In a case like this, we say that I1 has been *consumed*. Figure 9 illustrates the consumption of an input and a *post-condition* indicating that one or the other of two outputs is produced.

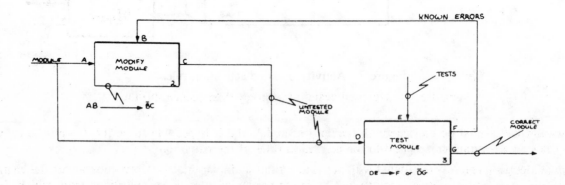

Figure 9: Consumption of an input

The detailed design diagram shown in Figure 10 is an example of a SADT diagram containing potential parallelism. The function 'Create Entry' could be performed in parallel with 'Determine Priority'. The notation makes the potential parallelism explicit, but the designer can impose a sequence on the diagram easily. For example, to indicate that 'Determine Priority' must be performed before 'Create Entry' the following two activation rules impose the desired sequence:

$$4/1 : DK \rightarrow SM$$
$$2/1 : SFG \rightarrow \bar{S}H$$

where S is an 'artificial' output of 'Determine Priority' indicating that the function has been performed. S is then consumed by 'Create Entry'. The 'artificial' output which was created only to impose sequence is shown as a dotted line on the diagram.

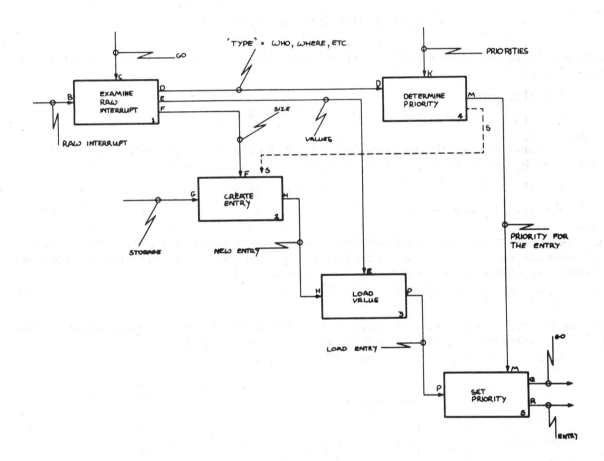

Figure 10: Detailed design diagram with sequence specified

Activation rules must be consistent throughout a model, and it is possible to verify that all the activation rules on a diagram correspond to the activation rules of the parent box.

Detailed design diagrams, annotated with activation rules and quantitative information about the characteristics of data and activities, provide the basis for producing module specifications from which code will be generated. A variety of different specification methods have been employed by SADT users to bridge between detailed SADT design diagrams and code, depending upon the programming language to be used, internal documentation standards, etc. Typically the module specifications have been used when the details of processing steps were the most important thing remaining to be specified. The SADT activity model shows the design structure, the interfaces between components, and the sequence in which components would be executed. The modules specifications would typically show the detailed processing logic and the data definitions which would be used in writing the program.

RELATIONSHIP OF SADT TO CONTEMPORARY DESIGN METHODOLOGIES

A design methodology should specify:

- How to recognize a 'good' design
- How to create a 'good' design
- How to communicate it.

Here 'good' depends upon a method's purpose or goals which, in turn, largely determine how 'good' modules will be selected and connected. The following definition for modularity has been given (012):

> Modularity deals with how the structure of an object can make the attainment of some purpose easier. Modularity is purposeful structuring.

We might characterize the purpose of three approaches which have been widely publicized:

- Structured Design (013)
      Purpose: emphasize functional decomposition
- Jackson Approach (014)
      Purpose: program structure should mirror the problem structure
- Parnas Approach (015)
      Purpose: hide design decisions (e.g., data structure representations)

All three methods are compatible with using SADT as the vehicle for communicating the design. Each of the three design methodologies (016) includes its own design documentation concepts, which are not actually integral to the aspects of the design methodology concerned with recognizing and recognizing and creating a 'good design'. This makes it possible to exploit the design guidelines of each methodology within the common framework of SADT. In most cases, SADT practitioners find the effectiveness of the methodologies is increased by the use of SADT thinking and notation instead of that promoted bys the original developers of each methodology.

For example, the Structured Design concepts have proven to be useful in guiding SADT authors in choosing among alternative decompositions (017). In particular the concept of coupling has been used to judge whether the arrows that connect diagrams are unacceptably complex. The concept of cohesion has helped authors judge whether a set of activities are related closely enough to belong on one diagram. The Structured Design structure charts and data flow diagrams represent information contained in SADT models but with less precision and without the capabilities provided by SADT data models and mechanism models.

The Jackson method documents the structure of input and output data with a graphical notation, which represents a part of the information contained in SADT data models. SADT also allows natural extension of the Jackson method to the cases where design structure should not follow exactly the given data structure.

The SADT mechanism notation also provides a concrete way of representing Parnas' information-hiding modules, as well as such abstractions as virtual machines, monitors, abstract data types and other useful design constructs. It also provides ready expression and control over virtually all of the aspects of software engineering that have been found to be of practical significance (012).

In summary, SADT does not force the designer to accept a new, or even any particular, design methodology. Rather it disciplines and directs a designer's thinking while enabling one directly to draw, see, compare and apply alternatives in any rational way that suits the specific design conditions. SADT offers a conceptual and a notational framework for expressing, evaluating, comparing and choosing among design alternatives. Proven design principles find a natural expression within SADT.

Finally, and perhaps most importantly, the rigor of SADT, enabled by the graphic language syntax and semantics, but enforced by the disciplined routine of the reader/author critique and correction cycle, allows full progress tracking throughout the design and implementation process. Visibility, understandability and confirmation of details throughout the process enable a higher and more comfortable degree of effective project management.

The discipline of SADT is not the discipline of the drill-sergeant, but the discipline of the dancer - smooth, flowing and expressive. Good design methodologies are enhanced and integrated when they are approached in a unified fashion.

REFERENCES

001 ROSS D T and BRACKETT J W *An approach to structured analysis* Comp Dec vol 8 no 9 pp 40-44 (1976)

002 ROSS D T and SCHOMAN K E *Structured analysis for requirements definition* Trans on Software engineering vol 3 no 1 pp 6-15 (1977)

003 HORI S *Human-directed activity cell model* CAM-1 Long Range Planning Final Report CAM-1 Inc (1972)

004 THOMAS M *Function decomposition: SADT* This volume page 355ff

005 ZIMMERMAN M *ICAM: Revolution in manufacturing* Machine Design vol 49 no 1 (1977)

006 MELICH M *Evolution of naval missions and the naval tactical data system* Proc Conf on *Managing the development of weapon system software p 26 (1976)*

007 PAYNE R *Calling for attention ... ITT's interesting telephone system* Computing Europe (June 1977)

008 ROSS D T *Structured analysis: a language for communicating ideas* IEEE Trans on Software engineering vol 3 no 1 pp 16-34 (1977)

009 HOARE C A R *Monitors: an operating system structuring concept* CACM vol 17 no 10 pp 549-557 (Oct 1974)

010 BRINCH HANSEN P *Operating system principles* Prentice-Hall Englewood Cliffs NJ (1973)

011 ROSS D T *Quality starts with requirements definition* Position paper for IFIP TC2 Working Conf on *Constructing quality software* Novosibirsk USSR (May 1977)

012 ROSS D T, GOODENOUGH J B and IRVINE C A *Software engineering: process, principles, and goals* Computer pp 17-27 (May 1975)

013 YOURDON E and CONSTANTINE L L *Structured design* Yourdon Inc New York (1975)

014 JACKSON M A *Principles of program design* Academic Press London (1975)

015 PARNAS D L *On the criteria to be used in decomposing systems into modules* CACM vol 15 no 12 pp 1053-1058 (Dec 1972)

016 McGOWAN C L and KELLY J R *A review of decomposition and design methodologies* Proc Infotech Conf on *Structured design* pp 117-143 (and discussion transcripts) (1977)

017 DICKOVER M E *Principles of coupling and cohesion for use in the practice of SADT* Tech publ no 039 SofTech Inc Waltham Mass (1976)

Discussed is a program design language—a form of pseudo-code—that has been developed and used to organize, teach, document, and develop software systems. An example of top-down program design illustrates the key steps in using the language: determining the requirements, abstracting the functions, expanding the functions, and verifying the functions.

Syntax and conventions of the language are given in an appendix.

Top-down development using a program design language

by P. Van Leer

The McDonnell Douglas Automation Company (MCAUTO™), which is a division of the McDonnell Douglas Corporation, provides data processing services to the other divisions within the corporation as well as nationwide commercial data-processing services. Each division of McDonnell Douglas has its own systems analysts for business applications. The systems analysts determine user requirements and develop appropriate application system designs. Specifications for the system designs usually include a prose overview, descriptions of input and output files, screen layouts, report layouts, and logic specifications. MCAUTO personnel may assist the divisional analysts with the specifications or may develop the system designs. In either case, MCAUTO personnel are responsible for refining the system design, program design as necessary, coding, testing, and writing documentation necessary for the operation and maintenance of the systems. Thus programmers in MCAUTO are presented with system specifications of varying levels of detail, in which any two systems may be defined at different levels of detail, especially with reference to program logic.

Early in 1973, MCAUTO established a pilot test task force to determine how and to what extent they could use various improved programming techniques that had been developed by that time. A result of that task force was the development and teaching of structured programming and other improved programming techniques. Most of the programming techniques that were known[1] in 1973 were tried simultaneously. The conclusion[2] was that the new techniques showed promise, but too

410

much had been attempted at one time. Accordingly, the instruction continued in 1974, concentrating on structured programming, top-down programming, structured walk throughs, and program design language, the latter being the subject of this paper. As a result of this further effort[3], use of these four techniques has become a stated policy at MCAUTO. This investigation into the other techniques continued in 1975, with Hierarchy plus Input Process Output (HIPO) also showing great promise as a system analyst tool.[4]

The logic specification standards that have been used at MCAUTO are roughly equivalent to detailed flowcharts, in which numbered English sentences are substituted for the various flowchart symbols. As detailed flowcharts were formerly used to create the required detail, so were logic specification standards. Although flowcharts and logic specification standards proved adequate for smaller and less complex applications, it was recognized in the early 1970s that more complex applications are correspondingly more difficult to describe and specify by the use of flowcharts. That increasing size and complexity of applications had gradually outgrown the capability and scope of earlier logic specifications was the primary condition that set the stage for the new technique of using a program design language.

Program design language

The program design language that is presented in this paper is a tool for designing programs in detail prior to coding. At MCAUTO, the program design language is used both as a language and as a program development methodology. The program design language is syntactically simple and supports structured control figures[5] tailored for PL/1 and COBOL. The syntax of the language is described in the Appendix. Top-down program development methodology and elements of stepwise refinement[6] and levels of abstraction are used with the program design languages.[7] The methodology is described in this paper. At MCAUTO, programmers use the program design language in conjunction with structured walkthroughs, top-down implementation,[5] and structured programming.[3,4] Although the value of the program design language has not been evaluated apart from the other techniques, the language is believed to be a major contributor to increased productivity.

The program design language, as a form of pseudocode, has the following characteristics:

- Notation is used to state program logic and function in an easy-to-read, top-to-bottom fashion.
- It is not a compilable language.

- It is an informal method of expressing structured programming logic.
- It is similar to a programming language (such as COBOL or PL/1), but is not bound by formal syntactical language rules.
- Conventions exist that pertain to the use of structured figures and indentation to aid in the visual perception of the logic.
- The primary purpose is to enable one to express ideas in natural English prose.
- The language permits concentration on logical solutions to problems, rather than the form and constraints within which the solutions must be stated.
- The language uses flowchart replacements, program documentation, and technical communication at all levels.
- Program design is expressed readably, and can be converted easily to executable code.

The program design language was initially used to teach structured programming to the programmers. As a teaching aid, the language helped the programmers make the transition to thinking in terms of a hierarchy of routines that consisted of basic structured figures.[4] When programmers started to implement application systems using flow charts and other earlier methods in which the programs were of the nonhierarchical and nonstructured type, the refining process included making hierarchical and structured program designs. Using the program design language rather than structured flowcharts or structuring the standard logic specifications proved to be the easiest way to improve the program design. Continued use and refinement of the language has established it as the medium of choice for either creating or refining a detailed program design. Although more experience with HIPO is needed, it presently appears that HIPO[4] may become the medium of choice for system design, and further become an excellent input for detailed program design. In time, HIPO may be as useful to analysts as the program design language is to programmers.

Top-down program design

Simplicity is a key attribute to the program design language syntax, conventions for which are given in the Appendix. In general, when the language is written according to the guidelines to be discussed in this paper, statements in the language are easy to transform into programs. More importantly, the simplicity frees the designer, who is usually a programmer, to concentrate on developing the detailed logic of a program. While the systematic application of the program design language facilitates program design, the language is not a simplistic means of doing the whole job of programming. Detailed program design is an iterative process, with the possibility that details discovered in the later stages of design may lead to modifications in previous portions. Although experience in using the language and familiarity with the application may reduce the impact of such incidents, one should usually plan to complete a detailed design before starting to code a program. Since the program design language is easier to change (or rewrite) than actual code, cleaning up a program design in that language is usually more cost-effective than cleaning up program code. The primary objective in defining a procedure for the systematic application of the program design language is to provide a general scheme of things to be done during detailed program design.

The systematic application of the language is to apply the principles of top-down programming to the detailed program design function, which we term "top-down program design." This implies that the process of program design can be described as a hierarchy of discrete functions, which further implies that the work product (the program design) should be a hierarchy of discrete units that ease program implementation in a top-down manner.

According to program design language conventions, the discrete units in the case of program design are one-entry-one-exit routines (as in structured programming) that are no larger than one page. In most cases, all the detailed logic for a program does not fit on one page, a fact that leads to a squeezing down of detail into lower-level routines, and results in a number of hierarchically related routines. The syntax and conventions of the program design language promote a program design that meets the objectives of top-down programming. An example that shows the squeezing of detail into lower-level routines and the formation of hierarchically related routines is given in the following section.

Top-down program design example

The top-down design process may be regarded as having the following three distinct phases:

- Determining requirements.
- Abstracting functions.
- Expanding functions.

Obviously, the time and effort needed for each of these phases depends on the designer's experience and ability. Likewise, the particular way in which the functions are designed depends on the amount and organization of the source information. If the source data for a program design do not include completed file designs, report layouts, and user input definitions, then the application system design is not ready to be expanded into a detailed program design. Moreover, a system design should include, as necessary, functions that the program should perform and any constraints on the program (such as field edits or sequences of calculations). Even after assuming that one has at least the minimum system-level specification for the program, there may still be wide variations in the level and volume of details and in the organization of those details. The optimum system specification is a hierarchy of user-oriented functions that includes only those details that are directly related to a user's requirements.

The establishment of practical guidelines for the optimal level of detail and organization for system-level specifications requires the active cooperation of both analysts and programmers. Whether done by analysts or programmers, the following three basic functions of detailed program design must still be performed: determine the requirements, abstract the functions, and expand the functions.

At the time of a detailed program design, the determining of program requirements consists primarily of studying the system specifications for the program. Any items that are vague, missing, undefined, or contradictory should be clarified before plunging into detailed program design. If the system specifications do not, at some point, provide a simple statement of user requirements, then write down such items as they become apparent. This point is crucial because the abstractive process should be in terms of the user's requirements. Likely sources are the definitions of output reports, files, screens, etc. The report specifications for a simple report generation program might yield the following functions:

determining requirements

- Accumulate total sales for each salesman.
- Accumulate total sales for each district.
- Accumulate total sales for all districts.

Examination of the input specification for the program might reveal the following constraints:

- The sales file has only one kind of record.
- Each sales record includes salesman name and number, and district number.
- Sales records are in order by salesman identification within each district.
- There may be several sales records for a salesman.

Additional constraints, such as "skip to new page after printing a district total" might be found.

If it is assumed that the specifications at the source specification level of detail do not express the user's requirements, the objective is to build a complete list at this level. It is not necessary to organize the list. Rather, one should concentrate on discovering all the functions that the user wants to be performed. Assuming this criterion, one might reasonably eliminate all the previously listed functions and constraints except the following:

- Accumulate total sales for each salesman.
- Accumulate total sales for each district.
- Accumulate total sales for all districts.
- Skip to new page after printing a district total.

At this point, a discussion with the analyst or user might be profitable. In any case, the requirements should be thoroughly understood, so that abstracting the functions—which is discussed in the following section—may be started.

abstracting functions   Abstracting the functions consists of discriminating between functions that are subfunctions and those that are main functions. To begin abstracting the functions, one first decides whether there is one function in the list that implies all the others. If there is none, then the programmer invents such a comprehensive function (i.e., he abstracts a general statement). For example, the report program function might be to "Summarize Sales," which implies that all the other sales functions are subfunctions. In that case, what are the relationships among the five functions on a main and subfunction basis? A good starting point for decision making is to organize the list by grouping all functions that have related inputs or outputs and by ranking each group in a most-general-to-most-detailed order. Since the report program has only one input file and one output report, grouping is not necessary. Ranking the sales functions yields the following general-to-detailed list:

1. Accumulate total sales for all districts.
2. Accumulate total sales for each district.
3. Skip to new page after printing district total.
4. Accumulate total sales for each salesman.

It appears that 2 and 3 are at the same functional level; that is, 1 implies 2 and 3 implies 4. This relationship suggests some minor reordering, which is brought out by the following list:

1. Accumulate total sales for all districts.
2.   Accumulate total sales for each district.
4.   Accumulate total sales for each salesman.
3.   Skip to new page after printing district total.

Compare the new list with the report layout and note that there is a good match-up, especially if the basic functions are expanded to designate the various totals that are to be printed as follows:

A1. Accumulate total sales for all districts.
B1.   Accumulate total sales for each district.
C1.   Accumulate total sales for each salesman.
C2.   Print total sales for each salesman.
B2.   Print total sales for each district.
B3.   Skip to new page after printing district total.
A2. Print total sales for all districts.

At this point, the following three functional levels have been identified: all districts, each district, and each salesman. Each functional level contains a mixture of relatively simple functions, e.g., print and skip; and more general functions, e.g., accumulate. Generally, one cannot code a program from abstractions of function at this level. Definitions of the too-general functions must be expanded until all functions are sufficiently defined.

The expanding of functions consists of repeating the following four basic steps until all functions in the design have been sufficiently simplified to be coded: selection, analysis, specification, and verification. The appropriate point at which to stop depends on a programmer's familiarity with the program design language, structured programming, and the functions. Usually, the greater a programmer's experience with the program design language, the higher will be the level of detail that he uses. That is, when a programmer first starts using the language, more detailed definitions are needed (and written) than are needed after he has become accustomed to using the language. If a next lower level of expansion of named functions results in program design language statements that are program code, then the current level of expansion is probably sufficient. Of course, if all the statements can already be transferred into code on a one-for-one basis, the design is complete.

expanding functions

Selecting a function is the first step in expanding the functions. Expansion should generally be accomplished in a top-down manner. That is, expand the highest level (as yet undefined) function next. When faced with a choice of undefined functions at the same level, the main-line, or most important function, is usually expanded first. In the program example used in this paper, the function labeled A1 is the natural candidate for being expanded first. Since the expansion of A1 may produce another function that needs expansion, it is premature to assert that B1 should be expanded next. After having selected a function, the next step is to analyze it.

Analyzing a function is the process of deciding what must be done to accomplish a given function. This is sometimes referred to as breaking a function down into subfunctions. In the event that major subfunctions have already been determined, analysis may consist of defining supportive subfunctions. For example, B1, B2, and B3 are major subfunctions of A1. Supportive subfunctions of A1 might be the following:

Set total for all districts to zero.
Add district sales to grand total.

Since A is the highest level in the program, the following data processing functions must also be done:

Open files.
Close files.

After the subfunctions have been identified, their relationships to one another can be specified.

Specifying relationships of the various subfunctions is accomplished by using the appropriate conditions and structured control figures. Specification may be done by using existing data variables, or it may require the definition of new data variables. New data variables should be noted as such, to facilitate both the eventual coding of a function and the expansion of lower-level functions during design. In effect, subfunctions and their relationships to one another should constitute a complete definition of function. For example, the A level might be specified as follows:

Summarize sales
Open files.
Set total for all districts to zero.
DO WHILE more sales data.
    Accumulate total for a district.
    Add total for district to total for all districts.
ENDDO
Print total sales for all districts.
Close files.

In this example, the statement "Accumulate total for a district" refers to the B- and C-level functions. We, therefore, proceed with the selection, analysis, and specification of the B- and C-level functions.

Accumulate total for a district
Set total for a district to zero.
Set current district to district in sales record.
DO WHILE current district matches district in sales record.
    And more sales data.
    Accumulate total for a salesman.

Add total for a salesman to total for a district.
ENDDO
Print total for a district.
Skip to a new page.

Accumulate total for a salesman
Set total for a salesman to zero.
Set current salesman to salesman in sales record.
DO WHILE current salesman matches salesman in sales record:
And current district matches district in sales record.
And more sales data.
Add sales data to total for a salesman
Read sales record
ENDDO
Print total for a salesman.

A programmer who is experienced in structured programming should find the specification and expansions just given relatively easy to code. Although some of the loop conditions have only been named (e.g., more sales data), their expansion into code should not pose a great problem. Before doing any coding, however, a little desk checking is often found to be of value.

Seldom can practical programs be completely defined on a single page using the program design language. More likely, the first page of material that is written in that language names the functions that are to be expanded on another page. The first- (or highest-) level page of program design language statements defines the environment of the lower-level function. After the completion of one page in that language, it is often useful to take a checkpont and verify the completeness and correctness of a function that is defined by the program design language. In doing the verification, it may be helpful to list the various combinations of inputs needed to test a routine, in effect, to define—at least in part—what must be done to test the program. In any event, one last thorough examination of a unit of design description before proceeding to lower-level design or coding may save subsequent rework. For example, attempting to process even one record by the example report program reveals the need for a read-sales-record statement before the first DO WHILE at the highest level, i.e., *Summarize sales.*

verification

Experience and conclusions

At MCAUTO, the following major advantages of using the program design language instead of traditional techniques for detailed program design have been observed:

• Ease of writing programs.

- Ease of changing programs.
- Transferability into structured code in a top-down manner.
- Ease of reading programs, especially by nonprogrammers.

The readability aspect contributes to the effectiveness of structured walkthroughs for nonprogrammers. Since the program design language is inherently hierarchical and structured, it also contributes to the success of top-down development and structured programming. Although further experience is needed, it appears that the functional orientation of HIPO also lends itself to expansion into the program design language. Thus the use of the language contributes to the successful use of the other programming techniques.

The systematic application of the program design language is not a cookbook checklist for designing programs. In practice, the individual steps—especially those involved in expanding a design—tend to be done simultaneously, rather than sequentially. Initially, the program designer may be slowed down by his unfamiliarity with manipulating DO WHILES and IF THEN ELSES to accomplish his purpose without recourse to GOTOs. With experience, program designs are usually created more readily than otherwise. The resultant designs are typically of better quality than traditional program designs. The better quality of programs designed using the program design language is reflected in relative ease of implementation and maintenance, and by the absence of production errors.

ACKNOWLEDGMENTS

The author extends his thanks and appreciation to the MCAUTO programmers for their interest and perseverence during our mutual learning period. He especially thanks Charles E. Holmes (MCAUTO St. Louis), John E. Hiles (MCAUTO West), and E. Jean Bland (IBM, St. Louis) for the imagination, dedication, and leadership that contributed to the successful adaptation of the methods discussed in this paper.

CITED REFERENCES

1. F. T. Baker, "Chief programmer team management of production programming," *IBM Systems Journal* 11, No. 1, 56–73 (1972).
2. C. E. Holmes and L. W. Miller, *Proceedings, 37th Meeting of GUIDE International*, Boston, Massachusetts, October 28–November 2, 1973 (560–575).
3. C. E. Holmes, *Proceedings, 39th Meeting of GUIDE International*, Anaheim, California, November 3–8, 1974 (689–700).
4. *HIPO—A Design Aid and Documentation Technique*, Order No. GC20-1851, IBM Corporation, Data Processing Division, White Plains, New York 10604.
5. *Improved Programming Technologies—An Overview*, IBM Systems Reference Library, Order No. GC20-1850, IBM Corporation, Data Processing Division, White Plains, New York 10604.

6. N. Wirth. *Systematic Programming: An Introduction*, Prentice-Hall, Inc., Englewood Cliffs, New Jersey (1973).
7. E. W. Dijkstra, "The structure of T.H.E. multiprogramming system," *Communications of the ACM* 11, No. 5, 341–346 (1968).

Appendix

The syntax of the program design language includes provisions for expressing the three basic logic constructs (or figures) of structured programming: SEQUENCE, IF THEN ELSE, and DO WHILE. In the program design language, these constructs have been augmented with the PERFORM UNTIL and CASE constructs. Each logic construct has a definite and simple syntax. In addition to the statement syntax, conventions have been established for the use of indentation and the size of self-contained units of the program design language. The SEQUENCE construct is used to describe any action or work that is followed by the next sequential construct. In control structure forms, SEQUENCE is represented by the function of a subroutine block as shown in Figure 1, where f is the action or work to be done. Syntactically, SEQUENCE represents a simple English sentence, with at least a verb and an object. In practice, the language is most meaningful when action-oriented statements with objects that are natural to the problem are used. Compare, for example, the following sentences: "Print." with "Print XYZ." and with "Print gross sales for salesman."

The IF THEN ELSE construct is used to describe binary decisions. In its most general form, that logic construct is used to describe the conditions under which one of two actions are to be taken. The control structure for IF THEN ELSE is given in Figure 2. The symbol is the predicate (or list of conditions), and f and g are alternative actions. Note that f and g may include any of the logic constructs, and are not limited to being the SEQUENCE construct. The general syntax of the IF THEN ELSE construct is as follows:

```
IF       p
THEN     f
ELSE     g
ENDIF
```

The IF, THEN, ELSE, and ENDIF should always be vertically aligned and displayed in all capitals for ease of reading. When p consists of multiple simple conditions, each condition should be written on a separate line, and all conditions should be vertically aligned, as, for example, in the following way:

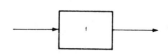

Figure 1 Control structure for the SEQUENCE logic construct

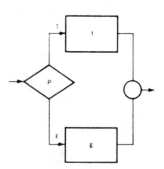

Figure 2 Control structure for the IF THEN ELSE logic construct

420

```
IF          No more data or
            Different department.
THEN        Print total department sales.
ELSE        Add sale amount to total department sales.
ENDIF
```

The IF and ENDIF conditions are required. When, however, either the THEN or the ELSE clause is not needed, they may be omitted. In other words, the following are syntactically valid forms of the IF THEN ELSE logic construct.

```
IF          p
THEN        f
ENDIF
and
IF          p
ELSE        g
ENDIF
```

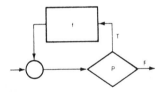

Figure 3 Control structure for the DO WHILE logic construct

The DO WHILE logic construct is used to describe the repetition of an action under prescribed conditions (looping). The control structure for DO WHILE is shown in Figure 3, where p is the predicate (or list of conditions) and f is the action to be taken. (Note that Figure 3 is a decision loop in which the action is taken when a condition is true.)

The program design language syntax of the DO WHILE construct is as follows:

```
DO WHILE      p
          f
ENDDO
```

where the DO WHILE and ENDDO conditions are vertically aligned and capitalized. Consider the following pseudo code sequence that is based on the example in the body of this paper:

```
DO WHILE      More data and
              Same district:
          Accumulate district sales total.
          Read next sales record.
ENDDO
```

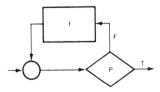

Figure 4 Control structure for the PERFORM UNTIL logic construct

The PERFORM UNTIL construct is used to describe looping, when COBOL is the target language for implementation. Control structure for PERFORM UNTIL is shown in Figure 4, where p is the predicate, and f is the action to be taken. PERFORM UNTIL differs from the DO WHILE in that the PERFORM UNTIL loop exits when p is true, rather than when p is false. In effect, DO WHILE p is equivalent to PERFORM UNTIL not p. By using a PERFORM

UNTIL in the program design language. p may be written exactly as it is written in COBOL. thus avoiding the errors that might occur in doing a Boolean inversion of p from the DO WHILE of the program design language to the PERFORM UNTIL of COBOL. The program design language syntax of the PERFORM UNTIL logic construct is given as follows:

```
PERFORM UNTIL     p
         f
ENDLOOP
```

where the PERFORM UNTIL and ENDLOOP are vertically aligned and capitalized. An example fragment taken from the text and expressed in the program design language is as follows:

```
PERFORM UNTIL     No more data or
                  Different district:
         Accumulate district sales total.
         Read next sales record.
ENDLOOP
```

In comparing this fragment with the DO WHILE example. note that the loop conditions have been inverted.

The CASE logic construct is used to simulate a branch table. In the appropriate situation. CASE can be an efficient and effective alternative to multiple levels of nested IF THEN ELSE statements. This construct may be applicable when one of n functions is to be executed. depending on the value of a single variable. The control structure for the CASE construct is shown in Figure 5A. Figure 5B is the IF THEN ELSE logical equivalent of the CASE construct.

The program design language syntax of the CASE construct is given as follows:

```
CASE     variable  OF
         Value 1:     f1
         Value 2:     Value 3:     f2
         Value 4:     f3
            •
            •
            •
         Value n:     fm
ENDCASE
```

Here. "variable" is the variable to be checked for the various "values." and "value i" is a specific value of the variable to associate with the execution of the function f_i. which appears on the same line. Note that there may be more values n than there

Figure 5   Control structure for the CASE logic construct
   A. General f_n case
   B. Functional equivalent f_n case

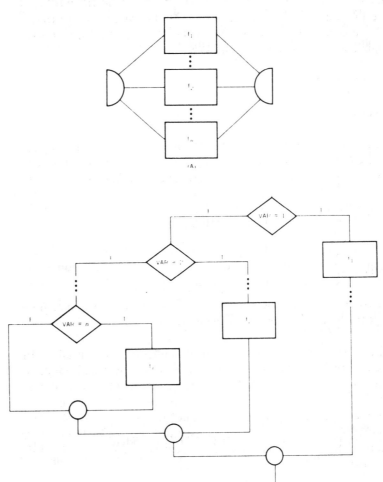

(A)

(B)

are unique functions m, and it is assumed that "variable" has been checked for valid values. Colons are used to delimit the values, as in the following example:

```
CASE          SALES CODE OF
     1:2:     CASH SALE
       3:     REVOLVING CHARGE SALE
       4:     DEFERRED PAYMENT PLAN SALE
       5:     MDSE DAMAGED RETURN
       6:     WRONG MDSE SENT AND RETURNED
ENDCASE
```

The keywords CASE and ENDCASE are vertically aligned and capitalized.

The indentation conventions in the program design language as used in this paper are to align vertically concatenated logic constructs and to indent any nested logic constructs. Two logic constructs are said to be concatenated when one immediately follows the other. The following fragments of program design language are concatenated:

```
IF          p
THEN        f
ELSE        g
ENDIF
DOWHILE     g
        h
ENDDO
```

where DO WHILE follows IF THEN ELSE.

Two logic constructs are said to be nested when one is contained within the other. For example, suppose function f were expanded, then we might have the following nested statements:

```
IF      p
THEN DO WHILE       q
          f2
      ENDDO
ELSE      g
ENDIF
```

where f2 is nested within a DO WHILE, which, in turn, is nested within the IF THEN ELSE. If f2 were expanded into two concatenated sequence constructs, the following structure might result:

```
IF      p
THEN    DO WHILE    q
          f21
          f22
        ENDDO
ELSE    g
ENDIF
```

In applying the indentation rules, a basic unit of indentation (usually three spaces) should be used consistently. These guidelines, coupled with the use of meaningful and application-oriented names help to make the design easy to read.

The idea of unit size of program design language has been mentioned in the body of the paper. It is based partly on convenience and partly on a perceived, but not well documented observation of human attention span and ability to abstract and synthesize information. A convention has, therefore, been adopted. Simply stated, the convention is that a single unit should not exceed one page of standard 8 1/2 × 11 inch paper. Furthermore, each logic construct should end on the same page on which it begins. In practice, this results in a package of one-page units where voluminous nested functions are represented by simple names — where they are used — that are then defined in detail on separate pages. Essentially, the program design consists of a number of subroutines that are hierarchically related.

Reprint Order No. G321–5032.

THE TOPD SYSTEM FOR COMPUTER-AIDED SYSTEM DEVELOPMENT

R. A. Snowdon
P. Henderson

INTRODUCTION

It is now widely accepted that current methods for producing software are not totally satisfactory. The evidence for this is all too familiar and ranges from error-ridden programs to complete project failures. A variety of tools and techniques have been proposed and been developed which attempt to alleviate the situation. In particular there have been advances in programming methods such as structured programming (001), serious attempts at program proving (002) and a number of improvements in programming language design. All of these advances respect the view that programming is a task that stretches the intellectual capacity of the human mind and therefore it is essential that ways be found which reduce rather than increase its complexity.

The TOPD system aims to assist in the programming process by tackling four areas in which complexity, not inherent in any particular task, frequently occurs in conventional programming environments. These problem areas are briefly referred to in (003) as:

- Ill-disciplined program design
- Inappropriateness of programming languages
- Disassociation of design and validation
- Bulk of information.

Ill-conceived programming disciplines are often of little more use than a complete lack of discipline. Individual programmers can find that adoption of a particular discipline provides obstacles to their work, possibly because of a lack of experience, but often because it is unsuited to the program being written. Some disciplines are simply unconstructive or require satisfaction of criteria which are inconsistent.

Conventional programming languages are most appropriate for the representation of the product in its final form, but, in general, are almost totally inappropriate for the representation of partially designed programs. Thus programmers use other notations which do not force unwanted decisions upon them. Use of these notations (e.g., natural language, pictures, pseudo-programming languages) can easily lead to misunderstanding, oversight or error simply because they lack the precision of a programming language.

It is generally the case that much design effort precedes that part of the programming effort that allows mechanical validation. This follows almost directly from the necessary use of imprecise linguistic forms. This effort and the associated investment in program code represents a considerable barrier against change and thereby encourages 'patching' to repair design faults.

The sheer bulk of information that even a modest software development needs introduces administrative problems of its own. These problems make the programming activity cumbersome and hence error-prone.

TOPD provides facilities which tackle each of these problem areas. The various features are introduced in the next section. More detailed descriptions of the major features of TOPD provide the bulk of the remainder of the report. Further, we discuss the relevance and place of such tools in a program development environment. In this discussion the report relates the facilities of TOPD to other endeavors in the area of programming support and attempts to show the kind of tools which may be provided in the future.

CONCEPTS OF TOPD

TOPD is aimed at providing support for the programming activity at the stage when the major software design is completed. It does not therefore attempt to provide facilities for problem analysis or system specification. It is oriented towards tackling programming problems at much the same level as is structured programming (001) or similar techniques (004).

Program development is based upon the design of *classes*. The concept of a class was originally described in SIMULA 67. In TOPD, however, the concept is much simplified and is based upon the presentation of Hoare (005). A class is used to introduce a new type of data object (e.g., a stack) along with all its associated properties. This approach to developing software can be seen also in systems such as CLU (006), Alphard (007) and GAMMA (008), although the name given to the basic unit of development may differ from 'class'.

The properties that are associated with a class include a set of *operations*. These are the unique set of operations (e.g., push, pop) which may be applied to data objects of the type described by class. Each operation is represented by a procedure declaration, identifying the operation by name and specifying any parameters it might have.

A list of *states* is also associated with a class. Each state describes a condition in which objects of the class may be found. Just as a class may be considered as defining an abstract type, a state may be considered as defining an abstract value for that type.

The states of a class are used to describe the expected behavior of a program. A definition of the action of each operation associated with a class is given by a *state transition*. This describes how the conditions of the objects manipulated by the operation change when the operation is called. A state transition is a model of the action of the operation. States and state transitions form the basis of the program validation and checking features of TOPD. The technique was rationalized in (009,010) and is further described in the section on Program Checkout in this paper. It is a scheme which allows a meaningful and exhaustive execution of abstract programs and plays a central role in the development of software using TOPD. Related but less powerful techniques have been described (011,012,013). These, however, are primarily concerned with allowing incomplete programs written in conventional programming languages to be tested (as opposed to exhaustively executed) and so lack both the abstract and complete nature of the TOPD scheme. (014) describes work in which assertional models are used in association with the axiomatic definition of the underlying programming language. Alphard (007) and EUCLID (015) are languages which try to combine program development schemes with concern for program proof.

A class is decomposed by relating it to a group of other classes, or instances of other classes. This decomposition represents a step in the process of adding detail to the transitions. The decomposition of a class is a process of showing in more detail how that particular part of the program is formed. In terms of a multi-level approach to program development the decomposition gives a basis of an implementation for the class as a whole. The detailing is continued by associating, with each procedure in the class, an algorithm. These algorithms describe how the actions represented by each procedure are implemented in terms of the procedures at the lower and more detailed (less abstract) level. To complete the decomposition process, the states of the class are each expressed in terms of the states of the lower-level classes.

The TOPD design notation provides a textual form in which the programmer may encode each class in his program, its properties and its decomposition.

A program development therefore is represented by a hierarchy of class definitions. However, the process by which this structure is developed is not well defined. The programmer is not constrained by the tools to progress in any particular fashion. Although it is likely that a top-down process will be most beneficial, there is no requirement that such an approach be followed. The design notation allows the programmer to encode classes or parts of classes and there are few rules as to the order in which this may be done. Each fragment of design is held in a central program development data base from which the various tools operate.

The use of a data base in program development is not unique in TOPD although its application to the support of programming is unusual. PEARL (011) and CADES (016) were early systems to make use of the idea of storing program information in a structure based on the logical content of the program being developed. More recently the GAMMA project (008) has proposed the concept of using such a data base to hold descriptions of program components while DREAM (017) is being developed to hold more complex information for software development. Other data bases (e.g., (018)) are being used to hold system design information.

The TOPD data base holds the fragments of text produced by the programmer during program development. The fragments are known as textual units and the data base also records the relationships that hold amongst the various textual units and which define the structure of the program being produced. The programmer can recall individual textual units from the data base, identifying them by their role, edit them and re-submit them is order to make program modifications.

The programmer can also request tools to act on the information in the data base. The tools provided in TOPD include one to carry out the exhaustive execution of an abstract piece of code, another which checks the behavior of an algorithm against its state transition model and one by which a COBOL source program is produced from the completed hierarchy of classes.

SYSTEM ORGANIZATION

TOPD is organized as a number of separate programs which service a principal file, called the scratch-pad, on which editing takes place. The process of moving text from the scratch-pad to the data base is known as *connection* and the program (invoked by a TOPD command) which accomplishes the task is called the *connector*.

Figure 1 shows the flow of information when the connector is invoked. Program text, placed on the scratch-pad is copied to the data base only if it is syntactically correct. This syntax check however refers only to information on the scratch-pad, not to information already stored in the data base. The scratch-pad is a standard text file as defined by the host operating system. (This has been the case for both the MTS and VM implementations of TOPD on IBM 360 and 370 systems.) This means that the text editor supplied by the host operating system can be used directly. Figure 2 shows the system with the editor incorporated.

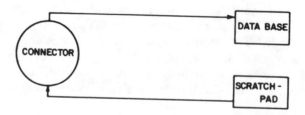

Figure 1: Invoking the connector

Text which is successfully connected to the data base remains on the scratch-pad and must be removed by using the editor or whatever facility the host operating system provides to delete information in a text file.

There is a system program called the *disconnector* which allows the movement of text from the data base to the scratch-pad. The disconnector has quite an extensive command language which enables the identification of the particular set of fragments of text to be moved. Again the process is a copying

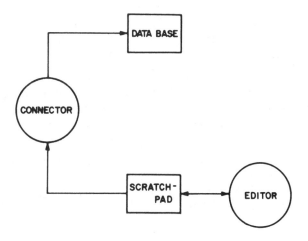

Figure 2: The use of the scratch-pad

one, the text remaining in the data base. The data base is so organized that it is able to keep multiple copies of parts of the program which could be incorporated in different versions of the final program. The process of removing text completely from the data base, called purging, is regarded an infrequent task and is accomplished by a special program intended to be run in batch.

The normal host operating system's capabilities for obtaining listing of the scratch-pad file enables the display of program fragments retrieved by the disconnector.

The complete text stored in the data base at some intermediate point in program development will represent a partially developed program. The data base will also hold however, details of models, as yet, undeveloped components and these models can be used to drive symbolic executions of the partially developed program. These executions are referred to as *'testing'* and *'checking'* and the programs which accomplish them for the user are referred to as the *tester* and the *checker*. As Figure 3 shows both the tester and the checker produce reports.

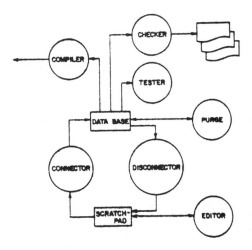

Figure 3: The elements of the TOPD system

Like all the programs shown in Figure 3 they will communicate information which requires immediate attention, directly to the user sitting at his terminal.

Figure 3 shows a notional tool called the compiler. This is not in fact a single program but, for the case of producing COBOL programs, is a sequence of preprocessors which expand the text in the data base into COBOL acceptable to a conventional COBOL compiler. (This tool exists only in rudimentary form in TOPD and hence is not described in detail in this report. Some discussion is included in the section TOPD as a development environment?)

THE DESIGN NOTATION

The program design notation resembles a conventional programming language, with some additional features which allow for the modelling of missing components.

The basic building block of program development is a *class*. Figure 4 shows the encoding of a FILEMERGE program (from (009)).

```
    CLASS FILEMERGE;
        MEMORY VAR(MFILE) F1,F2,F3
            VAR (MRECORD) R1, R2
            VAR (LOGICAL) INORDER;
        MERGE PROCEDURE;
            BODY F1.OPEN; F2.OPEN; F3.OPEN;
                F1.READ(R1);
                F2.READ(R2);
                WHILE R1  = INFINITE OR R2  = INFINITE DO
                BEGIN INORDER. COMPARE (R1, R2);
                    IF INORDER = TRUE THEN
                    BEGIN F3. WRITE (R1);
                        F1.READ (R1)
                    END
                    ELSE
                    BEGIN F3.WRITE(R2);
                        F2.READ (R2)
                    END
                END;
                F1.CLOSE; F2.CLOSE; F3.CLOSE
        END;
```

Figure 4: The FILEMERGE program

The class FILEMERGE represents a high-level abstraction of the problem of file merging. The actual merging algorithm is given as the body of the merge procedure. This describes how the result file (F3) is produced from the input files (F1, F2) by reading and comparing records. The logical, INORDER, records the result of a comparison and determines which record (R1 or R2) is written to F3. The various objects (variables) manipulated within the procedure body are listed as the memory of the class FILEMERGE. This represents the decomposition of the class into more detailed (less abstract) objects.

The notation for representing algorithms is statement based. Except for conditions in control structures, such as the WHILE repetitive construct and the IF alternative construct, statements are of the form,

$$V.p(V_1,...,V_n)$$

being a procedure call where $V, V_1,...,V_n$ are program variables and p is a procedure identifier. The meaning of the statement is, 'call the procedure p and allow it to operate on the variables $V, V_1,......,V_n$. The variable V is specially designated as being the 'owner' of p. Such a variable will have been specified as being of a particular class whose definition will include the specification of the procedure p.

Thus, for example, the statement,

F1.READ (R1)

represents a call on the READ procedure defined in the class MFILE (of which F1 is an instance) acting upon the variables F1 and R1.

The expressions appearing in control structures are boolean expressions testing the condition of the program variables. The notation provides tests for equality ($=$) and non-equality (i.e., satisfying a condition and not satisfying a condition). This notation is taken directly from (005).

It is clear that the program of Figure 4 leads to the identification of other program components. There must exist 3 further classes, namely MFILE, MRECORD, and LOGICAL. (TOPD, and hence the design notation, does not predefine classes such as LOGICAL. The user must provide his own definitions.) Various procedures are associated the these classes. Similarly some conditions are identified for the classes MRECORD and LOGICAL. In TOPD these conditions are represented by *states*.

Figure 5 shows these various observations encoded in the design notation. The design notation allows such skeletal definitions. Here, for example, all the procedure bodies are omitted. These occur quite naturally in an ordered development. Some additional assumptions have been made in Figure 5. Procedure parameters are designated as being VALUE, RESULT or VALUE RESULT. Intuitively the parameter for the READ procedure is a RESULT, whilst that of the WRITE procedure is a VALUE. A state NORMAL is shown for the class MRECORD in addition to the state INFINITE to indicate that there does exist some condition for an MRECORD which is not INFINITE. Similarly a complementary state FALSE is identified for the class LOGICAL. We have used these states in tests in Figure 4.

- CLASS MFILE;
  OPEN PROCEDURE;
  READ PROCEDURE((MRECORD)RESULT R);
  WRITE PROCEDURE((MRECORD)VALUE R);
  CLOSE PROCEDURE;

- CLASS MRECORD;
  STATES INFINITE, NORMAL;

- CLASS LOGICAL;
  STATES TRUE, FALSE;
  COMPARE PROCEDURE((MRECORD)VALUE R1, R2);

Figure 5: The MFILE, MRECORD and LOGICAL classes

The intention of the FILEMERGE program shown in Figure 4 is reasonably clear. However, to indicate more precisely how the program fulfils its function some kind of definition should be provided for each of the procedures it calls. In TOPD such definitions are provided in the form of finite state models.

The actual identification of states for a class has been seen already in Figure 4. The notation also provides for the expression of the state transition model for procedures. An example appears in Figure 6.

This models the COMPARE procedure of the class LOGICAL by describing the transition of states that will occur if the procedure is called. Each part of the transition specifies a condition to be met by the variables being operated upon and the condition in which those variables will be left when the operation is complete. The specification is allowed to be non-deterministic in the sense that the same condition on the input variables can specify different conditions as the result of the operation. In the notation the owning class object is understood within the transition. Thus in Figure 6 the COMPARE procedure is defined whenever the parameters R1 and R2 are in any combination of their states NORMAL and INFINITE and whatever the state of the owning, LOGICAL, object. Invocation of the procedure does not change the state of either R1 or R2 (confirming the use of VALUE in the procedure heading) but

```
LOGICAL.COMPARE PROCEDURE ((MRECORD)VALUE R1,R2);
          TRANSITION
               R1=NORMAL,R2=NORMAL → TRUE:
               R1=NORMAL,R2=NORMAL → FALSE:
               R1=NORMAL,R2=INFINITE → TRUE:
               R1=INFINITE,R2=NORMAL → FALSE;
```

Figure 6: State transition notation

does set the state of the owning, LOGICAL, object. The setting is not uniquely determined for the case when R1 and R2 are both in the state NORMAL. The transition specifies both FALSE and TRUE results in this case. A more complete description of the use of this technique in program development is given in the section on Program Checkout below.

Data structures can be built using the array feature, where, instead of declaring with VAR the form

$$ARRAY \ a : b \ (c) \ v$$

is used.

The FILEMERGE program being used as a vehicle for discussion does not readily provide an example of the use of this feature so Figure 7 gives an illustration from a separate source. This is the representation of a small set of integers (see (005)) by an array of 10 ELEMENTS and a variable COUNT to indicate the number of elements in the set.

```
CLASS SMALLINTSET;
     MEMORY
          ARRAY 1 : 10 (INTEGER) ELEMENTS
          VAR (1 : 10) COUNT
```

Figure 7: The array facility

The array feature introduces the one primitive 'type' whose meaning is understood by TOPD. This is the sub-range type, used here to indicate the domain of the array. The upper and lower bounds are given in the declaration. The variable COUNT is an instance of sub-range and may be used to index the array ELEMENTS.

Sub-range type program variables are considered to have the states

UNDER, a, NORMAL, b, OVER

where a and b represent the limits of the range. An ordering is defined for these states and comparisons can be expressed which appear to this (i.e., expressions which use $>$, $<$, $>=$, $<=$). There are also defined operations associated with sub-ranges to allow initialization etc.

The decomposition of a class also requires that each state of that class is described in terms of states of the classes of which it is composed. This is similar to the association of an algorithm with a procedure except in this case it is the association of an expression with a state.

Figure 8 shows this in the implementation of the class LOGICAL by means of an 0:1 sub-range.

The state TRUE of class LOGICAL is equivalenced to the state 1 of the FLIPFLOP and the state FALSE of class LOGICAL to the state 0 of the FLIPFLOP. The process of decomposition described so far has been purely one of the invention of classes. A notational scheme is provided by which use can be made of concepts from an existing programming language. For example, instead of associating a MEMORY with a class, a COMEMORY may be given whose content expresses the decomposition purely as text from a programming language. Figure 9 shows an example where a class OUTPUTLINE is described by a COMEMORY written in COBOL.

- LOGICAL MEMORY
    VAR (0 : 1) FLIPFLOP;

- LOGICAL.TRUE EQUIV FLIPFLOP = 1;

- LOGICAL.FALSE EQUIV FLIPFLOP = 0;

Figure 8: The use of the EQUIV feature


```
CLASS OUTPUTLINE;
COMEMORY
01      PRINTLINE.
    02      ASA PICTURE X DISPLAY.
    02      TEXT PICTURE X(132) DISPLAY. ;
```

Figure 9: Decomposition expressed in COBOL

THE DATA BASE

As described above the development of a program in TOPD comprises the development of a set of class definitions. Each class definition has the form

Class heading
    states declaration
    states equivalence
    memory declaration
    procedure declaration
    procedure declaration ...
    procedure declaration

and each procedure declaration has the form

    procedure heading
        procedure transition
        procedure body

The programmer, as we have seen, develops class definitions in distinct steps. The development of the FILEMERGE program in the previous section commenced (see Figure 4) with the definition of a class FILEMERGE whose form followed that given above but did not include everything. As development proceeded further classes were recognized (Figure 5) and their definitions extended (Figures 6 and 8). Such a development is typical and illustrates the fact that each of the text fragments which go to make up a class definition are generated at different times.

The TOPD data base is capable of receiving the various text fragments individually or as a group. Each fragment of text (*textual unit*) is stored separately. The relationships between textual units and between textual units and identifiers (the names of classes and procedures) are derived from the input and held in relations in the data base. These relations record the structure of individual class definitions purely as relations amongst pieces of text.

The figure describing the system organization (Figure 3) shows how information is entered into the data base. The user encodes information in the scratch-pad file as text according to the design notation. The connector tool is then invoked to determine the structure of this text and store the information in the appropriate form in the data base.

The figures of the previous section show how the design notation allows both the explicit identification of a relationship between a name and a textual unit and the implicit (contextual) identification of such relationships using the nested definition of class and procedure definitions. For instance, consider the FILEMERGE example (Figure 4).

When this text is submitted to the data base, the connector will recognize a number of textual units and will derive relationships by context. Thus the BODY of the MERGE procedure is recognized as such because it immediately follows the heading of that procedure. That the MERGE procedure is part of the class FILEMERGE is likewise determined by the context of its declaration.

Figure 6 shows the assignation of the COMPARE procedure in the class LOGICAL together with its transition model. Here the relationship between the procedure and the class textual unit representing the transition is contextual.

The data base allows multiple versions of information, time-stamping the arrival of each textual unit and each relationship to provide a distinction mechanism. Thus a procedure may be related, according to the relations held in the data base, to more than one procedure body. It is not, however, possible for one procedure body to be related to more than one procedure. The connector enforces a strict hierarchy.

The programmer may copy information from the data base to a scratch-pad or produce reports by use of the DISCONNECTOR (Figure 3). This tool is driven by appropriate commands which specify, by content, what is to be retrieved.

Figure 10 illustrates the retrieval of the states of the class LOGICAL. The user command is echoed and followed by the appropriate text retrieved from the data base. The information to the left identifies the test uniquely in the data base as there may be more than one textual unit which qualifies as being the 'states of logical'.

```
DATA BASE DISCONNECTION : AUG29, 1975 @ 14:18:27

** COMMAND : STATES LOGICAL

AM AUG-28-10:16    LOGICAL
AM AUG-28-10:16        STATES TRUE, FALSE;
AM AUG-28-10:16    .

** COMMAND : EOF
```

Figure 10: Retrieval of the states of class LOGICAL

The actual textual units, class and procedure names (if appropriate) are also directed to the scratch-pad file. Here the information may be edited by whatever means are provided for text editing by the host operating system and re-connected to the data base. This mode of operation provides a flexible and effective means of program modification.

The disconnector can be directed in its retrieval according to the time-stamps added when information is first stored. This allows the programmer the ability to look at old versions of his program, or to ignore old information. Disconnection (despite its name) does not destroy information held in the data base. A purge facility is provided for this purpose (see Figure 3), its main use being to release space in the data base.

PROGRAM CHECKOUT

The method of program checkout used in TOPD is referred to as finite-state testing. The technicalities of the method are fully described in (009) and (010) which extend and rationalize the concept of executing a partially developed program shown in (011,012).

The checkout feature is based upon the idea of executing the bodies of procedures using only the symbolic values for the variables which are manipulated. The symbolic values used are, in fact, just the states described for the classes of which the variables are members. For this purpose, the states defined for each class are considered to be mutually exclusive. In terms of these states it is possible to specify (or model) the behavior of a procedure by listing the possible changes to the variables it manipulates. This section describes the use of these ideas in TOPD by a pair of tools, the tester and the checker. The FILEMERGE program whose development was started in the preceding sections will be used to illustrate these features.

As shown in Figure 3, the checkout tools operate from information held within the data base. The tester allows the user to nominate a procedure to be tested and to supply a set of starting conditions for the variables operated upon by that procedure.

Figure 11 shows the result of a text execution of the procedure MERGE in the class FILEMERGE considered previously (see Figure 4). No initial values are supplied. The tester carries out an exhaustive 'execution' of the procedure body. The effect of each procedure call appearing in the body is determined by both

- The state transition model for that procedure as defined in the data base, and
- The particular states of the variables acted upon by the call.

Figure 12 defines the state transition models used to define the procedures called by the procedure MERGE.

As an example, the call on the COMPARE procedure at the start of the loop within the body of the MERGE procedure (identified as POINT 5 in the report shown in Figure 11) may be invoked, at different times in the execution, with the variables R1 and R2 being respectively in the states NORMAL and NORMAL, or NORMAL and INFINITE, or INFINITE and NORMAL. The effect in each case will be as defined in the transition for COMPARE for that particular combination of values of its parameters. The report generated by the tester shows this as the set of state combinations associated with POINT 10 immediately following the invocation of COMPARE. Expressions appearing in WHILE loops or IF statements have the effect of partitioning the set of state combinations which appear immediately before the expression according to the acceptability or not of each state combination under the evaluation of the expression. Such partitioning may, of course, be non-deterministic. Examples of deterministic partitioning appear in Figure 11.

The test of the procedure MERGE shown is apparently in order. Three separate results may be produced by the program, namely the two situations where the final record in the output file (F3) was written from either of the input files (F1 and F2), plus the case where neither input file contained any records.

The tester is capable of reporting on a number of different types of 'error' situations. These include checks on unexecuted code (i.e., branches of **if** statements or loops which are never entered and thus have no valid combination of states associated with them), checks on loops which, once entered, will never be left and execution sequences which result in a combination of state values being presented to an operation whose transition does not define an effect.

The tester is a tool by which demonstrations of the execution behavior of a procedure body can be given. An extension of this capability is a tool which checks whether this behavior is acceptable with an expression of the required behavior. In TOPD such checking capability is provided by a tool called the checker. The checker determines whether the transition and the body of a given procedure are consistent in the following sense. A transition defines, for each allowed input, what outputs are produced. Similarly a procedure body defines, for a given input, what are the outputs. The major difference in the case of a procedure body is that the body must be executed in order to determine those outputs. The TOPD terms the necessary exhaustive execution of a procedure body for a given input is exactly fulfilled by the tester tool. The body and the transition of a procedure are said to be consistent if the outputs described by the body for each input defined in the transition are exactly those specified for that input in the transition, except where the state of a variable is not specified in the output in the transition.

In order to illustrate the use of the checker it is necessary to continue the development of the FILEMERGE program a little further. The example which will be given is a check on the procedure READ of the class MFILE.

Figure 13 therefore gives a body to this procedure as part of a detailing process of the class MFILE. The procedure body includes calls on the newly invented procedures READ in the class READER and IOBECOMES and SETINFINITE in the class MRECORD. (The parameter of the MFILE.READ procedure is of the class MRECORD.) States are assigned to the new classes and transitions given to define the effect of the new procedures. To complete this stage of the development, the states of the class MFILE are expressed in terms of the states of the variables in the MEMORY of MFILE.

- MFILE
  MEMORY VAR(READER) RDR
       VAR (WRITER) WTR
       VAR (IOREC) IOBUFFER
       VAR (LOGICAL) E.KFILEFLAG;

- MFILE.READ
  BODY RDR.READ (IOBUFFER,E.KFILEFLAG);
     IF E.KFILEFLAG = TRUE THEN
          R.IOBECOMES(IOBUFFER)
     ELSE
          R.SETINFINITE
  END;

- CLASS READER;
  STATES READY,EXHAUSTED,CLOSED;
  READ PROCEDURE ((IOREC) RESULT R;
                   (LOGICAL) RESULT EOF);
       TRANSITION
          READY → READY, R=VALID,EOF=FALSE:
          READY → EXHAUSTED, R=VALID,EOF=TRUE;

- CLASS WRITER;
  STATES READY,CLOSED;

- CLASS IOREC;
  STATES VALID,INVALID;

- MRECORD.IOBECOMES PROCEDURE ((IOREC)VALUE IOR);
  TRANSITION
       IOR=VALID →   NORMAL;

- MRECORD.SETINFINITE PROCEDURE;
  TRANSITION
  → INFINITE;

- MFILE.OPENED EQUIV RDR=READY AND WTR=READY;

- MFILE.READEXHAUSTED EQUIV RDR=EXHAUSTED;

- MFILE.CLOSED EQUIV RDR=CLOSED AND WTR=CLOSED;

Figure 13: Detailing of the class MFILE

The READ procedure of MFILE can now be checked. The report of this check is shown in Figure 14.

Firstly, a listing of the body is given showing program points for possible later reference. Next the checker invokes a test using as input the first input specified in the transition (i.e., that MFILE =

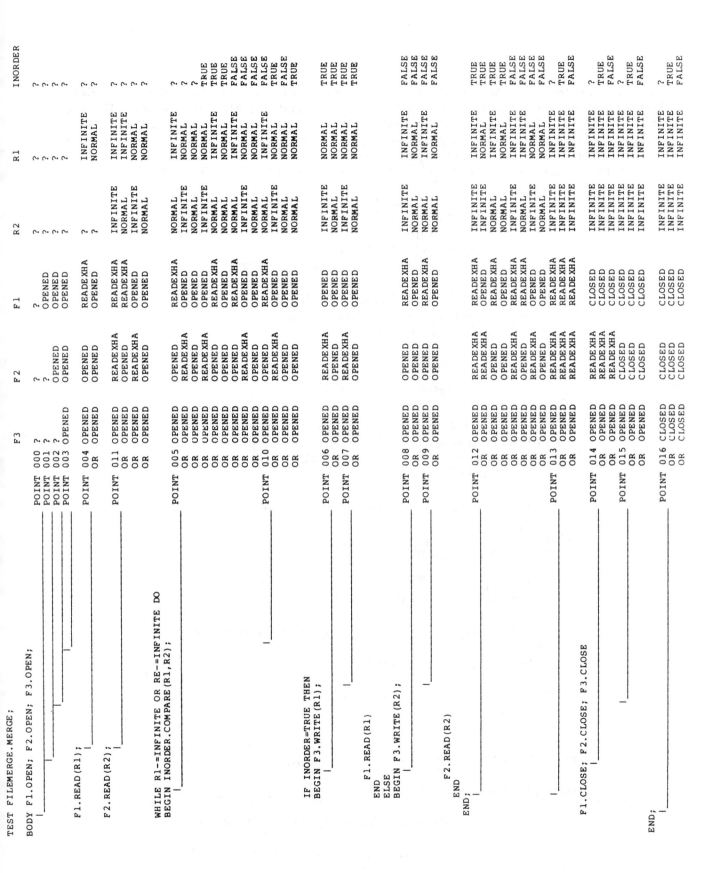

Figure 11: Test execution of the MERGE procedure

437

```
CLASS MFILE;
        STATES OPENED, READEXHAUSTED,CLOSED;
        OPEN PROCEDURE;
          TRANSITION
            → OPENED;
        READ PROCEDURE ((MRECORD) RESULT MR);
          TRANSITION
            OPENED → OPENED,MR=NORMAL;
            OPENED → READEXHAUSTED,MR=INFINITE;
        WRITE PROCEDURE ((MRECORD)VALUE MR);
          TRANSITION
            OPENED,MR=NORMAL → OPENED;
        CLOSE PROCEDURE;
          TRANSITION
            OPENED → CLOSED;
            READEXHAUSTED → CLOSED;


    CLASS MRECORD;
        STATES NORMAL, INFINITE;


    LOGICAL.COMPARE PROCEDURE ((MRECORD)VALUE R1,R2);
            TRANSITION
                R1=NORMAL,R2=NORMAL → TRUE:
                R1=NORMAL,R2=NORMAL → FALSE:
                R1=NORMAL,R2=INFINITE → TRUE:
                R1=INFINITE,R2=NORMAL → FALSE;
```

Figure 12: State transition model for procedures called by MERGE

OPENED). This output condition is transformed by using the appropriate equiv (see Figure 13) to an input condition over the variables manipulated in the body (i.e., RDR=READY). The test is carried out and a report given. In this case the report consists solely of the 2 vectors of state values produced by the body as output. (In other cases various tester messages may be given.) Next the checker returns to the transition to determine what outputs had been described for this input. In this case there are 2 possible outcomes and each is transformed as above so as to be re-specified in terms of the variables in the body. A check is now made to ensure that:

```
CHECK MFILE.READ:
*** LISTING OF BODY WITH PROGRAM POINTS ***
      BODY RDR.READ(IOBUFFER,ENDFILEFLAG);
            |_____POINT 000
                                                          |__POINT 003
            IF ENDFILEFLAG=TRUE THEN
                        |_____POINT 001
                  MR.IOBECOMES(IOBUFFER)
            ELSE
                  |_____POINT 002
                  MR.SETINFINITE
         END;
            |_____POINT 004
```

```
** ENTRY SPECIFICATION: MFILE=OPENED,MR=?
      EQUIVALENT TO:     RDR=READY,IOBUFFER=?,ENDFILEFLAG=?,MR=?


** EXERCISE REPORT

   EXERCISE PRODUCES:    RDR=READY,IOBUFFER=VALID,
                         ENDFILEFLAG=FALSE,MR=NORMAL
                      OR RDR=EXHAUSTED,IOBUFFER=INVALID,
                         ENDFILEFLAG=TRUE,MR=INFINITE

** RESULT REQUIRED:      MFILE=OPENED,MR=NORMAL
      EQUIVALENT TO:     RDR=READY,IOBUFFER=?,ENDFILEFLAG=?,
                         MR=NORMAL
   REQUIRED RESULT PRODUCED

** RESULT REQUIRED:      MFILE=READEXHAUSTED,MR=INFINITE
      EQUIVALENT TO:     RDR=EXHAUSTED,IOBUFFER=?,ENDFILEFLAG=?,
                         MR=INFINITE
   REQUIRED RESULT PRODUCED

                  * * * * * * * * * *

** BODY AND TRANSITION ARE CONSISTENT
```

Figure 14: Checking of the READ procedure

• Each of the outputs specified in the transition is produced by the body

• No other outputs are produced by the body.

As Figure 14 shows, everything checks out satisfactorily in this case, there only being the one input specified in the transition. If there had been more inputs specified in the transition the whole cycle of testing the body and checking of the outputs produced would be repeated.

The checker tool provides the means by which the behavior of the whole program under development can be maintained as the behavior of its parts. The test of the MERGE procedure described above demonstrated a behavior which assumes the behavior of the procedures it invoked as being as described by their transitions. The checker is a tool which demonstrates that the behavior of some implementation of one of these procedures is consistent with this assumption. That is, if the MERGE procedure was executed and the procedures it called properly invoked rather than modelled, then the behavior would be similar.

Program checkout in TOPD allows the testing of programs which use arrays and sub-ranges. Array bound checking, for example, is carried out by checking that the sub-range index is not in either of the states UNDER or OVER.

TOPD AS A DEVELOPMENT ENVIRONMENT?

The tools provided by TOPD are of most use in the later stages of program development. Since they support abstract programming and, in particular, hierarchical development, they can be used (more easily) at an earlier stage than the tools of more conventional environments. It is, however, worthwhile considering how much the various tools do contribute to improving the program development process and to generalize such comment to include and relate to other approaches and systems that are available. Comment is also necessary about the things that TOPD itself does not support but which might be desirable in such an environment.

The design notation is capable of a useful compromise between the precision of expression that is usually required in programming languages and the abstract expression which is a necessity when a program is being designed. It is however, not ideal and on occasion it is necessary to make use of abstractions which are neither completely obvious nor natural. For example it is not clear in Figure 13 that the procedure IOBECOMES should belong to the class MRECORD. It could be argued that this procedure belongs to the class IOREC or that the procedure should belong to neither. There are other restrictions which arise from the purely hierarchic program decomposition process. Such restrictions are a result of the particular method of development for which TOPD was intended to provide support. Currently this approach has the major benefit of being reasonably well understood and accepted whilst remaining acceptably close to what the good programmer usually does.

The notation allows a full mechanical interpretation along with a degree of naturalness of expression. This does, however, mean that the notation introduces a level of rigidity that is not always seen in examples of structured programming. As the tools are programming tools rather than design aids this is correct. As is argued in (003), one of the failings of many conventional programming languages is that they are inappropriate to represent the developing program. This should not mean that the only appropriate medium for expression is a completely free language devoid of more than passing resemblance to any programming language. Such expression can only have its place much earlier in the software design process.

Use of TOPD does not demand a top-down programming method although the tools encourage it. The tools do provide an environment in which disciplined development can easily take place and by which the quality of the program being developed can be improved. That the discipline is very much concerned with the actual program design activity is apparent when methods such as (019) or (020) are considered. These approaches tend to find their place much earlier in the development process.

The use of a data base to hold information about the developing program and from which the various tools operate provides many benefits. The scheme is not unique and may be seen in other program development support systems (016,008). In particular in TOPD the retention in the data base of information by its logical position in the program structure makes it unnecessary for the programmer to concern himself about file names or other schemes by which such information is conventionally stored. This not only reduces clerical effort but removes a source of typical programming error. The granularity of the information held by TOPD was chosen to be large enough to allow a reasonable degree of syntactic check to be made on data base update, but not so large as to require large amounts of program design to be carried out before text can be inserted. In practice the allowed textual units represent a reasonable division of a class into its constituent parts. Holding development information in a data base provides a degree of uniformity in the way that information is represented and, in large developments is a good means of control. The TOPD data base itself is not a particularly good example of such use. Systems which provide more include (021) and (018).

Experience with TOPD (022) has shown that it is probably necessary that there be a tool operating on the data base which checks for completeness and consistency in the information on a wider scale than is provided by the program checkout facilities. It would report on missing information (e.g., procedures without bodies, classes without memories) as well as inconsistencies such as mismatched parameter types. In large-scale use of program development data bases the usefulness of such a tool is readily apparent.

The data base support for versions of a program is useful, especially in the context of modelling where different models can be held to allow checks to be made on different aspects of the program and also for developing families of programs, members of which differ in some detail. However, the actual mechanism provided by TOPD (a time window) is altogether too naive. In large systems development the problem of versions demands very special attention (023).

The program checkout features of TOPD are a practical compromise between conventional testing techniques and complete automatic program proving. As is described in (010) and (022), the finite state modelling technique tends to err on the side of caution in detecting program 'faults', due to the local context of any model. However, TOPD has demonstrated that the technique does not require explosive amounts of machine time or space to complete its task. This is, probably, because the design notation discourages the use of elaborate models allied to the fact that in developing programs in TOPD testing is performed as each new component is added. Modelling offers significant advantages over schemes for testing incomplete programs which involve intervention by the programmer (011,012,013) in an interactive environment or the provision of 'dummy' procedures which simulate the incomplete parts (024). These advantages include the not insignificant one of providing a well-defined behavioral model against which implementations can be checked. Riddle (017) is experimenting with a set of program support tools based on TOPD but including more sophisticated modelling and checking techniques.

TOPD does not provide very powerful tools for generating a complete program from the data base. COBOL programs may be produced provided that the programmer has encoded class memories and procedure bodies in COBOL language statements. These are then compounded together in the appropriate manner to form a COBOL program (022). Such a scheme does not provide any flexibility in the way the various components are compounded. The major structure of the program is, of course, defined by the class hierarchy. A program development data base could, however, be viewed as a store of software objects which can be structured to form many programs, each structure also being contained in the data base. This is the view taken by the GAMMA project (008). The CADES system (016) currently provides some flexibility in program composition and it is being developed (023) to allow more.

The TOPD environment could also be considered deficient in terms of the facilities that could be provided. More sophisticated program analysis aids and maintenance of data describing development status (e.g., tested, excepted) are particular areas where assistance may be worthwhile. These and others are described in (025).

SUMMARY

TOPD is a system of tools designed to assist in the structured development of programs. In particular the tools are a notation for writing abstract programs, a data base for maintaining the program during development and a scheme for modelling which enables partially developed programs to be checked by symbolic execution. TOPD is aimed at reducing the complexity of program development by providing support in those areas where the source of complexity is not derived primarily from the problem area of the program. Some of these areas are covered more completely than others, the most notable deficiencies being the control of large amounts of information and the flexible generation of completed programs ready for execution.

REFERENCES

001 DIJKSTRA E W, *Notes on structured programming* In *Structured programming* O-J Dahl, E. W. Dijkstra, and C. A. R. Hoare (eds) Academic Press London (1972).

002 LONDON R L, *A view of program verification* Proc Intl Conf on *Reliable software* pp 534-545, (April 1975).

003 HENDERSON P and SNOWDON R A, *A tool for structured program development* Proc IFIP Congress Stockholm Information Processing '74 North-Holland Publ Co pp 204-207 (1974).

004 WIRTH N, *Program development by stepwise refinement* CACM vol 14 no 4 (April 1974).

005 HOARE C A R, *Proof of correctness of data representations* Acta Informatica vol 1, (1974).

006 LISKOV B H, *An introduction to CLU* In *New directions in algorithmic languages* S. A. Schuman (ed) IRIA Paris, (1975).

007 WULF W A, LONDON R L and SHAW M, *Abstraction and verification in Alphard* In *New directions in algorithmic languages* S. A. Schuman (ed) IRIA Paris, (1975).

008 FALLA M E, PEARCE D J and PIERCE R H, *The GAMMA design and programming system* EUROCOMP '76 on *Software systems engineering* On-line Uxbridge UK (1976).

009 HENDERSON P and QUARENDON P, *Finite state testing of structured programs* Colloque sur la Programmation Paris, (April 1974) Programming Symposium Lecture Notes in Computer Science vol 19, Springer-Verlag.

010 HENDERSON P, *Finite state modelling in program development* Proc Intl Conf on *Reliable software* '(April 1975).

011 SNOWDON R A, *PEARL. a system for the preparation and validation of structured programs* In *Program test methods* W C Hetzel (ed) Prentice-Hall Englewood Cliffs NJ (1973).

012 SNOWDON R A, *Interactive use of a computer in the preparation of structured programs* PhD Thesis Univ of Newcastle-upon-Tyne, (1974).

013 CUNNINGHAM R J and PUGH C G, *A language-independent system to aid the development of structured programs* Software P&E vol 6 pp 485-503, (1976).

014 CUNNINGHAM R J and PUGH C G, *An approach to the support of successive refinement in the construction of verified programs* Publ no 77/6 Dept of Computing and Control Imperial College, London, (1977).

015 LAMPSON B W, HORNING J J, LONDON R, MITCHELL J G and POPEK G J, *Report on the programming language EUCLID* SIGPLAN Notices vol 12 no 2, (Feb 1977).

016 PEARSON D J, *CADES - Computer-Aided Design and Evaluation System* Computer Weekly (July/Aug 1973).

017 RIDDLE W E, SAYER J H, SEGAL A R and WILEDEN J C, *An introduction to the DREAM Software Design System* RSSM/33 Dept of Computer and Communication Sciences Univ. of Michigan, (May 1977).

018 TEICHROEW D and HERSHEY E A, *PSL/PSA: a computer-aided technique for structured documentation and analysis of information processing systems* IEEE Trans on Software engineering vol SE-3 no 1 (Jan 1977).

019 JA.KFON M A, *Principles of program design* Academic Press London (1975).

020 DIJKSTRA E W, *A discipline of programming* Prentice-Hall Inc Englewood Cliffs NJ (1976).

021 FALLA M E and BURNS D, *Software development systems* Datafair '73 Conf Papers vol 1 Business Papers pp 166-173 British Computer Society (1973).

022 HENDERSON P, SNOWDON R A, GORRIE J D, and KING I I, *The TOPD System* Computing Laboratory Univ. of Newcastle-upon-Tyne Tech Rep TR77 (Sept 1975).

023 PRATTEN G D and SNOWDON R A, *CADES - support for the development of complex software* In *Software systems engineering* EUROCOMP 1976 On-line Uxbridge UK

024 BAKER F T, *Chief Programmer Team management of production programming* IBM Syst J vol 11 no 1 pp 56-73 (1972).

025 BOEHM B W, *Software engineering* IEEE Trans on Computers C-25 no 12 pp 1226-1241 (1975).

BIBLIOGRAPHY OF TUTORIAL PAPERS

1. Jack R. Distaso, "Software Management—Survey of the Practice in 1980," *Proceedings of the IEEE,* Vol. 68, No. 9 (September 1980), pp. 1103-1119.

2. William C. Cave and Alan B. Salisbury, "Controlling the Software Life Cycle—The Project Management Task," *IEEE Transactions on Software Engineering,* Vol. SE-4, No. 4 (July 1978), pp. 326-334.

3. Barry W. Boehm, "Software Engineering," *IEEE Transactions on Computers,* Vol. C-25, No. 12 (December 1976).

4. *Structured Walk-Throughs: A Project Management Tool,* IBM Corporation (August 1973).

5. Edward Yourdon, "Top-Down Design and Testing," in *How to Manage Structured Programming,* Chapter 3, Yourdon, Inc., New York (1976), pp. 31-52.

6. David Gries, "On Structured Programming," in *Programming Methodology,* Springer-Verlag, New York (1978), pp. 70-74.

7. F. Terry Baker, "Structured Programming in a Production Programming Environment," *IEEE Transactions on Software Engineering,* Vol. SE-1, No. 2 (June 1975), pp. 241-252.

8. David L. Parnas, "Designing Software for Ease of Extension and Contraction," *IEEE Transactions on Software Engineering,* Vol. SE-5, No. 2 (March 1979), pp. 128-137.

9. Michael A. Jackson, "Constructive Methods of Program Design," *Lecture Notes in Computer Science,* G. Goos and J. Hartmanis, eds., Springer-Verlag, New York (1976), pp. 236-262.

10. Michael A. Jackson, "Information Systems: Modelling, Sequencing and Transformations," *Proceedings of the Third International Conference on Software Engineering,* Atlanta, Georgia (1978), pp. 72-81.

11. John R. Cameron, "Two Pairs of Examples in the Jackson Approach to System Development," *15th Hawaii International Conference on System Sciences,* Honalulu, Hawaii (January 1982).

12. Kenneth T. Orr, "Introducing Structured Systems Design," Infotech State of the Art Report, *Structured Analysis and Design,* Vol. II, Infotech International, Maidenhead, England (1978), pp. 3-23.

13. Kenneth T. Orr, "Using Structured Systems Design," in *Structured Systems Development,* Yourdon Press, New York (1977), pp. 81-106.

14. W. P. Stevens, G. J. Myers, and L. L. Constantine, "Structured Design," *IBM Systems Journal,* Vol. 13, No. 2 (1974), pp. 115-139.

15. Meilir Page-Jones, "Transform Analysis," in *The Practical Guide to Structured Systems Design,* Yourdon Press, New York (1980), pp. 181-203.

16. Meilir Page-Jones, "Transaction Analysis," in *The Practical Guide to Structured Systems Design,* Yourdon Press, New York (1980), pp. 207-219.

17. David Gries, "An Illustration of Current Ideas on the Derivation of Correctness Proofs and Correct Programs," *IEEE Transactions on Software Engineering,* Vol. SE-2, No. 4 (December 1976), pp. 238-244. Correction, *IEEE Transactions on Software Engineering,* Vol. SE-3, No. 3 (May 1977), p. 262.

18. Jay M. Spitzen, Karl N. Levitt, and Lawrence Robinson, "An Example of Hierarchical Design and Proof," *Communications of the ACM,* Vol. 21, No. 12 (December 1978), pp. 1064-1075.

19. Gilles Kahn and David B. MacQueen, "Coroutines and Networks of Parallel Processes," *IFIP Congress Proceedings,* Toronto, Canada (1977), pp. 993-998.

20. C. A. R. Hoare, "Communicating Sequential Processes," *Communications of the ACM,* Vol. 21, No. 8 (August 1978), pp. 666-677.

21. Per Brinch Hansen, "Distributed Processes: A Concurrent Programming Concept," *Communications of the ACM,* Vol. 21, No. 11 (November 1978), pp. 934-941.

22. Glenn D. Bergland, "A Guided Tour of Program Design Methodologies," *Computer,* IEEE Computer Society, Los Alamitos, California (October 1981).

23. Lawrence J. Peters and Leonard L. Tripp, "Comparing Software Design Methodologies," *Datamation,* Vol. 23, No. 11 (November 1977), pp. 89-94.

24. S. N. Griffiths, "Design Methodologies—A Comparison," Infotech State of the Art Report, *Structured Analysis and Design,* Vol. II, Infotech International, Maidenhead, England (1978), pp. 133-166.

25. E. L. Ivie, "The Programmer's Workbench—A Machine for Software Development," *Communications of the ACM,* Vol. 20 (October 1977), pp. 746-753.

26. Mack W. Alford, "Software Requirements Engineering Methodology (SREM) at the Age of Four," *Computer Software and Applications Conference,* Chicago, Illinois (October 1980), pp. 866-874.

27. Daniel Teichroew and Ernest A. Hershey, III, "PSL/PSA: A Computer-Aided Technique for Structured Documentation and Analysis of Information Processing Systems," *IEEE Transactions on Software Engineering,* Vol. SE-3, No. 1 (January 1977), pp. 41-48.

28. Douglas T. Ross, "Structured Analysis (SA): A Language for Communicating Ideas," *IEEE Transactions on Software Engineering,* Vol. SE-3, No. 1 (January 1977), pp. 16-34.

29. M. E. Dickover, C. L. McGowan, Douglas T. Ross, "Software Design Using SADT," Infotech State of the Art Report, *Structured Analysis and Design,* Vol. II, Infotech International, Maidenhead, England (1978), pp. 101-114.

30. P. Van Leer, "Top-Down Development Using a Program Design Language," *IBM Systems Journal,* Vol. 15, No. 2 (1976), pp. 155-170.

31. R. A. Snowdon and P. Henderson, "The TOPD System for Computer-Aided System Development," Infotech State of the Art Report, *Structured Analysis and Design,* Vol. II, Infotech International, Maidenhead, England (1978), pp. 285-305.

PROGRAM DESIGN LIBRARY

The Program Design Library is a collection of current texts which cover in detail the areas of programming management, software design strategies, and support tools. Those wishing to pursue in greater detail the topics introduced in this tutorial may wish to consult the following texts. Together, these books attempt to cover the complete spectrum of ideas on program design strategies.

3rd International Conference on Software Engineering. IEEE, Inc., New York, 1978.

Aho, Alfred V., Hopcroft, John E., and Ullman, Jeffry D., *The Design and Analysis of Computer Algorithms.* Addison-Wesley Publishing Co., Reading, 1977.

Anderson, Robert B., *Proving Programs Correct.* John Wiley & Sons, Inc., New York, 1979.

Anderson, T., and Randell B., eds., *Computing Systems Reliability.* Cambridge University Press, New York, 1979.

Aron, Joel D., *The Program Development Process* Part I—The Individual Programmer, Part II—The Programming Team. Addison-Wesley Publishing Co., Reading, 1974.

Basili, Victor R., and Baker, Terry, *Structured Programming: A Tutorial.* IEEE, Inc., New York, 1977.

Biggs, C. L., Birks, E. G., and Atkins, W. A., *Managing the Systems Development Process.* Prentice-Hall, Inc., Englewood Cliffs, 1980.

Boehm, Barry W., Brown, John R., Kaspar, Hans, Lipow, Myron, Macleod, Gordon J., and Merrit, Michael J., *Characteristics of Software Quality.* Elsevier North-Holland, Inc., New York, 1978.

Bauer, F. L., ed., *Software Engineering,* Springer-Verlag, New York, 1975.

Brinch Hansen, Per, *The Architecture of Concurrent Programs. Prentice-Hall, Englewood Cliffs, 1977.*

Brooks, F. P., Jr., *The Mythical Man-Month: Essays on Software Engineering.* Addison-Wesley Publishing Co., Reading, 1975.

Dahl, O. -J., Dijkstra, E. W., and Hoare, C. A. R., *Structured Programming.* Academic Press, Inc., New York, 1972. (see also Knuth, Donald E., *A Review of "Structured Programming."* Stanford University, Computer Science Department, STAN-CS-73-371, June 1973)

DeMarco, Tom, *Structured Analysis and System Specification.* Yourdon, Inc., New York, 1979.

Dijkstra, E. W., *A Discipline of Programming.* Prentice-Hall, Inc., Englewood Cliffs, 1976.

Donaldson, Hamish, *A Guide to the Successful Management of Computer Projects.* John Wiley & Sons, Inc., New York, 1978.

Freeman, Peter, and Wasserman, Anthony I., *Tutorial on Software Design Techniques.* IEEE, Inc., New York, 1977.

Gane, Chris, and Sarson, Trish, *Structured Systems Analysis: Tools & Techniques.* Improved System Technologies, Inc., New York, 1977.

Glass, Robert L., *Software Reliability Guidebook.* Prentice-Hall, Inc., Englewood Cliffs, 1979.

Gries, David, ed., *Programming Methodology—A Collection of Articles by Members of IFIP WG2.3.* Springer-Verlag, New York, 1978.

Hice, G. F., Turner, W. W., and Cashwell, L. F., *System Development Methodology,* Elsevier North-Holland, Inc., New York, 1978.

Holt, R. C., *et. al., Structured Concurrent Programming with Operating Systems Applications.* Addison-Wesley Publishing Co., Reading, 1975.

Horowitz, Ellis, *Practical Strategies for Developing Large Software Systems.* Addison-Wesley Publishing Co., Reading, 1975.

Hughes, J. K., and Mitchtom, J. I., *Structured approach to programming.* Prentice-Hall, Inc., Englewood Cliffs, 1977.

Jackson, Michael A., *Principles of Program Design.* Academic Press, New York, 1975.

Jensen, R. W., and Tonies, C. C, *Software Engineering.* Prentice-Hall, Inc., Englewood Cliffs, 1979.

Kraft, P., *Programmers and Managers: The Routinization of Computer Programming in the United States.* Springer-Verlag, New York, 1977.

Katzan, Harry J. Jr., *Systems Design and Documentation: An Introduction to the HIPO Method.* Van Nostrand Reinhold Co., New York, 1976.

Metzger, Philip W., *Managing a Programming Project.* Prentice-Hall, Inc., Englewood Cliffs, 1973.

Miller, E., and Howden, W. E., *Software Testing and Validation Techniques.* IEEE, Inc., New York, 1978.

Miller, E., *Tutorial on Program Testing Techniques.* IEEE, Inc., New York, 1978.

Miller, E. *Tutorial: Automated Tools for Software Engineering.* IEEE, Inc., New York, 1979.

Myers, Glenford J., *Reliable Software through Composite Design.* Van Nostrand Reinhold Co., New York, 1975.

Myers, Glenford J., *Software Reliability, Principles & Practices.* John Wiley & Sons, Inc., New York, 1976.

Orr, Kenneth T., *Structured Systems Development*. Yourdon Press, New York, 1977.

Page-Jones, Meilir, *The Practical Guide to Structured Systems Design*, Yourdon Press, New York, 1980.

Peters, Lawrence J., *Software Design: Methods and Techniques*, Yourdon Press, New York, 1981.

Ramamoorthy, C. V., and Yeh, Raymond T., *Tutorial: Software Methodology*. IEEE, Inc., New York, 1978.

Riddle, W. E., and Wileden, J. C., *Tutorial on Software System Design: Description and Analysis*. IEEE, Inc., New York, 1980.

Structured Programming—Independent Study Program. IBM, Corp., Poughkeepsie, New York, 1975.

Structured Programming. Infotech State of the Art Report. Infotech International, Maidenhead, England, 1976.

Software Engineering Techniques. Infotech State of the Art Report. Volume 1: Analysis and Bibliography; Volume 2: Invited Papers. Infotech International, Maidenhead, England, 1977.

Structured Analysis and Design. Infotech State of the Art Report. Volume 1: Analysis and bibliography; Volume 2: Invited Papers. Infotech International, Maidenhead, England, 1978.

Swann, G. H., *Top-down Structured Design Techniques*. Petrocelli/Charter, Inc., New York, 1978.

Tausworthe, Robert C., *Standardized Development of Computer Software* Part I—Methodology, Part II—Standards. Prentice-Hall, Inc., Englewood Cliffs, 1979.

Turski, W. M., *Computer Programming Methodology*. Heyden and Son, Ltd., Philadelphia, 1978.

Warnier, Jean Dominique, *Logical Construction of Programs*. Van Nostrand Reinhold Co., New York, 1974.

Wasserman, Anthony I., and Freeman, Peter, *Software Engineering Education*, Springer-Verlag, New York, 1976.

Weinberg, Gerald M., *The Psychology of Computer Programming*. Van Nostrand Reinhold Co., New York, 1971.

Weinberg, Victor, *Structured Analysis*. Yourdon, Inc., New York, 1978.

Weiss, Paul A., *Hierarchically Organized Systems in Theory & Practice*. Hafner Publishing Co., Inc., New York, 1971.

Wirth, Niklaus, *Systematic Programming: An Introduction*. Prentice-Hall, Inc., Englewood Cliffs, 1973.

Wirth, Niklaus, *Algorithms + Data Structures = Programs*. Prentice-Hall, Inc., Englewood Cliffs, 1976.

Yeh, Raymond, T., ed., *Current trends in Programming Methodology.* Volume I: Software Specification and Design; Volume II: Program Validation; Volume III: Software Modeling; Volume IV: Data Structuring. Prentice-Hall, Inc., Englewood Cliffs, 1977.

Yourdon, Edward, *Techniques of Program Structure and Design.* Prentice Hall, Inc., Englewood Cliffs, 1975.

Yourdon, Ed, *How to Manage Structured Programming.* Yourdon, Inc., New York, 1976.

Yourdon, Edward, and Constantine, Larry L., *Structured Design.* Yourdon Press, New York, 1978.

Yourdon, Edward, *Structured Walk-Throughs.* Yourdon, Inc., New York, 1978.

Zelkowitz, M. V., Shaw, A. C., and Gannon, J. D., *Principles of Software Engineering and Design.* Prentice-Hall, Inc., Englewood Cliffs, 1979.

AUTHOR AND PERMUTED TITLE INDEX

References to selected articles published during 1979 and 1980 in the area of software design strategies are listed in the following indices. A complete reference to the article is given in the first index. The second index contains the permuted title index; the third provides an alphabetical list of all authors whose papers were referenced. A unique sequence number, listed with the complete reference in the first index, is used to identify the articles within the second and third indices.■

0001   AFIPS CONFERENCE PROCEEDINGS. 1980 NATIONAL COMPUTER CONFERENCE.
                 SAC 1981: 005529

0002   SOFTWARE DESIGN AND TESTING.
         MANAGE INF NO 7-8: 427-32 (JULY-AUG 1980) (IN ITALIAN)
                 SAC 1981: 005221

0003   TESTING LAB CUSTOMIZES MINI, DESIGNS PROGRAMS FROM END USER PERSPECTIVE.
         DATA MANAGE 18(7): 19-20 (JULY 1980)
                 SAC 1981: 002533

0004   PROCEEDINGS OF THE SYMPOSIUM ON FORMAL DESIGN METHODOLOGY. 1979.
                 SAC 1980: 024228

0005   MEDICAL INFORMATICS BERLIN 1979.
                 SAC 1980: 022035

0006   AGARD CONFERENCE PROCEEDINGS NO. 272. ADVANCES IN GUIDANCE AND CONTROL SYSTEMS USING DIGITAL TECHNIQUES.
         1979.
                 SAC 1980: 020878

0007   SOFTWARE DESIGN METHODOLOGY IN ITALY.
         SIST AUTOM NO 197 SUPPL: 32-5 (OCT 1979) (IN ITALIAN)
                 SAC 1980: 012816

0008   PDL (PROGRAM DESIGN LANGUAGE).
         SIST AUTOM NO 197 SUPPL: 29-30 (OCT 1979) (IN ITALIAN)
                 SAC 1980: 012813

0009   JACKSON METHOD.
         SIST AUTOM NO 197 SUPPL: 26-7 (OCT 1979) (IN ITALIAN)
                 SAC 1980: 012811

0010   WELL MADE SYSTEM DESIGN METHODOLOGY.
         SIST AUTOM NO 197 SUPPL: 23-4 (OCT 1979) (IN ITALIAN)
                 SAC 1980: 012809

0011   COLLOQUIUM ON TEACHING SOFTWARE DESIGN TECHNIQUES FOR MICROPROCESSORS. 1979.
                 SAC 1980: 006968

0012   PROGRAM DESIGN TECHNIQUES.
         EDP ANAL 17(3): 1-13 (MARCH 1979)
                 SAC 1979: 024245

0013   TRENDS IN ONLINE COMPUTER CONTROL SYSTEMS.
                 SAC 1979: 011869

0014   IMPLEMENTATION OF THE CDCA-NICE SOFTWARES PACKAGE IN SOME ITALIAN INSTITUTES.
         ACAMPA E + FALCIANI R + PITTELLA GC + SAMBUCO AM
         MEM SOC ASTRON ITAL 50(3): 359-61 (SEPT 1979) (IN ITALIAN)
                 CAPODIMONTE ASTRON OBS, NAPLES, ITALY
                 SAA 1980: 098561

0015   ENHANCING EASE OF USE OF ARRAY PROCESSORS THROUGH SOFTWARE DESIGN.
         ALEXANDER P
         IND RES/DEV 22(5): 11-14 (MAY 1980)
                 CSP INC, BILLERICA, MA,
                 SAC 1980: 032850

0016   A FORMAL DESCRIPTION OF THE DTE PACKET LEVEL IN THE X.25 RECOMMENDATION (FOR COMPUTER NETWORKS).
         ALFONZETTI S + CASALE S + FARO A
         ALTA FREQ 48(8): 513-22 (AUG 1979)
                 ISTITUTO ELETTROTECNICO, UNIV DI CATANIA, CATANIA, ITALY
                 SAB 1979: 048408

0017   FOLLOW THREE SIMPLE RULES TO IMPROVE SOFTWARE PRODUCTIVITY.
         ALLISON A
         EDN 25(6): 167-71 (20 MARCH 1980)
                 SAC 1980: 030810

0018   A MODEL FOR AUTOMATING FILE AND PROGRAM DESIGN IN BUSINESS APPLICATION SYSTEMS.
         ALTER S
         COMMUN ACM 22(6): 345-53 (JUNE 1979)
                 STEVEN ALTER AND ASSOCIATES INC, SAN FRANCISCO, CA,
                 SAC 1979: 024274

0019   EFFECTIVENESS OF A COMPUTER BASED FEEDBACK SYSTEM FOR WRITING.
         ANANDAM K + EISEL E + KOTLER L
         J COMPUT-BASED INSTR 6(4): 125-33 (MAY 1980)
                 MIAMI-DADE COMMUNITY COLL, MIAMI, FL,
                 SAC 1981: 006240

0020   POWER SYSTEM MONITORING AND CONTROL SOFTWARE FOR THE CEGB.
         ANNESS DL + PETERS GC + WARD SD + FLEMING M
         P170-4 OF INT CONF ON POWER SYSTEM MONITORING CONTROL LONDON, ENGLAND, 24-26 JUNE 1980, IEE, LONDON,
         ENGLAND, 1980
                 SAB 1980: 042116

0021   A NEW SWITCHING PROCESSING ARCHITECTURE AND ITS OPERATING SYSTEM FOR A DISTRIBUTED HIERARCHY SOFTWARE
        STRUCTURE.
        ARIMA T - KOBAYASHI H - MAKINO H - ASO T
        P943-7 OF INT SWITCHING SYMP, PARIS, FRANCE, 7-11 MAY 1979 COLLOQUE INT DE LA COMMUNICATION, PARIS,
        FRANCE, 1979
                    NEC, TOKYO, JAPAN
                    SAB 1981: 002687

0022   SOFTWARE FOR MICROPROCESSOR CONTROL OF MECHANICAL EQUIPMENT.
        AUSLANDER DM - DORNFIELD D - SAGUES P
        P71-7 OF PROC OF THE 1979 JOINT AUTOMATIC CONTROL CONF, DENVER CO, 17-21 JUNE 1979, AMERICAN INST CHEM
        ENGRS, NEW YORK, 1979
                    UNIV OF CALIFORNIA, BERKELEY, CA,
                    SAC 1980: 001063

0023   SOFTWARE DOCUMENTATION AND MANAGEMENT IN SPC SWITCHING SYSTEMS FOR TELECOMMUNICATIONS.
        BAGNOLI P + SARACCO R
        ALTA FREQ 49(3): 239-46 (MAY-JUNE 1980)
                    SIP, ROME, ITALY
                    SAB 1980: 054792

0024   DATABASE SOFTWARE.
        BAKER G
        DATA PROCESSING 21(4): 28-9 (APRIL 1979)
                    SAC 1979: 025047

0025   A SOFTWARE DESIGN METHODOLOGY FOR AN INDUSTRIAL ENVIRONMENT: EARLY EXPERIENCES.
        BAKER JD + VESTAL SC
        P101-13 OF WORKSHOP ON RELIABLE SOFTWARE, BONN, GERMANY, 22-23 SEPT 1978 RAULEFS, P(ED), CARL HANSER
        VERLAG, MUNCHEN, GERMANY, 1979
                    HONEYWELL INC BOSTON, MA,
                    SAC 1980: 005671

0026   SPECIFYING THE SYSTEM.
        BAKER K
        MICROPROCESS MICROSYST 4(7): 259-61 (SEPT 1980)
                    SAC 1981: 005219

0027   MICROPROCESSORS AND SOFTWARE DESIGN TOOLS.
        BAKER K
        MICROPROCESS MICROSYST 3(2): 87-93 (MARCH 1979)
                    SCHOOL OF ENGNG AND APPL SCI, UNIV OF SUSSEX, GUILDFORD,
                    ENGLAND
                    SAC 1979: 033818

0028   HANDLING MICROPROCESSOR SOFTWARE MODULES.
        BAKER K
        P5/1-3 OF COLLOQUIUM ON TEACHING SOFTWARE DESIGN TECHNIQUES FOR MICROPROCESSORS, LONDON, ENGLAND, 21 NOV
        1979, IEE, LONDON, ENGLAND, 1979
                    SCHOOL OF ENGNG AND APPL SCI, UNIV OF SUSSEX, BRIGHTON,
                    ENGLAND
                    SAC 1980: 012881

0029   SHORT-TIME TESTING OF SYNTHETIC MATERIALS BY THE APPLICATION OF PROCESS COMPUTERS.
        BARDENHEIER R
        MASCHINENMARKT 85(34): 665-8 (27 APRIL 1979) (IN GERMAN)
                    DEUTSCHEN KUNSTSTOFF-INST, DARMSTADT, GERMANY
                    SAA 1979: 061822

0030   AUTOMATED SOFTWARE DESIGN.
        BARINA H + COBEY W + ROSENBAUM J + WHITE S
        P384-91 OF PROC OF COMPSAC THE IEEE COMPUTER SOCIETY S THIRD INTERNATIONAL COMPUTER SOFTWARE AND
        APPLICATIONS CONF, CHICAGO, IL 6-8 NOV 1979, IEEE, NEW YORK, 1979
                    SAC 1980: 012868

0031   GALILEO FLIGHT SOFTWARE MANAGEMENT: THE SCIENCE INSTRUMENTS.
        BARRY RC + REIFER DJ
        P684-90 OF COMPUTER SOFTWARE AND APPLICATIONS CONF, CHICAGO, IL, 27-31 OCT 1980, IEEE, NEW YORK, 1980
                    JET PROPULSION LAB, PASADENA, CA,
                    SAC 1981: 012898

0032   A NOTE ON SYNTHESIS OF INDUCTIVE ASSERTIONS.
        BASU SK
        IEEE TRANS SOFTWARE ENG SE-6(1): 32-9 (JAN 1980)
                    DEPT OF COMPUTER SCI, UNIV OF NEBRASKA, LINCOLN, NE,
                    SAC 1980: 016284

0033   WHAT DOES A TP-MONITOR DO.
        BAUER M
        ONLINE-ADL-NACHR NO 5: 420-3 (MAY 1979) (IN GERMAN)
                    SAC 1979: 030489

0034   A GENERALIZED IMPLEMENTATION METHOD FOR RELATIONAL DATA SUBLANGUAGES.
        BECK LL
        IEEE TRANS SOFTWARE ENG (USA) VOLSE-6NO2152-62 MARCH 1980
                    DEPT OF COMPUTER SCI, SOUTHERN METHODIST UNIV, DALLAS,
                    TX,
                    SAC 1980: 021760

0035   P2 AND PLUS: A PRAGMATIC APPROACH TOWARDS SOFTWARE RELIABILITY THROUGH DOCUMENTATION CONSIDERATIONS.
        BEIDLER J
        P221-33 OF WORKSHOP ON RELIABLE SOFTWARE, BONN, GERMANY, 22-23 SEPT 1978 RAULEFS, P(ED), CARL HANSER
        VERLAG, MUNCHEN, GERMANY, 1979
                DEPT OF COMPUTER SCI, UNIV OF SCRANTON, SCRANTON, PA,
                SAC 1980: 005676

0036   EXPERIMENTS WITH SOFTWARE MODIFIABILITY.
        BELADY LA
        P1-12 OF LIFE-CYCLE MANAGEMENT, STATE OF THE ART REPORT, INFOTECH MAIDENHEAD, ENGLAND, 1980
                IBM THOMAS J WATSON RES CENTER, YORKTOWN HEIGHTS, NY,
                SAC 1981: 005232

0037   ADVANTAGES AND CHARACTERISTICS OF THE PHOS METHODOLOGY. PART-2.
        BETTINAZZI + MASERATI - MONZANI - SPOLETINI + TOSCANI
        MANAGE INF 19(2): 109-19 (FEB 1980) (IN ITALIAN)
                SAC 1980: 026928

0038   MICROPROCESSOR TESTING USING A MINIMAL INSTRUCTION COVER.
        BHUJADE MR + DESHPANDE SR
        P182-6 OF AUTOTESTCON 79 INT AUTOMATIC TESTING CONF MINNEAPOLIS, MN, 19-21 SEPT 1979, IEEE, NEW YORK,
        1979
                COMPUTER CENTRE, INDIAN INST OF TECHNOL, BOMBAY, INDIA
                SAC 1980: 006637

0039   UNIFIED DESIGN SPECIFICATION SYSTEM (UDS(2)).
        BIGGERSTAFF TJ
        P104-118 OF PROC OF SPECIFICATIONS OF RELIABLE SOFTWARE, CAMBRIDGE MA, 3-5 APRIL 1979, IEEE, NEW YORK,
        1979
                BOEING COMPUTER SERVICES CO, SEATTLE, WA,
                SAC 1979: 021507

0040   DESIGN OF SOFTWARE OF DISTRIBUTED CONTROL SYSTEMS.
        BISHOP PG
        EUROMICRO J 5(6): 358-62 (NOV 1979)
                CENTRAL ELECTRICITY RES LABS, CEGB, LEATHERHEAD, ENGLAND
                SAC 1980: 019413

0041   DESIGN OF SOFTWARE FOR DISTRIBUTED COMPUTER CONTROL SYSTEM.
        BISHOP PG + BREWER C + JERVIS P
        P58-62 OF TRENDS IN ONLINE COMPUTER CONTROL SYSTEMS, SHEFFIELD, ENGLAND 27-29 MARCH 1979, IEE, LONDON,
        ENGLAND, 1979
                CERL, LEATHERHEAD, ENGLAND
                SAC 1979: 013834

0042   SUCCESSFUL DEVELOPMENT OF HIGH QUALITY SOFTWARE FOR MICRO PROCESSOR SYSTEMS.
        BLUM A + BUCHER K
        P111-18 OF PROC OF THE JOURNEES D ELECTRONIQUE 1979 MICROPROCESSORS: A TOOL FOR THE FUTURE, LAUSANNE,
        SWITZERLAND, 2-4 OCT 1979 SWISS FEDERAL INSTITUTE OF TECHNOLOGY, LAUSANNE, SWITZERLAND, 1979
                BROWN, BOVERI AND CO, TURGI, SWITZERLAND
                SAC 1980: 018828

0043   PERFORMANCE OPTIMIZATION OF SOFTWARE SYSTEMS PROCESSING INFORMATION SEQUENCES MODELED BY PROBABILISTIC
        LANGUAGES.
        BOOTH TL
        IEEE TRANS SOFTWARE ENG SE-5(1): 31-44 (JAN 1979)
                DEPT OF ELECTRICAL ENGNG AND COMPUTER SCI, UNIV OF CONNECTICUT,
                STORRS,
                CT,
                SAC 1979: 009837

0044   PERFORMANCE ABSTRACT DATA TYPES AS A TOOL IN SOFTWARE PERFORMANCE ANALYSIS AND DESIGN.
        BOOTH TL + WIECEK CA
        IEEE TRANS SOFTWARE ENG SE-6(2): 138-51 (MARCH 1980)
                DEPT OF ELECTRICAL ENGNG, UNIV OF CONNECTICUT, STORRS,
                CT,
                SAC 1980: 021584

0045   MICROPROCESSOR ARCHITECTURE, SYSTEMS AND SOFTWARE DESIGN: TRENDS AND EXPECTATIONS.
        BOUTE RT
        J A 21(4): 153-60 (OCT 1980)
                BELL TELEPHONE MFG CO, ANTWERP, BELGIUM
                SAC 1981: 008498

0046   WELLMADE.
        BOYD D
        P60-93 OF PROC OF THE SYMP ON FORMAL DESIGN METHODOLOGY CAMBRIDGE, ENGLAND, 9-12 APRIL 1979, STANDARD
        TELECOMMUNICATION LABS LTD HARLOW, ENGLAND, 1979
                SAC 1980: 024231

0047   DEADLOCK PREVENTION FOR ATE INSTRUMENT ALLOCATION.
        BUCHAN W
        P143-52 OF AUTOMATIC TESTING 80 CONF PROC, PARIS, FRANCE 23-25 SEPT 1980, NETWORK, BUCKINGHAM, ENGLAND,
        1980
                SAB 1981: 021327

0048   AN ACADEMIC PROGRAM PROVIDING REALISTIC TRAINING IN SOFTWARE ENGINEERING.
        BUSENBERG SN + TAM WC
        COMMUN ACM 22(6): 341-5 (JUNE 1979)
                HARVEY MUDD COLL, CLAREMONT, CA,
                SAC 1979: 024238

0049   EVOLUTION OF THE SSSP SCORE EDITING TOOLS.
        BUXTON W + SNIDERMAN R + REEVES W + PATEL S + BAECKER R
        COMPUT MUSIC J 3(4): 14-25,60 (DEC 1979)
                UNIV OF TORONTO, TORONTO, ONTARIO, CANADA
                SAC 1980: 022349

0050   IDEAS BEHIND THE JACKSON STRUCTURED PROGRAMMING (JSP) METHOD OF PROGRAM DESIGN AND ITS DEVELOPMENT.
        CAMERON J
        P2/1-50 OF PROC OF THE SIXTH EUROPEAN DATAMANAGER USER GROUP CONFERENCE, ZURICH, SWITZERLAND, 19-21 MAY
        1980 EUROPEAN DATAMANAGER USER GROUP, LONDON, ENGLAND, 1980
                MICHAEL JACKSON SYSTEMS LTD, LONDON, ENGLAND
                SAC 1981: 002280

0051   OPERATIONAL SYSTEMS EVOLUTION.
        CAPOGROSSO F
        SIST AUTOM 26(204): 345-59 (MAY 1980) (IN ITALIAN)
                SAC 1980: 033072

0052   METHODOLOGY OF PROGRAM DESIGNING.
        CARDA A
        AUTOM SYST RIZENI 13(2): 73-8 (1979) (IN CZECH)
                SAC 1979: 033796

0053   STRUCTURING OF MANAGEMENT PROGRAMS IN A CONVERSATIONAL ENVIRONMENT.
        CARREZ C
        RAIRO INF/COMPUT SCI 14(2): 185-210 (1980) (IN FRENCH)
                SAC 1980: 033070

0054   DESIGNING STATISTICAL SOFTWARE FOR THE NEW COMPUTERS.
        CHAMBERS JM
        P99-103 OF PROC OF THE COMPUTER SCIENCE AND STATISTICS 12TH ANNUAL SYMPOSIUM ON THE INTERFACE, WATERLOO,
        ONTARIO, CANADA, 10-11 MAY 1979 UNIV WATERLOO, WATERLOO, ONTARIO, CANADA, 1979
                BELL LABS, MURRAY HILL, NJ,
                SAB 1980: 017991

0055   LOGICAL CONSTRUCTION OF SOFTWARE.
        CHAND DR + YADAV SB
        COMMUN ACM 23(10): 546-55 (OCT 1980)
                GEORGIA STATE UNIV, ATLANTA, GA,
                SAC 1981: 005192

0056   APPLICATION OF SOFTWARE ENGINEERING TECHNIQUES TO ESS.
        CHANG HY + HORNBACH TS + SCANLON JM
        P1390-5 OF INT SWITCHING SYMP, PARIS, FRANCE, 7-11 MAY 1979 COLLOQUE INT DE LA COMMUNICATION, PARIS,
        FRANCE, 1979
                BELL LABS, NAPERVILLE, IL,
                SAB 1981: 002722

0057   SOFTWARE ENGINEERING: AN APPLICATION.
        CHANG NY + HORNBACH TS + SCANLON JM
        SIST AUTOM 26(207): 607-16 (SEPT 1980) (IN ITALIAN)
                BELL LAB, NAPERVILLE, IL,
                SAC 1981: 012024

0058   REFLECTION ON THE IMPLEMENTATION OF A SOFTWARE DESIGN.
        CHEN TLC
        P69-73 OF PROC OF COMPSAC THE IEEE COMPUTER SOCIETY S THIRD INTERNATIONAL COMPUTER SOFTWARE AND
        APPLICATIONS CONF, CHICAGO, IL 6-8 NOV 1979, IEEE, NEW YORK, 1979
                SPERRY UNIVAC, ROSEVILLE, MN,
                SAC 1980: 009149

0059   ROLE OF TESTING TOOLS AND TECHNIQUES IN THE PROCUREMENT OF QUALITY SOFTWARE AND SYSTEMS.
        CHERNIAVSKY JC + ADRION WR + BRANSTAD MA
        P309-13 OF CONF RECORD OF THE THIRTEENTH ASILOMAR CONF ON CIRCUITS, SYSTEMS AND COMPUTERS, PACIFIC GROVE,
        CA, 5-7 NOV 1979, IEEE NEW YORK, 1979
                INST FOR COMPUTER SCI AND TECHNOL, NBS, WASHINGTON, DC,

                SAC 1980: 029899

0060   I M ALRIGHT JACK, OLD SON: ONE LAYMAN'S VIEW OF THE JACKSON PROGRAM DESIGN METHODOLOGY.
        CLARKE R
        AUST COMPUT BULL 4(5): 8-11 (JUNE 1980)
                SAC 1981: 005189

0061   SOFTWARE BASICS FOR COMPUTATIONAL MATHEMATICS.
        CODY WJ
        SIGNUM NEWSL 15(2): 18-29 (JUNE 1980)
                APPL MATH DIV, ARGONNE LAB, ARGONNE, IL,
                SAC 1980: 032885

0062   PROBLEMS OF TEACHING SOFTWARE DESIGN.
        COHEN B
        P4/1-5 OF COLLOQUIUM ON TEACHING SOFTWARE DESIGN TECHNIQUES FOR MICROPROCESSORS, LONDON, ENGLAND, 21 NOV
        1979, IEE, LONDON, ENGLAND, 1979
                APPL SOFTWARE RES GROUP, STANDARD TELEVOMMUNICATION LABS,
                HARLOW, ENGLAND
                SAC 1980: 006971

0063   MANAGEMENT OF LARGE SOFTWARE (SYSTEM DEVELOPMENT FOR STORED PROGRAM SWITCHING SYSTEMS.
        DALY EB + MNICHOWICZ DA
        P1287-91 OF INT SWITCHING SYMP, PARIS, FRANCE, 7-11 MAY 1979 COLLOQUE INT DE LA COMMUNICATION, PARIS,
        FRANCE, 1979
                GTE AUTOMATIC ELECTRIC LABS, NORTHLAKE, IL,
                SAB 1981: 002711

0064   MANAGEMENT OF SOFTWARE DEVELOPMENT FOR STORED PROGRAM SWITCHING SYSTEMS.
        DALY EB - MNICHOWICZ DA
        TELEPH ENG MANAGE 84(9): 120,122,124,126 128 1 MAY 1980
                SAB 1980: 050283

0065   MANAGEMENT OF LARGE SOFTWARE DEVELOPMENT FOR STORED PROGRAM SWITCHING SYSTEMS.
        DALY EB - MNICHOWICZ DA
        GTE AUTOM ELECTR J 17(5): 155-60 (SEPT 1979)
                GTE AUTOMATIC ELECTRIC LABS, NORTHLAKE, IL,
                SAB 1980: 010980

0066   A SOFTWARE DESIGN FOR A COMPUTER BASED IMPEDANCE RELAY FOR TRANSMISSION LINE PROTECTION.
        DAVALL PW - AU YEUNG G
        IEEE TRANS POWER APPAR SYST PAS-99 NO1235-45 JAN-FEB 1980
                SASKATCHEWAN POWER CORP, REGINA, SASKATCHEWAN, CANADA
                SAB 1980: 032527

0067   SOLID-STATE CARTRIDGE SYSTEM.
        DAVIS MI
        IBM TECH DISCLOSURE BULL 23(5): 1748-50 (OCT 1980)
                IBM CORP, ARMONK, NY,
                SAC 1981: 008480

0068   EDP SYSTEMS CONCEPTS: THE FIRST PROBLEM IS AN ANALYSIS.
        DE CINDIO F + DE MICHELIS G + SIMONE C
        SIST AUTOM 26(201): 119-26 (FEB 1980) (IN ITALIAN)
                UNIV DI MILANO, MILANO, ITALY
                SAC 1980: 024195

0069   AN INTEGRATED SYSTEM TO SUPPORT PROGRAM DESIGN, DEVELOPMENT AND ANALYSIS.
        DEGANO P + PACINI G + TURINI F + LEVI G + SIROVICH F
        RIV INF 9(4): 353-66 (OCT-DEC 1979)
                ISTITUTO DI SCIENZE DELL INFORMAZIONE, UNIV DI PISA, PISA,
                ITALY,
                SAC 1980: 018801

0070   DESIGN OF A SOFTWARE DEVELOPMENT METHODOLOGY EMPHASIZING PRODUCTIVITY.
        DELFINO AB + BEGUN RA
        P159-64 OF IEEE 1980 IECI PROC APPLICATIONS OF MINI AND MICROCOMPUTERS, PHILADELPHIA, PA, 17-20 MARCH
        1980, IEEE, NEW YORK 1980
                CENTRAL ENGINEERING LAB, FMC CORP, SANTA CLARA, CA,
                SAC 1980: 021284

0071   COURSE MANAGEMENT USING A DATABASE STRUCTURE.
        DETMER RC + SMULLEN CW
        COMPUT EDUC (GB) VOL3NO3211-34 1979
                DEPT, OF MATH, UNIV OF TENNESSE, CHATTANOOGA, TN,
                SAC 1979: 034766

0072   SOFTWARE MANAGEMENT: A SURVEY OF THE PRACTICE IN 1980.
        DISTASO JR
        PROC IEEE 68(9): 1103-19 (SEPT 1980)
                TRW DEFENSE AND SPACE SYSTEMS, REDONDO BEACH, CA,
                SAC 1981: 000071

0073   SOFTWARE TECHNOLOGY-KEY ISSUES OF THE 80'S.
        DISTASO JR + MANLEY JH + STUCKI LG + MUNSON JB
        P387-9 OF COMPCON SPRING 80 VLSI: NEW ARCHITECTURAL HORIZONS SAN FRANCISCO, CA, 25-28 FEB 1980, IEEE, NEW
        YORK, 1980
                TRW DEFENSE AND SPACE SYSTEMS GROUP, REDONDO BEACH, CA,

                SAC 1980: 025336

0074   SOME PROBLEMS OF SOFTWARE DESIGN.
        DRAZEK Z + SZYJEWSKI Z
        INFORMATYKA 14(5): 12-13 (MAY 1979) (IN POLISH)
                OSRODEK OBLICZEN EKONOMICZNYCH, WROCLAW, POLAND
                SAC 1979: 030335

0075   ECONOMIC CRITERIA FOR MORE EFFICIENT SOFTWARE DESIGN METHODS.
        DUKE C
        ELETTRON OGGI NO 5: 75-6,78,80-2 (MAY 1980) (IN ITALIAN)
                SAC 1980: 032866

0076   STANDARDISATION OF DESIGN AND PROGRAM ELEMENTS IN ADMINISTRATIVE DATA PROCESSING AND THEIR EFFECTIVE
        EXPLOITATION.
        DVORAK B
        MECH AUTOM ADM 19(6): 221-5 (1979) (IN CZECH)
                SAC 1979: 034049

0077   MANAGEMENT OF SOFTWARE ENGINEERING. PART-4: SOFTWARE DEVELOPMENT PRACTICES.
        DYER M
        IBM SYST J 19(4): 451-65 (1980)
                FEDERAL SYSTEMS DIV, IBM CORP, BETHESDA, MD,
                SAC 1981: 012010

0078   COMPLETE PASCAL. PART-7: PROCEDURES AND FUNCTIONS.
        EISENBACH S + SADLER C
        PERS COMPUT WORLD 3(3): 68-9,72-3,101 (MARCH 1980)
                SAC 1981: 005375

0079   DLP, A DESIGN LANGUAGE PRE-PROCESSOR.
        ELLIOT IB
        SIGPLAN NOT 14(3): 14-20 (FEB 1979)
                HONEYWELL, INC, ST LOUIS PARK, MN,
                SAC 1979: 013058

0080   AFLC EMBEDDED COMPUTER SYSTEM SOFTWARE MANAGEMENT: THE FOREIGN MILITARY SALES CONCEPT.
        EMBERTON RW
        P394-9 OF PROC OF THE IEEE 1979 NATIONAL AEROSPACE AND ELECTRONICS CONFERENCE NAECON 1979, DAYTON, OH,
        15-17 MAY 1979, IEEE, NEW YORK, 1979
                HEADQUARTERS AIR FORCE LOGISTICS COMMAND, WRIGHT-PATTERSON,
                AFB, OH,
                SAC 1979: 028177

0081   METHODS AND DEVICES FOR DESIGNING DIGITAL SYSTEMS BASED ON MICROPROCESSORS.
        ERENI I
        PRIB SIST UPR NO 8: 1-3 (1980) (IN RUSSIAN)
                SAC 1981: 008388

0082   CRITERIA FOR THE ORGANISATION AND MANAGEMENT OF PROGRAM TESTING: EXPERIENCES AND POSSIBLE GENERALISATION.
        FOUILLOUZE O + LANZARONE GA + SCRIGNARO D + ZAFFERRI G
        P59-70 OF AICA 79 CONF, BARI, ITALY, 10-13 OCT 1979 ASSOCIAZIONE ITALIANA CALCOLO AUTOMATICO, BARI,
        ITALY, 1979 (IN ITALIAN)
                SOC ITALIANA TELECOMUNICAZIONI SIEMENS, MILAN, ITALY
                SAC 1980: 021677

0083   SOFTWARE DESIGN FOR DIGITAL DATA SWITCHING SYSTEM.
        FUTAMI K + OTA T + HARA T + IMAI K
        REV ELECTR COMMUN LAB 28(5-6): 350-60 (MAY-JUNE 1980)
                NIPPON TELEGRAPH AND TELEPHONE PUBLIC CORP, TOKYO, JAPAN
                SAB 1980: 050191

0084   ITT 1230 DIGITAL EXCHANGE. SOFTWARE DESIGN FOR DIGITAL EXCHANGES.
        GARDINER A + KATZSCHNER L + VAN DER STRAETEN C
        ELECTR COMMUN 54(3): 199-204 (1979)
                INTERNAT TELECOMMUNICATIONS CENTER, BRUSSELS, BELGIUM,

                SAB 1980: 001719

0085   JACKSON STRUCTURED PROGRAMMING: A CORRECT EXAMPLE.
        GEORGE W
        ANGEW INF 22(3): 91-5 (MARCH 1980) (IN GERMAN)
                MATH BERATUNGS- UND PROGRAMMIERUNGSDIENST GMBH, DORTMUND,
                GERMANY
                SAC 1980: 018776

0086   UNIVERSAL RELATION ASSUMPTION AND DECOMPOSITION STRATEGIES FOR SCHEMA DESIGN (SOFTWARE ENGINEERING).
        GEWIRTZ WL
        P136-40 OF PROC OF COMPSAC THE IEEE COMPUTER SOCIETY S THIRD INTERNATIONAL COMPUTER SOFTWARE AND
        APPLICATIONS CONF, CHICAGO, IL 6-8 NOV 1979, IEEE, NEW YORK, 1979
                BELL LAB, MURRAY HILL, NJ,
                SAC 1980: 009154

0087   INSTRUMENTAL MEANS FOR THE DESIGN OF PROGRAMS FOR PROCESSING MATHEMATICAL TEXTS.
        GLUSHKOV VM + KAPITONOVA YUV + LETICHEVSKII AA
        KIBERNETIKA 15(2): 37-42 (MARCH-APRIL 1979)
                SAC 1980: 016702

0088   UNTRADITIONAL SOFTWARE DESIGNING SERVES UNTRADITIONAL MINI MICRO MARKET.
        GRAYSON YA
        DATA MANAGE 17(3): 24-5 (MARCH 1979)
                COUNTRY PROGRAMMERS INC, FAIRLEE, VT,
                SAC 1979: 031327

0089   A SYSTEMATIC APPROACH TO PROGRAM DESIGN.
        HAMPSHIRE N
        PRACT COMPUT 3(3): 113-16 (MARCH 1980)
                SAC 1980: 021558

0090   A DESIGN PROCESS FORMALIZATION.
        HARADA M + KUNII TL
        P367-73 OF PROC OF COMPSAC THE IEEE COMPUTER SOCIETY S THIRD INTERNATIONAL COMPUTER SOFTWARE AND
        APPLICATIONS CONF, CHICAGO, IL 6-8 NOV 1979, IEEE, NEW YORK, 1979
                DEPT OF INFORMATION SCI, UNIV OF TOKYO, HONGO, TOKYO, JAPAN
                SAC 1980: 012865

0091   DESIGNING TRANSLATOR SOFTWARE.
        HECKEL P
        DATAMATION 26(2): 134-8 (FEB 1980)
                INTERACTIVE SYSTEMS CONSULTANTS, LOS ALTOS, CA,
                SAC 1980: 025186

0092   DESIGN OF A MEDICAL COMPUTER OFFICE SYSTEM-LONG RANGE VIEWPOINT.
        HEISTERKAMP C
        P758-60 OF PROC OF THE THIRD ANNUAL SYMP ON COMPUTER APPLICATION IN MEDICAL CARE, WASHINGTON, DC, 14-17
        OCT 1979, DUNN RA(ED), IEEE, NEW YORK, 1979
                BIOMEDICAL ENGNG, LANCASTER, PA,
                SAC 1980: 009432

0093   STRUCTURED DESIGN AND ASPECTS OF ITS APPLICATION.
        HELLNER J
        RECHENTECH DATENVERARB 16(2): 6-10 (FEB 1979) (IN GERMAN)
                VEB DVZ, KARL-MARX-STADT, GERMANY
                SAC 1979: 018930

0094   USE OF A MODULE INTERCONNECTION LANGUAGE IN THE SARA SYSTEM DESIGN METHODOLOGY.
        HELOISA PENEDO M - BERRY DM
        P294-307 OF PROC OF THE 4TH INT CONF ON SOFTWARE ENGINEERING, MUNICH, GERMANY, 17-19 SEPT 1979, IEEE, NEW
        YORK, 1979
                    COMPUTER SCI DEPT, UNIV OF CALIFORNIA, LOS ANGELES, CA,

                SAC 1980: 005810

0095   PDI IQ BUILDER SOFTWARE.
        HEUER R
        CREATIVE COMPUT 5(5): 70-1 (MAY 1979)
                SAC 1979: 034760

0096   PROGRAM DESIGN AND CONSTRUCTION.
        HIGGINS DA
                SAC 1980: 018811

0097   SOFTWARE DESIGN: FROM THE EXPERIENCE TO THE METHOD.
        HOCIEJ T
        SIST AUTOM NO 197SUPPL : 3-7 (OCT 1979) (IN ITALIAN)
                SAC 1980: 012799

0098   A PRODUCTION SYSTEM APPROACH INTERACTIVE GRAPHIC PROGRAM DESIGN.
        HOPGOOD FRA + DUCE DA
        P247-63 OF METHODOLOGY OF INTERACTION PROC OF THE IFIP WORKSHOP ON METHODOLOGY OF INTERACTION, SEILLAC,
        FRANCE, MAY 1979, GUEDJ, RA, TEN HAGEN PJW, HOPGOOD, FRA, TUCKER, HA, DUCE, DA(ED), NORTH-HOLLAND,
        AMSTERDAM NETHERLANDS, 1980
                    ATLAS COMPUTING DIV, RUTHERFORD LAB, DIDCOT, ENGLAND
                SAC 1980: 034425

0099   A MICROCOMPUTER BASED VIDEO MOTION DETECTION SYSTEM.
        HOWINGTON LC
        P127-32 OF PROC OF THE 1979 CARNAHAN CONF ON CRIME COUNTERMEASURES, LEXINGTON, KY, 16-18 MAY 1979,
        JACKSON, JS, DE VORE RW(ED), UNIV KENTUCKY, LEXINGTON, KY, 1979
                    NUCLEAR DIV, UNION CARBIDE CORP, OAK RIDGE, TN,
                SAC 1979: 033491

0100   DESIGNING TRANSPORTABLE SOFTWARE.
        HUG R + PRESSER L
        MINI-MICRO SYST 13(5): 120-1,123-4,126-8,130 (MAY 1980)
                    SOFTOOL CORP, GOLETA, CA,
                SAC 1980: 029703

0101   A FORMALIZATION AND EXPLICATION OF THE MICHAEL JACKSON METHOD OF PROGRAM DESIGN.
        HUGHES JW
        SOFTWARE-PRACT EXPER 9(3): 191-202 (MARCH 1979)
                    COMPUTATION DEPT, UNIV OF MANCHESTER, MANCHESTER, ENGLAND
                SAC 1979: 015491

0102   MICROCOMPUTER EDUCATION: A CHALLENGE FOR THE FUTURE.
        HUGUENIN F
        P251-67 OF PROC OF THE JOURNEES D ELECTRONIQUE 1979 MICROPROCESSORS: A TOOL FOR THE FUTURE, LAUSANNE,
        SWITZERLAND, 2-4 OCT 1979 SWISS FEDERAL INSTITUTE OF TECHNOLOGY, LAUSANNE, SWITZERLAND, 1979
                    GROUP FOR AUTOMATIC CONTROL, SWISS FEDERALINST OF TECHNOL,
                    ZURICH,
                    SWITZERLAND
                SAC 1980: 017256

0103   A MICROPROCESSOR-BASED PSYCHOPATHOLOGY LABORATORY. PART-5: SOFTWARE DESIGN.
        HUNTZINGER RS + SPACE LG
        BEHAV RES METHODS INSTRUM 11(2): 253-6 (APRIL 1979)
                    UNIV OF ROCHESTER, ROCHESTER, NY,
                SAC 1980: 018200

0104   PROGRAM GENERATION TECHNIQUES.
        ITO Y + FUJITA S + KIMIJIMA T + YONEDA T
        REV ELECTR COMMUN LAB 28(3-4): 280-93 (MARCH-APRIL 1980)
                    ELECTRICAL COMMUNICATION LABS, YOKOSUKA, JAPAN
                SAC 1980: 029879

0105   MASCOT.
        JACKSON K
        P40-58 OF PROC OF THE SYMP ON FORMAL DESIGN METHODOLOGY CAMBRIDGE, ENGLAND, 9-12 APRIL 1979, STANDARD
        TELECOMMUNICATION LABS LTD HARLOW, ENGLAND, 1979
                SAC 1980: 024230

0106   MJSPDT.
        JACKSON M
        P172-190 OF PROC OF THE SYMP ON FORMAL DESIGN METHODOLOGY CAMBRIDGE, ENGLAND, 9-12 APRIL 1979, STANDARD
        TELECOMMUNICATION LABS LTD HARLOW, ENGLAND, 1979
                SAC 1980: 024234

0107   A TECHNIQUE FOR THE ARCHITECTURAL IMPLEMENTATION OF SOFTWARE SUBSYSTEMS.
        JAGANNATHAN A
        P236-44 OF CONF PROC OF THE 7TH ANNUAL SYMP ON COMPUTER ARCHITECTURE, LA BAULE, FRANCE, 6-8 MAY 1980,
        IEEE, NEW YORK, 1980
                    BELL LABS, HOLMDEL, NJ,
                SAC 1980: 035343

0108   PROGRAM DESIGN METHODOLOGY FOR INTERACTIVE SYSTEMS.
        JASTRZEBSKI S
        INFORMATYKA 15(5): 7-10 (MAY 1980) (IN POLISH)
                MIEDZYNARODOWE CENTRUM INFORMACJI NAUKOWEJ I TECH, MOSKWA,
                USSR
                SAC 1980: 032869

0109   SOFTWARE ENGINEERING.
        JENSEN RW + TONIES CC
                SAC 1980: 029715

0110   HEURISTIC CONTROL OF DESIGN-DIRECTED PROGRAM TRANSFORMATIONS.
        JETTE CL
        P1071-7 OF AFIPS CONF PROC VOL48 1979 NATIONAL COMPUTER CONF, NEW YORK, 4-7 JUNE 1979 AFIPS, MONTVALE, NJ,
        1979
                UNIV OF WASHINGTON, SEATTLE, WA,
                SAC 1980: 016196

0111   SYSTEM IMPLICATIONS OF PRIVACY LEGISLATION.
        JOHNSEN K
        INF PRIVACY 2(2): 60-8 (MARCH 1980)
                NORWEGIAN RES CENTER FOR COMPUTERS AND LAW, OSLO UNIV,
                OSLO, NORWAY
                SAC 1980: 022506

0112   APL AS A SOFTWARE DESIGN SPECIFICATION LANGUAGE.
        JONES WT + KIRK SA
        COMPUT J 23(3): 230-2 (AUG 1980)
                UNIV OF LOUISVILLE, LOUISVILLE, KY,
                SAC 1980: 029789

0113   DESIGN OF ABSTRACT PROGRAMS IN AN INTERACTIVE ENVIRONMENT.
        KAHN L
        DATA 9(7-8): 47-54 (AUG 1979)
                SAC 1980: 005613

0114   APPLICATION SOFTWARE'THE PROBLEM CHILD OF THE 80'S.
        KANNGIESSER J
        ONLINE-ADL-NACHR NO 12: 1006,1008-10 (DEC 1979) (IN GERMAN)
                SAC 1980: 019813

0115   COOP: A NEW CONCEPT IN SWITCHING SOFTWARE ENGINEERING.
        KELLY WJ + OTT KW
        P1037-40 OF INT SWITCHING SYMP, PARIS, FRANCE, 7-11 MAY 1979 COLLOQUE INT DE LA COMMUNICATION, PARIS,
        FRANCE, 1979
                ITC, BRUXELLES, BELGIUM
                SAB 1980: 054853

0116   IMPROVED SWITCHING PROGRAM FOR D20 ELECTRONIC SWITCHING SYSTEM.
        KIMURA S + SAITO T + TOMURA M + MATSUURA H
        REV ELECTR COMMUN LAB 27(5-6): 415-22 (MAY-JUNE 1979)
                NIPPON TELEGRAPH AND TELEPHONE LAB, MUSASHINO-SHI, TOKYO,
                JAPAN
                SAB 1979: 039637

0117   ONE APPROACH TO SOFTWARE DESIGN FOR CENTRAL CONTROL SYSTEMS (MANAGEMENT INFORMATION SYSTEM).
        KIRSHTEIN BKH + SHAPIRO YUZ
        AVTOM TELEMEKH 41(3): 178-86 (MARCH 1980)
                SAC 1981: 012385

0118   SOFTWARE DESIGN TECHNIQUES.
        KLEIN M
        ELEKTRON PRAX 15(1): 8,10-11 (JAN 1980) (IN GERMAN)
                SAC 1980: 021544

0119   TERMINAL DATA COMMUNICATION CONTROL.
        KOJYO S + IWAMOTO Y + TOYOSHIMA S + KATSUMATA M + OHBAYASHI K
        ELECTR COMMUN LAB TECH J 28(12): 2793-809 (1979) (IN JAPANESE)
                NIPPON TELEGRAPH AND TELEPHONE PUBLIC CORP, TOKYO, JAPAN
                SAB 1980: 050136

0120   SOFTWARE DESIGN FOR FAULT TOLERANCE.
        KOPETZ H
        P591-5 OF COMPUTER SOFTWARE AND APPLICATIONS CONF, CHICAGO, IL, 27-31 OCT 1980, IEEE, NEW YORK, 1980
                TECH UNIV BERLIN, BERLIN, GERMANY
                SAC 1981: 012059

0121   AN ANALYSIS OF THE PERFORMANCE OF A SOFTWARE DEVELOPMENT METHODOLOGY.
        LATTANZI LD
        GTE AUTOM ELECTR WORLD-WIDE COMMUN J 18(2): 41-6 (MARCH 1980)
                GTE AUTOMATIC ELECTRIC LABS, NORTHLAKE, IL,
                SAB 1980: 041035

0122   AN ANALYSIS OF THE PERFORMANCE OF A SOFTWARE DEVELOPMENT METHODOLOGY.
        LATTANZI LD
        P7-11 OF PROC OF COMPSAC THE IEEE COMPUTER SOCIETY S THIRD INTERNATIONAL COMPUTER SOFTWARE AND
        APPLICATIONS CONF, CHICAGO, IL 6-8 NOV 1979, IEEE, NEW YORK, 1979
                GTE AUTOMATIC ELECTRIC LABS, NORTHLAKE, IL,
                SAC 1980: 009146

0123   SOFTWARE METHODOLOGIES FOR A SYNTHESIS-BY-RULE SYSTEM.
        LESMO L - TORASSO P - MEZZALAMA M
        ALTA FREQ 49(3): 196-205 (MAY-JUNE 1980)
                UNIV DI TORINO, TORINO, ITALY
                SAB 1980: 054548

0124   SOFTWARE MAINTENANCE MANAGEMENT.
        LIENTZ BP - SWANSON EB
                SAC 1980: 030847

0125   MANAGEMENT OF SOFTWARE ENGINEERING. PART-3: SOFTWARE DESIGN PRACTICES.
        LINGER RC
        IBM SYST J 19(4): 432-50 (1980)
                FEDERAL SYSTEMS DIV, IBM CORP, BETHESDA, MD,
                SAC 1981: 012009

0126   STRUCTURED PROGRAMMING TECHNIQUES.
        LLOYD M
        ELECTRON NO 194: 15-19 (11 SEPT 1979)
                SAC 1980: 021542

0127   DO YOURSELF A FAVOR-USE A BASIC STRUCTURE (PROGRAMMING).
        LUNN K
        DATALINK (GB) 8-9 5 FEB 1979
                SAC 1979: 018946

0128   A MICROCOMPUTER SYSTEM DESIGN AND SOFTWARE FOR DISTRIBUTED CONTROL APPLICATIONS.
        MARGETICH SJ + JEFFERIS RP
        P65-73 OF PROC OF MICRO-DELCON 80 THE DELAWARE BAY MICROCOMPUTER CONFERENCE, NEWARK, DE, 11 MARCH 1980,
        IEEE, NEW YORK, 1980
                WIDENER UNIV, CHESTER, PA,
                SAC 1980: 022189

0129   PARALLELISM IN ADA: PROGRAM DESIGN AND MEANING.
        MAYOH BH
        P256-68 OF INT SYMP ON PROGRAMMING PROC OF THE FOURTH COLLOQUE INT SUR LA PROGRAMMATION, PARIS, FRANCE
        22-24 APRIL 1980, ROBINET, B(ED), SPRINGER-VERLAG, BERLIN, GERMANY, 1980
                COMPUTER SCI DEPT, AARHUS UNIV, AARHUS, DENMARK
                SAC 1980: 032912

0130   AN EXPERIMENT IN PARALLEL PROGRAM DESIGN.
        MCKEAG RM + MILLIGAN P
        SOFTWARE-PRACT EXPER 10(9): 687-96 (SEPT 1980)
                DEPT OF COMPUTER SCI, QUEEN S UNIV OF BELFAST, BELFAST,
                NIRELAND
                SAC 1980: 035669

0131   SOFTWARE DESIGN REPRESENTATION USING ABSTRACT PROCESS NETWORKS.
        MEKLY LJ + YAU SS
        IEEE TRANS SOFTWARE ENG SE-6(5): 420-35 (SEPT 1980)
                TELETYPE CORP, SKOKIE, IL,
                SAC 1980: 035655

0132   HARDWARE AND SOFTWARE DESIGN OF THE FAULT TOLERANT COMPUTER COPRA.
        MERAUD C + BROWAEYS F + QUEILLE JP + GERMAIN G
        P167 OF NINTH ANNUAL INT SYMP ON FAULT-TOLERANT COMPUTING MADISON, WI, 20-22 JUNE 1979, IEEE, NEW YORK,
        1979
                SAC 1979: 033582

0133   HOW TO MAKE EXCEPTIONAL PERFORMANCE DEPENDABLE AND MANAGEABLE IN SOFTWARE ENGINEERING.
        MILLS HD
        P19-23 OF COMPUTER SOFTWARE AND APPLICATIONS CONF, CHICAGO, IL, 27-31 OCT 1980, IEEE, NEW YORK, 1980
                IBM CORP, FEDERAL SYSTEMS DIV, BETHESDA, MD,
                SAC 1981: 011999

0134   MANAGEMENT OF SOFTWARE ENGINEERING. PART-1: PRINCIPLES OF SOFTWARE ENGINEERING.
        MILLS HD
        IBM SYST J 19(4): 414-20 (1980)
                FEDERAL SYSTEMS DIV, IBM CORP, BETHESDA, MD,
                SAC 1981: 009884

0135   FUNCTION SEMANTICS FOR SEQUENTIAL PROGRAMS.
        MILLS HD
        P241-50 OF INFORMATION PROCESSING 80 PROC OF THE IFIP CONG 80 TOKYO, JAPAN, 6-9 OCT 1980, LAVINGTON,
        S(ED), NORTH-HOLLAND, AMSTERDAM NETHERLANDS, 1980
                FEDERAL SYSTEMS DIV, IBM INC, BETHESDA, MD,
                SAC 1981: 004592

0136   A DESIGN OF SOFTWARE MONITOR AND ITS APPLICATION.
        MIYAZAKI M + OBATA S + MATSUZAWA S
        TRANS INF PROCESS SOC JPN 20(1): 53-60 (1979) (IN JAPANESE)
                TOHOKU UNIV COMPUTER CENTER, SENDAI, JAPAN
                SAC 1980: 009299

0137   SOFTWARE DESIGN FOR SMALL BUSINESS SYSTEMS.
        MOONEY RC
        INTERFACE AGE 4(6): 77-9 (JUNE 1979)
                SAC 1980: 002339

0138   SOFTWARE IN ITS ENGINEEERING CONTEXT.
        MORALEE D
        ELECTRON POWER 26(6): 443-9 (JUNE 1980)
                SAC 1980: 029671

0139   APPLICATION VERSATILITY OF THE BASIC SOFTWARE OF THE HZG 4/A UNIVERSAL X-RAY DIFFRACTOMETER.
        MORAS K + LANGER R
        JENA REV NO 4: 173-5 (1979)
                SAA 1980: 052375

0140   DEX-A113 TS, TLS PROGRAM DESIGN AND EVALUATIONS.
        MORISAWA T + KIMURA S + YAMAKI T
        REV ELECTR COMMUN LAB 27(5-6): 469-81 (MAY-JUNE 1979)
                NIPPON TELEGRAPH AND TELEPHONE LAB, MUSASHINO-SHI, TOKYO,
                JAPAN
                SAB 1979: 039638

0141   A SOFTWARE DEVELOPMENT METHODOLOGY FOR REAL-TIME APPLICATIONS.
        MOTT DR
        P423-9 OF COMPUTER SOFTWARE AND APPLICATIONS CONF, CHICAGO, IL, 27-31 OCT 1980, IEEE, NEW YORK, 1980
                PHANTOS RES INC, CAMILLUS, NY,
                SAC 1981: 012380

0142   DESIGN OF SOFTWARE FOR TEXT COMPOSITION.
        MUDUR SP + NARWEKAR AW + MOITRA A
        SOFTWARE-PRACT EXPER 9(4): 313-23 (APRIL 1979)
                NAT CENTRE FOR SOFTWARE DEV AND COMPUTING TECHNIQUES,
                TATA INST OF FUNDAMENTAL RES, BOMBAY, INDIA
                SAC 1979: 016890

0143   A TECHNIQUE FOR COMPARATIVE ASSESSMENT OF SOFTWARE DEVELOPMENT MANAGEMENT POLICIES.
        MULHALL BDL + JACOBS SM
        P687-93 OF AFIPS CONF PROC 1980 NATIONAL COMPUTER CONF ANAHEIM, CA, 19-22 MAY 1980, AFIPS, ARLINGTON, VA,
        1980
                JET PROPULSION LAB, CALIFORNIA INST OF TECHNOL, PASADENA,
                CA,
                SAC 1981: 003312

0144   MEASUREMENT AND MANAGEMENT OF SOFTWARE RELIABILITY.
        MUSA JD
        PROC IEEE 68(9): 1131-43 (SEPT 1980)
                BELL LABS, WHIPPANY, NJ,
                SAC 1981: 002245

0145   COMMUNICATION MANAGEMENT PROGRAM.
        NAEMURA K + TERASHIMA N + SASAKI M + MUKOUSAKA H + YAMAZAKI H
        ELECTR COMMUN LAB TECH J 28(12): 2775-80 (1979) (IN JAPANESE)
                NIPPON TELEGRAPH AND TELEPHONE PUBLIC CORP, TOKYO, JAPAN
                SAB 1980: 050134

0146   MANAGEMENT OF SOFTWARE ENGINEERING. PART-2: SOFTWARE ENGINEERING PROGRAM.
        O NEILL DO
        IBM SYST J 19(4): 421-31 (1980)
                FEDERAL SYSTEMS DIV, IBM CORP, GAITHERSBURG, MD,
                SAC 1981: 009885

0147   COMMUNICATION CONTROL METHOD IN COMPUTER NETWORKS.
        OHASHI K + IWATA K + ITOH H + SUMIDA T
        ELECTR COMMUN LAB TECH J 28(12): 2781-92 (1979) (IN JAPANESE)
                NIPPON TELEGRAPH AND TELEPHONE PUBLIC CORP, TOKYO, JAPAN
                SAB 1980: 050135

0148   STRUCTURAL REQUIREMENTS TO A FREE TEXT RETRIEVAL SYSTEM.
        ORE T
        DATA 9(10): 39-46 (OCT 1979)
                SAC 1980: 016277

0149   HARDWARE AND SOFTWARE SYSTEMS RESEARCH ON THE RAP DATABASE MACHINE.
        OZKARAHAN EA
        P894-8 OF PROC OF THE IEEE INT CONF ON CIRCUITS AND COMPUTERS ICCC 80, PORT CHESTER, NY, 1-3 OCT 1980,
        IEEE, 1980
                DEPT OF COMPUTER ENGNG, MIDDLE EAST TECH UNIV, ANKARA,
                TURKEY
                SAC 1981: 004913

0150   DESIGNING SOFTWARE FOR EASE OF EXTENSION AND CONTRACTION.
        PARNAS DL
        IEEE TRANS SOFTWARE ENG SE-5(2): 128-37 (MARCH 1979)
                DEPT OF COMPUTER SCI, UNIV OF NORTH CAROLINA, CHAPEL HILL,
                NC,
                SAC 1979: 015992

0151   A SYSTEMATIC APPROACH TO INTERACTIVE PROGRAMMING.
        PEI HSIA + PETRY FE
        COMPUTER 13(6): 27-34 (JUNE 1980)
                UNIV OF ALABAMA, HUNTSVILLE, AL,
                SAC 1980: 029683

0152   DESIGN OF SOFTWARE TOOLS FOR MICROPROGRAMMABLE MICROPROCESSORS.
        PERSSON M
        P119-27 OF MICROPROCESSORS AND THEIR APPLICATIONS, GOTEBORG, SWEDEN 28-30 AUG 1979, TIBERGHIEN, J,
        CARLSTEDT, G, LEWI, J(ED), NORTH-HOLLAND AMSTERDAM, NETHERLANDS, 1979
                DEPT OF NUMERICAL ANALYSIS AND COMPUTER SCI, ROYAL INST
                OF TECHNOL,
                STOCKHOLM, SWEDEN
                SAC 1980: 024386

O153   REQUIREMENTS OF A NAVAL DISTRIBUTED PROPULSION CONTROL SYSTEM.
        PIRIE IW + FRENCH C + FINDLAY DGE
        P1/1-8 OF COLLOQUIUM ON MICROPROCESSOR APPLICATIONS IN MARINE CONTROL SYSTEMS, LONDON, ENGLAND, 10 MARCH
        1980, IEE, LONDON, ENGLAND, 1980
                SHIP DEPT OF MINISTRY OF DEFENCE, BATH, ENGLAND
                SAC 1980: 018132

O154   EXPERIENCE IN THE CONVERSION OF SOFTWARE SYSTEMS FOR TR440 (SPSS, SCSS, NAG, IMSL).
        POEHLE U + KOLBE W - LUAGGER J - ROITZSCH R
        P 37-7 OF PRACTICE IN SOFTWARE ADAPTION AND MAINTENANCE PROC FOR THE SAM WORKSHOP, BERLIN, GERMAN, 5-6
        APRIL 197, EBERT, R, LUGGER J, GOECKE, L(ED), NORTH-HOLLAN, AMSTERDAM, NETHERLAND, 198
                GROSSRECHENZENTRUM FUER DIE WISSENSCHAFT IN BERLIN, BERLIN.
                GERMAN
                SA 19C8: 003289

O155   ALGORITHMS AND PROGRAMS FOR THE HANDLING AND SOLVING OF BINARY EQUATIONS.
        POSTHOFF C + STEINBACH B
        NACHRICHTENTECH ELEKTRON 30(3): 92-6 (1980) (IN GERMAN)
                TECH HOCHSCHULE KARL-MARX-STADT, KARL-MARX-STADT, GERMANY
                SAC 1980: 021048

O156   SOFTWARE DESIGN METHODOLOGIES APPLIED TO REMOTE PROCESS CONTROL.
        POULO R
        AUTOM CONTROL (NEW 10(3): 39-42 (1980)
                SAC 1981: 009709

O157   COMPILATION OF STRUCTURAL PROGRAMS IN A DIALOGUE MODE WITH CONCURRENT TEST GENERATION.
        PRAVIL SHCHIKOV PA + SHCHEPIN VS
        AVTOM TELEMEKH 40(8): 129-38 (AUG 1979)
                SAC 1980: 024365

O158   MANAGEMENT OF SOFTWARE ENGINEERING. PART-5: SOFTWARE ENGINEERING MANAGEMENT PRACTICES.
        QUINNAN RE
        IBM SYST J 19(4): 466-77 (1980)
                FEDERAL SYSTEMS DIV, IBM CORP, BETHESDA, MD,
                SAC 1981: 009886

O159   CURRICULUM 78-IS COMPUTER SCIENCE REALLY THAT UNMATHEMATICAL
        RALSTON A + SHAW M
        COMMUN ACM 23(2): 67-70 (FEB 1980)
                STATE UNIV OF NEW YORK, BUFFALO, NY,
                SAC 1980: 014220

O160   DIMS FOR EHV SUBSTATION CONTROL HARDWARE AND SOFTWARE DESIGN EFFICIENCY.
        REISS L
        P217-22 OF IEEE 1980 IECI PROC APPLICATIONS OF MINI AND MICROCOMPUTERS, PHILADELPHIA, PA, 17-20 MARCH
        1980, IEEE, NEW YORK 1980
                INST OF POWER SYSTEMS AUTOMATION, GDANSK, POLAND
                SAC 1980: 027500

O161   PREDICTION AND MANAGEMENT OF PROGRAM QUALITY.
        REMUS H + ZILLES S
        P341-50 OF PROC OF THE 4TH INT CONF ON SOFTWARE ENGINEERING, MUNICH, GERMANY, 17-19 SEPT 1979, IEEE, NEW
        YORK, 1979
                SANTA TERESA LAB, IBM GENERAL PRODUCTS DIV, SAN JOSE, CA,

                SAC 1980: 003345

O162   TOWARDS A COMPREHENSIVE AND HOMOGENOUS SOFTWARE DEVELOPMENT METHODOLOGY.
        RENAULT JP
        P217/19 OF ICC 79 1979 INT CONF ON COMMUNICATIONS BOSTON, MA, 10-14 JUNE 1979, IEEE, NEW YORK, 1979
                CIT ALCATEL, PARIS, FRANCE
                SAB 1980: 001744

O163   DESIGN OF SOFTWARE FOR USE ON MACHINE TOOLS.
        RINCON ARCHE M
        METAL ELECTR 44(511): 98-100 (APRIL 1980) (IN SPANISH)
                SAC 1980: 032827

O164   A MICROPROCESSOR FOR THE REVOLUTION: THE 6809. PART-3.
        RITTER T + BONEY J
        BYTE 4(3): 46-8,50,52 (MARCH 1979)
                MOTOROLA INC, AUSTIN, TX,
                SAC 1980: 004996

O165   CODE GENERATION AND STORAGE ALLOCATION FOR MACHINES WITH SPAN-DEPENDENT INSTRUCTIONS.
        ROBERTSON EL
        ACM TRANS PROGRAM LANG SYST 1(1): 71-85 (JULY 1979)
                INDIANA UNIV, BLOOMINGTON, IN,
                SAC 1980: 016407

O166   SOFTWARE DESIGN PROCESSOR.
        ROMANOS JP
        P380-3 OF PROC OF COMPSAC THE IEEE COMPUTER SOCIETY S THIRD INTERNATIONAL COMPUTER SOFTWARE AND
        APPLICATIONS CONF, CHICAGO, IL 6-8 NOV 1979, IEEE, NEW YORK, 1979
                SAC 1980: 012867

O167   COMPUTER SOFTWARE DESIGN FOR AN AERIAL REFUELING TRAINER.
        ROSENGARTEN SJ
        P1261-9 OF PROC OF THE IEEE 1979 NATIONAL AEROSPACE AND ELECTRONICS CONFERENCE NAECON 1979, DAYTON, OH,
        15-17 MAY 1979, IEEE, NEW YORK, 1979
                HYBRID SIMULATION DIV, ASD COMPUTER CENTER, WRIGHT-PATTERSON
                AFB, OH,
                SAB 1979: 044608

0168   DESIGN STRUCTURE DIAGRAMS: A NEW STANDARD IN FLOW DIAGRAMS.
        ROTHON NM
        COMPUT BULL (GB) SER2, NO 19: 4-6 (MARCH 1979)
                SAC 1979: 024240

0169   A SOFTWARE MANAGEMENT SYSTEM.
        ROUGEOT B + SALEMBIER D
        P1402-8 OF INT SWITCHING SYMP, PARIS, FRANCE, 7-11 MAY 1979 COLLOQUE INT DE LA COMMUNICATION, PARIS,
        FRANCE, 1979
                CNET, LANNION, FRANCE
                SAB 1981: 002724

0170   VERIFICATION AND VALIDATION OF AVIONIC SIMULATIONS.
        SAIB SH
        P6/1-6 OF AGARD CONF PROC NO268 MODELING AND SIMULATION OF AVIONICS SYSTEMS AND COMMAND, CONTROL AND
        COMMUNICATIONS SYSTEMS, PARIS FRANCE, 15-19 OCT 1979, AGARD, NEUILLY-SUR-SEINE, FRANCE, 1980
                GENERAL RES CORP, SANTA BARBARA, CA,
                SAB 1980: 051469

0171   COMPUTER SUBSYSTEM OF AN AUTOMATIC TEST LABORATORY FOR SPECIAL BATTERIES.
        SANCHEZ J + ALBERDI J + GONZALEZ J + GOTZ H
        MUNDO ELECTRON NO 81: 53-6 (JAN 1979) (IN SPANISH)
                SAB 1979: 025661

0172   ROLE OF THE FUNCTIONAL APPROACH IN THE DESIGN OF SOFTWARE.
        SANTONI M
        MANAGE INF NO 5: 353-5 (MAY 1980) (IN ITALIAN)
                SAC 1980: 032876

0173   DOCUMENTATION RULES IN SOFTWARE PRODUCTION.
        SANTONI M
        SIST AUTOM 25(199): 809-17 (DEC 1979) (IN ITALIAN)
                ELEA SPA, FIRENZE, ITALY
                SAC 1980: 016242

0174   AN EXPERIMENT IN SOFTWARE ERROR DATA COLLECTION AND ANALYSIS.
        SCHNEIDEWIND NF + HOFFMANN HM
        IEEE TRANS SOFTWARE ENG SE-5(3): 276-86 (MAY 1979)
                NAVAL POSTGRADUATE SCHOOL, MONTEREY, CA,
                SAC 1979: 021467

0175   SOFTWARE DESIGN TECHNIQUES: A COMPARISON BETWEEN THE LITOS TECHNIQUE AND JACKSON METHOD.
        SCHULTZ A
        ANGEW INF 21(1): 23-34 (JAN 1979) (IN GERMAN)
                INST FUR STATISTIK UND INFORMATIK, JOHANNES KEPLER UNIV,
                LINZ-AUHOF,
                AUSTRIA
                SAC 1979: 009824

0176   SOFTWARE DESIGN METHODS. A COMPARISON OF THE JACKSON PROGRAM INVERSION AND PARNAS PROBLEM-ORIENTED PROGRAM
        MODULARIZATION.
        SCHULZ A
        ANGEW INF 22(9): 371-9 (SEPT 1980) (IN GERMAN)
                INST FUR INFORMATIK, JOHANNES-KEPLER-UNIV LINZ, LINZ, AUSTRIA
                SAC 1981: 002250

0177   SOFTWARE DESIGN METHODS: A COMPARISON OF THE LITOS METHOD WITH THE JACKSON METHOD; REPLY TO A LETTER TO
        THE EDITOR.
        SCHULZ A
        ANGEW INF 22(3): 96-100 (MARCH 1980) (IN GERMAN)
                INST FUR INFORMATIK, JOHANNES-KEPLER-UNIV LINZ, LINZ, AUSTRIA
                SAC 1980: 018777

0178   DATA ORIENTED PROGRAM DESIGN.
        SHARP JA
        SIGPLAN NOT 15(9): 44-57 (SEPT 1980)
                DEPT OF COMPUTER SCI, UNIV COLL OF SWANSEA, SWANSEA, ENGLAND
                SAC 1980: 035673

0179   EXPERIMENTAL EVALUATION OF ONLINE PROGRAM CONSTRUCTION.
        SHEPPARD SB + MILLIMAN P + CURTIS B
        P505-10 OF COMPUTER SOFTWARE AND APPLICATIONS CONF, CHICAGO, IL, 27-31 OCT 1980, IEEE, NEW YORK, 1980
                SOFTWARE MANAGEMENT RES, GENERAL ELECTRIC CO, ARLINGTON,
                VA,
                SAC 1981: 012054

0180   A SOFTWARE DESIGN SYSTEM BASED ON A UNIFIED DESIGN METHODOLOGY.
        SHIGO O + IWAMOTO K + FUJIBAYASHI S
        INF PROCESS SOC JPN (JOHO 21(5): 528-38 (1980) (IN JAPANESE)
                CENTRAL RES LAB, NIPPON ELECTRIC CO LTD, TOKYO, JAPAN
                SAC 1980: 032870

0181   SL10 SOFTWARE PRODUCTION, TESTING AND UPDATING.
        SHORROCKS WB
        P1277-82 OF INT SWITCHING SYMP, PARIS, FRANCE, 7-11 MAY 1979 COLLOQUE INT DE LA COMMUNICATION, PARIS,
        FRANCE, 1979
                BELL NORTHERN RES, OTTAWA, ONTARIO, CANADA
                SAB 1981: 002709

0182   SOFTWARE IN COMMUNICATIONS TECHNOLOGY.
        SIMMEN A
        BULL ASSOC SUISSE ELECTR 71(21): 1177-80 (1 NOV 1980) (IN GERMAN)
                AUTOPHON AG, SOLOTHURN, SWITZERLAND
                SAC 1981: 009664

0183   SUGGESTIONS FOR COMPOSING AND SPECIFYING PROGRAM DESIGN DECISIONS.
        SINTZOFF M
        P311-26 OF INT SYMP ON PROGRAMMING PROC OF THE FOURTH COLLOQUE INT SUR LA PROGRAMMATION, PARIS, FRANCE
        22-24 APRIL 1980, ROBINET, B(ED), SPRINGER-VERLAG, BERLIN, GERMANY, 1980
                    PHILIPS RES LAB, BRUXELLES, BELGIUM
                    SAC 1980: 032334

0184   ASPECTS OF SOFTWARE DESIGN ANALYSIS: CONCURRENCY AND BLOCKING.
        SMITH C + BROWNE JC
        PERFORMANCE EVAL REV 9(2): 245-53 (SUMMER 1980)
                    DEPT OF COMPUTER SCI, UNIV OF TEXAS, AUSTIN, TX,
                    SAC 1981: 002127

0185   PROGRAM DESIGN METHODS COMPARED.
        SNEED H
        ONLINE-ADL-NACHR NO 9: 716,718-21 (SEPT 1979) (IN GERMAN)
                    SAC 1980: 002072

0186   SINGLE-BOARD COMPUTERS AND SINGLE-CHIP MICROCOMPUTERS. SOME DO'S AND DON'TS.
        SNIGIER P
        DIGITAL DES 10(3): 48-50,52,54,56 (MARCH 1980)
                    SAC 1980: 026677

0187   MEASUREMENT AND ANALYSIS CENTRES: SOFTWARE DESIGN.
        SPIEGELHALTER BR + BROWN RS
        POST OFF ELECTR ENG J 71(4): 233-8 (JAN 1979)
                    TELECOMMUNICATIONS DEV DEPT, TELECOMMUNICATIONS HEADQUARTERS,
                    LONDON,
                    ENGLAND
                    SAB 1979: 013929

0188   STRUCTURED PROGRAMMING AT AECI.
        STEPHENS RE
        SYSTEMS (S 9(5): 20,22-4 (MAY 1979)
                    SAC 1979: 033826

0189   DATA STRUCTURES KEY TO PROGRAM DESIGN.
        STEWART M
        COMPUT WKLY 26(651): 4, 20 (3 MAY 1979)
                    SAC 1979: 027454

0190   APPROACHING GAME PROGRAM DESIGN.
        STUCK HL
        BYTE 4(2): 120,122,124,126 (FEB 1979)
                    SAC 1980: 003159

0191   DESIGN TECHNIQUES WHICH SAVE TIME AND REDUCE EFFORT.
        SWINDELLS B
        PRACT COMPUT 3(11): 90-1 (NOV 1980)
                    SAC 1981: 005225

0192   SOFTWARE DESIGN FOR PCM-B TRIAL EXCHANGE.
        TAT TN + VAN DEN BRANDE F
        ELECTR COMMUN 54: NO289-92 (1979)
                    COMPAGNIE GENERALE DE CONSTRUCTIONS TELEPHONIQUES, PARIS,
                    FRANCE
                    SAB 1979: 048538

0193   DESIGNING PORTABLE SOFTWARE.
        THEAKER CJ
        P247-61 OF LIFE-CYCLE MANAGEMENT, STATE OF THE ART REPORT, INFOTECH MAIDENHEAD, ENGLAND, 1980
                    UNIV OF MANCHESTER, MANCHESTER, ENGLAND
                    SAC 1981: 005245

0194   EXPERIENCES WITH A SCHEMATIC LOGIC PREPROCESSOR.
        TRIANCE JM + YOW JFS
        SOFTWARE-PRACT EXPER 10(10): 791-800 (OCT 1980)
                    COMPUTATION DEPT, UNIV OF MANCHESTER, INST OF SCI AND TECHNOL,
                    MANCHESTER, ENGLAND
                    SAC 1981: 005407

0195   SOFTWARE DESIGN PROCEDURE FOR INTELLIGENT TERMINALS.
        TSURIN OF
        PRIB SIST UPR NO 7: 3-4 (1980) (IN RUSSIAN)
                    SAC 1980: 034729

0196   CHOOSING THE SOFTWARE PACKAGE THAT S RIGHT FOR YOUR NEEDS.
        VAUTHIER T + ASNER M
        CAN DATASYST 11(7): 70-2 (JULY 1979)
                    LABATT BREWERIES OF CANADA LTD, LONDON, CANADA
                    SAC 1980: 000012

0197   DESIGNING A PORTABLE PROGRAM.
        WALLIS PJ
        P295 OF LIFE-CYCLE MANAGEMENT, STATE OF THE ART REPORT, INFOTECH MAIDENHEAD, ENGLAND, 1980
                    UNIV OF BATH, BATH, ENGLAND
                    SAC 1981: 005248

0198   STRUCTURED TEST OF COBOL PROGRAMS.
        WALSH DA
        SIST AUTOM 25(196): 591-600 (SEPT 1979) (IN ITALIAN)
                    SAC 1980: 005595

0199   VERIFICATION OF SP-1 4WIRE/TOPS IN TORONTO.
        WATSON RA
        P465/1-5 OF ICC 79 1979 INT CONF ON COMMUNICATIONS BOSTON, MA, 10-14 JUNE 1979, IEEE, NEW YORK, 1979
                BELL CANADA, TORONTO, CANADA
                SAB 1980: 001705

0200   SYSTEM-INDEPENDENT PROGRAM DESIGN WITH DATABASE SYSTEMS.
        WEDEKIND H
        ELEKTRON RECHENANLAGEN 21(2): 55-60 (APRIL 1979) (IN GERMAN)
                FACHGEBIET INFORMATIONSSYSTEME UND DATENVERARBEITUNG,
                TECHNISCHE HOCHSCHULE DARMSTADT, DARMSTADT, GERMANY
                SAC 1979: 019029

0201   DESIGNING A TEST PROGRAM.
        WILKINSON AR
        ELECTRON NO 175: 13 (1 MAY 1979)
                CIRRUS COMPUTERS, FAREHAM, ENGLAND
                SAB 1979: 046281

0202   SOFTWARE DESIGN FOR APPLICATION OF MICROPROCESSORS IN SUGAR-MAKING INDUSTRY.
        WINDAL G
        REV GEN ELECTR 89(6): 454-6 (JUNE 1980) (IN FRENCH)
                SAC 1981: 001287

0203   AN APPROACH TO DISTRIBUTED COMPUTING SYSTEM SOFTWARE DESIGN.
        YAU SS + CHEN-CHAU YANG
        P31-42 OF PROC OF THE 1ST INT CONF ON DISTRIBUTED COMPUTING SYSTEMS, HUNTSVILLE, AL, 1-5 OCT 1979, IEEE,
        NEW YORK, 1979
                DEPT OF ELECTRICAL ENGNG AND COMPUTER SCI, NORTHWESTERN
                UNIV, EVANSTON,
                IL,
                SAC 1980: 009300

0204   P-NOTATION: HIGH LEVEL DESCRIPTION LANGUAGE FOR SOFTWARE DESIGN.
        YOUNG S
        MICROPROCESS MICROSYST 4(8): 307-11 (OCT 1980)
                UNIV MANCHESTER INST SCI AND TECHNOL, MANCHESTER, ENGLAND
                SAC 1981: 008817

0205   P-NOTATION: HIGH LEVEL DESCRIPTION LANGUAGE FOR SOFTWARE DESIGN.
        YOUNG S
        MICROPROCESS MICROSYST 4(7): 267-72 (SEPT 1980)
                DEPT OF COMPUTATION, UNIV OF MANCHESTER INST OF SCI AND
                TECHNOL,
                MANCHESTER, ENGLAND
                SAC 1981: 005220

0206   STRUCTURED DESIGN. FUNDAMENTALS OF A DISCIPLINE OF COMPUTER PROGRAM AND SYSTEMS DESIGN.
        YOURDON E + CONSTANTINE LL
                SAC 1980: 024198

A

                                D

E

F

G

M

BIOGRAPHIES

Glenn D. Bergland received the B.S., M.S. and Ph.D. degrees in electrical engineering from Iowa State University in 1962, 1964, and 1966 respectively. In 1966 he joined Bell Telephone Laboratories in Whippany, N. J. where he conducted research in highly-parallel computer architectures. In 1972 he became head of the Advanced Switching Architecture Department in Naperville, Illinois, and later head of the Software Systems Department which was involved in feature development for the No. 1 Electronic Switching System (ESS). He is currently head of the Digital Systems Research Department in Murray Hill, New Jersey. His principal research areas are software design methodologies, digital telecommunications services, and personal computing.

Dr. Bergland is a member of the Association for Computing Machinery and the Institute for Electrical and Electronics Engineers.

Ronald D. Gordon received the B.A.S. degree in Computer Science from Southern Methodist University in 1973. His M.S. and Ph.D. degrees in Computer Science were earned at Purdue University in 1976 and 1977. After completing his doctorate, he joined the Department of Computer Science at Purdue University as an Assistant Professor.

Currently, he is employed as a member of the technical staff at Bell Laboratories in the Digital Systems Research Department. His current research interests are in the areas of software systems design and analysis, with particular emphasis upon the development of a methodology to aid in the development of switching systems software.

Dr. Gordon is a member of the Association for Computing Machinery.